HYMAN ☑ W9-AXS-212

DIRECTORY OF BUYERS

How and Where to Easily Sell
Collectibles, Antiques & Other Treasures
Found Around Your House & Neighborhood

Dr. Tony Hyman

Nationally known authority on
buying and selling collectibles by mail

Treasure Hunt Publications
Shell Beach, California 93448

Hyman's Where To Sell Directories
are published by
Treasure Hunt Publications
PO Box 3028
Shell Beach, CA 93448

For more information, tune in "Trash or Treasure" on radio
every weekend on United Broadcasting Network
Saturday at 3-4 and Sunday at 10-noon Eastern.
Heard live at those times on the internet at <audionet.com>

Cover design: Steve Gussman, Santa Fe, NM
Cover photos: Hyman and courtesy of various listees
Proofreading: Cecilia Fleischauer and Karen Woodruff

Printed in the United States of America.

        5   6   7   8   9   10

ISBN: 0-937111-06-6

Table of contents

Congratulations. You have in your hand everything you need to get accurate information about millions of antiques and collectibles. With that information, you should be able to sell any collectible items you might own for fair prices.

This book was written to be used by everyone, not just antique dealers. Even if you don't care about antiques or collectibles, you can cash in on the high prices paid today without leaving the comforts of your own home.

This edition adds 150 exciting categories of buyers and updates more than 300 address and phone number changes. We've crammed a lot of information into these 640 pages. If you spend a few minutes to read the next few pages, you'll learn the exact steps taken by me and by tens of thousands of readers before you. You too can easily put money in your pocket by getting "old things" into the hands of people who want them.

Trash or Treasure is based on two principles:

• **It pays to deal with experts who know what they're doing.** When you want something done right do business with experienced, knowledgable, helpful people. As a general rule, the more expert and the more experience, the better.

• **It pays to deal with honest people.** Yes, there are many greedy dishonest ethical-corner-cutters in the world, but there are also a lot of decent, honest, hardworking nice people who try to treat you fairly.

I believe you should ask experts to evaluate what you have, then, based on that information, decide whether or not to sell. By letting experts set the value I've had less hassle and more profit than when attempting to research on my own, then sell locally.

Inside, you will find valuable tips and strategies I've learned during my 45 years as a successful buyer and seller of collectibles. These tips are marked with a drawing of my head or various symbols. Reading them will help you be successful too.

Two boxes full of mail from people who have happily used what I call "the fast system" of selling are sitting at my feet as I write this. I look forward to reading about your success stories. Good luck.

Tony Hyman
Shell Beach, CA 93448

HOW TO USE THIS BOOK

The FAST way to get fair prices

The letters **F-A-S-T** stand for **Find** something that might be valuable, **Ask** an expert, **Send** the item, **Take** the money. That's my shorthand way of making it easy for you to remember an important strategy for getting information, assistance, and cash.

THE VALUE PYRAMID

Value isn't something found in a Price Guide or book. There is no giant grocery-checker sitting up in Heaven stamping an absolute value on goods. Every situation is different, but ultimately it's buyers and sellers alone who determine what something is "worth." Money talks.

The more that someone wants a particular item, the higher the price that person is willing to pay.

Doesn't it make sense to sell something to the person who wants it the most?

Find something that might be valuable

Most Americans already have valuable things among their possessions. That's because so many things made in the 1940's, '50s, '60s and '70s have become collectible.

The key to finding things is knowing what to look for. Valuables are all around you. People discard items worth thousands of dollars because they don't recognize their new collector value. You live in a time when $5 toys made in the 1960's bring $1,000 from some buyers. So do fishing lures, children's marbles, and plastic 40's jewelry. **It's time to be careful.** There can be a lot of money at stake every time you clean house. **The best way to protect yourself is to read and use this book.**

In the back of this book you'll find a list of all the things you own that are collectible today. Starting on 593 is a 25 page double column list of 2,200 categories worth money to you.

Most of you reading this book already have found something you'd like to know about. Whether it's one thing or a household, the Trash or Treasure "Things You Can Sell" Index is an important key to learning whether any item has value. **The Index tells you where to find the people who know.**

The "Things You Can Sell" Index is easy to use and **saves you days of research** in libraries and hundreds of price guides. Read the **tips** on page VIII to increase your odds of success.

Ask a buyer what it's worth

Since value is determined by a buyer and seller, your next step is to find a buyer. A real buyer is someone willing to hand you money in exchange for whatever you have. No other person is a buyer. Advice from anyone else is suspect.

A primary purpose of this book is to put you in touch with one or more buyers to help you determine the desirability and value of what you have.

This is my personal "little black book." Actually, it's a greatly expanded version of my actual address book first published by World Almanac back in 1980 under the title *Where To Sell Anything and Everything*. This is the 8th and largest edition of that ground breaking reference book.

Over the past 45 years I've bought from, sold to, and asked questions of thousands of people in every state and province. My address book is filled with authors, newsletter editors, club presidents and other officers, auctioneers, and prominent collectors. These are people with whom I do business. They are the buyers and experts I turn to when I need help answering a question in my column or on the air. These are the people I sell to confidently, quickly, easily, discretely and profitably.

Since I personally use the information in Trash or Treasure for interviews and referrals in my column and on my radio show, every effort has been made to be accurate and comprehensive. If you know a prominent buyer who is not included, I either have not met them yet or they didn't choose to open themselves to contact by large numbers of amateur sellers.

One expert bragged he became an expert so he *could* take advantage of people's ignorance. I don't knowingly do business with people like that. You shouldn't find him or his ilk in here.

USING THE INDEX

This index makes it easy to locate a discrete, reliable, expert buyer faster, with fewer mistakes, fewer dead-ends, and better resulting prices than any other list anywhere.

Turn to page 593 **and look at the "Things You Can Sell" index.** This index is a detailed list of more than 2,200 types of items buyers are seeking. Many entries are obvious, like dolls and coins, but did you know that lace and toasters were also worth money?

Take a moment to read all the boldface items in the index. Readers often discover they are richer than they thought when they take a minute to read this list carefully. The bold items are the ones I get asked about most often. Everything listed in the index can be sold.

Increase your chances of making money by looking under several categories. For example, an art glass cigar box with a label depicting Lincoln playing poker in a railroad car would be desirable to buyers of art glass, cigar boxes, labels, advertising, card playing, Lincoln, gambling and railroads. A buyer may be under any of those categories. Circle possibilities as you go.

If you can't find your item in the index on the first try, it might be rewarding to look it up in a different way. Any item you own might be sold because of

- What it is (perfume bottle, knife, clothing, art, etc.);
- Who made it (John Deere, Maytag, Planters, etc.);
- Where it was made (Salem bottles, NY guns, etc.);
- What it is made of (ivory, glass, china, silver, etc.);
- Where it was sold (Disneyland, Walgreens, etc.);
- What it is shaped like (dog, cat, reptile, etc.);
- Who painted it (Vargas, Norman Rockwell, etc.);
- Who owned it (gangsters, celebrities, etc.);
- Who signed it (ball players, Presidents, artists, etc.).

Creativity in using the index to find a buyer can pay off big. Buyers in one category might pay two or three times more than buyers in another.

How to find a buyer in this book

Where do you find a buyer and or expert?   Remember that 25 page list in the back of this book?   One or more buyers is identified for everything in that list. Each of those thousands of items is followed by page numbers.   Turn to those pages, and you'll find from one to a half dozen entries, each of which introduces you to a buyer.

Each buyer's entry begins with bold type telling you the main category of things that person wants. Read the entire entry because it may contain info about other things the person wants, how to describe what you have, what the buyer pays, what books are available and what the buyer doesn't want. The more entries you read, the more likely you are to learn about things you own, but did not know had collector value.

Entries are grouped so that buyers with similar wants are on the same or nearby pages. You may find three or four people interested in something you have. From reading each entry, you should have a fair idea of whether or not your item fits what that buyer wants. When in doubt, ask.

Buyers listed in Trash or Treasure are a mix of private collectors, universities, museums, auctioneers, and specialty dealers. They have been selected for experience, knowledge, and willingness to give information to me and to amateur sellers, and their commitment to pay fair prices.   No one has paid a fee to be included in this book.

Contacting a buyer

The majority of buyers prefer you to state clearly in your first letter what you have and its condition. They want you to set a price or to request an offer. Buyers want sellers, not pen pals.

Before you contact a buyer, read the entry carefully. If an entry reads "No tribbles," you will not be able to sell your tribble to that buyer.   Don't waste your time asking. If an entry reads "Tribbles considered," it means that tribbles are not a specialty, but if your tribble is particularly scarce and in fine condition, the buyer may make an offer.

If you believe you own something a buyer might want, it is easy to ask him or her by mail or by telephone. Each entry in Trash or Treasure gives you the buyer's name and address and, in many cases, their phone and fax number. A few e-mail addresses are new to this edition. Although you will frequently be dealing with the top people in their field, you'll find them to be "just plain folks," friendly, and easy to talk to.

Most buyers provide their phone number. Phone calls are fast, easy, and let you get the most information to the buyer with the least effort. The telephone gives the buyer an opportunity to ask questions, **so have your item in front of you when you call**, if possible, and be prepared to discuss details, including size, color, maker, distinguishing characteristics, and damage. An expert can often tell what you have based on a few simple questions.

A few buyers indicate specific hours during which they'd like you to call. Respect their wishes and you'll get off to a good start. If no hours are suggested, call during normal business hours for the time zone in which they live. If you don't reach them, try between 7 and 8 p.m. their time. Folks in California hate 6 a.m. calls from eager Easterners, just as Easterners don't appreciate 2 a.m. calls from Western night owls.

When leaving a message on an answering machine, be brief and specific about what you have. Say your name and phone number slowly so it can be understood and written down when your message is played back. Repeat your phone number.

Many items can't be adequately described over a phone. The advantage of contacting a potential buyer by mail is that you can send pictures or Xerox™ copies. Buyers are much more likely to pay well for things they can see.

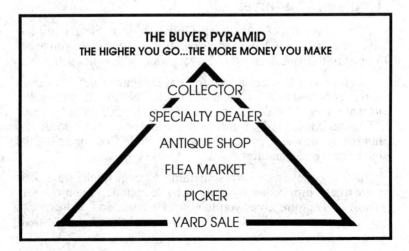

THE BUYER PYRAMID
THE HIGHER YOU GO...THE MORE MONEY YOU MAKE

COLLECTOR

SPECIALTY DEALER

ANTIQUE SHOP

FLEA MARKET

PICKER

YARD SALE

WHO PAYS THE MOST?

The typical collectible changes hands 7-9 times as it moves up the pyramid from the original owner to the final collector. Each person who handles it raises the price. If the collector at the top of the pyramid pays 100% of value, what do others pay?

Collectors tend to pay 50% to 100% of retail value. They pay the highest percentage for rare and expensive items.

Specialty dealers typically pay from 30% to 75% of an item's retail value. How much they pay depends on how anxious he/she is to add your item to inventory, and how quickly your item is likely to resell. The more expensive the item, the higher percentage of retail you should get.

Auction houses exist at all levels of skill and clientele. The price you get at auction will depend upon the quality of your item, its history, what is being auctioned with it, when and where the auction is held, and, most important of all, who will be attracted to bid in the auction. Most sales at auctions are to **dealers**, who will raise, double, or triple the auction price when they sell to their customers. Prices range from a typical 15% to 60%. Only rare goods under perfect conditions in important auctions will sell for 75% - 100% of value, or more. Remember to deduct the auction house charges, typically 15% to 25% of the bid.

Antique Shop owners come in all sizes, shapes, specialties and skill levels, but generally try to pay from 5% to 30% of retail to survive, with higher prices paid only for fast moving quality goods. Shop owners make many mistakes because their experience is usually limited to a few fields. When they buy outside their specialty, you may be paid only 1% to 5% for a rare item.

Mall dealers' profits are low, so the prices they pay must be low too. They do best when they pay under 5% and seldom pay you more than 20%.

Flea market dealers generally pay in the same range as pickers, from 1% to 15%. Their knowledge and markets are limited. They try to buy estates, paying as little as 1%.

Pickers who buy from yard sales pay from 1% to 20% of dollar value, often less. Picking can be very profitable

Yard sale buyers pay well for children's clothes, but few other items fare as well. Items worth $300 to $10,000 may get from 1¢ to 6¢ for each $20 of value.

Specialty dealers and collectors pay the most
and make deals with the least fuss.
That's why I deal with them.

When writing to a possible buyer, Sell-a-grams make contacting a potential buyer as simple as filling in the blanks. This handy form letter (seen on the opposite page) gives you easy to follow guidelines, so you're never in doubt as to what  you should say and what information you should provide. Many Sellers give special attention to Sell-a-grams. Some buyers normally charge for services they will provide free only to my readers or listeners. If you don't use a Sell-a-gram, whether you write or call, identify yourself as a reader of Trash or Treasure.

To get the most from a Sell-A-Gram, blow it up to a full size 8 1/2" x 11" page on a copy machine. Use that page as a master. You have my permission to make as many copies of this © form as you need for your personal use. I print the Sell-A-Grams I use on yellow paper, as it's an attention getting color.

Ask for an offer

When I sell something, I almost never set the price. I ask the buyer to set a fair price. Forty-five years experience taught me that I make more money easier by dealing with experts qualified to decide what I have and what fair value is. If you deal with reputable people, you'll get a fair offer. That is the heart of my FAST system.

One reader asked buyer Mickie Zekley for $200 for her oboe rather than asking him to set the price. Since she set the price, he could have legally and ethically paid it. But he instantly recognized it as a valuable instrument and paid her $7,000 instead. That's why I deal with him. That's why I deal with experts.

SASE

When you ask someone for information or an offer, take a long business size #10 envelope, address it to yourself, put a stamp in the corner. This is called a Self-Addressed Stamped Envelope or SASE. **Include one with every request.** Use a long envelope because many buyers have brochures, wants lists, and other informative material they'll send you free. Buyers are under no obligation to answer mail without an SASE.

SELL-A-GRAM   from one of Tony Hyman's readers

TO: _____

FROM: _____

Phone: ( )_____

I have the following item:

Remember to include the (1) shape, (2) colors, (3) dimensions, and (4) all names, dates, and marks.

It's condition is:

List all chips, creases, cracks, dents, scratches, rips, tears, holes, stains, fading, and foxing.
Note any missing pages, parts, or paint.   Describe any repairs that have been done.

C
H
E
C
K

O
N
E

☐ The item is for sale for $_____ plus shipping.

☐ The item is for sale. I am an amateur seller and would like you to make an offer.

☐ The item may be for sale if the price is sufficient. Would you like to make an offer?

☐ The item is not for sale, but I am willing to pay a fee to learn its value.

To assist you to evaluate the item, I am enclosing a:
☐Sample ☐Photocopy ☐Photo ☐Tracing ☐Sketch ☐Rubbing ☐Nothing

This is to certify that, to the best of my knowledge, the item is genuine and as described.
Buyer has a 5 day examination period during which the item may be returned for any reason.

Signature: _____   Date: _____

☐ Answer Requested (SASE enclosed).   ☐ No answer needed.

BUYER'S RESPONSE:

SECRETS OF SUCCESS

Although most buyers prefer you to set the price you want, most have agreed to share their knowledge and make certain you receive fair market value. One buyer expressed the sentiments of many when he said, "I am not interested in doing free appraisals but I will help any amateur genuinely uncertain about what price to ask." **If you are an amateur, ask for help.** Since I am an amateur in most fields, I ask buyers to price *my* items. If you are a dealer, most buyers expect you to price your goods.

Buyers whose entry reads NO OFFERS mean exactly that. You must tell them in the first letter what price you want. Buyers who refuse to make offers are inevitably people who have bad experience dealing with the public.

If you describe your item well and it is something the buyer wants, you will receive an offer, often in the form of a check. Because they are making an offer based on your description, and many folks do not describe things well, buyers may have to see your item before making a firm offer or making final payment. This is not unusual. **Condition is always important,**

If a buyer decides that your item is not of interest, don't waste time arguing. If you're talking on the phone, ask if the buyer can recommend another collector or dealer who might be interested. If your item is in good condition, but not wanted by specialists, you can safely sell it at a yard sale, donate it to a charity, or sell to a local antique dealer.

How do you know the offer is fair?

You ultimately decide whether to accept an offer or not. When I sell things about which I know little, I try to deal with people with reputations for integrity who will make that offer a fair one. Experience has taught me that dealing with experts is usually quicker, easier, and more profitable than selling at yard sales, flea markets or to local dealers and auctioneers.

Experts and people with experience can recognize what you have, and, if they are listed in here, have pledged to treat you fairly. Seventeen years of putting buyers and sellers together has shown that it is more likely a reader will cheat one of my buyers than the other way around.

Since 1980 I've asked readers to report any bad experience with someone I recommend. Less than two dozen complaints and five people dropped is an outstanding record!

Send the item

If you have accepted a buyer's offer, or a potential buyer has requested you to send the item for inspection, you will need to ship your item. Shipping is easier than you think. In the case of large items like furniture and juke boxes, the buyer will probably arrange to have all shipping done for you.

When packing smaller items you sell, always use sturdy boxes. You can buy boxes at most post offices , stationery

---

CONDITION, CONDITION, CONDITION

It is vital that you examine and accurately describe the condition of your item. Some items lose 40-50% of their value with their first scratch or dent. Stains, tears, wear, fading, foxing, thin spots, fraying, nicks, handwriting and brittleness all affect value.

Low or medium quality items in only fair condition almost never have buyers at any price. Neither dealers nor collectors want to tie up cash in poor goods. Chips and cracks in most china, pottery and glass make values drop to almost nothing. Postcards, comic books, and sheet music are among paper collectibles which become nearly valueless if not in excellent condition.

On the other hand, some less-than-perfect paper will sell. "Rock & roll concert posters and handbills found in the drawers of aging hippies are rare enough to be a cash windfall in any condition," reports one expert.

Mechanical items will sell with parts missing. Radios, jukeboxes, slot machines, radios, etc., can be restored, although buyers warn you should never try restoration of anything you want to sell.

Whatever your item's condition, if you don't describe it accurately, the buyer will return it, costing you and the buyer money and wasted effort.

Amateur sellers are notorious for overestimating the quality of condition. As a result, many dealers and collectors will ask to see the item before they make a final offer. This is particularly true of buyers of paper goods like postcards, trade cards, match covers, sheet music, and stamps. Paper dealers want to see what you have, because very small variations in condition mean substantial difference in price. For example, paper money worth $50 in very fine condition might be worth only $5 in circulated condition. Postcards with creases, or match covers with their strikers removed, are worth little or nothing.

---

stores, and packing companies, but heavy duty boxes can often be obtained free from book stores. Don't ship anything, even shoes, in shoe boxes.

If you are shipping a breakable item, double boxing is the preferred method. Pack your item carefully in the smallest box that leaves an inch or two of protection around your item. Write the name and address of the recipient on that box, then pack it inside a larger box, with two or three inches of padding.

When packing breakables, never let two items touch. Wrap each item separately in Styrofoam sheets, bubble wrap, or clean paper. Never leave lids on cookie jars, sugar bowls, and the like. They are likely to chip or break if you do.

Never pack your item in direct contact with newspaper. Newsprint smears and can damage clothing and ruin items like porous china. Wrap breakables in tissue, paper towel or plain unprinted paper, then use newspaper wads to fill the carton.

Flat items should be shipped between two or more sheets of cardboard approximately one inch bigger on all sides than what you are sending. Put the grain of the two pieces at right angles. That makes your package less likely to bend.

Ship by First Class mail or by private carrier. Do not use Parcel Post. The difference in price between Parcel Post and first class is so small, the few pennies you save aren't worth the time delay and increased risk. If your package weighs under two pounds, you can send it anywhere in America for only $3.

When an item is worth more than $300, I ship it Registered Mail, because registered items receive special security handling. Registered Mail can also be insured for up to $25,000 and must be signed for by the addressee. All this for one fee from $5 to $10 (which will be paid by the buyer). You should consider using Registered Mail for anything valuable that is one-of-a-kind or cannot be replaced.

If using Registered Mail, there are a few special rules. You must use a clean box with no damage or printed advertising. The address and return address must be written directly on the box, not on an applied label. Each seam of the box must be covered with brown paper tape. No plastic tape is allowed.

Insure what you ship. Insurance on a First Class package is about $5. Insurance on Registered Mail costs much less, because of the strict security under which Registered Mail is handled.

If a deal is made and you ship your item, **a buyer has a three to five day inspection period and may return it for a refund**. You must return the full amount of their check, although most buyers are willing to pay postage both ways, unless you mis-represented what you were offering. The most common reason for an item to be returned is its condition was not as good as you described.

If a buyer moves or dies

If you discover that one of my recommended buyers has moved or died, please tell me. In general, collectors are more stable than average, but we live in a very mobile society, changes do occur, and busy folks sometimes forget to notify us. When you tell me about any changes, I'll send you a free update sheet listing all changes reported by other readers since the last printing if you include a long SASE with your information. This offer is good as long as this edition is in print. You can get an update sheet any time by sending a long SASE and two one dollar bills.

Share your experiences

If you'd like to tell me about your experiences selling to these folks by mail, drop me a line. I don't have time to answer personally, but I listen well, and I'll take what you say into consideration when doing radio, TV and future editions of Trash or Treasure

If you know other buyers you think should be included, please don't be shy. I'm always glad to meet more folk who are expert in their fields, honest in their dealings and fair in their pricing.

Special symbols

Pay attention each time you see the drawing of my head or one of the other symbols that mark tips, advice and warnings. The information they spotlight is important to your success.

Top ten most asked questions

My F.A.S.T. system has worked so well for buyer and seller alike that I have been invited to appear on TV shows like Donahue, Vicki!, and Mike & Maty plus 1,800+ radio shows to teach it. Letters pour in at the rate of 350 per week as a result of my monthly advice column about collectibles and the weekly syndicated "Trash or Treasure" radio show heard on 150 stations nationally. Each year, I answer thousands of questions about the disposition of antiques and collectibles. People everywhere share the same questions and concerns.

1 "Why bother? Why not simply give it away?"

A fine idea. But it's smart to know what you are giving away and what its cash value is. Items worth $10,000 turn up in charity shops far more often than you realize. When toys less than 30 years old can be sold for 300 times what you paid for them, I urge you to be cautious about what you give away. Instead of donating an item, why not sell it properly, and donate part or all of the proceeds? You'll be giving your church or charity a lot more, and getting a healthy tax break as well.

2 "Why not sell at a yard sale?"

Great idea, as long as you sell things appropriate to a yard sale: children's clothing, modern kitchen items, and newer household do-dads. Beware of selling anything fifteen or more years old at a yard sale.

The problem with selling at a yard sale is that you must set the price, and most people reading this are not qualified to do that. Do you know what lace is $100 an inch? Which marbles are $1,000? Which postcards and photographs have value? Most people don't. That's why antique dealers shop at your yard sales. One properly sold collectible could make more money than all the rest of your yard sale.

3 "Why not sell to a local dealer?"

Sell to a local dealer only after you have made certain you don't own an item wanted by one of the specialty dealers or collectors.

The problem with selling to anyone other than an expert is that the buyer may not know exactly what your item is. One dealer in a thousand might recognize the rarest Indian stone spear point; fewer yet would pay you the $10,000 you'd get by dealing with someone who knows and appreciates Indian stone. Dealing with an expert will require a phone call, a letter, and perhaps a photocopy or photo. Selling your spear point to the dealer around the corner will take about the same amount of time, but the difference in price could be substantial.

4 "Will I get cheated?"

What is to keep a buyer from cheating you and saying your $5,000 watch is worth $5? Honesty, for one thing; reputation for another. This book represents the people I personally do business with. Experience has taught me I seldom go wrong dealing with authors, club presidents, newsletter editors, and people like that. The world of collectibles is a small one. Word gets around fast, and dishonest buyers seldom stay in business long. "Why would I risk a reputation it took me thirty years to build, just to cheat some old lady out of $500? It doesn't make sense," explains one veteran pro.

Some people believe a conflict of interest exists when the same person evaluates and sets the price. To some extent, that may be. But when you deal with people who have reputations for knowledge and integrity, you're likely to get fair prices and be many dollars ahead of selling at a yard sale, flea market, or local auction.

Dishonesty, misunderstandings, and disagreements are possible in any human interactivity. I don't worry about that because I've known some of these people personally for 20 years. I've featured them in books, newspapers, radio and television since 1980. Hundreds of thousands of transactions have taken place between readers and these buyers. I've received less than a two dozen letters of complaint, all but five of them minor. Buyers who fail to treat my readers and listeners with respect and honesty are dropped from my files immediately.

5 "If I wait, won't prices go up more?"

Maybe. Maybe not. Many items sell for less today than they did a few years ago. Just as the value of gold or the stock market goes up and down constantly, so does the value of antiques and collectibles.

Items sold during the inflation of 1987-89 are frequently resold now at 50% to 75% of what the cost then, and in a few hobbies only the very best items are selling at all. It's true that over the long haul, prices tend to rise. But they often rise far less than the benefits you gain by converting those items to cash now.

6 "Can I make money as a picker?"

People in their '60s and '70s tell me they're having fun and making money the Trash or Treasure way. They report adding income by reselling things they buy from yard sales and flea markets run by people who have not read Trash or Treasure. If you would like to become a successful part time seller of collectibles with a minimum of effort, Trash or Treasure is the single most important book you can own.

7 "I wrote to a buyer. Why didn't I get an answer?"

If you offer something rare for sale, you'll get an answer from any collector or dealer.

If you don't get a response to your inquiry from one of the people in Trash or Treasure, it may mean that your item was not collectible, or you didn't include a self-addressed stamped envelope, or the buyer hasn't had time to respond. Perhaps you wrote the wrong person, or offered something the buyer specifically said was not wanted. It's also possible your letter got lost in the mail or that the buyer is out of town or sick. Remember, you're writing to real people. Like you, they have families, work long hours, and sometimes travel. You may not have gotten an answer because the person to whom you wrote has moved and mail was forwarded slowly, or not at all. If you discover that a phone has been disconnected, try writing, requesting it be forwarded.

8 "Why aren't there pictures and prices in this book?"

In the last 150 years more than a billion different items have been manufactured. A book which pictures them all would be taller than the World Trade Center, an obvious impossibility. For me to include a few hundred pictures in this book would help no one and make it more expensive to bring you this valuable reference book.

Pictures are essential only in price guides used by amateurs curious about the "worth" of their item and by novice antiques and flea market dealers. **You get accurate prices from expert buyers, not books.** Trash or Treasure explains how and to whom you sell the items pictured in other books. It introduces you to the people who write price guides instead of other amateurs who read them.

Not one of the seven most valuable things known to have been sold by my readers was pictured or listed in any price guide, yet they got as much as $200,000 for what they had. Photos seldom exist of the most valuable items.

9 "How often do you update Trash or Treasure?"

We never stop. The first address or phone change usually arrives about the time a Directory rolls off the press. By September of 1997 expect 20 or so changes, by Spring of 1998 there may be 50 to 60. By the time an edition of our Directory has been out for two years, 15% to 20% of the addresses will have changed. At that time, we quit providing update sheets and produce an all new edition.

You can write us for a current list of changes at any time. Send a long Self-Addressed stamped envelope and two one dollar bills to Buyer Update, Box 3028, Pismo Beach, CA 93448. Please, no checks.

10 "How do we get you on the radio?"

Two ways. "Trash or Treasure" is heard on 150+ stations every Saturday from 2 p.m. to 3 p.m. and every Sunday from 10 to noon. It's available free off a satellite and any station or homeowner may request information on receiving "Trash or Treasure" by calling United Broadcasting Network in Florida at (904) 397-2000.

If you have a computer with a soundcard and are an internet surfer, tune in audionet.com at those times, select UBN, and I'll be live in living digital sound.

I'm also a frequent guest on radio and TV stations all over America. If you have a favorite radio or television talk show, have them call (805) 773-6777 after noon Eastern and arrange an interview.

Special money-saving bonus question

11 "Can I save money when I buy Trash or Treasure as gifts for friends?"

Sure can. One is $24.95 (save $10) and two are $49.90 (save $20). The best deal of all is three for $59.85. That's right! You get the same discount the bookstores get *and* your friends and relatives will receive the price guide and Sell-A-Grams as well. Neither of those two important bonuses are available in stores.

Yes, I'd like to order additional copies of Trash or Treasure

Regularly $34.95 (29.95 + $5 s/h). With this Coupon:
☐ **One for $29.95** postpaid (save $5)
☐ **Two for $49.90** postpaid (save $20)
☐ **Three for $59.90** postpaid (save $35...like getting one free)
  California residents add $1.60 sales tax for each book

Send to_____

_____

_____

Treasure Hunt Offer, Box 3000, Pismo Beach, CA 93448

TIPS ON SELLING FURNITURE, RUGS AND LAMPS BY MAIL

If you own "furniture store" bedroom or dining room suites made after 1920 they probably have little if any collector value. Sell factory furniture from this period through classified ads in your local newspaper. Read the next few pages to see what you can sell. Many pieces have been reproduced or copied, so a good clear photo is essential.

Some ordinary looking furniture can have value. Be especially careful with hand carved items, mission oak, and designer furniture from the 1930-1960 period. Before contacting a possible buyer, examine the legs and underside looking for signatures, maker's marks, or labels. They can make a big difference in selling price.

Damaged rugs lose value, but very old Oriental rugs should be evaluated by an expert, no matter what their condition. The finest Oriental rugs are not thickly piled, but are rather thin so don't think your carpet has no value just because the threads aren't long and lush. One reader found a $2,000 carpet (3'x5') used as a mud rug outside a mountain cabin. All you need to avoid expensive mistakes is a good photo and the buyers in Trash or Treasure.

If sending a photo is not possible, you may wish to phone the buyer and discuss your item. Always call with the item in front of you. Be prepared to answer questions about colors, dimensions, type of wood, labels, etc. It is very difficult to sell a rugs, lamps, or furniture without a photo, however.

Make certain when selling large or heavy items that you and the buyer agree who has responsibility for packing and shipping. This cost is normally born by the buyer, but sellers make the arrangements. If this will be difficult for you, ask the buyer to help. Generally, you should request the buyer to have large items picked up as part of the sale. This is particularly important if you are elderly, have difficulty getting around, or if you live outside a big city.

FURNITURE

★ **Entire estates which include furniture and accessories from the American colonial period,** art, or important collections of toys, dolls, guns, decoys, miniature lamps, art glass, advertising, or other specialties. Your estate or collection must have a value in excess of $50,000 to be handled by this important firm. No interest in minor collectibles, limited edition plates, or common items.

James D. Julia Auctioneers
PO Box 830
Fairfield, ME 04937
(207) 453-7904   Fax: (207) 453-2502

★ **Heavily carved or decorated American furniture made between 1820-80** including fancy Empire, Gothic revival, rococo, American Renaissance, etc., especially furniture made by *Belter, Roux,* or *Meeks.* Also **gas chandeliers and *Argand Astral* lamps.** This prestigious dealer does not make offers so research is in order since many of these pieces can be very valuable. Send her a photo of the furniture plus a copy of every label or maker's mark you can find. She will help an amateur "if they are really *selling* and not fishing for free appraisals."

Joan Bogart
PO Box 265
Rockville Centre, NY 11571
(516) 764-5712   Fax: (516) 764-5712

★ **Furniture and accessories from the Arts and Crafts or "Mission" period.** Buys oak furniture, light fixtures, and metalwork by *L. & J.G. Stickley, Gustav Stickley, Roycroft, Limberts, Lifetime, Charles Stickley, Rohlfs, Stickley Brothers,* and *Dirk Van Erp*, especially unusual pieces, custom made pieces, and items inlaid with silver, pewter or copper. Also textiles, various publications, and catalogs from these firms. "If you have any doubts, please call. I will be glad to help."

Robert Berman
Le Poulaille
441 South Jackson Street
Media, PA 19063
(610) 566-1516

Do not even think about refinishing oak furniture that you plan to resell. Collectors want that dark original finish found on most Mission pieces. An original finish is worth more than what you or your local refinisher will do.

★ **Furniture that is square in appearance,** made of oak, and characterized by square spindles, cut out designs, and/or inset tiles. Wants chairs with adjustable backs, benches, beds, couches, dressers, desks, library tables, book stands, cabinets, sideboards, etc. Examine the piece carefully for woodburned maker's marks or paper labels. A photo is strongly suggested. Does not want refinished pieces. Call if in doubt.

>Gary Struncius
>PO Box 1374
>Lakewood, NJ 08701
>   (800) 272-2529

★ **Arts & Crafts or "Mission" style furniture** but only signed pieces by *Gustav Stickley, L. & J.G. Stickley, Roycroft, Limbert* and other important makers. "I DON'T WANT furniture by generic makers." A *Gustav Stickley* inlaid armchair with rush seat and in its original black finish can bring as much as $10,000. Send a photo and include the dimensions, and a drawing of the mark. Marks on furniture can be on legs, underneath, on the back, and elsewhere so look carefully for labels or woodburned names. This well known expert in the Arts & Crafts period has agreed to make offers to amateur sellers who learn about him through this book if they are serious about selling what they own, but states clearly that he "does not wish readers to price fish or to involve him in bidding wars with other buyers." If you need an appraisal for estate or insurance purposes, the fee is $10 per item.

>David Rago
>333 North Main Street
>Lambertville, NJ 08530
>   (609) 397-9374   Fax: (609) 397-9377

★ **Furniture and accessories from the Arts & Crafts or "Mission" period.** Buys oak furniture, lamps, light fixtures, and hammered copper metalwork by *L. & J.G. Stickley, Gustav Stickley, Roycroft, Limberts, Lifetime, Charles Stickley, Rohlfs, Stickley Brothers, Jarvie, Albert Berry, Onondaga Metal Shop, Karl Kipp, Harry Dixon* and *Dirk Van Erp*, especially Morris chairs, case pieces (like dressers), bedroom and living room furniture, and benches. Smaller items include desk sets, bookends, lamps, vases, trays, and candle holders. Prices can be high, as lamps often bring $2,000 up. Photo is helpful as part of your description. Note the maker and any repairs or damage. Note whether the original finish is still there. "I expect sellers to give me a minimum acceptable price. If their item is worth a great deal more, I'll let them know." Bruce wrote *The America Arts & Crafts Movement in Western NY, 1900-1920*, available for $16 postpaid.

>Bruce Austin
>RIT College of Liberal Arts
>Rochester, NY 14623
>   (716) 475-2879   (716) 387-9820 eves   BAAGLL@rit.edu

★ *Roycroft* **furniture and accessories.** Buys and sells lamps, waste baskets, clocks, frames, art, pottery, china, glassware, and all books and paper ephemera associated with the *Roycroft* company or its founder, Elbert Hubbard. When you write, make certain to state honestly whether the item is for sale or whether you are seeking identification and appraisal. Please give the source of the item for sale and include any stories or history you know about the piece(s).

> Tom and Rosaline Knopke
> House of Roycroft
> 1430 East Brookdale Place
> Fullerton, CA 92631
>   (714) 526-1749

★ **Wicker furniture and luggage.** "I'll consider any good condition old wicker, but am most interested in Bar Harbor Victorian characterized by curled arms and an open weave that you can see through. Pieces can be in any color, but natural is usually best. **Wicker luggage** can have either leather or brass trim, but should be in fine condition, inside and out, suitable for resale. Give the dimensions, status and color of the lining, condition of the wicker, hardware, and the leather trim."

> Joan Brady
> 834 Central Avenue
> Pawtucket, RI 02861

★ **Designer furniture from the 1940's through the present** by Herman Miller, Knoll, Eames, Nelson, Gilbert Rohde, Frank Lloyd Wright, **Heywood Wakefield**, Noguchi, Thonet, and other national and international designers. Also interested in unusual plastic and fiberglass designer furniture. Most pieces are signed on the bottom. Primarily interested in **bent plywood chairs and fiberglass arm chairs** with no upholstery made by Herman Miller.

> Jay Novak
> Modernica
> 7366 Beverly Boulevard
> Los Angeles, CA 90036
>   (213) 933-0383   Fax: (213) 683-1312

★ **Blond furniture by Heywood Wakefield** from the 1930's through 1960's. Please send a photo along with information about any markings or labels. Describe condition accurately. Also interested in buying **catalogs** of Wakefield furniture.

> Don Colclough
> 231 North Elmwood Street
> Oak Park, IL 60302
>   (800) 775-5078   Fax: (708) 848-9124

★ **Adirondack and other rustic twig furniture.** "Please let me hear from you if you have large quantities of rustic furniture to sell or if you have individual pieces of excellent quality. I can handle any size deal and am experienced at both buying and brokering the contents of any rustic camp. summer home, motel or hotel that contains fine rustic furniture and accessories."

       Barry Friedman
       PO Box 55492
       Valencia, CA 91385
          (805) 255-2365   BarryF@fishnet.net

★ **Twig furniture.** "I'm interested in any type of rustic or Adirondack furniture. This includes pieces by *Old Hickory* and *Twig Furniture*. The wilder the style, the more I will want it. As always the better the condition, the more I will pay. If you have any doubts, call."

       Robert Berman, Le Poulaille
       441 South Jackson Street
       Media, PA 19063
          (610) 566-1516

★ **Unusual furniture** made of twigs (Adirondack), horn, horse shoes, found objects and other "wild, eccentric, and unusual stuff" like small **folk art chairs and tables** in original paint. A photo is essential because of the nature of these items.

       Matt Lippa and Elizabeth Schaaf
       Artisans
       PO Box 256
       Mentone, AL 35984
          (205) 634-4037   artisans@folkartisans.com

★ **Furniture made with or decorated with steer horns** is sought by this long time scholar of the genre. "I'll buy chairs, tables, hat racks, etc., made from cattle or buffalo horn. I prefer pieces that have the appearance of being artfully or creatively constructed with as many horns as possible, and made between 1880 and 1920. I have no interest in contemporary horn furniture. The fabric on most horn furniture is in poor condition, so we are mostly concerned with the condition of the horns themselves so make sure you check for cracks and bug damage. These pieces can be fairly valuable, so it is worth your time to take pictures from the front, back and sides. Give the dimensions of the furniture you have. I also want furniture which is decorated with inlaid horn, particularly fine examples of which can be worth in the multiple thousands of dollars."

       Alan Rogers
       1012 Shady Drive
       Kansas City, MO 64118
          (816) 436-9008

★ **Unusual "fantasy" chairs and other furniture** made between 1880 and 1980. Please call or send photos along with asking price.

> Charles Martignette
> PO Box 293
> Hallandale, FL 33008
>   (954) 454-3474

★ **Folding chairs with advertising on the back.** Interested in everything dealing with folding chairs with advertising on the back, including photos of chairs in use in lodges, churches, picnics or other events. Send a photo or photocopy of items offered.

> Richard Bueschel
> 414 North Prospect Manor Ave.
> Mt. Prospect, IL 60056

RUGS

★ **Rugs with advertising logos, cartoons or images** such as Buster Brown, *Coca-Cola*, etc.

> Charles Martignette
> PO Box 293
> Hallandale, FL 33008
>   (954) 454-3474

★ **Grenfell hooked mats and rugs.** "I'll buy any tightly hooked mat, rug, or purse labeled GRENFELL LABRADOR INDUSTRIES as long as it is in excellent condition. These always depict Northern scenes like polar bears, hunters, Eskimos, etc. Please send dimensions and a photo with your first letter. Dealers are expected to price their goods, but amateurs may request an offer."

> Barry Friedman
> PO Box 55492
> Valencia, CA 91385
>   (805) 255-2365   BarryF@fishnet.net

ORIENTAL RUGS & TAPESTRIES

★ **High quality rugs and tapestries.** Oriental, Chinese, European, American Indian, and large hooked rugs are of interest if of sufficient quality and condition. Buys Art Deco, Art Nouveau, and Arts & Crafts rugs and textiles as well. Worldwide interest in fine tapestries, textiles, embroideries, and weavings as well as paisley and Kashmir shawls. A good clear color photograph is important. Make certain to mention wear or stains. Appraisals and offers are made *only* after actually seeing your rug. Gallery open by appointment only.

> Renate Halpern Galleries
> 325 East 79th Street
> New York, NY 10021
>   (212) 988-9316   Fax: (212) 988-2954

★ **Oriental rugs.** Claims "highest prices paid" for Oriental rugs of all types: "antique, semi-antique, used, or just plain old, regardless of size or condition." Also buys American Indian rugs, hooked rugs, tapestries, and miscellaneous textiles.

> David Tiftickjian, Jr.
> 260 Delaware Ave.
> Buffalo, NY 14202
>   (716) 852-0556   (716) 634-8835

★ **Oriental rugs** made by hand before 1950 in any size or condition. A good sharp photo plus the dimensions is essential for this dealer/appraiser with 24 years experience to make an offer. Aaron's buys, sells, cleans and repairs antique Oriental rugs.

> Robert Anderson
> Aaron's Oriental Rug Gallery
> 1217 Broadway
> Fort Wayne, IN 46802
>   (219) 422-5184

Damaged rugs lose value, but very old Oriental rugs should be evaluated by an expert, no matter what their condition. The finest Oriental rugs are not thickly piled, but are rather thin so don't think your carpet has no value just because the threads aren't long and lush. One reader found a $2,000 carpet (3'x5') used as a mud rug outside a mountain cabin. All you need to avoid expensive mistakes is a good photo and the buyers in Trash or Treasure.

LAMPS

★ **Lamps and lamp parts of all types from all periods.** Buys a wide range of wall, floor, and table lamps from the Betty lamps of the 1700's right through to the 1950's. Will buy kerosene, whale oil, electric, *Aladdin*, organ, marriage, student, desk, and other lamps. Also interested in *Tiffany* and other high quality leaded and painted lamps. This major Western dealer can be very helpful to amateurs with just about any type of lamp to sell. **Especially wants *Aladdin* lamps and parts** including galleries, chimney cleaners, bug screens, flame spreaders, wick cleaners, wick raisers, finials, and anything else made by *Aladdin*. Also buys parts from other lamp makers. If you have lamps or parts for sale, please note whether they are brass or nickel plated and give all numbers and wording. A photo is very helpful if asking for an offer.

> Richard Melcher
> PO Box 1812
> Wenatchee, WA 98807
> (509) 662-0386

★ **Lamps and light fixtures from the early 1800's to the early 1940's** are wanted by this veteran lighting restoration dealer. He buys old iron, brass, or tin electric, gas or kerosene fixtures, wall sconces, chandeliers, colored glass shades from fixtures, and damaged fixtures suitable for scavenging parts. He will buy inside or **outside lighting fixtures** (including street lights) and has particular interest in those from commercial buildings as well as homes. He notes that large fixtures can be disassembled and shipped at his expense. Note all cracks or chips in glass. He is not interested in reproduction shades or in any fluorescent fixtures, but is strongly interested in **old catalogs from manufacturers** or retailers which depict large numbers of lighting fixtures from before 1920.

> Robert Daly's Historic Lighting Restoration Sales & Service
> 10341 Jewell Lake Court
> Fenton, MI 48430
> (810) 629-4934   LDALY1@aol.com

Lamp collectors want to know if your lamp is original and complete, and if there is anything wrong with it. You should mention if it shows any signs of repair or of being a marriage of parts from different lamps. Describe the quality of the finish on the base and whether the glass shows any cracks or chips. A signature on the base or shade usually makes a lamp worth more. Look carefully, as signatures can be hard to locate on some valuable lamps.

★ **Reverse painted, leaded glass, or art glass lamps** including table lamps, boudoir lamps, and floor lamps. "I am interested in buying **shades, bases or parts** for lamps of these types. I have a special interest in *Moe-Bridges*, *Classique Studios*, or *Phoenix Light Co.* I am also interested in catalogs from lamp and lighting fixture manufacturers (not retailers) before 1935." Does not want oil lamps, hurricane lamps, Gone With the Wind lamps, etc. No lamps after 1920's. Give all names and numbers found anywhere on the lamp or shade, and all dimensions. Please set the price you want for your lamp and include a photo.

>Merlin Merline
>PO Box 16265
>Milwaukee, WI 53216
>(414) 871-6261

Many leaded lamps have been reproduced. These reproductions sell new for around $250 and are worth only $20 to $100 in local markets. If you have original leaded or painted lamps from before 1930, however, the value can top a thousand dollars, so don't be hesitant to ask an expert for assistance.

★ *Tiffany* **and other high quality glass lamps.** "I believe we are the only auction firm in North America that conducts specialty auctions for rare lamps only." Collections, large or small, of *Tiffany, Handel, Jefferson, Pairpoint,* and other quality lamps, lamp bases, and lamp shades from both **large and small oil and electric lamps** will be considered by this record setting auctioneer. Photos are a must. Telephone if you have a large group of lamps to sell.

>James D. Julia Auctioneers
>PO Box 830
>Fairfield, ME 04937
>(207) 453-7904   Fax: (207) 453-2502

★ *Tiffany* **lamps, lamp parts, chandeliers,** windows, art glass, and enamel pieces in addition to other maker's **high quality glass lighting fixtures.** Please include photos and your phone number.

>Carl Heck
>PO Box 8416
>Aspen, CO 81612
>(970) 925-8011

Broken lamps and lamp parts before 1930 almost always can be worth some cash to you.

★ **Lamps and light fixtures from the "Mission" or Arts & Crafts period.** Anything signed by *L. & J.G. Stickley, Gustav Stickley, Roycroft, Limberts, Lifetime, Charles Stickley, Rohlfs, Stickley Brothers,* and *Dirk Van Erp*, especially unusual pieces, custom made pieces, and items inlaid with silver, pewter or copper. Also **catalogs from these firms**. "If you have any doubts, please call. I will be glad to help."
Robert Berman
Le Poulaille
441 South Jackson Street
Media, PA 19063
(610) 566-1516

★ *Emeralite* **lamps,** 1909 to 1940's, wall, desk, table, and floor models. Buys green-shaded, acid etched or painted models. These are found with brass, metal, marble or glass bases.
Bruce Bleier
73 Riverdale Road
Valley Stream, NY 11581
(516) 791-4353 (call collect)

★ **Student lamps,** lamp shades, and lamp burners, 1870-1890, are wanted, especially lamps made by *Griffin*. A double *Griffin* can be worth $1,500 in fine condition and a single up to $450. "Make certain your lamp has an oil or kerosene tank that lifts out of the lamp, as many reproductions do not." Note if your lamp has been electrified, as well as any other damage which may have occurred.
Jerry and Marsha Ritch
8357 Bridlewood Drive
East Amherst, NY 14051
(716) 741-9580

★ *Bellova* **lamps,** 1920's and 1930's. Boudoir, table, and floor models but frequently found with green-shaded, acid etched or painted shades. These are found with brass, metal, marble or glass bases. *Bellova* lamps are frequently signed on the base and shade. May be marked with a dime size 4 leaf clover in a circle. May be marked CZECHOSLOVAKIA.
Bruce Bleier
73 Riverdale Road
Valley Stream, NY 11581
(516) 791-4353 (call collect)

★ **Miniature oil lamps** made of metal, art glass, or milk glass. Give the size, and indicate all names and numbers you can find on the lamp. A photo is appreciated.
Carl Cotting
1441 Crowell Road
Vienna, VA 22182
(703) 759-5646

★ **Revolving radio and TV lamps** from the 1930's, 40's, and 50's that are driven by the heat of the light bulb. These were made by *Econolite Corp, Scene In Action,* and *Rev-O-Lite* among others. "I will pay $350 for the scene in a fish bowl, and other substantial amounts for mermaids, motorcycles, snow skiers, sailing ships, water skiers, Santa Claus, and many others. Please call if you have one for sale." The Montgomerys wrote *Animated Motion Lamps Price Guide,* available from them for the bargain price of only $13 postpaid.

> Bill and Linda Montgomery
> 12111 SE River Road
> Milwaukee, OR 97222
>   (503) 652-2992

★ **Revolving TV lamps with pin-up girls** made by Econ-o-lite. Please call or send photos along with asking price.

> Charles Martignette
> PO Box 293
> Hallandale, FL 33008
>   (954) 454-3474

If you shop at yard sales to make money, revolving lamps are good to watch for. They are often found for $5 or so. Don't buy a lamp with broken glass or plastic parts if you want to resell it.

★ **Lamp shades of cloth or beaded silk** from 1890 to the 1930's that are in near perfect condition. He'd like you to send a photo, the dimensions, and your asking price.

> Charles Martignette
> PO Box 293
> Hallandale, FL 33008

★ **Catalogs from lamp and lighting** fixture companies published before 1935, especially catalogs which show lamps with leaded or scenic glass shades. Especially interested in catalogs from one of the many companies based in Milwaukee. Does not want department store catalogs with lighting sections. Xerox© the cover and send a page count and an indication of how many color illustrations are included.

> Merlin Merline
> PO Box 16265
> Milwaukee, WI 53216
>   (414) 871-6261

CLOCKS

★ **Old wall and shelf clocks.** This family business describes itself as "a clock adoption agency, looking for nice items in need of a good new home." They buy a wide range of 18th and 19th century shelf and wall clocks, but are especially interested in the following:
  • **Victorian shelf and wall clocks.** Wants ornate ones, with busts, teardrops, cherubs or side mirrors;
  • **Reverse painting on glass pillar and scroll clocks** about 36" high with free standing wooden pillars and curved scroll ("swan's neck") tops;
  • **Steeple or beehive shelf clocks,** but *only* if the veneer is perfect, or nearly so. "These are plentiful with poor veneer. I want those in beautiful condition;"
  • **Any American carved clocks.** "I'm a pushover for clocks with carved columns or splats, eagles or fruit baskets;"
  • *Eli Terry* clocks or those by any of his sons;
  • *Seth Thomas* clocks;
  • **French, German** and **English clocks** from the 18th and 19th century. "Some excellent 20th century German clocks were made, but no matter how good the clock we don't buy 20th century," he cautions, so don't ask;
  • **Cuckoo clocks** if very old, very heavily carved, and in perfect condition. "I'm afraid I'll open a floodgate if I mention I'll buy cuckoos, because there are so many junk ones around. I only want those that are very early and very ornate." No souvenir clocks. Photo a must;
  • **Black Forest trumpeter clocks.** These are like cuckoos, but instead of a bird, a man plays a tune on a trumpet. "These are valuable, and we'll travel to pick yours up if it's a nice one."
"We buy clocks with walnut or cherry cases. We buy spring driven clocks but especially like to find older weight driven clocks. We buy clocks with wooden works only if in running condition," they say, "but there are a few exceptions, so it's worth inquiring. We don't buy any 20th century clocks, oak gingerbread kitchen clocks, electric clocks, or Mission (Arts and Crafts) clocks. We also do not buy plain ogee clocks (rectangular veneered clocks with fronts that look like picture frames). We almost never buy clocks that have undergone restoration or modification. We don't want to spend lots of time restoring the clocks. We prefer to buy them in nearly perfect condition."
Mark Kenley
Old Timers
PO Box 392
Camp Hill, PA 17001
    (717) 761-1908   Fax: (717) 761-7446

*To describe a clock, answer as many
of the following as you can:*

> *What name is on the dial?*
> *What name is on the movement?*
> *How tall and wide is the case?*
> *What is the case made of?*
> *Is the case decorated?*
> *Is there a label inside the case?*
> *Is there a serial number?*
> *Is there anything unusual about its looks?*
> *How is it wound or activated?*
> *Do you have the key and weights?*
> *Is it presently running?*

★ **American wall and mantle clocks** from the 1700's through the Arts & Crafts movement of the early 20th century. "I'll buy, sell, or trade a wide range of clocks, but my specialties are weight driven calendar and regulator clocks that hang on a wall. I also buy interesting, unusual, and better grades of shelf (mantle) and other wall clocks of the 1800's. Especially like clocks with multiple dials or faces in either plain or fancy cases." Some of the many names to look for include *Simon-Willard, E.N. Welch, Howard, Ithaca, Waterbury, Seth Thomas, New Haven*, and other early Connecticut makers. Bruce is well versed in clocks of all types so can be helpful to the amateur seller. "If I'm offered something I can't use, I try to refer folks to someone who might like to buy it. Early electric clocks don't interest me much, but I may be able to give readers some help in identifying or evaluating them." Bruce says, "For my own collection, I like to find ones that are a little out of the ordinary." Some interest in **European clocks with porcelain dials, or with fine cases with gilt, inlay, or marble.**

> Bruce Austin
> RIT College of Liberal Arts
> Rochester, NY 14623
> (716) 475-2879 (716) 387-9820 eves BAAGLL@rit.edu

★ **Grandfather clocks both European and American.** "I prefer 100+ year old grandfather clocks made in the United States, especially in Pennsylvania, but will also consider fine grade European and English clocks. If you have something good in the way of an old tall case clock, we will be glad to hear from you."

> Mark Kenley
> Old Timers
> PO Box 392
> Camp Hill, PA 17001-0392
> (717) 761-1908 Fax: (717) 761-7446

★ *Howard Miller* **clocks** from the 1950's and 60's. These are usually metal or metal and wood and marked on the back (and sometimes the front). A photograph or sketch is helpful.

> Jay Novak
> Modernica
> 7366 Beverly Blvd.
> Los Angeles, CA 90036
> (213) 933 0383   Fax: (213) 683-1312

★ **Winking eye clocks.** "I'll buy any good specimens of these 19th century figural cast iron clocks which wink their eyes as the hands go around. Made in Connecticut during the 3rd quarter of the 19th century by *Bradley and Hubbard*, figures include dogs, owls, lions, elves, Topsy, a man on a barrel, and others. They bring $1,000 up in fine condition and paint, but I'll buy them in any condition, including broken, missing paint, or incomplete. Take photos from more than one angle or phone me with the item in front of you."

> Gregory "Dr. Z" Zemenick
> 1350 Kirts Blvd. #160
> Troy, MI 48084
> (810) 244-9426   Fax: (810) 244-9495

★ **Advertising clocks** made by *Baird*.

> Jerry Phelps
> 8012 Deronia Avenue
> Louisville, KY 40222
> (502) 425-2561

In most cases, buyers will want to inspect your timepiece before making a final offer.   Always discuss exact shipping procedures with the buyer.

★ **Alarm clocks**, 1880-1910. These battery driven "tin can" clocks usually have a bell on top, but he's looking for unusual varieties that strike the hour, have calendars, play music, or are in unusual shapes. *Parker, Terry, Darche* and *Kroeber* are among the important early brands. He does not want anything that plugs in, or any modern wind-up clocks like *Big Ben, Little Ben* and *Ingersoll*. Give the brand name and any other info you can find on the clock. Everyone must include a photo and price their items. Will not make offers.

> Steve Cunningham
> 3200 Ashland Drive
> Bedford, TX 76021
> (800) 991-0165   Fax: (800) 991-0166

MISCELLANEOUS ACCESSORIES

Accessories is a word used to describe many useful things around our homes. Collectors seek accessories because of what they are made of, who made them, or the style in which they were made.

★ **Arts & Crafts period lamps and accessories** made by *Van Erp, Roycroft, Limberts, Stickley*, and others. Lamps are often copper and colored glass, as are **cigarette boxes, bookends, ashtrays, humidors, desk sets**, and other items. Better pieces are often inlaid with silver. This active Arts & Crafts expert also buys **furniture** by these makers, whose work tends to be massive square oak furniture, often with dark finishes, visible pegs and hinges, and simple unornamented lines. Many people call it "mission oak." Send a photo or call if you think you have one of these pieces, as some can be quite valuable.

> David Rago
> 333 North Main Street
> Lambertville, NJ 08530
> (609) 397-9374   Fax: (609) 397-9377

★ **Accessories from the Mission or Arts & Crafts period** including light fixtures and metalwork by *L. & J.G. Stickley, Gustav Stickley, Roycroft, Limberts, Lifetime, Charles Stickley, Rohlfs*, and *Dirk Van Erp*, especially unusual pieces, custom made pieces, and items inlaid with silver, pewter or copper. He is also interested in catalogs from these firms. "If you have any doubts about what you have, please call. I will be glad to help."

> Robert Berman
> Le Poulaille
> 441 South Jackson Street
> Media, PA 19063
> (610) 566-1516

Always check accessories for maker's marks, as signed pieces are usually of better quality and more likely to be collected. You should look for quality of workmanship, fine materials, and good design. Deciding what is good design is difficult, especially when artistic judgment comes into play. I'm sure you've seen valuable things you thought were ugly. I know I have. Many of these items may not appeal to you personally, but that shouldn't keep you from profiting when you find them. Good luck!

★ **Hammered copper** and other Arts and Crafts period items such as:
  • Lamps with mica or glass shades;
  • Vases and candlesticks by *Roycroft, Van Erp, Jarvie* and
    others working in the Arts & Crafts style;
  • Silver by *Kalo*;
  • Metal with applied or cut-out squares by *Roycroft*;
  • Arts & Crafts jewelry.
Descriptions are difficult without a photo. Since some of these pieces
are fairly valuable, it could be worth your time. Describe all maker's
markings, damage, and give dimensions.
  Gary Struncius
  PO Box 1374
  Lakewood, NJ 08701
    (800) 272-2529

★ *Roycroft* accessories such as bookends and other small items. A
photo or Xerox™ is a good idea if requesting an offer.
  Richard Blacher
  209 Plymouth Colony/Alps Road
  Branford, CT 06405

★ **Art Deco accessories.** "I'll buy Deco items to compliment my radio
collection." Ed wants a wide range of distinctive Deco items, so give
him a try for items like clocks, **picture frames**, and **lamps**. If you are
the original owner, he'd appreciate the item's history. He prefers you to
set your price but will make offers to amateurs intending to sell.
  Ed Sage
  PO Box 13025
  Albuquerque, NM 87192
    (505) 298-0840

★ **Standing picture frames** made of wood, brass, silver plate, celluloid, copper, ivory and bronze, usually from 3" to 15" high. "Larger
OK, smaller even better. Missing glass OK, too, but the frame itself
must be in fine condition and made before 1930, preferably with the
easel in back. Best frames are marked *Gorham, Tiffany, Germany* or
Aspreys. Porcelain or ivory pictures in the frame add greatly to value,
but ordinary portraits do not. Photocopies and good description will
bring a cash offer.
  Carol Payne
  Carol's Gallery
  14455 Big Basin Way
  Saratoga, CA 95070
    (408) 867-7055

★ **Bookends** made before 1940 that are three dimensional figures of men or women that are at least 4" high. Metal are preferred, but glass, wood and plaster will be considered, as will metal bookends with interesting designs that are not necessarily figural. Do not offer small bookends, singles, or newer items. Picture preferred, along with dimensions. Point out any cracks, flaws, or wear. "This is a new hobby for me, so you must price what you have so I can decide whether it appeals to me at your price. Don't contact me with things not for sale."

> Susan Mast
> 849 Almar Avenue #C-270
> Santa Cruz, CA 95060
>   (408) 423-9786 eves   Fax: (408) 423-7001

★ **Victorian era boxes** which held collars, cuffs, gloves, brush and mirror sets, shaving sets, neckties, etc. "The boxes we collect have a picture on the front or top that is covered with a thin layer of celluloid. Our favorite lithos are of women and children, and we do not buy those picturing French or Colonial attired folks. Boxes are usually covered with celluloid. Nothing will be considered that isn't in top condition, that has cracked celluloid, split seams, or missing hardware." Interior condition is not as critical. Color photo needed. Note all damage. Pays finder's fees. For more info, request their illustrated wants list.

> Mike and Sherry Miller
> 303 Holiday Avenue
> Tuscola, IL 61953
>   (217) 253-4991

★ **Photo and autograph albums.** "The albums we collect have a lithograph on the cover that is coated with a thin layer of clear celluloid. Our favorite lithos are of women and children, and we do not buy those picturing people in French or Colonial dress. Musical albums are particularly desirable; we pay from $100 to $250 for nice ones. Nothing will be considered that isn't in top condition, that has cracked celluloid, split seams, or missing hardware. Interior condition is not as critical." Color photo needed. Note all damage. Wants list available.

> Mike and Sherry Miller
> 303 Holiday Avenue
> Tuscola, IL 61953
>   (217) 253-4991

★ **Gold bearing quartz items.** Masculine items made from or decorated with quartz containing gold veins are sought. Items include matchsafes, cane handles, watch fobs, watches, pocket knives, boxes, etc. Sandra doesn't have much interest in jewelry, "unless it's exceptional." A Xerox™ or photo is the best way to sell.

    Sandra Whitson
    PO Box 272
    Lititz, PA 17543
        (717) 626-4978   Fax: (717) 626-7625

★ **Items made of banded agate.** Will purchase pens, button hooks, snuff boxes, and small decorative items made mostly of banded agate. If you want to sell, give dimensions and condition.

    Stanley Block
    PO Box 51
    Trumbull, CT 06611
        (203) 261-0057

★ **Indian motif sterling silver items made for men** by *Unger Bros.* Items she seeks include **desk sets, clothes brushes, matchsafes**, etc. Has only limited interest in women's items and jewelry by *Unger*, but will buy some items.

    Sandra Whitson
    PO Box 272
    Lititz, PA 17543
        (717) 626-4978   Fax: (717) 626-7625

★ **Peter Max designs on any household item or article of clothing** such as shoes, tights, pants, shirts, jackets, scarves, ties, jewelry, sheets, furniture, pillows, glassware, posters, clocks, ashtrays, dishes, bowls, and anything else. Condition is important. Items must be clean, with no wear, tears, stains or chips. Send a photo or Xerox@ along with an accurate description for her offer.

    Judy Polk Harding
    1701 60th Street
    Des Moines, IA 50322
        (515) 279-7099 voice and fax   THEFIVEJS@aol.com

MISCELLANEOUS HOUSEHOLD ITEMS

★ *Glascock* **stoves and other ephemera.** "We want cook stoves, heaters, ranges and other items (whether complete or not) produced by G.T. Glascock & Son[s] or Glascock Stove & Mfg. Co. of Greensboro, NC. Also want all advertising, catalogs, and other items related to Glascock. I'd even like a photo of your stove if it's still in use!" There were many models, and stoves were produced under many names, such as *Carolina, Charter, Carbon Banner, Blue Ridge, Victor, Tar Heel* and many more. This company historian is interested in everything you have. Do not try to repair or repaint anything, please. Please send a photo, and anything you know about the piece's history and use.

> Nollie Neill, Jr.
> PO Box 38
> Ennice, NC 28623
> (910) 657-8152 eves   Fax: (910) 657-8084

★ **Gas kitchen stoves** from before 1930 are preferred, but I will consider all types of stoves, including heating type) as long as they are early models. Also want all related industry memorabilia such as catalogs and advertising signs. "The earlier the better." Photo, please.

> Paul Schoenharl
> Cincinnati Stove & Range Museum
> 3940 Spring Grove
> Cincinnati, OH 45223
> (513) 541-0450 days

★ **Washing machines.** "I buy old and unusual washing machines, usually wooden, galvanized, or copper tubs with wringers, although some hand-operated varieties did not have wringers. What may look worse than junk may be quite restorable and indeed an exciting machine so you are encouraged to inquire. I usually do not buy machines with porcelain tubs. If you have something I want, I'll pick it up so send a good sharp photo and any information."

> Lee Maxwell
> 35901 WCR 31
> Eaton, CO 80615
> (970) 454-3856

★ **Early Victorian terrariums and aquariums.** Please send a photo or description. Include your phone number.

> Mark Miller
> PO Box 52261
> Philadelphia, PA 19115
> (215) 464-3561 voice and fax   70176.1153@compuserve.com

★ **Pressing irons**. "I'll buy unusual pressing irons of all types including goffering irons, crimping irons, fluters, charcoal heated irons, slug irons, *Pyrex* glass irons, miniature irons of any material, irons with animals or other figures for handles, ruffle irons, hat irons, and flower irons used in making artificial flowers." He also buys advertising for irons by various companies and some smoothing boards. He does not want common cast iron sad irons or ordinary electrics. Dave is author of *Irons by Irons*, available for $44 postpaid, and *Pressing Iron Patents,* available for $23 postpaid.

> Dave Irons
> 223 Covered Bridge Road
> Northampton, PA 18067
> (610) 262-9335

★ **Miniature sad (flat) irons.** Wants irons smaller than 4 inches only. No electric irons, no matter how early.

> George Fougere
> 67 East Street
> North Grafton, MA 01536

★ **American sewing machines from before 1875,** especially rare early treadle machines with low serial numbers for which he will pay from $1,000-$10,000. Small hand operated machines in the shape of animals are of particular interest. Also photographs of sewing machines in use before 1890. Tell him the maker and the serial number as well as the condition. If there is no name, send a photograph. Carter does not buy *Singer, White, Wheeler & Wilson, Willcox & Gibbs*, or other machines with that turn-of-the-Century *Singer* look, nor does he buy treadle machines in oak cases, or any sewing machine with a chrome or nickel plated flywheel. "High serial numbers on your machine mean it's a common one and of no collector interest." His beautiful *Encyclopedia of Early American Sewing Machines* is available for $49.

> Carter Bays
> 143 Springlake Road
> Columbia, SC 29206
> (800) 332-2297

★ **Sewing items** such as old tape measures, sewing birds, thimbles and thimble cases and other items from a 19th century sewing box. Fine condition only. "I don't want anything common or easily found, anything made after 1960, or any reproduction." Making a Xerox™ is the best way to describe what you have.

> Betty Bird
> 107 Ida Street
> Mt. Shasta, CA 96067
> (916) 926-2231

★ **Miscellaneous household items** including:
- Glass, not ceramic, **wall pocket vases** in any color;
- Reamers, especially figurals, fine china, and precious metals;
- Two-piece china **tea strainers** as long as they are complete;
- **Napkin doll ladies;**
- **Stringholders** made of china or chalkware, but not metal;
- **Children's cups** that are whimsical, with whistles or figures on the handle or writing on the cup like "Whistle for milk";
- Figural **egg timers;**
- Ceramic figural **tea balls;**
- **Laundry sprinkler bottles** in the shape of people.

They do not not damaged items. Please give the color, size, and a description of the material, figure, and any marks. A photo is a good idea and an SASE is a must. You're on your own as these folks insist that both amateurs and dealers set the price wanted. No offers.

Bobbie and Alan Bryson
1 St. Eleanora's Lane
Tuckahoe, NY 10707
(914) 779-1405

★ **Victoriana.** "I'll buy anything likely to have been in Sherlock Holmes' apartment in 1895. This includes but is not limited to the following items specifically mentioned in stories:
- **Bull's eye hand held oil lantern** with focusing lens, 1859-1900
- **Dark lantern** hand held lamp which has a sliding cover that blocks out the light without having to extinguish it.
- **Gasogene.** "These devices make soda water and consist of two glass globes, one sitting above the other, usually with metal mesh encasing both globes/"
- **Tantalus 'decanter stand".** "These are stands containing cut glass decanters which, though apparently free, can not be removed until the bar which engages the stoppers is raised.
- **Wall gas lamps;**
- **Settee style couch, coal scuttle, floor safe, etc.**

"When in doubt, please contact me with information on any items you hope will interest me."

Rev. Sherlock "Yes, it's my real name" Holmes
Private Letter Box 3
Worcester, MA 01613
(508) 754-9907

★ **Gadgets.** "I'll buy interesting old small mechanical devices such as:
- **Pocket typewriters or sewing machines**;
- Pocket size **calculators**;
- Miniature cameras;
- Small optical devices, like **sundials** and instruments;
- Trick, tool, gadget or **special purpose knives**;
- Lighters, compacts, and other pocket items combined with other tools;
- Things that fold, hide-away or look like things they aren't;
- **Personal check protectors** and other small business devices;
- Scientific instruments;
- Combination pen-pencil-rulers;
- Adding machines.

I'm interested in everything that whirs, buzzes, clanks, or just looks interesting." Darryl is particularly fond of typewriters and adders, paying $1,500 for important pocket typewriters. A photo is generally a good idea, and your description should include a detailed statement of condition. Will respond promptly to all offers.

Darryl Rehr
2591 Military Ave.
Los Angeles, CA 90064
(310) 477-5229   Fax: (310) 268-8420

★ **Light bulbs** (1880-1905) with ball or other tips on the end of the glass bulb. Also wants bulbs with dimmers inside and those with figural filaments (Masonic emblems, Fraternal lodges, Worlds Fair, etc.) but not bulbs with flowers or peace signs for filaments. Also wants **old catalogs** from light bulb companies.

Steve Cunningham
3200 Ashland Drive
Bedford, TX 76021
(800) 991-0165   Fax: (800) 991-0166

★ **Figural light bulbs and neon glow lights** are wanted by this long time collector. Christmas figurals are preferred, but all types of novelty light bulbs, such as *Playboy* bunny, Abraham Lincoln and the Statue of Liberty will be considered. Also buys all types of advertising and display materials for figural bulbs. Send a description with a photo. Cindy wrote *Neon Glow Lights* and runs a bimonthly auction of Christmas collectibles.

Cindy Chipps
4027 Brooks Hill Road
Brooks, KY 40109
(502) 955-9238   Fax: (502) 957-5027

★ **Victorian celluloid household items**. Wants pictorially decorated celluloid **photo albums, autograph albums, shaving mirrors, and boxes** that held collars, cuffs, jewelry, brush sets, neckties, etc in the Victorian era. Large boxes in very fine condition can bring $500. She does not want pins, buttons, jewelry, toys, brush and comb sets, or celluloid items other than those requested above. Nothing made of hard plastic. Send a photo along with dimensions. Note condition carefully. Dealers must price their goods. Amateurs may request an offer.

> Judith Rubin
> This Time Around
> 8515 Troutman Court
> Manassas, VA 20110

★ **Thermometers,** pre-1920, especially ornate Victorian desk or mantle types. "I buy just about every *non advertising* one I can locate," but outdoor and decorative models are particularly prized, as are those from Russia and Eastern Europe. "I have the largest antique thermometer collection in the world but am always looking for more." Not wanted: commercial, industrial, clinical, advertising or "cutesy" thermometers. No barometers or souvenir key chain thermometers. Send a photo, accompanied by information regarding the maker, any dates or numbers, condition and whether mercury or red liquid is in the bulb. "Many of the items go to the American Thermometer Museum in Baker, CA." Thermometer catalogs and other ephemera are sought.

> Warren Harris
> 6130 Rampart Drive
> Carmichael, CA 95608
> (916) 654-2097 days   Fax: (916) 966-3490

★ *Louis Vuitton* **trunks and hard case luggage**, the older the better, especially in early cloth designs other than the typical *LV* pattern. "We'd pay $4,000 for a mint condition steamer trunk, but we do not want things in less than fine condition and we do not buy any soft sided luggage." Send a photo, dimensions and history of the item, if possible.

> Duane and Eunice Bietz
> Les Meilleurs
> 6461 SE Thorburn
> Portland, OR 97215
> Fax: (503) 233-1602

★ **Vacuum cleaners** that are hand powered. "I'll travel anywhere, buy one or a collection, and will pay finder's fees for information leading to my obtaining a fine scarce item."

> Peter Frei
> PO Box 500
> Brimfield, MA 01010
> (800) 942-8968   (413) 245-4660   Fax: (413) 245-6079

★ **Strap type watch fobs picturing machinery or advertising products.** No lodge, American Legion, VFW or similar fobs. He'd like you to tell him how much wear it shows and the name of the stamper, usually found at the bottom. No fakes or modern fobs.

> Albert Goetz
> 1763 Poplar Ave.
> South Milwaukee, WI 53172
>   (414) 762-4111

★ **Hotwater and enema bottles**, rubber syringes, bulbs, pumps, irrigators, and other similar home devices that are in complete as-found condition, with clamps, tubes, instructions, box, etc. U.S. or foreign, complete in wooden box they bring $45-75. More unusual ones made of pewter, brass, or other materials are also sought. Does not want modern plastic items, or anything made after 1965. Does not want ice caps, throat bags, atomizers, and other home health devices that don't involve insertion. When describing, give maker, color, size, accessories, info on the box, and where you obtained it. Would also like any stories of personal experiences with these home remedy/treatment devices.

> Ms. Brunswick
> Box 9729
> Baltimore, MD 21284

★ **Baby and child care manuals**, books, booklets, magazines, films and articles **that contain illustrated information on using enemas** as part of sick care and treatment, This 30+ year veteran researcher also wants diaries, hand written notes, and family reminisces in letter form revolving around this particular treatment.

> Ms. Brunswick
> Box 9729
> Baltimore, MD 21284

★ **Flashlights.** Old flashlights, advertising, and catalogs are wanted, especially anything early marked *Eveready*.

> Bill Utley
> PO Box 4095
> Tustin, CA 92781
>   (714) 730-1252

★ **Flashlights.** Old unusual and ornate flashlights, and advertising and catalogs of flashlight companies are wanted. Schneider is author of numerous books, including one on flashlights.

> Stuart Schneider
> PO Box 64
> Teaneck, NJ 07666
>   (201) 261-1983

FANS

★ **Desk, ceiling, or pedestal fans** that are antique or unusual. Wants brands like *G.E., Westinghouse, Emerson, Peerless, Diehl* and others, but especially those made before 1920 or with unusual mechanisms. These early fans are usually cast iron and brass. Also wants literature, catalogs, ads and other information about fans and the companies that made them. If you want to sell your fan, include the brand, nameplate information, dimensions of the blades, number of blades, and what the various parts are made of, if you can. When describing condition, indicate whether your fan operates. Michael is president of the American Fan Collectors Ass'n and editor of its bimonthly newsletter.

>Michael Breedlove, Antique Fans of Indiana
>15633 Cold Spring Court
>Granger, IN 46530
>   (800) 858-3267

★ **Mechanical fans** of all types are wanted, including:
- Electric and battery fans before 1920;
- Water fans before 1900;
- Belt driven fans before 1920;
- *Gyro* ceiling fans from the 1920's;
- Bank teller fans from the 1920's;
- GE and Robbins & Myers Art Deco fans from 1930's;
- Photos of fans in use before 1910;
- Advertising signs, posters and banners for fans.

Prices paid range from $10 to $2,000, depending on the model and condition. Please don't inquire about newer fans. To describe a fan, tell him the the brand name and model number and how many blades it has. Then answer the following questions: Are the blades shaped like dogs' ears or pizza slices? Is the base round or footed? Are the blades brass or steel? Is the cage brass or steel? Is it complete? Does it work?

>Richard Padron
>1005 East Idlewild Avenue
>Tampa, FL 33604
>   (800) 320-FANS   (941) 688-6800

★ **Fans** with brass blades and cages. Also wants loose brass blades and cages, name tags, motors, oscillating mechanisms, advertising for fans as well as fan and motor catalogs. Does not want fans with steel cages or steel blades, but will buy **parts** of non-working old fans. Give the size of the blade and cage, the information on the motor tag, and the condition. Dealers, price your goods. Amateurs may request offers.

>Steve Cunningham
>3200 Ashland Drive
>Bedford, TX 76021
>   (800) 991-0165   Fax: (800) 991-0166

EYEGLASSES & CANES

★ **Eyeglasses,** but *only* old, rare, and unusual ones. Not interested in any common eyeglasses or in buying them for their gold content. "I only want pre-1850 glasses with unusual lenses, frames, or history." Describe all writing on frames. Also wants any eye-related ephemera, display advertising, eyeglass trade signs, and "eye quackery."
W.H. Marshall
PO Box 1339
Melrose, FL 32666
(352) 475-5990

★ **Antique eyeglasses and spectacles** are sought. Also would like to purchase early catalogs and trade cards featuring eyeglasses, unusual reading glasses, antique ophthalmoscopes, and any material from the *McAllister Optical Co.* He has some interest in textbooks on ophthalmology from before 1890. Please describe the condition thoroughly.
Charles Letocha
444 Rathton Road
York, PA 17403
(717) 846-0428

A photocopy machine will take a good picture of most eyeglasses or cane tops. Remember to give standard bibliographic information when describing books

★ **Canes.** Especially likes dual purpose, container, weapon, gadget, and fancy carved canes made with ivory, gold, or silver. "Any cane or walking stick that does something, or has something enclosed or attached to the shaft for purposes other than support, is of interest, as are well executed hand-carved canes." Describe the tip of the cane and indicate whether it gives any evidence of having been shortened. Is there a hole in the shaft? What materials?
Arnold Scher
1637 Market Street
San Francisco, CA 94103
(415) 863-4344   Fax: (415) 863-4399

FOUNTAIN PENS

★ **Unusual quality fountain pens,** pre-1940, by makers such as *Eversharp, Waterman, Swan, Dunn, MacKinnon, Laughlin, Shaeffer, Chilton, Wahl, Moore, Camel* and many others. Some of these can be worth several hundred dollars. She also buys old **quill cutters**, **stylus pens**, and **glass pens**. **Advertising related to pens** is also wanted, including signs, trade catalogs, repair manuals, and spare parts. Also wants packaged powdered ink. To sell your pen, tell her the maker's name, model, color, and length of your pen. Describe the pen point and all decorations on the pen. Best to make a photocopy. Pens will have to be inspected before final price offered. No unbranded pens, *Wearever, Esterbrook,* ball point pens, or magazine ads. She gets a lot of mail, so include an SASE with all inquiries, please.

Mrs. Ky
PO Box 957
Port Jefferson Station, NY 11776
(516) 584-4246 voice or fax

Pen collectors want to know the brand name. Less than 12 brands are considered premium but a great many others are also collected.

Pen collectors want any and all numbers you find anywhere on your pen. Check the end of the barrel, the clip, etc.

Pen collectors want to know the color. Color is very important in determining value. The earliest pens are black, red, or swirled red and black.

The size of your pen is important. Men's pens sell for more than smaller ladies' pens. Measure the length with the cap on. Pens longer than 5" sell for more than pens shorter than 5".

Pen points are best if wide and gold. Points that say WARRANTED or WARRANTED 14k are cheap. Write down what it says on the point.

Condition is important to collectors of pens. Take off the cap and run your fingernail around the rim, feeling for hairline cracks. More than 50% of the value is gone if you find one. Inspect the two halves looking for fading. Make sure the clip, fill lever, and any gold banding is still there. Roll the barrel of the pen on a flat surface to see if it is warped.

Is it worth your time to do all this for a fountain pen? Someone who didn't do all this...someone who didn't contact one of my recommended buyers...donated a $15,000 pen to a rummage sale in Hartford. The rummage sale folks sold it for $55. **Don't let that happen to you.**

★ **Fountain pens, quill pens, desk sets and inkwells.** "I want better quality items in excellent condition only." Does not want pencils or ball point pens. Please send a Xerox™ of what you have, along with a description of color, any markings, and condition. Glen is publisher of *Pen World* magazine, available for $42/year and author of *Collectible Fountain Pens*, available for $25. He has other publications as well.

    Glen Bowen
    2240 North Park Drive
    Kingwood, TX 77339
        (713) 359-4363 Fax: (713) 359-4468

★ **Fountain pens** in fine condition are sought by the head of the Pen Collectors of America ($25/year to join), who provided the info on the previous page. Check condition carefully and don't forget an SASE.

    Boris Rice
    11319 Wickersham Lane
    Houston, TX 77077
        (713) 496-7152 Fax: (713) 496-2290

★ **Inkwells,** either U.S. or foreign, figural or traveling, whether made of pottery, glass, or wood. Especially would like one made by *Tiffany*. He does not buy desk sets or fountain pens.

    Eli Hecht
    19 Evelyn Lane
    Syosset, NY 11791

★ **Pencil sharpeners.** Wants small hand-held figural pencil sharpeners made of metal, celluloid or *Bakelite*. She is only looking for those made in Germany or Japan during the 1930's and 40's. Don't offer her the small bronze colored sharpeners from Hong Kong made in the shape of various antiques. To sell your sharpener, give the shape, condition, country of origin, size, condition of the blade, and price.

    Martha Crouse
    4516 Brandon Lane
    Beltsville, MD 20705

★ **Pencil sharpeners,** but *only* figural hand-held sharpeners made of metal, celluloid, or Bakelite in Germany, Japan and the USA during the 1920's, 30's and 40's. Also wants metal souvenir type sold for last 20 years at tourist spots around the country. "I do not want plastic sharpeners or common die-cast antiqued sharpeners found at every flea market. Detailed description of condition is important. Dealers must set price wanted. Amateurs may request offers. I will gladly share my knowledge with beginning collectors."

    Bernice Kraker
    9800 McMillan Avenue
    Silver Spring, MD 20910

KITCHEN TOOLS

★ **Apple parers**, but only specific ones. He will pay from $200 to $500 for the following brands only: *Bergner, Browne's Nonpareil, Buchi, Champion, Climax by Brokaw, Dandy, Eagle, Electric, Empire State, Eureka, Excelsion, GEM, Jersey, Little Giant, Mammoth, Maxam, Monarch, Nonpareil, Oriole, Oscillator, Parker, Peerless, Returntable, Rices, SS Hersey, Selick's, Star (Foster & Cotton), Standard, Thompson, Tripp Bros., Victor, Wiggins,* and *Yankee.* He does not buy other brands or rusted or broken parers. Give the name and date, if marked, the material from which it's made, and the number of gears.

John Lambert
117 East High
Mount Vernon, OH 43050
(614) 393-2508

★ **Butter molds** that are hand carved of wood, ivory or clay. Will consider all sizes and forms, especially those with carvings of people, animals, or things rather than abstract patterns. Does not want machine carved items or anything new. Give the shape and size, material, and make a Xerox™ of the design.

Carl Cotting
1441 Crowell Road
Vienna, VA 22182
(703) 759-5646

★ **Hand can openers.**
Craig Dinner
PO Box 4399
Sunnyside, NY 11104
(718) 729-3850

★ **Tin can openers.** Will consider wall, counter, or hand operated kinds, but he wants old ones (1810-1940), not modern openers. There are more than 1,200 patents for can openers! Give all information that is stamped on the opener.

Joe Young
PO Box 587
Elgin, IL 60121
(847) 695-0108   Fax: (847) 695-1679   istamp2@msn.com

★ **Fancy or unusual nutcrackers,** big or small, made of iron, brass, wood, or any other material. A sketch or photocopy is suggested. Include dimensions, colors, and all writing or marks.

C. J. Davis
East 4400 English Point Road
Hayden Lake, ID 83835

★ **Toasters.** "I buy early electric toasters with unusual mechanisms and/or design, especially those made of porcelain in whole or in part and those with buttons or cranks that flip the toast. I do not want toasters in poor condition, or most pop-up types." Please give the make, model, color, and condition. Dealers, price your goods; amateurs may ask for offer. Will pay $600-$750 for a *Pan-Electric* porcelain toaster.

Dan Lunzmann
PO Box 482
Auburn, NE 68305
(402) 274-4555

★ **Toasters.** "I'll buy old or unusual electric toasters in good, non-corroded condition, as long as there are no pieces missing. I am especially interested in very old or very unusual toasters, porcelain models and ones with toast racks. Prices vary greatly, according to rarity. Mint condition examples and ones with original boxes bring the best prices, but toasters do not have to work to be desirable. Please call or write if you have specific questions." Give the maker's name and model number. A sketch is helpful, but a photo is best. An accurate description of condition is essential. Toasters bring $15 and up, with rare ones bringing you $1,000.

Joe Lukach
7111 Deframe Court
Arvada, CO 80004
(303) 422-8970 eves   Fax: (303) 623-2262

☆ **Egg beaters, cream whips and glass bottomed mixers** are wanted. Old cast iron beaters and or beaters with unusual mechanical actions are most sought after. Please describe the condition, size, markings, etc. A clear photo, sketch or photocopy is extremely helpful. Will buy some undamaged parts, but the better the condition of the mixer, the better the price. Most are valued $5 to $100/ Please, no beaters with plastic or stainless steel. Also no electric mixers except early *Horlicks*.

Reid Cooper
32942 Josheroo Court
Temecula, CA 92592
(909) 506-3348

★ **Egg beaters.** "I'll buy pre-1910 cast iron rotary crank egg beaters, the older the better, the more unusual the better." Also buys rotary cranks that came with jars, especially looking for the *E-A-S-Y* and *Family* brands. Does not want any beaters after 1910. Descriptions should include the height and any markings. He is author of the excellent *Beat This: The Eggbeater Chronicles* which you can order from him for $29.

Don Thornton
1345 Poplar Avenue
Sunnyvale, CA 94087

★ **Tunbridge Ware** is attractive woodware with geometric or mosaic designs, or with embedded pictures created with cut woods of different colors. She buys boxes, candlestick holders, tea caddies, etc. made in Tunbridge. These pieces are rarely marked. If in doubt, send a good photo or a photocopy of the patterned portion of the item.

> Lucille Malitz, Lucid Antiques
> PO Box KH
> Scarsdale, NY 10583
> (914) 636-7825

★ **Russian samovars** from before 1930. Please send picture with descriptive information and a statement of condition. He needs to know the size, shape, type of metal, markings, condition, and whether there are any additional matching pieces. He prefers you to price what you have. Wants written material on samovars, especially catalogs.

> Jerome Marks
> 120 Corporate Woods #260
> Rochester, NY 14623
> (716) 475-0220   Fax: (716) 475-0208

COOKBOOKS

★ **Hard and soft covered cookbooks,** especially soft cover advertising recipe books published by various food companies, such as *Jell-O, Rumford* baking powder, etc., especially fine condition ones from before 1900. Will pay $50 each for the 1930's *Jell-o* cookbooks based on the OZ books by Frank Baum. The founder of the Cook Book Collectors Club, and editor of its newsletter, does not want appliance company recipe books, diet books, or other modern health cookbooks such as heart and cholesterol related cookbooks. As with all books for sale, sellers should give complete bibliographic information. Sellers must price the books they offer.

> Col. Bob Allen
> Cookbook Collectors Club of America
> PO Box 56
> St. James, MO 65559
> (573) 265-8296 anytime

★ **Spiral bound church, community, charity, fund raiser, ethnic and other privately published cookbooks** with limited distribution.

> Bob Roberts
> PO Box 152
> Guilderland, NY 12084

TEA & COOKIES

★ **Figural cookie jars.** "I'll buy amusing, colorful jars in the shape of various people and animals dating before 1950. Especially want those depicting fairy tales, nursery rhyme and cartoon characters." Also buys **teapots and pitchers from the Art Deco era.** "I'll buy solid color Deco era teapots and pitchers that exemplify the streamlined, geometric designs of the late Art Deco/moderne period." Makers to look for are *Fiesta, Riviera, Harlequin,* and *Hall.* No items with gold trim or other decoration. No damage. Wants a photo or good description.

    Kier Linn
    2591 Military Avenue
    Los Angeles, CA 90064
       (310) 477-5229   Fax: (310) 268-8420

★ **Figural cookie jars** are wanted by Chicago's only shop devoted exclusively to kitchen counter novelties. Wants figural ceramic jars and jar tops, but nothing cracked or repaired. Jars that aren't figural aren't of interest. She also buys **figural salt and pepper shakers.** She declares a photo to be essential, plus wants you to describe all markings on the bottoms of jars or salt sets. Make certain to mention every chip! Prefers you to price what you want to sell. She charges $10 per jar to make appraisals for insurance or estate purposes.

    Mercedes DiRenzo, Jazz'e Junque
    3831 North Lincoln Avenue
    Chicago, IL 60613
       (312) 472-1500   Fax: (312) 472-1552

★ **Figural cookie jars,** especially featuring Disney, comic characters, advertising, Negroes, unique animals, etc. Brands to look for include *Poppytrail, Metlox, Brayton Laguna, USA, Abbingdon, McCoy,* others. Prefers no damage, but will consider some restoration. Please include a good description and sketch or photo for this major jar dealer.

    Loretta Hamburg
    PO Box 1305
    Woodland Hills, CA 91365
       (818) 346-9884   Fax: (818) 346-0215

★ **Teapots, tea tins and tea related items.** Check out your teapot as values range from $1 TO $1,000+. Items not of interest include teapots made in Japan since WWII and tea sets with sugars, creamers and trays. Dealers set your price but amateurs may request offers. No damage. Photo showing the decoration is helpful. Or you may reference it to her book *Teapots, A Collector's Guide* which is only $16. SASE a must.

    Tina M. Carter
    882 S. Mollison Avenue
    El Cajon, CA 92020
       (619) 440-5043

KITCHEN CERAMICS & GLASS

★ **Jadite green (a milky light green) or delphite blue (a similar blue) kitchen ware.** Wants bowls, reamers, canisters, **salt and peppers** and "anything else." A wide range of items, often in a variety of shapes, were made. Green pieces start at $4, with rare pieces reaching $100, whereas the blue is much more scarce with most pieces starting around $75. Tell what piece you have, its size, whether it is marked on the bottom (most weren't), and the condition, indicating any flakes or chips in the rim and base, and the condition of the painted decoration on canisters, salts, etc. There are other similar glass makers, and very little is marked, so it's best if Steve looks at a photo of what you have. "I feel badly for your readers," he says, "because most of what I'm offered isn't what I'm looking for, but I urge them to keep trying."

> Steve Kelley
> PO Box 695
> Desert Hot Springs, CA 92240
> (619) 329-3206

★ **Older fruit (canning) jars with unusual closures or in unusual colors** other than aqua or clear. Colors wanted include amber, brown, deep green, and shades of cobalt blue. Is willing to pay up to $400 for a pint sized embossed Cadiz jar with a glass screw top. Also wants pre-1960 **advertising**, promotional brochures, letterheads, signs and paper-weights from jar and bottle manufacturers, including **wooden canning jar boxes** or box ends, which generally bring $10-$30. Give the size and color, and report *exactly* what is embossed on the jar. Note all cracks, chips, dings, or unwashable stains.

> Tom and Deena Caniff
> 1223 Oak Grove Avenue
> Steubenville, OH 43952
> (614) 282-8918

★ **Pie birds.** Old pie funnels (often called birds) are decorative ceramic figures which sit in the center of a pie and allow the steam to be released. Invented in England for meat pies they have been used in the US for a century for fruit pies as well. A set of three decorated with cherries, apples and peaches could put over $100 in your pocket. Common ones to ignore are modern English ones stamped ENGLAND in the shape of clowns, police, frogs, and blackbirds. Tell this pioneer collector the shape, colors, and condition. Dealers price your goods, Amateurs may request offers. She edits *Piebirds Unlimited* newsletter.

> Lillian Cole
> 14 Harmony School Road
> Flemington, NJ 08822
> (908) 782-3198

★ **Glass knives** are wanted in most configurations and colors. Values run from $8 to $200 or more. It's worth having her check out your knife because it's difficult for amateurs to tell the rare from the common. Send a photocopy and describe color. She edits a quarterly newsletter about glass knives. If you want a reply, send an SASE.

> Adrienne Escoe
> 4448 Ironwood Avenue
> Seal Beach, CA 90740
> (310) 430-6479

★ **Salt and pepper shakers.** "I buy novelty figural shakers. I special-ize in Black Americana, Disney and other comic characters, Kewpies, advertising, and figural nodders which rock back and forth on a stationAry base. I also like German porcelain and shakers that are part of a condiment set (on a tray with mustard jar, etc.), especially those with comic characters, baseball, nursery rhyme, dinosaurs, and outer space themes. Anthropomorphic sets (animals or inanimate objects dressed as people) are of particular interest. Value is determined by condition, desirability, quality and rarity. Topic and form are more im-portant in determining value than age or country of origin. I don't buy non-figural glass or wooden sets, but there are hundreds of shakers I'll buy that aren't mentioned here. Please supply a description and or pho-tos."

> Judy Posner (May to Oct)   Judy Posner (Nov to April)
> Route 1   Box 273 W   4195 S Tamiami Trail #183W
> Effort, PA 18330   Venice Fl 34293
> (717) 629-6583 in PA   (941) 497-7149 in FL   judyandjef@aol.com

★ **Salt and pepper shakers.** "After 35 years, I'm looking only for fine condition novelty shakers, especially those featuring Negro stereo-types, but I also buy animals, people, and other types of objects. I'll buy your collection, no matter how large or small. Also want German-made **condiment sets with mustard jars**. About the only thing I don't want is reproductions or shakers made of wood. Please send a photo or video of your collection. I would like the seller to tell me the price they'd like for their collection." Larry is president of the Novelty Salt and Pepper Shakers Club ($20/year) and co-author of *Salt and Pepper Shakers: Over 1001 Shakers* (available from him for $22) as well as other books. Inquire as to what is currently available.

> Larry "The Salt & Pepper Man" Carey
> PO Box 329
> Mechanicsburg, PA 17055
> (717) 766-0868

CAST IRON COOKWARE

★ **Cast iron muffin pans,** gem pans, popover pans, and maple sugar molds in unusual patterns and shapes. Also interested in old catalogs, etc., which list multi-sectioned baking or muffin pans. Buys *any* cast iron item marked *Griswold*. Will pay $500+ for *Griswold* #13, 50, and 2800 muffin pans. Publishes a bimonthly 8 page newsletter, *Kettles 'n Cookware*, for $20. Author of the excellent *The Book of Griswold and Wagner*, autographed copies of which are $33 postpaid.

> David "The Pan Man" Smith
> PO Box B
> Perrysburg, NY 14129
> (716) 532-5154   DGSpanman@aol.com

★ **Early kitchen items made of cast iron** or of wood which has been folk carved or decorated are wanted by this important dealer.

> Louis Picek
> PO Box 340
> West Branch, IA 52358
> (319) 643-2065

★ **Iron pans and broilers in odd or decorative shapes,** including pans for muffins, popovers, rolls, and maple sugar molds. Roll pans shaped like hearts bring $100 and up, while those shaped like fruits and vegetables are worth $150. Pans made by *GF Filley* start at $75. Cast iron broilers look like strange frying pans with grid work, slots, and holes. Not interested in reproductions (they have rough surface and grind marks) or in tin pans of any type. Trace your pans or photocopy. Dave write the excellent *Book of Griswold and Wagner*, autographed copies of which are $33 postpaid.

> David "The Pan Man" Smith
> PO Box B
> Perrysburg, NY 14129
> (716) 532-5154   DGSpanman@aol.com

★ **Griswold brand cast iron.** This veteran collector is interested in muffin pans, molds, skillets with lids, sad irons, kettles with lids, rectanglular and French style waffle irons, etc., but only those by Griswold. Buys only less common items in excellent condition.

> Alan Stone
> PO Box 500 or 5170 County Road 33
> Honeoye, NY 14471
> (716) 229-2700

OTHER CAST IRON

★ **Useful items made from cast iron.** Many types of household items are wanted including:
- **Trivets** from pre WWII;
- **Miniature or unusual irons,** "not ordinary sad irons" he says;
- **Small stoves,** either toys or salesmen's samples;
- **Sprinklers;**
- **Stringholders;**
- **Doorstops, paperweights** and **bookends** with figures or ads;
- **Banks and toys.**

"I'm interested in anything unusual that isn't extremely heavy, like andirons" but I don't want reproductions. Since it may be hard for you to know what's common and what's not, ask by sending a photo and description along with an SASE. Jim is co-author of *Collector's Guide to Trivets and Stands.*

      Jim Ellwood, Irontiques
      7077 East Main #4
      Scottsdale, AZ 85251
        (602) 947-9679 days

★ **All useful items made from cast iron** in the shape of figures. "I'll buy doorstops, bottle openers, lawn sprinklers, paperweights, pencil holders, match holders, string holders, windmill weights, horse weights, shooting gallery targets, and firemarks. I have no interest in buying modern reproductions and castings but I will buy some non figural cast iron cookware." Include your phone number and an SASE.

      Craig Dinner
      PO Box 4399
      Sunnyside, NY 11104
        (718) 729-3850

★ **Cast iron doorstops and windmill weights** are sought by this prominent dealer. No reproductions or modern pieces.

      Louis Picek, Main Street Antiques
      PO Box 340
      West Branch, IA 52358
        (319) 643-2065

★ **Cast iron lawn sprinklers, doorstops, windmill weights, shooting gallery targets, croquet wickets** and other figural cast iron. Does not want reproductions, damaged and repaired items, items with new paint or "small shooting gallery targets such as ducks and birds." Please include color photo, phone number, and price range you'd like.

      Richard Tucker, Argyle Antiques
      PO Box 262
      Argyle, TX 76226
        (817) 464-3752   Fax: (817) 464-7293

SILVERWARE & TABLE ITEMS

★ **Sterling flatware and serving pieces** are wanted by the nation's largest buyer and seller of second hand sterling tableware. "If a customer sends a SASE and the name of their pattern and its maker, we will send a written offer." If you do not know the name of the pattern, make a picture on a copy machine and list how many pieces you have. "Most sterling is standard, so if you know the name of the pattern, we know exactly what you have. As a result, we do not need to see what you have before buying. Please note, we do not make offers on non-standard items. We don't offer on coin silver, souvenir items, old unmarked tea sets, and the like, although we will consider them for purchase if you send a photograph or photocopy and set the price you want. We only make offers on standard items." If an item is damaged, worn, or monogrammed, be certain to note that fact. MidweSterling also repairs and restores flatware.

    Thomas Ridley, Head Buyer
    MidweSterling
    4311 NE Vivion Road, Dept HY
    Kansas City, MO 64119
       (816) 454-1990   Fax: (816) 454-1605

★ **Sterling and silver plated flatware,** especially made by *Holmes & Edwards, 1847 Rogers,* and *Community.* Also all old grape patterns. Send the information on the back of your silver, and a photocopy if you don't know the name of the pattern. An SASE will get you a pattern guide. Particularly interested in more unusual pieces such as pie forks, punch ladles, ice tongs, sardine forks, etc. "We do not want monogrammed, damaged or worn silver except large serving pieces or very rare patterns." A 30 year veteran of buying through the mail.

    L.C. Fisher
    Silver Exchange
    Route 8 Box 554 (Hwy 190 East)
    Huntsville, TX 77340
       (409) 295-7661

★ **Sterling silver flatware and serving pieces** as well as novelty items such as goblets, mint julep cups, and trays, especially in elaborate antique patterns. You should take photos of larger pieces, and make photocopies of flatware. Everything must be in fine condition, cautions this 25 year veteran dealer. Their *Silver Flatware: An Illustrated Guide to Pieces, Manufacturers and Care* is helpful in identifying what you have for sale. It is available from the authors for only $15 postpaid.

    Helen & Duncan Cox
    As You Like It Silver Shop
    3025 Magazine Street
    New Orleans, LA 70117
       (800) 828-2311   Fax: (504) 895-4149

★ **Modern European sterling silver** from French, Scandinavian, Italian, and U.K. companies like *Christfofle, Buccellati, Puiforcat, Ricci, Puiforcat, Jensen Cohr, Frigast, Bruckmann,* etc. Buys and sells.
> Russ Burkett
> PO Box 4231
> Mission Viejo, CA 92690
>   (714) 364-3844

★ **Pickle castors** and other castor sets for the Victorian table. Sets must be complete and in fine condition, with no missing or broken parts. A photo is suggested.
> Betty Bird
> Antiques, Etc.
> 107 Ida Street
> Mt. Shasta, CA 96067
>   (916) 926-2231

★ **Unusual condiment sets.** Combination salt, pepper, and mustard sets are wanted if they are unusual and figural. Wants pieces without chips or repairs, but will consider slightly damaged goods if the piece is extremely unusual. Especially likes German sets, and those with designs related to water. A picture is important.
> Sylvia Tompkins
> 25-C Center Drive
> Lancaster, PA 17601
>   (717) 569-9788

★ **Victorian figural silverplate napkin rings.** Wants old figural napkin rings. Describe your rings to her well, including all markings, and "I'll probably know what you have."
> Sandra Whitson
> PO Box 272
> Lititz, PA 17543
>   (717) 626-4978   Fax: (717) 626-7625

★ **Napkin rings and other small silver objects** such as **children's rattles**, which are made of silver in the shape of animals, people or other objects. Must be in fine condition. A photo is suggested, Make sure to list all names, numbers and other marks.
> Betty Bird
> Antiques, Etc.
> 107 Ida Street
> Mt. Shasta, CA 96067
>   (916) 926-2231

★ **Open salt cellars.** Salt cellars are small open bowls, often with a tiny spoon, that were used instead of salt shakers at the table. They can be almost any material or shape, including human, animal, and other figures. "I am especially looking for art glass, colored glass, pressed pattern glass and silver with colored glass liners, and pay from a few dollars to hundreds, depending on the quality and rarity. I do not want plain clear glass (except in sets), but I will buy individual salt spoons. To sell to me, you need to provide a clear photo, dimensions and a description of any markings you find on the piece. Condition is vital. Any chips, cracks, flakes, or nicks may drop the value by 70% or more. Every major glass company, china manufacturer and potter, as well as many silversmiths, made these so there are plenty out there somewhere." Buys collections or individual cellars. Will also buy **condiment sets and salt and pepper sets which contain open salt cellars.**

> Betty Bird
> Antiques, Etc.
> 107 Ida Street
> Mt. Shasta, CA 96067
> (916) 926-2231

★ **Toast racks** (silver, pewter, copper or ceramic frames, often footed, with 4-8 wire racks to hold toast upright at the table). Values from $25 to $175 depending on fanciness and rarity. Good condition only. Please draw a picture of any maker's marks and give measurements.

> Carol Payne
> Carol's Gallery
> 14455 Big Basin Way
> Saratoga, CA 95070
> (408) 867-7055

★ **Tea caddies** are boxes for holding loose tea at the table and are made of wood, silver, ceramic, tortoise shell, or other materials Values vary from $50 to $300 depending on rarity and quality. Photos helpful. Describe size, shape, decoration, and condition. Xerox™ the bottom to show marks if you can't draw accurately.

> Carol Payne
> 14455 Big Basin Way
> Saratoga, CA 95070
> (408) 867-7055

SPOONS

★ **Sterling silver souvenir spoons**, U.S. or foreign, particularly those made between 1890 and 1920. "Almost any spoon which is a turn-of-the-century quality souvenir will be considered for purchase or accepted on consignment for my auctions." Of most interest are spoons with:
  • Enameled bowls, especially *Gorham;*
  • Figural handles;
  • Special topics like Negroes, Indians, military, coins, music,
      historic sites, etc.;
  • Famous persons, especially on European spoons;
  • World's Fair themes before 1920.
"I only want old, pre-WWI souvenir spoons, not modern spoons which are typically sold in airports and tourist shops." Values range from a few dollars for some, $20-$30 for most, to more than $300 for top items like the *Gorham* spoon with their factory depicted in the bowl. Please make a photocopy of your spoon(s) and make a drawing or copy of the markings on the back. If you don't Xerox™ the spoon, please give the total length.
  Chris McGlothlin
  "The Original Spoon Auctioneer"
  780 Rock Springs Road
  Kingsport, TN 37664
    (423) 239-6776

★ **Sterling spoons with "cute" Negro figures.** Will pay up to $150 for enameled teaspoons and $100 for enameled demitasse spoons.
  Elijah Singley
  2301 Noble Avenue
  Springfield, IL 62704
    (217) 546-5143 eves

★ **Silver spoons with advertising** on them. Either sterling or plate.
  W.T. Atkinson
  1217 Bayside Circle West
  Wilmington, NC 28405

Spoons are similar to all other antiques and collectibles in that you should not attempt to clean, polish, or repair them prior to offering them for sale.

HOW TO SELL CHINA

The first thing to do if you plan to sell china is to take a long hard look at what you have. *Then ask yourself, "Would I want to buy this and use it?"*

No one wants chipped, stained, or damaged items. *Dishes less than 150 years old must be in perfect condition to find a buyer. Don't waste time offering items with chips and/or cracks, crazing, heavy knife scratches and pattern wear. Pay particular attention to gold trim. If the gold is worn to where you can see the china underneath, you must tell a buyer that. Don't be surprised if the value of your china drops by 60% to 80% if gold is worn.*

Your set does not have to be complete to sell. *That's the big advantage to selling to matching services. Since their goal is to fill in someone else's china, your set doesn't have to be complete to have some value.*

Serving pieces and items with lids are worth the most. *Serving pieces, especially large pieces and those with lids (like soup tureens) are harder to find and as a result worth more than ordinary table settings. The more unusual the piece, the more likely it is to have a market. Cups and saucers are the most common pieces.*

You can sell your china with a few simple steps. *Begin by listing the pieces, and how many of each you have. Do not list damaged pieces. If you don't know the pattern name, don't despair. It is easy to tell buyers what you have, even when you don't know yourself.*

A photocopy (Xerox™) machine is a seller's best friend. *Send a photocopy of the front and back of a small plate and indicate the colors in your pattern and the color of the maker's mark on the back (as some companies use color codes). Photocopies usually give excellent detail, so will give an expert an accurate look at what you have. Many china companies have similar names. There are many Wedgwood and Haviland companies. The marks on the bottom tell experts what you have.*

If possible, take a close up 35mm photograph. If you are able to take sharp, close-up 35mm photographs, include a photo which shows the shape of a cup handle. If you can't take photos, a sketch which shows the shape of the handle and base of the cup compared to the bowl of the cup can be very useful.

Keep your expectations of value reasonable. Don't expect to be paid a fortune for old china just because it belonged to great granny. China patterns and companies fall in and out of favor. Recent trends toward informality mean you can't assume people are waiting to purchase your old china, silver, or glassware, no matter how lovely. If your set is reasonably complete, or not a popular pattern, consider giving it to a friend or relative who has admired it and would use it.

Packing china is not difficult as long as two pieces never touch. The buyer will provide packing instructions. If packed properly, china can be shipped around the world safely as long as two pieces of china don't touch while packed. Padding such as bubble pack, styrofoam sheets, or similar material must separate every packed piece. Lids will chip or break if they are left on sugar bowls or other covered dishes while they are being shipped. Never wrap china in newspaper as the ink can rub off onto the china are ruin its value.

Remember these simple steps:

• List how many of each type item (plates, saucers, cups, and other items) you have;

• Include a color photograph or a b/w photocopy which indicates the colors and patterns;

• Include a drawing or Xerox™ of all marks on the bottom of the china, remembering to indicate the color of the marks.

CHINA

★ **China, crystal, and flatware** is sought for resale. More than 65,000 different patterns from 1,200 American, European, and Japanese manufacturers will be purchased if in fine condition. Chips, cracks, stains, or serious knife marks are not acceptable. Pieces with some pattern or gold wear may be purchased if the pattern is rare or in high demand. Provide the maker's name, pattern name and/or number, and an accurate count of what and how many pieces are available. If you do not know the pattern or the manufacturer, make a Xerox™ of a small plate and describe the colors, or make a copy of a place setting of silverware along with any serving pieces you have, and include whatever is written on the back of your silver. A good sharp photo is always helpful, particularly with stemware. They have 3,200,000 pieces in stock and will try to fill your china, crystal, or silverware needs.

> Robert Page
> Replacements, Ltd.
> 1089 Knox Road or PO Box 26029
> Greensboro, NC 27420
> (800) 737-5223 Fax: (910) 697-3100 ReplaceLtd@aol.com

★ *Wedgwood*, *Adams*, *Coalport*, and *Midwinter* **dinnerware** in discontinued patterns is wanted by one of the leading experts on discontinued *Wedgwood* dinnerware in the United States. All pieces must be in mint condition, with no chips, cracks, crazing (age lines), stains, or severe scratches. Please list the mint condition pieces only, and how many of each type. Give the dimensions of plates and bowls. Note the maker and the pattern, if you can. If you do not know the maker or the name of the pattern, please send a photocopy or photo of one of the plates, front and back. She does not want *Johnson Brothers* or *Franciscan* dinnerware (two other companies owned by *Wedgwood*) nor does she want *Waterford* crystal. Note that *Enoch Wedgwood* and *Wedgwood, Ltd.* are not the same as *Wedgwood* and ARE NOT WANTED.

> Gloria Voss Beyer, A Wedgwood China Cupboard
> 740 North Honey Creek Parkway
> Milwaukee, WI 53213
> (414) 259-1025

★ **American and English china and earthenware** by the following makers: *Booths, Castelton, Coallport, Franciscan, Flintridge, Gorham, Hammersley, Hohnson Brothers, Lenox, Minton, Pickard, Royal Albert, Royal Doulton, Royal Winton, Royal Worcester, Shelley, Spode,* and *Wedgwood.* Dinnerware must be in like new condition.

> Jacquelynn Ives, China Matching
> 219 North Milwaukee Street
> Milwaukee, WI 53202
> (414) 272-8880 Fax: (414) 272-0361

★ **Sets and pieces of obsolete dinner china.** Primarily interested in English china, but buys American, European and Japanese patterns. Buys *Adams, Aynsley, Coalport, Minton, Paragon, Rosenthal, Spode, Royal Albert, Royal Crown Derby, Royal Doulton, Royal Worcester, Shelley, Wedgwood* and others. European chinas wanted are *Bernardaud & Co, Elite, M. Redon, MZ, Schumann, T&V* and *Vignaud. Oxford, Castleton, Theodore Haviland, Haviland & Company, Franciscan, Syracuse, Pickard, Flintridge-Gorham, Lenox* and some crystal is also of interest. They do business worldwide and will make offers for items they can use. Items *must* be in excellent condition. If you wish china or stemware appraised, there is a fee, which is refundable if and when they buy your dishes. Send a Xerox™ of the pattern and the markings on the underneath. Note the colors of the markings and all pattern elements. They do not buy giftware, figurines, or floral arrangements. Remember, no SASE to foreign countries.

    Old China Patterns Limited
    1560 Brimley Road
    Scarborough, ON
    M1P 3G9 CANADA
       (416) 299-8880   Fax: (416) 299-4721

★ **Discontinued English and American china patterns** in perfect condition, produced by *Castleton, Franciscan, French Haviland, Lenox, Spode, Minton, Pickard, Royal Doulton, Royal Worcester, Syracuse, Wedgwood,* etc. "We buy sets or incomplete sets consisting of ten pieces or more. For patterns in demand we buy outright; others are listed in our computer system and customers notified as to availability and prices." They do not want to buy Japanese china or *anything* imperfect. Prefers you to set the selling price, but will make offers.

    J. Warren Roundhill
    Patterns Unlimited TOT
    PO Box 15238
    Seattle, WA 98115
       (206) 523-9710   Fax: (206) 524-1252

★ **French, American, or English china and stemware,** especially pieces by *Haviland, Castleton, Franciscan, Oxford, Royal Doulton, Lenox, Spode, Syracuse,* and *Wedgwood.* Wants **stemware** by *Cambridge, Duncan, Fostoria, Heisey, Imperial, Lenox, Rock Sharp,* and *Tiffin.* List only the perfect pieces, and give the measurements of all serving pieces. She does not buy German or Japanese china. Medley has been a dealer for 20+ years.

    Laura Medley
    Laura's China & Crystal
    2625 West Britton Road
    Oklahoma City, OK 73120
       (405) 755-0582

★ *Wedgwood* **commemorative transfer print china.** Earthenware or bone china plates, hollow ware, trivets, tiles, etc., that contain American scenes, views of historic places, children's topics, or scenes from literature. "We mainly want items of American interest, but will also buy some Canadian and Australian scenes." These pieces bear backstamps marked JOSIAH WEDGWOOD & SONS, WEDGWOOD ETRURIA or ETRURIA & BARLASTON. Calendar tiles are from 1879 to 1929. Those before 1890 are worth in excess of $200. Jugs such as the Washington Light Infantry depicting the Civil War are worth in excess of $400 each. "It's hard to tell what we don't want. People are better off to inquire by giving a good description or sending a photo or Xerox™ of the item and its marks. Some items will have to be seen before we can make an offer."

    Benton and Beverly Rosen, Mansion House
    9 Kenilworth Way
    Pawtucket, RI 02860
        (401) 722-2927 winter   (508) 759-4303 summer

★ *Haviland* **china for resale.** Buys sets or single unusual pieces. Especially wants jardinieres, claret jugs, unusual tea or toast sets, free form salads, syrup jugs, spoon trays, tea caddies, lemonade sets, and other unusual pieces. No individual saucers. If your Limoge china isn't marked *Haviland*, she doesn't want it. Pieces must be in mint condition with no wear or scratches. To sell your dishes, give the pattern name on the back-stamp, a photocopy of the pattern, and note the colors. Holly has 22,000 pieces in stock and has a computerized search service to help customers find other dishes.

    Holly B. Thomas, Auld Lang Syne
    6321 Delta Court
    Magalia, CA 95954
        (800) 709-8060

★ *Royal Doulton, Royal Worcester,* **and** *Fitz and Floyd* **fine china and crystal by** *Fostoria, Gorham, Lenox, Royal Doulton* and selected patterns of *Mikasa* **and** *Noritake* are purchased for stock. Buys whole or partial sets. Some *Spode, Wedgwood* and *Willeroy and Boch* will be "purchased if I have a ready customer." She cannot use worn, damaged, or repaired pieces. "If an item is in fine condition, but I do not wish to buy it, I will try to refer the seller to someone else who may." Give the maker and pattern name and number. Send a Xerox™ if convenient for you. Connie has inherited the family business from her mom, Freda Bell, a lady whom we have recommended for years.

    Connie Stolz, China Match & Crystal Match
    72 Longacre Road
    Rochester, NY 14621
        (716) 338-3781

★ **Series Ware by *Royal Doulton*** includes hundreds of shapes and patterns of pitchers, mugs, plates, and other useful but highly decorated items. This popular transfer ware with a hand-painted look includes a wide variety of themes such as motoring, golfing, fishing, and coaching. Value is dependent on the rarity and desirability of the form and the image. There have been four books written on *Doulton* Series Ware, so you can get information at your local public library. If your item is for sale, call Ed, who has edited price guides to *Royal Doulton*. Also buys *Royal Doulton* **figurines, figural bottles and red animals** (see his listings in this book under Animals, Whiskey, and Figurines for more information). He is not interested in buying dinnerware, and does not do pattern matching.

      Ed Pascoe, Pascoe & Co.
      101 Almeria Avenue
      Coral Gables, FL 33134
         (800) 872-0195   Fax: (305) 445-3305

★ **Grandmother's Ware - Chelsea - Applied Sprigware...** Whatever you call it, this mid 1800's English china, ironstone, stoneware and porcelain is sought by this veteran collector-dealer who is currently writing a book on this white ware with applied blue/lavender sprigs (grape, thistles, etc) accompanied by other design elements. She wants mugs, tureens, toilet sets, vases, and more. "I do not buy common items with chips on rims, major cracks, or bad stains (hairline cracks make most items worth less than $10) but will buy very rare items in less than perfect condition." She does not want common cups and saucers with simple sprigs. Tell her the type of item, size, pattern, and maker's mark. Photo if possible. Xerox™ copy of the pattern is a good idea. "I am trying to document as many makers and motifs as possible, and would love to hear from other collectors."

      Stephanie Schnatz
      17 Tallow Court
      Baltimore, MD 21244
         (410) 944-0819

★ **Dishes with dark blue decoration** made in England or the U.S. before 1900. Especially wants pieces with impressed marks such as CLEWS, ADAMS, or HALL. Teapots, sugars, creamers, cups and saucers are particularly wanted, Staffordshire, flow blue, *Spode, Wedgwood* and historical patterns are all desirable, although items marked E.WEDGWOOD are not *the* Wedgwood and are a lot less valuable. Xerox™ flat pieces, photograph others. Send photo, description of condition and accurate drawing of marks found on the bottom if you'd like an offer.

      Carol Payne, Carol's Gallery
      14455 Big Basin Way
      Saratoga, CA 95070
         (408) 867-7055

★ *Noritake* **china in "Azalea" or "Tree in the Meadow"** patterns in any quantity from single pieces to entire sets, as long are there are no chips, cracks, or worn gold or paint. Azalea pieces are backstamped "#19322." Tree in the Meadow pieces must have blue water in the foreground and a tree in the rear of the house. Serving pieces, children's sets, and salesmen's samples are the most desirable and will bring from $100 to $1,000. Does not want "Azalea" pattern with a blue backstamp that reads NIPPON. Include the dimensions of your pieces.

    Ken Kipp or Gloria Munsell
    PO Box 116
    Allenwood, PA 17810
    (717) 538-1440

★ **Nippon and** *Noritake* **china**. "We're seeking large vases, urns, portrait pieces, dolls, chocolate and tea sets, jugs, wall plaques, smoke sets, humidors, and anything else that's quality and perfect. We'll buy *Coralene, Moriage*, blown-outs, rectangulars, pieces with silver overlay, you name it! We're also in the market for *Noritake* with Art Deco decorations of men and women. Call or write if you have any."

    Mark Griffin and Earl Smith
    1417 Steele Street
    Fort Myers, FL 33901
    (800) 726-1489   Nippononly@aol.com

★ **Chintz china** with an all-over floral design made in England. All except damaged items or items in the "Winter Summertime" pattern.

    Russell Mascieri
    13 Running Water Court
    Medford, NJ 08055

★ **Sets or pieces of German, Bavarian, Czechoslovakian, and Austrian china** in fine condition. Companies stocked include *Johann Haviland, Bavarian, Heinrich, Fronconia, Meissen, Rosenthal Thomas, Royal Heidelberg, Krautheim,* and many more. China need not be old, just discontinued. Also buys **a few French patterns**, but no *Haviland*, Japanese china, or English china. "We buy no china with cracks, crazing, chips, or with the color in a pattern worn off, although we will accept pieces with a slight amount of gold wear. Please send a colored photocopy of a 6" or 8" plate. Copy the front for the design and the back so we can see the hallmark. We also need a color photo of a plate and a cup in silhouette to see the shape of the cup handle and base. We will quote a fair price for any items we can use. If we cannot use what you have, we will try to tell you how to sell it in your locality."

    Joan Nackman
    56 Meadowbrook
    Ballwin, MO 63011
    (314) 227-3444

★ **Phoenix bird china,** both English and Japanese, is wanted. As an advanced collector, she is interested **only** in serving pieces and unusual shapes not normally found in a dinner set. She does not want cups, saucers, small sauce dishes, bread & butter plates, or 7 1/4" salad plates. Please give condition, noting any hairline cracks. Give the diameter of plates or bowls, and describe any markings on the bottom. She wants you to set the price, so you might want to look at her books on Phoenix, available at $16 each.

    Joan Oates
    685 South Washington
    Constantine, MI 49042
      (616) 435-8353

★ **Flying phoenix china.**
    Carl Cotting
    1441 Crowell Road
    Vienna, VA 22182
      (703) 759-5646

★ *Clarus Ware* **plates, bowls, vases and other china.** "We also buy old pieces of *Pope Gosser China Ware* and want any vase, bowl, plate, or other china signed AST VAN HISE."

    C.W. and Hilda Roderick
    27858 TR 31
    Warsaw, OH 43844
      (614) 824-3083

★ *Clarice Cliff Bizarre Ware.* This English hand painted pottery is decorated with fanciful, geometric, and floral themes. Most pieces are marked, often with the name of the artist, but usually CLARICE CLIFF or BIZARRE. Does not want transfer patterns, only painted ones such as Crocus, Fantasque, Delecia, Caprice, Ravel, and many others. A photo or photocopy is very important as the company made so many patterns, it's almost impossible to know which you have without seeing it.

    Darryl Rehr
    2591 Military Avenue
    Los Angeles, CA 90064
      (310) 477-5229   Fax: (310) 268-8420

★ *Warwick* **china, especially portrait items.** Include a photo with your complete description, and he'll return it. Promises to answer every letter regarding the work of this fine American china maker. Prefers you to set the price wanted, but "amateurs should still write."

    Jeff Mauck
    1900 Warwood Avenue
    Wheeling WV 26003
      (304) 277-2356

★ **Autumn Leaf** (*Jewel Tea*) **china** and other items marked with *Jewel Tea's* red, orange, and brown leaf pattern. There are 300+ different pieces of Autumn Leaf china; it takes an expert to tell the difference between a $10 piece and a $100 piece. Common cups, saucers, plates, and mixing bowls are only a dollar or two, but items like candle holders, teapots, bud vases, and butter dishes can bring $40 to $500 each, with a few worth more than $1,500. **Silverplated and stainless steel *Jewel Tea* tableware** is also highly collectible, bringing $10/$15 per item, with some as much as $100. **Other Autumn Leaf products**, including canisters, bean pots, and linens are also worth an inquiry. "If your item is in good condition, but it's not something I want to buy, I've got a dozen friends whom I can route you to." Send an SASE. Dimensions are a good idea. Annual membership in the National Autumn Leaf Collector's Club includes a 40+ page newsletter and is only $20.

> Tom Whipple
> National Autumn Leaf Collector's Club
> 62200 East 236 Road
> Wyandotte, OK 74370
>   (918) 786-7632   twhippl@inworks.net

★ *Buffalo Pottery* or *Buffalo* **china.** "I'll buy almost any marked piece made in that factory," he says.

> Seymour Altman
> 8970 Main Street
> Clarence, NY 14031
>   (716) 634-4488

★ *Coors* **pottery and porcelain**, including lines of dinnerware, art pottery, older ashtrays, Colorado State Fair memorabilia, spittoons, malted milk containers, advertising (including paper), etc. "I also buy other *Coors* Malted Milk and dairy items such as labels, boxes, back bar containers, milk bottles, and all advertising related to them." Does not want small vases, common mugs with lions on them, newer bar ashtrays, *Coors Beer* ads, or anything newer than 1950. "You may call my toll free number, workdays 9-5 MST, to get an estimate or offer on *Coors* pottery. I cannot answer questions about brewery items, but if you have something very old, I may be able to recommend a buyer."

> Jo Ellen Winther
> 8449 West 75th Way
> Arvada, CO 80005
> (800) 872-2345 days   (303) 421-2371 eves   Fax: (303) 431-5302

★ **Oyster plates.** Nothing damaged, please.

> Sheldon Katz
> 211 Roanoke Avenue
> Riverhead, NY 11901
>   (516) 369-1100

★ **Eggcups.** If you have a fine eggcup to sell, the *Eggcup Collectors Corner* may be your best source of information. Sample copies of this club newsletter cost only $5 and will give you insights into cups and their prices, plus a bibliography. When you order your sample, tell Joan why you want one and she'll pick an appropriate issue. Eggcup Collectors' Club members share information about buying and selling.

> Joan George, editor
> *Eggcup Collectors Corner*
> 67 Stevens Ave.
> Old Bridge, NJ 08857
> (908) 679-8924

★ **Roseville Juvenile china** designed for children not dolls.

> Bill and Linda Montgomery
> 12111 SE River Road
> Milwaukee, OR 97222
> (503) 652-2992

★ **Children's dishes.** "Any china used by children to eat or drink" is sought, "but I prefer American items, and I prefer those made by *Roseville* (both unmarked and those marked R on the bottom), *S.E.G., Paul Revere* or *Dedham.* No damaged pieces."

> Steve Kelley
> PO Box 695
> Desert Hot Springs, CA 92240
> (619) 329-3206

Packing china for shipment is not as hard as you think, but does require some care. Never allow two pieces to touch. Ask your buyer for specific packing instructions.

★ **Old pictorial souvenir china** with views of various towns, streets, and places of interest before 1930. "I prefer cups, vases, unusual shapes, and three dimensional figures, but some plates are OK. I am especially interested in pictorial china with New England views, but all old U.S. pictorial souvenir china will be considered. I don't want 1950's and 60's church plates." Indicate what the scene is, where the item was made, and whether there are any cracks or chips. Gary publishes *Antique Pictorial Souvenirs Buyer's Guide.*

> Gary Leveille
> PO Box 562
> Great Barrington, MA 01230
> (413) 528-5490

★ **College plates** depicting scenes or seals of universities and colleges. Prefers those made by *Wedgwood, Spode* and *Lamberton*. Items must be in perfect condition without cracks or chips, even if they have been professionally restored. They prefer you to set the price you want, but will make offers.

> Pat or Bill Klein
> PO Box 262
> East Berlin, CT 06023
>   (860) 828-3973 eves

★ **Calendar plates.** This relatively new collector/dealer wants all calendar plates, 1875 to 1949, especially those that were advertising giveaways. He does not buy those that are damaged, chipped or worn, however. Give the date, condition and the scene depicted on the plate. He offers $150 for a 1900 *Wedgwood* plate and $2,000 for a 1909 by *Deldare*. He publishes a quarterly newsletter, *The Calendar*.

> Alan Gumtow
> Odd Things
> 710 North Lake Shore Drive
> Tower Lakes, IL 60010
>   (847) 526-5319 voice and fax

★ **Presidential and patriotic English urns, vases and mugs** with American historical motifs, pictures of political figures, battles, or famous events. May be any type of china by any maker. A delft teapot advocating NO STAMP ACT would bring around $8,000.

> Rex Stark
> 49 Wethersfield Road
> Bellingham, MA 02019
>   (508) 966-0994

★ **Advertising china made by *Royal Doulton*.** All types including ashtrays, jugs, mugs, bottles, ginger beers, display signs. Old and rare pieces do not have to be in perfect condition to be considered for purchase, but you must indicate any flaws in your description. Make sure to mention the item, the product being advertised, size, color, condition, and any markings.

> Diane Alexander
> 20834 San Simeon Way #70-C
> North Miami Beach, FL 33179
>   (305) 770-4422

TIPS ON SELLING POTTERY AND GLASS

Pottery, porcelain, china, bisque, parian, and stoneware are names which confuse amateur sellers. Fortunately, to sell the **Trash or Treasure** *way, you need to know only the simplest basics about pottery.*

All these names describe ceramics or earthenware made from one form or another of clay. The different names signify the quality and colors of the raw materials and the processes by which they are fired and decorated. You don't need to know too much more than that, because I'm going to steer you to people who care about those distinctions and can make them for you. If you want to explore the topic, head for your local public library.

Pottery ranges in value from a few pennies to thousands of dollars. *Collectors often pay well for items once thought ordinary, so take caution when disposing of pottery items of all types. Valuable pottery is not always easy for the untrained eye (that's you) to detect.*

The output of a few 20th century factories such as Rookwood, Roseville, Cowan, Fulper, and Weller are popular, *while the work of other makers is ignored by collectors. Some one-person operations, like that of eccentric George "The Mad Potter of Biloxi" Ohr, created unusual pottery in great demand today.*

Stoneware crocks were made in unimaginative shapes, but their folksy decorations (usually in blue on a gray crock) make them desirable. Prices can reach $20,000 or more, although most sell for less than $300 A reader reports being told by his local antique dealer his crock was worth about $50. He turned to a previous edition of **Trash or Treasure** *and found crock expert Dick Hume who paid $4,800 for the same crock. You'll meet Dick in a few pages.*

Determining the value of earthenware is not easy. The quality of the clay and the delicacy of the painting do not guarantee collector interest and high prices. Popularity and scarcity do.

TIPS ON SELLING POTTERY AND GLASS (CON'T)

The same is true of glass. *The work of some companies and periods is hotly sought after, while other older and more rare glass goes relatively ignored.*

Glass, like clay, is manufactured into many forms and colors, some worth tens of thousands of dollars, others only worth recycling! Advice in selling glass is essential since it is difficult for the amateur to tell the good from the bad, the common from that worth $100 or more.

Because color has so much to do with value of both glass and earthenware, a photo is almost essential to sell anything. An otherwise identical piece of glass or pottery can be worth fifty times as much in one color as in another. If you can't send a photo, "at the very least," advises Majolica buyer Denise Sater, "accurately describe the color, give the dimensions, patterns, and marks, along with a statement of condition."

When purchasing earthenware or glass, buyers seldom want chipped, stained, or damaged items, although a few very large and/or rare "bruised" pieces may find a market at a small percent of the price of a perfect one.

Always inspect glass and pottery carefully for damage. Look along all rims, including the base, lid and inside lip. Check the top and bottom for cracks. The best way to do this is to run your fingernail along the top and other edges. Your fingernail will find cracks your eye will miss.

Pottery and glass can be shipped safely. Buyers will give you specific instructions telling you how they want their newly purchased items packed. If you double box your breakables you'll usually be safe.

A number of the buyers you'll meet in the next few pages have written books, price guides, and catalogs. Others edit newsletters or are officers in clubs.

They are all valuable sources of information capable of putting money in your pocket. I recommend them.

POTTERY & CERAMICS (earthenware)

★ **American art pottery of all types.** Buys pottery from *Fulper, Paul Revere, Rookwood, Grueby, Dedham, TECO, Tiffany, Clewell, Marblehead, Saturday Evening Girls, Newcomb College, George Ohr, Van Briggle, Cowan, Grand Feu, Losanti, New Orleans Art Pottery, Robineau,* and other quality American art pottery. Also buys good **quality European pottery** such as *Martin Bros, Moorcroft,* and others. Especially likes large and unusual pieces, and has been known to consider damaged pieces if they are important. "If you have any doubts, phone me and I will be glad to be of assistance."

> Robert Berman, Le Poulaille
> 441 South Jackson Street
> Media, PA 19063
> (610) 566-1516

★ *Rookwood* **and other art pottery** is wanted by the world's largest dealer in *Rookwood,* who also buys other American and European art pottery, both production and artist-signed pieces. Brand names they will buy include *Grueby, Teco, Van Briggle, Newcomb, Marblehead, Weller, UND, Roseville, Fulper, Overbeck,* and *Cowan* among American companies. European pottery makers of interest include *Moorcroft, Massier, Amphora, Gustavsberg, Bock, Freres, Deck, Lachenal, Haviland, Robj, Longwy, Delaherche, Picasso, Zsolnay, Lauger, Rorstrand, Clarice Cliff* and *Ruskin.* Pieces made between 1890 and 1950 are generally the most desirable. Quality *Rookwood* pieces will be considered even if damaged, although value is reduced. "If you have any questions about the value of your art pottery, *Rookwood* or other, please write or call for information at no charge." When writing, include a photo and describe all markings found on the bottom. Please give the dimensions of each piece, and mention any damage no matter how tiny. This well-known dealer has bought, sold, and auctioned high quality pottery for more than twenty years, and offers beautiful illustrated catalogs of past and future auctions at prices ranging from $20 to $50.

> Riley Humler
> Cincinnati Art Galleries
> 635 Main Street
> Cincinnati, OH 45202
> (513) 381-2128   (513) 381-7527

Because color has so much to do with value of both glass and earthenware, a photo is almost essential to sell anything other than a stock item from a well-known factory ✔

★ **Hand decorated art pottery**, American or European, is sought, but David emphasizes that his interest as a dealer is exclusively in "hand decorated" pottery, such as that by *Newcomb College, Grueby, George Ohr, Robineau, Overbeck,* and *Marblehead.* Artist signed *Rookwood* is also of interest, but "we are not looking to buy factory production *Rookwood* or *Roseville.*" He needs to know the maker, condition, size, shape, decoration, and markings on the bottom, so including a photo is a good idea. This well known expert in the Arts & Crafts period has agreed to make offers to amateur sellers who learn about him through this book if they are serious about selling what they own, but states clearly that he "does not wish readers to price fish or to involve him in bidding wars with other buyers." If you need an appraisal for estate or insurance purposes, the fee is $10/ item. Dave writes a monthly column on pottery, and publishes *Arts and Crafts Quarterly*, an attractive and informative magazine available by subscription for $25/year. His book on Fulper may be purchased from him for $35. Other books, catalogs, and materials on art pottery are available. SASE for more information.

David Rago
333 North Main Street
Lambertville, NJ 08530
    (609) 397-9374   Fax: (609) 397-9377

★ *Van Briggle* **and other American art pottery.** A variety of fine pottery will be considered, including *Rookwood* that is artist signed, *North Dakota School of Mines* pottery "with good color contrast," *Hylong, Newcomb,* decorated *Marblehead,* and the like. But his primary interest is in pre-1913 *Van Briggle* pottery, the man who created it, and the company that produced it. Wants company records and catalogs, as well as paintings and pots signed by Van Briggle. Will even accept damaged pre-1913 pieces "if priced accordingly." Is not interested in undated *Van Briggle* or in *ND School of Mines* that is plain. Describe the size, shape, colors, glaze quality, bottom markings, and condition. Scott is a former president of the American Art Pottery Association and author of *The Collector's Guide to Van Briggle*, available from him for $35 and a *Van Briggle Price Guide* for $6.50. He does appraisals for a fee, and expects you to price your own goods.

Scott Nelson
PO Box 6081
Santa Fe, NM 87502
    (505) 986-1176

★ **John Bell pottery** made in the 19th century in Waynesboro, especially fancy pieces, which can bring $1,000 or more.

Ken Broyles
PO Box 42
Waynesboro, PA 17268
    (717) 762-3068

★ *Stangl* **pottery.** "We especially want the following dinnerware patterns: Blueberry, Bittersweet, Chicory, Colonial #1388, Country Garden, Country Life, Fruit, Fruit and Flowers, Garden Flower, Garland, Grape, Holly, Jeweled Christmas Tree, Lyric, Magnolia, Mediterranean, Newport, Ranger, Rooster, Thistle, Blue & Yellow Tulip, Wild Rose and Town and Country spatterware. We don't want brown stains, chips, or cracks, but minor flaws are acceptable. We'll buy any pieces of Kiddieware, even 'as is' especially Wizard of Oz and Flying Saucer. *Stangl* artware, vases, and lamps are desired, as are perfect condition *Stangl* birds and animals, animal planters, and piggy banks. We also buy specialty pottery by *Stangl* such as flower pots, flower ashtrays, political pitchers and mugs, cigarette boxes, etc., as well as any advertising or promotional pieces for this pottery company.

   Bob and Nancy Perzel, Popkorn Antiques
   PO Box 1057
   Flemington, NJ 08822
      (908) 782-9631

★ *Fulper* **art pottery,** especially bullet vases, cabinet vases, candles, figural flower frogs, bookends, door stops, wall pockets, porcelain figural perfume lamps, powder jars and more. Also wants catalogs and advertising from the *Fulper* pottery. Send photos, along with all marks.

   Bob and Nancy Perzel, Popkorn Antiques
   PO Box 1057
   Flemington, NJ 08822
      (908) 782-9631

★ *TECO, Weller* **and other American art pottery.** "*TECO* pottery is my favorite. I'll buy geometric and organic vases with square or built in handles. Sculptural leaves and plant forms, usually in matte finish with green tones, but also brown, yellow, gray, etc. This is often highlighted in a black/gray gunmetal color. I am also a strong buyer of *Weller* vases with raised figures, lizards, snakes, nudes, etc. *Weller* also comes in strong geometrics. Colors are rose, pink, blue, gray, yellow, brown and matte green, often mixed, often veined with gunmetal. Normally signed. I buy a great deal of *Weller*, including many of their other lines." He also buys a wide range of other art pottery including *Grueby, Saturday Evening Girls, Newcomb College, University of North Dakota, Jervis, American Art Clay, Fulper, George Ohr, Arequipa, California Faience, Chelsea Keramic, Clewell, Clifton* (large vases only) and many more. Strongly advise you take a picture since the form and color of pottery determines value. When you send your photo, write down carefully all the marks on the bottom.

   Gary Struncius
   PO Box 1374
   Lakewood, NJ 08701
      (800) 272-2529

★ **Pottery by** *Hull, McCoy, Weller, Watt, Red Wing* **and** *Shawnee.*
She buys vases, wall pockets, pitchers, candlesticks, bookends, bowls,
and most other forms. **She does not buy** items with chips, cracks or repairs. She does not buy items that are not marked with the name of a
maker. Please send a photo along with any numbers or words on the
bottom of your item.

> Sharon Vohs-Mohammed
> PO Box 7233
> Villa Park, IL 60181
> (630) 268-0210   Fax: (630) 268-0282

★ *Shawnee* **pottery**, 1937 - 1961, especially figural cookie jars and
water pitchers such as Chanticleer the rooster, Smiley Pig, Winnie Pig,
Puss 'n Boots, etc. Also salt and pepper shakers, planters, and any item
that has been decorated with gold trim and/or decals. Has a special interest in Valencia dinnerware and kitchenware in good condition (look
for bright yellow, cobalt, green, tangerine and maroon). "All Shawnee
items for sale that are brought to my attention could end up in good
homes eventually as I have a national network of collectors, and will
often refer sellers to potential buyers if I am not interested in the item
offered. I am not interested in the more common planters and shakers."
Your descriptions must note chips and hairline cracks. Include your
phone number along with the color and marks on the bottom. Dealers
must price your goods. If you are really an amateur seller, you may request an offer, "but I'd like an idea of what you think its value is."
People with large collections for sale are encouraged to join the club
for $25 and advertise in their folksy, illustrated and very informative
Exclusively Shawnee newsletter for free.

> Pamela Curran, Shawnee Pottery Collectors Club
> PO Box 713
> New Smyrna Beach, FL 32170
> (904) 760-6600   Fax: (904) 760-5004

★ *Roseville* **pottery** in many patterns in both their Rozane and production lines. Does not want "brown florals." Photo urged.

> Gary Struncius
> PO Box 1374
> Lakewood, NJ 08701
> (800) 272-2529

★ *Roseville* **pottery,** especially in Sunflower, Pinecone and Jonquil
patterns. No cracks or chips. Please send photo and dimensions plus
any markings you find on the bottom.

> Leda Andrews
> 2110 Staples Avenue
> Key West, FL 33040
> (305) 296-4195   Fax: (305) 293-0904

★ *Roseville* **and** *Clarice Cliff* **pottery.** "I'll make an accurate offer for any marked piece if you send me a clear sharp photo and the dimensions." Items must have no chips or cracks.

> Rosemary Pietraszewski
> 60 Grant Street
> Depew, NY 14043
> (716) 681-2339

★ *Roseville* **and other children's dishes.** "Any china used by children to eat or drink" is sought, "but I prefer American items, and I prefer those made by *Roseville* (both unmarked and those marked R on the bottom), *S.E.G., Paul Revere* or *Dedham.* No damaged pieces.

> Steve Kelley
> PO Box 695
> Desert Hot Springs, CA 92240
> (619) 329-3206

★ *Cowan* **pottery** flower vases and frogs decorated with women (especially in colors other than white), bookends ($250+), vases (up to $500 depending on the artist, design and skill of execution). Black sculptures trimmed in gold can go even higher. Pieces are usually marked but COWAN can be hard to read under the glaze, so he advises you to look closely. Many *Cowan* artists including Thelma Frazier Winter, Waylande Gregory, and Viktor Schreckengest continued to make pottery and ceramic sculpture on their own after *Cowan* closed in 1931. These are also wanted by this *Cowan* researcher who notes, "bowls and candlesticks are of little interest unless they have an unusual design, such as those shaped like women." He requests you give the height of your piece along with a photo. The color of the glaze is so important in valuation, it's impossible to give values without a clear sharp photo. Examine the piece carefully for chips, repairs, or hairline cracks as well as worn patches or scratches in the finish.

> Mark Bassett
> PO Box 771233
> Lakewood, OH 44107

★ **Ceramic flower frogs and candelabra** depicting ladies dancing or posing in the Art Deco style. "I'm especially interested in those made by the Ohio company called *Cowan*, but also buy European makers." He especially seeks *Cowan* frogs number 708, 717, 803, 804, 805, 812, and 853 as well as the figural dancing candelabra #752. These can bring from $150 to $600, depending on the figure, colors, and condition. To sell your frog, note all the markings you can find.

> William Sommer
> 9 West 10th Street
> New York, NY 10011
> (212) 260-0999

★ **California ceramics by *Madison* or *Florence*.** Sharon requests you send a description (including all info on the bottom) along with a photo whenever possible if you have figural ceramics made by Madison Ceramic Art Studio or Florence Ceramics.

    Sharon Vohs-Mohammed
    PO Box 7233
    Villa Park, IL 60181
       (630) 268-0210   Fax: (630) 268-0282

★ **Buffalo Pottery.** "I'll buy almost any marked piece."

    Seymour "Si" Altman
    8970 Main Street
    Clarence, NY 14031
       (716) 634-4488

★ **Head vases.** These are small vases shaped like human heads, mostly made during the 1940's, 50's and 60's. She wants ladies (the most common), children, clowns, Indians, Orientals, and whatever. Please send a photo along with any numbers on the bottom of your item. "Please, no damaged vases."

    Sharon Vohs-Mohammed
    PO Box 7233
    Villa Park, IL 60181
       (630) 268-0210   Fax: (630) 268-0282

★ **Pottery and glass with a corn motif.** Wants rare glass or pottery items which are shaped like corn, have corn patterns, depict corn or corn growing. Not interested in Shawnee corn-shaped pottery but especially wants Majolica and pottery by *Stanford* or *Vallona Star*. She also buys **lamps** and other items with corn motif. It's worth your inquiry because "previously unknown items are found regularly." State your item's condition, and if it is for sale what you would like for it. She is the editor of the Corn Items Collectors Association's newsletter.

    E. Eloise Alton
    613 North Long Street
    Shelbyville, IL 62565
       (217) 774-5002

☆ **Decorated stoneware crocks and jugs.** Especially likes pottery with clear markings from NY, NJ, OH, PA, and New England. "I'll pay top dollar for unusual forms decorated with people, animals, ships, trees, houses, strong blue florals, etc. Dated pieces are particularly desirable. I pay from $100 to as much as $10,000 for the right items." He emphasizes that he is interested only in stoneware that is blue decorated, not brown or white. Also buys inkwells, flasks, and unusual small items made of blue decorated stoneware. Needs to know the size of the piece in quarts or gallons if marked, in inches if not. Take a photo or make a good sketch of the decoration because the more unusual the decoration, the more he pays. Mention the darkness of the blue. He will help amateur sellers determine what they have. "If you are interested in joining a stoneware collectors club, call me."

    Richard Hume
    1300 North Stream Parkway
    Point Pleasant, NJ 08742
      (732) 899-8707

★ **Spongeware, stoneware, and redware pottery and crockery.** Note all markings on the sides and bottoms, please, if you'd like this important dealer to evaluate what you have. These are often incised with the name of the maker or user, and their city and town, as well as the size of the container. Minor damage and cracks are acceptable in very rare pieces, but you must note all damage, no matter how small. The decoration is the key to value, so photos are essential.

    Louis Picek
    Main Street Antiques and Art
    PO Box 340
    West Branch, IA 52358

☆ **Redware plates, bowls, and other pieces.** "We buy decorated redware from the Mid-West and Eastern/Southern United States. Multicolors are the more desireable pieces, as are those decorated with animals or people, or with verses written on them. We'll pay $1,000 or more for the best pieces." Please take photos or make a sketch of any markings on the bottom and take a photo or make a sketch of the pattern, indicating what part of the pattern is what color. Make certain you note if there are any cracks or chips or other damage.

    Richard Hume
    1300 North Stream Parkway
    Point Pleasant, NJ 08742
      (732) 899-8707

EUROPEAN POTTERY & CERAMICS

★ **Art pottery of Eastern Europe**, especially pottery made in Art Nouveau or Secession style by *Zsolnay* in Pecs (Hungary), *Fischer* in Budapest, *E. Whaliss* in Vienna and *Amphora* in Turn Teplitz (Czechoslovakia) between 1890 and 1920. The names of these makers are typically incised into the bottom of the items, the values of which can range from $50 to more than $1,000. "Though we do buy rare examples that are damaged, the value is diminished." They do not buy *Zsolnay* made after 1940. Please send a photo, the size, and markings on the bottom.

Federico Santi
The Zsolnay Store
PO Box 641
Newport, RI 02840
(401) 841-5060   Fax: (401) 848-0953   santi39@mail.idt.net

★ **European pottery and porcelain** of the following types:
- French **quimper** from the 19th century especially vases and jardiniere which can be worth $1,000 or more;
- Italian colorful pottery;
- **Gold banded dinnerware**, vases, serving pieces, with or without other colors;
- English **Staffordshire** blue and white historical pieces;
- Italian **porcelain by Richard Ginori**.

"I am not interested in common dinnerware or anything with chips, cracks, hairlines, or restorations. Please send a photo, and include a photo or drawing of the markings on the back/bottom."
Dealers should price their goods; amateurs may ask for offers.

Rita Armstrong
393 Main Street
Los Altos, CA 94022

★ **European ceramic flower frogs and candelabra** depicting ladies dancing or posing in the Art Deco style. These can bring from $50 to $500, depending on the figure, colors, and condition. To sell your frog, note all the markings you can find.

William Sommer
9 West 10th Street
New York, NY 10011
(212) 260-0999

★ **Italian pottery (Majolica)** of all types: flower pots, vases, dinnerware, bottles, lamps, tiles, dishes, figurines, pockets, etc. "The pieces are all hand-painted in bright colors, often on a white background. There are hundreds of types of decoration: fruit, flowers, people, mythical and religious themes, architecture, etc, but always in bright reds, blues, yellows, greens, and rose (usually all of the above!). Many are reproductions of pieces created during the Renaissance, others are more modern and look like souvenirs. I am interested in all types marked MADE IN ITALY on the bottom. Sometimes the markings also identify the region where they were made, such as GUBBIO, DERUTA, ASSISI, etc." A photo is "very helpful," but at the very least, give the dimensions, patterns, colors, and marks, along with a statement of condition. The price you'd like is "helpful" but not required.

> Denise Sater
> 871 Holly Tree Road
> Manheim, PA 17545
> (717) 665-2229

★ **Quimper** ("kam-pair"), a form of antique French peasant pottery, is sought, especially older large examples such as candlesticks, chargers, jardinieres, and figures. New pieces are not wanted. Send a clear photo, the dimensions, and a statement of condition. It is important to describe the markings on the bottom (most pieces are marked), including the color. Among other books, the Bagdades wrote *English and Continental Pottery and Porcelain: An Illustrated Price Guide* and a similar guide to American pottery and porcelain, each available for $22.95. Send an SASE for more information about books written by these popular columnists.

> Susan and Al Bagdade
> The Country Peasants
> 3136 Elder Court
> Northbrook, IL 60062
> (847) 498-1468

GLASS

★ **Antique and 20th century art glass.** This well known auctioneer conducts cataloged auctions of art glass, so can handle collections and fine individual pieces of *Daum Nancy, Steuben, Galle, Tiffany* and other art glass, as well as collections and fine pieces of *Wedgwood* and other fine porcelain.

> James D. Julia Auctioneers
> PO Box 830
> Fairfield, ME 04937
>   (207) 453-7904   Fax: (207) 453-2502

When a listee says he or she is not interested in a particular item, please do not waste his or her time and yours by offering what they do not want.

★ **Black glass** has been Marlena's passion for 30 years, so she says "I am not interested in common pieces made by L.E.Smith I am looking for truly unusual pieces such as figurines, animals, Victorian pieces, creamers, and glass made by *Fenton* that is white or pink with black glass edging around the top ruffles. There is little known about black glass (which often looks a very deep violet when held to bright light) so I can't tell you exactly what I want...just unusual pieces." She does say she isn't interested in the octagonal black dinner sets made in France and sold in discount stores today, nor does she want dishes and plain vases. Because there are so many different pieces, a picture and dimensions are a must, as it's the only way she can identify what you have. She is the author of *Collector's Guide to Black Glass*, available from her for $20 postpaid.

> Marlena Toohey
> 703 South Pratt Parkway
> Longmont, CO 80501
>   (303) 678-9726

★ **Black amethyst glass** (looks black until you hold it to the light and find it's really purple). This advanced collector will buy only the odd and rare, especially dinner plates with silver or gold overlay, large bowls, water and juice glasses, lamp bases, candlesticks with three or more candles, and figurines. She will answer all mail that includes a photo, dimensions, and SASE. As with all glass, condition is crucial.

> Judy Polk Harding
> 1701 60th Street
> Des Moines, IA 50322
>   (515) 279-7099 voice and fax   THEFIVEJS@aol.com

★ **Ruby glass.** This 30 year veteran collector is looking for the more rare and unusual items made in this distinctive deep red glass, such as candle sticks and other pieces with leaf pattern made by Cambridge. She does not want "common Anchor Hocking glass (look for an anchor in a circle on the bottom) or nondescript foreign made glass." Please send her a picture of what you have (glass is very difficult to describe). You may be able to find it in her book *Ruby Glass of the 20th Century*, available from her for $25 postpaid.

> Naomi Over
> 8909 Sharon Lane
> Arvada, CO 80002
> (303) 424-5922

★ **Victorian glassware.** "We pay cash for collections, estates, or single pieces of the following:
* Decorated glass;
* **Cobalt blue** glass;
* **Ruby-stained** glass;
* **Cranberry** glass;
* **Blown opalescent** glass;
* Fancy art glass.

Buys all types of Victorian glass including pitchers and tumblers, salt shakers and sugar shakers, syrup jugs, and **milk glass vases** in silver-plated holders. He does *not buy* depression glass, bottles, clear glass (without color), or anything that is chipped, cracked or damaged. Please give a detailed description and tell how you came to own it. A picture is important. Dealers should price their goods; amateurs ready to sell may ask for offers."

> Scott Roland
> Glimmer Glass Antiques
> PO Box 262
> Schenevus, NY 12155

★ **Coin glass dated 1892.** "I'll buy glass bowls, lamps, and other items with clear or frosted glass coins attached or inset. Coins should be dated 1892. It's important to give exact height and diameter." If I don't want your piece of coin glass, I'll try to suggest another collector who is looking for it. Tim pays $500 and up for lamps, and will send you a price list of what he pays for all pieces. Watch for reproductions (most of them have a ribbon above the eagle's head on the reverse side of the coin). Tim wrote *US Coin Glass: A Century of Mystery* which pictures nearly all known coin glass, available from him for $20.

> Tim Timmerman
> 11655 SW Allen Blvd #31
> Beaverton, OR 97005
> (503) 646-8300

★ **Many kinds of glassware and china** are sought by one of the country's larger auction firms specializing in post-Victorian glass. He buys outright or accepts on consignment for auction:
  • **Carnival glass,** especially pitcher sets, tumblers, whimsies, opalescent pieces, and common items in rare patterns and colors. He encourages you to contact him with one item or a giant collection since there are many valuable pieces that only an expert will recognize;
  • **Victorian pattern glass;**
  • **Cameo glass vases,** plates,urns, and other glass items made by the *Phoenix Glass Co.*;
  • **RS Prussia china** with scenes, portraits, or pearlized florals;
  • *Noritake* **china** with geometric designs;
  • **Nippon china humidors** and large high relief "blown out" vases depicting birds, animals, or figures;
  • **Mandarin red glassware** by *Fenton Glass Company.*
Include your phone number if the piece is for sale. Tom has a reputation for being slow to respond, but helpful with amateur sellers. Phone him midweek if you think you have something good.
> Tom Burns
> Burns Auction Service
> PO Box 608
> Bath, NY 14810
>   (607) 776-7942

★ **Carnival glass** is wanted "in any amount and any color." Prefers dealers to price, but warns that some of the standard price guides are highly overpriced. This 25 year veteran collector is willing to help amateurs "who are actually selling, not just calling everyone fishing for free appraisals and the highest price."
> Dick Hatscher
> 142 Walnut Hill Road
> Bethel, CT 06801
>   (203) 743-1468

★ **Carnival glass.** "I'll buy one piece or a collection, in any colors." Prefers you to set the price.
> W. J. Warren
> 38 Mosher Drive
> Tonawanda, NY 14150
>   (716) 692-2886

Don't take chances with carnival glass.
Differences in color or pattern can
result in dramatic differences in value.
Do not trust what you read in a price guide.

Don't underestimate the value of the colored glass dinnerware of 1910-1940, called "depression glass." A few pieces are surprisingly valuable. Covered butter dishes, for example, usually bring you $100 - $400 each. Candy dishes and water pitchers also bring better than average prices.
Expert advice is essential, because *pieces with no value in one color or pattern can be worth $100 in another.*

Be careful setting a price on carnival glass, which ranges from $10 to $10,000. Work with the buyer when it comes to pricing, as rarities are very hard for anyone but an expert to recognize. A North Carolina woman sold a carnival glass plate for $1 to a picker who came to her home. The picker who bought it resold it by phone for $10,000 to Tom Burns, a buyer listed in this book. Tom paid $10,000 for a pitcher owned by someone who called in to my radio talk show.

★ **Depression glass** in various colors and patterns. A Xerox© copy is very helpful if you don't know the pattern. Do not count pieces that have chips. A photo helps if your item is colored. "I'll pay fair prices for any depression glass I can resell in my shop."

Nadine Pankow
PO Box 207
Willow Springs, IL 60480
(708) 839-5231

★ *Fostoria* **glass and memorabilia** are wanted by the founder of the *Fostoria* Glass Society in Southern California. "I'll buy dealer signs, dealer catalogs from before 1940, postcards, displays, trade cards, calendars, magazine ads (1924 to 1931 only), and any other *Fostoria* Glass Company memorabilia that's in mint condition." His glass wants are more restricted as he only buys frosted or clear **Victoria** (pattern #183) and rare pieces of pattern #2412 called **Colony**. He is not interested in common Colony glassware or other *Fostoria* patterns, but finding a Victoria oil lamp is high on his list. "All items must be in mint condition or don't bother."

Gary Schneider
18864 J & J Lane
Yorba Linda, CA 92886
(714) 777-8823   Fax: (714) 693-5508

★ **Glass toothpick holders** in mint condition. She seeks numerous patterns. Make a photocopy or photo of your holder if you don't know the name of its pattern, and describe the color as best you can. There are many reproduction holders, so she may have to examine yours before making a final offer. Will also consider interesting holders made of metal or china. Judy is founder of the National Toothpick Holder Collectors Society and has published their newsletter for 23 years.

    Judy Knauer
    1224 Spring Valley Lane
    West Chester, PA 19380
       (610) 431-3477

★ **Early American pressed glass in Willow Oak pattern** in amber, blue, or Vaseline colors.

    Audrey Buffington
    Box 386
    South Thomaston, ME 04858
       (207) 594-2683

 Color is so important in the value of glass that it is almost essential to send a photo. Condition is also critical. Buyers seldom want glass that is chipped or cracked.

★ **Crystal stemware.** Buys English, American, Japanese and European manufacturers, but is only interested in named and numbered patterns. Indicate the maker and pattern, and how many of each item you have. Do not count anything damaged.

    Old China Patterns Limited
    1560 Brimley Road
    Scarborough, Ontario
    M1P 3G9, CANADA
       (416) 299-8880　Fax: (416) 299-4721

★ **Fine crystal stemware.** Buys crystal for resale, and **repairs glass, crystal, porcelain, bisque, and figurines**. He also buys damaged and undamaged figurines and *Hummels* for resale.

    David Jasper
    46508 267th Street
    Sioux Falls, SD 57106
       (605) 361-7524　Fax: (605) 361-7216

**See "China" section in Trash or Treasure
for other buyers of fine crystal stemware.**

PAPERWEIGHTS

★ **Antique glass paperweights,** 1845-1900. "I will buy fine French (*Pantin, Baccarat, Clichy, St. Louis*), American (*Boston Glass Co., Sandwich Glass Co., New England Glass Co., Gillinoer, Mt. Washington*), English (*Bacchus, Whitefriars*), Russian and Bohemian paperweights. I am especially looking for *Pantin* paperweights from the late 1870's for which I will pay from $2,000 to $35,000. I also seek early *Clichy* bouquet on a moss background which can be worth as much as $40,000. I don't want paperweights with blobs of colored glass or with large bubbles in the design." A close up color photo of your weight is important and should be accompanied by a good description, including the diameter. This well known author and collector does not send out a wants list because, he explains, "I will purchase all top quality weights." Paul's book *The Jokelson Collection of Antique Cameo Incrustation* is available with price guide for $60.

> Paul Dunlop
> The Dunlop Collection
> PO Box 6269
> Statesville, NC 28687
> (800) 227-1996   In NC: (704) 871-2626

★ **Paperweights**. "I pay the highest prices for both antique and modern art glass paperweights of all types," says this 25 year veteran Please send him a photo with your name and phone number. Call for information about the International Paperweight Society and full-color magazine. Selman is the country's largest auctioneer of valuable art glass weights and the author of numerous books on paperweights, available through him.

> Larry Selman
> 761 Chestnut Street
> Santa Cruz, CA 95060
> (800) 538-0766   Fax: (408) 427-0111

★ **Antique glass paperweights and other items** including art glass, **glass pens**, and whimsies. "I'm looking for the old and rare." Make certain to note all damage, no matter how small or send close up pix. Semi-annual paperweight auctions are conducted. Write for info.

> Stanley Block
> PO Box 51
> Trumbull, CT 06611
> (203) 261-3223

CLOTHING

★ **Vintage clothing and hats.** "I buy and sell mint condition men's, women's, children's and fancy baby clothing dating from the 1890's through the 1940's, especially flapper dresses, stylish women's suits and jackets, 1940's rayon dresses, evening suits and dresses. Both day wear and evening wear are desirable.
- **Stylish hats** from the early 1930's or before with full lining;
- **Old draperies**, and old bolts of material;
- Early **bridal clothing** and headpieces;
- Accessories such as **shoes, hats, belts,** etc.;
- Jewelry, compacts, etc.;
- **Handbags and parasols**;
- **Lace**.

Individual prices run from $10 to $75, with only "absolutely incredible" items bringing more. "I do *not* want things that are ripped, faded, have underarm stains, too small for today's wearers (with tiny neck or arm holes), worn out, or that have poor craftsmanship. Nor do I want anything from the 1950's or 60's except designer clothes. I do not buy fur. If you want to sell clothing, you must tell me the period, give the size and color, indicate whether it has a zipper or buttons, identify the material if possible, and list any defects." Note whether hats have lining. Amateur sellers may request an offer, which will be made after seeing the item. Dealers must price their goods. Photo a good idea. Call her about shipping on approval to make it easy on everyone.

> Pahaka September
> 19 Fox Hill
> Upper Saddle River, NJ 07458
> (201) 327-1464 eves

 Stained or torn clothing is not wanted. Always describe the style, color, material, size, and label. Clothes with designer labels are very desirable, but Levis *may have value.*

★ **Vintage clothes made before 1950** such as beaded sweaters and **beaded purses and bags**, evening gowns, prom dresses, men's tuxedos and hats, etc. Also buys **parasols** and **piano shawls**. No damaged or stained items as items are purchased for resale in her 2,000 sq.ft. shop. Price your goods when possible.

> Bird In the Cage
> 110 King Street
> Alexandria, VA 22314
> (703) 549-5114

★ *Levis, Lee,* and *Wrangler* **jeans and jackets** for resale. "I'll buy all pre-1970 *Levi Strauss* jeans and jackets and some older *Wrangler* and *Lee* jeans and jackets." The *Levis* he wants all have a small red tag on the front pocket (jackets left, pants right) which spells out LEvis. That capital "E" makes these called "Big E" jeans, and they are a hot fad item in Asia today. Jackets from 1920-1949 bring $500 to $1,500; if they're heavily worn, they're still worth $100 to $300. Other jackets, with two front pockets, bring from $25 to $500. Does not want *Levis* with tags of any color other than red. Does not want pants with waists larger than 34" either. If you have a red Big E *Levis* tag in one of your front pockets and want an immediate cash offer, describe condition carefully noting stains, holes, wear, the condition of the leather ID tag. The serial number on the back pocket leather ID tag would be helpful. Also buys **advertising signs and figures** from *Levi Strauss,Wrangler* and *Lee* products.

> David Bailey
> Aloha
> 517 Kapahulu
> Honolulu, HI 96815
> (808) 734-7628

★ **Vintage Hawaiian shirts, 1930-1955.** The label, size, coloration, and pattern are important, as is the material, so include all that when you write. Shirts can be made of cotton, rayon, or silk. A silk shirt with a fish pattern (his personal favorite) could bring as high as $500. Most are considerably less, but well worth your time. "I'm willing to answer questions and provide information to people who are not sure if their shirts are old enough." A photograph or photocopy is helpful.

> Evan Olins, Hula Heaven
> 75-5744 Alii Drive
> Kailua-Kona, HI 96740
> (808) 329-4122   (808) 329-7885   Fax: (808) 326-2110

★ **Hawaiian shirts made before 1960.**

> David Bailey
> 517 Kapahulu Avenue
> Honolulu, HI 96815
> (808) 734-7628

★ **Men's and women's clothing and accessories,** 1900-1940. Wants average sizes in good condition. Very interested in old warehouse stock and in **rayon yardage**. Open by appointment only.

> Doris Raymond
> The Way We Wore
> 1094 Revere Ave #A-29
> San Francisco, CA 94124
> (415) 822-1800 voice and fax 10 a.m. to 5 p.m.

★ **Men's clothing from 1880-1895**, either original or reproduction, in specific sizes. Including accessories, like **top hats, watch chains**, other items that are appropriate to the English gentleman of that period. "Please contact me for a list of sizes for each specific item."

> Rev. Sherlock "Yes, it's my real name" Holmes
> Private Letter Box 3
> Worcester, MA 01613
>   (508) 754-9907

★ **Men's old clothes**, with an emphasis on sport, casual and work clothing from 1920 through the 1960's. Items wanted are:
- *Levi's* **jeans and jackets** (age, size, and condition determine the value...from $100-$3,000);
- **Military khakis;**
- **Flight jackets** and **Military tour jackets;**
- **Decorated sweat shirts** with interesting designs and logos;
- **Hawaiian shirts** ($50-$200);
- **Bowling shirts** ($50-$200);

"We do NOT want women's jeans, newer jeans with problems, polyester jeans, colored jeans, or jeans with chemical treatment (like acid wash or stone wash)." Please give specific information about the size, color, any defects. To get the best offer, make sure to include a good color photo, especially on expensive items with colors or designs.

> Dan Kelley
> Experienced Denim
> PO Box 239
> Fayetteville, AR 72702
>   (501) 444-7541   Fax: (501) 521-8331

★ **Leather mini skirts, micro skirts and hot pants** from the 1960's. "I buy leather only. No suede or vinyl, please." Describe the condition, any tears, stains, dirt, smells. Give the label and size, too, please.

> Steve Hannan
> 141 East Central Street
> Natick, MA 01760

★ **Women's rubber undergarments** including girdles, panty girdles, garter belts, sanitary garments, corsets, corselettes and all-in-ones. They can be U.S. or foreign made, perforated or solid, gum rubber or sheet rubber, and in any color. The more unusual the better. Original boxes are a plus, as is any original counter advertising for the product. DOES NOT WANT cracked, melted or hopelessly stuck together items or those that have hardened. Your description should include what it is, the size, color, and condition. "The price you'd like helps."

> Ms. Brunswick
> PO Box 9729
> Baltimore, MD 21284

★ **Women's rubber boots,** both rain and fashion type, especially those from 1940 to 1970 in odd colors, decorated, thigh highs, Cuban heels and other less ordinary boots. Wants U.S. or foreign made in any color except black, but will consider black ones if unusual. Original boxes are a plus as is any counter or display material. DOES NOT WANT vinyl or plastic "unless they're high white or other dramatic colors." Your description should include what it looks like, size, color, and condition. Photo helpful, as is the price wanted (usually $20-$50).
>
> Ms. Brunswick
> PO Box 9729
> Baltimore, MD 21284

★ **Handpainted neckties.** "Most are 1940's vintage wide ties in silk or rayon blend with various scenes or abstracts. Especially wants nudes, lusty women, and hula dancers (worth up to $100 each), but also cowboy and fishing themes (which can bring to $75). Does not want narrow ties. Include maker's name and a Xerox™. Condition critical.
>
> Don Colclough
> 231 North Elmwood Street
> Oak Park, IL 60302
> (800) 775-5078   Fax: (708) 848-9124

☆ **Antique fancy buttons.** Wants those with metal pictures, Oriental, pearl, *Bakelite*, etc. The way to tell whether she wants your buttons is to ask yourself two questions before contacting her:
   (1) Does the button have holes through it? If yes, she is not
        interested in your button. If no, ask question #2.
   (2) Is it fancy or unusual? If yes, she wants it. If not, she doesn't.
She does not want shirt buttons or ordinary plastic buttons with visible sewing holes. Almost all the buttons she buys are shank type. Please price your buttons for resale. Photocopies or approvals are suggested.
>
> Barbara Bronzoulis, Barbara's Button Bracelets
> 3700 Kingwood Drive #321
> Kingwood, TX 77339
> (281) 358-7640

★ **Buttons,** especially U.S. military, Confederate, military school, and uniform buttons with state seals. He also buys "**high quality clothing buttons** of porcelain, satsuma, or with pictures." He does not want WWI or WWII buttons or "simple clothing buttons made of plastic or bone." Please describe the design, and note anything stamped on the back. This former director of the National Button Society prefers that you ship for inspection prior to final offer.
>
> Warren Tice
> PO Box 8491
> Essex, VT 05451
> (802) 878-3835 voice and fax

LACE & NEEDLEWORK

★ **Handmade lace** from 1500-1900. "Unless you are a lace scholar or have access to important reference books on lace, the best thing is to photocopy as much of the piece as possible. From a photocopy I can often tell whether a full appraisal is warranted or if it is a piece I might like to buy. Even small pieces are worth your attention." She does not want lace known to be machine made or ordinary crochet and tatting. She prefers sellers to set the price, but will assist genuine amateurs to identify what they have "if it's for sale." Produces an interesting newsletter for lace fanciers for $10 a year.

    Elizabeth Kurella
    Lace Merchant
    PO Box 222
    Plainwell, MI 49080
       (616) 685-9792   Fax: (616) 685-5043

A great deal of valuable lace is lost each year because people don't take time to inquire. Small pieces of high-quality lace can bring up to $100 and large pieces a great deal more.

★ **Lace, trimmings, embroidery** and **stitchery.** Wants assortments of pre-1920 rosettes, fabric or ribbon trims for clothing or hats, tatted items that are more than 5" in size (including doilies), white on white stitchery, red stitchery on white, **beaded clothing and accessories**, and clothing (including pantaloons, skirts, and dresses) with decorative handiwork. Also buys quilt tops, crazy quilts, and other handmade cloth items. Send a good photograph or photocopy of what you wish to sell. "Items can be partially damaged if I use them to make other things. Please, no hankies or crochet items." Include SASE for response.

    Linda Gibbs, Heirloom Keepsakes
    10380 Miranda
    Buena Park, CA 90620
       (714) 827-6488

★ **Samplers and vintage needlework and linens.** "I'll consider rugs, coverlets, needlepoint and other fine quality handiwork." Send a photo or photocopy, along with dimensions and a clear description of damage or wear. Include an SASE.

    Denise Hamilton
    899 Latta Brook Road
    Elmira, NY 14901

★ **Old material, cloth scraps, patterned flour and feed sacks**, and other material useful for old style quilting. Send a sample or make a Xerox™ of what you have to offer.
> Judy Speezak
> 425 5th Avenue
> Brooklyn, NY 11215
> (718) 369-3513

★ **Blankets with Indian or cowboy patterns.** "I buy commercially made wool blankets by *Beacon, Buell, Candelario, Capps, Esmond, Hamilton, Oregon City, Pendleton, American Indian Blanket Mills, Provo Woolen Mills, Knight Woolen Mills*, and *Racine (Badger State)*. Don't worry if your blanket has lost its label; if old, it's still worth money to me. I also buy Indian material patterned bathrobes, jackets, pillows, couch covers, etc. I prefer all material to be priced, but will make offers to people who are not dealers. I answer calls and letters promptly." A photograph or photocopy is a must, and you are requested to list all flaws, holes, etc., in your first letter. Because blankets are often washed improperly, shrunk, and therefore undesirable, dimensions are a must.
> Barry Friedman
> PO Box 55492
> Valencia, CA 91385
> (805) 255-2365   BarryF@fishnet.net

★ **Chenille bedspreads, rugs and houserobes.** These come in a variety of designs. They can can be solid colors or a mix of colors in interesting designs. She especially wants animals, bright florals, Art Deco geometrics, birds, cowboys and other characters as well as various themes designed for infants. Chenille is made of soft tufted cords of silk, cotton or worsted and was very popular in the 1950's (sold by *Ward's* among others). Condition must be excellent with no tears, stains or visible wear.
> Judy Polk Harding
> 1701 60th Street
> Des Moines, IA 50322
> (515) 279-7099 voice and fax   THEFIVEJS@aol.com

★ **Quilting and patchwork patterns, books** and **tools** before 1950.
> Judy Speezak
> 425 5th Avenue
> Brooklyn, NY 11215
> (718) 369-3513

Buyers of quilts and samplers are also found in the section on folk art beginning on page 490.

TIPS ON SELLING COSTUME JEWELRY

You must get all jewelry into the hands of someone trained and experienced in old jewelry. If you try to evaluate it yourself, you could make costly mistakes. Diamonds and other precious and semi-precious stones are often mistaken for glass in old jewelry. You cannot rely upon local jewelers and diamond merchants for accurate appraisals of antique jewelry.

A certified gemologist and costume jewelry expert said, "Few dealers know who the important makers of costume jewelry are. If they sell good pieces at junk prices, that means they paid junk prices for them. The original owner lost money. Sellers should always go to jewelry experts."

19th century gemstones were cut differently than is popular today. *A reader showed me a two and a half carat diamond ring he bought at a yard sale for a quarter. I hope he wasn't shopping at your house!*

Jewelry buyers want to know:

(1) *The basic material from which your item is made, such as silver, gold, brass, plastic, etc.*
(2) *All names, numbers, and markings. The right mark can put hundreds of dollars in your pocket.*
(3) *Shape, color, and number of any stones.*
(4) *Dimensions are helpful; values can be influenced by size. Photocopying is a good way to describe hatpins, brooches, bracelets and other jewelry.*

Be prepared to ship your jewelry with a five day return privilege. *Buyers want to inspect jewelry before committing to buy. If they do pay first, you must give the money back if the buyer isn't happy for any reason with what you send.*

When mailing items worth more than $500, send them Registered Mail. *It costs between $5-$10 to mail safely throughout the U.S. with insurance as high as $25,000. All recipients must sign for Registered Mail. Ask your post office because some minor restrictions apply.*

JEWELRY

★ **Old and antique jewelry,** especially:
- **Karat gold pieces**, particularly signed pieces with Art Nouveau
  and Art Deco designs;
- **Sterling silver items** signed by *Unger Brothers* or *Kerr*,
  mostly Art Nouveau brooches featuring female faces;
- **Designer costume jewelry** signed by *Trifari, Mariam
  Haskell, Hattie Carnegie, Coro* or *Eisenberg Original;*
- *Georg Jensen* **jewelry**;
- **Silver puffed heart fancy charms**.

Describe your items completely, or make a photocopy. If you know the
item's ownership history, please give it. Note all markings.

Arnold Reamer
Timepiece Antiques
PO Box 26416
Baltimore, MD 21207
(410) 944-6414   (410) 486-8412   Fax: (410) 265-7877

★ **Antique and collectible jewelry** from the 1700's to 1940's "with a
preference for precious metals but I do deal in some costume jewelry."
Her special interests include:
- Victorian jewelry;
- Enameled pieces;
- Hair jewelry;
- Old cut diamonds;
- Unusual jewelry;
- High grade wrist and pocket watches.

Send her a description of the item, including its size. A photo of both
the front and back is highly advisable. Dealers must price their goods.
Amateurs may ask for an appraisal or an offer. Appraisals are for a fee.
"If I do an appraisal, I will not make an offer to buy. If I make an offer,
I will not appraise." Ms. Bell is a Graduate Gemologist and certified to
evaluate fine gems and jewelry. She has been in the business of antique jewelry for 30 years and is author of *Answers & Questions about
Old Jewelry 1840-1950*, obtainable from her for $25 postpaid. Inquire
about her instructional video on jewelry and her bimonthly newsletter.
She is available to share her knowledge of jewelry at various gatherings
for a fee.

C. Jeanenne Bell
Jewelry Box Antiques
4035 Broadway
Kansas City. MO 64111
(816) 472-1760   Fax: (816) 531-3942

★ **Costume and other jewelry** is sought, but only particular kinds:
  • **All signed designer pieces** by B.David, Boucher, Ciner, Cini,
    Corosterling, DeRosa, Dior, Eisenberg, Gerrys, J.J., Joseff,
    Ledo, Matisse, Mazer, Pennino, Pinnetta, Renoir or Reja;
  • **Rhinestone jewelry** with red or purple stones in any size or style,
    especially large and gaudy pieces;
  • **Czech jewelry** (especially bracelets, brooches and necklaces with
    drop pendants); pieces tend to be large, intensely colored, and
    have brass filigree often marked CZECH or CZECHOSLOVAKIA;
  • **Hair jewelry and wreaths.** During the mid 1800's, human hair
    was braided or interlaced into rings, bracelets, necklaces,
    lockets, watch fobs or large wreaths;
  • **Mood rings** from the 1970's that change color while you wear
    them. Must be in working condition;
  • **Hand hammered aluminum** bracelets, pendants, brooches,
    key chains and money clips;
  • **Aluminum souvenir jewelry** marked as being a souvenir of a
    particular place;
  • **Copper jewelry** marked MATISSE, RENOIR or REBAJE, many of
    which have an enamel overlay;
  • **Holiday pins** with a Christmas, Halloween, Easter or other
    holiday theme or character;
  • **Animal and insect pins**, especially those with Lucite bellies;
  • **Pins depicting humans or animals;**
  • **Charms and charm bracelets** made of gold, sterling, silver plate,
    plastic or Mexican silver in a variety of themes: novelties,
    awards, animals, people, animated characters, souvenirs, and
    realistic objects, especially those with wheels that turn or other
    moving parts;
  • **Cuff links** pre-1940 made of gold or silver, plain or ornate,
    especially with precious or semi-precious stones; single cuff
    links welcome;
  • **Men's watch chains and fobs** in a variety of themes;
  • **Award pins** designed to be worn on a lapel or shirt-front, made of
    14k, 10k, sterling or gold filled only, with or without a pearl or
    other stone; all types (years of service, attendance, activities)
    issued by any group, fraternal organization, church, school or
    service organization;
  • **Broken pieces of good jewelry;**
  • **Ladies' non-working 14k wrist watches** priced for craft use.
"I'll buy one piece or a showcase full," she says. Please send a photo
or photocopy, along with a description and the history if known. Deal-
ers must price their goods, but amateur sellers may request an offer.

> Judy Polk Harding
> 1701 60th Street
> Des Moines, IA 50322
>   (515) 279-7099 voice and fax   THEFIVEJS@aol.com

★ *Bakelite* and *Catalin* **jewelry.** This nationally known expert buys bangles, bracelets, pins, brooches, necklaces, earrings, and buckles made of *Bakelite* or *Catalin*, phenol plastics from the 1920's, 30's and 40's. *Bakelite* comes in black, dark brown and muddy wine, whereas *Catalin* comes in red, orange, yellow, amber, butterscotch, green, blue, purple, pink, turquoise, white and ivory. This plastic jewelry is frequently made of one color, with black and red the most popular, but single colored bangles are usually $20 or less unless heavily carved or painted in some interesting way. Multi-color jewelry can bring up to $500. As a general rule, the more complex the color, the more valuable. Some particularly interesting forms of plastic jewelry are:

- One color molded on top of another so that the carving discloses the underneath color ($100 up);
- Two or more colors laminated together so colors appear as stripes or rings that run around the bracelet ($150 up);
- Colors appear like polka dots or circles ($150 up);
- Translucent bracelets are sometimes undercarved so the carved part lays against your arm; often hand painted ($200 up);
- Big gaudy multi colored pins ($50 up);
- Elaborate sets of 5-8 pieces with necklace, earrings, brooches, etc., in colors will bring premium prices ($1,000 up);
- Pins with people, hands, faces, bugs, birds, animals (horses and dogs the most common) and other topics can put from $50 to $500 in your pocket;

Bigger is usually better, especially in pins. Complexity and rarity of the pattern are the final determiners of price. As a dealer, she pays 30% to 70% of retail, depending on the quality and value of the piece. Dealers MUST price your goods. If you are an amateur seller with no idea of the jewelry market, say so in your initial letter containing your description and she will make offers. To see some of the finest available plastic jewelry, order her *The Best of Bakelite and Other Plastic Jewelry* which can help train your eye to recognize the good stuff. It's $42 from the author.

   Dee Battle
   9 Orange Blossom Trail
   Yalaha, FL 34797
    (352) 324-3023

To tell if you have Bakelite/Catalin or a newer plastic, feel it. A slightly oily feel is characteristic of the older plastics. So is its weight as it's heavier than modern plastics. Look for mold seams as Bakelite/Catalin jewelry does NOT have them. Touch new plastic with a red hot needle and it will melt or give off a puff of smoke. Bakelite can't be hurt with a hot needle (it's so tough it's even hard to drill).

★ **Old jewelry before 1930,** garnets, black jets, cameos, rings, **lockets**, **charms,** filigree beads, glass beads, and glass buttons. Craftsmanship and detail ("ornate and unusual") is more important than whether it's made of gold or not. **Lockets, hearts,** stars, flowers and other keepsake jewelry is wanted in gold or silver. "I look for all unusual items of clothing, jewelry, and accessories." Photocopy is suggested. Jewelry may be broken and need repair. SASE a must.

> Linda Gibbs
> 10380 Miranda Avenue
> Buena Park, CA 90620
> (714) 827-6488

★ **Mexican sterling jewelry.** Wants "strange or unusual eye-catching pieces, especially very heavy ones from the 1920's to 1940's. "A photo or photocopy will tell me a lot" but you should also list anything marked on the piece. This 40 year veteran prefers you to indicate a price range, but will make offers.

> Marilyn Baseman
> Birdcage Antiques
> PO Box 268
> South Egremont, MA 01258
> (413) 528-3556

★ **Old Taxco (Mexico) jewelry, flatware and holloware**, especially pieces by William Spratling, Hector Aguilar, Fred Davis, Hubert Harmon, Antonio, Mat'l, and other well known artists. These pieces are decorated with a variety of stones, including onyx, garnet and amethyst and are almost always marked with the maker's name or symbol. A good sharp photo is essential. Please copy the mark if you can't take a photo of it.

> Daniel Brown
> PO Box 149
> Davenport, CA 95017
> (800) 492-6786

★ **Photo keepsake jewelry** with real photos mounted in pendants, lockets, brooches, etc., from the 1800's. He does not want photo jewelry if the original photo has been removed. "I can give an estimate of value, although not enough reference material is available. Prices are largely determined individually based on the esthetic value of the piece [how attractive it is...ed.]. In general, jewelry made with Daguerreotypes or ambrotypes is more valuable than that made with ferrotypes (tintypes). If possible, a color picture in closeup, both front and back is helpful. Indicate any inscriptions or markings as well as any damage. If you want your photos back, please include an SASE. Dealers price your goods. Amateur sellers may ask for help.

Ed Clark, Texas Photo Center
215 West Camp Wisdom #6
Duncanville, TX 75116
(972) 780-5735 Fax: (972) 780-0937 camera35@aol.com

★ **Woodburned glove and jewelry boxes** are purchased for resale, as are **jewelry boxes made of cast iron,** particularly those that are silk lined. Please give a thorough description. SASE a must.

Linda Gibbs
10380 Miranda Avenue
Buena Park, CA 90620
(714) 827-6488

★ **B & D barrettes** made of inexpensive colorful plastic in the early 1980's by the Buch and Deichmann company in Denmark. "They are only worth a few dollars each, but please let me know if you have any for sale." A Xerox™ is an effective way to tell her.

Holly Lyall
34 Meadowbank Road
Winnipeg, MB
R3Y 1N8 CANADA

★ **Gold scrap.** "I buy all marked and unmarked gold and silver rings, wedding bands, and scrap," says this giant dealer in coins, medals, and tokens. Hartzog says you may ship whatever you have for his offer.

Rich Hartzog
PO Box 4143 BVT
Rockford, IL 61110
(815) 226-0771

Jewelry buyers want to know:
  (1) The basic material from which your item is made, such as silver, gold, brass, plastic or material you don't recognize.
  (2) All names, numbers, and markings. Try to record these accurately. A magnifying glass may help.
  (3) Shape, color, and number of any stones.
  (4) Size of your brooch, pendant, etc.

TIPS ON SELLING WATCHES

Watches have been made by the hundreds of millions for a century!

A great variety of watches exist and a great variety of collectors seek them. Values can range from a dollar or two to prices over $100,000.

Whenever a great deal of money is at stake, it is smart to get expert advice.

Be cautious about selling watches locally. Your local jeweler is probably not qualified to evaluate and price old watches even though he sells new ones. You may put five or ten times as much money in your pocket when you deal with watch buyers who keep up with the international used watch market.

If you wish to sell your watch, be prepared to tell a potential buyer the following information:

> *What is the case made of?*
> *What is the size of the case?*
> *Is the case decorated or engraved?*
> *What name is on the dial?*
> *What name is on the movement?*
> *Does it say how many jewels?*
> *Is there a serial number?*
> *How is it wound?   Do you have the key?*
> *Is it running?*
> *Is there anything unusual about the case or watch?*

Watch buyers will want to inspect your timepiece before making a final offer.   Send watches via Registered US Mail, insured. This is usually a safe way to ship, and requires the recipient to sign for the package.

Always discuss exact shipping procedures with the buyer.

WATCHES

★ **Pocket watches and high grade wristwatches.** Especially seeking *Patek Philippe, Howard, Illinois, Hamilton, Rolex* and signed railroad dials and RR movements. Also buys keywinds, watches that chime, Civil War watches, enameled watches, calendar watches, moonphases, historical watches, gold cases, novelty character watches, sports related watches, unusual American and European watches and chronographs. "I always buy any American made pocket watch 21 jewels or higher." Pays finders fees for leads to purchase of collections, estates, and good accumulations. He does NOT buy *Timex* or inexpensive watches made after 1965, nor does he buy any lady's watches. Please describe your watch as per Dr. Hyman's instructions at the beginning of this section, and include an SASE along with a Xerox™ of the watch front and back if possible. Watches do not need to run. 33 years of experience.

> Maundy International
> PO Box 13028 TH
> Shawnee Mission, KS 66282
> (800) 235-2866

★ **Wrist and pocket watches,** both men's and women's, in gold, silver, or gold fill. Pocket watches may be in other metals if they date before 1940. Doesn't matter whether running or not. Describe all markings and give dimensions.

> Arnold Reamer
> Timepiece Antiques
> PO Box 26416
> Baltimore, MD 21207
> (410) 944-6414   (410) 486-8412   Fax: (410) 265-7877

★ **High quality and collectible watches** by *Patek Phillipe, Rolex, Cartier, Tiffany, Audemars* and types of watches like chronographs, re- peaters, alarm, doctor's watches, two time zone, and rectangular faces made between 1870 and 1960. **Also advertising items relating to watches.** Irv deals in watches from rare to common. Buys parts, cases, boxes, movements, dials, and bands from all *Rolex, Patek* or *Cartier* watches. If you are thinking of auctioning watches or **antique gold jewelry**, Irv says, "We will buy any piece that interests us at 95% of anticipated net sellers hammer proceeds." Irv promises: "Fair prices, next day payment, postage refunded, and free appraisals," adding "I will come to you if what you have is very valuable or if you have many good pieces." Describe metal, shape, details, all names and numbers, as indicated on previous page. Irv offers a priced wants list.

> Irv Temes
> Temes and Co.
> 338 North Charles Street
> Baltimore, MD 21201
> (800) 722-5274   (410) 882-0580   Fax: (410) 685-3299

★ *Hamilton* **men's electric wristwatches** watches and mechanical watches with unusual case styles. An electric watch repairman, he also wants dealer's stock, parts, movements, **advertising materials, catalogs**, and anything else related to the *Hamilton Watch Co.* No *Hamilton Electronic* watches. Only American made pre-1970 watches. Rene's comprehensive book on *Hamilton* electric watches is $30.

> Rene Rondeau
> 120 Harbor Drive
> Corte Madera, CA 94925
> (415) 924-6534   Fax: (415) 924-8423   rrondeau@prodigy.com

★ **Racing stopwatches, pocket watches, dashboard clocks, and schoolhouse clocks with the name of a horse,** horse race, carriage company, or automobile manufacturer on the face. "If in doubt, inquire. Send your watch on approval for an immediate response."

> Donald Sawyer
> 40 Bachelor Street
> West Newbury, MA 01985
> (508) 346-4724 days   Fax: (508) 346-4841

★ **Watches and clocks with cartoon characters or products on the face.** Any items mint in their original box are particularly desirable. Tell whether face is round or rectangular, any wording on the face or back, defects (including scratches), the condition of the box (if any), and whether it is working. Don't overwind! Free appraisals for amateur sellers. Maggie both buys and sells these pop-culture watches.

> Maggie Kenyon
> One Christopher Street #14G
> New York, NY 10014
> (212) 675-3213

★ **LED calculator watches** from the early 70's. These lit up, usually in red, when you pressed a button. He most wants a *Hewlett-Packard* HP-01 combination watch/calculator in gold or stainless steel, especially if complete with original stylus. List make and model and indicate if it works. Please indicate type and condition of strap.

> Guy Ball
> 14561 Livingston Street
> Tustin, CA 92780
> Fax: (714) 730-6140

★ **Ladies 14k wristwatches that no longer work.** "Any maker, any year, any style, with or without a band...I'm buying for craft use not as jewelry. Please send a Xerox™ and your asking price.

> Judy Polk Harding
> 1701 60th Street
> Des Moines, IA 50322
> (515) 279-7099 voice and fax   THEFIVEJS@aol.com

LOCKS & KEYS

★ **Antique and unusual padlocks.** "We'll buy padlocks of all kinds and types, those that are oddly shaped, made of cast iron or brass, figural, *Wells Fargo, Winchester*, railroad, miniature, and many others." If you want so sell your lock, a photocopy will help them know what you have. Indicate whether your lock has a key with it.

> Joe and Pam Tanner
> Tanner Escapes
> 3024 East 35th Street
> Spokane, WA 99223
> (509) 448-8457 voice and fax

★ **Padlocks and keys** are wanted, especially American locks marked with patent dates or the name of the maker. Some English and other European locks are of interest as well. Locks can be worth hundreds of dollars apiece, so it's worth your while to inquire, although he has no interest in modern locks made after 1930. A good rule of thumb is "the older and more unusual the better." A Xerox™ is a good idea. Note all dates, words, or symbols found on the lock, and indicate whether you have the key or not "as a lock without a key is acceptable, but definitely worth a lot less" for obvious reasons. Bob is secretary of the West Coast Lock Collectors, whose quarterly newsletter is $15/year.

> Bob Heilmann
> Ace Lock & Key
> 1427 Lincoln Boulevard
> Santa Monica, CA 90401
> (310) 454 7295 eves

SCALES

★ **Antique scales** of any type, in any condition and quantity, are sought by this 20 year veteran collector/dealer who also buys toy scales, signs, advertising scales, scale catalogs, postcards showing scales, scale parts, and "anything else" related to scales. Provide the brand name, model, serial number and condition. Note whether the scale is complete.

> Bill and Jan Berning
> PO Box 41414
> Chicago, IL 60641
> (815) 784-3134

KNIVES

★ **Pocket, hunting, and military knives.** A few of the good brands to look for: *New York, Canastota, Remington, Wabash, Winchester, Honk Falls, Napanoch, Henry Sears, Shapleigh, Union Cut, Keen Kutter, Bingham, American, Bridge, Capitol, Case, Cattaraugus, Phoenix, James Price, Platts, Press Button, Wallkill, Walden, Van Camp, Union Razon, Standard, Zenith, Northfield, Crandall*, and others. "I love large bone-handled knives made in the U.S." **If your knife is one of the following brands, it is not of interest:** *Ambassador, Atco, Camco, Colonial, Executive, Frontier, Hit, Ideal, Klien, Richards, U.S.A., Pakistan,* and *Sabre*. For an evaluation of your knife and an offer, photocopy knives with the blade(s) open, write down everything found on the blades and handles, identify the handle material and include an SASE.

Charles Stapp
7037 Haynes Road
Georgetown, IN 47122
(812) 923-3483

★ **Knives of all types**, but especially pocket knives, Bowie knives, hunting knives, commemorative knives, and custom knives. "We are primarily interested in older and higher grade items, but we do have a market for the junk as well. We will purchase entire collections without cherry-picking. If it's a knife, we're interested."
• Handmade knives by Wm. Scagel ($1,000-$5,000)
• Handmade knives by RW Loveless ($800-$2,500)
• Antique **Bowie knives** ($200-$25,000)
• Older Randall knives ($200-$1,000)
• Old American made pocket knives ($20-$500)
They also buy pre 1940 **advertising related to knives**. Photos or Xerox© copies are needed. Give a brief description and include your phone number.

Tom Clark
Blue Ridge Knives
Route 6 Box 185
Marion, VA 24354
(703) 783-6143   Fax (703) 783-9298

★ **Knives less than 1" long** are wanted, especially multi-bladed knives with mother-of-pearl, sterling, stag or horn handles. To sell your knife, give as much information as possible, including number of blades, maker, condition, etc. Old knives only. No new items or reproductions. Says he also "buys and trades swords and razors."

Jim Kegebein
6831 Colton Blvd.
Oakland, CA 94611
(510) 339-1147   Fax: (510) 339-1146   njak@aol.com

★ **Knives, tools and other items** by selected makers: *Keen Kutter, Winchester, Simmons, Shapleigh, Norvell-Shapleigh,* and various combinations thereof. "They made thousands of different things. Look at your tools carefully, as the names are often hard to read or find. I pay most for items in their original box. I don't want scissors or meat grinders that clamp on the table. I don't buy broken items, reproductions, heavily worn knives, or items that have been modified. If you call with an item made by one of these companies in front of you, I can usually evaluate it over the phone. Some items have been reproduced. When in doubt, call." He also buys catalogs, advertising, promotional items, signs, showcases, postcards, cookbooks, clocks, radios and other products marked with the name of one of those companies. Send photocopy or tracing, the exact wording of the mark and any other numbers or words. Include an SASE and your evening phone number. Tom is currently president of the Winchester, Keen Kutter and Diamond Edge Collector's Club.

Tom Basore
715 West 20th Avenue
Hutchinson, KS 67502
(316) 665-3613 eves

★ **Antique pocket knives of all kinds** in excellent to mint condition. "I will consider buying all kinds of knives as I buy for resale as well as for my own collection. I personally collect quill knives, whittler pattern knives and hobo (slot) knives. Value of knives depends on maker, age, rarity, condition, and desirability. A knife can range from $50 to $1,000 just on condition. I generally pay 40% to 60% of full market value when buying for resale. How much I pay for things for my own collection depends on how badly I want it. I will tell the seller what I think fair market value is, then explain my offer." He DOES NOT WANT broken blades, deep rust, or *Case* knives made after 1980. Tell this 25 year veteran knife buyer the number of blades, the maker's markings on the blades, the handle material, the size and the condition. SASE. Bob is the ex-veep of the Southern California Blades.

Robert Berman
Robert Berman Gallery
9540 Sylvia Avenue
Northridge, CA 91324
(818) 349-3926   Fax: (818) 349-3923

STRAIGHT & SAFETY RAZORS

★ **Straight razors with handles of sterling, rough bone, mother-of-pearl, or aluminum.** Celluloid or pressed horn razors with several characters are also wanted. Good razors generally bring from $50-$75, with some higher, some less. Please provide all information found on the blade or handle. He does not want plain handled razors from Solingen, Germany. Make photocopies with the blade(s) open. Indicate the material from which the handle is made.

    Charles Stapp
    7037 Haynes Road
    Georgetown, IN 47122
       (812) 923-3483

★ **Straight razors with fancy handles** made of gold or sterling silver. Also razors with figural handles, multiple blades, fancy etching on the blade, or with fraternal emblems or advertising on the handle. Handles may be made of horn, mother-of-pearl, or multi-colored celluloid. Rare razors will be considered even if they are slightly damaged. Also **razor and cutlery advertising** and memorabilia, catalogs, trade cards, etc., including oversize displays.

    William Campesi
    PO Box 140
    Merrick, NY 11566
       (516) 546-9630

Value of straight razors lays almost all in the handle. When buyers ask for unusual handles, they really mean it!

Ordinary black handled straight razors have little if any value. Don't ask.

★ **Safety razors and accessories.** This 20 year veteran collector wants to buy odd safety razors and advertising for razors including posters, magazine ads, and signs. He'd love to find oversize store display razors or oversize shaving mugs or brushes. Give all colors and metals and note "all writing on the items. A good clear photo is best," he says, but photocopies will suffice.

    Cary Basse
    6927 Forbes Avenue
    Van Nuys, CA 91406
       (818) 781-4856

★ **Razor blade collections or accumulations.** Photocopies are good, but even better is a sample of each cap, with the number you have of each written on the back lightly in pencil.

David Wampler
1808 Hidden Harbor Road
Hixson, TN 37343
(423) 843-1693   (423) 875-7315   dwampler@mindspring.com

★ **Safety razors,** stropping machines, **packs of blades**, blade banks, and other early or unique shaving items, "with highest prices paid for safety razors with unusual or oddly shaped blades." Phil wrote *The Complete Gillette Collector's Handbook* available from him for $24.

Phillip Krumholz
PO Box 4050
Bartonville, IL 61607
(309) 697-1120

★ **Safety razor shaving memorabilia**, 1880-1930, including safety razors, mechanical blade sharpeners, razor blade banks, advertising signs and buttons, counter and window displays, giveaways, catalogs, and miscellaneous paper associated with any of the above. Also wants figural shaving mugs in the shape of animals, people, or birds and shaving brushes with figural handles. Shaving mugs and barber bottles which appear to be covered with imitation bark are also of interest. The following brands of safety razor are NOT WANTED: *Rolls, Durham, Valet* or *Gillette* (if the serial number is higher than 500,000). Blade sharpeners that are too common to have value are *Kriss Kross* and *Twinplex.* Blade banks given away by *Listerine* are also very common. Please provide as much detail as possible, including all names, letters, dates, colors, etc. A drawing is helpful.

Lester Dequaine
155 Brewster Street
Bridgeport, CT 06605
(203) 335-6833

★ **Razor blades and blade sharpeners.** "I'll buy U.S. or foreign blades, in singles, packages, or on cards as well as interesting advertising signs, posters, and displays related to razor blades." Describe your sharpener carefully, pointing out all damage, and noting any words or numbers on it.

Cary Basse
6927 Forbes Avenue
Van Nuys, CA 91406
(818) 781-4856

PERFUME

★ **Perfume bottles**. Wants high quality commercial, miniature and other perfume bottles from 1700 to 1950. Especially wants elaborate 18th and 19th century scent bottles and 20th century bottles made by famous glassmakers like Lalique and Baccarat. She does not want anything made by *Avon*. Please indicate the size in inches, color of the glass and stopper, whether or not the original label and box are present, and if the bottle is signed (look very closely at both bottle and stopper with a magnifying glass as signatures and markings can be very small). If the stopper does not seem to match the base, it may be OK as many valuable bottles have unusual stoppers which seem mismatched. Photos or Xerox© copies of your bottle are helpful. Ms. Parris is a founding member of the Perfume & Scent Bottle Association and their membership chairperson. Please contact her only if your bottle is old, in perfect condition, and for sale, or if you would like to join the club. SASE.

    Jeane Parris
    Sugarplums, etc.
    2022 East Charleston Boulevard
    Las Vegas, NV 89104
        (702) 385-6059 days   Fax: (702) 388-1202

Collectors seek many perfume bottles from the 1920's, 30's, and 40's. Since these bottles were designed and made by top European art glass companies, they are frequently worth $100 and up. Record prices of over $10,000 have been paid, so advice is essential.
Look for pretty shapes, silver trim, atomizers, glass stoppers, and anything unusual, figural, or particularly decorative.

Avon *perfume and toiletry bottles have no resale value at this time. They are widely offered at $1 and $2 each retail.*

★ **Perfume bottles, decanters, and vases with silver overlay.** Describe all markings and give dimensions and colors.

    Arnold Reamer
    Timepiece Antiques
    PO Box 26416
    Baltimore, MD 21207
        (410) 944-6414   (410) 486-8412   Fax: (410) 265-7877

★ **Perfume bottles.** "I collect, buy and sell perfume bottles, from 1900 to the 1960's, in good to mint condition. I'm looking for unusual bottles, ceramic bottles with metal crown stoppers, and unusual shapes as well as "testers" with daubers. A photo of your bottle would be appreciated, accompanied with a description. Please include an SASE if you want photos returned. I pay fair market prices, and will make offers when necessary, but prefer you to set the price wanted."
    Sue Murphy
    29668 Orinda Road
    San Juan Capistrano, CA 92675
        (714) 364-4333

★ **Perfume bottles made of blown or cut art glass,** singles or matching sets. Wants fine beautiful bottles including those with atomizers. Some important makers include *DeVilbis, Daum Nancy, Galle, Baccarat, Webb, Moser, Czechoslovakian, Lalique,* and *Steuben.* Also English scents, bottles with sterling overlay, and figural perfume bottles. The proprietor of this unusual shop for women does not make offers, nor does she buy *Avon* bottles.
    Madeleine France
    Past Pleasures for the 20th Century Woman
    PO Box 15555
    Plantation, FL 33318
        (954) 921-0022 days   Fax: (954) 584-0014

★ *DeVilbis* **atomizers,** with or without original bulb and cord. Describe the size, colors, and condition. A detailed sketch or close up photo is essential. Please, no commercial or medicinal atomizers as he wants only the pretty ones that were used for perfume.
    Bruce Bleier
    73 Riverdale Road
    Valley Stream, NY 11581

★ *California Perfume Company* **(CPC) products made between 1886 and 1920,** especially *Natoma Rose* fragrances. He also wants CPC products marketed as *Goetting and Company, Savoi Et Cie, Marvel Electric Silver Cleaner,* and the *Easy Day Automatic Clothes Washer.* Please give a complete description of the item you have for sale, including its condition and whether or not it has its original box. Is there a label and/or a neck band? Are there cracks or chips? Photocopy is helpful. Be prepared to leave a message stating exactly what you have, its condition and the price you'd like for it. Dealers price your goods. Genuine amateurs may request help in setting prices. Dick does not want anything with AVON or PERFECTION on the label.
    Dick Pardini
    3107 North El Dorado Street, Dept TH
    Stockton, CA 95204
        (209) 466-5550 7am to 11pm

COMPACTS, MAKEUP & PURSES

★ **Women's sterling silver dresser sets, hair brushes, mirrors and other boudoir items**. The proprietor of this unusual shop for women does not make offers, so you'll have to price what you have.

> Madeleine France
> Past Pleasures for the 20th Century Woman
> PO Box 15555
> Plantation, FL 33318
>   (954) 921-0022 days   Fax: (954) 584-0014

★ **Women's powder compacts,** from before 1950. All types of good looking, fine condition compacts are wanted, as long as the compact is complete. Unusual, Art Deco and precious metals are preferred.

> Bird In the Cage
> 110 King Street
> Alexandria, VA 22314
>   (703) 549-5114

★ **Women's figural compacts.** "We buy compacts that are in the shape of an object like a padlock, Christmas ornament, miniature stuffed animal, etc. Compacts must be in very fine condition, with no scratches, dents, or worn finish. It is best if the original rouge, powder and mirror are intact, but the more unusual the compact, the more forgiving we are. We do not collect conventional round or square compacts even if they have an embossed, engraved or applied figure on the lid." A clear close-up photo is needed, or a good Xerox™ if possible. Your description should indicate the condition of the mirror, the puff, and the contents. "Small markings stamped into the metal on the inside are critical to mention." An illustrated wants list is available.

> Mike and Sherry Miller
> 303 Holiday Ave.
> Tuscola, IL 61953
>   (217) 253-4991

★ **Ladies' compacts.** "I am a buyer and seller, always looking for the unusual, enameled, novelty, in the shape of other items, or compacts that are part of purses of other items. I prefer items in good to mint condition, but have been known to buy lesser condition, but priced accordingly. Please include an SASE if you want photos returned. I do ask you to set the price wanted but will make offers when necessary."

> Sue Murphy
> 29668 Orinda Road
> San Juan Capistrano, CA 92675
>   (714) 364-4333

★ **Purses** from before 1930. Primarily seeking:
  • Enameled mesh purses in bright colors, scenic designs, etc.
      from the late 1920's, especially with jeweled frames or
      in odd shapes or made with unusual mesh;
  • **Beaded purses**, with interesting patterns, scenes of people,
      pictures of places, Persian carpet or Egyptian motifs;
  • *Bakelite* purses;
  • **Plastic compacts** which are actually small purses;
  • Trinity plate very small purses made of brass with
      complex filigree work and stones, often with tassels.

Good purses must be without wear in mint to near mint condition and
will bring prices from $50 to $300 depending on style, rarity and condition. "I'm looking for the out of the ordinary." Your description
should include the style, design, and color. A photo or Xerox™ is a
good idea. Dealers should price their goods. Amateurs may request an
offer from this veteran collector. If she is not interested in your item,
she will be happy to tell you what an appropriate price should be.

> Leslie Holms
> PO Box 596
> Los Gatos, CA 95031
> (408) 354-1626

★ **Metal mesh purses** with colorful designs painted into the mesh.
Prefers mint condition items but will consider some with minor wear
or a few disconnected links. Among items sought are:
  • Very large bags, 6" x 10" or larger;
  • Very small bags, 2" x 3" or so;
  • Bags with designs portraying scenes, animals or people;
  • Bags with cartoon characters;
  • Bags with ornate frames set with polished stones, fake jewels,
      or enameled decorations;
  • Bags with elaborate Art Deco designs on the mesh and or frame;
  • Mesh vanity bags which combine a compact and a purse (these
      usually bring the highest prices);
  • Beaded purses, but only older bags with very small glass beads
      (18 to 22 beads to the inch) which are strung into a scene, a
      figure, or into the design of an Oriental rug.

Must be in mint or nearly mint condition. A Xerox™ copy is a good
way to describe your purse. Illustrated wants list available for SASE.

> Mike and Sherry Miller
> 303 Holiday Ave.
> Tuscola, IL 61953
> (217) 253-4991

★ **Compacts.** Wants unusual compacts:
- Shaped like phone dials, pistols, hot air balloons, suitcases, hands, drums, guitars, lady bugs, flying saucers, etc.;
- Enameled Art Deco designs;
- **Jeweled vanities**;
- Molded plastic Bakelite vanities;
- Mesh and beaded purses with compact tops;
- **Canes** or **hat pins** concealing compacts.

"I don't buy 1940's and 50's carryalls (usually 3"x5" or 4"x6"), nor am I interested in plain brass, sterling, or silver plate without color." No compacts with damaged enamel. Photo helpful.

> Lori Landgrebe
> 2331 East Main
> Decatur, IL 62521
> (217) 423-2254

★ **Fancy lipsticks and compacts**, especially those in combination with purses, bracelets, etc. Wants gold, sterling or enameled pieces only. Will consider **vanity cases, chatelaines** and **cigarette holders.** Values range from $15 to many hundreds" but items must be near mint with no chips, dents, or broken hinges. Make a Xerox™ copy.

> Rita Berman
> 9540 Sylvia Avenue
> Northridge, CA 91324
> (818) 349-3926   Fax: (818) 349-3923

Avon bottles are everywhere, and I have not been able to locate a buyer for collections of Avon items. You may wish to subscribe to Avon Times, a monthly newsletter with 8 pages of "Buy and sell" ads for $21 (PO Box 9868, Kansas City, MO 64134). A sample newsletter is $3. A price guide to Avon is advertised as being available from them for $26.

In my experience it's difficult to find buyers for common items. They generally sell one at a time, for $1 or $2 at flea markets. Only a few are sought after and bring higher prices.

TIPS ON SELLING DOLLS AND TEDDY BEARS

Doll collecting is the second largest hobby in the United States. Doll lovers spend one-half billion dollars each year. Collectors want all types from the high priced 19th century mechanicals and French fashion dolls which cost many thousands of dollars to modern plastic dolls worth a fraction as much. Because you are more likely to have the more modern dolls, a greater emphasis has been placed on them in this book.

Buyers of most dolls want the following information:

(1) Length of the doll, important because some dolls made in multiple sizes have different values;

(2) How big around the head is, important on old dolls; use a seamstress's tape or string to measure;

(3) Material from which the head, hair, hands, feet and body are made (may be from different materials);

(4) Type of eyes (painted, button, glass), their color and whether or not they move;

(5) Whether the mouth is open and whether teeth (molded, painted, or attached) show;

(6) Marks incised into the scalp, neck, shoulders, or back of the doll;

(7) How the doll is dressed and whether the clothes seem to be original;

(8) Any chips, cracks, repainting, or other repairs.

When offering a doll for sale, a photo can be helpful, but you can often get better results faster, easier, and cheaper with a photocopy machine. Photocopies are particularly useful for showing how a doll is dressed.

The original box for your doll may add as much as 50% to the doll's value. When describing modern dolls such as Barbie™ whose accessories are frequently marketed in plastic bubble packs mention packages that are un-opened and unfaded as they make a doll worth two or three times the value of loose dolls or accessories.

ANTIQUE DOLLS

★ **Dolls, antique and modern.** Buys:
  - Dolls of bisque, china, wood, cloth, papier-maché, composition
      and hard plastic from the beginning of time to the 1960's;
  - **Kewpies, bears, and other animals**;
  - **Doll accessories** like shoes, clothing, wigs, purses, combs,
      opera glasses, and the like;
  - **Small props** like **buggies, furniture, tea sets**, and the like.
"I prefer things priced, but will make offers."
> Madalaine Selfridge
> Hidden Magic Doll Museum
> 33710 Almond Street
> Wildomar, CA 92595
> (909) 674-9221

★ **Character dolls.** Buys a variety of character dolls:
  - **Barbie dolls** from 1964 and before, especially the Color-Magic
      and "American Girl" models. Also buys factory-made
      Barbie clothes, but not home-made ones;
  - **Raggedy Ann and Andy** and related items, including
      Beloved Belindy. She emphasizes a willingness to pay
      top prices for very early high quality dolls;
  - **Howdy Doody** dolls and marionettes. Also interested in dolls
      of all other characters on the show: , Clara Belle, Mr. Bluster,
      Princess, Flubba Dub, and Dilly Dally;
  - **Little Lulu & Tubby** dolls and related items in all sizes;
  - **Red Riding Hood** and related items;
  - **Cinderella** and related items.
Follow the basic rules for describing what you have to sell, including
dimensions and an accurate statement of condition. "I don't want re-
productions, common items, or junk."
> Gwen Daniel
> 18 Belleau Lake Court
> O'Fallon, MO 63366
> (314) 978-3190 anytime   gdaniel@mail.win.org

★ **Collections of antique dolls** are sought for cataloged specialty
auctions by this well known New England auctioneer. No junk,
reproductions, or dolls made after 1940 will be considered.
> James D. Julia Auctioneers
> PO Box 830
> Fairfield, ME 04937
> (207) 453-7904   Fax: (207) 453-2502

★ **Old dolls and their parts.** "I buy, both as a collector and as a dealer, a large variety of old dolls and their parts.
• Old **German dolls** (a particular favorite);
• **Cloth comic characters** such as Lulu, Tubby, Nancy, or Sluggo;
• **Raggedy Ann or Andy** dolls, but only old ones;
• Bisque **snow babies**;
• Wooden jointed creche-type dolls for display at Christmas;
• **Damaged dolls** if priced reasonably;
• **Accessories for old dolls,** such as shoes, clothing, wigs, purses;
• **Doll carriages** and quality furniture;
• **Buster Brown china dishes**.
I have no interest at all in Japanese bisque or currently made dolls. Send a Xerox™ or photo of what you have."
    Patricia Snyder, My Dear Dolly
    PO Box 303
    Sparta, NJ 07871
        (201) 729-8087

★ **Dolls.** This 30 year veteran doll dealer wants collections or single:
• **Antique dolls** from France, Germany or the U.S. made from
        bisque, wood, china, composition or other material;
• **Shirley Temple dolls**;
• 1950's and 60's dolls such as *Ginny, Terri Lee, Buddy Lee*, etc.;
• *Barbie* **dolls** and accessories, especially those made before 1970
        all limited edition *Barbies*, porcelain *Barbies,* Mackie designer
        dolls, store specials, convention dolls, or other special issues;
• **Kewpie** dolls;
• Doll **buggies, furniture and dishes**.
"I pay especially well for these dolls in their original packages." Prices vary widely depending on the individual doll, its rarity and its condition. "I do not want any dolls that are still available in stores or any new reproduction porcelain or artist dolls. In most cases, I need you to tell me the size, any marks or identifications, and what you know of its history. Dealers, price your goods; amateurs may request an offer."
    Donna and Al Purkey, All About Dolls
    1238 South Beach Blvd. #D
    Anaheim, CA 92804
        (714) 828-5909   (714) 826-4699 days

★ *Skookum* **Indian dolls wearing colorful Indian pattern blankets** from the smallest sizes up to those five feet tall, if in perfect condition. Some dolls marked SKOOKUM and/or BULLY GOOD under the feet. He does not want *Skookums* with plastic parts. Send a photo for offer.
    Barry Friedman
    Box 55492
    Valencia, CA 91355
        (805) 255-2365   BarryF@fishnet.net

★ **Dolls of all types.** This active dealer will consider a wide range of good looking fine condition dolls made of papier-maché, wood, china, or bisque, including:
- Expensive **French fashion dolls**, character dolls, etc.;
- Early **cloth dolls**;
- **Teddy bears**;
- **Steiff character and animal dolls**;
- **Vogue Ginny** dolls;
- Kathe Kruse, Chase, Madame Alexanders, or Izannah Walker;
- **Doll houses**.

Follow guidelines on page 110 for describing dolls correctly.

> Valerie Zakszewski
> 61 6th Street
> Cambridge, MA 02141
>   (800) 897-2933   (617) 576-0796

★ **Teddy bears that are fully jointed with glass or shoebutton eyes.** "I'll pay the best prices for early German bears in very fine condition." Follow basic rules for describing.

> Gwen Daniel
> 18 Belleau Lake Court
> O'Fallon, MO 63366
>   (314) 978-3190 anytime   gdaniel@mail.win.org

★ **Teddy bears that are fully jointed with glass or shoebutton eyes.** Wants pre-1920 *Steiff* bears in any condition and will pay $1,000+ for those larger than 20" long. Not interested in any non-jointed bears or bears made after 1940. Also teddy bear books, postcards, photos, trays, etc. Polly also buys **stuffed animal toys on cast iron wheels**.

> Polly Zarneski
> 5803 North Fleming
> Spokane, WA 99205
>   (509) 327-7622

★ **Mohair teddy bears with long arms and big feet** made between 1903 and 1915 are wanted in all sizes as long as they are fully jointed. Also wants perfume and compact bears in various colors and any unusual mohair teddy or teddy related items. Also looking for early *Steiff* **cats and dogs** with printed ear buttons. Also wants **Billy Possum stuffed dolls with shoebutton eyes** and all Billy Possum items including doll dishes and silverware, banks and postcards. Mimi wants you to know your dolls are going to a "loving home, not a dealer."

> Mimi Hiscox
> 12291 St. Mark
> Garden Grove, CA 92645
>   (310) 598-5450

MODERN DOLLS

★ **Cabbage Patch Kids** are wanted but only a select few. Ann, who is a collector not a dealer, wants 1983 *Colecos* (black signature) with freckles, boy dolls with fuzzy or shag hair, dolls from molds 4, 6, 19 or 30. She also wants UT tags, dolls sold in foreign countries, and mint clothing accessories. A color photo and SASE is a must. Ann is the author of an inexpensive ($7) book that describes the types and variants of CPK's. If you have Kids for sale other than those listed above, you are encouraged to obtain her book, then advertise your CPK's for sale in the monthly Newsletter which she edits. Ads are 25¢/word.

You must be aware that there are many types of CPK's:
- Xavier Roberts' soft sculptured originals (1978 on);
- Mass market dolls by *Coleco* and *Hasbro* with vinyl heads
  and yarn or nylon hair (1983-present);
- Porcelain dolls by *Applause* or *Shader* (1985-86);
- Porcelain figurines by *Extra Special* (1984-85);
- Vinyl figurines and "numerous accessories."

Many CPK's sell below issue price but some originals bring $200-$300 and rare models by *Coleco* bring $150 and up. If you want to sell your doll, determining its value requires expertise and a lot of information. If your doll is in its original box, open it from the bottom and untwist the wire holding the CPK in place. Your letter should contain the following information for an accurate response:
- Head mold number impressed on the back of the neck;
- Hair style and color;
- Eye color and whether there are freckles or not;
- Description of the clothing (look for a tag and CPK logo);
- Color of the Xavier Roberts signature found on the left butt;
- If the CPK's butt has a date, please give it as well;
- The name of the manufacturer and the factory ID letters in the
  circle on the body tag found under the diaper on the left side
  (letters should be J, P, IC, KT, OK, PMI or UT);
- And lastly, whether the box and birth papers are present.

Sounds like a lot...and it is, but that's what it takes. These once fanatically popular collectibles haven't skyrocketed, and values remain stable compared to many other dolls.

Ann Wilhite
The Cabbage Connection
610 West 17th
Fremont, NE 68025

★ *Barbie* **dolls.** Wants to buy all *Barbie* dolls, fashions and accessories, 1959-1972. "Anything *Barbie* related," she says, especially prototypes, gift sets, licensed Mattel products, watches, ponytails, color magic, bendable leg *Barbies*, and the rest of *Barbie*'s family, especially Francie, introduced in 1966. Will pay $1,000 for a mint in box airplane and $500 for a MIB *Barbie* boat. She does buy Bob Mackie *Barbies*, porcelain, holiday, Xmas, and FAO Schwartz *Barbies* too. It's worth your time to look for early dolls, especially for the clothes and accessories in their original boxes, because some were made for a very short time or sold in very limited markets. Some inside tips:

The first *Barbie* sleep eyes were introduced in 1964.

If the knees bend, the doll was made after 1965.

Rooted eyelashes came into use in 1966.

Talking *Barbie* family arrived in 1968.

Black Barbies Julia and Christie arrived the same year.

Dolls that are easy to pose, and those with growing hair, are both products of the 1970's and too late to interest most *Barbie* collectors. To describe a *Barbie*, you must give the name of the doll, hair color, lip color and condition. "Please," she asks, "do not send or write about *Barbies* because they say 1966 on their back. Today's dolls still say 1966 on them." Marl offers an important clue about how to tell if your *Barbie* is old. "If it does not say JAPAN on the buttocks or foot, I don't want it." Marl buys dolls for her personal collection and for resale.

Marl Davidson, WS8
10301 Braden Run
Bradenton, FL 34202
(941) 751-6275   Fax: (941) 751-5463   marlbe@aol.com

The first Barbie *wore a black and white swimsuit and had copper tubes set in holes in the bottom of her feet. Barbie stood on a round black plastic disk. Her white irises and black eyeliner looked Oriental.*

The second Barbie was like the first except the stand holes were gone. Barbies three through six had blue eyes.

The first (ponytail) Barbie from the late 1950's and early 60's had MCM LVIII embossed on her behind. This remains until 1962. For 20 years, beginning in 1966, Barbie was tush marked "1966."

Barbie was made worldwide, and tush marked accordingly. Only those marked JAPAN *are sought by most collectors.*

★ *Barbie* **dolls and accessories from 1958 through 1966** are wanted, especially items still in their original box. "I'll also buy other members of the *Mattel* family of dolls from that era, and clothing for them all. HINT: *Barbie's* clothing is numbered. The earliest clothing is in the 900 series, but I also want the 1600 series outfits sold in the early 1960's. Call even if your outfit isn't all there, because you may have just the parts I need to complete a set. Of all the *Barbie* items, the one I'd like to find the most is the case of 30 or 31 Barbies that was carried by salesmen in 1958 in an effort to sell the doll to toy stores. It contains #1 *Barbies* wearing the old outfits that were going to be available. If you have one of these in perfect condition it could be worth as much as $100,000. Pink display box dolls that retailers used in the early 60's containing dressed *Barbies* are also sought, and can put from $3,000 to $5,000 in your pocket if in fine condition. In 1964 when *Mattel* introduced the bendable *Barbies*, they tried a variety of hair styles, so *Barbie* came with bubble cuts, pony tails, and page boys. The American girl dolls with side-parts in their hair are among the rarest of the *Barbie* dolls, and can be worth $2,000 to $4,000 or more if in their original boxes." She is not buying *Barbies* from the 1970's and 80's, or earlier dolls with serious flaws such as damaged toes or missing limbs or fingers. Describe your *Barbie* and accessories thoroughly, paying particular attention to condition. Describe the condition of the box as well. You may set the price wanted or request an offer if your doll is for sale.

Linda Brundage
2717 West Olive Avenue #200
Burbank, CA 91505
(818) 843-8616

Most amateurs trying to research dolls are limited by what is available in their local public library. If you have 20th century dolls, books by Pat Smith may be of help. Ask the reference librarian to obtain these and other doll books through interloan if you can't find what you need in your local branch.

Researching dolls on your own can be frustrating. A specialty book like Barbie Rarities *by Florence Theriault is excellent, but at $45 is for the serious collector. For most other types of dolls, there is no single book certain to help you.*

☆ *Nancy Ann Storybook Dolls* were created in the mid 1930's. These early dolls were bisque (unglazed china) made in Japan, and usually marked with a sticker reading NANCY ANN DRESSED DOLL. After 1942, dolls were "frozen legged." *Nancy Anns* were the number one selling girls' toy in the 1940's. In 1947 they introduced plastic arms, then all plastic bodies. In 1949, eyes opened and shut. Many different series were created including Sports, Masquerade, and Famous pairs like Hansel and Gretel (all desirable). You may also find:

- Nursery rhymes, days of the week, and months of the year (the most common of her dolls);
- *Margie Ann* is same doll but dressed as a little girl in a suit;
- *Audrey Ann* in an organdy dress and white boots is hard to find;
- *Geraldine Ann* with eight outfits and a "movie set" with a director's chair, lights, etc., is fragile and very desirable;
- *Judy Ann*/USA dolls, which are very scarce;
- *Muffie* and *Debbie*, 8" and 10" hard plastic dolls, were the tops of the line, and came with many matching outfits.

Nancy Ann made a great many dolls, so values range from $20 to $175 with a few over $500. Dolls must be individually evaluated, however, because there are so many different costumes. In general, the frozen leg and plastic dolls are less valuable, but boy (male) dolls are rare and desirable in any form as is some furniture. *McCalls* pattern #811 for making cardboard furniture at home is $50+ to you! All Nancy Ann dolls have a hat or ribbon in their hair. A missing hat reduces the value of a doll by more than half, and "you can't put just any old ribbon in the hair." To sell a *Nancy Ann*, you must tell whether it's plastic or bisque, has moving or frozen legs, has eyes that move or not (and their color), and the height. Make a photocopy of the doll which shows the dress. If you have the original box, copy that too, since some boxes are more valuable than others.

Elaine M. Pardee
7909 Walerga Road #112
Antelope, CA 95843
(916) 725-7277   Fax: (916) 725-7447

★ *Annalee* **dolls.** Wants 1950's, 60's, 70's and 80's versions of these felt dolls with painted faces, most of which have internal wires for positioning arms and legs. All types considered, including human, animal, and holiday, especially those with feather or yarn hair. Look for embroidered (or woven) tags as tags, more than copyright dates, are indicators of when a doll was made, although early dolls didn't always have tags, and doll owners often cut them off. Dating dolls by their tags is a job for experts, and never foolproof, as many different tags appear on the oldest dolls. Some *Annalee Dolls* were custom made, some limited production, and others factory made in fairly large quantities, so Sue will often need to talk to you or inspect the doll before giving an offer. Dolls tend to be worth $20 to $150 with a very few worth more. "I'll analyze your doll and will always give you a fair price." Pictures are helpful, but "if you can't send a photo, you must tell me what the doll is (human or animal) and what it's doing and how it's dressed. I also need to know the height of the doll, as they come in many different sizes. Condition is important in determining price. If you have an *Annalee Doll*, I want you to call with the doll in front of you. Before you call, please make a careful inspection for moth and silverfish damage in the form of holes, pock-marks, etc., and for any signs of fading in the doll or clothing." Sue is willing to train pickers who regularly shop at yard sales and flea markets if you send a Stamped Self-Addressed Envelope. Please include your phone number. If you're a picker, her detailed informative wants list is a must.

Sue Coffee
10 Saunders Hollow Road
Old Lyme, CT 06371
(860) 434-5641

★ **Dolls of the 1950's,** but only in excellent condition with original clothes. Call, fax, or write a description if you have the following:
- *Nancy Ann Storybook* dolls, particularly Muffie;
- *Vogue Ginny* dolls;
- *Betsy McCall* dolls;
- *Alexanderkins*;
- *Hard plastic dolls* in interesting costumes, such as cowboys, Hawaiians, ethnic dress, etc. "The costume's the thing."
- **Doll houses and furniture** from before 1960.

A complete description of the doll, costume, and box is helpful, but a photo is the best. Dimensions from head to toe are also helpful.

> Leda Andrews
> 2110 Staples Avenue
> Key West, FL 33040
> (305) 296-4195   Fax: (305) 293-0904

★ **Betsy McCall dolls and clothing** in original package or loose, one item or an entire collection. The "Designer Studio" and "A Day at the Ranch" gift sets are particularly sought, as are puzzles, cookie cutters, coloring books, figurines, etc. "I'm interested in anything and everything *Betsy McCall.*" Marci produces a *Betsy-On-Line* newsletter.

> Marci Van Ausdall
> PO Box 946
> Quincy, CA 95971
> (916) 283-2770   Dreams707@aol.com

★ *Madame Alexander* **dolls of the 1950's.** Mid 1920's dolls were cloth, then composition. The 1950's Alexanders were made of hard plastic jointed at neck, shoulders and hips, and often knees, elbows, and even ankles! In the early 1960's, these hard plastic dolls gave way to squeezable vinyl dolls with rooted hair. "I want **good condition hard plastic dolls with glued wigs and original clothes.**" Wants all sizes, from 8" to 21", but they must be in good condition with original clothes. The same doll might have 80 or more different costumes, and a variety of hair. "Some that don't look too exciting may actually be rare and valuable because they didn't sell and were only offered for a short time." The 1950's dolls she seeks were generally tagged and marked. To sell your doll, give her the information on the clothing tag, a description of the costume, and a statement of condition. Note whether you have the original box. Have the doll in hand if you call. Lia says, "I will consider older composition or cloth *Alexander* dolls, but only if in mint perfect condition. They don't have to be in the original box, but must be like new."

> Lia Sargent
> 74 The Oaks
> Roslyn Estates, NY 11576
> (800) 421-9912   Fax: (516) 621-7517

★ *Topper Dawn* **and other dolls from the 1960's and 70's.** "I am interested in *anything* Dawn doll related, especially the Aladdin Dawn Brunch Bag and catalogs and other printed Dawn material. I am also looking for the following dolls:
  * Hasbro *Love, Leggy, Jem* and *Disco Girls*;
  * Kenner *Blythe and Darcy*;
  * Mattel *Liddle Kiddles, Talk-Ups, Major Matt Mason* and *Upsy Downsys*;
  * *Galoob Baby Face*;
  * American Character *Emerald the Witch*;
  * Ideal *Flatsys* (but only boxed or carded).

"I am also interested in any **catalogs** that include toys and dolls, thingmakers, *Oily Rubber Creatures* and the like.
>   Joedi Johnson
>   PO Box 565
>   Billings, MT 59101
>   (406) 248-4875 voice and fax

★ **Doll houses and furniture circa 1900,** but *only* wooden houses covered with colorfully lithographed paper, especially made by *Bliss*.
>   Jerry Phelps
>   8012 Deronia Avenue
>   Louisville, KY 40222
>   (502) 425-2561

★ **Doll houses and miniatures,** especially *Schoenhut* and *Bliss* houses for which they pay $500-$1,500. "We are one of the oldest and most experienced companies in the doll house and miniatures industry," Bob says, "and we will consider buying anything in miniatures that is old and in good condition." Their catalog of new doll house parts is fascinating, and well worth the $5.50 charge.
>   Robert Dankanics, The Dollhouse Factory
>   PO Box 456
>   Lebanon, NJ 08833
>   (908) 236-6404

★ **Chinese Door of Hope dolls** sold by Christian missionaries to raise funds between 1909 and 1947. Also **china or bisque headed dolls** less than 12" high made before 1925. Will buy **doll parts**, bodies, heads, and old clothes, but will make no offers. Everyone price your goods.
>   Marjorie Gewalt
>   3900 North Main Street #114
>   Racine, WI 53402
>   (414) 639-2346

TIPS ON SELLING TOYS AND GAMES

*Games and toys are often treasures,
especially if they are colorful, in their
original box, and in excellent condition.
There is a market for lesser items, but*
prices drop to nothing for anything shabby.
*It seems as if nearly every toy is collected by someone, and
you'll find the very best buyers in the following pages.*

If you carefully read sections in **Trash or Treasure** *about
Toys, Dolls, Games, and Pop Culture, you will see a wide
range of small and seemingly insignificant items sought by
collectors. Games based on movies and TV usually find
ready buyers in the $20 to $100 range (see pp111-126).
You will also find a buyer for nearly all toy vehicles made
from tin, steel or cast iron. The market is not good for
plastic vehicles, though some other plastic toys, especially
comic characters will sell. Baby boomer toys of the 1960's
and 70's are particularly popular right now.*

**Common games with names you recognize are seldom
collectible,** *unless they are prototypes or hand made.*

*To sell something, you should provide the potential
buyer with a complete description, including the following
information:*

(1) *What you have, including its size, color, and the
material from which it is made;*
(2) *Names, dates, and numbers printed, embossed,
stamped, or labeled on the item;*
(3) *Condition, including mention of any damage,
missing parts or pieces, or missing paint;*
(4) *Whether it has the box and/or instructions, especially
important when selling games.*

Wooden, tin, and iron toys were usually painted. **The
amount of paint that still remains is vital information,** *as is
any evidence that the toy might have been repainted.
You should estimate what percentage of original paint
remains.*

Don't forget your Self-Addressed Stamped Envelope.

MISCELLANEOUS TOYS

★ **Fine old kaleidoscopes** made of wood and/or brass especially elaborate inlaid or complex instruments from the mid 19th century. No cardboard toys.

> Lucille Malitz
> Lucid Antiques
> PO Box KH
> Scarsdale, NY 10583
> (914) 636-7825

★ **High quality kaleidoscopes** from the 1800's, made of wood and/or brass by makers such as *Bush, Brewster, Carpenter,* or *Leach.* Prefer perfect original condition brass instruments in wooden cases with the Royal seal, but will consider less. He does not buy cardboard or other inexpensive kaleidoscopes. Nothing made in the 1900's. Include your phone number and time you're home so he can phone.

> Martin Roenigk
> Mechantiques
> 26 Barton Hill
> East Hampton, CT 06424
> (203) 267-8682 Fax: (203) 267-1120

★ **Polyramapanoptiques and megalethescopes.** The former are early 19th century cardboard or wooden boxes with flaps for slides, which permit viewing of hand painted or pin-pricked scenes. Megalethescopes, invented in 1860, are large wooden cabinets, often heavily carved, also devices for slides, usually seen as day and night views of the same scene in 3D. Lucile also buys and sells slides for these early optical toys.

> Lucille Malitz
> Lucid Antiques
> PO Box KH
> Scarsdale, NY 10583
> (914) 636-7825

19th century toys with moving parts regularly bring more than $2,500 and top the $500 mark often. At least one Trash or Treasure find resulted in an $18,000 sale. Be very careful how you dispose of any old toy in fine condition. Be careful not to over-emphasize the importance of "old." Many toys from the 1960's are worth $1,000.

★ **Antique toys** including cars, carousels, character and comic wind-ups. German and American tin toys, penny toys, nested blocks, still banks and pop-up books are all sought. Special interest in toys by Gibbs, Arcade, TootsieToy, Buddy L, Hubley (motorcycles), and 1950's Matchbox. Has no interest in dolls or trains. List manufacturer, size, and condition. Fine condition items only. Photo desirable.

James Conley
2758 Coventry Lane NW
Canton, OH 44708
(330) 477-7725

★ **Collections of fine tin and iron toys** are sought for cataloged specialty auctions by this well known New England auctioneer. No junk, reproductions or items made after 1940.

James D. Julia Auctioneers
PO Box 830
Fairfield, ME 04937
(207) 453-7904   Fax: (207) 453-2502

★ **Cast iron bell toys,** working or not. He will consider incomplete specimens of these early toys which move and ring a bell when pulled on a string. Send clear photos taken from more than one angle, or phone with the item in hand.

Gregory "Dr. Z" Zemenick
1350 Kirts Blvd. #160
Troy, MI 48084
(810) 642-8129   (810) 244-9495

★ **Victorian toys:** Jack-in-the-boxes, animals on rolling platforms, nine pins bowling games, and other traditional toys, especially those with nursery rhyme tie-ins. He does not want anything made after 1920. This 25 year veteran requests a photo or photocopy of what you'd like to sell. Prefers to find toys in like-new condition, because they are frequently used as part of Christmas theme displays.

Dolph "Father Christmas" Gotelli
PO Box 188977
Sacramento, CA 95818
(916) 456-9734   (916) 457-1559

★ **Antique toys** of many different types:
  • **Mechanical banks,** pre-1920, made of tin or iron;
  • Cast iron **bell toys**, circa 1890;
  • **Figural clockwork toys**, in tin or iron, from the 1870's;
  • **Political campaign toys** and banks;
  • European **tin toys** and large boats;
  • Colorful **paper on wood boats and trains** from the 1890's;
  • Colorful **Victorian children's games** and **block sets**;
  • **Hand painted tin wind-up toys**.

He's not interested in anything after 1940, nor does he want banks marked BOOK OF KNOWLEDGE, repainted items or things that have been dug up. Broken mechanical banks or rare toys that are incomplete may be of minor interest. Give the size, condition of the metal, and the condition of the paint including fading. List all repairs and note if the item has been lacquered or refinished. This 17 year veteran insists you set the price you want for your items.

Mark Suozzi
PO Box 102
Ashfield, MA 01330
   (413) 628-3241   Fax: (413) 628-3241

You should give the following information:

  (1) What you have, including its size, color, and the material from which it is made;
  (2) Names, dates, and numbers printed, embossed, stamped, or labeled on the item;
  (3) Condition, including mention of any missing parts, pieces, or paint, or damage to what remains;
  (4) Whether it has the box and/or instructions.

Don't forget your Self-Addressed Stamped Envelope.

★ **Tin wind-up toys** made in Germany or Japan, as well as a "few select American wind-ups" are sought by this collector/ dealer who says he 'prefers automotive and character toys. He does say that **some battery operated and non operating toys will also be considered, especially cast iron cars and motorcycles as well as "carnival ride" toys**. He does not buy plastic items or anything in poor condition. He'd like to know if your toy is complete, how much paint is missing, whether it works and if you have its box. If it's newer than 1960, it's not wanted.

Richard Trautwein
Toys n' Such
437 Dawson Street
Sault Ste. Marie, MI 49783
   (906) 635-0356

★ **Clockwork (wind-up) toys** from before 1910, made of tin or iron, working or not, complete or not. "I want wind-up cars, boats, horses and buggies, people, and what have you, with particular interest in large ocean boats and steamships." Send a good clear sharp photo of both sides of the toy and include your telephone number.

Greg "Dr. Z" Zemenick
1350 Kirts Blvd. #160
Troy, MI 48084
(810) 642-8129 eves   (810) 244-9426 days   Fax: (810) 244-9495

★ *Schoenhut* **circus animals,** milk and bread wagons, trolleys, and other other toys, games and dolls made by Schoenhut. No pianos. He asks for pictures and an accurate description. No offers, so research is in order before making any inquiry.

Harry McKeon, Jr.
18 Rose Lane
Flourtown, PA 19031
(215) 233-4094

★ **Clockwork German or French tin clockwork toys** by makers such as Martan, Lehman and Marklin. He asks for pictures and an accurate description. No offers.

Harry McKeon, Jr.
18 Rose Lane
Flourtown, PA 19031
(215) 233-4094

See also: Teddy bears and Dolls for other buyers of early toys.

★ **Old one of a kind kites from before 1940** especially those made by important inventors. Names on desirable kites include *Hargrave, Lecornu, Saconney, Conyne, Perkins, Bell,* and many others including *Barrage Kite, Target Kite,* and the *U.S. Weather Bureau.* Also wants prototype models of production kites. Also traditional kites of Europe, the Orient, Malaysia, or South America. If it's old, interesting, or unusual, she'd like to hear about it. As publisher of *Kite Lines,* Valerie says she can act as a contact person to help you sell your kite if it's something she doesn't want. Rare and important kites are scarce but the market is small. They bring from $100 to $500. Give the history of your kite if you can.

Valerie Govig, Kite Lines
PO Box 446
Randallstown, MD 21133
(410) 922-1212   Fax: (410) 922-4262

★ **Baby rattles** from 1950 or earlier in gold, silver, wood, celluloid, plastic or rubber. "I am particularly interested in Art Nouveau baby rattles as well as Georgian, Victorian and early American examples. I would like to find Oriental rattles, too. I am not interested in reproductions or the most common types of rattles, since I already have more than 600. I need a good photo and a complete description. You must price what you have for sale. I do not make offers."

Marcia Hersey
106 West 69th Street
New York, NY 10023

★ **Any sand-operated self contained toys,** including the "not very old" enclosed boxes with figures set in motion by flipping over the box. Also **small toy scales** made of tin.

Donald Gorlick
PO Box 24541
Seattle, WA 98124
(206) 824-0508

★ *Erector* **sets** by *A.C. Gilbert*. Will buy complete sets, partial sets, manuals, signs, and sales catalogs. Give model numbers and dates whenever it's possible.

Elmer Wagner
28 East Willow Street
Carlisle, PA 17013
(717) 258-0839

★ **Colorforms** are 1960's toys with colored plastic pieces to make people and scenes of the time. Subjects included *Star Trek, Popeye, The Jetsons, Flintstones, Munsters, Beverly Hillbillies, Addams Family, Roy Rogers & Dale Evans, Little Orphan Annie* among the most sought after. Complete sets in crisp boxes bring the best prices. A full description of the box and contents along with a photo will bring an offer.

Carol Ann Osman
PO Box 16383
Pittsburgh, PA 15242
(412) 922-0117

When you ask someone for information or an offer, include a long business size #10 envelope, address it to yourself, and put a stamp in the corner. This is a Self-Addressed Stamped Envelope (SASE). Use a long envelope because many buyers will send you information which won't fit into smaller envelopes.

TOY BANKS

★ **Cast iron mechanical banks**, 1870-1920, and **Japanese tin battery operated banks**, 1946-1960. Include a bottom tracing. Indicate whether it works or not and if you still have the original box. Battery banks *must* be in near mint condition. No plastic banks.

     Rick Mihlheim
     PO Box 128
     Allegan, MI 49010
       (616) 673-4509

Tin and iron toys were usually painted. The amount of paint that remains is vital information to a collector. So is evidence that the toy might have been repainted. You should estimate the percentage of paint remaining.

Toy banks are desirable, particularly 19th century originals. These were sold in boxes, which can add hundreds of dollars to the value. Banks marked BOOK OF KNOWLEDGE on the bottom are not of interest. Advertising cards which depict banks sell for $200 to $1,000 each!

Here's a couple pages of people who pay that!

★ **Mechanical and still banks made of cast iron, tin, or wood.** Especially any mechanical bank with its original box, packing, and receipt. Also buys painted and stenciled cast iron or tin still banks shaped like buildings. Will consider incomplete, broken and non-working specimens, if old and genuine. No banks made after 1930, especially those which say BOOK OF KNOWLEDGE on the bottom. Also buys trade cards, catalogs, empty packing boxes, advertising depicting mechanical banks and photos of children with banks. Send sharp photos of the bank from different angles, or phone with it in front of you. Greg is the former president of a club for bank collectors.

     Gregory "Dr. Z" Zemenick
     1350 Kirts #160
     Troy, MI 48084
(810) 642-8129 eves   (810) 244-9426 days   Fax: (810) 244-9495

★ **Cast iron or tin banks, still or mechanical.** Also buys original boxes and color trade cards for mechanical banks. No banks after 1950. Indicate any repairs, repaints, and give the dimensions. Prefers you to set the price you want.

Virginia Jensen
22410 Wilson
Dearborn, MI 48126

★ **Still banks made of cast iron or metal** with special emphasis on unusual or rare examples in excellent to near-mint condition. Letters should include an accurate description including an estimate of how much of the original paint is still there. Carefully measure the length, width, and height. Photos are appreciated. Private collector answers all letters which include SASE.

Ralph Berman
3524 Largo Lane
Annandale, VA 22003
(703) 560-5439

★ **Banks, both still and mechanical** made of cast iron, tin, or zinc alloy before 1935. Also wants bank related items such as the wood boxes used to package banks by the manufacturer, ads, **trade cards**, and flyers depicting mechanical banks. Also photos of children with mechanical banks. Does not want reproductions or rusted items. Tell him the condition and exact size of the bank. He notes it is impossible to make a firm offer without seeing a good sharp color photo. Sy writes a monthly column on banks for *Antique Toy World.*

Sy Schreckinger
PO Box 104
East Rockaway, NY 11518
(516) 536-4154

★ **Mechanical banks in the form of rocket ships** used by Financial and Insurance Companies as promotional giveaways. "I want banks with all the original parts in excellent condition. Photo is helpful."

Anthony Glab
4154 Falls Road
Baltimore, MD 21211
(410) 235-1777   Fax: (410) 889-1937   glab@aol.com

TOY SOLDIERS & TOY GUNS

★ **Toy soldiers, farm figures and zoo animals and related buildings and vehicles** made of metal, composition or plastic. "I buy single pieces, sets, and entire collections. Prices vary widely, but complete sets of toy soldiers mint in their box will bring from $50 to $1,500. I am not interested in reproductions or damaged figures. Please send a photograph, an accurate description, or a sample figure."

    Dave Francis
    PO Box 16
    Wadsworth, OH 44281
       (330) 335-3717   Fax: (330) 335-3617

★ **Toy lead soldiers** and related items by the following companies, especially when packed in original boxes: *Britains, Mignot, Heyde, Lineol*, and *Elastolin*. When writing, please give a brief description of the soldiers, the name of the maker whenever possible, whether or not you have the original box, the number of soldiers and include a photo.

    Bob Fisher, Old Toy Soldier's Home
    977 South Santa Fe Avenue #11
    Vista, CA 92083
       (619) 758-5481 voice and fax

★ **Toy soldiers of all types** including dime store soldiers, 1930-50, made in the USA of painted lead, boxed sets of fine British soldiers, or German composition soldiers of WWII. Xerox™ gets a free appraisal.

    Larry Bruch
    PO Box 121
    Mountain Top, PA 18707
       (800) 549-TOYS

★ **BB Guns.** Older BB guns with cast iron parts, and USA made spring-air BB guns in excellent condition. Many brands are wanted, although *Daisy* guns are preferred from the Plymouth, MI, factory. Does not want recently made guns, or those that are damaged, broken or in less than very good condition. You must list everything broken or missing. Is the stock, forestock, or grip broken, cracked or worn? Describe the finish on all metal and wooden parts. Include all names, numbers and addresses found on the gun. Indicate if it works or not.

    James Buskirk, Toy Gun Collectors of America
    3009 Oleander Avenue
    San Marcos, CA 92069
       (619) 599-1054

Minor differences in castings, handles, or decoration can put extra money in your pocket. Accurate descriptions are important.

★ *Quackenbush* **air guns.** Send a complete description, including a sketch or photo. Will make offers, but appraisals are for a fee.

Charles Best
11523 Pinevalley Drive
Franktown, CO 80116
(303) 660-2318

★ **Cap pistols.** Especially interested in cast iron guns by *Kilgore, Stevens, Hubley* and *Kenton.* Premium paid for character guns such as the *Kilgore Long Tom, Big Horn, Roy Rogers, Lone Ranger* or *American,* the *Kenton Lawmaker,* the *Stevens Cowboy King,* or any of the many different models of *Gene Autry* guns made by *Kenton.* Also interested in the 1950's and 60's die cast guns. Buys any guns marked *Gene Autry, Roy Rogers, Dale Evans, Trigger, Lone Ranger, Tonto, Paladin, Alan Ladd, Hopalong Cassidy, Hoppy,* or *Shane.* Particularly seeks character guns made in Los Angeles by the *Schmidt Company* or by *LATCO.* Must give all identifying marks, numbers, etc., found on the guns and a complete accounting of damage or wear to the gun, finish, or handles (grips). Buys only guns in fine condition. Publishes the *Toy Toy Gun Collectors Newsletter,* available with club membership for the bargain price of $15/year.

James Buskirk, Toy Gun Collectors of America
3009 Oleander Avenue
San Marcos, CA 92069
(619) 599-1054

★ **Cap pistols made of cast iron,** especially animated guns from the 1800's or guns featuring movie cowboys and other Pop Culture heroes before 1940. A magnet *must* stick to your gun or he's not interested.

George Fougere
67 East Street
North Grafton, MA 01536
(508) 839-2701

★ **Cap pistols.** "I'll buy Western style cap guns made before 1965 by *Kilgore, Hubley, Stevens, Leslie-Henry, Chas. Schmidt, Nichols, Mattel,* and others. Especially looking for *Kilgore* "disc cap" guns such as the American, Big Horn, Long Tom and Roy Rogers models. Also seeking any cap gun or holster sets associated with cowboy movie and TV actors like Gene, Hoppy, Paladin, the Lone Ranger, etc. Condition is important. Guns must be complete, working, and have little wear. Top prices paid for guns or holster sets in their original box. Photo if possible. Xerox™ your gun if you don't know what it is.

Bill Hamburg
PO Box 1305
Woodland Hills, CA 91365
(818) 346-1269   Fax: (818) 346-0215

GAMES & PUZZLES

★ **Games.** Buys children's and adult games in colorful pictorial boxes copyrighted before 1970 including:
* Victorian games before 1900;
* Comic character games;
* Television games from the 1950's and 60's;
* Sports games with famous players named on the box;
* Space and science fiction games before 1970;
* Games based on children's book series;
* Lesser known games with colorful names or pictures.

Does not want generic games, or any common game. Condition of games is very important as he buys for resale. Give the name of the game, the maker, copyright (©) date, and list all missing pieces, if any.

> Paul Fink's Fun & Games
> PO Box 488
> Kent, CT 067547
> (860) 927-4001

★ **Antique and collectible board and card games** made in the U.S. from 1840-1950's. Any game before 1860 is wanted, especially those made by *Ives, Crosby, Magnus,* or *Adams*, for which they will pay $500 and up. Other items of particular interest are baseball games before WWI and games about cartoon characters, space exploration and pop culture (including movies) of the 1930's-1950's. They also buy **wooden jigsaw puzzles, blocks**, and **paper toys**. No chess, checkers, *Pit, Lotto, Rook, Flinch, Autobridge, Parcheesi, Touring,* variants of *Bingo,* TV "game show" games, or "kiddie" games like *Chutes and Ladders.* Give the name of the game, the maker, size, condition, copyright date, and the degree of completeness.

> Dave Oglesby and Sue Stock
> 57 Lakeshore Drive
> Marlborough, MA 01752
> (508) 481-1087

★ **Almost any complete playable game,** especially out-of-print titles by *Avalon Hill, 3M, SPI,* pre-1964 *Parker Bros.,* war games, sports games, political games, and TV related games. Include the name of the manufacturer and copyright date. Please thoroughly check the contents and note if anything, no matter how small, is missing. Describe how much wear shows on the box and pieces. Also buys **gaming magazines** such as *The General, Wargamer, The Dragon,* and *Games & Puzzles.* Please, no checkers, chess or common children's games like *Authors.*

> H.M. Levy
> PO Box 197-TH
> East Meadow, NY 11554
> (516) 485-0877   gamers@pipeline.com

★ **American boxed games,** all types and all years. "I buy:
  • **Board games;**
  • **Card games;**
  • **Skill and action games;**
  • **Jigsaw puzzles;**
  • **Mechanical puzzles;**
  • **Paper games** published in magazines and newspapers;
  • **Games with themes reflecting American history and culture**, sports, politics, social issues, fads or leisure;
  • **Mystery games;**
  • **Space games;**
  • **Games depicting specific events or persons;**
  • **Games with fictional or cartoon characters;**
  • **Games based on radio, television, movies or books;**
  • **Games which have advertising** or were sponsored by products;
  • **Games made in upstate New York;**
  • **Games with colorful illustrations on the box** or game board;
  • **Game boards, parts and pieces before 1900;**
  • **Advertising or ephemera** related to game companies.
"Specific games I want include *Philo Vance, Charlie Chan, Boom or Bust, Star Reporter, Red Barber's Baseball, Troque,* and *Elvis* but I buy most games by McLoughlin Brothers and E.G. Selchow, and pre-1920 games by Parker Brothers, Selchow & Righter, Milton Bradley, Singer, Bliss, Ives, Cadaco, National, Games of Fame, Jim Prentice Electric Game Company, and others, especially small regional companies.
I do not want games that don't indicate the manufacturer, or common games such as *Authors, Backgammon, Beano, Bingo, Bridge, Charlie's Angels, Checkers, Chess, Chinese Checkers, Doctor Busby, Fish Pond, Flinch, Jack Straws, Keno, Kojak, Lost Heir, Lotto, Monopoly, Old Main, Parcheesi, Peter Coddles, Pick-Up-Sticks, Pit Rook, Snap, Tic-Tac-Toe, Tiddly Winks, Touring* or *Whist* unless there is something very striking or unusual about your edition. **Please don't offer games that are not complete and in near mint condition unless** they are before 1900 or priced so cheaply that I can buy them for parts." When describing a game, give the name, date, manufacturer, box size, box contents, and the material from which the pieces are made. Tell whether the game has all parts and instructions. Make a Xerox™ of the cover of the box and board. Bruce charges a fee for appraisals. Dealers should price their goods, but amateurs may request offers with the understanding that Bruce buys for resale. Bruce has written more than 100 articles on games, past president of the American Game Collectors Ass'n and author of the definitive price guide to games: *American Boxed Games and Their Makers, 1822-1992* which you can order for $23.

Bruce Whitehill
The Big Game Hunter
620 Park Avenue #202
Rochester, NY 14607
 (716) 442-8998 days   clue@netacc.net

★ **Chess sets.** "I'll buy rare and unusual chess sets of all sorts, but primarily those with *themes* such as Disney, Watergate, etc. I like historical, literary, fictional, and mythological." If it's out of the ordinary in theme, design, material, or whatever, give him a call. He would especially like to find the 3-D chess set from *Star Trek* in the late 1960's. No plastic or "typical wooden sets," he warns. "I'm looking for works of art or imagination." Describe the board if one accompanies your set. Provide whatever background you can about the history of the set, including when and where it was bought and the price paid. Describe condition in detail and the height in inches of a king and pawn. Photo and SASE are essential for an accurate answer.

> Dennis Horwitz
> PO Box 301
> Topanga, CA 90290
> (310) 455-4002

★ **Chess sets, as well as books and art related to chess.**
- "I'll buy figural or very ornate sets" made of ivory, bone, amber, wood, silver, metal, glass, or porcelain. Sets from before 1900 are preferred. Artist signed sets are of particular interest as are ivory sets from 19th century Europe or Russia. Standard looking sets are not wanted.
- Art sought includes paintings, prints, figurines, and anything else with a chess related theme.
- Books related to playing chess, chess pieces, or chess history. "Will consider any book related to chess" including those on other topics with chess sections.
- Ephemera such as photos, autographs, postcards, score cards of well known players, medals, souvenirs from chess Olympiads, and what have you.

Chess sets should be complete, but early and rare items will be considered even if damaged. A photo or Xerox™ is helpful. When offering a set for sale, note the material from which it is made and measure the height of a pawn and the king. Note whether pieces are boxed or loose. Dealers, price your goods. Amateurs may request an offer.

> Jeffrey Litwin
> PO Box 5865
> Trenton, NJ 08638
> (609) 275-0996   Fax: (609) 275-1427

★ **Checker ephemera,** primarily books about checkers or draughts, but also old checker sets made of wood, rubber, Catalin™ or Bakelite™. Call about anything unusual related to checkers.

> Don Deweber
> 3520 Hillcrest #4
> Dubuque, IA 52002
> (319) 556-1944

★ **Mechanical and dexterity puzzles.** Wants all types of mechanical and dexterity puzzles. Not interested in jigsaw or paper and pencil puzzles. Please send a photocopy, sketch, or clear photo of your puzzle.

>Cary Basse
>6927 Forbes Avenue
>Van Nuys, CA 91406
>(818) 781-4856

★ **Mechanical puzzles of all types** including **trick locks** and matchsafes "and all others." Also expresses some interest in advertising for trick locks and puzzles. A photocopy, photograph, or good sketch is appreciated. Dealers should price their goods, but he will help amateurs to determine the value of what they have.

>"Mr. Slocum"
>PO Box 1635
>Beverly Hills, CA 90213
>(310) 273-2270   Fax: (310) 274-3644

★ **Games and jigsaw puzzles with sentimental or sexy themes** dating from 1920-1959, such as pin-ups, children and animals, parents and children, patriotism, etc. Must be in the original box.

>Charles Martignette
>PO Box 293
>Hallandale, FL 33008
>(954) 454-3474

Pencil and paper puzzles like rebuses and crosswords are sought by a different type of collector. You will find this type of puzzle in the section on paper. Look in the index under "crossword puzzles" and you'll be steered to pages 460, 506 and 517.

MARBLES

★ **Marbles and marble related ephemera.** Will buy postcards, magazine covers, ads, trade cards, stories, calendars, or "anything depicting or written about kids playing marbles."

>William Nielsen
>1379 Main Street
>PO Box 1379
>Brewster, MA 02631
>(508) 896-7389

★ **Better quality marbles** are sought, as are marble related items such as original boxes, tournament trophies and medals, and marble literature. "We run quarterly marble auctions, and if you send a detailed description or close-up color photo, we'll give you an idea of what your items will bring at marble auction and what we will pay you to purchase them outright." Stan is the chairman of the Marble Collectors Society of America, publishers of *Marble Mania*. Son Robert is author of the excellent *Marbles Identification and Price Guide* available from them for $24 postpaid.

    Stan and Robert Block
    PO Box 51
    Trumbull, CT 06611
       (203) 261-0057   BWVR62A@Prodigy.com

★ **Marbles and marble-related toys.** Wants old marbles including clay, china and porcelain marbles decorated with flowers, people, animals or geometric designs. He also buys Indian swirls, German swirls, clam broth, sulfides and machine made marbles if before 1940. "I'll pay up to $2,000 for colored sulfide marbles with unusual objects or people in them and up to $1,000 for porcelain or china marbles decorated with flowers, ships, birds, or people and animals." He also wants, and will pay well for, early boxed sets of marbles made by *Christensen Agate Co., Peltier Marble Co.,* or *Akro Agate*. Toys related to marbles are also often of interest. He does not want *Chinese Checker* marbles and boards or any cat's-eye marbles. If you know your marble's history, tell him. Otherwise a good description should include what is on or in the marble and its diameter.

    Edwin Snyder
    PO Box 156
    Lancaster, KY 40444
       (606) 792-4816 eves

★ **Marbles and marble-related items.** "I'll buy marbles with pontil marks (from where they were hand-blown), toys or games using marbles, marble bags, tournament pins and medals, and boxes of marbles. Also pictures, magazine ads, and postcards which depict marble games." He does not buy "beat up" or chipped marbles, machine made marbles, homemade games, or *Chinese Checkers*. When selling marbles, it is important to give the diameter as part of your description.

    Larry Svacina
    7812 NW Hampton Road
    Kansas City, MO 64152
       (816) 587-1203

TOY & ELECTRIC TRAINS

★ **Toy trains and accessories, U.S. or foreign, made between 1900 and 1970.** Will buy any maker and gauge except HO gauge trains. Items do not have to be in perfect condition to be considered. **Also buys train catalogs and literature**. A wind-up *American Flyer* train with cars marked *Coca-Cola* is worth $350 in mint condition. This 40 year veteran will make offers **only if you're serious about selling**. Lazarus is past president of the Toy Train Operating Society. Make certain to include a stamped envelope for a reply.

> Hillel Don Lazarus
> 14547 Titus Street #207
> Panorama City, CA 91402
> (818) 762-3652 eves

When describing electric trains, give the brand name, any model numbers found on the engine, and a list of the cars. It's worth your time to indicate the color of each car, its purpose, and RR line name, since minor variations can affect value. If the car has been repainted or otherwise modified by someone other than the factory, be certain to note that fact.

If you have the original box, describe its condition. Make a list of any accessories, noting the condition of the paint of each. Some buildings and other items will bring you $100 or more.

★ **All makes of old toy trains except HO gauge and hand made scale models.** Buys *Lionel, American Flyer, Ives, Marx* and all foreign trains larger than HO. "I'll buy engines, cars, accessories, signals, and incomplete sets that are new, like new, used, and even incomplete but useful for parts. No layouts, rusty junk or other toys." This 45 year veteran hobby shop owner offers a large price guide to trains for $7, which is refunded on your first purchase.

> Allison Cox
> 18025 8th Avenue N.W.
> Seattle, WA 98177
> (206) 546-2230 Fax: (206) 546-0114

★ *Marklin* **and other European toy trains and metal toys.** "I'll buy trains powered by clockwork, electricity, or live steam." Other toys such as airplanes, boats, circus toys, and others made by *Marklin* will also be considered for purchase. Most *Marklin* toys are marked with the company name, but some have an entwined GM or GERMANY. "I want anything by *Marklin* before 1955 in decent condition." Also wants *Bing, Schuco, Doll, Lehmann, Carette* and other European trains and metal toys in very good or better condition. "I will buy common items in excellent condition, but don't want repros, fakes, or toys with pieces missing. I'm a collector so prefer people not contact me unless they actually want to sell or trade what they have. I pay fair prices and am willing to travel to inspect collections." *Marklin* trains from before WWII are worth $500 to as much as $10,000 to Ron so check carefully.

Ron Wiener
Packard Bldg #1200
111 South 15th Street
Philadelphia, PA 19102
(215) 977-2266   Fax: (215) 977-2334

★ **Toy trains in all gauges and types** are wanted, including electric, wind-up, floor type, etc. "Age is not the main consideration, but I do want items from before World War II. I like to buy large collections, but will buy smaller units, and consider properly priced junkers, but no reproductions." Wants to know the train's gauge, maker, condition, the number of pieces and the markings on each, and how many of the original boxes you have.

Jay "The Chicago Kid" Robinson
PO Box 529
Deerfield, IL 60015
(847) 945-8691   Fax: (847) 940-7579

★ **HO and N gauge trains and accessories,** preferably in running order, but they don't have to be old. He also buys **railroad books and magazines**.

Cliff Robnett
7804 NW 27th
Bethany, OK 73008
(405) 787-6703

★ **Trains and other vehicles.** Will make an offer on trains in any gauge, especially HO, Standard, and O. He is also in the market for any fine old toys, but especially **steam engines, tin plate toys, and airplanes.** A color photo must accompany your description if you wish to sell to this long time dealer.

Heinz Mueller, Continental Hobby
PO Box 193
Sheboygan, WI 53082
(414) 693-3371   Fax: (414) 693-8211

★ **Electric trains by** *Marx* with metal or plastic cars that have eight wheels. Especially wants complete sets in original boxes. "I'll pay $100 for *Marx* Pennsylvania RR car #53941. Not interested in plastic engines numbered #400 or #490 or plastic cars." When writing, give him all numbers you find on boxes or cars.

> Robert Owen
> PO Box 204
> Fairborn, OH 45324

If toy trains interest you, join the Toy Train Operating Society. Their Bulletin is one of the truly fine club publications. For information write to the Society at 25 West Walnut Street, Room 408, Pasadena, CA 91103. They'll send complete information and a sample copy.

TOY MOTORS & ENGINES

★ **Toy outboard motors,** either battery or wind-up, alone or mounted on toy boats. "I'll buy motors by *K&O Fleetline* made between 1952 and 1962 with names of popular manufacturers of real outboard motors." Pays $75-$400 for your toy depending on the model. Describe the decals and color. Author of *Toy Outboard Motors*.

> Jack Browning
> 214 16th Street NW
> Roanoke, VA 24017
> (540) 982-1253   (540) 890-5083   Fax: (540) 342-1283

★ **Toys run by live steam or hot air** wanted, as are accessories and catalogs related to steam and hot air toys. "I'll pay $100 to several thousand dollars for steam engines or for boats, trucks, cars, trains or tractors, American, English or German made. Makers include *Weeden, Buckman, Union, Bing, Marklin, Carette* and others. I don't want modern steam toys made by *Wilesco, Mamod,* or *Jansen*." Give dimensions and markings. Some *Marklin* power plants were 4' tall and can be worth up to $10,000. "I usually require a photo before I buy, since most people do not understand the technical aspects of steam toys."

> Lowell Wagner
> 10585 Knight Avenue
> Waconia, MN 55387
> (612) 442-4036

★ **Model airplane engines**, both foreign and domestic, built between 1930 and 1970. Buys both spark and glo plug ignitions as well as diesel. "I am particularly interested in .15 cubic inch (2.5 cubic centimeter) displacement glo and diesel engines." Generally, engines with ball bearings are more valuable than those with plain bushings. Engines should be complete with proper carburetor and no disfiguring marks. Engines can be worth from $5 to $400, depending on rarity and condition. Does not buy model boat engines, steam engines or stationery engines, but a few small **car engines** may be acceptable. Give the name of the engine if known, and all markings stamped on the crankcase. Give serial numbers, if any. A picture is preferred. SASE is a must. Dealers price your goods; amateurs may request an offer or appraisal

Jim Dunkin
29805 East Ryan Road
Blue Springs, MO 64014
(816) 229-9671 voice or fax

★ **Toy electric battery driven motors** for kids, 1910 to 1930, made by *Ajax, Lil Hustler, Porter, Kent, Edison, Leavitt* and others. These range in size from lemons to large apples and had a variety of applications. Send complete information and the price wanted.

Steve Cunningham
3200 Ashland Drive
Bedford, TX 76021
(800) 991-0165   Fax: (800) 991-0166

★ **Miniature outboard marine motors** used on model boats before 1970. Wants fuel type motors only. No electric motors or boats. Condition must be described carefully. Offers made only on items sent for examination. Owner pays postage for return of my offer not accepted.

Sven Stau
240 Knox Avenue
West Seneca, NY 14224
(716) 825-5448

★ **Toy outboard boat motors made of metal** labeled *Gale, Oliver, Mercury, Evinrude, Scott, Johnson, Fuji, Sea-Fury, Orkin* and the like. A *Gale* Sovereign 60HP toy metal outboard will bring $200 as will an *Oliver* 35HP. Boxes are worth an additional 10%. No plastic motors. Please send a photo (not a Polaroid™) and describe the condition.

Richard Gronowski
140 North Garfield Avenue
Traverse City, MI 49686
(616) 941-2111

PLASTIC MODEL KITS

★ **Plastic model kits** especially from the 1950's made by *Monogram, Hawk , Aurora, Bachman, Comet, ITC, Frog, Allyn, Monogram, Revell, Strombecker*, and others. Models can be autos, airliners, commercial ships, spacecraft, TV and movie subjects, and science fiction and other figures. Also manufacturers catalogs and store display models. Kits must be complete and unbuilt, with minimal damage to the box. Sealed unopened kits are best. He offers to send a copy of the grading system used by kit collectors for an SASE. He'll pay $100 for a perfect condition *Athearn* **gas-powered flying model** of the *Convair XFY-1 Pogo*. Bob publishes *Vintage Plastic*, the journal for kit collectors.

Bob Keller's Starline Hobbies
PO Box 38
Stanton, CA 90680
(714) 826-5218 days   Email: GQYGOIA@prodigy.com

★ **Plastic model kits** of airplanes, tanks, ships, figures, cars, buildings, or what have you *if complete, unbuilt, and in original box.* Include the manufacturer and kit number. John publishes *Kit Collector's Clearinghouse*, a bimonthly newsletter for kit collectors and is the author of *Value Guide for Scale Model Plastic Kits,* available for $30, and other model books.

John Burns
3213 Hardy Drive
Edmond, OK 73013
(405) 341-4640

★ **Plastic 1/25th scale model car kits,** built or not. Also buys dealer promotional materials, **model car books and magazines,** if pre 1975. Does not want anything currently available. Give the name of the maker and model number. If you have **dealer promotional models**, note the color, condition, and whether the original box is present.

Rick Hanson
PO Box 161
Newark, IL 60541
(815) 695-9484 voice and fax

TOY VEHICLES

★ **Metal vehicles and toys,** pre-1959, including cars, trucks, boats, airplanes, trains and construction equipment:
  • **Large steel toys** by *Buddy-L, Sturditoy, Turner, Kingsbury, Sonny, Keystone,* and *Structo*;
  • *Tootsietoys* with white rubber tires or all metal wheels;
  • **Old tin toy boats,** the larger the better;
  • **Children's pedal cars** and trucks made before 1940;
  • *Smith-Miller* or *M-I-C* **trucks** made of steel in California between 1945 and 1957;
  • **Tin windup automotive, aviation, or comic toys,** U.S. or European, working or not. Will pay $8,000 for an 8" truck with "Aunt Eppie Hogg" in perfect condition;
  • *Dinky* toys, pre-1964, from England or France;
  • **Any metal motorcycle** 8" or longer, especially *Hubley Indian* delivery cycle, worth $2,500 in original condition;
  • **Japanese scale models of U.S. cars;**
  • **Cast iron toys** by *Hubley, Arcade, Kilgore,* and *Williams.*
Plastic, rubber, or wooden vehicles are not wanted. Describe the condition carefully, paying particular attention to the quality of the paint and whether or not all the parts and pieces are present. Describe the condition of the wheels and tires. Dimensions are helpful.
> Larry Bruch
> PO Box 121
> Mountaintop, PA 18707
> (800) 549-TOYS

★ **Cars, trucks and race cars** made of metal before 1960 are wanted.
  • Toy cars by *Hubley, **Dinky**, Arcade, Kilgore, Williams, Tootsietoy, Sun Rubber,* and *Auburn Rubber* are wanted;
  • Race cars, with or without engines, are wanted made by *Cox, Thimbledrome, Ohlson and Rice, Rodzy,* and others;
  • Trucks by *Smith-Miller, MIC, Tonka, Marx* and others are sought.
Please send a photo and good description. "Prompt response assured."
> Bill Hamburg
> PO Box 1305
> Woodland Hills, CA 91365
> (818) 346-1269   Fax: (818) 346-0215

★ *Tonka, Doepke,* and *Smith-Miller* **toy trucks** and catalogs, ads and photos depicting them. He does not want *Tonka's* "Mighty" or "Mini" series trucks or anything repainted. Photos of both sides are necessary.
> Nollie Neill, Jr.
> PO Box 38
> Ennice, NC 28623
> (910) 657-8152 eves   Fax: (910) 657-8084

★ **Larger pressed steel toy cars and trucks** are wanted by this 10 year veteran collector-dealer. "I'll buy *Smith Miller, Doepke, Tonka, Buddy-L, Keystone, Arcade* and other makes of toy vehicles including construction types, boats, airplanes, and farm tractors." To sell your vehicles, tell him [1] the maker if you can, [2] what it looks like, including what type of vehicle it is, [3] how many you have, and [4] the condition of each. Make an estimate of what percentage of the original paint is left. "I prefer not to buy rusty or damaged vehicles, but this policy is not written in stone."

> Jay "The Chicago Kid" Robinson
> PO Box 529
> Deerfield, IL 60015
>   (847) 945-8691   Fax: (847) 940-7579

★ **Toy tin automobiles** made in France and Germany before WWI that run by steam, batteries, or clockwork. "The item, its size, and the condition all determine value. "Some early autos by *Bing* are worth thousands of dollars. A photo is almost a must."

> David Bausch
> 252 North 7th Street
> Allentown, PA 18102
>   (610) 432-3355   Fax: (610) 820-9368

★ **Toy garbage trucks** in any size or condition. Please give the maker, size, and condition of tires and paint.

> A.J. Perez
> 5408 North Diversey
> Whitefish Bay, WI 53217
>   (414) 964-5399

★ **Hard rubber toys,** especially **vehicles**, motorcycles, trains, airplanes, ships, **animals, soldiers, football and baseball players**, especially by *Rainbow Rubber Co.* Hard rubber toys only. No vinyl. Hard rubber is painted. Vinyl is made in the color of the toy and is the same color throughout. Give the maker, size, colors, condition, and description of features. Also buys **all toy vehicles of all sizes, from** *Dinky* **to pedal cars** made before 1950. "Photos are best."

> Steve Kelley
> PO Box 695
> Desert Hot Springs, CA 92240
>   (619) 329-3206

★ **Toy farm tractors and equipment** from 1980 or older, including the large cast metal riding tractor toys. "I want toys with real farm equipment company names like *John Deere, Farmall, Oliver, Ford, Allis-Chalmers* and the like, in plastic or metal, and pay over $200 for some tractors. Even broken ones are wanted for parts." Also wants *Caterpillar* **dozers and heavy equipment toys.** Does NOT want anything made after 1980. Give the color, size, brand, model, condition, and the status of the original box, if available. "A photo is helpful."

Dave Nolt
PO Box 553
Gap, PA 17527
(717) 768-3066 voice and fax

★ **Toy firetrucks and fire related toys.** This veteran collector/dealer wants U.S. made fire toys built prior to 1960. Buys all types, all sizes, all styles as long as they are in good condition. Is particularly interested in finding *Ahrens Fox* and *Bulldog Macks* and other large steel firetruck toys, some of which can be worth $700 or more. Buys **toy fire stations,** firemen, and other toys and **games that are fire related.** Requests color photos, the price you'd like, and a statement of condition. Include your phone number. Will assist amateurs to set price. No Japanese tin toys or anything made after 1965.

Luke Casbar
Big Boy's Fire Toys
22 Garden Street
Lodi, NJ 07644
(201) 478-5535

★ *Hot Wheels* are hot. With more than 700 basic body styles, 5,000 color combinations, and 10,000 minor variations it's important to get expert advice before disposing of these toys. Values begin at a few dollars, but some can be worth more than $1,000 each! If you want to sell your cars, give the name of the car, the color, and the condition, including an estimate of the percent of original paint remaining. If all you want is an estimate of value, Mike wrote *Price Guide to Hot Wheels,* available from him for $30. He edits *Hot Wheels Newsletter,* available for only $20. "I give honest evaluations and pay fair prices," says this 20 year veteran collector/dealer, "but condition is important in the value of cars, and sellers really don't know how to properly evaluate condition, so I will never send money without seeing the cars first."

Mike Strauss
26 Madera Avenue
San Carlos, CA 94070
(415) 591-6482 after 6 PST   Fax: 571-7935   hwnewsltr@aol.com

★ *Dinky* **toys** of all types except army vehicles. Also wants to buy all types of **toy motorcycles.**

> Don Schneider
> PO Box 1570
> Merritt, BC
> V1K 1B8 CANADA
> (604) 378-6421

GASOLINE & ELECTRIC CARS

★ **Gasoline powered toy cars.** Wants all types of race cars made by *Dooling, Rexner, Morrison, Bremer, Duesenberg, JL Special, BB Corn, Popp*, etc., as well as **all Mite cars** such as *Thimbledrome, O&R, McCoy*, etc. Also buys damaged cars, 60 size racing engines, parts, coils, condensers, spark plugs, ignition leads, etc. Also buys **toy diesel engines, steam engines, and home made engines.**

> Richard Gronowski
> 140 North Garfield Avenue
> Traverse City, MI 49686
> (616) 941-2111

★ *Aurora Thunderjet* **and** *AFX* **1/87 electric race cars/slot cars** in 1/87 HO scale. Wants cars, track, accessories, parts, complete sets, and collections of miscellaneous pieces. Original boxes not necessary, but welcome. Photos requested, "or give me a call." Also buys HO trains.

> Pat Jacobsen
> PO Box 791
> Weimar, CA 95736
> (916) 637-5923

★ *Atlas* **and** *Aurora* **electric race cars.** "No limit," he says, but prefers to buy entire collections. He particularly wants items in complete sets and original boxes or **store displays** and stock, but "will consider any *Atlas* and *Aurora* electric race cars you have." Photos are requested, but if you have a large collection for sale, you are encouraged to phone him. "I also collect colorful **hockey related games**, preferably complete in original box, but will consider incomplete sets if the boxes are good."

> Joe Bodnarchuk
> 62 McKinley Avenue
> Kenmore, NY 14217
> (716) 873-0264 voice or fax

PEDAL CARS

★ **Pedal cars.** "I'll buy any pre-WWII pedal car, pedal plane or pedal truck, and will consider some from the mid-1950's. I'm a most generous buyer, as I buy to keep not to resell. Condition is not a problem. I'll even buy half a vehicle if that's all you have. Please send photos." Will also purchase large (bigger than 12") metal cars, trucks, and planes made by *Keystone, Buddy-L, Dayton,* etc. No interest in *Tonka.*

     Sandy Weltman
     39 Branford Road
     Rochester, NY 14618
        (716) 442-8810

★ **Pedal car and planes, three fender tricycles, and tricycles with sidecars** in any condition. I will pay over $1,000 for the better examples." Also wants any **pedal car advertising**, sales catalogs, and the like as well as **photos of kids with their pedal cars**. He does not want pedal cars with plastic wheel covers and/or plastic steering wheels, as they are considered too new by collectors. The *one* exception to that rule is the *Ford Mustang* pedal car which he does want. Give the name of the manufacturer and the length of the vehicle. "I prefer to make offers only if you include a good clear color photo of both sides."

     Frank Martin
     7669 Winterberry Drive
     Youngstown, OH 44512
        (330) 758-4470

★ **Pedal cars** and other child-propelled vehicles including boats, planes, trucks, tanks, etc., made before 1940 "I prefer complete original toys but will consider units requiring restoration, but I'm not interested in basket cases. I especially want pedal airplanes and will pay from $1,500 to $4,000 for excellent originals. Perfectly restored planes will also be considered. I do not want any vehicle that has any plastic parts. Please give the maker if you can and note all missing parts."

     Stan Phillips
     438 8th Street
     Oakmont, PA 15139
        (412) 828-7351

SELLING POP CULTURE: THE TRASH THAT CAN BE TREASURE

Pop Culture is called "the fun stuff in life."
When folks talk about Pop Culture, they mean
radio, television, music, magic, celebrities,
personalities, cartoons and comic characters.
Pop Culture is Little Lulu, Donald Duck and
Superman. Pop Culture is Tom Mix, G.I. Joe,
and Star Wars. It's Elvis, P.T. Barnum, and Batman.
It's Frankenstein! And Gilligan.

Advertising has become part of pop culture. More 7
year olds recognize Mr. Clean *than Santa Claus.* Aunt
Jemima, Speedy Alka-Seltzer, *The* Campbell's Soup *kids,*
and Reddy Kilowatt *are among advertising icons that have*
become collector favorites.

Lots of this stuff is only worth $10 or $20, but someone
paid $1,000 for a cardboard cereal box and $2,000 for a
plastic model less than 30 years old. Prices for Pop Culture
reflect the law of supply and demand perfectly. Desirabili-
ty (demand), not rarity, drives the market place.

Pop Culture collectors want rare, brightly colored items
in original boxes and mint condition. Sometimes, but not
always, they will settle for less. Depends on how highly
sought after the item is. That's the advantage of dealing
with the people I'm suggesting. They know what you have
and what it is worth; they know what the market is, and
they're committed to paying you fair prices for good items.

Whether you already own this stuff, or whether you want
to make money by finding it at other people's yard sales,
the best way for you to cash in is to read all the Pop Culture
entries as well as those in the closely related Entertainment
and Advertising sections to see what's hot. By selling to
buyers in **Trash or Treasure** *you can cash in.*

Good close-up photos or Xerox© copies are important
since many vehicles, dolls, robots, and other Pop Culture
toys and games are worth $100+ and a surprising number
bring $1,000 or more. Buyers want to see exactly what you
are offering, as the condition affects value greatly.

POP CULTURE

★ **Americana and Pop Culture of all sorts** is wanted by Ted Hake, the longest established mail dealer and auctioneer of pop collectibles. The wide range of items Ted buys includes:
- **Pin back buttons** for politics, advertising products, sports, gum, Scouts, comic characters, movies, radio shows and all else;
- **Premiums from radio, TV or cereal**;
- **Disney** characters from before 1970;
- **Animation art** from Disney and other cartoons;
- **Battery or wind up toys,** especially comic and movie characters;
- **Television related toys,** games, lunchboxes, etc., 1950's to 60's;
- **Singing cowboys** and other western film heroes' guns, etc.;
- **Robots and space toys**;
- **U.S. Space Program** items;
- **Elvis Presley** pre-death items;
- *Beatles* and other famous rock and roll personalities;
- **Movie posters**, lobby cards, etc.;
- **Toys of the 1960's** like *GI Joe, Capt. Action, Batman,* etc.

"I'll buy almost any item related to a famous character or personality." Ted wants to know the material your item is made from, its size, any dates you can provide, and general condition. Firm offers are made only after inspection of your item. Hake has written four books on pin back buttons which are the basic reference works in the field. No reproductions are wanted, nor are political items after 1968.

> Ted Hake
> Hake's Americana Dept. 333
> PO Box 1444
> York, PA 17405
>   (717) 848-1333 10-5 Eastern M - F

To sell Pop Culture items, give the following information:
   (1) What it is, its size, color, and the material from which it is made;
   (2) Names, dates, and numbers found on the item;
   (3) Accurate statement of condition, noting missing parts, pieces, or paint and all other damage;
   (4) Description of all repairs or repainting;
   (5) Whether the original box, packaging and paper work are included and in good condition.

It's not hard, and a Xerox™ machine can be a big help.

★ **Radio premiums** associated with superheroes, fictional detectives, movie heroes and villains are sought by this well known mail order dealer of high quality collectibles. Rex DOES NOT BUY things made after 1960. No exceptions.

- **Maps** from radio shows: Sherlock Holmes' map of London, *Gang Busters, Flash Gordon Macy's Commandos* map, and others from *Mickey Mouse, Sea Hound, Tarzan,* etc.;
- **Rings** with lightning bolts, skulls, scarabs, spiders, and similar images, including **rare decoders** like *Red Ryder, Buck Rogers* and *Don Winslow.* "No common *Orphan Annie* or *Captain Midnight* decoders, please."
- **Guns** from the *Jr. G-Men* in the original mailer, *Crusade Against Crime Gang Busters* submachine gun in its original box and condition, *Dick Tracy* rapid fire tommy gun in its box;
- **Pins:** Ellery Queen, *Chandu, Ace Drummond, Sky King, The Shadow, Flash Gordon Movie Club, Tarzan, Fu Manchu* and others, but no *Pep* pins;
- **Store displays** involving heroes or comic characters.

"I do not want *Hopalong Cassidy* and other 1950's cowboys, nor do I buy lunchboxes, movie *Batman* or *Dick Tracy,* beat up lobby cards, coverless comics, or junk...just fine condition items, please. I pay more than anyone for the top range items, but if you want to sell to me it has to be on my terms. You must write first, providing a full description of the item and its condition." If Rex is interested he will request that you ship for inspection. Rex pays postage both ways on items he does not buy. "I have bought and sold this way for 20 years," he adds, pointing out numerous awards he has won for dealer integrity. Do not contact him with anything except perfect items. If you have something really good, "call between 10 and 10."

> Rex Miller
> Route 1 Box 457-D
> East Prairie, MO 63845
>   (314) 649-5048

★ **Comic character toys and collectibles from the 1930's and 40's,** made of any material from cardboard to cast iron, especially **Disneyana**, radio premiums, and all **children's play suits** from western heroes to sailor suits. No Halloween costumes. There are also many pieces of **comic character related sheet music** Ralph is seeking.

> Ralph Eodice
> Nevermore
> 161 Valley Road
> Clifton, NJ 07013
>   (201) 742-8278

★ **Pop culture items**, including:
  • **Radio premiums from children's adventure programs** such as
    *The Lone Ranger, Jack Armstrong, Tom Mix, Sky King, The
    Shadow, Doc Savage, Buck Rogers, Dick Tracy*, etc.;
  • **Cereal boxes offering premiums** from the 30's through the 60's;
  • **Superhero action figures,**
  • **Space adventure items;**
  • **Disney.** "I'll buy anything that isn't pictured in one of the price
    guides to Disney that I wrote."
  • *Mickey Mouse* **from the 1930's** ONLY (the "rat" Mickey) in all
    materials and forms: wind-up, dolls, figurines, etc.;
  • **Any odd Pop Culture item** in its original box.
Prefers items to be priced, but will make an offer only after seeing the
item in person. Write first, with complete details and photo.
> Tom Tumbusch
> 3300 Encrete Lane
> Dayton, OH 45439
> (513) 294-2250   Fax: (513) 294-1024

To sell Pop Culture items,
    you should give the buyer
    the following information:

(1) What it is, its size, color, and the
    material from which it is made;
(2) Names, dates, numbers found
    anywhere on the item;
(3) Accurate statement of condition, noting missing
    parts, pieces, or paint. Mention scratches, dents,
    dings, tears, stains, etc.
(4) Be certain to describe all repairs or repainting;
(5) Mention if the original box, packaging and paper
    work are included and in good condition.

It's not hard, and a Xerox™ machine can be a big help.

★ **Comic character pin back buttons,** 1896-1966, from the earliest
Yellow Kid to all comic strip and comic book characters since then except no *Pep* pins, please. This *Star Trek* actor (Chekov) pays up to
$1,000 for rare buttons like the *Buck Rogers 25th Century* and *Wash-
ington Herald Mickey Mouse*. Ask and he'll send an illustrated wants
list. Include your phone number.
> Walter Koenig
> PO Box 4395
> North Hollywood, CA 91607

★ **Pop Culture toys** related to radio, television or movie characters and superheroes including :
- **Western movie & TV toys**, watches and premiums from riders of the range like: Roy Rogers, Gene Autry, Hopalong Cassidy, *The Lone Ranger, Red Ryder* and Tom Mix;
- **Western style cap guns** made of metal;
- **Disney and other comic character toys**;
- **Doll houses** of tin in fine condition and *Renwall* plastic doll houses and accessories;
- **Toy vehicles** by *Smith Miller, Tonka, Doepke, Dinky, Renwall* (plastic), *Auburn* (rubber), *Arcade, Marx*, and *Wyandotte*;
- *G.I. Joe* **dolls**, accessories, pre-1970, in the 12" size;
- **Toys which advertise** nationally known products.

Condition is critical and only excellent condition items are wanted. Items in original box always preferred. Descriptions should include dimensions. Photo helpful. "Generous prices paid, but all offers not final until I've seen the item in person." Will answer all inquiries that have an SASE. Calls welcome.

William Hamburg
PO Box 1305
Woodland Hills, CA 91365
(818) 346-1269 Fax: (818) 346-0215

★ **Pop Culture treasures,** especially made of paper, including:
- **Comic books**, 1890's-1980's, but only hero comics after 1963;
- **Sunday comics** from the 1890's to 1959;
- **Original comic strip art**;
- **Walt Disney** books and anything else before 1960;
- *Big Little Books*, 1933-1950;
- **Movie magazines,** 1920-1945;
- **Television collectibles,** 1948-1970;
- **Radio and cereal premiums** and giveaways pre-1960;
- **Song magazines**, 1929-1959, like *Hit Parader* and *400 Songs;*
- **Popular music magazines** 1920-1959 like *Downbeat, Billboard*;
- **Pulp magazines**, 1930-49, except love, Westerns, and crime.

Wants nothing in poor condition. Ken has been in business 25 years. He pays Americans in U.S. dollars and drafts for quick payment.

Ken Mitchell
710 Conacher Drive
Willowdale, Ontario M2M 3N6 CANADA
(416) 222-5808

Pop rings worth 2¢ and rings worth $1,500 can look quite similar to the inexperienced. Don't take chances. Deal with my buyers.

★ **Comic, cartoon, TV and other Pop Culture items** such as:
- **Advertising product figures** Mr. Clean, Speedy Alka-Seltzer, and others can be worth up to $500 or more;
- **Original animation and comic strip art** from before 1970, with a particular interest in Disney films;
- **Watches and clocks** but only if pre-1978 and in original box $1,000 for Betty Boop pocketwatch, 3 pigs wristwatch or the Donald Duck wristwatch from the 1930's;
- **Empty boxes** for toys, watches, and models;
- **Cereal, gum, candy and food wrappers and boxes**, some of which, like the *Kix* atom bomb box, are worth $500+;
- **PEZ candy dispensers**, premiums, and store displays (worth up to $1,500 for rarities);
- **Premiums from radio and TV shows, comic books or cereal**, 1920-70's; pays $10,000+ for *Superman of America* member rings or *Superman* secret compartment rings, and $2,000+ for *Superman* and *Captain Marvel* wooden statues;
- **Monster toys and games** of Frankenstein, The Creature, others;
- **1960's TV characters** such as *Munsters, Addams Family, Jetsons, Flintstones, Lost in Space, Batman* and the like;
- **Children's books** (coloring, sticker, paper doll, cut-out, pop-up) that feature TV, movie, cartoon, or pop personalities before 1975, if they are in near mint condition. $2,500+ for *Mickey Mouse* or *Wizard of Oz* Waddle Books;
- **Celluloid, battery, wind-up or friction toys,** especially Disney and *Popeye*; pays $10,000+ for German *Mickey* and *Minnie* on a motorcycle or celluloid *Horace Horsecollar* pulling *Mickey* in a cart;
- *Captain Action* **and** *G.I. Joe* **dolls** with painted hair, their accessories and vehicles, but **only if in their original boxes** ("I'll pay $3,500 for a boxed *Capt. Action Spiderman* outfit");
- **Trash cans** made of metal with colorful pictures of cartoon or advertising characters from the 1960's if in perfect condition;
- **Robots** made before 1970 only, with a primary interest in metal robots from the 1960's or earlier (some boxed robots are worth $10,000); *Marx's Big Loo* and a few other older plastic robots may be of interest ("Watch out for reproductions");

Condition is crucial. Make certain to note all damage and if there are missing parts. Make certain to mention if item is in its original box or wrapper since they can be "worth more than the item they held." Photos are "very helpful." Does not buy reproductions. David stresses, do not sent items without first contacting him. David is the author of two books on *Pez* dispensers, both available through him.

David Welch
PO Box 714
Murphysboro, IL 62966
(618) 687-2282   Fax: (618) 684-2243

★ **Robots and space toys** made of tin before 1965, either wind-up or battery operated, are wanted. "I'll pay $2,000 for *Mr. Atomic* and $750 for the *Robby Space Patrol* vehicle. Condition is important with these toys, so I'll pay an extra 10% for any toy in its original box." Also buys tin wind-up **comic character toys** made in the USA or Europe, whether working or not, and any **Disney toys,** especially celluloid toys from the 1930's. **Santa Claus toys** are also of interest.

> Larry Bruch
> PO Box 121
> Mountaintop, PA 18707
> (800) 549-TOYS

The cheaters of the world have built so many fakes that most dealers will not make final payment until they have actually held the item. This is not unreasonable.

★ **Disneyana from before 1946,** especially:
- *Mickey* or *Donald* painted **plaster lamps;**
- **Waddle Books** from the 1930's (these have been reproduced);
- **Animation cels** from before 1960, including drawings and background paintings;
- *Mickey, Minnie,* and *Donald* **costume dolls** in Western, Mexican, Russian or bandleader outfits;
- *Vernon Kilns* **ceramic figurines;**
- **Tin or celluloid plain or wind up toys** of Disney characters;
- **Wood or porcelain figurines;**
- **Original art** for WWII combat insignia and other wartime items;
- Cartoon movie theater posters.

Items can be foreign or domestic, but nothing newer than the 1950's is of interest. "Do the best you can in describing the dimensions, color, maker's markings, condition (mention all damage or missing parts)." Dennis will make offers for items "only when I'm holding it in my hand," preferring you to set the price. Include your phone number when you write.

> Dennis Books
> Comic Characters
> PO Box 99142
> Seattle, WA 98199
> (206) 283-0532

★ **Pop Culture toys,** including
  • Older **comic books;**
  • **Marilyn Monroe** memorabilia;
  • **Elvis** memorabilia from before 1977;
  • **Disney** paper collectibles;
  • **Non-sports cards;**
  • **Rock 'n' Roll records** and memorabilia from before 1970;
  • **B-movie cowboy collectibles.**

This well known magazine collector/dealer has expanded into the above related ephemera. Please describe what you have fully. Items are purchased for resale.

>   Stan Gold
>   7042 Dartbrook
>   Dallas, TX 75240
> (972) 239-8621   Fax: (972) 239-9622   record@unicomp.net

★ **Baby Boomer toys and pop culture items,** such as:
  • *Pez* **dispensers** without feet;
  • *Barbie* **dolls** from before 1966;
  • **Robot toys;**
  • **Monster toys;**
  • **Cereal boxes** with premium offers;
  • **Howdy Doody;**
  • **Advertising characters;**
  • **James Bond;**
  • **Kiss rock and roll items;**
  • **Flintstones toys and games.**

Describe what you have carefully as condition is important. Indicate whether you have the original boxes or blister packs.

>   Mark Blondy
>   35952 North Valley Court #207
>   Farmington Hills, MI 48335
> (810) 442-7335   Fax: (810) 442-7554   GROOVEDEN@aol.com

**Dealers make their living buying and selling.
They can't and don't stay in business long
if dishonest. The world of collecting is small.
Word gets around fast.**

★ **Comic character and science fiction toys** made in Germany, Japan, or the U.S. Also merry-go-rounds and airplanes (no jets). "I'll pay over $1,000 for a *Mr. Atomic* robot or *Mickey the Magician*, two battery toys." He does not want common items like the Charlie Weaver bartender toy, plastic toys, wind-up dogs, toy trains, dolls, items with missing parts, or toys made in the third world. Tell this toy consultant and restorer the condition of the item and box, and about any restoration or repainting.

> Don Hultzman
> 5026 Sleepy Hollow Road
> Medina, OH 44256
> (330) 225-2668

To sell Pop Culture items, tell the buyer:

(1) What it is, its size, color, and the material from which it is made;
(2) Names, dates, numbers found anywhere on the item;
(3) Accurate statement of condition, noting missing parts, pieces, or paint. Mention scratches, dents, dings, tears, stains, etc.
(4) Description of all repairs or repainting;
(5) Whether the original box, packaging and paper work are included and in good condition.

It's not hard, and a Xerox™ machine can be a big help.

★ **Playsets and plastic figures** from the 1950's to early 1970's by *Marx, Archer, Auburn, Giant Plastics, Lido, MPC, Multiple, Remco, Ideal* and others.. These toys came with metal buildings and loads of plastic people and accessories. Particularly desirable are boxed sets of **Lost in Space, Batman,** *Justice League,* **Gunsmoke,** *Wells Fargo, The Civil War,* **Disneyland, The Untouchables,** *Alaska, Ben Hur, Johnny Ringo,* and the *Revolutionary War.* If clean and complete in the original box, these can be worth up to $2,000. If yours isn't in perfect shape, inquire anyway as a few rare individual parts can be worth $500. Condition is extremely important, as damaged pieces have no value. Small TV and cartoon figures from one inch to six inches tall that were sold individually rather than in boxed sets are are also wanted.

> David Welch
> PO Box 714
> Murphysboro, IL 62966
> (618) 687-2282   Fax: (618) 684-2243

G.I. JOE & OTHER ACTION FIGURES

★ *G.I. Joe figures and accessories.* "I'll buy anything related to all eras of *G.I.Joe* from 1964 to the present day. The most valuable items are from the 1960's, however fuzzy headed and small *G.I. Joe* items are of interest as well. Many boxed *G.I.Joe* items can bring over $1,000." Mike buys for his collection as well as for resale, and requests you call with what you have. If it sounds good, you will be asked to send it to him at his expense for inspection and for an offer. Do not send things unannounced. "For large collections, I'll come to you." Mike is the promoter of the official HASBRO sponsored *G.I.Joe* Convention.

>Michael Herz
>Whiz Bang! Collectibles
>952 East Semoran Blvd.
>Casselberry, FL 32707
>   (407) 260-8869   Fax: (407) 260-2289

★ *G.I. Joe* toys produced between 1964 and 1969 including dolls (dolls from this period have molded/painted hair not flocked hair), guns, uniforms, vehicles and accessories. Items associated with the Vietnam War are particularly sought after, including the Airborne Military Police, Marine jungle fighter, and the Air security helmet and radio, all of which can be worth several hundred dollars. Among vehicles he particularly wants the crash crew fire truck and desert patrol jeep among others and will pay up to $500 for complete sets, more with boxes. A complete Canadian Mountie set would be worth from $150 to $300 even without its box. Items must be marked GI JOE or HASBRO. "I'll buy one or a collection and am happy to identify your items over the phone. When you call, have the items handy and be ready to answer questions about colors, letters stenciled on them, and the condition of the box. Original packaging is a plus. If you write, send photos when possible. I insist on return privileges if the item is not exactly as described. If I do not wish to buy what you have for sale, I will refer you to another collector whenever possible." Condition is very important. An item worth hundreds of dollars mint and packaged can be worth nothing when stained, ripped, damaged or missing pieces. "Some items can be repaired. Call if you have questions." He does not buy the small figures made in the 1980's.

>Matthew McKeeby
>149 Lake Hill Road
>Burnt Hills, NY 12027
>   (518) 384-0893

★ *G.I. Joe* **action figures.** "I'll buy figures, uniforms, vehicles and accessories." Prefers items from the 1964-69 era, but "will consider anything in good condition whether boxed, carded or loose." Especially seeks store displays and stock, dolls, novelties, puzzles, games, vehicles, and carded stock but will buy nearly anything. He notes that painted headed dolls are more valuable than fuzzy headed ones, and that a 1967 nurse doll, mint in her box, could bring $2,000. Purchases both for his personal collection and for resale.

> Joe Bodnarchuk
> 62 McKinley Avenue
> Kenmore, NY 14217
> (716) 873-0264 phone and fax gijoe@bodnarchuk.com

★ **Superhero, action and cartoon character figures** especially *Captain Action*, *G.I.Joe* and *Mego Superheroes*. "I buy, sell, and trade most any character collectibles including superheroes, cartoon characters, and action figures like *Star Wars* and *G.I. Joe*. I specialize in premiums, rings, and superhero items from the 1940's through the present such as Superman, Batman, etc." He does not buy books except comics. He requests you call with what you have. If it sounds good, you will be required to ship it at his expense for inspection and an offer. Do not send things unannounced. "For large collections, I'll come to you."

> Michael Herz
> Whiz Bang! Collectibles
> 952 East Semoran Blvd.
> Casselberry, FL 32707
> (407) 260-8869 Fax: (407) 260-2289

Experienced dealers make their livings buying and selling. They can't and don't stay in business long if dishonest. The world of collecting is very small. Word gets around fast.

★ **Action figures** by *Marx*, 1965 to 1976. These 8" and 12" fully jointed figures had solid color plastic bodies and soft flesh colored heads and hands. They were made as cowboys, Vikings, and knights and came with soft plastic accessories. "I will buy large or small lots of these figures in any condition, whole or in parts, if they are reasonably priced. Horses must be complete. I am particularly interested in finding the *Noble Knight and Horse* in black armor." When describing your item, tell the color of the plastic. "Price sought is helpful," he says, "but not necessary."

> Arnie Starkey, Starkey Art
> 11054 Otsego Street #5
> North Hollywood, CA 91601

SCIENCE FICTION & SPACE TOYS

★ **Toy robots and *Erector* sets** are sometimes purchased by this specialist in toy vehicles.
>Jay "The Chicago Kid" Robinson
>PO Box 529
>Deerfield, IL 60015
>(847) 945-8691   Fax: (847) 940-7579

★ **Space toys and ray guns** from the 1930's through the 1950's, particularly *Buck Rogers, Flash Gordon, Tom Corbett, Capt. Video,* and *Space Patrol.* Fine condition toys of all types are wanted, even rocket shaped pedal cars. He does not want *Star Wars, Star Trek,* the new *TV Buck Rogers* and other characters from after 1960. Leslie is author of the award-winning *Zap! Ray Gun Classics* available for $16 postpaid.
>Leslie Singer
>103 West Capitol #1104
>Little Rock, AR 72201
>(501) 375-1860 voice and fax

★ **Space theme games, puzzles,** coloring books, clothing, bedspreads, records, greeting cards and drinking glasses. Pop culture, not real life space themes are wanted. Only wants items made in the 1950's in nice condition. No items from the real moon landing. No toys.
>Don Sheldon
>PO Box 3313
>Trenton, NJ 08619
>(609) 588-5403

To sell Pop Culture items, you should give the buyer the following information:

(1) What it is, its size, color, and the material from which it is made;

(2) Names, dates, numbers found anywhere on the item;

(3) Accurate statement of condition, noting missing parts, pieces, or paint. Mention scratches, dents, dings, tears, stains, etc.

(4) Description of all repairs or repainting;

(5) Whether the original box, packaging and paper work are included and in good condition.

It's not hard, and a Xerox™ machine can be a big help.

★ **Monster items** of all types including:
  • **Gum cards, display boxes and wrappers** such as *Mars Attack,*
    Outer Limits, Terror Tales, Spook Stories, etc.;
  • **Plastic model kits** of Frankenstein's monster, wolfman, mummy,
    King Kong, Rodan, The Munsters, and so on, built or unbuilt.
    Will even purchase some broken models for parts, and pay up
    to $50 for some empty boxes;
  • **Toys and games,** puzzles, novelties, and the like that feature any
    movie, TV, or comic book monsters or creatures. Will pay
    $75 for the board game, *Outer Limits*;
  • **Halloween masks** of monsters, especially masks by Don Post;
  • **Comic books** by *Zenith, E.C.* and other 10¢ monster titles;
  • **Magazines and record albums**, especially *Famous Monsters,*
    Castle of Frankenstein, World Famous Creatures, Monster
    Parade and similar titles.

"I welcome any calls or letters, and am always happy to talk with
anyone who has monster items." If you write, include where you got
the item. Don't forget your phone number.

Joe Warchol
Small World
5345 North Canfield
Chicago, IL 60656
    (847) 843-2442 days   (773) 774-1628 eves

★ **Model kits of human, monster, comic, or science fiction characters** from before 1975 are sought. Kits were produced by *Aurora,
Hawk, Revell, MPC, Multiple,* and *Lindbergh.* Any kit containing
figures (not cars and boats) may be of interest **as long as it is unbuilt
in its original box**. Will also buy empty boxes, factory promos, store
displays and advertising and manufacturer's catalogs. A few items like
Godzilla's Go-Cart or *King Kong's Thronester* can bring $3,500 if still
factory sealed. Has a special interest in gift sets with two or more kits
in the same box made by any model company in the 1950's or 60's.

David Welch
PO Box 714
Murphysboro, IL 62966
    (618) 687-2282   Fax: (618) 684-2243

*Science fiction collectibles may also be of interest to
general pop culture dealers found in the beginning of
the Pop Culture section.*

POP CULTURE FOOD

★ **Plastic advertising and comic characters** by *F and F Mold and Die Works*. This Dayton company was responsible for an enormous number of Pop characters including *Aunt Jemima, Uncle Mose, Keebler Elf, Dennis the Menace, Yogi Bear, Bugs Bunny* and the like. They made cups, bowls, cookie jars, salt and pepper shakers and other items. Pieces are marked, usually on the bottom or lower back, and the mark can sometimes be hard to see. "I do not want broken items or those with excessive paint chipping (though some chipping is to be expected). *Aunt Jemima* has been reproduced, but without the *F and F* logo. I am not interested in repros. I pay from $5 to $30 for items and have paid as much as $400 for rare cookie jars. Pictures are helpful or phone with the item right in front of you."

Tom Basore
715 West 20th Avenue
Hutchinson, KS 67502
  (316) 665-3613 eves

★ *PEZ* **candy items.** "I'll buy any-thing related to *PEZ*: old candy or dispensers without feet, premiums, paperwork, store displays, ads, etc.) premiums and store displays. Pays up to $2,000 for *Make-A-Face* dispenser if the package is unopened; $1,000 for the full body shiny gold robot; and $1,500 for the shooting star lighter with no head. Dave is author of *A Pictorial Guide to Plastic Candy Dispensers* ($22) and *Collecting PEZ* ($44) .

> A PEZ dispenser without feet on the character is likely to be worth at least $10, perhaps a lot more.

David Welch
PO Box 714
Murphysboro, IL 62966
  (618) 687-2282   Fax: (618) 684-2243

★ **Cereal boxes, 1930-1959, depicting comic characters or give-aways.** A series of 1940's *Cheerios* boxes featuring Disney characters is particularly desirable as is the 1946 atom bomb ring box of *Kix*.

John Fawcett
PO Box 1156
Waldoboro, ME 04572
  (207) 832-7398 before 8pm Eastern

Many other food and drink related items are collected. You'll find buyers listed in Trash or Treasure under Liquor, Beer, Advertising, and Soft Drink as well as among the general Pop Culture dealers you can find at the beginning of the Pop Culture section.

❖

POP CULTURE COWBOYS

★ **Tom Mix collectibles** including *Shredded Ralston* cereal boxes from the 1930's and 40's with Tom Mix markings, arcade and gum cards, postcards, unusual photos, feature films, short subjects, various radio premiums, and the 1930's Tom Mix *Ingersoll* pocket watch. This 40 year veteran is author of *The Tom Mix Book*, available from him for $24.95. Note that he does not want lobby cards, movie posters, newly made items, common photos, *Big Little Books,* clothing, video tapes or any material that is not in good condition. He insists that sellers price what they have.

> Merle "Bud" Norris
> 1324 North Hague Ave.
> Columbus, OH 43204
> (614) 274-4646

★ *Hopalong Cassidy* **collectibles.** Offer any in good condition.

> Ron Pieczkowski
> 1707 Orange Hill Drive
> Brandon, FL 33510

★ *Lone Ranger* **items.** Wants wide range of 1933-55 items including cereal boxes, dolls, games, posters, premiums, gun sets, carnival plaster figures, books with dust jackets, autographs, and other items associated with the Lone Ranger's radio days.

> John Fawcett
> PO Box 1156
> Waldoboro, ME 04572
> (207) 832-7398 before 8 pm Eastern

★ *Gunsmoke* **items from both radio and TV.** "I'll buy nearly anything associated with either show except magazines and recently made stuff. I want autographs, contracts, production documents, scripts, advertising, gifts, awards, belt buckles, toys, promotional items, props, and anything personalized belonging to a cast member. I don't buy anything severely damaged." He can send you a list of nearly 30 cast members whose autograph and photo he wants. He's a collector and dealer who charges to make appraisals and expects you to tell him what you want him to pay for your item.

> Hank Clark
> PO Box 812
> Waterford, CA 95386
> (209) 874-2640   Fax: (209) 529-8678

TV, movie and radio cowboy collectibles may also be of interest to general pop culture dealers found in the beginning of the Pop Culture section. ❖

SUPERHEROES

★ *Superman* **items.** Buys all rare or unusual *Superman* items, particularly dating from 1938 to 1966, but "I purchase interesting items from all years." Seeks toys, figurines, puzzles, watches, games, buttons, advertising, etc. "Please write me about any good *Superman* item because I buy duplicates and quantity." No comic books, except free premiums. No homemade items. Give a complete description, including *every* defect, and include its color, manufacturer, copyright date and country of origin. Photo or photocopy is appreciated. Danny has collected *Superman* for 30 years and is co-author of *The Adventures of Superman Collecting.*
> Danny Fuchs
> 209-80 18th Ave.
> Bayside, NY 11360
> (718) 225-9030 Fax: (718) 225-3688

★ *Captain Marvel, Captain Marvel Jr.*, **and** *Mary Marvel* **memorabilia** including toys, buttons, posters, comic books, mechanical items, and statues produced between 1940-1953. Also items related to similar *Fawcett Comics* characters.
> Michael Gronsky
> 10328 Royal Woods Court
> Gaithersburg, MD 20879
> (301) 445-9088

★ *James Bond 007* **and Ian Fleming memorabilia** including first edition hard and soft cover books, magazines with articles about Bond, movie posters, record albums, toys, dolls, plastic model kits, beer cans, clothing, games, comic books, and much more. Especially wants books autographed by Fleming, the British 1st edition of *Casino Royale,* and one of the signed and numbered limited editions of *On Her Majesty's Secret Service.* Give standard bibliographic information on any books, paying attention to the condition of the dust jacket (or the covers on paperbacks). On other items, indicate whether you have the original packaging for the item or not, and if you do, describe its condition as well as that of the item itself. He does not want *Saturday Evening Post, Life* or *Look* magazines. Neither does he want *Signet* paperbacks after 1961 or U.S. Book Club editions.
> Gary Pimenta
> 64 Lakeside Drive
> Tiverton, RI 02878

❖

Super Hero, literary and comic strip character collectibles may also be of interest to general pop culture dealers found in the beginning of the Pop Culture section.

★ *Green Hornet.* "I have one of the world's largest collections, and I buy for resale and for my collection. A mint *Green Hornet Captain Action* suit in a mint box could be worth as much as $4,500, and some posters and premiums can bring as much as $2,000."

Michael Herz
Whiz Bang! Collectibles
952 East Semoran Blvd.
Casselberry, FL 32707
    (407) 260-8869   Fax: (407) 260-2289

★ *Tarzan* and **Edgar Rice Burroughs memorabilia** including books, magazines, and collectibles. This enormous library collection still seeks items, such as the 1915 edition of *Return of Tarzan* with a dust jacket for which they'll pay over $1,000. Also seeking early *Tarzan* movies, foreign editions, Armed Services Editions and many smaller items associated with Burroughs or any of his characters. George advises, "Don't waste your time if your items aren't in fine to mint condition, including dust jackets. Please describe what you have carefully, give a guarantee, and tell us in what form you'd like payment."

George McWhorter
Burroughs Memorial Collection
University of Louisville
Louisville, KY 40292
    (502) 852-8729

★ *Tarzan* toys, games, movie items and autographs. Describe condition of the book, include standard bibliographic information (that includes publisher and date), and note whether dust jacket is there.

Jim Gerlach
2206 Greenbrier
Irving, TX 75060
    (214) 986-5233

Super Hero, literary and comic strip character collectibles may also be of interest to general pop culture dealers found in the beginning of the Pop Culture section.

COMIC CHARACTER COLLECTIBLES

★ **Comic character items from the 1920's and 30's** are wanted, especially Disney but also *Betty Boop, KoKo the Clown, Felix the Cat, Maggie and Jiggs, Mutt & Jeff, Krazy Kat and Ignatz, Little Nemo, Barney Google*, and more. Wants figurines, masks, toys, premiums, posters, dolls, pins, original art, lamps, radios, store displays, etc.
> John Fawcett
> PO Box 1156
> Waldoboro, ME 04572
> > (207) 832-7398 before 8pm Eastern

★ *Yellow Kid* **memorabilia.** Wants tins, toys, buttons, postcards, advertisements, "and anything else with the Kid on it."
> William Nielsen
> PO Box 1379
> Brewster, MA 02631
> > (508) 896-7389

★ **Felix the Cat** pictured on china, or anything else, as long as it's from the 1930's or before. She is not interested in any of the Felix items reproduced in the 1950's. Please include a clear photo as she will be able to tell old from new in most cases.
> Marilyn Baseman
> Birdcage Antiques
> 47 Main Street in the PO
> South Egremont, MA 01258
> > (413) 528-3556

★ **Cartoon and comic character books** such as *Big Little Books*, *Pop-Up Books, Fast Actions, Fawcett Dime Action Books, Cupples and Leon*, and other early **comic reprint books** from 1910's, 20's and 30's. Also **coloring books**, *Whitman* hard cover children's books with dust jackets, *Whitman Penny Books, Nickel Books, Buddy Book*s, and any similar books published by *Salsfield, Mclaughlin, Lynn Publications, Engel Van Wiseman*, etc. "Let me know what you have and what you want for it, or ship for my immediate offer."
> Alan Levine
> PO Box 1577
> Bloomfield, NJ 07003
> > (201) 743-5288

Cartoon and comic strip character collectibles may also be of interest to general pop culture dealers found on pages 132-139.

★ *Dick Tracy, Sparkle Plenty* and *Bonny Braids* **collectibles.** "I'm buying toys, games, premiums, original art, store displays, posters, books, paper, figures...anything! SASE gets his FOR SALE list. "I will give free appraisals if you send a description, good photo and an SASE.
>   Larry Doucet
>   2351 Sultana Drive
>   Yorktown Heights, NY 10598
>   (914) 245-1320

★ *Peanuts* **cartoon character toys and memorabilia** of all types and characters including advertising, music boxes, ceramics, jewelry, etc., as long as it is marked UNITED FEATURES SYNDICATE and in fine condition. Especially wants a musical ice bucket and the *Ansi* and *Schmidt* music boxes made of wood. Not interested in *Avon*, squeak toys, or other common items, though. A picture is appreciated. This top collector is author of the price guide to *Peanuts* collectibles; send her $12 if you want one. She reminds you not to assume the © date is the date the item was produced. "It's not," she says.
>   Andrea Podley
>   Peanuts Collector Club
>   539 Sudden Valley
>   Bellingham, WA 98226
>   (360) 733-5209   Fax: (360) 733-5239   acpodley@nas.com

★ *Snoopy* **and** *Peanuts* **toys and memorabilia** such as ceramics, music boxes, advertising, pins, buttons, books, magazines, toys. Especially wants a *Snoopy Says See and Say* game, *Charlie Brown's Talking Book*, and wooden or older *Peanuts* music boxes. She also wants any catalogs (including Sear s, Wards, etc.) containing *Peanuts* items. All items *must* be marked UNITED FEATURES SYNDICATE or UFS. Freddi co-authored the price guide to *Peanuts* collectibles, and says about *Peanuts* items, "If I don't have it, I want it."
>   Freddi Karin Margolin
>   12 Lawrence Lane
>   Bay Shore, NY 11706
>   (516) 666-6861   Fax: (516) 665-7986

★ *MAD* **magazine collectibles**, dolls, busts, straight jackets, bookends, jewelry, and all collectible items related to Alfred E. Newman. Wants only first printings of softcover books and hardcover books only if complete with dust jacket and all inserts. Does not want anything in poor condition. Also wants original art by any of the *MAD* artists. Promises to answer all letters accompanied by an SASE.
>   Dr. Gary Kritzberg
>   PO Box 47
>   Yorkville, IL 60560
>   (630) 553-7653 eves

★ *MAD* **magazine collectibles:** dolls, jewelry, hand puppets, busts, straight jackets, bound volumes, and other EC comic items. Also wants any and all pictorial representations of Alfred E Neuman's face from pre-*MAD* days. Nothing made after 1974 or in poor condition.
Grant Geisman
Box 56773
Sherman Oaks, CA 91413
(818) 501-0884   Fax: (818) 501-0886

★ **Walt Kelly and Pogo** items. This dedicated collector/historian seeks items produced by and associated with Kelly and his work, not only on Pogo, but as an illustrator for Disney, Peter Wheat, advertising, and various children's books. Of interest are first edition books, comics, records, plastic and porcelain figures, pin-back buttons, magazines, newspaper strips, original artwork, and what have you. Prices can be high for items like the 1968 button set, porcelain figures, plastic figures, records, and other scarce items. Books other than first editions are not wanted unless they are signed by Kelly. Photocopies are helpful. Complete bibliographic information should be provided for all books. Give specific information about all flaws. Steve publishes a wide variety of Kelly originals and reprints, including a bimonthly newsletter (membership is $20/year) and the *Walt Kelly Collector's Guide* (with prices) available for $16.50 postpaid.
Steve Thompson
6908 Wentworth Avenue South
Richfield, MN 55423
(612) 869-6320   thomp030ms/our.tc.umn.edu

Cartoon and comic strip character collectibles may also be of interest to general pop culture dealers found in the beginning of the Pop Culture section. ❖

RADIO PROGRAM COLLECTIBLES

★ **Radio show giveaways,** membership cards, pins, photos, games, rings, toys, etc. from *Lone Ranger,* Tom Mix, *Sky King, Capt. Midnight, Charlie McCarthy*, Gene Autry, etc.

> John Fawcett
> PO Box 1156
> Waldoboro, ME 04572
> (207) 832-7398 before 8pm Eastern

★ **Radio show giveaways** such as rings, badges, decoders, etc. Wants *Captain Midnight, Superman, Little Orphan Annie, Buck Rogers, Howdy Doody, The Shadow, Sgt. Preston, Doc Savage, Sky King*, and other characters. Also buys the manuals from old radio, TV and cereal advertising campaigns. "Please advise what you have and what you want for it, or ship for offer."

> Alan Levine
> 292 Glenwood Avenue or PO Box 1577
> Bloomfield, NJ 07003
> (201) 743-5288

★ **Jimmie Allen radio show giveaways** from the 1930's. "I will pay $100 each for certain Jimmie Allen wings and premium prices for other items." Since dozens of different types of wings, membership cards, and certificates were given away, it is important to make a photocopy and indicate which sponsor's name is printed on the item. Manuals, model kits, I.D. bracelets, and "other rare and/or unusual Jimmie Allen premiums" are sought. Include your phone number when you write.

> Jack Deveny
> 6805 Cheyenne Trail
> Edina, MN 55439
> (612) 941-2457

Radio show premiums and advertising may also be of interest to general pop culture dealers found in the beginning of the Pop Culture section. ❖

TV SHOW COLLECTIBLES

★ **TV related memorabilia.** "I'll buy toys, puzzles, games, lunchboxes, etc., but specialize in all types of records and fan magazines associated with television." Wants records in all speeds, adult and children's, serious or funny, as long as it is related to television. Also TV fan type magazines like *TV-Radio Mirror, TV Fan, TV Carnival, TV Western* and the like as well as paperback books spun off from TV series. Items from before 1970 only, please. Examine your fan magazines carefully and note if they have had pictures clipped. **No movie fan mags.** When describing, give the date, volume and issue number and condition of magazines. Record info should include title, label, condition, and whether or not it has a sleeve.

> Ross Hartsough
> 98 Bryn Mawr Road
> Winnipeg, MB R3T 3P5 CANADA
> (204) 269-1022

★ *Star Wars toys,* action figures and related memorabilia. "I'll buy anything related to *Star Wars* in decent condition. Items do not have to be in their original packaging, but packaged items bring a much higher value. A loose action figure can be worth from $1 to $300, whereas carded figures can be worth over $1,000." He is interested in loose and carded action figures, dolls, vehicles, posters, or any other *Star Wars* items, except he does NOT want vehicles that are broken or missing parts. Mike requests you call with what you have. If it sounds good, you will be asked to send it to him at his expense for inspection and for an offer. Do not send things unannounced. "For large collections, I'll come to you."

> Michael Herz
> Whiz Bang! Collectibles
> 952 East Semoran Blvd.
> Casselberry, FL 32707
>   (407) 260-8869   Fax: (407) 260-2289

★ **Television private detective and spy memorabilia.** Wants to buy games, puzzles, toys, books, photos, gum cards, wrappers, dolls, model kits, autographs, comic books, and just about everything else you can think of from shows like *77 Sunset Strip, Dragnet, Surfside 6, Peter Gunn, I Spy, The Man from U.N.C.L.E., The Wild Wild West, Secret Agent, Hawaiian Eye, Adventures in Paradise, The Untouchables* and others. This relatively new collector/dealer says he's interested in everything in good condition. Include photocopy or good description as condition is very important. Describe the package if you still have it.

> Gary Pimenta
> 64 Lakeside Drive
> Tiverton, RI 02878

★ *Bewitched* TV series scripts, games, puzzles, comics, dolls, autographed photos, press releases, taped episodes with commercials intact, tapes of show promos, gum cards, and much more. "If it's Bewitched, I'd like it, and will also consider material dealing with the actors or actresses before or after the show." Cels from the opening credit animation could bring $1,000 or more and a Samantha doll in its original box, $500+. Describe condition and completeness carefully. SASE.

  Carol Ann Osman
  PO Box 16383
  Pittsburgh, PA 15242
  (412) 922-0117

★ *Charlie's Angels* **and Farrah Fawcett memorabilia** including cups, puzzles, walkie-talkies, pillows, Halloween costumes, radios, store displays for dolls, etc. Also wants original photos, magazines, posters, displays, videos, etc. Does not want lunchboxes, dolls, doll outfits, games, models or bubble gum cards. He prefers items in absolute mint condition, never used or played with, with no bends, crushes, or tears. Wants list available.

  Jack Condon
  PO Box 57468
  Sherman Oaks, CA 91403
    (818) 789-0862   Fax: (818) 501-1004

★ *I Dream of Jeannie* items, especially board games, comic books, scripts, photos, or original film. Wants the *Libby* Majorette doll but none by *Remco*. Send a photo or Xerox™ and include your phone number. He is author of the 450 page *Diary of a Genie: A History* available from him for $35. Send SASE for more information.

  Richard Barnes
  1520 West 800 North
  Salt Lake City, UT 84116
    (801) 521-4400   Fax: (801) 292-1947

★ *Gilligan's Island* **collectibles.** "I'll buy or trade for all *Gilligan's Island* TV show items, including cast photos and videos of episodes." Especially interested in the 1965 *Gilligan's Island* bubblegum cards and the box they came in. Will also pay for video recordings of the cartoons *The New Adventures of Gilligan* or *Gilligan's Planet*. His club also produces a newsletter with classified ads for people who want to buy, sell, or trade *Gilligan* ephemera.

  Bob Rankin
  Gilligan's Island Fan Club
  PO Box 25311
  Salt Lake City, UT 84125
    (801) 272-5729

★ **Lucille Ball and Desi Arnaz memorabilia** from any era associated with the *I Love Lucy* show, Desilu productions, their movies, records, and other activities, including toys, dolls, board games, magazines, comic books, paper dolls, advertising, scripts, tickets, props, costumes, autographs, and the like. If if says Lucy or Desi on it, he probably wants it. No newspaper or magazine clippings, please. He is the author of *For the Love of Lucy*, available though bookstores for $35.

> Ric Wyman
> 408 South Highland Avenue
> Elderon, WI 54429

★ **Lucille Ball memorabilia** related to any of the many Lucy TV shows: dolls, comics, magazines, etc.

> Cari Purkey
> 5 Massier Lane
> Foothill Ranch, CA 92610
> (714) 588-8585

★ **Pee Wee Herman items** such as props from his TV show, movie promotional items, souvenirs, ads, fan club newsletters, giveaways and other toys. Also any size clothing put out by *JC Penny Stores* with the Pee Wee Herman label and designs. Especially large displays! He does not want small dolls, including the ventriloquist one. Xerox™.

> Everen T. Brown
> PO Box 296
> Salt Lake City, UT 84110
> Fax: (801) 364-2646

★ *Howdy Doody* **memorabilia** is wanted, including all items related to any character on the show. Especially seeks items in original boxes. Runs *Howdy* auctions, "so will buy anything in fine condition."

> John Andreae
> PO Box 156
> Granger, IN 46530
> (219) 272-2337   Fax: (219) 271-1146

★ **Smurfs**, especially those produced in Europe before 1979.

> Suzanne Lipschitz
> Smurf Collectors' Club Dept TH
> 24 Cabot Road West
> Massapequa, NY 11758
> (516) 799-3221   NYSmurf@aol.com

TV show and personality collectibles may also be of interest to general pop culture dealers found in the beginning of the Pop Culture section. ❖

MISCELLANEOUS CHARACTERS

★ *Smoky Bear* **items** of all sorts are wanted by this ten year veteran collector who asks for "very descriptive detailed data on your item, including the condition." He points out Smoky items have been produced in great variety and he'll consider anything. Dealers price your goods. Amateurs may request offers.

    Ken Laaker
    1109 South 22nd Street
    Quincy, IL 62301
       (217) 222-5691

★ *Smokey the Bear* **ephemera.**

    Thomas McKinnon
    PO Box 86
    Wagram, NC 28396
       (910) 369-2367

CHILDREN'S LITERARY CHARACTERS

★ *Uncle Wiggily* **items** including books, toys, empty boxes, buttons, Sunday comics, puzzles, mugs, dishes, games, and "all other memorabilia." Especially wants *Uncle Wiggily's* paint books, drums, *Put-Together* puzzles, candy tins, *Animal Crackers* boxes, kid's tea sets, and wind-up toys. Does not want *Uncle Wiggily Game* or books published by American Crayon Company or by Platt-Munk. Pays you a fee if you find something he wants and report it to him.

> Martin McCaw
> PO Box 9
> Prescott, WA 99348
>   (800) 451-9755

★ *Uncle Wiggily* **items** including toys, paper dolls, comics, dishes, handkerchiefs, fabric, and any unusual items.

> Audrey Buffington
> PO Box 386
> South Thomaston, ME 04858
>   (207) 594-2683

★ **Red Riding Hood toys**, books, and other items.

> Wes Johnson, Sr.
> 106 Bauer Avenue
> Louisville, KY 40207
>   (502) 899-3030 extension 228 days only

★ *Alice In Wonderland* **books and memorabilia** including films, figurines, tins, toys, games, puzzles, posters, greeting cards, dolls, etc. Especially wants a *Beswick* china figurine of the Cheshire Cat, but encourages all inquiries. Also wants other Lewis Carroll items, including **books, letters, and personal articles associated with Carroll**. No books published by *Whitman* or illustrated by John Tenniel but would love the Alice published by *Appleton* in 1866, worth at least $1,000!

> Joel Birenbaum
> 2765 Shellingham Drive
> Lisle, IL 60532
>   (630) 637-8530

★ *Alice In Wonderland* **memorabilia** including dolls, figurines, tins, cookie jars, coffee mugs, and "anything else" is wanted, especially editions of **books in obscure languages**, or editions with lesser known illustrators like Allen, Adams, Appleton, McEune, Norfield, or Sinclair. Alice encourages you to "quote all Alice items."

> Alice Berkey
> 127 Alleyne Drive
> Pittsburgh, PA 15215
>   (412) 782-2686

LUNCHBOXES

★ **Children's lunch boxes and/or** *Thermos©* **bottles**, metal or vinyl, in excellent condition, especially radio, TV and space characters from the 1950's and 60's. "Call about any fine condition item as I am always glad to talk to anyone any time about lunch boxes, and will be happy to give a reasonably accurate assessment of the value of your old character lunchbox." Joe has prepared guidelines for describing the condition of your box and information on cleaning which he will send if you include a long SASE with your inquiry. If you telephone, first inspect your box carefully for a date.

> Mark "Joe Lunchbucket" Blondy
> 35952 North Valley Court, #207
> Farmington Hills, MI 48335
> (810) 442-7335   Fax: (810) 442-7554   GROOVEDEN@aol.com

★ **Comic character children's lunch boxes,** both metal and vinyl, from 1975 or before. Must have pictures depicting space, cartoon, TV, sports, western, or other kid-related themes. Condition is very important. Boxes and bottles should look as if they were only slightly used, with no rust, bad rubbing, dents, serious scratches, or names written on the outside of the box. The most sought after boxes bring over $500, with *Matt Mason's Space Diver* a hot $1,000+.

> David Welch
> PO Box 714
> Murphysboro, IL 62966
> (618) 687-2282   Fax: (618) 684-2243

★ **Lunchboxes from any TV show or movie** such as *Hopalong Cassidy, Brady Bunch, Green Hornet, Land of the Giants, James Bond, The Beatles,* etc. Condition is very important.

> Paul Scharfman
> Chic-a-Boom
> 6817 Melrose Avenue
> Los Angeles, CA 90038
> (213) 931-7441   Fax: (213) 930-2990

*Children's metal lunchboxes with interesting pictures
may also be of interest to pop culture dealers found in
the beginning of the Pop Culture section
of Trash or Treasure, pp 132-139.*

CARTOON & CHARACTER GLASSES

★ **Cartoon and character glasses** issued by restaurants, fast food chains, TV shows, and others. Peter buys outright, and also accepts items on consignment from pickers, dealers and private parties for his twice a year auctions of glasses, **mugs, steins** and related items. Some cartoon characters bring as much as $100. He does not want foreign glasses, anything issued in the last 10 years, or anything not in mint condition. He suggests you send a picture whenever possible. His 60+ page auction catalogs are $11 each and come with prices realized for over 1,600 auctioned items. Back issues are available.

> Peter Kroll
> Glasses, Mugs & Steins Auction
> PO Box 207
> Sun Prairie, WI 53590
> (608) 837-4818 eves   Fax: (608) 825-4205

★ **Cartoon and character glasses.** "We buy drinking glasses that have cartoon characters, superheroes, sports personalities, fast-food logos, soft drink company logos, horse racing, grand openings, world's far, advertising, and convention decorations. We particularly want cartoon character and horse racing glasses from 1930-79. We don't want common glasses that are out there by the millions like *Camp Snoopy, Smurfs, Care Bears, Popples* and *Holly Hobbie*. We buy collections, accumulations, and singles but don't want anything faded or chipped." Best if you can send a photo, but not essential if you describe height, picture, and condition of the picture. They've promised to help amateurs, but dealers are expected to price their goods. Note any missing paint or misprinting. Mark and Mike are authors of *Collectible Drinking Glasses*. They also publish *Collector Glass News*, a bimonthly devoted to glasses, for $15 a year.

> Mark Chase and Mike Kelly
> Collector Glass News
> PO Box 308
> Slippery Rock, PA 16057
> (412) 946-2838   Fax: (412) 946-9012   cgn@nauticom.net

Cartoon glasses may also be of interest to general pop culture dealers found in the beginning of the Pop Culture section of Trash or Treasure 8, pp 132-139.

BOBBING HEAD DOLLS

★ **Bobbing head sports and non-sports dolls of all types,** especially composition/papier-maché dolls from the 1960's. Wants all types of dolls from all sports, but especially miniature bobbing heads about 4" tall and real player dolls. When you write, give the color of the base.

    Dale Jerkins
    1647 Elbur Ave.
    Lakewood, OH 44107
        (216) 226-7349   RJER16@aol.com

Rising prices in recent years has led to increased attention for all these kitschy collectibles, now considered among Pop Culture icons. When you describe a nodder for sale, give the height of the figure and the colors of the clothing, hat (helmet) and base. Decals must be in fine condition.

★ **Bobbing head sports and non-sports dolls,** Japanese ceramic or composition models only, no plastic dolls or dolls made in Taiwan or Korea. Indicate team or character portrayed. Also give the size, color, and shape of the base. Will pay $150 for any Blackface bobbing baseball doll in perfect condition and $600 for a perfect Roberto Clemente. Also wants **sports and non-sports plastic statues by Hartland.** Will pay between $100 and $700 for excellent and complete statues, depending on the character.

    Chip Norris
    PO Box 235
    Leonardtown, MD 20650
        (301) 475-2951

★ **Bobbing head and nodder dolls.** Prefers people or famous characters. Special wants include the *Pillsbury Doughboy, Elsie* the *Borden's* cow, *Popeye*, Presidents Eisenhower and Kennedy, *Minnie Mouse*, and *Elmer Fudd*. Also wants double **nodder salt and pepper shakers**, nodder ashtrays and other unusual nodders.

    Roxanne Toser
    4019 Green Street
    Harrisburg, PA 17110
  (717) 238-1936   Fax: (717) 238-3220   nsumag@aol.com

★ **Bobbing head "nodder" dolls.** Wants sports, advertising, political, comic and character dolls made of papier mache or ceramic. Plastic dolls are NOT wanted. Dolls must be in nice condition with no head or shoulder cracks ("Look carefully," he cautions, "because they can be hard to see"). Decals must be complete, and there should be no other damage. Generic Oriental figures (that represent no particular identifiable celebrity) are NOT wanted, nor are animals except cartoon animals like Sylvester the Cat. Top dollar is paid for Black/Negro athletes, which start at $350. With the exception of Col. Sanders, nodder figures which advertise a product are $250 and up. Celebrity figures are $50 and up, with some as high as $200. Tim will be happy to sell you a handy small guide to sports nodders for only $6. The country's biggest nodder dealer, he pledges to pay "an honest 60% of retail for any doll."

    Tim Hunter
    1668 Golddust Drive
    Sparks, NV 89436
        (702) 626-5029   Fax: (702) 626-4423

GUM CARDS

★ **Non-sports gum cards from 1930-49.** This *Star Trek* star (Chekov) wants cards featuring pirates, WWII, Indians, cowboys, and comic strip characters. Especially wants comic cards cut from 1930-50 candy boxes. Cards must be in fine condition.

    Walter Koenig
    PO Box 4395
    North Hollywood, CA 91607

★ **Non-sports gum cards** are priced in *Non-Sport Update* magazine, a slick bimonthly with a pull-out Price Guide, edited by Roxanne Toser and available for $21 a year. Ms. Toser, whom we have recommended for more than ten years, no longer personally buys cards or wrappers.

    Roxanne Toser, editor
    Non-Sport Update Magazine
    4019 Green Street
    Harrisburg, PA 17110
        (717) 238-1936

Sports and non-sports cards have been packed in tobacco, candy, gum, etc., for 100 years. Thousands of non-sports card sets depicting every imaginable topic from animals to zeppelins exist. Expect to get from 10¢ to $4 for most cards. 19th century cards occasionally bring more from Tobacco or pop culture collectors.

SELLING COMICS AND COMIC ART

Comic strips and books have been around since the turn of the century. Approximately 17,000 comic titles have been published, but only 300± of these have serious collector interest. Age has little to do with the value of comic books, and almost all comics, 1930's and 40's included, sell for $10 or less.

__The popularity of the artist who drew the comic has more to do with value than any other characteristic.__ Other things that go into determining how much money you get are the popularity of the character, the popularity of the publisher, the historical significance of the series or specific issue, the condition and the current demand.

__Comic collectors are fussy folks.__ Every tiny crease, tear, wrinkle, misprint, and off-center or rusty staple affects the value. Collectors tend to follow the grading standards suggested in Overstreet's The Comic Book Price Guide, the reference used by most folks as it contains values for nearly every American comic book. It is available at bookstores, public libraries, and by mail order.

__Expect buyers to pay you from 30% to 70% of prices quoted in Overstreet.__ As a general rule, the more valuable the comic you are selling, the higher the percentage of the value listed in Overstreet's guide. Dealers don't want to buy lots of inexpensive comic books. They know top items move quickly. Low priced items don't sell. Badly worn comics, even rare titles and issues, are nearly impossible for you or for dealers to sell.

__Buyers will usually ask you to send comics for inspection prior to payment__ since the value of comics is linked to condition. Ask your post office for "return receipt requested" which costs about one dollar. Always include a list of what you are sending and keep a copy of the list for yourself. Cautious sellers photocopy the covers of what they send, since the creases on the cover are like a finger-print and can identify your comic should it become necessary.

COMIC BOOKS

★ **All 10¢ comic books**, for which Gary has "unlimited funds" to pay 50% to 100% of price guide values. Send a list of titles and issue numbers along with a brief description of condition. This nationally recognized comic book expert and historian is not interested in any comics which originally sold for more than a dime. Gary is also interested in **comic strip original art** for daily or Sunday strips.

Gary Colabuono
Pop Culture Resources, Inc.
PO Box 117
Elk Grove Village, IL 60009
    (847) 806-1130   (800) 344-6060   Fax: (847) 806-1158

☆ **Comic books** originally costing 10¢ or 12¢, especially superhero, Western, science-fiction, and movie or TV related. Particularly looking for comics published by the following companies: *E.C., Dell, Marvel),* *DC, Fawcett, Fiction House, Quality,* and *Harvey.* He does not need more Classics Illustrated comics. The comics most wanted are by *Timely Titles* including *Captain America, Marvel Mystery, Mystic, All Winners, Human Torch, Sub-Mariner, USA,* and *Young Allies.* He will pay up to $1,000 for early issues of *Marvel Mystery.* He does not want any comics newer than 1966 or any comics without covers, no matter how old or rare they are. When writing or calling, give the title, publisher, and issue number (usually found on the cover, inside front cover, or first page). Describe condition including cover gloss, creases, stains, tears, tape, and damage to the spine. Note loose or missing pages, bends, and folds, as well as browning of the pages. A photocopy of the covers is very helpful. Joe has been in the mail order comics business since 1978 and promises to answer all inquiries if you include a Self-Addressed Stamped Envelope.

Joe Hill
Phoenix Toy House
223 Fairview Road
Erin, NY 14838
    (607) 796-2547   jrhillerin@aol.com

☆ **Comic books** from 1938 to 1969 that originally cost 10¢ or 12¢ on the cover. Seeking crime, horror, romance, science fiction, super hero, war and western titles. "I'll buy in fair+ or better condition, but no brittle, damaged or incomplete comics." Geoff offers to pay you cash or, if your prefer, to trade movie memorabilia for your comics. Geoff deals in movie memorabilia.

Geoffrey Mahfuz
30 Phoebe Avenue
Lowell, MA 01854
    (508) 458-0095 7a.m. to 9p.m.

★ **Comic books** from 1930 to 1970, whether you have single issues or large collections. "Call or write for a quote if they're before 1970." says this large West Coast auctioneer of sports, movie and comic items.

  Steve Applebaum
  3444 Via Lido
  Newport Beach, CA 92663
    (714) 673-1742   Fax: (714) 673-5327

★ **All comic books in fine condition 1900 to 1969** are wanted by this active Canadian dealer. He also buys *Big Little Books* and *Better Little Books* from 1932 to 1950. He has no interest in anything brittle or damaged. Pays in U.S. dollars and bank drafts.

  Ken Mitchell
  710 Conacher Drive
  Willowdale, Ontario
  M2M 3N6 CANADA
    (416) 222-5808

★ **Comic books** from before 1960 are wanted. Hugh has been buying and selling comic books for 27 years.

  Hugh O'Kennon
  2204 Haviland Drive
  Richmond, VA 23229
    (804) 273-6365

★ **Comic strip books, 1897-1922.** "These are large books with cardboard covers measuring approximately 10.5" x 16" and have colorful graphics. Characters featured include Buster Brown, Happy Hooligan, Katzenjammer Kids, Little Nemo, Pore Little Mose and several others. By 1915, a new format of black and white books measuring 5.5" x 15" were introduced. Condition is very important, with prices ranging from $50 to $250 for most items. I am not interested in items other than the above or in reprints. Please give the name of the book, the dimensions, the publication date and the condition of the covers and pages, making sure that all pages are present."

  Robert Quesinberry
  Route 3 Box 265
  Hillsville, VA 24343
    (540) 728-0919 days   (540) 728-4576 eves

★ **Cartoon and comic character books** such as *Big Little Books*, *Pop-Up Books, Fast Actions, Fawcett Dime Action Books, Cupples and Leon*, and other early **comic reprint books** from 1910's, 20's and 30's. Also *Whitman* hard cover children's books with dust jackets, *Whitman Penny Books, Nickel Books, Buddy Books*, and any similar books published by *Salsfield, Mclaughlin, Lynn Publications, Engel Van Wiseman*, etc. "Let me know what you have and what you want for it, or ship for my immediate offer."

Alan Levine
PO Box 1577
Bloomfield, NJ 07003
    (201) 743-5288

★ **Flip books** from any period, in any style or size. These are small booklets whose pictures seem to move when the pages are flipped. Will pay $200 for *Santa Claus Play Pictures* and *Mother Goose Play Pictures*, which had pages to be cut out and assembled into flip books. He does not want *Big Little Books* with flip illustrations in the upper corner, nor does he want the recent reproductions by *Merrimack* or *Shackman & Co*. Photocopy the cover and give a brief description of the action. Give the dimensions, whether illustrations are color or b/w and whether cartoons or photos. Describe condition.

Jeff Jurich
175 South Jersey Street
Denver, CO 80224
    (303) 393-7210

Selling comic pages and original comic art is no different than selling other paper goods. Make a photocopy of what you have and send it to one of the potential buyers along with your Self-Addressed Stamped Envelope. You only need to copy the cover of your comic books.

SUNDAY COMIC PAGES

★ **Sunday comic sections,** 1895-1970. Prefers to purchase runs of several years, not singles. He especially wants the color comics from the Saturday issues of the Chicago or the NY *Journal American,* from 1934 to 1964 but buys all very good condition sections before 1970.
Claude Held
PO Box 515
Buffalo, NY 14225

★ **Sunday and daily adventure comic strips, 1930-60** such as *Tarzan, Prince Valiant, Flash Gordon, Terry and the Pirates* and *Casey Ruggles.* No single daily panels, humor strips or torn items.
Carl Horak
1319 108th Ave.
SW Calgary, Alberta
T2W 0C6 CANADA
(403) 252-0878

★ **All Sunday comic sections in fine condition** from 1929 to 1959 *but nothing brittle or damaged.* Pays in U.S. dollars and bank drafts.
Ken Mitchell
710 Conacher Drive
Willowdale, Ontario
M2M 3N6 CANADA
(416) 222-5808

ORIGINAL COMIC ART

★ **Original artwork for animation, comic strips and cartoons,** 1920-1960, especially animation cels from Disney and Warner Brothers, for which this 30 year veteran has paid as much as $50,000. Jerry also buys original art from comic strips and magazine cartoons. Information he wants includes title, artist, description, the year, and any documentation you might have. In your description of condition, note any yellowing, folds, tears, cracked or missing paint, paste overs, etc. He does not want reproductions from newspapers or magazines, nor does he buy posters or prints of any type. Museum Graphics publishes a free bimonthly newsletter and price list.
Jerry Muller, Museum Graphics
PO Box 10743
Costa Mesa, CA 92627
(714) 540-0808

★ **Original comic book and animation art** especially but not exclusively from Disney studios. "Call or write for a reasonable quote."
> Steve Applebaum
> 3444 Via Lido
> Newport Beach, CA 92663
>   (714) 673-1742   Fax: (714) 673-5327

★ **Original art used in creating comic books and strips.** Please make a photocopy of what you have.
> Charles Martignette
> PO Box 293
> Hallandale, FL 33008
>   (954) 454-3474

Most comic art sells for $50 to $2,000, but some Disney pieces have sold for more than $200,000. Value depends upon age, artist, subject matter, and condition. Carl Barks at Disney is particularly popular as is Walt Kelly, George Herriman, Hal Foster and a few other artists who bring premium prices.

★ **Comic strip art by any noted cartoonist.** Dennis issues an illustrated annual catalog which you may write for.
> Dennis Books, Comic Character Shop
> PO Box 99142
> Seattle, WA 98199
>   (206) 283-0532 eves

★ **Original artwork** by Walt Disney studios, Walt Kelly (Pogo), or George Herriman (Krazy Kat). Some others may be of interest.
> John Fawcett
> PO Box 1156
> Waldoboro, ME 04572
>   (207) 832-7398 before 8 pm Eastern

★ **Original comic book or comic strip art**. This well-known Canadian Pop Culture dealer pays in U.S. dollars or drafts.
> Ken Mitchell
> 710 Conacher Drive
> Willowdale, Ontario
> M2M 3N6 CANADA
>   (416) 222-5808

SELLING MOVIE AND ENTERTAINMENT ITEMS

Nearly everything associated with entertainment is Treasure to someone. Movie related items are the most popular entertainment collectible, but entertainment includes anything done on a stage, Disneyland, World's Fair souvenirs, and the like. Distinctions between entertainment, music, toys, advertising, sports and Pop Culture are arbitrary, so when selling an entertainment collectible, also try looking in these sections of **Trash or Treasure** *whenever it seem appropriate.*

Stars like James Dean and Marilyn Monroe are hot and genuine autographed photos can be worth $1,000 or more, but most star photos and production stills from films bring a few dollars at most. Many movie star autographs and photos are signed by secretaries or machines. Real signatures on hand-written letters and on scripts are of much more interest to collectors.

Posters from popular stars and important or cult films can bring hundreds, even thousands, of dollars. Contact more movie poster buyers in the section on Posters.

Items sought by more than one type of collector are called "cross-over collectibles." A signed photograph of Marilyn Monroe would find buyers in movie, photo, and autograph categories. Cross-over items are often priced very differently by the different types of collectors.

Radio and television sets are popular with a different breed of collector than the "Entertainment" collector. Set collectors will often collect decorative "go-withs" to display with their sets. Go-withs are photos, catalogs, signs, and advertising related to a collector's main specialty. A photo of the interior of a radio store in 1923 would be a fine go-with for a radio collector. That some photo would also be of interest to a collector of photos of store interiors, or to a collector of something else pictured in the store. Many entertainment collectibles make attractive go-withs, so consider all possibilities when looking for a buyer.

MOVIE MEMORABILIA

★ **Kinetoscopes and peep machines from old arcades and amusement parks.** He does not buy a great many machines, but is instead selectively looking for a few fine examples with historical or intrinsic value. "Amateurs can't tell one machine from another. An expert should look at all old arcade machines." Pays $7,500 for an Edison Kinetoscope from 1894. He suggests you shoot a roll of high speed 35mm film, covering all aspects of whatever machine you wish to sell. Send him the roll and he'll process it and reimburse you for your film. That's a good deal so it's not fair to waste his time with junk or late model machines. "It is very important for me to know where you got your machine." Richard is author of numerous books on slot machines, trade stimulators, pinball and arcade machines.

    Richard Bueschel
    414 North Prospect Manor Avenue
    Mt. Prospect, IL 60056
       (847) 253-0791

★ **Commercial motion picture and magic lantern projectors** and associated films, slides and other ephemera related to theatrical history such as tickets, programs, and posters from early performances. Especially wants to find cameras and projectors made by Sigmund Lubin Co. of Philadelphia, and will play $500 and up. Also buys old "persistence of vision devices" such as zoetropes, praxinoscopes, and outfits used by traveling itinerant showmen at the turn of the century. He emphasizes, "I have **no interest at all in toy magic lanterns or toy slides**, nor do I want any 8mm or 16mm film or projectors." When offering something for sale, indicate the maker's name, the model number, and other relevant data. Describe condition accurately.

  George Hall
  Professor Hall's Ragtime Show
  835 East Windsor
  Tucson, AZ 85719
     (602) 888-2490

Professional lantern slides are usually 3 1/4"" square or 3 1/4" x 4" and were either hand-painted, mechanically printed, or made from photographs. Some were mounted in 4" x 7" wooden frames with moving parts which changed the picture in some way. Children's slides are usually 1" to 2" high and 5" to 12" long.

★ **Magic lanterns and their glass slides.** He buys these early glass slide projectors from all countries in all sizes and shapes, colors and makes. Also wants all related materials such as glass slides, accessories, books, catalogs, handbills, and broadsides. "The older the better," with prices varying from $10 to more than $1,000." Does not want reproductions or small black magic lanterns with "EP" on them. Send a photo and indicate all markings found on the lantern. Dealers must price their goods; amateurs only may request an offer.

> Jack Judson
> Magic Lantern Castle Museum
> 1419 Austin Highway
> San Antonio, TX 78209
>   (210) 805-0111   Fax: (210) 822-1226

★ **Magic lantern glass slides.** These slides are usually 3 1/4" square or 3 1/4" x 4" and were either hand-painted, mechanically printed, or made from photographs. Some were mounted in 4" x 7" wooden frames with moving parts which changed the picture in some way. "I give old-time magic lantern shows as a hobby and am always looking for interesting or entertaining slides to add to my repertoire. I don't want church hymn or scripture slides or the small, long ones for children's toy magic lanterns. I would be grateful if you could state the price that you would like."

> Lindsay Lambert
> 41 Bellwood Avenue
> Ottawa, ON
> K1S 1S6 CANADA

★ **Silent movie memorabilia** including coming attraction slides, posters, lobby cards, figurines, sheet music, pin back buttons, paper dolls, and spoons by *Athens* or *Rogers Bros.* (but not *Oneida*). Has a specific interest in *Our Gang* handkerchiefs, Artamo needlework, star garment hangers, and the standee for *Robin Hood* shoes. Nothing from the talkies or from later stars. No autographs or photographs from any period are wanted.

> Richard Davis
> 9500 Old Georgetown Road
> Bethesda, MD 20814
>   (301) 530-5904   Fax: (301) 530-8532

★ **Silent movie programs.** Please Xerox™ the cover and describe the condition of the contents, including how many photos it has. Complete items, please.

> Gary Bart
> 620 Siena Way
> Los Angeles, CA 90077
>   (310) 471-6980   Fax: (310) 471-1910

★ **Projectionist's manuals and catalogs,** pre 1925.
  Lindsay Lambert
  41 Bellwood Avenue
  Ottawa, ON
  K1S 1S6 CANADA

★ **Movie ephemera** including posters, lobby cards, **souvenir booklets** and standees, both American and European. "I guarantee a fast decision and faster check."
  George Theofilis
  Miscellaneous Man
  PO Box 1776
  New Freedom, PA 17349
      (717) 235-4766 days   Fax: (717) 235-2853

★ **Movie memorabilia,** including lobby cards (especially from B movies 1930-1960), theater souvenirs, tickets, programs, **photos of theaters,** and materials sent by studios to theater owners. Also wants **magazines** such as *Motion Picture Herald, Box Office, The Exhibitor,* and others aimed at theater owners and will buy them in any condition. This 20 year veteran collector does not buy items made after 1960.
  Chris Smith
  26 Ridge Avenue
  Aston, PA 19014
      (610) 485-0814

★ **Movie posters** of all sizes, with particular interest in collections of pre-1940 posters. All posters printed in color will be considered. Give the film title, general description of the image and the *exact* outside dimensions (the size) of the poster. One sheet posters that he particularly wants include *Public Enemy* for which he'll pay $12,000 and *Flying Down to Rio* worth a cool $10,000. But the original *Dracula* or *Frankenstein* one sheet poster could put ten times that much in your pocket!
  Dwight Cleveland
  PO Box 10922
  Chicago, IL 60610
      (312) 525-9152   Fax: (312) 525-2969

★ **Movie posters,** foreign or domestic, from 1900 to the present. Give the title of the movie, size, description of the image, year of release, and the condition of the poster. Jon wrote *Warren's Movie Poster Price Guide* at $22.50 and publishes *Collecting Hollywood* magazine.
  Jon Warren
  American Collectors Exchange
  2401 Broad Street
  Chattanooga, TN 37408
      (423) 265-5515   Fax: (423) 265-5506

★ **Movie posters and Hollywood memorabilia.** Seeks quality posters in any size (11"x14" lobby cards, window cards, and larger posters) in any genre (type of movie) including classics, western, horror, sci-fi, etc. Also buys autographs, **props and garments seen on screen** and "anything else interesting" associated with Hollywood movie industry.
> Steve Applebaum
> 3444 Via Lido
> Newport Beach, CA 92663
> > (714) 673-1742   Fax: (714) 673-5327

★ **Cartoon posters from silent movies.** "I buy posters featuring cartoon characters like *Felix the Cat, Out of the Inkwell,* and other silent films, but will consider other silent movie posters as well."
> Richard Davis
> 9500 Old Georgetown Road
> Bethesda, MD 20814
> > (301) 530-5904   Fax: (301) 530-8532

★ **Paper movie ephemera,** 1925-1959, including movie **magazines,** pressbooks, heralds, posters, trade journals, studio rehearsal discs and "almost anything else having to do with movies."
> Buddy McDaniel
> 2802 West 18th Street
> Wichita, KS 67203
> > (316) 942-3561

★ **Original studio production movie scripts** with original binders or covers when possible. "I am not interested in photocopies, TV scripts, or unproduced scripts unless the latter are by very important writers." Indicate author's name, whether script has its cover, what draft (or the date), whether all pages are present, and whether there are notations.
> Grayson Cook
> 367 West Avenue 42
> Los Angeles, CA 90065
> > (213) 227-8899

★ **Movie memorabilia** including autographs of stars, promotional stills, lobby cards, and posters. This dealer wants bulk rather than single items from private parties, unless the single item's unusually good. Everything is purchased for resale.
> Ralph Bowman's Paper Gallery
> 5349 Wheaton Street
> La Mesa, CA 91942
> > (619) 462-6268 voice and fax

★ **Movie memorabilia** 1920-96, including **posters** of all sizes, inserts, and lobby cards. Also wants movie **autographs** and **magazines**. Stars of particular interest include Jean Harlow, Marlene Dietrich, Bette Davis, Errol Flynn, James Cagney, Humphrey Bogart, James Dean, and Marilyn Monroe. Condition is important. Include your phone number.

> Gary Vaughn
> Cinemonde
> 138 2nd Avenue North #106
> Nashville, TN 37201
>   (615) 742-9256   Fax: (615) 742-1268

★ **Movie memorabilia.** Buys posters, lobby cards, pressbooks, heralds, fan photos and other memorabilia from 1898 to 1970. Also movie **magazines** before 1950. "Please let me know what you have and what you want for it, or just ship for my immediate offer."

> Alan Levine
> 292 Glenwood Avenue   or   PO Box 1577
> Bloomfield, NJ 07003
>   (201) 743-5288

★ **Autographs of film, TV, and Rock and Roll stars, song and script writers,** including both minor and major figures. "I do not want Country & Western performers or current sports figures. Photocopies are recommended. Tell me where you got the item and set the price wanted as I do not bid on items." SASE. Jim sells inexpensive books containing current addresses of movie, music, sport and sex celebrities.

> Jim Weaver
> 405 Dunbar Drive
> Pittsburgh, PA 15235

★ **B Western cowboy star memorabilia** from Hopalong Cassidy, Tom Mix, Ken Maynard, Roy Rogers, Tex Ritter and especially Gene Autry. "I'll buy buttons, photos, games, toy guns, radio giveaways, autographs, and most anything else that has to do with these stars." He is interested only in B westerns, not the epics. Has only minor interest in paper items, and does not buy "damaged or overpriced goods."

> Dennis Schulte
> 8th Avenue NW
> Waukon, IA 52172
>   (319) 568-3628 after 7 pm

★ **Stereoviews of Hollywood**, old movie theaters, movie stars, and anything else that is movie industry related.

> Chris Perry
> 7470 Church Street #A
> Yucca Valley, CA 92284
>   (619) 365-0475   Fax: (619) 365-0495

ACTORS & ACTRESSES

★ **Celebrity memorabilia.** "I buy, sell and collect celebrity memorabilia by mail. I'm looking for personal belongings of entertainment stars and historical figures, **including movie costumes, props, and autographed photos.** I'm not interested in most mass produced items, except very rare items like movie posters." Your description should include what the item is, its condition, and its history, including how you came to own it. Make certain to describe what authentication you have.

Richard Wilson
Norma's Jeans
3511 Turner Land
Chevy Chase, MD 20815
(301) 652-4644 Fax: (301) 907-0216

★ **Sherlock Holmes and Dr. Watson actors.** "I want anything about the actors who have portrayed Holmes and Watson, including Basil Rathbone, Nigel Bruce, Jeremy Brett, David Burke, Edward Hardwicke, William Gillette, Ellie Norwood, Arthur Wontner, Peter Cushing, Christopher Plummer, et al. Please describe and include a photograph or Xerox™ of what you have whenever possible.

Rev. Sherlock "Yes, it's my real name" Holmes
Private Letter Box 3
Worcester, MA 01613
(508) 754-9907

★ **Shirley Temple** items are always wanted by this specialty collector.

Rita Dubas
8811 Colonial Road
Brooklyn, NY 11209
(718) 745-7532 Fax: (718) 921-6444

★ **Humphrey Bogart memorabilia**, including film or video copies of early movies. *Broadway's Like That, A Devil with Women* and *Body and Soul.* He does not want sheet music.

Dennis Horwitz
PO Box 301
Topanga, CA 90290

★ **James Dean memorabilia** including magazines, photos, records, sheet music, lobby cards, autographs, posters, scrapbooks, plates and novelties. Description should include size, year, and condition.

David Loehr
PO Box 55
Fairmount, IN 46928
(317) 948-3326 Fax: (317) 948-3389

★ **Three Stooges memorabilia** of all types, especially related to their tour of England in 1939. Buys items associated with any Stooge except Joe Besser and Joe Derita, including toys, contracts, posters, tickets, autographs, checks, personal items, coloring books, records, puppets, etc., and will pay as high as $3,000 for some rare items. He does not want comic books, gum cards, or things made after 1968, but has strong interest in animation cels from cartoons in which they appeared.

> Neil Teixeira
> PO Box 20812
> Oakland, CA 94620
> (510) 658-9938   Fax: (510) 658-8757

★ **Three Stooges and other comedy team memorabilia.** Frank buys and sells items associated with all the classic teams.

> Frank Reighter
> 10220 Calera Road
> Philadelphia, PA 19114
> (215) 637-5744

★ **Ginger Rogers memorabilia:** posters, lobby cards, autographs, photos, sheet music, magazines with her on the cover, advertising, *Old Gold* cigarette ads, and "anything else pertaining to this great actress." All items must be in good condition.

> Thomas Morris
> PO Box 8307
> Medford, OR 97504
> (541) 779-3164

★ **Jack Benny collectibles.** "I'll buy any items pertaining to Jack Benny, and have for 15 years." Please describe your item, indicate the condition and set a price. If she doesn't buy what you have, she might run an ad for it in their newsletter so other collectors can see it. She sells a complete log of Benny's films, records and books for only $15.

> Laura Lee, International Jack Benny Fan Club
> 4749 Wilkie
> Oakland, CA 94619
> Fax: (510) 210-3699

★ **Lucille Ball and Desi Arnaz memorabilia** from any era associated with the *I Love Lucy* show, Desilu productions, their movies, records, and other activities, including toys, dolls, board games, magazines, comic books, paper dolls, advertising, scripts, tickets, props, costumes, autographs, and the like. If if says Lucy or Desi on it, he probably wants it. No newspaper or magazine clippings, please. He is the author of *For the Love of Lucy*, available though bookstores for $35.

> Ric Wyman
> 408 South Highland Avenue
> Elderon, WI 54429

★ **Marilyn Monroe and other sex symbol movie star memorabilia.**
He not only wants Marilyn, but also will buy ephemera related to Jayne
Mansfield, Mamie Van Doren, Diana Dors, Anita Ekberg, and Brigitte
Bardot. He asks that you quote prices for any pre-1962 items, inclu-
ding U.S. and foreign magazine covers, in excellent condition.

    John Van Doren
    60 Wagner Road
    Stockton, NJ 08559
        (609) 397-4803   Fax: (609) 397-2407

★ **Marilyn Monroe.** Wants "anything and everything" U.S. and foreign including lobby cards, press books, sound track albums, collector
plates, dolls, and the like. Will buy magazines with Marilyn on the
cover if they are in uncut condition. He does not want scrapbooks, new
posters, or new pictures. Photocopies are helpful.

    Clark Kidder
    3219 East County Road North
    Milton, WI 53563
        (608) 868-4185   Fax: (608) 868-6808

★ **Marilyn Monroe paper items** are wanted by this 10 year veteran
collector. She especially wants foreign magazines with Marilyn on the
cover, and various issues of popular magazines with important Marilyn
features or covers. Her most wanted item is a digest size copy of the
So-Rite Fashion Catalog for Fall of 1949. You'll be $500 richer if you
can find a mint one for her. She DOES NOT WANT nudes, *Playboy, Life,
Look, Modern Screen, Screen Stories,* American books about Marilyn,
nor does she want dolls or plates. She will consider sheet music, some
newspaper features, and 3D items.

    Ann Bartoli
    1230 Woodridge Court
    Princeton, IL 61356
        (815) 875-8925

★ **8"x10" studio glosses of sexy starlets** and actresses, 1920-1990.

    Charles Martignette
    PO Box 293
    Hallandale, FL 33008

❖
   *If you don't find a buyer for your movie memorabilia in
this section of Trash or Treasure, try the General Pop Culture
dealers you'll find at the beginning of that section.*

FAMOUS MOVIES

★ *Gone With the Wind* ephemera associated with the book, movie, stage play, or its author Margaret Mitchell, including items from her newspaper career, as well as various editions of her novel and promotional material for the book over the years. Will buy catalogs, pressbooks, lobby cards, programs, record albums, candy boxes, scarves, jewelry, neckties, games, bookends, buttons, clothing, hats, and many other items. He'd love to find an admittance card to Mitchell's 1949 funeral, but *does not want* anything made after 1980 such as plates, figurines, music boxes, dolls, reproduction posters, etc. Please give the dimensions and an "honest description" of its condition. Edits *The Scarlett Letter*, available for $15/year.

> John Wiley, Jr.
> 1347 Greenmoss Drive
> Richmond, VA 23225
>   (804) 771-3561 days   (804) 330-5484 eves

★ *Gone With the Wind* items associated with the film or the book such as tickets, posters, autographed books, magazines, scarfs, buttons, handkerchiefs, candy boxes, dress patterns, hair nets, bow ties, lockets and you name it. "I'd love to find a ticket to the premier," he says. He expects you to price what you have. NO OFFERS.

> Robert Buchanan
> 277 West 22nd Street #2B
> New York, NY 10011
>   (212) 989-3917

★ *Gone With the Wind* items associated with the film, the book, or its author. Wants book and Mitchell related items 1936-1965, foreign language editions of the book, movie scripts, movie posters, banners, props from the film, and all the promotional items such as dolls, games, scarfs, book ends, figurines, jewelry, nail polish, paint books, paper dolls, and more. Nothing printed after 1965. Herb no longer does free appraisals or make offers.

> Herb Bridges
> PO Box 192
> Sharpsburg, GA 30277
>   (770) 253-4934

★ *Castle* newsreels from 1937 to 1975, sound or silent, 16mm or 8mm, as long as they are complete. No shortened 50' or 100' versions are wanted. Will also buy selected titles of *Castle* space and moon flight films. Private party requests you list the film number if possible.

> Art Natale, Newsreels
> PO Box 295 TH
> Cliffside Park, NJ 07010

★ *Wizard of Oz* **items** from 1900 to the present whether associated with the books, the movie or various stage productions including posters, lobby cards, pressbooks, toys, games, magazine and newspaper features and original movie merchandise marked LOEW'S INC. The only exception: "No 50th anniversary movie merchandise unless it is foreign or a prototype." Your description should include all defects. Give the history you know. Dealers, price your goods; amateurs may request offers. *The Wizard of Oz Collector's Treasury* is available for $63.

Jay Scarfone and William Stillman
PO Box 167
Hummelstown, PA 17036
(717) 566-5538   Fax: (717) 566-7718   TheBBugle@aol.com

★ *20,000 Leagues Under the Sea.* "I collect anything and everything associated with the Disney movie version of the novel. That includes movie props, costumes, scripts, cast and crew autographs, banners, posters, standees, and other promotional items from the original 1954 release. There are many toys, games and children's items I'm seeking like the Captain Nemo hat, the electric quiz game by Jacmar, the Whitman coloring book (if yours is uncolored), the Pressman periscope with cardboard backing, the school bag, jigsaw puzzles, and many many other items. I am not interested in any items that are not Disney. Please give an accurate description and a price if you can."

David Enter
23851 Windmill Lane
Laguna Niguel, CA 92677
(714) 363-8113

★ **16 mm films** made before 1970 including educational, documentary, training, promotional, cartoons, features, musical shorts, burlesque, sex films, and **home movies**. Will **consider 8mm and 35mm** but NO Super8. Also want **movie projectors** from the 1950's, 60's and 70's, but not interested in toys. "We have fun splicing odd things together and putting on performances at our Lawn Chair Drive-In."

Todd & Kristin Kimmell
Box 43737
Philadelphia, PA 19106
(215) 925-2568

*If you don't find a buyer for your movie memorabilia
in this section of Trash or Treasure, try the
Pop Culture dealers you'll find on pages 132-137.
If you have movie posters, also see Posters on p. 522.*

WORLD'S FAIR EPHEMERA

★ **International expositions and fairs, 1851-1940.** The library buys print and photographic materials including reports from various governmental and official bodies relating to the construction, exhibits, awards, and demolition of expositions. Also interested in letters, sheet music, tickets, passes, award medals, maps, and photos (both commercial and non-commercial). The library does not collect exposition artifacts or souvenirs. "Purchase offers are made based on the value to the collection rather than on any other consideration."

> Tammy Lau
> Head of Special Collections
> Madden Library
> Calif. State University Fresno
> Fresno, CA 93740
> (209) 294-2595   Fax: (209) 278-6952   tammy_lau@csufresno.edu

★ **World's Fair ephemera from before 1940.** "I'll buy everything: tickets, official and unofficial stationery, postcard sets, badges, pin back buttons, tokens, medals, elongated coins, toys, and souvenirs. Please write or ship for offer." Hartzog does not buy single items after 1940 except unusual items. Newer pieces are wanted only in large collections. Rich runs numerous auctions and invites your consignments.

> Rich Hartzog
> PO Box 4143 BVT
> Rockford, IL 61110
> (815) 226-0771

★ **1876 Centennial** collectibles such as tokens, books, textiles, trade cards, tickets, posters, broadsides, pamphlets, medals, plates, and all other souvenirs of the exposition. Describe fully, noting all damage. Will make offers only on items he requests you send on approval.

> Russell Mascieri
> 13 Running Water Court
> Medford, NJ 08055
> (609) 953-7711   Fax: (609) 953-7768

★ **1895 Atlanta Cotton States Exposition** memorabilia, especially medals, tokens, and postcards. No glassware, please. **Agriculture medals from Georgia state fairs and expos** are also wanted.

> R.W. Colbert
> 4156 Livsey Road
> Tucker, GA 30084
> (404) 938-2596

★ **1893, 1901 and 1904 Expositions (Columbian, Buffalo, St Louis).**
"I am particularly interested in mugs, pitchers, china items, banks,
watches, clocks, toys, games, trays, spoons with enamel bowls, celluloid buttons and mirrors, postcards, sheet music, passes to the Expo or a
specific exhibit, stereo views, magic lantern slides, advertising and anything else unusual." Mugs will bring $75 up, banks $100 up, enamel
spoons $75 up, and some postcards with metallic glitter up to $100.
There are many items which he DOES NOT WANT including view
books with b/w photos, items referring to Mckinley's assassination,
postcards marked OFFICIAL SOUVENIR MAILING CARD, pot metal or
brass trays, aluminum items, decSks of cards or buttons picturing two
women representing North and South America, ruby glass items (except in a set), and silver plated spoons. A photo or Xerox™ is preferred. Give the size, color and condition. Please include an SASE for
prompt response.

> Fred Lavin
> 1 Fir Top Drive
> Orchard Park, NY 14127
>   (716) 662-5261   Fax: (716) 667-3234

★ **Tennessee Centennial and Exposition of 1897.** "I'll buy postcards, china plates, paperweights, booklets, tokens, medals, and just
about any other item you can name, if it was a souvenir of the fair. I
will pay $50 for the *Guide to the Tennessee Centennial* which depicts
the buildings and describes the exhibits." A typical complete description will be enough: size, material, colors, marks, and condition.

> Paul Jarrett
> 611 West Main
> Waverly, TN 37185
>   (615) 296-3151

★ **Tennessee Centennial Expo of 1897.** This major token collector
asks that you describe your item well, including its condition.

> Joe Copeland
> PO Box 4221
> Oak Ridge, TN 37831
>   (423) 482-4215

★ **Tennessee Centennial Expo of 1897.**

> Peggy Dillard
> PO Box 210904
> Nashville, TN 37221
>   (615) 646-1605 eves

★ **1904 World's Fair in St. Louis** and other U.S. expositions from 1876 to 1940. Especially wants *Ingersoll* souvenir watches, clocks, banks, lamps, steins, lithopanes, hold-to-light postcards, china and ceramic souvenirs picturing fair scenes, ribbons and badges from judges and officials, full sets of stereo cards, photographs, complete decks of playing cards, and more. "I have less interest in fairs after 1940."

> Doug Woollard, Jr.
> 11614 Old St. Charles Road
> Bridgeton, MO 63044
> (314) 739-4662

★ **World's Fair ephemera from 1904 or before** including china, wood, metal, textiles, paper, souvenirs, and glass. "Any and all items from a fair from 1851 to 1904 will be considered," although he has a particular interest in 1851, 1876, 1893, 1901, and 1904 fairs. A photo is requested, especially of any possibly expensive items. He requests you indicate the price you'd like for your item, although he will make offers on "things genuinely for sale."

> Andy Rudoff
> PO Box 111
> Oceanport, NJ 07757
> (908) 542-3712

★ **1907 Jamestown Exposition memorabilia** of all types is sought, except "no postcards, please."

> W.T. Atkinson, Jr.
> 1217 Bayside Circle West
> Wilmington, NC 28405

★ **1933-34 Chicago Century of Progress World's Fair.** "I want employee items such as uniforms badges and certificates, but also buy tickets for specific days (ie. "Oak Park Day"), souvenirs, toys, banks, models, replicas of buildings, statues, signs, posters, paintings, pins, and the like. I'd also like 16mm home movies and personal photos of the Fair, as well as quilts made for the Sears quilt contest. I am a collector and also run the Century of Progress Collector's Show which is held each year to commemorate the Fair."

>Rick Rann
>PO Box 877
>Oak Park, IL 60303
>   (708) 442-7907

★ **Trylon and perisphere at the 1939-40 NY World's Fair** pictured on paper items is sought by this major NY stamp dealer, in business for 50 years. Send a photocopy of what you have.

>Harvey Dolin
>5 Beekman Street #406
>New York, NY 10038

★ **1964 New York World's Fair.** Especially wants fabrics, jewelry, toys, and unusual items.

>Sue Stock
>57 Lakeshore Drive
>Marlborough, MA 01752

★ **World's Fair memorabilia suitable for resale or auction.** All fairs before 1940 are wanted, especially very early ones. Rex is one of the larger mail order dealer/auctioneers in the country. He offers a large quarterly auction catalog, and constantly needs new quality items in outstanding condition. No items valued under $50 are wanted, but "the very rare always is!"

>Rex Stark
>Americana
>49 Wethersfield Road
>Bellingham, MA 02019
>   (508) 966-0994

**World's Fair souvenirs and other items will
also be purchased by dealers in Pop Culture found
at the beginning of the Section in Trash or Treasure 8
devoted to Pop Culture.**

MAGIC APPARATUS & EPHEMERA

★ **Magic posters and memorabilia** including posters, books, lithographs, autographed photos and letters, and **children's magic sets**, particularly *Mysto*. Ken buys items from the famous and not so famous, including Kellar, Thurston, Blackstone, Nicola, Raymond, Germain, and especially **Houdini**. Prices offered will depend on the rarity and condition of what you have, so it is often necessary to inspect your item before a final offer can be made. Ken promises top dollar and prompt response to any item you offer that is of interest.

> Ken Trombly
> 1825 "K" Street NW #901
> Washington, DC 20006
> (800) 673-8158   (301) 320-2360   Fax: (202) 457-0343

★ **Magic apparatus of all sorts** including all paraphernalia and props, **escape devices**, tokens, programs, books, and other ephemera. Has a particular interest in pre-1900 posters, original photos of **Houdini**, and a complete set of Houdini letters, one on each of his twelve letterheads (worth $5,000 if you have it). A complete set of *Thayer Manufacturing's* wooden turned devices (1910-20) is worth $12,000 to some lucky seller. No items after 1950, newspaper clippings, radio premiums, or pulp books issued by *Wehman Bros*. An illustrated catalog of magic books and devices is available for $5 from this veteran collector dealer.

> Mario Carrandi, Jr.
> 122 Monroe Avenue
> Belle Mead, NJ 08502
> (908) 874-0630   Fax: (908) 874-4892

★ **Magic and magicians.** "I'm looking for everything related to magic and magicians, especially apparatus, pre-1940 books, posters, programs, advertising, newspaper and magazine articles, **toy magic sets** (particularly *A.C. Gilbert's Mysto Magic* sets), battery or windup toys with a magic theme, radio premiums with magic theme, and paintings and prints about magic." Will buy items associated with **mind readers, escape artists, ventriloquists, and Punch & Judy shows**, as well. Please send a photo of your item, along with notation about condition. He does not buy foreign language books, current magazine articles, or books that are severely damaged. Be certain to describe books using proper bibliographic information. Dealers, price your goods. Amateurs may request offers.

> Frank Herman
> 710 Anchor Way
> Carlsbad, CA 92008
> (619) 434-2254

★ **Harry Houdini memorabilia** of all types, including apparatus, posters, letters and books.

> Joe and Pamela Tanner
> Tanner Escapes
> 3024 East 35th Street
> Spokane, WA 99223
> (509) 448-8457 voice and fax

★ **Magic posters, memorabilia**, tricks, and books printed before 1940. Describe condition and include a photo or Xerox™. If you are a dealer, price your goods. Amateurs may request an offer.

> Marvin Yagoda
> Marvin's Marvelous Mechanical Museum
> 31005 Orchard Lake Road
> Farmington Hills, MI 48334
> (810) 626-5020   Fax: (810) 626-7945

★ **Harry Houdini memorabilia** including book, magazine and newspaper articles, photos, handbills, pamphlets, autographs, posters, personal apparatus and personal belongings. Anything relating to Houdini will probably be of interest. He especially wants to find copies of his silent movies (including home movies) except *The Man From Beyond*. If you are offering personal apparatus or effects you must explain why you know it is from Houdini. You may price or he will make offer. Provide bibliographic information for books. Arthur is a 15 year veteran collector and happy to provide free appraisals and make offers.

> Arthur Moses
> 4205 Hildring Drive East
> Ft. Worth, TX 76109
> (817) 294-2494   Fax: (817) 732-3339

STAGE & THEATER MEMORABILIA

★ **Minstrel memorabilia of all sorts.** "I'll buy playbills, autographs, letters written by minstrels, news clippings, postcards, posters, radio and TV programs, rare book and magazine articles, recordings, and miscellaneous artifacts." He can send you a lengthy multi-part wants list which details books, TV shows, movies, phonograph records and other items he seeks. If you have **anything related to minstrels** or minstrel shows, give Norm a call. Norm recreates minstrel shows and is a serious historian of this entertainment profession.
>Norman Conrad
>PO Box 184
>East Walpole, MA 02032
>>(508) 668-6926 eves

★ **Burlesque and vaudevill memorabilia,** 1870's to 1950's. Wants photos and film, posters, handbills, flyers, sequined costumes, comic shoes, routines on cylindrical or disk records, sheet music, scrap books for any stage act except "legitimate theater," such as strong men, animal acts, minstrels, and odd musical performances.
>Todd & Kristin Kimmell
>Box 43737
>Philadelphia, PA 19106
>>(215) 925-2568

★ **Ventriloquist's memorabilia** including:
- Old **puppets** used professionally by ventriloquists;
- **Photos** of ventriloquists;
- **Books** about ventriloquism printed before 1970 (there are a goodly number of these that he seeks, so inquire);
- **Event posters** depicting ventriloquist's performances;
- **Movie posters** featuring ventriloquists.

Not interested in items made after 1970. He DOES NOT BUY phonograph records of any sort, nor is he interested in toy puppets. He asks you to describe the item's condition and asks that you price what you have. He will make offers to amateur sellers only.
>Nick Pawlow
>4547 Milnor Street
>Philadelphia, PA 19124
>>(215) 537-0558

★ **Ventriloquist's dummies,** ephemera, photos and other items related to early ventriloquism. Frequently closed, they can be difficult to reach; don't count on phone calls being returned too quickly.
>Ann Roberts, Vent Haven Museum
>33 West Maple Ave.
>Ft. Mitchell, KY 41011
>>(606) 341-0461 and leave message

★ **Theater programs**. Please send a Xerox™ of the cover and indicate the date of the performance if you can (and if it's not shown on the cover). Clean complete items only, with a preference for the NY stage.

Harvey Dolin
5 Beekman Street #406
New York, NY 10038
(212) 267-0216

★ **Theater programs and souvenirs** especially items related to an anniversary such as 50th performance, 100th performance, closing performance, and the like. In general, he is mostly interested in theatrical productions from before 1920, but will consider others.

Drew Eliot
400 West 43rd Street #25-T
New York, NY 10036
(212) 563-5444

★ **Follies Bergere** programs and other items from before 1940. Make a photocopy of the cover, and "tell me how many photos it has" as part of your description. He only wants to buy "complete items, with nothing removed, please."

Gary Bart
620 Siena Way
Los Angeles, CA 90077
(310) 471-6980   Fax: (310) 471-1910

★ **Theatrical lighting from the gaslight era.** "I'll buy anything relating to 19th century gas, oil or candle stage lighting. This includes actual lamps and parts, **prints** showing them in use, **manuals, catalogs**, or other written material containing lighting information up to about 1940. I am especially interested in limelight spotlights, also called calcium lights. Limelight burners from old movie or slide projectors are also wanted, as are some carbon-arc lamps and carbon rods, but most electrical stage lighting is too new to interest me. I am gathering materials for educational purposes and would be grateful if people could set the price they want." Lindsay says he would pay as much as $400 for a complete limelight spotlight from the 1890's.

Lindsay Lambert
41 Bellwood Avenue
Ottawa, ON
K1S 1S6 CANADA

CIRCUS & OTHER AMUSEMENTS

★ **Wild West show items** including posters, handbills, letterhead, photos, and cowboy and cowgirl outfits. Will buy anything in fine condition that can be tied to a show or one of its famous performers like **Annie Oakley or Buffalo Bill** including belt buckles, watch fobs, holsters, etc., except he does not want saddles, and specifies that he is not interested in rodeo items. You must send a photo or Xerox™ of what you wish to sell. Dealers price your goods. Amateurs may request offer.

> Emory Cantey, Jr.
> Our Turn Antiques
> 1405 Ems Road East
> Fort Worth, TX 76116
> (817) 737-0430 voice and fax

★ **Circus ephemera.** "I'll buy anything directly related to circuses, especially Barnum & Bailey, but other tented shows as well. I want posters, programs, photos, route books, etc."

> Al Mordas
> 66 Surrey Drive
> Bristol, CT 06010

★ **Circuses, carnivals, freak shows, tattoo artists and daredevils.** "I'll buy postcards, pamphlets, books, banners, and **photos**, especially those featuring fringe performers. I'm also interested in some paraphernalia, including items from **tattoo parlors**. I'm also interested in oddballs of all types including **vaudeville**, **magicians**, jugglers, **ventriloquists**, **minstrels**, **outlaws**, and criminals. Prices of real photo cards start at $5 and can go as high as $500. He warns "there are thousands of photos available which have on the back rubber stamped names of the dealer or collector who distributed them. They are not of interest, nor are programs, posters, tickets, or route cards after 1920."

> David Denholtz
> 1089 Brevity Lane
> Ft. Myers, FL 33919
> (941) 437-3830 Fax: (941) 437-3894

★ **Emmett Kelly and Emmett Kelly, Jr., items** related to their "Weary Willie the Clown" character including **porcelain figurines**, dolls, souvenirs, advertising, books, photos, posters, programs, and what have you. Does NOT WANT Emmett Kelly Senior items currently being made by Staton Arts, or Dave Grossman. A photograph "makes sure we are all talking about the same item." No other clowns.

> Nollie Neill, Jr.
> PO Box 38
> Ennice, NC 28623
> (910) 657-8152 eves Fax: (910) 282-8132

★ **Chalk carnival prizes**. Wants cartoon characters like Popeye, Wimpy, Olive Oyl, Barney Google, etc., as well as movie and radio stars, hula girls, nudes, fan dancers, sailors, cowboys, etc. Seeks figures marked *Jenkins, Rainwater, Venice Dolls*, or *Gittins*. No animals are wanted unless they are part of a larger collection containing desirable figures. His two volume illustrated price guiude to *The Carnival Chalk Prize* are available for $15 each.

> Thomas Morris
> PO Box 8307
> Medford, OR 97504
> (541) 779-3164

★ **Amusement park memorabilia:** catalogs, brochures, photos, tickets, stationery, sheet music, letterheads, pennants, tokens, advertisements, books, postcards and anything else.

> Jim Abbate
> 1005 Hyde Park Lane
> Naperville, IL 60565
> (630) 416-3543 AmusPark@aol.com

★ **Ferris Wheel memorabilia** related to the **Columbian Expo** (1893) and the **St. Louis World's Fair** (1904), including folders, guide books, photos of the wheel (even in the background), sheet music, drawings, newspaper or diary accounts of first time riders. He will pay $1,500 for blueprints of the wheel.

> Richard Bueschel
> 414 North Prospect Manor Ave.
> Mt. Prospect, IL 60056

★ **Roller coaster and amusement park memorabilia** including official or amateur photos, prints, blueprints, postcards, souvenirs, home movies and *anything* else, no matter how small or odd, that is remotely related to roller coasters or amusement parks.

> Thomas Keefe
> PO Box 464
> Tinley Park, IL 60477
> Fax: (708) 349-0722

★ **Disneyland souvenirs and memorabilia** from the California park before 1980. Wants maps, guidebooks, tickets, food wrappers, brochures, ceramic items, special event programs, posters, passes, postcards, your personal color or b/w snapshots, and what have you.
Nothing from Florida's Walt Disney World is wanted.

> Linda Cervon
> 10074 Ashland Street
> Ventura, CA 93004
> (805) 659-4405 Fax: (805) 659-4776

★ **Mardi Gras souvenirs, tokens, and other ephemera** are wanted, especially pre-1900 ball invitations and colorful Carnival Bulletins originally printed in local newspapers. Hardy and his wife are always looking for photographs, postcards, early magazine articles, and other items from New Orleans before 1940 which they can reproduce in their annual *Mardi Gras Guide*. Please inquire about all illustrated items and this prominent New Orleans collector will help you with pricing.

    Arthur Hardy
    PO Box 19500
    New Orleans, LA 70179
       (504) 838-6111   Fax: (504) 838-0100

★ **Mardi Gras.** Specializes in Mardi Gras invitations and dance cards before 1960 from New Orleans and other cities, but also buys newspaper bulletins, postcards, and other paper ephemera. "If you need any assistance, please write or call."

    Marilyn Bordelon
    Enoch's Gallery
    1750 St. Charles Avenue #303
    New Orleans, LA 70130
       (504) 899-6686

★ **Disneyland souvenirs.** Dean will buy all types including ceramic figurines, guidebooks, maps, buttons, pins, coins, postcards, employee materials, etc. All items should be marked DISNEYLAND. Also will buy *Disneykins*, tiny one to two inch high plastic figurines of Disney characters sold by *Marx* in the 1950's and 60's. Also will buy anything related to *Tinker Belle*. Special wants include Disneyland items from 1955-59, a *Tinker Belle* glow-in-the-dark wand, and Walt Disney's autograph. Everything must be in mint to near mint condition. Items may be sent on approval or described in writing if you want an offer.

    Dean Mancina
    PO Box 2274
    Seal Beach, CA 90740
       (310) 431-5671 voice/fax   Email: DSNELND@aol.com

★ **Carnegie Hall memorabilia.** Seeking relics of its own past, the Carnegie Hall Corporation wants especially to find programs and stagebills from 1892-98, 1929-31 and 1944-45. Also photos of the building in construction, or any interior shots of performers or speakers on stage. Also recordings, films and posters of events as well as any historical records. Interested in ephemera from any type of performance.

    Gino Francesconi, Carnegie Hall Corporation
    881 Seventh Ave.
    New York, NY 10019
       (212) 903-9629

TIPS ON TURNING RADIOS AND TV SETS INTO TREASURE

Valuable radios and television sets are difficult for most people to recognize. Radios worth $500 are sometimes thrown away by people who keep other radios worth $50 because they looked more valuable.

"Get advice," is good advice.

The folks who buy old radios and televisions like to know the brand name, model name and number and cosmetic condition (what does the radio look like?). Describe whether it is scratched, faded, dented, chipped, cracked, or the paint or veneer is peeling. Examine the chassis carefully for missing parts or damage. If the chassis has blank spots where a component or tube might have originally been, tell the potential buyer.

Radios and TV sets are among those few collectible items that do not have to be in perfect condition to find a buyer. Certainly, the better the condition, thebetter the price, but scarce radios and television sets will sell in almost any condition, because parts are always in demand by people who enjoy rebuilding them.

Plastic table model radios can bring from $50 to $1,000 and even transistor radios can top $100. The most valuable radios are those covered with blue or other color of glass. Large glass radios are $10,000 and up.

Do not test old electric equipment. Plugging it in may cause damage because insulation around wires deteriorates, resulting in short circuits or fire.

Buyers will arrange for packing and shipping of these bulky yet fragile items.

Look for TV sets that have channel one, or that have no channels higher than seven. The very earliest sets (1923-1939) are hard to identify as they don't look much like TV's. You are most likely to find early TV's in those cities where TV began: Los Angeles, New York, Chicago, Philadelphia, and Schenectady. We're a mobile society and they could turn up anywhere, however.

RADIOS

★ **Radios of many types 1905-40,** including crystal sets, wireless receivers and transmitters, battery operated radios 1914-1928, and small electric table models 1928-35. Buys radios in wood, metal, or plastic cabinets. Especially interested in large collections of usable speakers, **tubes and parts** for radios from this period. No large console models of the 30's except those with chrome plated interiors. Also radio **magazines, catalogs, service manuals, sales literature, and advertising,** pre-1935, including novelties, radio dealer **promotional items, and anything shaped like or depicting a radio** such as banks, toys, pin back buttons, games, postcards, and dealer promotional items. Gary formerly published *Antique Radio Classified.*

Gary Schneider
14310 Ordner Drive
Strongsville, OH 44136
(216) 251-3714 days   (216) 582-3094 eves

★ **Radios of many types** including crystal sets, battery sets of the 1920's (usually in long rectangular boxes), wireless sets and parts, WWI military radios, unusual cathedral radios by *Grebe* or *Ozarka,* grandfather clock style, odd shapes, and all luxury models like *Zenith* Stratosphere (pays $6,000+). Other names and models to watch for are *Atwater Kent, McMurdo Silver, Marconi, De Forest, Leutz, Wireless Specialty, Norden Hauck, E.H. Scott, Grebe,* and *RCA Radiolas.* Also novelty radios like *Snow White* or the World's Fair. In addition, he likes radio dealer indoor and outdoor **advertising signs,** point of purchase displays, brochures, instruction books, service manuals, parts and **radio magazines.** Not interested in plastic radios of any kind. Don is former editor of *Radio Age* magazine. Don is a collector rather than a dealer but will consider buying large collections.

Donald Patterson
636 Cambridge Road
Augusta, GA 30909
(706) 738-7227

★ **Old radios, tubes, test equipment, open frame motors, generators** and other electrical apparatus, switch board meters, knife switches, **neon signs, fans,** Tesla coils, **quack medical devices,** and **electric trains** and accessories, as well as early books on radio and electrical theory and practice. Give info from the item's ID plate. Include a sketch or photo.

Hank Andreoni
504 West 6th Street
Beaumont, CA 92223
(909) 849-7539

★ **Radios from the 1900 to 1955,** including:
- **Crystal** and 1 or 2 tube radios, factory or home made;
- Radios with comic or pop-culture characters;
- Brightly colored **Bakelite radios** from the 1930's and 40's;
- **Mirrored radios** ($1,000 to $40,000 for a like new floor model);
- Black and **chrome radios** made by *RCA* or *Majestic;*
- 1950's **pocket transistor radios**;
- Tuners and other **quality audio equipment** by *Scott, MacIntosh,* and others. "If it's too heavy to pick up, I want it."

Harry says he'll buy the **complete contents of a ham shack, radio collector or Radio/TV shop**. "If you send a photo and an SASE, I'll give you a free evaluation. If I want it, I'll pay to have it picked up."

Harry Poster
PO Box 1883
South Hackensack, NJ 07606
(201) 794-9606   Fax: (201) 794-9553   hposter@WORLDNET.ATT.NET

★ **Wireless, crystal sets, and battery radios** from before 1930 such as *Atwater Kent, Crosley, Amrad, Deforest, Federal, Grebe, Kennedy, Firth, Paragon, Marconi, R.C.A.,* and *Zenith.* Also early vacuum tubes with brass or *Bakelite* base. Also *Jenkins* **scanning disc television**. Also all wireless and radio books and magazines printed before 1930. Also radio advertising, parts, relays, earphones, horn speakers, amplifiers, batteries, meters, etc. Will pay $500 for a *Marconi CA294,* $600 for a *Marconi 106,* $800+ for a *Pacific Wireless Specialty* audio receiver, and some others to $2,000. "I do not want anything made after 1940, floor model radios, or transistor radios."

David Shanks
115 Baldwin Street
Bloomfield, NJ 07003
(201) 748-8820

★ **Mirrored glass radios.** "I'm especially fond of green mirrored glass radios and forever trying to acquire *Sparton* floor model mirrored glass radios (model 1186). I pay through the nose if I have to." That translates to as much as $35,000 for a perfect condition peach colored glass and up to $30,000 for a perfect blue glass radio. Glass covered radios do not have to work and the glass may be cracked as "I don't turn down mirrored glass radios offered to me." He claims to outbid anybody, and points out that he will either come pick up any radio or have it professionally moved so you don't have to worry about shipping. He also buys **colorful plastic radios** of the 1930's and 40's. He prefers you to price but will make offers if you seriously intend to sell.

Ed Sage
PO Box 13025
Albuquerque, NM 87192
(505) 298-0840

★ **Radios with wood cabinets.** Give make and model number, condition, and price. Does not make offers.
Alvin Heckard
Route 1   Box 88
Lewistown, PA 17044
(717) 248-7071

★ **Radio manuals, handbooks, and sales literature** pre-1940.
Alan C. King
PO Box 86
Radnor, OH 43066

★ **Microphones,** 1940-1960, but only the short stand-up desk type mics used by broadcasters and radio stations. Especially wants to find microphones with the station or network letters still attached.
Charles Martignette
PO Box 293
Hallandale, FL 33008
(954) 454-3474

HI-FI EQUIPMENT

★ **Early tube high fidelity equipment** 1947-1960 especially monaural but also some early stereo from companies such as *Dynaco, Marantz, Fisher, McIntosh, Scott, Eico, Altec Lansing, JBL,* etc. Most makes and models are wanted, working or not, complete or for parts, as well as tubes, loudspeakers, schematics, manuals and **hi-fi magazines.** Of special interest are all **early** *McIntosh* **amps.** Nothing after 1970, "but I'll buy a wide range of things relating to early audio, from broadcast equipment to home systems."
Jack Smith
288 Winter Street
North Andover, MA 01845
(508) 686-7250

★ **Early tube-type stereo and hi-fi equipment** made by *McIntosh, Marantz, Dynaco, H.H. Scott, Western Electric, Heath, Leak, Harman Kardon, Acrosound, Altec-Lansing.* Also any manuals or literature for this equipment. Also want large **audio transformers** by *Acrosound* like their model TO-300. **Old microphones** from the 1930's to 50's by *RCA, Shure, Western Electric, Astatic, Turner,* and *Electrovoice.*
Jeff Viola
784 Eltone Road
Jackson, NJ 08527
(908) 928-0666

★ **Early tube high fidelity equipment** including stereo and mono amplifiers, pre-amps, tuners (especially *McIntosh, Marantz, Western Electric* and *Quad*), large old speakers (especially *Altec, JBL, Tannoy, Western Electric,* and *Jensen*). Also radios before 1920, vacuum tubes, homemade amplifiers and kits by *UTC, Dynaco,* and *Heath*, movie theater sound equipment (including amps, speakers, and microphones), **antique electrical, electronic, telephonic, and telegraphic items**. Also wants old **hi-fi magazines**, books, and other literature. Does not want "department store console stereos" from *Sears, Silvertone, Wards*, etc., television tubes, or any TV's made after 1940. Give the maker's name, model number, cosmetic condition (what it looks like in terms of scratches, dents, etc.), and whether the original literature is included.

> Vernon Vogt
> 330 SW 43rd Street #247
> Renton, WA 98055
> (206) 382-5571

★ **Tube-type hi-fi amplifiers,** pre-amps, and tuners are wanted as are "some old guitars and **guitar amps**. There isn't anything special I'm looking for, as I like it all, but the more unusual the better. I love talking about this old stuff, so welcome calls, as long as they are ready with the name of the manufacturer and the model number." He also buys **homemade hi-fi equipment**.

> Steve Sebra
> 6839 Amigo Avenue
> Reseda, CA 91335
> (818) 708-9612

★ **Tube-type hi-fi equipment** including:
- Amplifiers by *McIntosh, Marantz, Dynaco,* or *Heathkit;*
- **Audio tubes**;
- **Audio tube testers** made by *Hickok;*
- **15" Hi-Fi speakers**;
- **Tube limiters**;
- **Record cutting machines** by *Fairchild* and many others.

Describe what you have fully, including all information on the ID plate. Note if any tubes are missing or if anything seems damaged.

> Kim Gutzke
> 7134 15th Avenue S
> Minneapolis, MN 55423
> (612) 869-4963   Fax: (612) 798-4169

TRANSISTOR RADIOS

★ **Pocket-size radios, 5" x 7" or smaller.** "If they fit in a shirt or coat pocket, I'm interested, whether they are tube, transistor, or crystal radios. I want the old ones made in the USA or Japan between 1954 and 1964. I collect for appearance and for history. I like cute colorful radios with interesting shapes on the front such as boomerangs, arrows, etc. I do not care if your radio works and will buy useful ones in any condition, but prefer they be complete and without chips or cracks. Radios with their original boxes and papers especially appeal to me." The most valuable radios are the *Regency TR-1*, a 1954 radio from Indianapolis, and the earliest *Sony* transistors, such as the *TR-55, TR-52, TR-2K, TR-33, TR-6,* and *TR-66.* A perfect condition *Sony TR-55* would bring $750 and you'd make $250 for a *Regency.* To sell your radio, give the brand name, model number, color, and country of origin. If your radio has no model number, Xerox™ the front. Important: he does not want radios made in Hong Kong, Taiwan or Korea or radios that claim to have 10 or more transistors.

Eric Wrobbel
20802 Exhibit Court
Woodland Hills, CA 91367
(818) 884-2282

★ **Pocket transistor radios.** Has a particular interest in the *Hoffman Trans-Solar*, offering to pay $250 each for fine specimens in various colors. "I don't want anything not in good cosmetic condition, but it doesn't matter whether they work or not. Give the make and model number (which you will probably have to open the case to get) or make a Xerox™ of the front of the radio and describe the color.

Mike Brooks
7335 Skyline
Oakland, CA 94611
(510) 339-1751   Fax: (510) 444-4010

★ **Novelty transistor radios** especially Japanese radios shaped like commercial products. Also wants radios shaped like, or related to, robots, rockets, household or personal items, media stars and heroes, TV and comic characters, food and drink, travel and transportation. He is *not* interested in radios shaped like animals, Sesame Street characters, or anything related to war or weapons. When describing a radio tell whether it has its battery cover and original box. Describe its condition carefully, noting scratches.

Bob Roberts
PO Box 152
Guilderland, NY 12084

TELEVISION SETS

★ **Early television sets.** "I'll buy old or unusual TV's, such as:
  • All 1920-1940 scanning disc or electronic (paying to $10,000);
  • 1940's sets with 3", 7" or 10" tubes ($50-$1,000);
  • 1950's sets in unusual shapes and styles;
  • 1946-1956 sets with 9" -19" tubes and color adapters;
  • 1960-1980 unusually shaped transistor TV's;
  • 1980's LVD TV's like *Epson Elf, Sony KV4000,* etc.;
  • Dealer displays for TV's, catalogs, signs, neon, promotions, etc.;
  • All books and manuals about TV printed before 1940.
"Mechanical TV's are often mistaken for early electronic junk," he cautions, "so look for 12" metal disks containing tiny holes that spin in front of a neon glow lamp. These early TV's drew their sound from radio sets, and most had no cabinets. Also interested in mirror-in-lid sets by *Pilot, Andrea, Philco, RCA, GE, Garod,* and *Zenith.* I also buy *Fada* and *Meissner* 5" kit televisions. "I am willing to buy an entire TV shop, attic, or estate to get one TV I want." Harry offers free evaluations of TV sets if you send him a good photo and SASE.
> Harry Poster
> PO Box 1883
> South Hackensack, NJ 07606
> (201) 794-9606   Fax: (201) 794-9553   hposter@WORLDNET.ATT.NET

★ **Television sets** from 1938 to 1950 especially those with a reflective mirror in the lid and only four or five channels such as the *RCA TT-5, RCA TRK-9* or *TRK-12, GE HM-225, GE HM-275* and the *GE HM 171* (worth $2,000 each). Television sets from 1946 to 1950 with screen sizes of 7" and 10" are worth from $75 to $250 for nice sets. Also wants sales literature and dealer promotions.
> Donald Patterson
> 636 Cambridge Road
> Augusta, GA 30909
> (706) 738-7227

☆ **Television literature,** including books, catalogs, and company pamphlets (either internal or intended for the public) from before 1940. SASE required.
> Harold Layer
> Box 27676
> San Francisco, CA 94127

TIPS ON TURNING MUSICAL ITEMS INTO TREASURE

Music collectibles fall into five categories, each type sought by different collectors.

*(1) **Musical instruments** can be valuable, especially quality guitars and violins. To sell any instrument, you need to state the maker and the model, and describe the type and quality of finish. Mention all cracks, dents, and the like. If you have a piano or organ to sell, no national market exists so it is best to offer it for sale in a local classified ad.*

*(2) **Mechanical music** refers to phonographs, record players, player pianos, music boxes, and other devices which play music by mechanical means. Describing what you have is usually a matter of taking a good photograph, listing all the information on the maker's ID plate, and describing the condition. Buyers of juke boxes, a form of mechanical music, are considered part of the "Coin-Op" world and are listed in Trash or Treasure on pages 196-200.*

*(3) **Sheet music** collectors are more concerned with the picture on the cover than with the musical content, so, classical music and school scores are not of interest. Music must be in exceptionally fine condition, free of significant tears, writing, or other damage.*

*(4) **Phonograph records** are seldom exceptionally valuable, with most records still selling for $5 to $10 retail. Don't let the fact your records are worth only a dollar or two discourage you. Records come in piles, and can add up! Record buyers want to know the title, artist, record label, and catalog number (there's one on every record). Note the condition of the record, the record jacket, and the paper sleeve. Records in mint condition are preferred by collectors, but a few early 78's have never been found in perfect condition. If it lists for more than $15 in Les Docks'* American Premium Record Guide, *collectors may want it even if it looks a little beat up.*

*(5) **Memorabilia** of music, musicians and singers is like other Pop Culture items. Rare, colorful, and in fine condition describes what collectors want.*

STRINGED MUSICAL INSTRUMENTS

★ **Fretted stringed musical instruments** such as banjos, guitars, mandolins, ukuleles, and the like. "A *Martin D-45* guitar made prior to 1942 could be worth as much as $100,000," so instruments are worth selling properly. Also **related memorabilia** such as manufacturer's catalogs, old photos of guitar shops and players, accessories, etc. State the preservation of your instrument. Examine carefully for repairs. Look for any signs that it might not be original. Mention the type and condition of the instrument's case. Offers a monthly 24 page catalog of used instruments for $15 per year. "We display more than 2,000 instruments and offer free catalogs of new merchandise."

> Stan Werbin
> Elderly Instruments
> 1100 North Washington Dept. TT
> Lansing, MI 48906

(517) 372-7890 ext 132   Fax: (517) 372-5155   swerbin@elderly.com

☆ **Most string, wood, and brass musical instruments** are of interest for trade or resale. "I'll buy **any museum quality instrument**." For his own collection he wants instruments that are rare, very old, pretty, unique, or hand crafted. He especially wants **trumpets or cornets** that have extra keys, fewer keys, or keys that are in unusual positions or shapes. Also **instruments of other cultures** including African, Asian, Pacific, etc., but no pianos or organs. A photo should go with a complete description, including all labels or markings.

> Sid Glickman
> 314 Park Hill Avenue
> Yonkers, NY 10705
>   (914) 476-5001 voice/fax

*To **sell any instrument, you need to***
   (1) State the maker and the model;
   (2) Describe the type and quality
       of the finish;
   (3) Give an indication of its condition.
       Include mention of all cracks,
       dents, and the like.

If some thing seems unusual to you, make a sketch or include a photo. If you have a piano or organ to sell, unless it's a concert grade Steinway, there is no national market and it is usually best to offer it for sale in a local classified ad.

TRASH OR TREASURE

★ **Stringed musical instruments** including electric and acoustic guitars, banjos, mandolins and ukeleles. No ukelins or mandolin-harps, please. He buys the following brands of guitar: *D'Angelico, Gibson Les Paul, Martin, Stromberg National, Epiphone, Fender, Gretsch*, and *Rickenbacker*. Many guitars purchased for $100-$300 in the 1950's are worth five to ten times as much today, and a *Martin D-45* would bring from $20,000 to $50,000. Buys gold plated four-string banjos and fancy five string banjos by *Fairbanks, Vega, Epiphone, Gibson, Weymann, Slingerland, Bacon & Day, Studio King, Recording King, Paramount*, and others. Mandolins by *Gibson, Martin* and *Washburn* are wanted, as are ukeleles by *Martin* and *Gibson*. Photos of the front and back of your instrument are requested. Pays all shipping costs. Appraisal services are available.

> Steve Senerchia
> The Music Man
> 300 Quaker Lane, #7
> Warwick, RI 02886
> (401) 821-2865 Fax: (401) 823-4728 musicman@tiac.net

★ **American guitars, banjos, and mandolins** made by the following: *C.F. Martin, Gibson, Fender* (older models only), *Dobro, National, D'Angelico, B&D (Bacon & Day), Epiphone* (older), *Paramount, Vega, Fairbanks, SS Stewart, Washburn, Lyon & Healy, Stromberg, Gretsch, D'Aquisto* and *Rickenbacker*. "If you have fine condition instruments for sale by these makers you may call us collect for an offer. Have your instrument in your hand. Be prepared to answer specific questions about condition, originality, serial number, color, and the type of case it has. Without this information, we cannot provide meaningful evaluation. *Serious sellers only may call collect.* All others are welcome to call for advice or information." Among instruments Jay would most like to find are the *Martin* D-45 with abalone inlay, the electric *Gibson* Les Paul Standard made in 1958-60, and *Gibson* Mastertone banjos made during the late 1930's. Dates and models are very important. "Another model made at the same time might be worth only 1/20 as much. Original condition matters a lot." Offers an interesting catalog of high quality new and used instruments. Wants list available.

> Stan Jay
> Mandolin Bros.
> 629 Forest Ave.
> Staten Island, NY 10310
> (718) 981-8585 (718) 981-3226 Fax: (718) 816-4416

★ **French and Italian violins, violas, and cellos.** "I'll pay high prices for quality instruments, both commercial and handmade from anywhere in the world, but especially France and Italy. I don't want children's or school violins nor any imitations of Stradivarius, Guarnerius, or other masters." Describe the label inside the instrument. Appraisal services are available.

 Robert Portukalian's Violin Shop
 1279 North Main Street
 Providence, RI 02904
 (401) 521-5145

Many readers own violins with labels proclaiming them to be made by Stradivarius in the 1700's. These are usually cottage industry pieces made in Germany at the turn of the century for Sears Roebuck, who sold them for $9 in their catalog. A few, although not genuine Strads, are quality instruments and can command good prices.

★ **High quality Italian violins and some of their imitators** are the prime interest of this 20 year veteran West coast dealer. Cremona school violins, 1650-1750, can be worth from $2,500 to $100,000 or more, but many copies exist. Jones will consider better French instruments and your fake "Stradivarius" violins. Most of the fake "Strads" sell for $100 or less, but a few more valuable "fake Strads" were made by fine craftsmen who affixed the Stradivarius label in an effort to sell the instrument. Others were high quality reproductions of the master's work, deliberately copied in homage to his craftsmanship. Many other **guitars, banjos, basses, violas, and mandolins** can be fairly valuable to Jones if you have one of better quality. It takes years of handling violins to be able to recognize originals or instruments of value. For this reason "it is difficult to buy through the mail, but not impossible." The reputation of the maker and the condition of the instrument are crucial in determining value. To sell a stringed instrument, you must describe all damage, the type and quality of finish, the bow, and give every word on the label. In many cases, he will request seeing the instrument before making a final offer. No Oriental instruments are wanted.

 David N. Jones' Violin Shop
 3206 32nd Street
 San Diego, CA 92104
 (619) 584-1505

BRASS MUSICAL INSTRUMENTS

★ **Brass musical instruments,** especially the unusual and obsolete. He wants "to know about all your old brass instruments since they all look the same to the untrained." Among other instruments, he especially wants a B-flat cornet with the bell pointing over the shoulder and a Schreiber horn with a straight up bell. He is attempting to assemble a representative collection of the hundreds of different brass instruments. Also interested in **band related memorabilia** such as photos of bands or individual musicians holding instruments, band programs, **catalogs** of instruments, mouthpieces, decorative or unusual **wooden music stands,** and old-style **conducting batons**. Also interested in your coffin shaped wooden instrument cases. If you regularly sell musical instruments, get his informative illustrated wants list.

> Jonathan Korzun
> 206 Michigan Avenue
> Dowagiac, MI 49047
> (616) 782-5594

★ **Saxophones made by** *Selmer, King, Buescher* or *Conn* especially from 1920 - 1970. The serial number of your instrument is important, so always include it as part of the description. Original finish, even if worn, is preferable to relacquered instruments. Large dents and heavy scratches take away most of the value. Some mouthpieces are collected, so tell him the maker of that, too. He asks you to write or call collect if you want to sell any good condition old sax.

> Ed Hakal
> 10126 Signal Butte Circle
> Sun City, AZ 85373
> (602) 972-3091 evenings

★ **Brass musical instruments** made in the United States during the 19th century, especially keyed bugles and instruments which hang over the shoulder, worth $600 and up. He does *not* want saxophones or modern brass instruments. Give the maker's name, the number of valves, the shape of the instrument and whether it is made of brass or silver. You should include a photo or drawing of the shape of the instrument. He also wants photos of bands and bandsmen as well as old instrument catalogs.

> Mark Jones
> PO Box 98
> Eden, NY 14057
> (716) 992-2074 voice and fax

OTHER MUSICAL INSTRUMENTS

★ **Rare and unusual musical instruments** including harps, bagpipes, hurdy-gurdies, wooden flutes, concertinas, ethnic instruments, and all manner of **brass and woodwinds**, stringed instruments, dulcimers, autoharps, and others. No keyboards except a folding "preacher's organ." Mickie repairs instruments and will purchase good ones in "any restorable condition." Can make arrangements for consignment selling of instruments he doesn't wish to buy. This 20 year veteran conducts annual seminars on musical instrument history and performance. He charges reasonable rates for insurance appraisals, and will make offers. An extensive illustrated catalog may be ordered for $3. **Has no interest in accordions, pianos, pump or electric organs, or ukelins.**

Mickie Zekley
Lark in the Morning
PO Box 1176
Mendocino, CA 95460
(707) 964-5569

★ **Drums and drum catalogs** from the early 1900's to 1970. Buys sets or single tom toms, bass drums, or snare drums, and buys uncracked **cymbals marked K.ZILDJIAN** but not those made by A.ZILDJIAN. "To save everyone effort, a thorough and complete inspection of your instrument should be done before contacting us. Check and note modifications and/or damage of any kind including scratches, cracks, peeling, bulging, holes drilled, rim warp, rust, pitting, stains, or discoloration." Information needed to evaluate your drum(s): the brand name, shape and color of the ID emblem, the diameter of the head(s), the depth of each drum's shell (not including the rims), and the color and type of finish of the drum(s) on both the outside and inside. Does not buy drums or drum catalogs produced after 1970, exotic or ethnic drums, or parade basses. He requests "serious inquiries only, please. Kindly keep in mind that we do not offer appraisals or estimates by mail or phone. If you have no idea of the value of your item(s), I'll give you a retail price range that your item sells for in the vintage drum market and then request you quote me your wholesale asking price. I'm willing to educate sellers so they can make an informed decision and determine a fair price, keeping in mind that we must recondition items, resell them, and make a profit." One of the world's largest dealers in collectible drums, Vintage Drum Center publishes a quarterly catalog, available free to drum buyers.

Ned Ingberman
Vintage Drum Center
2243 Ivory Drive
Libertyville, IA 52567
(800) 729-3111 ext 5 (buy or sell) Fax: (515) 693-3101

★ **Harmonicas** and related items. Seeking unusual ones other than the standard 10 hole 4" long instrument: harmonicas with attached horns, bells, or whistles, those joined together with other harmonicas, those mounted in brass funnel-shaped resonators, and instruments that are smaller than 2" long or larger than 12" long. He also wants:
- Toy instruments with harmonicas built inside;
- Canes with built-in harmonicas;
- Blow accordions (clarinet-like instruments with keys
    which when depressed make a harmonica note or chord);
- Advertising, display cases, posters, magazines;
- Catalogs with pages of harmonicas pictured;
- Records (old), sheet music, lapel pins, and what have you.

No instruments in poor playing condition or that have bad rust or dents. Provide the maker, model, number of holes, length, width, whether it is double sided, whether all notes play, physical condition and (very important) whether the box is included. Photocopy of both sides helpful. Dealers must price your goods. Amateurs who are actually selling may inquire as to value before shipment.

> Alan Bates
> 495 Dogwood Drive
> Hockessin, DE 19707
>   (302) 239-4296   76367.1760@compuserve.com

★ **Cigar box musical instruments.** Any musical instrument made from a cigar box is wanted. When describing your item, please include any of the instrument's history you know. Mention whether strings, pegs, bow and carry bag are present, and describe any applied or painted decorations. Photo is helpful. Also buys **toys and other items made from boxes**, especially items which retain their basic "boxness" rather than items made from cut up pieces of boxes.

> Tony Hyman
> PO Box 3028
> Pismo Beach, CA 93448
>   (805) 773-6777   Fax: (805) 773-8436

MECHANICAL MUSIC

★ **Any pre-1930 device that plays music mechanically** including disk and cylinder music boxes, clocks and watches that play tunes, disk players, automata dolls, player organs, monkey organs, nickelodeons, horn phonographs in any condition from perfect to incomplete. Especially a barrel operated monkey organ with pipes ($2,000-$4,000), large disc music boxes that play more than one disc at a time ($10-$12,000), and cylinder music boxes with more than 175 teeth, and early musical watches. **No player pianos are wanted,** but most other mechanical devices bring $300 up. Give measurements of any disk or cylinder. Please include your phone number with correspondence.

> Martin Roenigk
> Mechantiques
> 26 Barton Hill
> East Hampton, CT 06424
> (203) 267-8682   Fax: (203) 267-1120

★ **Musical instruments that "play themselves"** by motor, springs, pneumatics or other means: **music boxes,** roller organs, cylinder music boxes, musical bird cages, nickelodeons, and organettes. Will buy rough condition items for parts or repair. Also musical disks, cylinders, piano rolls, old photos, postcards or paper ephemera depicting anything in mechanical music. Doug does not make offers.

> Doug Negus, Phonograph Phunatic
> 215 Mason Street
> Sutherland, IA 51058
> (712) 446-2270   (712) 446-3746

★ **Horn phonographs in any condition.** Will buy complete machines or parts from any machine. Especially seeking: *Berliner Gramophone, National Gramophone, Universal Talking Machine, Zonophone* or *Victor.* Photos are helpful. All inquiries answered promptly.

> Charlie Stewart
> 900 Grandview Avenue
> Reno, NV 89503
> (702) 747-1439 days

★ **Edison 4-minute recorder** to fit a phonograph, and a **sapphire shaving knife** for an *Ediphone* or *Dictaphone* dictation cylinder shaving machine. "Inexpensive only, please, as I used these for classroom demos of early recording procedures."

> Lindsay Lambert
> 41 Bellwood Avenue
> Ottawa, ON
> K1S 1S6 CANADA

★ **Phonographs, music boxes, and related ephemera.** Would like to hear from you regarding all disc and cylinder phonographs with outside horns, especially those with wooden horns. Also floor model wind-up phonographs in deluxe or fancy cabinets. Also antique disc or cylinder music boxes, especially those that sit on the floor. Will pay from $200 to $10,000, depending on type, style, and condition. "I am also interested in purchasing old record catalogs, posters, metal signs, *Victor* dogs, needle tins, and the like. Phonograph related paper items before 1910 are especially desirable, particularly **items associated with Thomas Edison.**" Send descriptions and photocopies.

> Kurt Nauck
> Nauck's Vintage Records
> 6323 Inway Drive
> Spring, TX 77389
> (281) 370-7899   Fax: (281) 251-7023   nauck@78rpm.com

★ **Antique music boxes and phonographs.** Wants all types, 1850-1920, including cylinder, disc, paper roll, and cob organs. Brands like *Regina, Mira, Stella, Symphonian,* and *Kalliope* are sought. Especially interested in a *Regina Changer,* a 15 1/2 inch upright music box which changes automatically. He'd pay $12,000 for a nice one. He wants to know the brand, model, size, and condition. Pictures are most helpful. Is not interested in "late miniature music boxes."

> Chet Ramsay
> 2460 Strasburg Road
> Coatesville, PA 19320
> (610) 384-0514

★ **Phonographs and related memorabilia** from before 1930 including cylinder and disc records, catalogs, needle tins, postcards, stereoviews depicting phonographs, toy phonographs, signs and other advertising except magazine ads. Also buys cylinder records of speeches by Taft, Teddy Roosevelt, and other famous people, for which he pays $10-$50. Also all **material related to Thomas Edison.** List make, model, and condition. Include label, artist, and title of records. SASE for offer.

> Steven Ramm
> 420 Fitzwater Street
> Philadelphia, PA 19147
> (215) 922-7050 eves

★ **Phonographs with outside horns,** complete or for parts. No Victrolas. Alvin doesn't want to be bothered unless you're serious about selling. Does not make offers.

> Alvin Heckard
> Rural route 1   Box 88
> Lewistown, PA 17044
>   (717) 248-7071

★ *RCA* or *Capehart* **radio-phonographs that automatically flip records over** to play the other side. Pays $500-$700 for these large complicated machines from the 1930's. "If your machine weighs less than 75 pounds, I'm probably not interested." Take a photo of the record changing mechanism or give him a call.

> Joseph Weber
> 604 Centre Street
> Ashland, PA 17921
>   (717) 875-4401 from 3 to 5 p.m.

★ **Catalogs of phonograph records and piano rolls** published by record and piano roll companies, 1890 to 1960. Prefers to buy collections or very early pieces. No records, magazine ads, or damaged items. Tim is past president of the Association for Recorded Sound Collections, a national club for recording historians.

> Tim Brooks
> Box 31041 Glenville Station
> Greenwich, CT 06831

★ **Phonograph needle clippers and sharpeners.**

> Don Gorlick
> PO Box 24541
> Seattle, WA 98124

★ **Record cutting machines** by *Fairchild* and many others. Describe what you have fully, including all information on the ID plate. Note if any tubes are missing or if anything seems damaged.

> Kim Gutzke
> 7134 15th Avenue S
> Minneapolis, MN 55423
>   (612) 869-4963   Fax: (612) 798-4169

SHEET MUSIC

★ **Old popular sheet music** from 1820-1970, with pictorial covers, especially music or songs from movies, shows, WWI or WWII. Wants ragtime, blues, Negro, ethnic music, political, historical, and particularly likes covers with baseball, cartoons, fire, aviation, and automobile songs. No classical, teaching or religious, please. **Also buys** *Downbeat, Metronome, Billboard* **and movie magazines.**

    Beverly Hamer
    PO Box 75
    East Derry, NH 03041
    (603) 432-3528

★ **Sheet music** in small or large collections or accumulations. Primary interest is in popular music of the 20th century (1890-1970). Movie and show tunes are of primary interest, but "also any music that falls into any of the main collectible categories, like presidential, political, patriotic, war, transportation, cartoon, baseball, *Coca-Cola,* advertising, historical, Black related, and anything else that has interesting cover art." Particularly likes to find music published by the *ET Paull Music Company*, and will pay between $10 and $300, depending upon the title and condition. **Does not want to buy classical music or sheet music designed for teaching.** "If the person wants to sell the music as a lot, I need to know quantity, condition, and the rough percentage of movie, show, and pop tunes. I also want to know the percentage of large format (11" x 14") and small format (9" x 12") music."

"Please don't describe sheet music as 'good for its age.' That means fair or poor condition. 'Excellent' and 'mint' are terms reserved for music that has almost never seen the light of day, music store stock, or publisher's remainder."

    Wayland Bunnell
    Clean Sheets
    199 Tarrytown Road
    Manchester, NH 03103
    (603) 668-5466

Sheet music collectors are very fussy about condition. **Don't waste their time and yours by offering items in poor condition.** *They won't buy them! When trying to sell a few pieces of sheet music, a photocopy is the best strategy, but with large quantities, follow Wayland Bunnell's suggestions, giving quantity, general condition, number of songs in each of the two sheet music sizes, and the percentage of the pile that are movie, show, and pop tunes.*

★ **Bound volumes of sheet music from before 1900.** Pays $1 or more per title for illustrated ones, but rare publishers bring more. Prefers bound books with no titles removed. Also **songbooks with oddly shaped notes.** "I'll pay $25+ for singing school books with notes that are oblong, triangular, rectangular or oddly shaped, especially those in good condition published before 1860. Authors of popular versions of these books include Funk, Carden, Davisson, Swan, and others."

    Jim Presgraves, Bookworm & Silverfish
    PO Box 639
    Wytheville, VA 24382

★ **Sheet music.** "I am a general sheet music collector who buys music in 500+ categories, so I look for whatever I don't have that interests me. What I don't need is the most popular songs of any era. I don't have much interest in "nice" music like love songs, moon songs, waltzes, etc. I'm more apt to buy music in major categories with strong illustrated covers such as movies, politics, cartoons, transportation, sports, or racism." To offer her your music, list the title, date, composer, name of the movie or show, condition, and what is on the cover.

"Don't expect to get rich on piles of old sheet music. Few pieces of sheet music have significant value...and those must be in outstanding condition. Some sheet are worth $100 or more, so it is important to check."

    Sandy Marrone
    113 Oakwood Drive
    Cinnaminson, NJ 08077
    (609) 829-6104

★ **Sheet music about WWI and WWII** in fine to mint condition. Also wants sheet music with pictures of Frank Sinatra or Presidents of the U.S. Also buys **music by Charles K. Harris and Irving Berlin.**
    Herman Rush
    10773 Ojai-Santa Paula Road
    Ojai, CA 93023

★ **Song books and sheet music** are sought **as donations.** If you can't find a buyer, but hate to see those musical treasures go to waste, consider donating to a public library specializing in music. They'll take any usable sheet music or song books, any language, up to the present. They don't need "how to" books. Donations must be unrestricted. No need to contact them; just ship and request a receipt for tax purposes.
    May Anstee, Helen Plumb Library
    110 West Maple
    Lombard, IL 60148
    (630) 627-0316

To sell hymnals, see Religion section, pp 308-312

CYLINDER AND 78 RPM PHONOGRAPH RECORDS

★ **Music cylinders.** The following cylinders (early phonograph recordings) are wanted by a well known music auctioneer:
• Cylinders colored brown, pink, purple, white or orange;
• Cylinders 6" long or 5" in diameter;
• Blue cylinders numbered 5000 to 5750;
• Cylinders with opera or historical content.
It is a plus if the cylinders are in their original boxes, but not necessary. Cylinders can bring from $5 to $200 each, depending on the size, color, and condition. List the title, artist, catalog number, color, length and diameter, and note whether you have the box. If your collection is very large, so listing is impractical, phone him to make other arrangements. "Cylinders break or scratch easily. Avoid touching the surface. Do not play them, even if you think you have the right equipment."
Kurt Nauck, Nauck's Vintage Records
6323 Inway Drive
Spring, TX 77389
(281) 370-7899   Fax: (281) 251-7023   nauck@78rpm.com

★ **Rare 78 rpm records.** Among his particular wants are:
• Jazz, blues, cajun and country records 1925-1935;
• Rock and roll records, 1948-1960;
• Records before 1903 (often 7" diameter with no paper labels);
• Speeches by historical figures on disk or cylinder;
• **Picture records** (transparent records w/ pictures under grooves);
• Advertising, promotional, and special purpose records, some of which are made of thin cardboard *(don't play them!)*;
• Classical and opera before 1908, especially smaller than 10";
• **Long play 78's** marked "longer playing," "five minute record;"
• Rare labels, of which he can supply you a long list, including *Black Patti, KKK, Sunshine, Marconi, Vitaphone,* and more;
• Puzzle, or multi-track, records;
• Unusual sizes and shapes of records.
He urges you to read Les Docks' *The American Premium Record Guide* and to list any records you have that catalog for more than $15 in that publication. Include the label, number, artist, and any noticeable defects. "If you have a large collection so that making a list is impractical, call me and we can discuss the possibility of evaluating your collection in person." Send a long SASE and $2 for his wants list. He DOES NOT WANT big bands, Hawaiian, popular songs, religious music, album sets, country music after WWII, home recordings, or later opera and classical, nor does he want 45's or LP records of any type.
Kurt Nauck, Nauck's Vintage Records
6323 Inway Drive
Spring, TX 77389
(281) 370-7899   Fax: (281) 251-7023   nauck@78rpm.com

★ **78 rpm recordings, 1900-1940,** including popular, dance orchestra, vocal, military band, classical, jazz, country & western, instrumental, spoken word, personality, humor, and recordings in foreign languages. Also seeks picture records. Highest prices are paid for records in good condition with no cracks or chips into the grooves. Values range from $1 to $1,000 with 80% of them under $5 each (but a pile of them adds up). When listing your records, include the label, artist and catalog (index) number. Song titles are not necessary. A Stamped Self-Addressed Envelope should be included if you wish records evaluated. David will **buy a wider range of items than most** record buyers. He is especially interested in entire collections and will travel anywhere in the East. Catalogs of record companies before 1930 are also sought.

David Alan Reiss
3920 Eve Drive
Seaford, NY 11783
(516) 785-8336   Fax: (516) 785-4490

When describing phonograph records the most important pieces of information are the record label and catalog number. Record experts like buyers recommended in **Trash or Treasure** *will know what you have without your even listing the artist and title. Condition is not as important, but still should be mentioned. Some rare 78rpm records will be purchased in any condition.*

If your record is of a very popular song, there are many copies available, so it doesn't have much value.

A leading record buyer once said, "If your records were bought by someone who is white and middle class, the odds are they have little value. Black, cajun, hillbilly and ethnic music is where the action is."

★ **American 78 rpm pop records, 1888-1949,** especially in quantity. Pays 10¢ to $1 apiece, less if records are not in fine condition. Buys disks, cylinders, and sapphire ball recordings at higher prices. Likes to find pre-1960 versions of *Froggy Went a Courtin'*, especially the *Victor* black label version from 1926, worth $100 in fine condition. Some interest in **sheet music for pop music and songs** from 1890-1925.

Ron Graham
8167 Park Ave.
Forestville, CA 95436
(707) 887-2856

★ **78 rpm, 45 rpm, and 33 rpm jazz, blues, big band, hillbilly, rock and roll, rhythm and blues, rockabilly, and celebrity records.**
• Jazz and dance bands from the 1920's and 30's;
• Jug and washboard bands;
• Radio transcription disks;
• Anything recorded on *Autograph, Black Patti,* and 50 other labels (send long SASE for a list);
• Records marked "Fox Trot," "Stomp," or "For Dancing."
He buys many rare, obscure and unpopular records but DOES NOT WANT easy listening, hit records, or pop singing stars like Al Jolson and Bing Crosby. If you have 78's to sell, send $2 for the *Shellac Shack's Wants List*, a 72 page book listing the prices they pay for thousands of records. Les is author of *American Premium Record Guide*, the basic reference book on phonograph records, available for $26 postpaid from him.
Les Docks
The Shellac Shack
PO Box 691035
San Antonio, TX 78269
(210) 492-6021 Fax: (210) 492-6489

★ *Vogue* **78 rpm picture records.** Will pay $500 for *Rum and Coca Cola*. Records must be clean and in excellent condition. Long SASE brings a list of other records John wants to buy.
John Widmar
Lake Side Towers
5800 3rd Avenue #515
Kenosha, WI 53140
(414) 654-6802

★ **Phonograph records, tapes, music videos, sheet music, books and magazines related to music,** 1900 to the present. Items must be in fine condition as they are purchased for resale. Buys in bulk, so indicate the type of record (78, 45, 33), the type of music (rock, country, classical, jazz, easy listening, spoken, soundtrack, etc.), and the number you have of each. SASE is a must. Produces *Record Finder*, a 56 page monthly for $12/year.
W.H. Smith
Memory Lane Records
PO Box 1047
Glen Allen, VA 23060
(804) 266-1154 Fax: (804) 264-9660 wsmith2761@aol.com

★ **Phonograph records** in all categories:
  • 78 rpm including popular, vocal, instrumental, personality,
      jazz, especially big band, country & western, dance
      orchestra and blues, 1900-1959;
  • 45rpm from 1947 to the present, especially rock and roll
      "gems" from 1954-1964;
  • 33rpm LP's both 10" and 12" of many types including
      popular, instrumental, jazz, folk, etc., from 1947-1990;
  • Novelty records..."I'm crazy about them!"
  • Radio Transcriptions on shellac or vinyl.
When listing your records, please include the label, artist, and catalog
number. If you want an offer, include a long SASE. Jamie buys large
quantities of records for 10¢ to $1 and up but he does not buy any Chil-
dren's records at all.
  Jamie Sager
  House of Golden Oldies
  3231 Edgeware Road South
  Memphis, TN 38118
      (901) 795-2739   Fax: (901) 795-4492

★ **Children's 78rpm records,** 1900's-1960's, in all sizes on all labels.
Children's records that do not have their original jackets or sleeves are
usually not of interest unless they are picture records (with pictures
right in the vinyl as these are usually not found in sleeves). Most items
are $1-$10 but a handful can bring $100 each. The condition of the
record and the sleeve should be described, along with the label name
and catalog number. He's compiling a discography of 78rpm children's records, so welcomes all information you have.
  Peter Muldavin
  173 West 78th Street, #5F
  New York, NY 10024
      (212) 362-9606

★ **Edison wax cylinder recording blanks** for making home recordings on a cylinder phonograph. Also buys badly scratched brown wax
cylinder records which can be shaved for recording. "I give talks on
phonographs and need the wax blanks to demonstrate how records were
made. Inexpensive only, please, as I used these for classroom demos of
early recording procedures."
  Lindsay Lambert
  41 Bellwood Avenue
  Ottawa, ON
  K1S 1S6 CANADA

33 rpm LONG PLAYING ALBUMS

★ **LP (long playing 33rpm) records** in the following categories may be of interest if they are in fine condition:
- **Modern jazz**, preferably from the 1950's (no Dixieland!);
- **Soul, doo-wop, blues, and rhythm & blues** from the 1950's and 60's; original albums only, not rereleases;
- *Bluenote* **and** *Prestige* jazz recordings in mono, not stereo;
- **Obscure Broadway original cast albums**, like *Clown Around;*
- **Soundtracks to obscure or unpopular movies**, or any **spoken soundtracks** such as *The Caine Mutiny* (especially desirable);
- **Classical stereo recordings** on *RCA Living Stereo, Mercury Living Presence Stereo, Decca FFSS* and *London* from the early days of stereo in the 1950's and 60's;
- **Classical recordings of solo performers** on piano, violin, cello, etc., especially of lesser known performers;
- **Oddities, including test pressings**, items never released, etc.;
- Some rare 1950's and 60's 45's;
- **Depression era 78's**, especially jazz, blues, and dance bands.

Many of these items are only a few dollars, but some are worth many hundreds, and a handful can bring $1,000 or more. There are some records which have no value and can be considered "yard sale" fare, including all easy listening, rock and roll recorded after 1960 (unless unusual in some way), and any LP's with no sleeves. If you want to offer records for sale, list the label, the catalog number, the title, artist, and condition to this 40 year veteran expert dealer.

> Rod Baum, Rare Records
> 1432 Queen Anne Road
> Teaneck, NJ 07666
>   (201) 833-4883 (10am to 6pm)   Fax: (201) 833-4874

★ **LP (long playing 33rpm) records** in the following categories are of interest if they are before 1975 and in very fine condition:
- Movie soundtracks;
- Children's TV cartoon characters;
- TV soundtracks or character albums;
- Weird, involving unusual characters or themes.

No 78's, Broadway sound tracks, cardboard records or generic children's records like nursery stories or Mother Goose are wanted.

> David Welch
> PO Box 714
> Murphysboro, IL 62966
>   (618) 687-2282   Fax: (618) 684-2243

★ **Jazz LP's from the 1950's and 60's.** Also buys "**jazz literature and magazines**, any years, and some other materials associated with jazz." No 45's or 78's. No music other than jazz. No records with poor condition covers. Please include your phone number.

> Gary Alderman
> PO Box 259164
> Madison, WI 53725
> (608) 274-3527   Fax: (608) 277-1999

★ **LP (long playing 33rpm) records** in the following categories may be of interest if they are in fine condition:

- **Jazz and soul,** "but no big hit records because I probably already have them;"
- **Classical albums from the 1950's in monaural**: Barylli, Enesco, Spalding, and "hundreds of other performers on dozens of labels are wanted" (can provide a list for SASE);
- **Obscure Rock & Roll bands** from the 1960's and 70's;
- **Christian Rock bands.**

When writing, please list the performer, album title, and the label. Records should look well cared for. "I do not want opera, or any sets which contain more than three records."

> Joe Flynn
> 274 West 12th Street, #1-R
> New York, NY 10014
> (212) 675-7440

When describing 33rpm phonograph records the most important pieces of information are the artist, title, record label and catalog number. Since many albums went through editions, mention the color of the label, too. It is also important to note whether it is a mono or stereo recording, as some records are common in one form and rare in the other.

Condition of 33's is very important. Buyers care about the condition of the cover as well as the record. Make certain to mention writing (like owner's names), banged corners, split seams, and missing inside sleeves. Poor condition 33's that look like licorice pizza will not find a buyer.

It is very difficult for you to know which albums have value, because of surprises like the Caine Mutiny *soundtrack worth more than $1,000, or the Bob Dylan album with the "missing song."*

45 rpm RECORDS

★ **45 rpm records in quantity** in unplayed or nearly unused condition. Looking for store stock or radio station collections, but will also buy small collections if they contain desirable records. Nothing worn or scratched. "Phone if you think you have what I'm looking for."

> Ken Clee
> PO Box 11412
> Philadelphia, PA 19111
> (215) 722-1979

★ **Odd 45's from the 1950's and 60's.** "I want little known performers on little known labels. I have no interest in Elvis and other popular artists or in labels like *Columbia, RCA, Capitol* and the like. I don't buy 78's, classical music or other instrumentals. Be specific in your descriptions, including label and catalog number."

> Otti Schmitt
> Finders-Keepers Collectibles
> 7724 Hayfield Road
> Alexandria, VA 22310
> (703) 550-1454

★ **Rhythm and Blues or Rock and Roll 45's from the 1950's.** Wants original recordings of groups like the *Flamingos, Robins, Wrens, Penguins,* etc. Will buy any 45's from race labels such as *Chance, Red Robin, Blue Lake, Harlem, Grand, Rockin, After Hours, Aladdin, Parrot, Flip, Allen, Rhythm, Club 51,* and *Swingtime.* No records that are reissues, bootlegged, or damaged. When writing, give the label, catalog number and condition.

> John Widmar
> Lake Side Towers
> 5800 3rd Avenue #515
> Kenosha, WI 53140
> (414) 654-6802

★ **Rock and roll, rhythm and blues, and country music records** from the 1950's and 1960's, especially 45 and 33 rpm:
- 45's with picture sleeves;
- Odd ball items;
- Disc jockey radio promos;
- **Rock, blues, or country sheet music and magazines.**

Nothing having to do with classical, big band, opera, or polka music is wanted at all, no matter how old or interesting.

> Cliff Robnett
> 7804 NW 27th
> Bethany, OK 73008
> (405) 787-6703

SELLING COIN-OPERATED MACHINES

"Coin-ops" is what collectors call slot machines, jukeboxes, arcade games, trade stimulators (games you play for product prizes), and other machines put into play by dropping a coin into a slot.

If you give the make, model, and serial number, most dealers will know what machine you have. A photo of older items is advisable, especially of vending machines and trade stimulators since unfamiliar ones turn up.

When writing about a coin-op, indicate whether it works and whether parts are missing or broken. Coin-ops do not need to be in perfect condition to sell. Most collectors and dealers restore them.

When describing pinball machines note how much paint is peeling off the back board illustration. If the illustration is not in perfect condition you must include a photo as the condition of the backboard is very important.

When taking photos of pinball machines, include the play field in one photo and back glass (vertical pictorial area) in another.

Because the machines are large, heavy, and valuable, buyers will usually make shipping arrangements.

★ **Coin-op machines** including jukeboxes, nickelodeons, arcade devices such as diggers and claws, view machines, coin-op fans and radios, and **vending machines** for gum, condoms, etc. Has particular interest in **slot machines** and **gambling devices that pay cash** rewards. These have a minimum value of $500 with the more unusual machines bringing considerably more. Pre-1910 gambling machines made on the west coast are very desirable. Also **paper ephemera** about coin-op machines including catalogs, brochures, advertising, and anything historical. No pinball, video, or service machines like washers.

> Fred Ryan, Slot Closet
> PO Box 83135
> Portland, OR 97203
> (503) 286-3597

★ **Coin-op machines,** especially early wood cabinet and cast iron machines 1885-1912, very rare pinball machines, kinetoscopes, and 1888-1905 peep machines. Offers $40,000 for the *Fey* 1906 Liberty Bell slot machine but has only minor interest in most other slots. Pays $7,500 for an *Edison* Kinetoscope from 1894. Particularly interested in paper ephemera about coin-ops including catalogs, advertising, letterheads, and anything else historical. Also photos of store or saloon interiors which depict machines. Also *The Coin Machine Journal, Automatic Age, Automatic World, Spinning Reels, The Billboard* (pre-1932), and other trade magazines devoted to coin-op machines. Bueschel is an editor of the bi-monthly *Coin-Op Classics* and responsible for dozens of guides to coin-ops. Since thousands of dollars are involved, he wants you to shoot a roll of 35mm film of details of your coin-op and ship the undeveloped roll to him. He'll reimburse. You *must* tell him where you got your machines.

> Richard Bueschel
> 414 North Prospect Manor Ave.
> Mt. Prospect, IL 60056
>   (847) 253-0791

★ *Gottlieb* **pinball machines,** 1948-58. Machines before 1948 don't have flippers and are not of interest. He explains that most of the games from before 1956 have wooden cabinets, trim, and legs; after 1956, they're metal. Will buy *Gottlieb* machines in any mechanical condition, but the back glass must be present and in good condition with little or no chipping, cracking, or paint flaking. Normal wear on the playing surface is expected, but severely damaged play fields make a game uncollectible. Damaged machines have some value for parts, but it's a fraction of what games in fine condition command. Pays $500 for *Gin Rummy* or *Mystic Marvel* games by *Gottlieb.* "I will consider games by other manufacturers, but only if they are in very good condition. No games which have revolving reels to record scores or that have metal cabinets. If you are in doubt, call and I will try my best to identify your game. When you describe your machine, pay attention to cosmetics, missing bumper caps, light shields missing, cracks, etc." He prefers amateurs to set the price wanted, but he will make offers, but only if you are serious about selling.

> Gordon Hasse, Jr.
> PO Box 1543 Grand Central Station
> New York, NY 10163
>   (212) 885-3619 days   (212) 996-3825 eves

★ **Coin-op machines,** especially pre-1940 slots and jukeboxes. No solid state pinball machines. Ted publishes the monthly *Coin Machine Trader* ($20/year) devoted to ads and information about coin-ops.
Ted Salveson
PO Box 602
Huron, SD 57350
(605) 352-3870   Fax: (605) 352-7590

★ **Coin-op machines** including 78 rpm *Wurlitzer* jukeboxes from 1938-48, **penny arcade machines** from before 1920, **vending machines** from before 1910, and all **slot machines**.
Martin Roenigk, Mechantiques
26 Barton Hill
East Hampton, CT 06424
(203) 267-8682   Fax: (203) 267-1120

★ **Jukeboxes,** jukebox speakers, wall boxes, remote equipment, literature and brochures are all wanted by this dedicated collector who also buys magazines associated with the coin-op world including: *Automatic Age* (1925-46), *Automatic World* (1927-57), *Cash Box Coin Machine Journal, National Coin Machine News,* and many others. His interest extends to all brands of jukeboxes, especially those made before 1946, and will consider them in any condition. Not particularly interested in those made after 1962. Only wants items he doesn't already have, but pledges to help you find a buyer if he doesn't want your item. When you write, include the brand name, the model number, and a photo or video. Wayne is author of the *Jukebox Speaker and Wallbox Guide,* available from the author for $30, and plans to open a jukebox museum. He can send you a list of specific items he is seeking.
Wayne Kline
20750 Ventura Boulevard #160
Woodland Hills, CA 91364
(818) 840-2296   Fax: (818) 840-2249   whkline@aol.com

★ **Table model jukeboxes.** He will buy *all* pre-1960 jukeboxes if you live close enough for him to pick them up. Also jukebox literature, advertising and parts. If you live far enough away that your machine must be shipped, he only wants the small ones. He doesn't want to ship the larger machines.
Alvin Heckard
Route 1   Box 88
Lewistown, PA 17044
(717) 248-7071

★ *Wurlitzer* and *Rock Ola* **jukeboxes,** working or not, especially *Wurlitzer* model 42 (worth up to $1,800) and model numbers 500 or above (which begin at $450 for a #500 and can go to nearly $12,000 for a nice condition model #950). Also **all slot machines, in any condition**, complete or not, working or not. All but the most common working machines will bring $500, many over $1,000. He advertises widely that $50,000 is waiting for the finder of a working *Fey* Liberty Bell slot machine. Will pick up machines anywhere in the U.S.

  Frank Zygmunt
  Antique Slot Machine Co.
  PO Box 542
  Westmont, IL 60559
   (630) 985-2742 Fax: (630) 985-5151

★ *Wurlitzer* **jukeboxes** with model numbers lower than 500. These 1930's machines predate the "plastic-and-bright-lights era" favored by most collectors. Also *Capehart* **radio-phonographs** and **jukeboxes from the 1930's that flip records over.** Pays $500-$700 for *Wurlitzer 416* or *Capehart C20-30*. He'll buy these in any condition, but condition does affect value. Will pick up anything east of the Mississippi and arrange for shipments in the West.

  Joseph Weber
  604 Centre Street
  Ashland, PA 17921
   (717) 875-4401 between 3 and 5 p.m.

★ *Wurlitzer* **jukeboxes** from the 1940's. Also **paper ephemera, service manuals, and advertising related to jukeboxes** of all types. Rick publishes the monthly *Jukebox Collector Newsletter* and is author of three books about jukeboxes, including *A Complete Identification Guide to the Wurlitzer Jukebox* available from him for $15.

  Rick Botts
  2545 SE 60th Court
  Des Moines, IA 50317
   (515) 265-8324

★ **All types of coin-operated machines,** including **slot machines, pin-ball machines,** pre-electronic **arcade games** made of oak and/or iron, and **trade stimulators**. The more unusual, the better. "Tell me what it is, its condition, and whether it works. Please send a photo." Dealers should price your goods, but amateurs may request offers.

  Marvin Yagoda
  Marvin's Marvelous Mechanical Museum
  31005 Orchard Lake Road
  Farmington Hills, MI 48334
   (810) 626-5020 Fax: (810) 626-7945

★ **Countertop coin-operated machines** including arcade machines, trade stimulators, and vending machines from the 1920's through the 1950's. You must send a photo and the price wanted. Ken is publisher of *Antique Amusements, Slot Machine and Jukebox Gazette.*

>Ken Durham
>909 26th Street NW
>Washington, DC 20037
>(202) 338-1342   www.GameRoomAntiques.com

★ **Penny arcade games** such as grip tests, target games, kicker and catcher, Pike's Peak, and the like. Prefers penny machines.

>James Conley
>2758 Coventry Lane NW
>Canton, OH 44708
>(330) 477-7725

★ **Mechanical coin-op kiddie rides** in any condition. "I prefer to make offers only when you send a good clear photo of both sides."

>Frank Martin
>7669 Winterberry Drive
>Youngstown, OH 44512
>(330) 758-4470

★ **Gumball and peanut vending machines** made of cast iron or porcelain before 1930, with glass globes that are faceted, shaped like light bulbs or otherwise unusual. He does *not* want machines with square globes from the 1940's to the present. List the make of machine, shape of the globe, material from which it is made, any decals, condition of the paint, and whether or not it is working. Dealers must price your goods, but amateur sellers may request offers.

>Don Reedy
>13 South Carroll Street
>Frederick, MD 21701
>(301) 663-4240 days   (301) 662-5503 eves   Fax: (301) 663-3478

★ **Various coin-operated machines**
- *Wurlitzer, Seeburg* and *Rockola* jukeboxes;
- Slot machines;
- *Popperette* popcorn machines;
- Arcade games with wood cabinets;
- Ten pin bowling machine by *Evans* or *Williams;*
- *Chicago Coin Basketball.*

A description of your item should include your asking price. He will help amateurs decide the value of what they have.

>Kim Gutzke
>7134 15th Avenue South
>Minneapolis, MN 55423

MUSIC, MUSICIANS & SINGERS

★ **Country music autographs, photos,** and other memorabilia. "What have you? Gary is general manager of a company specializing in movien and country music memorabilia in the heart of Nashville.
>Gary Vaughn
>Cinemonde
>138 2nd Avenue North #106
>Nashville, TN 37201
>>(615) 742-9256   Fax: (615) 742-1268

★ **Opera and classical music concert programs, autographs and photos.** Please give title, date, and other information. Xerox™ helpful.
>Steve Jabloner
>7380 Adrian Drive #23
>Rohnert Park, CA 94928
>>(707) 795-3081   jabloner@marin.cc.ca.us

★ **Ephemera associated with the history of pianos** including advertising signs, posters, catalogs, photos of factory and store interiors, models of pianos and mechanisms, tools used by piano tuners and builders, and piano trade publications. He is not interested in magazine ads. Your description should include size and condition as well as noting the materials from which your item is made. Photo or photocopy helpful. "The history of pianos and of their manufacture fascinates me." **He does not want to buy your piano. No exceptions!**
>Phillip Jamison III
>17 Sharon Alley
>West Chester, PA 19382
>>(610) 696-8449 voice & fax

★ **Eubie Blake or Sissle and Blake memorabilia** and records, especially a 10" recording called *Jammin' at Rudi's*.
>Steven Ramm
>420 Fitzwater Street
>Philadelphia, PA 19147

When you ask someone for information or an offer, include a long business size #10 envelope, address it to yourself, and put a stamp in the corner. This is a Self-Addressed Stamped Envelope (SASE). Use a long envelope because many buyers will send you information which won't fit into smaller envelopes.

★ **Big Band memorabilia from the 1930's and 40's** especially of Glenn Miller or Bunny Berigan. John buys phonograph records, home recordings, tapes of concerts or radio performances, transcription disks, autographs, photographs, newspaper articles, magazine articles, movie short subjects, home movies, posters, and sheet music if it has to do with big bands. This 30 year collector will negotiate an item's value.
> John Mickolas
> 172 Liberty Street
> Trenton, NJ 08611
> (609) 599-9672   (609) 530-5568 days

★ **Bobby Breen phonograph records and song sheets** dating from the late 1930's.
> Ralph Eodice
> 161 Valley Road
> Clifton, NJ 07013

★ **Frank Sinatra memorabilia** including records, sheet music with his picture, radio items, stuff from TV shows, scrap books, and what have you. Please send Xerox™ copies or good description.
> Herman Rush
> 10773 Ojai-Santa Paula Road
> Ojai, CA 93023

★ **Alvin & the Chipmunks and creator David Seville.** "I want anything from the Chipmunks, Chipettes, Clyde Crashcup or David Seville including records (especially picture sleeves), books, comics, dolls, plush toys, clothes, posters, cups and mugs, figures, lunchboxes, puzzles, games, etc. Alvin items are dated from 1958 to the present, while **Chipette** items start in 1983. Pre-1961 items are especially rare. Because they are common, I am not looking for Soakies, Christmas albums, cassettes or CD's recorded in the 90's, and the 1983 10" tall chipmunks. When writing, make sure to include the date and and copyright holder (Bagdasarian, Karman/Ross or Monarch). Please describe the condition and the dimensions. Some of the items on her wants list were made as late as 1990.
> Kim Shriner
> 236 Lakeside Drive
> Little Egg Harbor, NJ 08087
> (609) 296-2322

★ **Rock concert T-shirts** from any band but must have a date from 1964 to 1975 *printed* on the shirt. They can be in any size, but must be clean and never worn. I will buy one or dozens." Send a brief description and your asking price. Will make offers to genuine amateurs.
> Judy Polk Harding
> 1701 60th Street
> Des Moines, IA 50322

ROCK & ROLL

★ **Rock & Roll memorabilia.** You name it, if it's rock and roll related and made between 1950 and 1990, he'd like to know about it...photos, instruments, jackets, rare recordings, posters, props...what have you? Fine condition only. The more rare and unusual the better. Among items sought are:

- **Guitars and accessories** used by name artists for practice, recording, or live performance. Will accept autographed guitars if accompanied by photos of the performer with the instrument. Also straps, capos, and broken parts. Hendrix, Presley, and Vaughan most sought.
- **Pianos** from the Beatles' studio work or those autographed for charity by Elton John;
- **Synthesizers and other small keyboards** if star use can be proven;
- **Drums** used on stage or studio by major artists;
- **Clothing worn on stage** that is colorful; must have photos of artist wearing the clothes on stage;
- **Cars and motorcycles** if still registered in the star's name, or if paper trail is compete, especially with photos of star with car or cycle;
- **Handwritten song lists, notations,** lyrics, etc.;
- **Contracts,** autographs, and other paper;
- **Awards, gold records, Grammys, etc.**
- **Posters from any live performance**, especially 1960's and early 70's. No hand bills. Movie posters with a rock and roll or motorcycle theme are wanted;
- **Unused concert tickets;**
- **Original artwork** for albums, posters, etc.

Send Danny a complete description, including a photo when appropriate. If it was a personal item belonging to a famous performer, you must include any and all documentation for authenticity. Danny has "runners" in all parts of the country, so he can usually have important items evaluaated or picked up within a matter of days. He buys for himself and as a representative of *The Hard Rock Cafe* chain and other commercial operations, so he can buy an unusual range of items, big and small. Include your phone number when you write.

Danny Perkins
17927 River Court
Pierrefonds, PQ
H9J 1A2 CANADA
(514) 624-8515   Fax: (514) 624-8942

★ **Rock and roll memorabilia** is wanted, including the **Beatles, Kiss, The Monkees and other headliners**. Autographs of rock singers and musicians are especially desired. He does not purchase rock and roll records unless you have studio dubs or tapes or radio station promotional copies. No other exceptions.

> Robert "Nostalgia Bob" Urmanic
> 199 Brookvalley Drive
> Elyria, OH 44035

★ **Beatles, Elvis, Kiss and the Rolling Stones** are wanted by this active West Coast pop-culture dealer.

- **Beatles items include t**oys, games, musical instruments paint sets, dolls, tickets, movie posters, talcum powder, hair spray, lunch pails. Has a particular interest in the movie *Yellow Submarine.*
- **Elvis** items must be marked EP ENTERPRISES 1956 and include sneakers, lipstick, dress, gloves, scarves, plastic guitar, sweatshirts, autographs, wallets, purses, etc.
- **Rolling Stones and Kiss items** similar to above.

Paul encourages you to ask about any authentic fine condition item, but cautions **he does not buy recordings**. He notes that there are many fake Beatles items and that a photo is essential. Elvis items marked other than 1956 are not wanted.

> Paul Scharfman
> Chic-a-Boom
> 6817 Melrose Avenue
> Los Angeles, CA 90038
> (213) 931-7441 Fax: (213) 930-2990

★ **Rock & Roll memorabilia** including ticket stubs, unused tickets, programs, posters, handbills, original negatives, slides and movies from concerts of Jimi Hendrix, Bob Dylan, The Doors, The Rolling Stones, Buddy Holly, Elvis, The Beatles, Janis Joplin, Bob Marley, The Cream, Led Zepplin and other important bands. Please mail or fax Xerox™ copies of what you would like to sell.

> Marty Novak
> 1150 Cushing Circle #334
> St. Paul, MN 55108
> (612)-646-5567 Fax: (612) 646-0624

★ **Rock star clothing and personal effects.** Give a complete description, including a history of the item, who used it, when, and how you came to own it. Photos are helpful.

> Paul Scharfman
> Chic-a-Boom
> 6817 Melrose Avenue
> Los Angeles, CA 90038
> (213) 931-7441 Fax: (213) 930-2990

★ **Elvis Presley collectibles.** After 30 years of avid collecting, Robin still buys Elvis items, especially:
  • Autographed photos, records, and other items;
  • 45rpm records in their original sleeve, 1950-1960;
  • Personal items, including clothing;
  • Tour books from 1955-1977;
  • E.P. ENT (Elvis Presley Enterprises) items from the 1950's;
  • Movie posters and lobby cards from Elvis films;
  • Store displays and promotions for Elvis products.
Prices vary according to the item, condition, authentication and rarity. Not interested in shot glasses, ash trays, postcards, or anything made after Elvis's death. Give the condition, and describe how you got the item. Robin's collection is featured in *All the Kings Things* available from her for $18 postpaid.
>
> Robin Rosaaen
> All The King's Things
> 101 Glen Eyrie Avenue #202
> San Jose, CA 95125
> (408) 297-0861 eves   kingthings@aol.com

★ **Elvis Presley memorabilia** dating from before his death, including all marked E.P. ENT 1956, such as lipsticks, skirts, perfume, gloves, and anything else out of the ordinary. He also buys posters and promo-tional items from Elvis movies, records, and appearances. He'd especially like to find a plastic guitar with pictures on it, and issues of 1950's magazines such as *Dig* and *Teen Stories* with all Elvis features. Autographs are always wanted. No records except promotional copies.
>
> Robert "Nostalgia Bob" Urmanic
> 199 Brookvalley Drive
> Elyria, OH 44035
> (216) 365-3550

★ **Michael Jackson or Jackson 5** backstage passes, phone cards, and lunch boxes. Wants only these items in official issues.
>
> Carolyn Jamison
> PO Box 111752
> Nashville, TN 37222
> (615) 252-4083

★ **The Runaways.** A fan wants anything: tapes, records, photos, and other memorabilia related to the group or members Lita Ford, Joan Jett, and Cherie Currie (Hays).
>
> Jessica "Lita" Smith
> 3502 Blue Coat Road
> Baltimore, MD 21236

★ **Beatles memorabilia** including toys, dolls, games, tickets, cartoon kits, model kits, *Yellow Submarine*, Halloween costumes, wallpaper, talcum powder, shampoo, ice cream wrappers, blankets, jewelry, china, toy musical instruments, fan club items, etc., especially items sealed in their original factory cartons. Rick also looks for hard-to-find albums such as *Beatles vs the 4 Seasons* or *Yesterday and Today* with the butcher block cover. "I'll pay $800 for a Beatles record player in mint condition, $500 for an unopened pomade, and $250 for a *Kaboodle Kit* like new." Rick also buys **The Monkees ephemera of all types.** Co-author of *The Beatles Memorabilia Price Guide* available for $28.

Rick Rann
PO Box 877
Oak Park, IL 60303
(708) 442-7907

★ **Beatles memorabilia** from before their 1970 breakup. Everything is wanted, including games, toys, dolls, posters, movie related items, candid photos, concert posters and programs, tickets, and ads for merchandise or concerts. Would love any Beatles toy musical instruments picturing the group, and will pay from $200-$500 for Beatles bongos or banjos. Buys common items as long as they are old and original. Wants to know where you got your item, and requests your phone number. Co-author of *The Beatles Memorabilia Price Guide.*

Jeff Augsburger
507 Normal Avenue
Normal, IL 61761
(309) 452-9376   Fax: (309) 664-1771

★ *Kiss* **collectibles.** Buys only items with the *Kiss* logo or that picture the band in make up. I'll buy any toy, tour book, guitar pick, drum stick, display, song book, poster, t-shirt, reel to reel tape, sealed 8 track, picture disc, American or foreign concert items. I DO NOT WANT bootleg videos, cassettes or unsealed 8 tracks, nor do I want concert photos or t-shirts without makeup." Xerox™ copies or photos are helpful.

Thomas Shannon
PO Box 25056
Lexington, KY 40524
(606) 272-7371 before 10pm EST

★ *Grateful Dead* **memorabilia** including cloth embroidered patches, t-shirts in very good or better condition, posters, backstage passes, and the like are wanted by this new collector. Send a photo or photocopy. "I DON'T WANT records, tapes, books or magazines. Please price what you have and don't offer expensive items."

David Kveragas
1943 Timberlane
Clarks Summit, PA 18411

SELLING SPORTS MEMORABILIA CAN BE PROFITABLE

This chapter is particularly important because of the large number of items you own or can find that have some value. I urge all readers to go through this chapter thoroughly. These are important people, good buyers...and mean profit for you.

Balls, gloves, bats, uniforms, programs, championship belts, trophies, photos... anything sports is collectible. *Professional championship rings, belts, and trophies brings top prices (within each category). Amateur sports, except The Olympics, generate little dollar interest.*

It is possible to cash in very large. *A Detroit listener followed my instructions and turned a baseball uniform into $176,000. Readers and listeners just like you have uncovered 14 Babe Ruth balls and thousands of other uniforms, bats, programs and other baseball items have turned up.*

In terms of dollar volume ,baseball leads all sports. Don't let baseball's high prices mislead you. ***Items you are likely to find in other sports categories may bring as little as 10% of the value of a comparable baseball item.***

Thousand dollar prices are not unknown in other sports, but prices of $20 to $500 are a lot more common. Fishing tackle brings the most money to **Trash or Treasure** *readers and listeners. Find one good tackle box, and you could be thousands richer. Buyer Rick Edmisten reports spending $100,000 a year with* Trash or Treasure *readers and listeners. Small plugs (wooden and metal baits) purchased in the 1920's and 30's for pennies sell for hundreds of dollars today. Some boxes they originally came in are worth $50! Don't let them gather dust. Rick or other fishing tackle buyer will give them a good home...and give you a fatter purse or wallet.*

Keep alert for strings of old decoys *laying unused in barns, basements and boat houses. These regularly bring over $1,000 each and once sold for more than $300,000. Millions of dollars worth of decoys are sitting around in New England alone.*

Baseball collectibles bring high prices because there are so many collectors. Competition is not as great in other sports (including minor league baseball) so prices remain generally reasonable.

For example, the top price for a baseball card is over $100,000 while top value basketball and football cards sell for only $300. Expert advice is essential in sports cards. Prices are down substantially from their over-inflated days, but really rare cards still can bring you $100 or more each. I personally don't like the long range prospects of cards, so would sell now and put the money to better use.

The importance of condition depends upon the item you have to sell. Card collectors require near perfection while collectors of other baseball items like wear because it shows proof of use during a game.

When offering items for sale, provide the following:

(1) What it is, its size, color and the material from which it is made;
(2) All names, dates and numbers embossed, incised, labeled or decaled on the item;
(3) An accurate statement of condition, noting missing parts, pieces, or paint;
(4) Mention whether the original box, packaging and instructions are included and in good condition.

Since many sports collectibles are paper, remember that a photocopy (Xerox™) machine is your best friend!

Pop culture dealers found on pages 122-127 also buy sports memorabilia of all types.

SPORTS EQUIPMENT & EPHEMERA

★ **Baseball, football, basketball, and Olympic memorabilia** is wanted including items such as:
- **Uniforms, trophies**, and medals and pins from famous athletes;
- **Baseball gum cards** pre-1920;
- **Posters** and **advertising** pieces related to sports, pre-1940;
- World Series (1903-30) scorecards, tickets, press pins, pennants and souvenirs;
- All star game programs, tickets, posters and press pins;
- **Black baseball bats**;
- **Autographed** balls, contracts and documents from sports greats;
- **Song sheets** related to sports pre-1930;
- **Games and toys** related to sports pre-1930.

"Unique and unusual" sports equipment and other material especially related to Hall of Fame baseball players from the 1920's and 1930's is sought. All items must be old, rare, and original. The gallery is now open to the public to see and to purchase rare sports collectibles.

Joel Platt
Sports Immortals Museum and Memorabilia Mart
6830 North Federal Highway
Boca Raton, FL 33487
(561) 997-2575   Fax: (561) 997-6949

★ **Baseball, football, and boxing memorabilia,** with particular emphasis on the Victorian era, including:
- **Baseball equipment** from before 1920, especially early fingerless gloves;
- **Paper ephemera**: books from before 1920, display posters, baseball scorecards pre-1900, baseball guides pre-1920, World Series programs, and early ads featuring baseball;
- **Uniforms** from any sport before 1960;
- Football guides and equipment, pre-1930;
- **Trophies** for any 19th century sports;
- **Gum and tobacco cards.**

"Premium prices paid for 19th century baseball items."   This 30 year veteran collector offers from $1,000 to $10,000 for posters depicting 1890's baseball cards, equipment, or sports figures. He does not want or buy *anything* after 1970. A clear photo is helpful.

John Buonaguidi
Monterey Bay Sports Museum
540 Reeside Ave.
Monterey, CA 93940
(408) 375-7345

★ **Baseball, football, and boxing memorabilia** especially autographs of dead Hall-of-Famers and other important players. Wants yearbooks of New York sports teams and programs from championship events in all three sports. Will buy tickets, pins, and advertising items which mention players or teams, but **not interested in sports cards.** "Sellers should be willing to send the item to me for inspection. In many cases a good photo or photocopy will do."

> Richard Simon Sports, Inc. TH
> 215 East 80th Street
> New York, NY 10021
> (212) 988-1349   Fax: (212) 288-1445   richards@aol.com

★ **Baseball memorabilia,** especially from before 1948. Wants gum and tobacco cards and silks picturing baseball players, postcards, photos, games, programs, yearbooks, guides, advertising, fans, sheet music and autographs from dead Hall-of-Fame players. This 25 year advanced collector-dealer does not buy anything after 1960. Be as accurate as possible with descriptions and include your phone number with your letter. Photocopies are helpful.

> William Mastro
> 12410 Ridge Road
> Palos Park, IL 60464
>   (708) 361-2117   Fax: (708) 361-3848

★ **Professional baseball and football equipment**, especially game worn jerseys, bats, and equipment. Does not want foreign items, other sports, paper ephemera, or cards. Each item must be evaluated individually as to value. For an offer, describe your item thoroughly, including age, condition, and history. David's *Vintage Baseball Glove Price Guide* is only $6. A pocket guide to collectible bats is $5.

> David Bushing
> Vintage Sports
> 217 Homewood
> Libertyville, IL 60048
> (847) 816-6847   (847) 816-6861 eves   Fax: (847) 816-0570

★ **Canadian sports memorabilia.** "I'll buy all items associated with **Canadian hockey** teams and players before 1960, **Canadian lacrosse** teams and players, and **Canadian basketball** teams and players. I'm particularly looking for game schedules and calendars, programs, autographed photos, gum cards, etc. If practical, a clear photocopy is best. Small items can be sent on approval as I will always refund postage."

> Michael Rice
> PO Box 286
> Saanichton, BC
> V8M 2C5 CANADA
>   (250) 652-9047 eves

★ **Early sports memorabilia.** "I'll buy sports ephemera, 1860-1970. I'm mainly interested in early baseball items such as pins, postcards, silks, leathers, advertising, and autographs, but will also buy paper and other ephemera from **boxing** and **football**." Describe the condition and indicate the price you have in mind.

> Steve Applebaum
> 3444 Via Lido
> Newport Beach, CA 92663
> (714) 673-1742   Fax: (714) 673-5327

★ **Babe Ruth material.** Send Xerox© to this major ephemera dealer.

> Harvey Dolin & Company
> 5 Beekman Street #406
> New York, NY 10038
> (212) 267-0216

★ **Philadelphia Phillies memorabilia,** especially pre-1930 programs and pre-1950 baseball player postcards.

> Gary Gatanis
> 3283-B Cardiff Court
> Toledo, OH 43606
> (419) 475-3192

★ **Baseball memorabilia from the Pacific Coast League** and selected other minor leagues. Most items wanted date from the 1920's to early 50's and include programs, selected team and League year books, postcards of ball parks, and team photos. Also buys programs and other ephemera associated with the **non-baseball use of Gilmore Field, Gilmore Stadium and Pan Pacific auditorium.**

> Jerry Mezerow
> 442 Via Porto Ave.
> Anaheim, CA 92806
> (714) 630-6198

★ **Baseball gloves** and other older items including bats, autographed balls, cut autographs, programs, ticket stubs, scorecards, and uniforms. Does not buy any baseball cards.

> Gary Alderman
> PO Box 259164
> Madison, WI 53725
> (608) 274-3527   Fax: (608) 277-1999

★ **Old sports equipment** suitable for restaurant, theme, model home, and other decorative purposes, including:

- **Balls** from various sports including pre-1950 leather footballs, baseballs, soccer balls, and basketballs. Seeks moderately priced old leather balls from before 1940 for decorator use. Not interested in balls autographed by famous persons.
- **Wooden skis and bamboo poles.** Brand name doesn't matter, and neither do bindings, as long as they are all wood and in reasonably good condition;
- **Leather football helmets;**
- **Lacrosse equipment** such as sticks, balls, and leather knee pads;
- **Snow shoes,** which are preferred intact with original gut, but empty frames in fine condition will be considered;
- **Croquet mallets** or complete boxed sets if old and if the paint is in good condition;
- **Cricket bats** and balls;
- **Riding equipment** including tall boots, leather whips, velveteen riding hats, English style ladies' side saddles;
- **Wicker creels** and inexpensive bamboo fishing poles, nets, etc.

All items should be pre-1940 and be fairly well cared for. Please give a general description of what you have, or telephone with the item in hand. "I am seeking low-end items suitable for decorating theme restaurants, not fine expensive antiques. If what you have is very valuable, take it somewhere else. If you find that it isn't valuable, but you want it preserved, offer it to me."

> Joan Brady
> 834 Central Ave.
> Pawtucket, RI   02861

★ **Older (pre-1950) sports equipment** is wanted, including:

- **Basketballs made of leather** with laces;
- **Football helmets** made of leather;
- **Golf clubs** with wooden shafts;
- **Tennis rackets** made of wood, especially unusual shapes, with names of old professional players;
- **Baseball gloves and bats** endorsed by players;
- Unusual items..."Tell me what you have."

Asks for a photo, along with a good description. Requests that you include your phone number with all correspondence.

> Gary Alderman
> PO Box 259164
> Madison, WI 53725
>   (608) 274-3527   Fax: (608) 277-1999

★ **Tickets from sports events**, both full tickets and ticket stubs. Wants **World Series, All Star games, Stanley Cup, NCAA final four, Super Bowl, Indy 500**, and other significant events from the world of sports, including golf, tennis, boxing, etc. Tickets for any major events, such as no hitters and historic games, are sought. No common tickets to ordinary games unless there was a milestone of some sort (1st game in the stadium, last game, Aaron's last homer, etc.). Value is closely related to condition. You must describe whether there is damage, creases, tears, tape, glue, etc. Give the game, seat location, and date. This 25 year veteran collector/dealer asks other dealers to price their goods. Amateurs may request an offer.

> Norman Segel
> Doubleheader
> 3447 5th Street
> Oceanside, NY 11572
>   (516) 536-7600   Fax: (516) 742-7209

★ **Rugby and soccer memorabilia** wanted for resale. Can be either U.S. or foreign. Wants prints, cigarette cards, stamps, postcards, and paper ephemera. Also buys large items like coin operated games and strength machines with soccer or rugby themes.

> Matt Godek
> PO Box 565
> Merrifield, VA 22116
>   (703) 280-5540   Fax: (703) 280-4543

★ **Soccer memorabilia** wanted for museum display. Especially interested in U.S. soccer, but will also consider World Cup relics. Wants uniforms, rule books, posters, photos, prints, home movies, etc. Particularly likes to find items from soccer played in places other than the Northeastern U.S. Also interested in games and coin machines with soccer themes that might be suitable for play in their museum. Describe what you have. It's helpful if you set the price you'd like.

> Al Colone
> National Soccer Hall of Fame
> 5-11 Ford Avenue
> Oneonta, NY 13820
>   (607) 432-3351

★ **Roller Derby memorabilia**, including programs, posters, uniforms, flyers, autographs and "anything collectible from any era." He requests that you set the price wanted whenever possible, but says, "I will entertain all offers."

> Royal Duncan
> 7600 North Galena Road
> Peoria, IL 61615
>   (309) 691-2772

★ **College football, basketball and hockey programs** from before 1970. "I want programs from historic games, or with famous players, or with colorful art work but don't want those that are damaged or have missing pages." When contacting him about programs give the sport, date, and colleges involved. Identify any famous players if you can. Generally prefers to make offers only after seeing the actual program.

Lee Goldstein
1610 Kilmer Avenue South
Minneapolis, MN 55426
(612) 545-8584

★ **Pro basketball ephemera** especially autographed team balls, All-Star balls, programs, yearbooks and older cards. Anything before 1990.

Gary Alderman
PO Box 259164
Madison, WI 53725
(608) 274-3527   Fax: (608) 277-1999

★ **Harlem Globetrotters ephemera** from before 1970 in good condition including uniforms, programs, advertising, pennants, and what have you. A few later items will be considered if they are unusual and in fine condition. "I don't want programs that are not in excellent condition...no missing covers, stains, rusty staples, etc. although I'll consider programs from the 1920's and 30's in somewhat lesser condition. If you have a uniform, tell how you came by it.

Lee Goldstein
1610 Kilmer Avenue South
Minneapolis, MN 55426
(612) 545-8584

★ **Pro hockey memorabilia**, especially autographed pucks, programs, and unusual items like the 1969 Rangers' paperweight/bottle opener.

Gary Alderman
PO Box 259164
Madison, WI 53725
(608) 274-3527   Fax: (608) 277-1999

★ **Croquet items.** Will buy distinctive full size mallets, pegs, wickets, table or parlor sets, books, pamphlets, catalogs, photos of people playing croquet, jewelry, and other items related to the game. Please send photocopies or photos, along with your description of condition. Prefers that you price what you have if possible.

Allen Scheuch
167 Warren Street
Brooklyn, NY 11201
(212) 645-2278

★ **Running memorabilia.** "I'll buy medals, ribbons, trophies, cards, annuals, magazines, programs, and books related to running, track & field, road races and **the Olympics.**" Not interested in items since 1960, but will consider reproductions of some posters and other printed material. Tell what you have and its condition. Ed is president of the Motor City Striders, has been director of numerous races, and writes for various running magazines.

> Ed Kozloff
> 10144 Lincoln
> Huntington Woods, MI 48070
> (810) 544-9099   Fax: (810) 544-4601

★ **Self defense** magazines, photos, books, courses, equipment, posters, trophies, etc., printed before 1975. Doesn't want anything currently published. Please send an SASE with inquiries.

> William Moore
> PO Box 20732
> Tuscaloosa, AL 35402

★ **Recreational and competitive horseback riding.** Wants books and paper ephemera related to Morgan horses, Arabians, saddlebred horses, polo ponies, sidesaddles, and Lippizzaners. She would especially like to find books by or illustrated by Paul Brown and George Ford Morris. Books and paper only!

> Barbara Cole, October Farm
> 2609 Branch Road
> Raleigh, NC 27610
> (919) 772-0482   Fax: (919) 779-6265

★ **Horseshoe memorabilia.** Seeks early pitching shoes with no hooks on the points or shoes that are smaller than normal. Shoes are only $3 to $5 each but cased travel sets can bring $75 or more. Catalogs, photos and advertising related to the game may also be of interest. Does not want modern or foreign made shoes. Give brand and model name and style (hookless or with hooks) and condition of shoes and box.

> Bob Dunn
> 6417 Georgia Ave North
> Brooklyn Park, MN 55428
> (612) 535-3884

★ **Diving** related items especially hard hat diving gear, old two-hose SCUBA regulators, manufacturer's catalogs and brochures depicting underwater gear, and all magazines (especially foreign) about any aspect of sport diving. Will also buy comic books such as *Sea Hunt* and *Primus* which focus on diving. No hardcover books, please.

> Thomas Szymanski
> 5 Stoney Brook Lane
> Stratham, NH 03885
> (603) 772-6372

★ **Surfboards and surfing related items,** from before 1970, such as magazines, posters, stickers, patches, etc. Pays up to $1,000 for round nosed pre-1970 foam longboards. All wood boards can bring up to $5,000. No name garage-made paddleboards are less than $200, but Tom Blake, Catalina, and Mitchell paddleboards can bring ten times that. If you phone, please have your board right there so you can answer questions about it. Would love to find a board made by the legendary Duke Kahanamoku.

> Wayne Babcock
> 4846 Carpenteria Avenue
> Carpenteria, CA 93013
> (805) 684-8148

★ *Flexible Flyer* **sledding.** Wants "anything" having to do with *Flexible Flyer* sleds, including membership cards, models, pins, advertising, company literature, and rare sleds. Thorough description, with a photocopy or photograph, is helpful.

> Joan Palicia
> 15 Canton Road
> Wayne, NJ 07470
> (201) 831-0527

★ **Dog fighting.** Wants to buy prints, paintings, and statuary, especially as related to bull terriers. Books on dog fighting also wanted. Provide standard bibliographic information.

> Ron Lieberman
> RD #1   Box 42
> Glen Rock, PA 17327
> (717) 235-2134   Fax: (717) 235-8765   rarebooks@pobox.com

★ **Loving cup trophies** from before 1950. May be awarded for sports, beauty, service, heroism, or anything else as long as they have handles on each side and are 8" high or taller. No other style of trophy is wanted, nor is anything dating after 1950.

> Joan Brady
> 834 Central Ave.
> Pawtucket, RI 02861

FOOTBALL MEMORABILIA

★ **Super Bowl memorabilia** including tickets, ticket stubs, programs, banners, press passes, and what have you. Greater interest in earlier Bowls, especially II through V.

Marty Novak
1150 Cushing Circle #334
St. Paul, MN 55108
(612)-646-5567 Fax: (612) 646-0624

★ **Green Bay Packers and other pro football ephemera** including autographed balls, programs and yearbooks from before 1990, and other items. No trading cards.

Gary Alderman
PO Box 259164
Madison, WI 53725
(608) 274-3527 Fax: (608) 277-1999

★ **Miami Dolphin memorabilia.**

Joe Copeland
PO Box 4221
Oak Ridge, TN 37831
(423) 482-4215

★ **Notre Dame football programs and other memorabilia** from pre-1960, especially Knute Rockne and George Gipp autographs and other items. Other Notre Dame sports items will be considered.

Michael Tiltges
2040 185th Street
Lansing, IL 60438
(708) 895-3222

★ **Football helmets, face masks, and helmet decals.** "I'm primarily interested in modern era college and pro helmets. especially game used ones. Give the maker's name, model, size, color and describe the face mask and any decals. Please also include how you came to own it. No youth football helmets.

James Mark
710 East Woodward Heights
Hazel Park, MI 48030
(810) 543-6275

Football items are also purchased by sports memorabilia dealers and museums at the beginning of this chapter and by many Pop Culture buyers found elsewhere.

THE OLYMPICS

★ **Olympic memorabilia of all types from 1896 to the present** such as programs, pins, medals, flags, tickets, uniforms and actual mementos from gold medal athletes. "We pay the highest prices!"

      Joe Platt
      Sports Immortals Museum
      6830 North Federal Highway
      Boca Raton, FL 33487
         (561) 997-2575   Fax: (561) 997-6949

★ **Olympic memorabilia** including all pins, badges, medals, torches, mascots, posters, and everything else Olympic. "Naturally, I'd rather collect items from before 1972, but when you come down to it, I like it all." Particularly interested in purchasing anything from 1904 St. Louis Games and winner's medals from any year. He warns that many items from the 1936 Berlin Olympics have been reproduced. When writing, tell what you know of the item's history.

      Jay Hammerman
      15630 Softwood Road
      Elbert, Colorado 80106
         (719) 495-8938 eves

★ **Olympic memorabilia from the 1932 games** held in Los Angeles, including tickets, programs, postcards, photographs, literature, patches, and souvenirs. The more colorful and unusual, the better. Please send a photocopy of what you have.

      Reed Fitzpatrick
      PO Box 369
      Vashon, WA 98070
         (206) 567-4391 eves 5-7 Pacific

★ **Olympic items** from any year they were played.

      Otti Schmitt
      Finders Keepers
      7724 Hayfield Road
      Alexandria, VA 22310
         (703) 550-1454

★ **Olympic pins**, medals and participant's medallions from Olympics prior to 1984 and the following sports from anywhere anytime: soccer, equestrian, swimming, figure skating, gymnastics, track & field and cheerleading. Please make a Xerox™ copy of what you have.

      Margarita Volker, Designs by Margarita
      19382 Woodlands Lane
      Huntington Beach, CA 92648
         (714) 536-9850   Fax: (714) 536-9908

GOLF EQUIPMENT & EPHEMERA

★ **Golf memorabilia of all sorts**, including:
  • Wooden shaft clubs and early golf balls;
  • Books, magazines and catalogs related to pre-1940 golf;
  • Paintings, prints and photos with a golf motif;
  • Golf trophies;
  • Paper ephemera, scorecards and programs, catalogs, etc.;
  • Miscellany, such as statues and ashtrays.
"If it has a golf motif, I'm interested, and will pay premium prices for premium pieces." Does appraisals for a fee. Accepts select high quality items on consignment for sale or auction.
>   Richard Regan
>   293 Winter Street #5
>   Hanover, MA 02339
>   (617) 826-3537

★ **Golf memorabilia from before 1930**, especially:
  • Wooden shaft golf clubs that are in some way unusual;
  • Books, magazines, and catalogs related to pre-1930 golf;
  • China and pottery with a golf motif by *Royal Doulton,*
      Lenox, and other fine makers;
  • Golf balls and golf ball molds from before 1930;
  • Miscellaneous items related to "the knickers era."
This 35 year veteran collector wants wooden shaft clubs and old bags. He does not buy trinkets, ashtrays, petty jewelry or reproductions. Frank prefers you set the price you want but makes offers on rare items.
>   Frank Zadra
>   N 5830 County Highway H
>   Spooner, WI 54801
>   (715) 635-2791

★ **Golf antiques and memorabilia.** Wants *unusual* wooden shafted clubs with patent numbers and *unusual* golf balls, such as the pre 1850 ball stuffed with feathers for which he will pay $5,000. "I also buy golf pottery, items of silver, golf medals, pre-1920 golf books, and original art featuring golfers. I do not want clubs with simulated wood grain shafts or anything made after 1920. I'm really interested only in the very old and rare." You should follow standard rules for describing, including condition.
>   Art DiProspero
>   Highlands Golf
>   PO Box 308
>   Watertown, CT 06795
>   (860) 274-8471

★ **Old golf books, magazines, and ephemera.** No paperback reprints or magazines published after 1950.

> George Lewis
> Golfiana
> PO Box 291
> Mamaroneck, NY 10543
> (914) 698-4579

★ **Golf award medals from before WWII** and other pre-1930 golf ephemera. "If it's early and in good condition, ship it insured for my top offer." Items are purchased outright or, if you prefer, taken on consignment for his international auctions. He does not want golf clubs.

> Rich Hartzog
> PO Box 4143 BVT
> Rockford, IL 61110
> (815) 226-0771   Fax: (815) 397-7662

★ **Golf ball markers**, especially markers advertising products or tournaments, those used by famous players, male or female, or markers used in major championships. Markers are worth from $1 to $5, depending on their text, picture, and association. Does not want large quantities of a single type, nor does he want those that do not have advertising of some sort. Other golf items such as postcards and medals will be considered.

> Norm Boughton
> PO Box 93262
> Rochester, NY 14692
> (800) 581-2665   Fax: (800) 901-6676

Sports collectibles of all types are increasingly of interest to Pop Culture dealers. If you don't find a buyer in the sports chapter, look for a buyer in the first 6 pages of Pop Culture.

BOXING MEMORABILIA

★ **Boxing memorabilia of all types.** "I'm the world's largest dealer in boxing memorabilia. I sell to boxing collectors all over the United States and Canada. As a result, I need to continually replenish stock, which means I am always willing to buy, sell, or trade." Please send a photograph or photocopy of what you have.

    Jerome Shochet
    6144 Oakland Mills Road
    Sykesville, MD 21784
        (410) 795-5879

★ **Boxing photos and autographs from before 1920.** Please photocopy what you have.

    Johnny Spellman
    10806 North Lamar Blvd.
    Austin, TX 78753
        (512) 836-2889 days   (512) 258-6910

★ **Boxing memorabilia of all types.** Private collector who operates a gym seeks posters, programs, tickets, films, photographs, books and magazines about boxing, boxing awards, medals, belts and trophies from any level, Golden Glove to World Championship. "If you have single items or a large collection, whether it's from the earliest days or the present champs, I'd like to hear about it."

    Fred Ryan's Arena Archives
    7217 North Jersey
    PO Box 83135
    Portland, OR 97203
        (503) 286-3597

★ **Championship boxing belts,** robes, trunks, or gloves worn by famous champions. Also wants items associated with famous championship fights. Posters, sheet music and games related to boxing. This giant museum buys only quality unusual items that are old and rare.

    Joel Platt
    Sports Immortals Museum and Memorabilia Mart
    6830 North Federal Highway
    Boca Raton, FL 33487
        (561) 997-2575   Fax: (561) 997-6949

★ **Boxing ephemera of all types** dealing with James J. Corbett, Jim Jeffries or John L. Sullivan. A clear photo or photocopy is helpful.

    John Buonaguidi
    Monterey Bay Sports Museum
    540 Reeside Ave.
    Monterey, CA 93940
        (408) 375-7345

TENNIS MEMORABILIA

★ **Tennis memorabilia** such as trophies, figurines, art, postcards, cartoons, tableware, trade cards, lighters, first day covers, and all sorts of other little tennis-related knickknacks from before 1940. He does *not* want to buy rackets, photos, newspaper clippings, books, autographs, or programs, but "I'll buy any quantity of other reasonably priced items if they send a photo or photocopy and price what they have."

    Sheldon Katz
    211 Roanoke Ave.
    Riverhead, NY 11901
       (516) 369-1100

★ **Tennis rackets**. "My primary interest is in rackets produced in the 1940's through the 1960's, but earlier ones are considered. Most desirable are frames that were high quality in their day, and that are in excellent condition. Prices range from $1 to about $25 each depending on the age and scarcity." Identify the maker, model, decals, signature, length, any warpage, and the condition of the grip and strings. Also interested in catalogs and other literature picturing or describing rackets. "I can also advise on ball cans and other tennis related items."

    Donald Jones
    24 Marvalingrove
    Savannah, GA 31406
       (912) 354-2133

★ **Tennis ball cans** made of metal.   Any can, foreign or domestic, made before 1970 with key type opener will be considered. "I'm not interested in any plastic ball cans or sleeves." Send photo if possible and indicate whether the can has been opened.

    Rusty McInroy
    1331 West Chapala Court
    Tucson, AZ 85704
       (520) 797-2030

★ **Tennis items**, especially ball cans with metal lids, ball boxes, and 12 ball cans, for which he will pay as much as $300 if mint and unopened. "If it had tennis balls in it and it's old, I'm interested." Also buys pre-1940 rackets, lawn tennis sets, tennis trophies, "plus much more." Describe condition carefully.

    Michael Murphy, J&J Coins
    47 East Downer Place
    Aurora, IL 60505
       (708) 896-9439 eves   Fax: (708) 892-7044

AUTO RACING EPHEMERA

★ **Auto racing memorabilia.** If it's related to auto racing, and in good condition, George will probably want it. He'll buy one piece or a large collection: awards, arm bands, dash plaques, entry forms, flags, goggles, helmets, magazines, models (built or unbuilt), movies, photographs, paintings, passes, postcards, posters, rule books, toys, board games, trophies, uniforms, and "anything else auto racing related." If you know any history of the item, let him know when describing what you have and its condition. This ex-race driver has been collecting 25 years and will travel "a reasonable distance" to buy collections.

> George Koyt
> 8 Lenora Avenue
> Morrisville, PA 19067

★ **Indianapolis 500** pit badges from before 1952 are wanted, as are race tickets from before 1950, racing programs from before 1941, and all rings or trophies, any year. Jerry will pay $500 for a 1946 pit badge.

> Jerry Butak
> 242 West Adams
> Villa Park, IL 60181
>   (630) 834-6913

★ **Auto racing ephemera,** including books, programs, posters, and what have you are purchased by this giant dealer in automobile parts, manuals, advertising, and ephemera.

> Walter Miller
> 6710 Brooklawn Parkway
> Syracuse, NY 13211
>   (315) 432-8282   Fax: (315) 432-8256

★ **Auto racing before 1916,** especially items associated with the Vanderbilt Cup races or with the Long Island Motor Parkway.

> George Spruce
> 33 Washington Street
> Sayville, NY 11782
>   (516) 563-4211

★ **Drag racing and hot rodding** from the 1940's through the 60's is wanted including: posters, programs, trophies, jackets, racing apparel, speed equipment advertising, car club plaques, hot rod movie posters, hot rod and custom car magazines and hot rod papers. Hot rod club jackets are especially wanted. "The older the better!"

> Michael Goyda, Car Crazy
> PO Box 192
> East Petersburg, PA 17520
>   (717) 569-7149   Fax: (717) 569-0909

HORSE RACING MEMORABILIA

★ **Thoroughbred racing** memorabilia including:
- Paintings, prints and photographs;
- Paper ephemera including racing and breeding books, programs,
    posters, tobacco cards, postcards, games and "the unusual";
- Kentucky Derby programs, glasses and anything unusual.
- Phar Lap memorabilia, especially from his 1932 race at Caliente.

All material from all racing thoroughbreds worldwide will be considered, with foreign material and older items preferred. Not interested in anything having to do with harness horses or harness racing.
>   Gary Medeiros
>   1319 Sayre Street
>   San Leandro, CA 94579
> (800) 227-6049   (510) 351-6193   PHARLAP2.aol.com

★ **Horse racing collectibles** including programs, glasses, books, magazines, posters, photos, postcards, art prints, decanters, parimutuel tickets, lapel pins, buttons, admission items, etc. "I do not want Kentucky Derby glasses after 1974, paper items in poor condition or newspapers except the *Daily Racing Form*." Give the year, condition, and description. He conducts auctions of horse racing items every year.
>   James Settembre
>   5115 Woodstone Circle East
>   Lake Worth, FL 33463
>   (561) 964-5434   Fax: (561) 964-1143

★ **Dan Patch memorabilia,** especially Dan Patch postcards and a Dan Patch coffee can. Also wants pre-1950 **Kentucky Derby programs** and **drinking glasses** featuring horse racing. He will consider other **horse racing programs** from the turn of the century**.**
>   Gary Gatanis
>   3283-B Cardiff Court
>   Toledo, OH 43606
>   (419) 475-3192

WRESTLING & STRENGTH

★ **Pro wrestling autographs and other items** are sought, especially signatures of Frank Gotch, Joe Stecher, Dan McLeod, Charley Cutler, Earl Caddock and Wayne Munn. When possible, please price what you have. He wrote *Wrestling Title Histories*, available from him for $40.
> Royal Duncan
> 7600 North Galena Road
> Peoria, IL 61615
> (309) 691-2772

★ **Women's pro and amateur wrestling.** Wants posters, magazines, film, trophies, autographs and what have you... good items from any era, but especially videos of any match after 1940. "I want real wrestling between women skilled at applying holds, executing aerial maneuvers, etc., not mud wrestling, nude wrestling and other degrading exhibitions." Selena wants information on more than 75 women pros.
> Selena Kyte
> PO Box 1022
> St. Ann, MO 63074

★ **Ephemera related to Frank Gotch,** a turn of the century wrestling champion. He wants posters, postcards, books, photographs, etc.
> Don Olson
> PO Box 245
> Humboldt, IA 50548

★ **Bodybuilding ephemera.** "I'll buy anything before 1975 related to strength, body building, physical culture, weight lifting, strongmen or women, etc. I buy books, magazines, training courses, photos, catalogs, posters, letters, trophies, medals, certificates and videos. I want (1) Weider magazines like *Your Physique,* etc., (2) anything *Milo Barbell Company*, and (3) anything by or about George Jowett or Eugen Sandow. No magazines after 1970, and nothing currently in print." Describe what you have, give date and condition.
> William Moore
> PO Box 20732
> Tuscaloosa, AL 35402

★ **Strongmen, weightlifters, and bodybuilders.** "I'll buy magazines, photos, books, posters, sculpture, and equipment from these fields."
> David Chapman
> 656 32nd Ave. East
> Seattle, WA 98112
> (206) 329-7573 voice and fax

POOL & BILLIARDS

★ **Pool tables** (fancier the better), cue sticks and racks, ball racks, antique advertising, catalogs and other items related to pool or billiard playing before 1940. Send a photo and dimensions.

> Ken Hash
> Classic Billiards
> 4302 Chapel Road
> Perry Hall, MD 21128
> (410) 882-7665 days

★ **Pool and billiard tables and related items.** Wants:
- **Pool tables** with inlaid designs on the legs or bodies, or with ornate carved or cast iron legs; will also consider tables with round legs and tables in any condition;
- Cue racks with mirrors or in generally Victorian style;
- Cue racks that lock or revolve;
- Ivory balls, with or without numbers;
- Ball boxes that are old or unusual;
- Cues that are ornate and 30+ years old;
- Billiard lights, either gas or kerosene;
- **Benches and chairs** from billiard parlors;
- **Prints, paintings, posters**, and other art featuring billiards, especially by Currier & Ives;
- **Books on pool**, snooker, or billiards before 1940;
- **Magazines** and newsletters before 1940;
- **Catalogs** before 1900, especially for *Brunswick & Balke* or *Brunswick Balke Collender*;
- **Newspapers** containing prints or articles on billiards before 1900.

He does not want "bar type" pool tables, tables made after 1940, or plain square legged tables with no inlay. Send a photo of your item and give complete bibliographic information on books.

> Tim Lawrence
> 2489 Bexford Place
> Columbus, OH 43209
> (614) 235-9472 eves

★ **Pool and billiard memorabilia.** Wants interesting and unusual items associated with pool such as light fixtures, cue sticks and racks. Also buys catalogs, advertising, prints and other related items.

> Dilworth Billiards
> 300 East Tremont
> Charlotte, NC 28203
> (704) 333-3021   (704) 377-9069

HUNTING & FISHING ITEMS

★ **Fishing tackle from before 1945** including:
- **Lures** (especially wood with glass eyes or made of hollow metal). Easiest way to describe these is to make a Xerox™ and pencil in the colors of the lures. If made of wood or metal, most lures are $2 and up...and some are way up!
- **Reels**: quality-made fly, bait-casting, and ocean reels that have serial numbers or people's names engraved. Brass or very large reels, especially wanted. There are too many quality reels to list, so ask about all reels except *South Bend, Pflueger, True Temper Shakespeare,* or *Penn.* Dozens of makers have value, some in excess of $1,000. Reels with no names or serial numbers are junk.
- **Bamboo rods** in three or four pieces, stored in cases made of wood, aluminum or cardboard, often packed in a carry bag. Give the name of the maker or owner, usually found in ink or engraved on a metal fitting near where the reel attaches. Does not want "no name" rods or rods made in Japan, no matter how pretty. Other common rods not of interest include *Shakespeare, Montague* and *South Bend.*
- **Tackle boxes**: "If you have a tackle box that contains items from the 1930's or before, you may ship it for my free inspection, evaluation, and offer."
- **Catalogs** of fishing tackle before 1925.

Give names, model, patent dates and numbers, and serial numbers on all equipment. If you have a great many items, you may call collect. Don't overlook empty lure and reel boxes, as some of them can be worth $50 or more. CAUTION: don't clean or polish fishing gear you'd like to sell.

"Most people can't tell good stuff from bad. I'll check it all for you."

"You're likely to damage it. Leave the cleaning to me."

Rick Edmisten
PO Box 686
North Hollywood, CA 91603
   (818) 763-9406   Fax: (818) 763-5974

★ **Old fishing lures,** especially *Heddon 7500* vamps. Also **odd fish scalers**. When writing, include a photocopy of your lures, and indicate their color. For a quick response, please include your phone number.

Thomas McKinnon
PO Box 86
Wagram, NC 28396
   (910) 369-2367

★ **Antique fishing tackle** including bait and fly reels, bamboo fly and bait casting rods, willow creels, wooden nets, fishing lures (especially those with glass eyes), and early tackle boxes made of leather. Wants to find brass *Snyder* bait casting reels from early 1800's. Also buys **fishing equipment catalogs and books**. Not interested in anything made in the last 25 years.

    Robert Whitaker
    2810 East Desert Cove Avenue
    Phoenix, AZ 85028
       (602) 992-7304   Fax: (602) 493-5598

★ **Antique and classic fishing tackle** and ephemera from before 1950. Among items wanted are:
- Wood or hard rubber **lures** in good condition with or without glass eyes, maker marked or not, as long as they're in good condition;
- Metal lures marked with the name of the maker or patent data;
- **Reels** of all types, especially high quality nickel silver or brass, or reels with unusual features, but **all will be considered except** modern spinning or spin casting reels;
- **Split bamboo rods** in excellent conditing in original bag or tube. They do not want metal rods, fiberglass rods, or any rods in poor condition;
- Flied and fly boxes, and other fly fishing accessories;
- Fishing paraphernalia, creels, tackle boxes, equipment catalogs, minnow traps, and other tools, boxes and instructions;
- Early **fishing licenses**;
- **Paintings and prints** related to fishing, including calendars, advertising, and cigarette cards, but no damaged artwork.

"**We do not want** lead sinkers, nylon line, anything made of plastic, clothing of any type, metal rods, fiberglass items or modern spinning reels. We do not want anything made in China, Korea or Japan. We will deal with experts or with novice sellers, but make offers only after inspecting what you have, but do not ship anything without our permission first. Provide photos and as much detailed information as possible. You may call, *not collect*, between 8am and 10pm Eastern.

    Ed and Carolyn Corwin
    PO Box 1119
    Hastings, FL 32145
       (904) 692-2037 voice and fax

★ **Antique and modern fishing tackle** is wanted by an "avid fisherman" who buys lures, rods, wooden tackle boxes, fly reels, large ocean reels, catalogs of hunting and fishing equipment, hardcover books on fishing, old calendars with fishing motif and early advertising items with fishing graphics. Fair value offers made. Make certain to include an SASE for reply.

> Lee Pattison
> 6 Christview Drive
> Cuba, NY 14727
> (716) 968-2458

★ **Hunting and fishing ephemera** including catalogs, posters, calendars, pin back buttons, trade cards, and **envelopes** decorated with advertising from before 1940. He is also interested in possibly buying any fishing and hunting images from before 1900, including prints, original art, and illustrated books. He will make offers, but only after personally inspecting what you have for sale.

> Russell Mascieri
> 13 Running Water Court
> Medford, NJ 08055
> (609) 953-7711   Fax: (609) 953-7768

★ **Hunting, fishing, and trapping licenses** and tags from all states up to the present. Also interested in entry and use permits for state and national parks. "Photocopies are very helpful."

> Bill Smiley
> PO Box 361
> Portage, WI 53901
> (608) 742-3714 eves

★ **Gun, trap, and ammunition company items** such as posters and calendars (worth to $4,000), catalogs (up to $1,000), empty cardboard shotshell boxes (up to $5,000), pinback buttons (to $500), glass target balls and traps (up to $5,000), gunpowder cans (up to $1,000) and anything decorative or informative from before 1940. Does not want paper items that have been trimmed. No NRA items. "I am fair and honest," he says, exhorting, "Try me!"

> Ron Willoughby
> 1072 Route 171
> Woodstock, CT 06281
> (860) 974-1226   Fax: (860) 974-1226   swillo@neca.com

DUCK & OTHER DECOYS

★ **Wooden decoys and calls for ducks, geese, crows, and fish.** Buys ice fishing decoys, wooden plugs, and early reels made by *Meek, Talbot, Milan,* or *KY Bluegrass* (for which he will pay $100 up). Joe quotes prices of $200+ paid for turkey calls made by Gibson. Also buys various advertising signs that are related to hunting or fishing. He suggests you send photos, but may require you to send the item for inspection before he purchases it.

    Joe Tonelli
    PO Box 130
    Spring Valley, IL 61362
       (815) 664-4580   (605) 337-2301

★ **Wooden decoys of all types** including duck, swan, goose, crow, owl, shorebird and fish. Only old wooden items are wanted, but will consider items in any condition including separate heads and bodies. You must include photos of your decoy with your inquiry.

    Art Pietraszewski, Jr.
    60 Grant Street
    Depew, NY 14043
       (716) 681-2339

★ **Old duck, crow, and goose calls and decoys.** "I'll buy wooden decoys and calls in any quantity." Send a note or call with the description and the price you'd like.

    Jack Morris
    821 Sandy Ridge
    Doylestown, PA 18901
       (215) 348-9561

TRAPS

★ **Traps of all types and sizes from fly to grizzly bear.** Wants fine examples of fly, mouse, rat, mole, and gopher traps, glass minnow traps and spring operated fish traps. Will purchase anything unusual in any material including plastic, wood, wire, cast iron, glass, cardboard, and tin. Is especially fond of old and unusual mouse traps. He also buys patent models, books, catalogs, and advertising (pre-1940) related to traps. Does not want rusty or broken traps unless they are odd 19th century items. Send a picture or drawing, a good description, and an SASE and he promises to answer.

    Boyd Nedry
    728 Buth Drive NE
    Comstock Park, MI 49321
       (616) 784-1513

★ **Animal traps.** Has a special interest in oddly shaped and unusual traps. Will buy all sizes and pay up to $2,500 for unusually large ones. Will also buy pre-1940 trap and fur company catalogs, calendars, advertising items and scent and lure containers. All inquiries will be answered and everyone will be treated fairly and honestly."

  Ron Willoughby
  1072 Route 171
  Woodstock, CT 06281
 (860) 974-1226 Fax: (860) 974-1226 swillo@neca.com

★ **Glass flytraps or flycatchers,** especially early or unusual ones. Will consider interesting traps in other materials. Also advertising and paper ephemera related to early flytraps.

  Maris Zuika
  PO Box 175
  Kalamazoo, MI 49004
  (616) 344-7473

★ **Mouse traps** made of wood, metal or glass, as long as they are unusual. Also buy fly traps and very large bear traps.

  Steve Kelley
  PO Box 695
  Desert Hot Springs, CA 92240
  (619) 329-3206

★ **Traps, both animal and insect.** "I'll buy all sizes and types of traps prior to 1940, from large bear traps to small mouse traps, glass and porcelain insect traps, and all literature, advertising, and posters related to trapping. Traps made before 1900 are the most desirable." Please provide the manufacturer's name and any information you can read on the trap, including all numbers. Indicate the amount of rust and the length and type of chain if there is any. "If you can't identify the trap, please send photos and measurements, and I'll respond quickly."

  Frank De Bolle
  1930 West Gunn Road
  Rochester, MI 48306
  (810) 652-9148 eves Fax: (810) 650-8358

Don't forget to include a stamped envelope when you write to someone and want them to answer. No stamped envelope means "don't reply unless interested in buying."

MAKING MONEY ON ALCOHOL, TOBACCO, SEX AND GAMBLING

If that title doesn't get your attention I don't know what will. You should pay attention, because this is another chapter crammed with great buyers of an incredible array of items... lots of things you already own or can find relatively easily.

*In tobacco and liquor collecting, top prices are paid for 19th century items with attractive pictorials, but **there are lots of items less than 50 years old that you can profit from.***

If making money is your goal, it's important for you to learn about tobacco and beer cans, both of which can put hundreds of dollars in your pocket in a single sale. Someone who wanted to make money would learn about lighters ($5 to $2,000), cigar boxes and labels ($5 to $500), and mugs, glasses, and steins given away by 20th century breweries and soda companies $5 to 250.

Briar pipes can be bought for pennies at yard sales and second hand stores. To make money, look for Dunhill, Barling and Caminetto. Worth $25 to $100 to collectors.

Thirty pages full of buyers are waiting to hear from you. Nice people, committed to helping you get a fair price and a quick, easy and private sale.

To sell, you should provide the following information:

(1) What is advertised and what is depicted;
(2) Size, color, and the material from which it is made;
(3) Names, dates, and numbers on the item;
(4) Statement of condition, noting missing chips, cracks, and missing parts, pieces, or paint.

When you offer paper goods, photocopy what you offer.

PLAYING CARDS

★ **Anything concerning playing cards and card games.** Unusual playing cards including transformation cards, **non-standard decks**, and decks with a different picture on the face of each card. Also **single cards in quantity** with colorful backs and unusual Jokers, Aces or court cards. Also **books, magazines**, and other items on the games of contract bridge, auction bridge, and whist. Will consider early or limited edition books on other card games as well as plates, figurines, and other artwork depicting card playing. Will pay $100 up for *Royal Beyreuth* **china in the pattern called "Devil and the Cards."** Photocopies almost essential. Include an SASE to get an answer.

     Bill Sachen
     927 Grand Ave.
     Waukegan, IL 60085
       (847) 662-7204

★ **Antique decks of playing cards** are wanted, complete with joker and box or wrapper. Wants decks before 1930, identifiable because they are 2 1/2" wide with no box and 2 5/8" wide if boxed. Robert is the founder of a club for antique playing card collectors, and wants new complete decks with those dimensions, but "might be interested" in open decks. Make a photocopy of the back of one card and the face of the Joker and the Ace of spades.

     Robert Harrison
     582 Woodlawn Avenue
     Glencoe, IL 60022
       (847) 835-0842

★ **Playing cards** and related ephemera. "I want complete decks of pre-1920 American cards in excellent to mint condition," she says, but indicates a willingness to consider "modern decks of original design." What she doesn't want is double decks of bridge cards, incomplete decks, or single decks of narrow (bridge size) cards without advertising on the Joker or Ace of spades. When contacting her, a Xerox™ of the Joker, Ace, any face card, and the back of the card is the best idea. If you can't do that, you'll need to tell her whether the deck is bridge or poker width, whether it has gilt edges or not, whether the corners are round or square, and the condition. She also wants **advertising for cards, and will consider depictions of card playing** on postcards, trade cards, and the like. She is secretary/treasurer of the 400 member 52 Plus Joker Collector's club.

     Rhonda Hawes
     204 Gorham Avenue
     Hamden, CT 06514
       (203) 288-6584   robertcard@aol.com

★ **Playing cards**, pre-1945, from the U.S. and other countries, as well as **advertising and other pieces with a card playing theme**. "Packs should be complete, including Joker(s) and other extra cards, and preferably in their original box. I am especially looking for non-standard cards, **unusual designs**, advertising, pin-ups, comics, political, souvenir, etc., on the faces of the cards. I'll occasionally have interest in a more **recent pack, if very unusual.** I am not interested in standard cards or in foreign cards after 1900. I am also not interested in packs with damaged or missing cards, unless they are extremely unusual. No airline or gambling casino decks. Make a Xerox™ of the Ace of spades, Jokers, and any unusual cards as well as the back. It will help me to appreciate what you have."

David Galt
302 West 78th Street
New York, NY 10024
(212) 769-2514

★ **Playing cards** made in the U.S., poker size (2.5" wide), complete in their original box, made before 1940. "**I don't much care what's on the back**, as long as it's a complete deck in fine condition." He does not want bridge cards (2.25" wide) or any made after World War II. He asks that you make a Xerox™ of the face of the Ace of spades and the joker and the back of any other cards.

Robert Eisenstadt
GPO 020767
Brooklyn, NY 11202
(718) 625-3553   Fax: (718) 522-1087

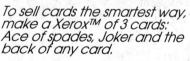

Buyers usually want "poker size" decks that are two and a half inches wide not "bridge size" decks that are two and a quarter inches wide. Bridge size decks date after 1930.

To sell cards the smartest way, make a Xerox™ of 3 cards: Ace of spades, Joker and the back of any card.

★ **Bridge tallies.** Please send a photocopy of bridge tallies and score cards dating from the 1920's through 1950's. May send on approval.

Fran Van Vynckt
7412 Monroe Ave.
Hammond, IN 46324
(219) 931-6813

POKER & CASINO CHIPS

★ **Casino chips, plaques, and poker chips** from around the world, old or new, as long as they are marked with the name of the casino or club, or the initials of the person for who they were custom marked. His favorites include chips from Cuba and closed Nevada and Atlantic City casinos. No plastic toy store chips, plain clay chips, or items currently in use in the U.S. Give the casino name, denomination, color, and how you came to own the piece. "Happy to give free appraisals."

John Benedict
PO Drawer 1423
Loxahatchee, FL 33470
    (561) 798-2520 voice and fax

To sell gambling chips, the best strategy is to make a Xerox™ copy. Send a list telling how many of each color you have. Count only those in fine condition

★ **Clay, ivory, or mother-of-pearl gambling chips** and selected other memorabilia. No plain, paper, or interlocking chips. Send a sample, rubbing or photocopy. Tell how many chips of each color. Dale wrote *Antique Gambling Chips*, available with a price guide for $20.

Dale Seymour, Past Pleasures
PO Box 50863
Palo Alto, CA 94303
    (415) 948-0949   Fax: (415) 941-3695

★ **Clay, ivory, mother-of-pearl and bone gambling chips** and "better chip racks and holders." No chips that are clay with no design, made of paper or plastic, or that interlock. Send a sample, rubbing or photocopy. Tell how many chips of each color.

Robert Eisenstadt
GPO 020767
Brooklyn, NY 11202
    (718) 625-3553   Fax: (718) 522-1087

SLOT MACHINES & OTHER GAMBLING ITEMS

★ **Slot machines,** especially pre-1940. Ted publishes *Coin Machine Trader* ($20/yr) devoted to ads and information about coin-ops.
>	Ted Salveson
>	PO Box 602
>	Huron, SD 57350
>		(605) 352-3870 Fax: (605) 352-7590

★ **Slot machines,** *Wurlitzer* **jukeboxes** (1938-48), **penny arcade machines** from before 1920, and **vending machines** from before 1910.
>	Martin Roenigk
>	Mechantiques
>	26 Barton Hill
>	East Hampton, CT 06424
>		(203) 267-8682 Fax: (203) 267-1120

★ **Slot machines.** Offers $40,000 for the *Fey* 1906 Liberty Bell slot machine but has only minor interest in most other slots. He does buy other **coin-operated gambling machines,** especially early wood cabinet and cast iron machines 1885-1912, including a few very rare **pinball machines**. Particularly interested in paper ephemera including **catalogs, advertising, letterheads, and anything else historical**. Also photos of store or saloon interiors which depict machines. Also *The Coin Machine Journal, Automatic Age, Automatic World, Spinning Reels, The Billboard* (pre-1932), and other trade magazines devoted to coin-op machines. Bueschel is an editor of the bi-monthly *Coin-Op Classics* and responsible for dozens of guides to coin-ops. Since thousands of dollars are involved, he wants you to shoot a roll of 35mm film of details of your coin-op and ship the undeveloped roll to him. He'll reimburse. You *must* tell him where you got your machines.
>	Richard Bueschel
>	414 North Prospect Manor Avenue
>	Mt. Prospect, IL 60056
>		(847) 253-0791

★ **Gambling items** including **slot machines**, poker chips, playing cards, and other early casino items and advertising. Says he seeks "any fine condition **advertising or ephemera on gambling**, including books and catalogs on poker, playing cards, and gambling that were produced before 1960." He requests you tell where you got the item, and include a photo. Also buys **billiard** items. Sellers must set the price they want.
>	Larry Lubliner
>	Re-Finders
>	737 Barberry Road
>	Highland Park, IL 60035
>		(847) 831-1102

Slot machines are also purchased by buyers of coin-operated machines. It might be worth your while to look in that section as well.

★ **Gambling equipment and related advertising and pop culture** such as:
- Small pieces of gambling equipment;
- Objects with gambling scenes like lighters, match safes, etc.;
- Tins and other packages featuring gambling;
- Lobby cards and other movie items featuring gambling;
- Catalogs and literature from makers of gambling supplies.

Please make photocopies or take photographs of what you have. No large or coin operated machines.

>Robert Eisenstadt
>GPO 020767
>Brooklyn, NY 11202
>(718) 625-3553   Fax: (718) 522-1087

★ **Punchboards** that are graphically interesting and unpunched. Give the condition and a photo or Xerox™ copy.

>Clark Phelps
>390 K Street
>Salt Lake City, UT 84103
>(801) 364-4747

★ **Mechanical punchboards** and **other gambling equipment**, including pre-1940 **slot machines**. Mechanical punchboards are made of metal and reusable, loaded by the owner. A photo is required of all gambling items.

>Roger Snowden
>PO Box 527
>Vashon, WA 98070
>(800) 327-6437   or   (206) 463-5656

★ **Bingo cages** and other interesting and early items or ephemera related to the game of Bingo. Primarily interested in professional items. When describing, include everything written on the item. For paper items, make a photocopy. No children's games are wanted.

>Roger Snowden
>PO Box 527
>Vashon, WA 98070
>(800) 327-6437   (206) 463-5656

★ **Books on gambling.** "We can give anyone information as to whether their book or gambling paraphernalia has value if they write, call, or preferably fax us." Not a bad bet, since Howard has been described elsewhere as the man who "knows more about gambling literature than anyone else alive."

Howard Schwartz
Gambler's Book Club
630 South 11th Street
Las Vegas, NV 89101
(702) 382-7555 (2 to 5pm)   (800) 522-1777   Fax: (702) 382-7594

LOTTERY TICKETS

★ **Scratch off type lottery tickets.** "I'll buy instant rub-off lottery tickets from the 1970's and 1980's."

Bill Pasquino
1824 Lyndon Avenue
Lancaster, PA 17602

★ **Lottery tickets.** "I buy instant scratch-off type lottery tickets from anywhere in North America, both used and unused, from before 1990. Special issue and short run tickets are most desirable, as are sets such as the Presidential Series, Landmarks, and Bicentennial sets issued by various states, especially if you have the complete set. Not every ticket is worth something, butt older complete tickets can bring up to original cost or more. If you have any questions or tickets for sale, call me and I'll take your phone number and call you back at my expense." Unusual, short run or special issue tickets from the 1990's are also purchased.

Jim Sheridan
PO Box 7
Tunkhannock, PA 18657
(717) 836-1626   JJSHERIDA@aol.com

Lottery tickets have been sold by two-thirds of all states. 10,000+ different instant games have been offered, each with a different ticket.

CORKSCREWS & WINE COLLECTIBLES

★ **Bottle openers and corkscrews,** especially those that contain advertising for a product or that have patent numbers. "I'm looking for antique items of quality. I don't want openers or corkscrews in poor condition, reproductions, or common modern advertising." He is editor of the newsletter, "Just for Openers" and author of *Handbook of United States Beer Advertising Openers & Corkscrews.* Send a photocopy and, if you're a dealer, the price. Amateurs may request an offer.

   John Stanley
   Just For Openers
   3712 Sunningdale Way
   Durham, NC 27707
      (919) 419-1546

★ **Corkscrews and wine related items.** Collects hand held and bar mounted corkscrews that are unusual in some way. Also wants wine related items such as wine tasters, **pre-1930 bottles, silver or ceramic bottle labels**, bottle cradles and **buckets**, etc. "I have little interest in paper labels." Make a photocopy of smaller items if possible. Describe the others. "I will answer all letters," says Joe.

   Joe Young
   PO Box 587
   Elgin, IL 60121
   (847) 695-0108   Fax: (847) 695-1679   istamp2@msn.com

★ **Corkscrews.** "I'm looking for older metal and/or mechanical types rather than the "basic-T" shape, although I will by those in silver or gold. Non "T-type" corkscrews bring $100 and up. Please give dimensions as part of your description." Xerox™ copies helpful.

   Mark Barlow
   3107-A Medlock Bridge Road
   Norcross, GA 30071
   (770) 449-7610 days   (770) 447-6649 eves   Fax: (770) 449-1839

★ **Wine-related items** such as corkscrews, wine tasters and coasters, holders, cradles, and other fine condition pieces. Give dimensions as part of your description." Photos or Xerox™ copies helpful. No labels or bottles, please.

   Mark Barlow
   Winetiques
   3107-A Medlock Bridge Road
   Norcross, GA 30071
   (770) 449-7610 days   (770) 447-6649 eves   Fax: (770) 449-1839

LIQUOR COLLECTIBLES

★ **Everything associated with saloons and speakeasies** including **photos of interiors** and exteriors, advertising, saloon equipment catalogs, letterheads, etc. Also trade magazines such as *the National Police Gazette* pre-1919, *Fair Play, Brewers Gazette,* and others.

> Richard Bueschel
> 414 North Prospect Manor Ave.
> Mt. Prospect, IL 60065
> (847) 253-0791 eves

★ **Prohibition artifacts of all kinds,** 1919-1933, related to gangster activity in Chicago and environs. Seeks relics from famous speakeasies such as *Colosimo's Cafe, Four Deuces, Red Lantern, Pony Inn, Cotton Club,* and *The Green Mill.* Also pamphlets, posters, and the like from the **Anti-Saloon League, WCTU, the Prohibition Party** and other groups for or against prohibition.

> Michael Graham's Roaring 20's
> 33133 O'Plaine Road
> Gurnee, IL 60031
> (847) 263-6285

★ **Ceramic *Jim Beam* type figural liquor bottles** from all makers. Your description should include the brand name, the figure, all marks on the bottom, the dimensions, and all colors. Bottles *must* have their original stopper. Fred buys and sells ceramic decanter bottles and offers a price guide to 6,000 different figural bottles for only $5.

> Fred Runkewich
> PO Box 1423-T
> Cheyenne, WY 82003
> (307) 632-1462

★ *Dewar's* **scotch figural liquor bottles made by** *Royal Doulton.* Called *KingsWare* by *Doulton* collectors, more than 100 different figural bottles were commissioned in the 1920's and 30's. These distinctive brown-glazed bottles feature various literary characters and English historical figures. He pays $300+ each, says this veteran *Royal Doulton* dealer, as long as the figure is not chipped or cracked. If you wish to sell yours, telephone with the item in front of you.

> Ed Pascoe
> Pascoe & Co.
> 101 Almeria Avenue
> Coral Gables, FL 33134
> (305) 445-3229   Fax: (305) 445-3305

★ *Green River Whiskey* **advertising** and that for J.W. McCulloch Distiller, Cliff Falls Distillers or the Oldetyme Distillers, Inc. "I want paper, cardboard diecut signs, display bottles, watch fobs, giveaways, counter displays, and company receipts, letterheads, etc. Will pay $250 for *Green River* shot glasses. Clear pencil rubbings of advertising coins and fobs is a must, as many types exist. I also buy **Whiskey or spirits trade magazines** such as *Wine & Spirits Bulletin* from before 1920. "No *Green River* soft drink or repro tin signs, please."
Elijah Singley
2301 Noble Avenue
Springfield, IL 62704
(217) 546-5143 eves (217) 786-2251

★ **China whiskey jugs marked KT&K** on the bottom. Also **miniature whiskey and apple vinegar jugs** with mottoes, product names or names of liquor stores on them. American pieces only, please.
Barry Friedman
PO Box 55492
Valencia, CA 91385
(805) 255-2365 BarryF@fishnet.net

★ *Jack Daniels, Green River Whiskey,* and *Lem Motlow* memorabilia including crockery jugs, embossed bottles, cork screws, shot glasses, lighters, and old paper advertising. Only older items are wanted.
Don Cauwels
3947 Old South Road
Murfreesboro, TN 37128
(615) 896-3614 Fax: (615) 896-3614

★ **Cocktail shakers and related memorabilia** made before 1960 are wanted by this 25 year veteran collector, especially unusually shaped shakers (golf bags, lady's leg, lighthouse) and designer shaker sets. Chrome sets by REVERE or MANNING BOWMAN are also wanted. "I also want anything to do with cocktails including **matches, ashtrays, recipe books, posters**, etc., from before 1930." Please include a photo or sketch. Measurements are very helpful. Stephen is author of *Vintage Bar Ware Identification & Value Guide.*
Stephen Visakay
PO Box 1517
West Caldwell, NJ 07007
(914) 352-5640

★ **Miniature whiskey bottles**, bourbons, blends, straights and ryes made in America from 1890 to 1960. Bottles should be two (2) ounces or less with most stating 1/10 pint. All bottles must have paper labels in good condition. Mike will buy one or a large collection, but warns that the price on large quantities may only average a dollar or two because many of the bottles, though old, are common and have minimal value. "Nothing made after 1960 is of interest," he says, pointing out that the date is often found embossed on the bottom of the bottle (often simplified to just two numbers). List the brand name and condition of the label. It's helpful to also give any dates, and the shape of the bottle ("most are flask shaped, he says). Indicate whether it is empty or full. He has no interest in figural ceramic whiskey bottles (*Jim Beam* type) or in wine bottles of any type from any period. A few of Mike's fellow collectors seek bottles of scotch, Canadian, vodka, and other booze although they are generally a lot less valuable. "I'll try to help you sell just about any good miniature liquor bottles, or **larger American whiskeys from Prohibition or before** if they are still sealed and full." More than 30,000 different mini liquor bottles range in value from 50¢ to $100, with half having no value at all. Mike says, "I don't know too much about large whiskey bottles as that's not my area of expertise." He adds, "If you recognize the brand name, it probably has no value."

Michael Olson, MELO
309 Knopp Valley Drive
Winona, MN 55987
(507) 454-1499

Liquor and beer advertising signs and premiums will often find a ready market among general Advertising collectors and with a few Pop Culture buyers.

If you have early ads for any liquor product...they'll sell!

BEER COLLECTIBLES

★ **Anything with the name of a beer on it.** It's called *breweriana*, and includes glasses, coasters, trays, calendars, label collections, signs, mugs, and anything else used to promote beer. Lynn particularly wants tin signs and other display advertising from the turn of the century. Lynn operates an auction service exclusively devoted to items associated with the golden brew. No *Billy Beer* or *J.R. Beer*.

> Lynn Geyer
> 300 Trail Ridge
> Silver City, NM 88061
> (505) 538-2341   Fax: (505) 388-9000

★ **Beer and soda cans from small regional companies** before 1965. Prefers cone top cans but also buys flat top cans, brewery advertising, signs, trays, statues and glasses from the same period. Especially likes to find items from the *Manhattan Brewing Company* owned by Al Capone and the *Grace Bros. Brewing Company* in California. Prices on cans from these two companies tend to start at $500. No rusty cans are wanted by this 10 year veteran collector/dealer, but "some light spotting and aging is natural. I do require cans be sent before a final purchase offer is made because condition so greatly affects the value and I need to examine cans closely."

> Tony Steffen
> 1115 Cedar Avenue
> Elgin, IL 60120
> (847) 741-9684   Fax: (847) 742-5778

★ **Beer bottles and jugs with painted labels.** American breweries only. Most of these are 6, 7 or 8 oz. Has particular interest in finding bottles from NY towns of Horseheads, Buffalo, Rochester, Syracuse and Tonawanda. *Stoney's Beer* and *Bald Eagle* are two PA brands he'd especially like to find. Describe whether the paint is scratched or faded and whether there are neck chips. No soft drink bottles, please, even if bottled in breweries.

> Jim O'Brien
> PO Box 885
> Sugar Grove, IL 60554
> (630) 466-4679

★ **Coasters with advertising, especially for beer.** "I buy U.S. coasters only. Ship any quantity for my fair offer by return check."

> Art Landino
> 88 Centerbrook Road
> Hamden, CT 06518

★ **Beer cans** from U.S. brands before 1950. "I'll buy all fine condi-tion conetop and flattop cans with no pulltabs. Price is dependent upon the condition and rarity. Mint cone-tops are worth $20 and up. I do not want pull-tab beer cans." Give the brand name, type (beer, lager, bock, etc.), can style and condition.

Steve Gordon
3821 Queen Mary Drive
Olney, MD 20832
(301) 774-7651 eves   Fax: (301) 434-7278   gono@clark.net

★ *Hamm's* **brewery memorabilia** including advertising, packaging and bottles, souvenirs, foam scrapers, coasters, bottle caps, kegs, glasses, signs and so on, for all of *Hamm's* brands. These include *Buckhorn, Velvet Glove, Matterhorn, Burgie, Right Time, Old Bru*, and *Waldech*. When selling glasses or cans, it is important to include *all* writing that appears on the object. Pete wants everything he doesn't al-ready have and says the areas around Houston, Los Angeles, San Francisco, Baltimore, and St. Paul "are particularly saturated with *Hamm's* breweriana."

Peter Nowicki
1531 39th Avenue
San Francisco, CA 94122
(415) 566-7506

★ **New Jersey breweriana** from the 1930's or older including signs, calendars, trays, tap knobs, coasters, labels, cans, foam scrapers and books. Collections or box lots of older "ball type" beer tap knobs are also wanted, as are pre-prohibition tip trays and foam scrapers from New York City. SASE is a must if you want an answer.

Paul Brady
32 Hamilton Street
Newton, NJ 07860
(201) 383-7204 voice and fax

★ **Beer uniform sew-on patches from anywhere in the world.** Jim wants any sewn patch: arm, cap, shirt, all ages, all sizes, all breweries. He isn't interested in beer club patches. Please describe condition not-ing whether it is used or unused, clean or not, and indicate whether it is a "second" or has been cut from a larger patch. Photocopy helpful.

Jim O'Brien
PO Box 885
Sugar Grove, IL 60554
(630) 466-4679

★ **Near beer advertising from the days of prohibition in Chicago** and items related to Chicago pre-prohibition beers and breweries like *Budweiser, Schlitz, Blatz, Old Milwaukee, Atlas, Keely, Schoenhoffen, Sieben's,* and *Manhattan.* Wants signs, beer barrels, bottles, etc.
>Michael Graham, Roaring 20's
>33133 O'Plaine Road
>Gurnee, IL 60031
>>(847) 263-6285

☆ **Pottery and glass ginger beer bottles,** metal signs, crates, and paper ephemera. Minor chips, scratches, surface crackling OK on most pottery bottles. Glass bottles must be mint (except for case wear on the shoulders). Offers made only on bottles shipped for inspection. If offer is refused, it's the seller's responsibility to pay return postage.
>Sven Stau
>851 Harlem Road #11
>West Seneca, NY 14224
>>(716) 823-0470

★ **American and foreign miniature beer bottles** especially pre-prohibition 1880-1920. The earliest are about 5" tall, filled with beer, and have a cork stopper.   These are desirable only if the labels are complete or the bottles are embossed. Post-prohibition bottles are smaller and of interest only if all labels are complete and in good condition. Foreign bottles must be in mint condition to be of interest. Also bottle openers with handles in the shape of mini beer bottles, wood or metal. There is a small group of post-prohibition mini beers which can be worth to $100 each. They include *Old Glory, Royal Pilsen, Wagner, Spearman, Ambrosia, Nectar, Frederick's 4 Crown, Citizens, Manro, Atlantic, Pennsy* and others. Alex will pay top price for sets of mini bottles in their original box. Condition of the label is crucial so describe every scratch or discoloration. Measure exact height. Also buys bottle shaped bottle openers. No Taiwan bottles.
>Alexander Mullin
>331 North Lehigh Circle
>Swarthmore, PA 19081
>>(610) 328-7381

★ *Dixie* **beer and the Lexington Brewery Company ephemera** including openers, trays, fobs, mirrors, letterheads, and what have you.
>Thom Thompson
>1389 Alexandra Drive, #7
>Lexington, KY 40504
>>(606) 255-2727 days

BEER STEINS & MUGS

★ **Antique beer steins** are sought, "but I want only quality steins. I am not interested in low end, common steins which sell under $100." Good steins have handles, lids, and decorations. They include:
* Regimentals, depicting military themes, 1860-1945;
* Character steins (shaped like people, animals, or things);
* Glass steins, sometimes heavily etched, often colored;
* Steins hand carved of wood, ivory, or unusual materials;
* Steins advertising early breweries;
* Porcelain steins, especially Meissen or Royal Vienna;
* Steins and **other items made by Mettlach**, including vases, plaques, humidors, and bowls.
* A few modern steins will be considered: limited editions, U.S. Military, made for **Anheuser Busch** before 1980, made by Villeroy & Boch, or made by **Ceramarte**.

Steins marked MADE IN OCCUPIED GERMANY or MADE IN WEST GERMANY are almost never wanted. Gary conducts about a half dozen stein auctions a year, in various cities around the country. Bidding by mail is allowed at these live auctions. Gary also conducts mail-only auctions of less expensive (under $500) steins. You can sell your steins to Gary outright. He also accepts steins on consignment for auction. Commissions are based on each lot sold (single stein, plaque, pair of plaques, etc.). The commission will be 2% of the selling price plus $30 per lot for mail bid only auctions and $40 per lot for live auctions. There are no other charges. They pay insurances, cataloging storage, transportation, etc. They will pick up large collections anywhere in the country. You will be paid within 40 days of the completion of the auction. Contact Gary before shipping anything for auction. Their UPS address (NOT A MAIL ADDRESS) is Gary Kirsner, 1940 Augusta Terrace, Coral Springs, FL 33071. "If you have steins for sale," says Gary, "contact us. We can discuss the best possible way for you to sell your steins." Gary is the author of numerous books on steins. Three with the most general interest are:

The Mettlach Book (376 pp, 1500 items illus, 1994, $35);
The Beer Stein Book (416 pp, 2400 items illus, 1985, $40);
German Military Steins (112 pages, 340 items illus, $18).

For information regarding auctions, books, etc., call or fax.

Gary Kirsner Auctions
PO Box 8807
Coral Springs, FL 33075
(954) 344-9856   Fax: (954) 344-4421

★ **Antique beer steins of all types,** from $10 to $10,000 as long as it was made before WWII. This active collector/dealer will buy one or a large collection. A photo is helpful, as are all markings, measurements, and a description of what is portrayed. Don't forget to note the condition of both the stein and lid. He offers free appraisals with no obligation and, if you telephone him with your stein in your hand, "I can usually tell you its wholesale and retail value over the phone."

> Les Paul
> 568 Country Isle
> Alameda, CA 94501
> (510) 523-7480   Fax: (510) 523-8755

★ **Beer mugs and glasses** are sought by this well known auctioneer.

> Lynn Geyer
> 300 Trail Ridge
> Silver City, NM 88061
> (505) 538-2341   Fax: (505) 388-9000

★ **Glasses and beer mugs of all sorts,** including:
- **Beer glasses**, mugs, and steins from closed U.S. breweries and older items from present breweries;
- **Horse racing glasses** from important races such as the Kentucky Derby, Belmont, and Preakness;
- **Etched shot glasses** with names of whiskeys;
- **Whiskey pitchers**;
- **Soda glasses and root beer mugs**, but only early ones;
- **Cartoon and character glasses** issued by restaurants, fast food chains, TV shows, and others.

Peter buys outright, and also accepts items on consignment from pickers, dealers and private parties for his twice a year auctions of glasses, mugs, steins and related items. *Budweiser* mugs from the 1970's bring $500+, early 1900's beer glasses $40+, and some cartoon characters as much as $100. He DOES NOT WANT foreign beer glasses, items issued by breweries in the last 10 years, or anything not in mint condition. He suggests you send a picture when possible. His 60+ page auction catalogs are $11 each and come with prices realized for over 1,600 items.

> Peter Kroll's Glasses, Mugs & Steins Auction
> PO Box 207
> Sun Prairie, WI 53590
> (608) 837-4818 eves   Fax: (608) 825-4205

★ **Beer mugs and steins** made in the 1970's and 80's by the Ceramate Brazil Company. "I'll buy lidded and unlidded varieties of *Budman, Busch Gardens*, Clydesdales, Olympics, etc."

> Tony Steffen
> 1115 Cedar Ave
> Elgin, IL 60120
> (847) 428-3150 days (847) 741-9684 eves   Fax: (847) 742-5778

CIGARETTE PACKS & EPHEMERA

★ **Cigarette packages and cartons** from any brand, 1920-1980, from anywhere in the world as long as they are unopened in fine unused condition. Xerox© copy helps, often not needed.

Paul Scharfman, Chic-a-Boom
6817 Melrose Avenue
Los Angeles, CA 90038
(213) 931-7441   Fax: (213) 930-2990

★ **Cigarette packs, tins, and cardboard boxes** from obsolete U.S. brands of cigarettes. No cards, premiums, silks, flat 50's tins, or cigar or tobacco items. Give the series number found on the tax stamp. Dick is president of the Cigarette Pack Collector's Association and editor of *Brandstand*, a monthly newsletter for cigarette pack collectors.

Richard Elliott
61 Searle Street
Georgetown, MA 01833
(508) 352-7377

★ *Philip Morris cigarette packs*, cartons, advertising, signs, premiums, counter displays from the 1920's to the 1960's. He especially wants items with Johnny the Bellhop. The one *Philip Morris* item he does not want is magazine ads of any type.

Charles Evarkiou
4223 Niagara Avenue
San Diego, CA 92107
(619) 222-8588

★ *Philip Morris* **ephemera** prior to 1955, including cigarette packs, tins, advertising, signs, stand-ups, matches, buttons, and what have you. This beginning collector does not want reprints, and expects you to price what you wish to sell.

Stuart Morrell
8925 Laureate Lane
Richmond, VA 23236

★ **Tire ashtrays.** Give the tire maker and the "size" printed on the tire. Note what is printed on the glass part of the ashtray.

Ed Natale, Jr.
PO Box 222
Wyckoff, NJ 07481
(201) 848-8485   Fax: (201) 891-4252

Other buyers of rubber tire ashtrays may be found in the automotive and tire section on p. 340-345.

★ **Ashtrays,** but *only* those shaped like people, animals or things, such as airplanes, frogs, etc., especially when combined with lighters or cigar cutters. No ordinary glass hotel or bar advertising ashtrays. Most are $5 to $15, but has paid $100+ for exceptional pieces. Send a clear photo or a good sketch. Sorry, no SASE, no answer.

> Tobacciana Resources
> 2141 Shoreline Drive #A
> Shell Beach, CA 93449

★ **Ashtrays with bronze nude dancers.** Ashtrays are usually marble or shells with figures from 3" to 6" high. "I'll pay retail price for them!" Nothing damaged, please. Photo or phone call almost essential.

> Tony Hyman
> Box 3000
> Pismo Beach, CA 93448
> (805) 773-6777   Fax: (805) 773-8436   thyman@tobacciana.com

CIGARETTE LIGHTERS

★ **Cigarette lighters and fire making devices.** Buys a wide range of items including:
- High quality *Dunhills, Ronsons,* and pre-1940 lighters, especially *Dunhills* with special features such as being built into a watch;
- Lighters with unusual mechanisms, burning lenses, etc.;
- Table lighters that are in the shape of people or things;
- Automatic lighters made before 1920 by *Thorens, Haway, RK*;
- Lighters consisting of cap, gear, and tinder cord;
- Flint and steel strikers and tinder pistols;
- Designer lighters made of 14K or 18K gold;
- Chemical lighters from 1790 to 1890.

Anything unusual. Has no interest in modern Japanese lighters, butane lighters, and most advertising lighters except those for political personages. Don't bother him with common or recent items. As a basic rule of thumb, he says, "If you've seen it before, I don't want it." Give a basic description including brand name, patent information, ornamentation, construction, and condition. This 20 year veteran collector says, "I'm happy to answer inquiries from beginners or advanced collectors."

> Tom O'Key
> 124 South Alice Circle
> Anaheim, CA 92806
>   (714) 630-8919   Fax: (714) 632-8275

★ **Lighters.** This veteran collector buys a wide range of quality lighters, but is especially interested in:
  • *Zippos* of all type which pre-date the Korean war, fancy or not;
  • Lighters made of gold, silver or platinum;
  • Enameled lighters;
  • Lighters with watches or clocks;
  • Lighters in canes or walking sticks;
  • Any highly decorated lighter with a complicated mechanism
      or that is in pristine condition;
  • Butane lighters made by *Dunhill, Dupont, Cartier* or
      Waterman, but only by those makers, no others.
  • **Catalogs, fluid cans, lighter displays, and advertising**.
What he doesn't want is silver plated *Ronson* table lighters, lighters made in Japan, Vietnam *Zippos,* and anything in poor condition or that has been tampered with. A complete description includes the name of the lighter, size, condition, color, material it's made of, and its history of ownership if known. Photocopies of the side and bottom are helpful. Terry is Vice President of the Pocket Lighter Preservation Guild and a contributor to *Flint and Flame*, its newsletter.
    Terry & Karen Cairo
    Box 1054
    Addison, IL 60101
        (708) 543-9120   Fax: (708) 834-4051

★ *Zippo* **lighters** with Navy and Marine Corps insignia, especially aircraft carriers, submarines, aircraft squadrons, and small craft like minesweepers and patrol boats. If the lighters have ZIPPO PAT 2032695 or ZIPPO PAT 2517191 they are more desirable. Square cornered *Zippos* are very rare. "If they are in fine to mint condition, I also buy **fancy lighters by *Dunhill* and lighters made by *Ronson*** which are marked ART METAL WORKS, AMW or LVA. Please send photocopies of your lighters along with your SELL-A-GRAM and an SASE." When in San Diego, you are encouraged to visit their free museums in Old Town State Historic Park and Old Town Train Station.
    Jeff Mogilner
    Racine & Laramine, Ltd.
    2737 San Diego Ave.
    San Diego, CA 92110
        (619) 291-7833   Fax: (619) 297-6653

TOBACCO & OTHER INSERT CARDS

★ **Cigarette and tobacco insert cards and other tobacco related paper.** Wants 19th and early 20th century U.S. tobacco and cigarette insert cards, tobacco advertising trade cards, counter stand-ups, hangers, posters, albums, giveaways, premiums, and cigarette slide packs. Will pay $25 each and up for many early American trade cards, and $700 for the Marquis of Lorne card from 1879. He DOES NOT WANT British or foreign cards, cigar bands, cigar labels, tobacco caddy labels, reproductions or reprints, matchbooks or badly damaged items. Give the size (vertical then horizontal), the maker, and condition. A photocopy is a good idea. Items must be in at least very good condition.

"I buy only cards that contain one of the following words printed on the card: tobacco, cigarette, smoking, cut plug, chewing, long cut, fine cut, scrap cut or navy cut."

> Peter Gilleeny
> 76 Rose Drive
> Fruitland Park, FL 34731
>   (352) 728-4819

★ **Cigarette cards and silks** for Canadian, British or U.S. cigarettes. He wants complete sets or albums of cards, but buys silks in odd lots. Sorry, but he does not want to buy a handful of odd cards from you unless they are 19th century U.S. cards in near mint condition. He will buy large lots of odd cards. Give the title of the set or album. Dealers must price their goods. Amateurs may request an offer.

> W.T. Brown
> 45 Park Avenue
> Carleton Place, ON
> K7C 2H9 CANADA
>   (613) 253-1790   NSTN2366@FOX.NSTN.CA

★ **Cigarette and other insert cards.** Wants all 19th century U.S. cigarette insert cards. This 50 year veteran also wants cards from *Brooke-Bond Tea Company* and the *Liebig Meat Extract Company.* He will consider *Liebig* cards in English, plus menu and calendar cards. Give quantities, and send a photocopy showing samples of the front and back of the cards you have for sale.

> Ron Stevenson
> 4920 Armoury Street
> Niagara Falls, ON
> L2E 1T1 CANADA
>   (905) 358-5497

★ **Cigarette and tobacco insert cards, silks** and **leathers.** Wants 19th century U.S. items primarily, such as cards by *Allen & Ginter*, but buys many 20th century pieces. Also buys **tobacco advertising trade cards** and tobacco related **match covers.** "Please describe and price, or send on approval. I pay all postage expenses and respond within 48 hours of receipt of your cards. Condition is important as I do not collect trimmed cards, badly creased or otherwise battered items." Does not want flannel flags (often erroneously called "felts").
>William Nielsen
>PO Box 1379
>Brewster, MA 02631
>(508) 896-7389

★ **Cigarette silks** given away by cigarette companies at the turn of the century. Has a particular interest in those illustrating Indians, actresses, colleges and rulers as well as those that are woven rather than printed. He does not want silks (which are actually satin) that are soiled, frayed, stitched or otherwise damaged. "When offering silks for sale, please describe the size and quantity and I will reply with an offer. Within 48 hours of receipt of the collection I will reply with a check for the agreed amount or return the items paying all postage. Xerox™ copies are helpful for estimating." He does not buy flannels (felts) or leather premiums except as part of a large collection of silks.
>Roland DeCesare
>11235 Valley Bend Drive
>Germantown, MD 20876

★ **Items made of cigarette silks or flannels** such as **pillows or quilts** are wanted by this prestigious quilt dealer. "No junk," she emphasizes, since everything is for sale in her shop. Please take a photograph or make a photocopy of your item. She also wants fine condition collections of silks or flannels. Please list how many flags and silks you have and their approximate size.
>Margaret Cavigga
>8648 Melrose Avenue
>Los Angeles, CA 90069
>(213) 935-6799

★ **Items made of cigarette silks or ribbons** such as **jackets, wall hangings, pillows or quilts** are wanted. Buying for resale. Please take a photograph or make a photocopy of part of your item. List how many silks of each size, counting only those in fine condition. Also buys high grade **American cigarette cards** and **advertising.**
>Tobacciana Resources Co.
>2141 Shoreline Drive
>Shell Beach, CA 93449

TOBACCO ADVERTISING

★ **All high grade tobacco related collectibles:** "We'll consider purchasing **tobacco jars, tobacco tins, cigar labels, catalogs, books about tobacco, cigar boxes, posters, advertising, humidors** and other tobacco related ephemera. We prefer collections, but buy individual items if value or collectible interest is sufficiently high. We buy for resale. SASE required for an answer; we regret sometimes unavoidably long delays in response. We have no interest in poor condition items, drug store pipes, pipe racks, common tins, magazine ads, flat 50 cigarette tins, cigarette packages after WWII, things covered with cigar bands, or cigar boxes dating after 1940."
> Tobacciana Resources Co.
> 2141 Shoreline Drive
> Shell Beach, CA 93449

★ **Tin and paper tobacco tags** and other advertising related to plug and chewing tobacco. Values of tin tags run from $1 to $5, but those with Blacks or political and military figures command more. "Most items from around the turn-of-the-century are sought." Include a brief description, name of the manufacturer and an accurate statement of condition for this 10 year veteran who buys, sells and trades tags.
> Chris Cooper
> Tin Tag Collector's Club
> Route 2 Box 55
> Pittsburg, TX 75686
> (903) 856-7286   Fax: (903) 856-6879

★ **Tin tobacco tags** and tag collections are bought, sold, and traded by this very active collector, who offers a free "suggestion sheet for new collectors" that will teach you all about tin tobacco tags. He also has the remaining stock of Gary Schild's basic book on tobacco tags, and is happy to sell you one for only $10. A colorful 2' x 3' poster picturing more than 100 tags in color is available for $17.50. Xerox™ your tags.
> Lee "Tagger Lee" Jacobs
> PO Box 3098
> Colorado Springs, CO 80934

★ *Seal of North Carolina* smoking and chewing tobacco advertising. Does not want tin cans, only lithographed ads. Fine condition a must. Photos appreciated.
> Lisa Van Hook
> PO Box 2666
> Spring Valley, CA 91979
> Fax: (619) 470-3430   Badblu22@aol.com

★ **Tin tobacco cans** from before 1940. Wants very fine condition **smoking tobacco, chewing tobacco and cigar cans and signs** only. Save time and effort by sending a photocopy of the top and front of your tin along with a description of the condition. SASE is a must. If you regularly pick or deal, he will send you an informative flyer listing some boxes and tins to look for. **Brands not wanted include** *Bond Street, Briggs, Buckingham, Bugle, Dial, Dills Best, Edgeworth, George Washington, Half & Half, Hickory, Holiday, John Middleton, Kentucky Club, Model, Philip Morris, Prince Albert, Red Jacket, Revelations, Sir Walter Raleigh, Stag, Target, Tuxedo, Twin Oaks, Union Leader, Velvet,* and *Willoughby Taylor.* "Please be aware," advises Tony, "that flat fifty cigarette tins such as *Lucky Strike* and *Chesterfield* have no value. My apologies, but response is often unavoidably slow except on very rare items."

Tony Hyman
PO Box 3028
Pismo Beach, CA 93448
(805) 773-6777   Fax: (805) 773-8436   thyman@tobacciana.com

To sell anything, you should provide the following information:

(1) *What is advertised and what is pictured;*
(2) *Size, color, and material from which made;*
(3) *Names, dates, and numbers on the item;*
(4) *Statement of condition, noting chips, cracks, and missing parts, pieces, or paint;*
(5) *Make a Xerox© whenever possible.*

When you ask someone for information or an offer, include a long business size #10 envelope, address it to yourself, and put a stamp in the corner. This is a Self-Addressed Stamped Envelope (SASE). Use a long envelope because many buyers will send you information which won't fit into smaller envelopes. If you do not include an SASE, you are telling buyers not to bother answering your letter if they are not interested in what you have to sell. "If my help isn't worth an envelope and stamp to the seller," said one expert, "it's not worth my time and money either."

CIGAR EPHEMERA

★ **Cigar boxes, labels, advertising, photographs**, counter lighters, **cigar store figures**, and everything else related to cigar making, selling, and smoking before WWII. Especially wants trade directories 1865-1940 (these are books which list cigar and tobacco factories). Want all materials relevant to the **Cigar Maker's International Union** or to **Samuel Gompers**, former CMIU officer. Condition is important. Please photocopy the inside lid of boxes. Pays from $5 to $50+ for cigar boxes, with top boxes bringing approximately $300. Send a long SASE for an informative priced wants list (which includes a useful list of common boxes). Tony's hardcover *Handbook of Cigar Boxes* is available with *Price Guide* for $18. He warns, "I have little interest in bands or items covered with cigar bands and pay little for them."

 Tony Hyman
 PO Box 3028
 Pismo Beach, CA 93448
 (805) 773-6777 Fax: (805) 773-8436 thyman@tobacciana.com

★ **Cigar bands** from before WWII, preferably sets of royalty, Presidents, playing cards, and other pictorials. No torn, damaged, or partial bands are wanted. Give the quantity, description, and an SASE. Myron heads the *International Label, Seal and Cigar Band Society* which you can join for only $6/year.

 Myron Freedman
 8915 East Bellevue Street
 Tucson, AZ 85715
 (602) 296-1048

★ **Cigar band collections** especially U.S. bands prior to 1920. Only items in good or mint condition wanted by this long time collector, owner of more than a quarter million bands.

 Joseph Hruby
 1511 Lyndhurst Road
 Lyndhurst, OH 44124
 (216) 449-0977

★ **Cigar band ashtrays** and other pieces of decoupage made by gluing cigar bands onto various items in a decorative manner. Send photos and dimensions, describing any damage, especially fading, most noticeable in the red. "Bands are red, not pink."

 Steve Davis
 Box 26192
 Birmingham, AL 35226
 (205) 979-8909

★ **Cigar bands** that are decorative and loose (not pasted into albums) as they are intended for artistic decoupage. This new collector also wants old **ashtrays and other glass items covered with cigar bands.** "If you send your item or bands for inspection, I will give you what I believe to be the wholesale and retail price of your item and make you an offer. If my offer is not accepted, I will return your item to you shipped COD. Current cigar bands are not of interest."

> Dennis Pecina
> 4865 Cardamon Lane
> Rockford, IL 61114
> (815) 637-1622

★ **Cigar humidors** by *Tiffany, Dunhill, Davidoff, Benson & Hedges* and *Meridan*, preferably in silver or exotic woods. Has less interest in glass or ceramic humidors, "although I will consider them." Will buy table top, free-standing, and travel styles, paying up to $5,000 for exceptional humidors. Prefers humidors with sporting motif, such as hunting dogs. Not interested in plain or damaged humidors. Give the maker's name, dimensions, and type of material. Photo if possible.

> Francis Lombardi II
> PO Box 181-TH
> Syracuse, NY 13208
> (315) 685-9806

★ **Cigar store Indians.** Wants full size wooden or metal figures, especially Punch, Captain Jinks, or Dandy. Take photos from more than one angle or phone with the item in front of you. Also wants items from **tobacco factories in Detroit:** signs, cans, advertisements, bills of sale, boxes, store figures, photos, cutters, lighters, match holders and trays. Especially wants *Hiawatha* by D. Scotten.

> Gregory "Dr. Z" Zemenick
> 1350 Kirts Blvd. #160
> Troy, MI 48084
> (810) 244-9426   Fax: (810) 244-9495

ANTIQUE & BRIAR PIPES

☆ **Antique smoking pipes and pipe parts.** Also buys **books and magazines** on pipes, tobacco, and related items. Primary interest is in **meerschaum,** but also buys other antique pipes, especially porcelains, and any historical or unusual items including pipes from any culture. Will purchase complete collections as well as individual pipes. Not interested in damaged pipes or reproductions. Give size (length and width), condition, and all other information you can provide.

> Frank Burla
> Box 446
> Lisle, IL 60532
>   (630) 271-1317   fpburla@aol.com

★ **High quality pipes of all type** are wanted, including:
- Name brand "pre-smoked" **used briar pipes**, especially *Dunhill, Charatan, Barling, Castello, Radich, GBD, Kaywoodie* and "others too numerous to mention";
- **Meerschaum pipes** in good to excellent condition;
- **Carved briar pipes;**
- **Clay pipes** that are very large or that have been carved into faces, animals, and other figures;
- **Pipe tobacco advertising and books**;
- **Lighters** of many different sizes and shapes.

Larger pipes are particularly desirable. When describing a pipe, include the brand name, its dimensions, shape, finish and all stampings. If you are not familiar with standard pipe shapes, make a photocopy of the pipe and list everything written on the pipe's shank. He does not buy *Medico, Yellow Bole, Dr. Grabow* or other drugstore pipes.

> Gary Donachy
> 801 West Sunset
> Steeleville, IL 62288
>   (618) 965-3189

★ **Antique pipes** including carved **meerschaums, opium pipes, water pipes, porcelain figural pipes,** early bas-relief and high-relief wood pipes and selected clays. Ben is a **specialist in the literature of tobacco**, and buys **books, magazines and pamphlets** on all aspects of tobacco culture and use, in any language, from any period. If you are seeking literature on tobacco, he has the world's largest selection on that topic. He has an extensive printed catalog, but please don't ask for it unless you are a buyer of tobacco literature.

> Ben Rapaport, Antiquarian Tobacciana
> 11505 Turnbridge Lane
> Reston, VA 20194
>   (703) 435-8133 until 10pm Eastern

★ **High quality pipes of all types** are purchased by one of the nation's largest and oldest tobacconists. Both modern and antique pipes are bought for resale or for display, but don't bother them with junk. *Dunhill, Comoy, Petersen* and *Sasieni* are among briars purchased. "If they are part of a large collection, we'll buy any pipes, including inexpensive ones, as long as they are in fine condition." Highly carved meerschaum will also be considered. A photocopy is a good idea. Check your item carefully for damage and mention any defects you find. Also buys antique cigar cutters, cigar cases, and *Dunhill* **lighters**, as well as other old lighters made of gold or silver.

    Charles Levi
    Iwan Ries & Co.
    19 South Wabash
    Chicago, IL 60603
  (312) 372-1306   Fax: (312) 372-1416   IWAN_RIES@ripco.com

★ **High grade briar pipes.** Brand names of interest include *Dunhill, Charatan, Barling, Comoy, Castello, Caminetto, Sasieni, Preben Holm,* and *Peterson.* "I'll buy them smoked or new, as long as they are in good looking condition, with no uneven surfaces on the rim, no tooth holes in the stem, etc." Wants collections of pipes, but will buy singles. He especially wants *Dunhills* with "ODA" or "ODB" and patent dates marked on the stem and *Peterson* pipes with IRISH FREE STATE or ERIE on the shank. Please, no "drug store pipes" like *Medico, Yellow Bole,* or *Dr. Grabow.* When offering pipes for sale, mention any writing on the pipe and its condition. There are dozens of standard pipe shapes, so if you don't know them, send a photocopy of your pipe.

    Marty Pulvers
    Sherlock's Haven
    275 Battery Street, Embarcadero Center West
    San Francisco, CA 94111
  (415) 362-1405   Fax: (415) 362-7048   MPulvers@aol.com

★ **Pipes and tobacco items** including:
- **Antique meerschaum** (ivory-like) pipes, carved or plain;
- Briar pipes, old or modern, new or smoked;
- Pipe tobacco, especially old English tins full;
- Full old boxes of cigars from Cuba or Tampa only;
- Books or catalogs about pipes or smoking;
- Advertising for pipes and smoking tobacco.

Please send photos or Xerox™ copies of what you have and include all information stamped on the pipe. "I am a 40 year collector and will offer more than a dealer." Include an SASE for an offer.

    Lee Pattison
    6 Christview Drive
    Cuba, NY 14727
        (716) 968-2458

★ **Clay pipes and clay pipe ephemera.** Especially wants figurals, faces, or political clay pipes. Prefers American pipes marked with the name of a city, but buys others. This author-historian buys **pipe molds, presses and anything else involved in the making of clay pipes.** Also wants billheads, letterheads, checks, catalogs, and other advertising before 1950 for any clay pipe maker. Generally not interested in plain white clay pipes with no markings or decoration. Please make a photocopy of your items, indicating any markings, and tell what you know about their origin or background. Send a long SASE for a list of publications Paul has produced on clay pipes.

> S. Paul Jung, Jr.
> PO Box 817
> Bel Air, MD 21014
>   (410) 569-8194

★ **Hookah (water) pipes.** "I'll buy one hose or multiple hose hookahs made of brass, ivory, or other materials. I'm seeking antique pipes, not head shop items, common glass bongs, and other drug paraphernalia. Please send a picture and information about the pipe's background. Dealers should price your goods but I will make offers for amateurs."

> Mark Rivkind
> 11265 NW 53rd Court
> Coral Springs, FL 33076

IF YOU GO TO YARD SALES LOOKING FOR PROFIT...

You can resell quality used briar pipes for $15 to $100 each, yet they are often found for under $5. As a general rule, only a handful of brands are resellable, with Dunhill the #1 favorite. Other good brands include Comoy, Barling, Charatan, Castello, Caminetto, Sasieni, Savinelli, and Peterson Irish Free State.

Most wooden pipes you will find are what collectors call "drug store pipes," because that's where they were most readily sold, usually for inexpensive prices. Some familiar drug store brands are Dr. Grabow, Medico, Wally Frank, Kaywoodie and Yello Bole among others.

ACCESSORIES, JARS & BOXES

★ **Cigar humidors and tobacco jars.** "I collect both plain and figural china, wood, copper or glass. Many jars without a tobacco motif are mistaken for cracker or cookie containers. A cone-shaped receptacle in the lid to hold a sponge is a clue you have a tobacco jar. Please send photo, including any china markings on the bottom. Sase for offer.

>Lee Pattison
>6 Christview Drive
>Cuba, NY 14727
>(716) 968-2458

★ **Tobacco jars.** "If you have old tobacco jars, I may be able to assist you to identify what you have and decide its relative rarity. If you would like to sell a tobacco jar, I can advise you how to go about it, and may be able to steer you to members who may be interested." Joe founded the international club for tobacco jar collectors and edits their newsletter. He has also written a book on jars which you can order through him.

>Joe Horowitz
>3011 Falstaff Road #307
>Baltimore MD 21209
>(410) 358-1323

★ **Snuff boxes** of all types, including early American, Civil War period, and Oriental.

>Eli Hecht
>19 Evelyn Lane
>Syosset, NY 11791

MATCHCOVERS & BOXES

★ **Matchcover collections,** match boxes, salesman's sample books, pamphlets, and other match industry ephemera. Send brief description and SASE to this head of the American Matchcover Collecting Club. Bill is author of the *Matchcover Collector's Price Guide,* available from him for $28 postpaid.

> Bill Retskin
> PO Box 18481
> Asheville, NC 28804
> (704) 254-4487   Fax: (704) 254-1066   MATCHCLUB@circle.net

★ **Paper matchcover collections.** Dave is a long time collector of matchcovers and past president of the Sierra Diablo Club. He collects many different types of matchcovers and buys accumulations and collections. Individual covers are not worth much, but collections of pre-WWII covers are worth your while. Dave is happy to hear from folks with questions or collections.

> David Hampton
> PO Box 1457
> Lower Lake, CA 95457
> (707) 995-1411

★ **Matchcovers and match boxes,** foreign or domestic. "I don't want damaged covers generally, but will consider those with *minor* damage if they're from the early 1930's or before." Wants to know approximately how many covers or boxes you have, whether they are U.S. or foreign, whether they are used or unused, whether the covers are in an album or loose, and whether the matches are present. John is secretary of the Rathkamp Matchcover Society.

> John Williams
> 1359 Surrey Road TH
> Vandalia, OH 45377
> (513) 890-8684

★ **Matchcovers and match boxes.** Wants interesting singles or entire estates. Hiller is a West Coast auctioneer who can handle large collections. The ideal condition for matchcovers is unused, open, with the staples carefully removed. No "grocery store" covers, "Thank You's," or covers not identified as to origin (like *Holiday Inn* covers that don't give a location). His favorite find would be a matchcover from the Lindbergh welcome home dinner, worth in excess of $100.

> Robert Hiller
> 2501 West Sunflower #H5
> Santa Ana, CA 92704
> (714) 540-8220

Matchcovers are not wanted if they are torn or dirty, or if their striker has been cut off. Collectors do not want matchcovers if they are glued, taped, or stapled into a book.

★ **Match box dispensers** from days gone by are sought by this dealer in contemporary advertising match boxes. Please give a thorough description of the item and indicate whether it works or not. Photo is helpful. As a relatively new collector, he'd appreciate your setting the price, but will make offers if necessary.

Ed Sabreen
907 Glenside Road
Cleveland, OH 44121
(216) 381-0100   Fax: (216) 382 0969

MATCH SAFES

★ **Match safes.** "I'll buy figural, fancy, trick and unusual match safes (pocket holders for loose matches) and related items such as catalogs, advertisements, and ephemera prior to 1915. I'll take one or a collection, but only quality items. Photograph or Xerox™ along with description and other information. Asking price helpful but not necessary. I will respond to all inquiries."

George Sparacio
PO Box 791
Malaga, NJ 08328
(609) 694-4167 eves

★ **Match safes.** Buys small pocket match safes **if they are figural (shaped like some object)** or if they advertise tobacco products. Xerox™ what you have, rather than take photos which show your safe as a small blur. Prefers you to price your safe(s), understanding that almost all are worth under $100 to him. Ordinary sterling match safes that are not figural will only bring $15 to $20 depending on the pattern. Buys quality **match box holders** in bronze or celluloid.

Tony Hyman
PO Box 3028
Pismo Beach, CA 93448

EROTICA & GIRLIE MAGAZINES

★ **Erotic art in all forms and formats** including statues, paintings, prints, post cards, photography, and three dimensional objects of all kinds from the days of the Roman empire up to the present. Especially seeks Oriental and European bisque or porcelain figures with hidden erotic scenes, revolving lamps from the 50's with pin-up shades, arcade "peep" machines, and photos of all types. Also **original art for pin-up calendars** or illustrations 1920-1970, especially work by **Alberto Vargas** and **George Petty**, but other artists are wanted including Earl Moran, Gil Elvgren, Zoe Mozert, Armstrong, Alk Buell, Al Moore and others. Also Vargas *Esquire* calendars and prints, other calendar pin-ups, and some homemade erotica, including obscene letters written by private parties. Describe condition. A photograph or photocopy is suggested. Include your phone number when you write.

> Charles Martignette
> PO Box 293
> Hallandale, FL 33008

★ **Erotica of all types,** including nude photos and photo books, original art and paintings, Oriental or European, and three dimensional materials of all sorts.

> Ivan Gilbert
> Miran Art & Books
> 2824 Elm Avenue
> Columbus, OH 43209
> (614) 421-3222   Fax: (614) 421-3223

★ **Erotica of all types, all languages, all eras**, including hard and soft cover books, sex newspapers, typescripts and mimeos, sex comics, original erotic art, films, photos, statuary, and sexually explicit objects of all types. Not interested in most magazines.

> C.J. Scheiner
> 275 Linden Blvd. # B2
> Brooklyn, NY 11226
> (718) 469-1089

★ **Girlie magazines published by *Parliament*** from the 1950's, 60's, and 70's. Buys *Playboy* from the 1950's only. Buys related girlie material, calendars, and paperbacks, but nothing from the 1980's. Fine condition items only. For $3 Warren offers a catalog of girlie magazines he has for sale.

> Warren Nussbaum
> 29-10 137th Street
> Flushing, NY 11354
> (718) 886-0558

★ **Girlie magazines published by *Parliament, Nuance, Marquis* or *Briarwood* from 1969 to 1989.** Will pay $1 each for magazines from these publishers and $2 each for a few issues. Will pay 25¢ to 50¢ for similar adult publications from the 1970's by other publishers. Pays $3-$5 each for *Puritan* and xxx magazines with cover price over $12. Wants complete clean copies. **"No embarrassment. No need to write or call.** Ship one or a hundred for immediate cash. Ship via Post Office 'Special 4th Class Book Rate' and I'll reimburse. Every shipment evaluated individually." No bondage, fat, or biracial. No *Playboy, Oui, Penthouse, Hustler, Chic, Club, Club International, Playgirl* or *Forum*.

> Hank Anthony
> PO Box 88
> Avila Beach, CA 93424

★ **Autographed *Playboy* playmate ephemera** including covers, gatefolds, and partial pages, but the photo must be from the magazine. Items may be dedicated ("To Bill," etc.) or not, but those without dedications are preferred, and bring from $20 to $50. Autographs of other women (actresses, models, celebrities) who have appeared in *Playboy* will be considered but only if they have signed the cover or photo spread in which they appear. Photocopy what you have.

> David Kveragas, McTieg Books
> 1943 Timberland
> Clarks Summit, PA 18411
> (717) 587-3429

★ **Alberto Vargas illustrations,** 1918-1960. "I'll buy magazine covers, Ziegfeld Follies posters, and other Vargas art depicting nudes, but only his work before he began drawing for *Playboy*." He does not want *Esquire* calendars unless they have their original jackets and is not interested in any of Vargas's *Playboy* art.

> David Kveragas
> McTieg Books
> 1943 Timberland
> Clarks Summit, PA 18411
> (717) 587-3429

★ **Explicit hardcover sex novels published in France in the 1920's through 1950's.** "Usually inexpensively bound, 4" x 6" or so, in English, there are many titles. I pay $40 to $100 each for all good condition usable titles, $50 to $150 in dust jacket. I am not looking for romance novels, but very explicit xxx-rated novels. Please ship first class mail for inspection and check by return mail. I'll pay post both ways."

> Hank Anthony
> PO Box 88
> Avila Beach, CA 93424

★ **Burlesque, strippers, and sexy dances.** Buys photos, posters, signs and any unusual items related to these skinful arts. Likes to find 3-D picture books and unusual pictorial items, especially art originals.

    Charles Martignette
    PO Box 293
    Hallandale, FL 33008
       (954) 454-3474

★ **Betty Brosmer photos** and other items related to this 1950's pin-up queen, including magazine covers and stories, newspaper articles, film loops, and videos of her TV appearances. Xerox™ copies of paper items are helpful. Date them if you can.

    Harold Forsko
    PO Box 57028-335
    Irvine, CA 92619
       (714) 261-6228

★ **Condom tins**, especially those with "nice colorful graphics" are wanted. The *Akron Tourist Tubes* tin which pictures a blimp is worth "about $250" but your old *Sheik, Ramses* and *Merry Widows* have no value nor do any tins in poor condition. Best if you make a Xerox™ of your tin to show its condition.

    Dennis and George Collectables
    3407 Lake Montebello Drive
    Baltimore, MD 21218
       (410) 889-3964

★ **Condom (prophylactic)** and **feminine hygiene** vending equipment, fine condition condom tins (the older and more colorful the better), and advertising relating to condoms or prophylactics, especially before 1960. Will buy single items or large lots.

    Mr. Condom
    1635 Acorn Ano Road
    Somerset, KY 42501
       (606) 274-4848

★ **Provocative or obscene photographs** including nudes, semi-nudes, candids, home made pictures, outdoor frolicking, etc., from teasing to hard core pornography. Also pin-up photos of dancers, starlets, and sexy ladies of all ages and periods.

    Charles Martignette
    PO Box 293
    Hallandale, FL 33008
       (954) 454-3474

MISC. HISTORIC EPHEMERA

★ **Immigration memorabilia.** "I'll buy documents, photos, pin-back buttons, ribbons, passports, pre-1920 naturalization certificates, books, postcards, and other material related to immigrants, Immigrant Aid Societies, Immigrant Social and Political Clubs, **Ellis Island**, Castle Garden, and ethnic festivals before 1950." Has particular interest in **Chinese immigration memorabilia**, and will consider purchase of anything having to do with movement of Chinese in the U.S. prior to 1950, including items related to **Chinese laundries** and Chinese social and political clubs. Also Immigration and Naturalization Service forms and documents from before 1930. Photocopy please.
>   K. Sheeran
>   PO Box 520251
>   Miami, FL 33152

★ **Radical movements' paper ephemera** from Tories of the American Revolution, the social and political radicals of the 1800's, the labor unionists, **women's suffrage**, etc., right down to and including the Black activists, **Peace movement**, and other "hippies" of the 1960's. Wants letters, documents, posters, broadsides, books, and pamphlets.
>   Ivan Gilbert
>   Miran Arts & Books
>   2824 Elm Avenue
>   Columbus, OH 43209
>   (614) 421-3222

★ **"The Beat generation" ephemera.** Wants items associated with "The Beat Generation" of the 1950's including books, records, posters, handbills, leaflets, underground newspapers, pins, comics, buttons, and the like, with a particular interest in the poets and authors associated with that era: Ginsburg, Rexroth, Burroughs, and Kerouac. Please state the condition, date, and how the item was stored.
>   Richard Synchef
>   16 Midway Avenue
>   Mill Valley, CA 94941
>   (415) 381-4448 days   Fax: (415) 381-4145

★ **Civil rights movement.** Wants buttons and paper ephemera, flyers, handbills, and pamphlets related to the civil rights movement.
>   Peggy Dillard
>   PO Box 210904
>   Nashville, TN 37221
>   (615) 646-1605 eves

★ **Civil Rights movement memorabilia** emphasizing **items relevant to Black Americans**, including **Jim Crow signs** (but only if authentic). Rare or one-of-a-kind items with strong provenance connected to a Black historical event or issue are most desired. "I DON'T WANT to buy books, sheet music, stereoviews, postcards, or any reproductions." Send a description, including the condition. You may set the price wanted or request offers. "I buy, sell, and trade."

> Elizabeth Meaders
> 94 Mersereau Avenue
> Staten Island, NY 10303
> (718) 727-0703

★ **Hippie items.** Wants items associated with the Counterculture of the 1960's including books, records, posters, handbills, leaflets, underground **newspapers** and **comics**, buttons, bumper stickers, etc., representative of 1960's student activism, the anti-war movement, Haight-Ashbury, the **1968 Democratic Convention**, Abbie Hoffman, Jerry Rubin, **Timothy Leary**, anti-LBJ, **anti-Nixon**, SDS, Yippies, Chicago Conspiracy Trial, the **Black Panthers**, drugs, **Woodstock**, Kent State, and the **Grateful Dead**. He DOES NOT WANT JFK items, jewelry, comic book reprints, Watergate, or common lp's. State condition, date, and how the item was stored.

> Richard Synchef
> 16 Midway Avenue
> Mill Valley, CA 94941
> (415) 381-4448 days   Fax: (415) 381-4145

★ **Political protest buttons** from the 1960's or before including civil rights, anti-war, leftist and student movements, etc. "I'm interested in any and all items, but their condition must be excellent. I do not want cracked, scratched or foxed items at *any* price." Send a Xerox of what you have along with a self addressed stamped envelope. Most buttons are from $3-$10.

> Michael Engel
> 29 Groveland Street
> Easthampton, MA 01027
> (413) 527-8733

★ **Slave tags.** These were small metal tags worn by slaves to indicate their status or occupation. Pays $200-$600 and up for tags reading SERVANT, PORTER, MECHANIC, SEAMSTRESS, FISHERMAN, FRUITERER, etc. Some rare types, dates, styles, or occupations can bring $1,500 or more. Call collect or ship insured for his offer. *Do not* clean the tags.

> Rich Hartzog
> Box 4143 BVT
> Rockford, IL 61110
> (815) 226-0771   Fax: (815) 397-7662

★ **Socialism and Communism in the U.S. before 1940.** "I'll buy anything pre-1940: books, magazines, leaflets, brochures, buttons, postcards, pennants, etc., that were produced by radical groups such as the Communist Party, Socialist Party, I.W.W. (Industrial Workers of the World), Socialist Labor Party, etc. Would especially like to find the magazines *Masses, New Masses,* and *International Socialist Review.*" Mike will purchase items written in Yiddish, Italian, and other foreign languages, but "I'm really not too interested in material not written in the U.S.A." What does Mike consider important? "Condition! Condition! Condition!"

Michael Stephens
2310 Valley Street
Berkeley, CA 94702
(510) 843-2780

★ **Labor union and Socialist material.** "I'll buy just about everything relating to organized labor, unions, and working people" including dues buttons and books, pins, convention and parade ribbons and badges, photographs of workers or unions, programs, contracts, labor trade cards, union magazines, books, and most any type of labor collectibles. "I'd like to find items about labor leaders, and the old and unusual from groups like the Knights of Labor, I.W.W., Railroad Brotherhood, AFL, and CIO. I'll consider anything but am most interested in learning about items before 1960."

Scott Molloy
550 Usquepaugh Road
West Kingston, RI 02892
(401) 782-3614

★ **Cigar Maker's Union and Samuel Gompers.** "I'd like to know about anything from or about the Cigar Maker's Union or any of its top officers, including stamps, pamphlets, regulations, photographs, and letterhead." Does anyone have a letter by **Samuel Gompers** on CMIU stationery? Or a copy of the papers that dissolved the Union into the Retail Clerks? Please include photocopies and price or ask for offer.

Tony Hyman
PO Box 3028
Pismo Beach, CA 93448
(805) 773-6777   Fax: (805) 773-8436   thyman@tobacciana.com

★ **Spy material.** Will consider anything you have related to real spies, from any country, any period: documents, signatures, photos, etc.

Keith Melton
PO Box 5755
Bossier City, LA 71171
(318) 747-9616

★ **British and European Royalty.** "Try me with whatever you have that's colorful, interesting, and in fine condition. No junk, no plastic, and nothing damaged."

    Pat Klein
    PO Box 262
    East Berlin, CT 06023
        (860) 828-3973 eves

★ **British Royal commemoratives.** Buys nearly any fine condition pictorial item, including ceramics, textiles, tins, plates, mugs, medals, busts, jewelry, paperweights, dolls, postcards, programs and more from various ceremonies and events involving British royalty from Queen Victoria to Queen Elizabeth Reign, including Prince Charles, Princess Diana, and Prince William. Will consider single items or large lots. Please send an SASE with complete descriptions, including condition. Photo or photocopy is desirable. Please do not send anything without prior approval. Audrey is the author of *British Royal Commemoratives*, available from her for $28 postpaid.

    Audrey Zeder
    6755 Coralite T
    Long Beach, CA 90808

★ **All fraternal order** materials that are small and flat, such as coins, tokens, medals, badges and ribbons. Especially interested in Masonic chapter pennies and hand engraved badges of precious metal. Will consider larger BPOE items or unusual fraternal items. If what you have is pre-1930, ship it to him for an offer. Hartzog will send you a check for the lot. He claims to pay higher prices than anyone else.

    Rich Hartzog
    PO Box 4143 BVT
    Rockford, IL 61110

★ **Odd Fellows items** including badges, medals, banners, posters, jewelry, furniture, arks, collars, signs, windows, lighting fixtures, rugs, and anything else with the three link emblem on it.

    Greg Spiess
    230 East Washington
    Joliet, IL 60433
        (815) 722-5639 days

★ **Mafia or organized crime items** including books, **magazines**, photographs, autographs, videotapes, recordings, government reports, and any other memorabilia or artifacts. "I'd love to find a poster from the Italian American Civil Rights League meeting of June 28th, 1971." Wants nothing fictional.

Ron Ridenour
PO Box 357
Moorpark, CA 93020
(800) 457-7473 days

★ **Newsboy memorabilia.** "In the 19th and early 20th century, street urchins and orphans spent their childhoods hawking newspapers for pennies a day. I want their badges, buttons, licenses, aprons and other memorabilia, including premiums and advertising which they distributed such as buttons, rulers, pocket mirrors, toys, etc., which advertised newspapers. Early badges can be worth $100 or more. I do not want the newspapers themselves, just the items used or given away by the children who sold them." A photo or photocopy is best, along with your description. Include an SASE for answer.

Tony Lee
PO Box 134
Monmouth Junction, NJ 08852
(201) 429-1531 eves

★ **Newsboy statues** around the U.S. including souvenir replicas, advertising for the figurines, and photos of any statue of a newsboy. Replicas of the statues bring $50 or more.

Gary Leveille
PO Box 562
Great Barrington, MA 01239

★ **3-D metal replicas of famous buildings and monuments.** Buys paperweights, banks, salt and pepper shakers, ashtrays...anything that is made of metal into a three dimensional representation of a famous place or structure. He does not want miniatures that you can buy today: Eiffel tower, US Capitol, Empire State building, Statue of Liberty, etc. Identify the building, give dimensions, and report any names or marks on the piece.

Dave Forman
1914 11th Street #3
Santa Monica, CA 90404
(310) 396-1272   Fax: (310) 392-1400

★ **Eastman Colleges.** "I'll buy anything you can find on Eastman Colleges, including postcards, books, paper ephemera, money, etc."

C.J. Meccarello
1572 Bowmans Trail
Lakeland, FL 33809

POLITICS

★ **Presidential political items of all sorts.** Will buy buttons, banners, ribbons, and paper material, especially from **candidates of the 1920's,** Coolidge, Davis, Harding, LaFollette, Cox, Hoover, Smith, and Debs, with a strong interest in **Calvin Coolidge**. Please don't send him any *Kleenex* button reproductions, other reproductions, or anything in poor condition. This well known collector/ dealer has been active for 30 years. He requests a Xerox™ and thorough description. The price you'd like is appreciated but "I will make a fair offer if you have no idea of an item's value."

> Larry L. Krug
> Americana Resources
> 18222 Flower Hill Way #299
> Gaithersburg, MD 20879
> (301) 926-8663   Fax: (301) 926-7648   larry.krug@amres.com

★ **Presidential campaign memorabilia made of paper or cloth,** from any campaign before 1976. *All* candidates are wanted including third party or those who lost in primaries, but **Lincoln** is a particular favorite. Small paper items from the 19th century are generally worth from $5-$15 and include pamphlets, posters, tickets, sample ballots, and cards of any kind. Cloth items such as bandanas, flags, ties, ribbons, and handkerchiefs are wanted, as long as they were used in a presidential campaign. He'll pay $75-$250 for bandanas picturing candidates. He does not buy buttons, bumper stickers, or daily newspapers. Prefers to buy piles of paper rather than single pieces, unless the items are early or unusual. When writing, indicate the candidate, the year (if you know), the size, any slogans or messages, and what's pictured.

> Charles Hatfield
> 1411 South State Street
> Springfield, IL 62704

★ **Abraham Lincoln presidential campaign memorabilia** including items related to **his various opponents**: Douglas, Bell, Breckinridge, McClellan, and Jefferson Davis. Will buy flags, banners, posters, tokens, ribbons, and photo badges. This 30 year veteran collector/dealer DOES NOT WANT autographs, engravings, newspapers, magazines, memorial items created after his death, or commemoratives of any sort. "I'll only buy items issued during an election or for Lincoln's two inaugurations." He wants a photocopy or photo, or a sketch with dimensions and information about material, inscriptions, and all defects. "I must see an item before I buy."

Don edits *The Rail Splitter* quarterly, available for $12.

> Donald Ackerman
> PO Box 3487
> Wallington, NJ 07057
>   (201) 779-8785 eves   Fax: (201) 744-1517

★ **Presidential memorabilia** including glass, china, campaign buttons and ribbons, **White House gift items**, inauguration medals, invitations, Xmas cards, etc. Will pay $4,000 for a mint condition Theodore Roosevelt inaugural medal. Author of *Collectors Guide to Presidential Inaugural Medals and Memorabilia.*

> H. Joseph Levine
> 6550-I Little River Turnpike
> Alexandria, VA 22312
> (703) 354-5454

★ **Political campaign items of all kinds.** Top priority given to better 19th century items, especially those associated with **Abraham Lincoln** and his contemporaries in the Civil War period. "I'll buy buttons, badges, ribbons, banners, tintypes, portrait flags, and three dimensional objects," says this 25 year veteran dealer /collector, but he is not interested in any buttons later than 1960 (Kennedy/Nixon), or in 20th century buttons that do not have pictures or something unusual. Except for political quilts, he does not buy commemorative items not actually issued as part of a campaign. A photocopy or photo "is of great help." **Third party candidates** from all eras are a special interest as well.

> Cary Demont
> PO Box 16013
> Minneapolis, MN 55416
> (612) 922-1617   Fax: (612) 922-3637

★ **Political buttons, tokens, and ribbons and other items from any election before 1925.** Consignments to his auction are invited. Send a Xerox™ or ship your item for his offer.

> Rich Hartzog, World Exonumia
> PO Box 4143 BVT
> Rockford, IL 61110
> (815) 226-0771

★ **Presidential, gubernatorial, and Congressional campaign memorabilia.** "I'll consider any and all items used in a political campaign for president, governor, U.S. Senate or the House of Representatives, including buttons, ribbons, banners, pennants, posters, and 3-D items like canes and hats." You are encouraged to inquire as " an item may look common but be very scarce." Send a Xerox™ copy. If this is not possible, this veteran of 21 years collecting and dealing asks you to give the size, color and condition of your item.

> David Quintin
> PO Box 800861
> Dallas, TX 75380
> (214) 934-1151 days   Fax: (214) 934-2660

★ **Presidential campaign memorabilia including political buttons** are wanted. Of special interest are:
- All **pre-1896 campaign items** including lapel badges, ribbons, bandannas, posters, cans, and "just about anything else" related to Presidential candidates;
- **Campaign buttons** and similar small items related to Presidential campaigns from 1896 through the campaign of 1972;
- **Buttons for 3rd part candidates, social issues, labor, anti-war, civil rights** and other causes from 1896 to 1972;

Ted would like to see Xerox™ copies and have you note any defects such as stains, scratches or cracks as all damage has an effect on value. For larger items, a photo is recommended, giving dimensions and again noting any damage. Ted does not buy buttons newer than 1952 that have only a candidate's name. You should check the inside of your button's edge and watch for the words KLEENEX, A-O 1972, OR REPRODUCTION, as a great many reproduction buttons exist. Tentative offers can be made from photocopies or photographs, but final evaluation depends upon personal inspection prior to payment. "Payments are made immediately upon receipt if condition matches the description." Ted is one of the country's largest buyers of campaign and pop culture items (*see his listing in that category*) and is author of numerous books on political buttons, campaign collectibles and pop culture which are considered standard references among collectors and dealers. You are encouraged to send an SASE for a catalog of available titles.

    Ted Hake
    Hake's Americana Dept 343
    PO Box 1444
    York, PA 17405
        (717) 848-1333 10-5 Monday-Friday

★ **Presidential campaign items**: buttons, badges, ribbons, tokens, canes, flags, china, posters, bandanas, banners, torches, lanterns, and novelty items. Does not want books. Has been buying and selling these items for 30+ years, and offers catalogs for $3 each.

    Historical Collections
    PO Box 42
    Waynesboro, PA 17268

★ **Presidential campaign** buttons, ribbons, and posters. This active collector does not want common buttons like "I Like Ike" or "Nixon's the One." Offers free appraisals, but an SASE is a must.

    Peggy Dillard
    PO Box 210904
    Nashville, TN 37221
        (615) 646-1605 eves

★ **Political buttons from state and local candidates** before 1930, the more odd and obscure, the better." Also buys other early campaign items, paper, ribbons, etc., used by mayors, congressmen, state legislators, county and municipal officials. Most desirable are buttons from famous persons and Presidents running for minor offices early in their career. "I'm interested in any and all items, but their condition must be excellent. Most buttons are $3-$10 with some much higher, but I do not want cracked, scratched or foxed items at *any* price." Send a Xerox of your button along with a stamped envelope.

> Michael Engel
> 29 Groveland Street
> Easthampton, MA 01027
> (413) 527-8733

★ **Election memorabilia of all types, 1780-1960**, for resale, especially higher quality items.. Wants china, ribbons, mirrors, clocks, glass, paintings, textiles, etc., that are **political or patriotic** in content. "I'll pay from $500-$5,000 for small historical medallions with pewter rims and lithographed portraits of military and political figures." Rex does not do free appraisals. Please don't contact him unless you want to *sell*. He does not want paper items after 1896.

> Rex Stark, Auctioneer
> 49 Wethersfield Road
> Bellingham, MA 02019
> (508) 966-0994

★ **Women's suffrage items:** "I'll buy anything related to the suffrage movement. I'm particularly interested in pinback buttons, badges, posters, ribbons, banners and 3-D items that say VOTES FOR WOMEN and related slogans. I Especially seek items that picture or mention Victoria Woodhull, Belva Lockwood, Susan B. Anthony, or Carrie Nation. If you send a photocopy, I'll pay top dollar."

> Cary Demont
> PO Box 16013
> Minneapolis, MN 55416
> (612) 922-1617   Fax: (612) 922-3637

★ **Women's suffrage and political campaign** items, especially 19th century buttons, ribbons, posters, and pennants.

> Ken Florey
> 153 Haverford
> Hamden, CT 06517
> (203) 248-1233

★ **William Jennings Bryan and Thomas Dewey memorabilia** of all types are wanted. Please send a Xerox™ or send your item for an offer.
>   Rich Hartzog
>   World Exonumia
>   Box 4143 BVT
>   Rockford, IL 61110
>   (815) 226-0771

★ **Personal and other memorabilia related to Harding, Coolidge, Hoover, FDR** and **Al Smith**. Documentation will be requested.
>   Michael Graham
>   Roaring 20's
>   33133 O'Plaine Road
>   Gurnee, IL 60031
>   (847) 263-6285

★ **Richard M. Nixon collectibles.** "I'll buy campaign collectibles, anti-Nixon items, and Watergate related ephemera including, but not limited to, buttons, jewelry, textiles, glassware, medals, coins, games, novelties, pens and pencils, pocket knives, keychains, stamps, stickers, caricatures, matchbooks, postcards, puzzles, headgear…almost anything picturing or referring to Nixon." He does not want magazines, posters, bumper stickers, and newspapers. He is interested in Nixon's entire history as a public figure. Please send a "crisp photocopy or photo of the item along with a description of all flaws such as foxing, chips, scratches, fading, etc." Include the price you'd like (although he will make offers to amateurs) and SASE if you want photos returned.
>   Eldon Almquist
>   975 Maunawili Circle
>   Kailua, HI 96734
>   (808) 262-9837 eves   nixco@aol.com

★ **Gubernatorial (governor) or U.S. Senate race political buttons** from any state. Pays $25-$50 each for those he can use. Photocopy. Describe condition if there are any problems not evident.
>   Dave Quintin
>   PO Box 800861
>   Dallas, TX 75380
>   (214) 934-1151   Fax: (214) 934-2660

❖
> *Some collectors pay for information where a particularly rare item might be found. So if you see something in an antique shop that you think is particularly nice, you may get a fee for reporting it. Give as much information as you can, but most important, don't forget the phone number of the antique shop in which the item can be found.*

★ **Illinois and Chicago politicians of the 1920's.** Wants posters, pamphlets, photographs, and buttons from Chicago politicians of the prohibition era such as mayors William Thompson, William Dever, and Anton Cermak. Also Illinois Governor Len Small, US Senator Charles Deneen, and Cook County States Attorney Robert Crowe. Especially wants items related to prohibition and gangsters. If offering personal items, documentation will be requested.

> Michael Graham's Roaring 20's
> 33133 O'Plaine Road
> Gurnee, IL 60031
> (847) 263-6285

★ **Tennessee and other Southern political items.** Interested primarily in races for Senate, Congress and Governor in any Southern state. Pictorial buttons a favorite. Xerox© what you have.

> Peggy Dillard
> PO Box 210904
> Nashville, TN 37221
> (615) 646-1605 eves

★ **North and South Carolina political buttons and ephemera** with a special interest in locating items from Taft's 1909 visit to Charlotte. Asks that you photocopy and describe all defects.

> Lew Powell
> 700 East Park Ave.
> Charlotte, NC 28203
> (704) 358-5229 or (704) 334-0902

★ **Canadian election memorabilia,** pin back buttons and badges from Canadian political campaigns before 1965, especially material on John MacDonald and Wilfred Laurier. Small items may be sent on approval. If Mike does not buy them, he will reimburse your postage.

> Michael Rice
> PO Box 286
> Saanichton, BC
> V8M 2C5 CANADA

POLITICAL SYMBOLS

★ **American flags.** "I'll buy cloth flags from 6" to huge. Prices depend upon the pattern in the stars, size, condition, construction technique, etc. "The following will give an idea of the minimum prices that this particular social studies teacher pays for flags:

- 13's are almost always reproductions and not wanted;
- 15 to 35 stars bring $85;
- 36, 37, 38, 40, and 41's bring at least $65;
- 43's and 47's are worth $95;
- 44's are only $45;
- 39, 42, 45, 46, and 48's are wanted *only* if they have an unusual configuration of stars or have pictures or advertising; these are definitely *not* wanted if the stars are in straight rows.

Sellers may add 50% more for unusual configurations such as circular, stars in stars, overprinted flags containing some message, or if they are all hand sewn. If the flag advertises a political candidate, prices should be multiplied by at least five times. Description should include the size, condition, and star pattern. No repros or pictures of flags."

Mark Sutton
2035 St. Andrews Circle
Carmel, IN 46032
(317) 844-5648

★ **Statue of Liberty.** Wants French bronzes of the statue, books from before 1890, advertising items depicting or satirizing the statue, tin signs or containers, bottles, thimbles, lamps, medals and tokens, and other 19th century items related to Liberty or sculptor **Auguste Bartholdi**. Wants U.S. Committee 6" or 12" pot metal models sold to raise money for the pedestal and will pay $300 to $1,000. Wants early ones only. Photo or photocopy requested. Not interested in postcards or centennial items.

Mike Brooks
7335 Skyline
Oakland, CA 94611
(510) 339-1751

★ **Statue of Liberty items.** What have you? Send a photo or photocopy of what you have to this well known stamp dealer.

Harvey Dolin & Company
5 Beekman Street #406
New York, NY 10038
(212) 267-0216

INDIAN ARTIFACTS

★ **Antique American Indian and Eskimo items.** Buys quality items made before 1920 by Indians and Eskimos: baskets, bead work, quill work, pottery, clothing, weapons, old Navajo rugs, and blankets. He'll even buy beaded souvenirs made by Indians (like match holders, picture frames, etc.). If you've got a 16 foot long birch bark canoe, he might buy that too. He does not buy any Indian jewelry, arrowheads and other stone, books, or modern items purchased ten years ago at a trading post on the Interstate. A photo is a must, and please list dimensions and any flaws the piece has in your first letter. Dealers, price your goods, as he makes offers to amateur sellers only. Answers inquiries promptly. This veteran collector is an advisor on Indian collectibles to several antiques publications, can handle any size collection, and is willing to refer you to other buyers. "If you have quality items to sell, chances are I can put a deal together for you."

> Barry Friedman
> PO Box 55492
> Valencia, CA 91385
> (805) 255-2365   BarryF@fishnet.net

★ **Indian artifacts** including arrowheads, stone axes, celts, pipes, flints, ceremonial pieces, bannerstones, birdstones, baskets, beaded items, pottery, rugs, blankets, masks, wooden bowls, and any other Indian related items. He will pay high prices ($500-$1,000) for ancient birdstones he can use for his own collection. Please list what you have and make a drawing or photocopy, giving all measurements. Include your home and work phone. This 40 year veteran holds 4-6 auctions a year of Indian artifacts and is always ready to buy or sell good items.

> Jan Sorgenfrei
> 10040 State Road 224 West
> Findlay, OH 45840
> (419) 422-8531 days

★ **Hopi and Zuni Pueblo Kachina dolls.** "I especially want those made between 1900 and 1940. Other Indian items, dance wands, costume parts, pottery, baskets, and jewelry from Southwest Indians are also of interest." Kachina dolls can range in value from $100 to $5,000 or more, but there are many fake Kachinas. "An expert can tell the difference." He'll need a photo and all background information.

> John C. Hill
> Antique Indian Art Gallery
> 6962 East First Ave.
> Scottsdale, AZ 85251
> (602) 946-2910   Fax: (602) 946-7410

The value of an Indian artifact depends

on its size, age, condition, workmanship,
eye appeal and authenticity.
Because values can be quite high,
it's a good idea to check out all
Indian items which have been in your
family since before World War II.

★ **Museum quality American Indian relics.** "I'll buy fine baskets, pre-1900 Plains bead work, quill work, weapons, Southwestern pots, pre-1940 jewelry, Kachinas, early Navajo weavings, blankets and rugs, Northwest Coast masks and carvings, Eskimo objects, old photos of Indians, and more. Some of these items can be worth $10,000 or more." Dan does not want arrowheads, stone material, anything modern, small pots, or reproductions of early work.

     Daniel Brown
     PO Box 149
     Davenport, CA 95017
         (800) 492-6786   (408) 426-0134

★ **Indian baskets, pottery and other art** are wanted by this nationally known folk art expert.

     Louis Picek
     PO Box 340
     West Branch, IA 52358

★ **North and South American Indian rugs** and weavings are sought by this major rug dealer. Color photo and dimensions, please.

     Renate Halpern
     Halpern Galleries
     325 East 79th Street
     New York, NY 10021
         (212) 988-9316   Fax: (212) 988-2954

★ **American Indian and Eskimo art and artifacts,** including rugs, crafts, baskets, pottery, weapons, and clothing, especially old beaded buckskin moccasins. The museum does not buy modern Indian items. Prefers a color photo be sent with your inquiry. Prefers you price what you have to sell, but "our appraiser will suggest a value for your item, but only after examination of it in person."

     Lynn Munger
     Potawatomi Museum
     PO Box 631
     Fremont, IN 46737
         (219) 495-2340

★ **Indian totems and carvings** from before 1950, including good quality items made for the tourist trade. Please provide a physical description, noting all obvious signs of damage. If you know the history of the ownership of the item, please give that information as well. Photos are helpful.

> Edwin Snyder
> PO Box 156
> Lancaster, KY 40444
> (606) 792-4816 eves

★ **Seminole Indian items** of all type made before 1930.

> Douglas Hendriksen
> Box 21153
> Kennedy Space Center, FL 32815
> (407) 867-2551 days   (407) 452-0633 eves

★ **Stone age artifacts,** including stone and bone tools, arrowheads, blades, pottery and other art and utilitarian objects. This 18 year veteran collector/dealer does not want modern American Indian items. Please include a photo with your description.

> Scott Young
> PO Box 8452
> Port St. Lucie, FL 34984
> (561) 878-5634

COWBOY ARTIFACTS

★ **Silver mounted parade saddles and spurs** by all makers, especially G. S. Garcia, Edward H. Bohlin or Visalia Stock Saddle Company. Always seeking quality cowboy items, such as fancy antique chaps and boots. Please send complete details along with a photo. This veteran collector is Indian/Western advisor to several antique publications.

> Barry Friedman
> PO Box 55492
> Valencia, CA 91385
> (805) 255-2365   BarryF@fishnet.net

★ **Antique cowboy regalia** such as chaps, holsters, belts, badges, hats, boots, saddles and lassos. Also buys *Colt* and *Winchester* guns and rifles pre-1900. No reproductions or fakes. You must include photo and your asking price, and will be expected to ship for inspection.

> Pierre Bovis, The Az-Tex Cowboy Trading Co.
> PO Box 13345
> Tucson, AZ 85732
> (520) 318-9512   Fax: (520) 318-0023

★ **Cowboy equipment and regalia** including:
* **Spurs** of all types except English and new military. Especially wants unusual spurs that are silver and maker marked;
* **Cuffs** made of leather, chaps, hats, scarves, and fancy boots;
* **Western saddles**, pre-1920, all types if maker marked, including black military McClellan saddles;
* **Saddle bags** with maker's marks;
* **Reatas, quirts,** and **bridles** that are marked, tooled, or carved;
* **Horse bits** more than 50 years old with silver mounts or inlay; some plain and/or foreign bought; inquire about any old bit;
* **Prison made spurs**, horse bits, quirts, belts, and lead ropes;
* **Catalogs for saddle makers** pre-1936;
* **Photographs** of old cowboy scenes;
* **Advertising related to the frontier**, especially watch fobs;
* **Movie posters** of cowboy movies;
* **Books by Will James**.

Especially wants marked spurs authenticated as having been made for some well known personality. Does not want anything made in the last 25 years or made in the Far East. In your description, make certain to describe all marks. Give dimensions and mention all damage or repairs. He prefers you to set the price, but will make offers to amateur sellers. No guns! Will buy single items or collections for resale.

Lee Jacobs
PO Box 3098
Colorado Springs, CO 80934
(719) 473-7101

★ **Cowboy gear** from before 1940 including Western guns, chaps, spurs, bits, brand books, law badges, saddles, reatas, quirts, cowboy hats, boots, vests, neckerchiefs, leather cuffs, early knives, beaded or embroidered gauntlets, and fine braided bridles or other items. Also wants old related catalogs, photos, documents, books, maps, and other items related to the life of the cowboy. He is most interested in spurs, holsters and cartridge belts which have maker's marks. Exceptional items can bring many thousands of dollars. Send a good photo and a description of your item, including a statement of condition. This 30 year veteran collector and museum curator, does not want horse collars, harnesses, and other farm related items. Bill's *Cowboy and Gunfighter Collectibles*, complete with price guide, is $22.

Bill Mackin
Museum of Northwest Colorado
1137 Washington Street
Craig, CO 81625
(970) 824-6717

★ **Cowboy clothing, gear, artifacts** and **ephemera.** Wants everything associated with both working cowboys and badmen and peace officers: clothing, trail maps and brand books, wanted posters, "historically important letters," photos of cowboys, badmen, and peace officers. Has strong interest in anything you have relevant to the lives of **Samuel Colt, Sam Houston** and **Benito Juarez.**

    Johnny Spellman
    10806 North Lamar Blvd.
    Austin, TX 78753
       (512) 836-2889 days   (512) 258-6910 eves

★ **Antique Western items** including boots, Stetson hats, gold-braided Mexican sombreros, chaps, leather cuffs, saddlebags, holsters, photos, letters of lawmen or gunfighters, rodeo pennants, tack catalogs, horsehair items made in prison, trunks covered with hide, and the like. This veteran price guide advisor will buy or broker any size collection. "If you've got good stuff, I can move it for you."

    Barry Friedman
    PO Box 55492
    Valencia, CA 91385
       (805) 255-2365   BarryF@fishnet.net

★ **Steer horns** from the 1930's or earlier. "Older horns are wrapped in various types of old cloth, buggy seat material, or natural hair. The wrapped center piece will usually be no more than 12" or 13" wide. Old horns will usually be various shades of yellow, brown, or dark green, frequently with black tips. Newer horns, **which I absolutely do not want**, are wrapped in tooled leather, vinyl or rope and are usually ivory or a mottled color. Newer ones also have wide, often 18" space between horns. The best old horns have heavy amounts of twist and curl, are mounted on a wood backboard, and are five to seven feet wide from tip to tip. The wrapping on most old horns is frequently in poor condition, so I am much more concerned with the condition of the horns themselves, with no cracks or serious bug damage. A photo is a must. Include the measurements from tip to tip and the measurements across the middle piece where the cow's skull would have been. If you can't send a color photo, make certain to describe the twist and the color of the horns, as well as the type of material." He also wants to buy **photographs of longhorn cattle.**

    Alan Rogers
    1012 Shady Drive
    Kansas City, MO 64118
       (816) 436-9008

WEIRD & MORBID THINGS

★ **Anything odd, unusual** or **morbid,** especially:
  • **Two headed calves** and other **freak animals,** natural or man-made, alive or mounted and preserved;
  • **Mummies, skeletons** and **human skulls;**
  • **Shrunken heads** and other **headhunter** and **cannibal items;**
  • **Funeral equipment,** coffins, embalming kits, and **tombstones;**
  • **Torture** and **execution devices** and photos of executions;
  • **Mounted reptiles, trophy heads** and **uncommon animals;**
  • **Man-made mermaids** (up to $300);
  • **Medicine show** photos and literature;
  • **Tattoo equipment,** tattoo photos, and tattooed skin;
  • **Voodoo** and **black magic** ephemera;
  • **Flea Circus** props and photos;
  • **Human oddity** photos and artifacts.

For 50+ years, this wheelchair bound vet has been buying odd, unusual, and bizarre items for public exhibit in his traveling and stationary museums. He does not buy furniture, clothing, plates, or jewelry. If you have something you think he might want, send a photo, a description, a statement of condition, and your lowest price.

Harvey Lee Boswell's Palace of Wonders
PO Box 446
Elm City, NC 27822
(919) 291-7181

★ **Human skulls,** preferably with more than 30 teeth. Send a photo or description, any background of it you know, and your phone number.

Mark Miller
PO Box 52261
Philadelphia, PA 19115
(215) 464-3561 voice and fax   70176.1153@compuserve.com

★ **Giant people.** "I'll buy postcards, pictures and other information about American giants (not the sports team, but real giants) including giant rings, souvenirs sold by giants, books by or about giants, etc."

Don Gorlick
PO Box 24541
Seattle, WA 98124
(206) 824-0508

★ **Skulls, skeletons, tusks, teeth, fossils, shrunken heads** and **mounted insects.** This relatively new dealer does not make offers.

Ronald Cauble, The Bone Room
1569 Solano Ave
Berkeley, CA 94707
(510) 526-5252   evolve@boneroom.com

★ **Animal trophies, skulls,** skins, fur rugs, teeth, claws, horns, antlers, and the like. Please give your phone number with your description.
David Boone, Boone Trading Company
562 Coyote Road
Brinnon, WA 98320
(206) 796-4330 (800) 423-1945 Fax: (206) 796-4511

★ **Shrunken heads from the Jivaro tribe.** Please send a photograph or description, including whatever history of the item which you know. Include your phone number.
Mark Miller
PO Box 52261
Philadelphia, PA 19115
(215) 464-3561 voice and fax 70176.1153@compuserve.com

★ **Funeral ephemera.** "I'll buy things having to do with funerals such as funeral parlor advertising, mirrors, ribbons, trays, badges, and other items issued by funeral parlors. I am not interested in caskets, funeral or embalming equipment, or cemeteries."
Rich Hartzog
PO Box 4143 BVT
Rockford, IL 61110
(815) 226-0771 Fax: (815) 397-7662

★ **Cemetery ephemera.** "I'll buy books, maps, magazines, photos, catalogs, deeds, etc., related to the cemetery business, especially:
• Cemetery advertising from before 1920;
• Maps and deeds of cemeteries, before 1900;
• Sales catalogs for mausoleums, before 1940;
• Photos and real photo postcards of mausoleums;
• Magazines like *The Cemetery Beautiful*;
• Burial society certificates, before 1940.
Since these are paper items, include a photocopy. "Do not confuse cemeteries with funerals. I am interested in land, monuments, and mausoleums, not funerals and embalming. The only funeral item I want is *The American Funeral Gazette* from the early 1880's." Not interested in colored photo postcards of famous tombs or cemeteries.
Steve Spevak
PO Box 3173
Winchester, VA 22604

★ **Death and postmortem photos,** casket photos, black bordered photos, hair lockets with photos, as well as dissection and other unusual medical photos.
Steve DeGenaro
PO Box 5662
Youngstown, OH 44504
(330) 757-7735

BLACK & NEGRO MEMORABILIA

★ **African-American historical memorabilia.** This serious historian/collector/dealer wants artifacts and paper associated with the history of African-Americans in the United States.
- **Black militaria.** "I will buy any and all items specific to African-American participation in wars from the Revolution through Vietnam, especially named medals, uniforms, equipment, documents, photos, and prints.
- **Books** dealing with Black military history;
- **Items associated with historically important Blacks**, including sports and entertainment figures, "the earlier the better;"
- **Slavery items;**
- **Jim Crow signs,** but only if authentic;
- Civil Rights movement memorabilia.

Rare or one-of-a-kind items with strong provenance connected to a Black historical event are most desired. "I don't want books, sheet music, stereo cards or postcards, or any reproductions." Send a good description, including the condition. You may set the price wanted or request offers. "I buy, sell, and trade."

Elizabeth Meaders
94 Mersereau Avenue
Staten Island, NY 10303
(718) 727-0703

★ **Items depicting Blacks in an exaggerated, comic or derogatory manner** "I'll buy anything made before 1920 with Black Americans (not African natives) such as minstrel posters, spoons, toys, advertising, figurines, sheet music, postcards, trade cards, and the like." Emphasizes that he does not want reproductions. This authority on Black American items wants a careful description of condition.

Sam Ginsberg
PO Box 24944
Ft. Lauderdale, FL 33307
(954) 566-3344 voice or fax   ginsberg@icanect.net

★ **Black memorabilia** that is comic or exaggerated including cookie jars, plates, lamps, clocks, salt and pepper shakers, table cloths, towels, plaster or ceramic items, and other household items depicting Blacks. "I also buy advertising pieces of all kinds that depict a Black person, including whiskey ads, *Aunt Jemima* items, *Cream of Wheat* packs, *Uncle Ben's Rice* memorabilia, etc."

Diane Cauwels
3947 Old South Road
Murfreesboro, TN 371298
(615) 896-3614   (615) 896-3614

★ **Items depicting Blacks in an exaggerated, comic or stereotypical way** including cookie jars, older dolls, toys, kitchen items, prints, Black folk art, children's books, *Uncle Remus*, advertising items, *Aunt Jemima, Cream of Wheat, Amos 'n Andy*, and "all items relating to Blacks in America. Buys one piece or a collection." Wants include **golliwogs, Little Black Sambo, Nicodemus, Pickaninnies**, etc. "I also buy literature, poetry, humor, and other books by or about Blacks. I want vintage entertainment related **minstrel material, Amos 'n' Andy, Josephine Baker, Hattie McDaniel**, etc. I DO NOT buy African art or artifacts, slave items, or KKK material. No magazine ads or reproductions. All offers welcome and will be answered if you include SASE."

Judy Posner (May to Oct)   Judy Posner (Nov to April)
Route 1   Box 273 W   4195 S Tamiami Trail #183W
Effort, PA 18330   Venice Fl 34293
(717) 629-6583 in PA   (941) 497-7149 in FL judyandjef@aol.com

★ **All items depicting Blacks** in a manner that is exaggerated, comic, or realistic including dolls, folk art, sewing items, walking sticks, miniature bronzes, jewelry, paintings, valentines, playing cards, games, children's books, cookie jars, string holders, spoons, *Golliwogs*, linens, jigsaw puzzles, candy containers, Christmas ornaments, and items associated with the *Our Gang* comedy's Farina. No postcards, sheet music, trade cards, photos, outhouse figures, ads, large signs, damaged items, or reproductions. This active dealer/collector does not make offers.

Jan Thalberg
23 Mountain View Drive
Weston, CT 06883
(203) 227-8175

★ **Popular portrayals of Black dancers** on sheet music, figurines, postcards, etc. Wants dancers doing the cake walk, jitterbug, etc.

William Sommer
9 West 10th Street
New York, NY 10011
(212) 260-0999

★ **K.K.K. items** of all type, including robes, swords, pamphlets, jewelry, knives, badges, medals, china, banners, books, letters, newspapers, magazines, figurines, rituals, etc. This buyer is a serious historian of this movement, not a Klan member. "Please, no hate mail."

Historical Collections
PO Box 42
Waynesboro, PA 17268

★ **Ku Klux Klan activity in the U.S.,** especially the 1920's Midwest.

Michael Graham's Roaring 20's
33133 O'Plaine Road
Gurnee, IL 60031

SCOUTING MEMORABILIA

★ **Scouting items from Boy Scouts, Girl Scouts and Lone Scouts**, especially before 1940.
- **Uniforms, badges**, and **pins**. Patches with WWW from Order of the Arrow lodges, and badges from Senior Scout and Explorer groups particularly needed;
- **Rank and Honor medals**: lifesaving medals, medals for war service, Eagle, Ranger, Silver, Ace and Quartermaster medals, and World Jamboree medals; he notes that some medals are worth $1,000;
- **Girl Scout uniforms** (either blue or khaki) with badges, Golden Eaglet pins, senior GS pins in blue or green, and leader pins;
- **Cub Scout items** marked CUBS USA, not with CUB SCOUTS BSA;
- **Girl and Boy Scout dolls,** soft or composition, in all sizes, if complete. *Kenner Steve Scout* dolls from 1975, if mint in box. All *Steve Scout* accessories, such as a summer uniform;
- **Scout toys and games**, including figures, boards, etc.;
- Scout table model *Bakelite* radios from the late 1930's;
- Official **books and other literature** including manuals and magazines before 1930, merit badge pamphlets and Cub Scout literature from before 1940, and "all Air Scout stuff".
- **Historical items** related to founders of Scouting, including Baden-Powell, Juliette Low, Seton, Beard, West, Boyce, and Robinson. Also wants books by or about these people.

When you are offering things to them for sale, they remind "a photo-copy is worth 1,000 words."
> Fran and Cal Holden
> PO Box 264-H
> Doylestown, OH 44230
> (800) 663-2793

★ **Girl Scout memorabilia.** "Try me for anything that says or means Girl Scout." She especially wants very old items, Mariner and Wing Scout items, Senior GS items, all pre-1945 items, World's Fair items, war time items, and items from Camp Edith Macy, Our Chalet, and Our Ark. Make certain to note condition and whether any-thing is missing. Asking price is appreciated. Since she will buy so many items, it is important to note she does NOT want the following: handbooks after 1918, 1940's green uniform, 1960's green cotton or Dacron Brownie and Intermediate uniforms, 1960's forest green two piece senior uniform, 1970's or 80's uniforms, any mess kits, canteens, back packs, sleeping bags, and other big camping gear after 1925.
> Phyllis Palm
> PO Box 5272
> Mt. Carmel, CT 06518

★ **Boy Scout memorabilia and patches,** especially Order of the Arrow patches with WWW on them (for which he will pay from $2.50 to $1,000+). Items from National Order of the Arrow conferences from 1948 and earlier are especially sought, although *staff* items from *all* NOAC's are needed. Early Order of the Arrow National Committee items are needed such as the red felt sash which is worth $2,000. Pre-1960 National Jamboree *staff* items are wanted, as are pre-1955 World Jamboree items. As a general rule, the older the patch, the better. However, this does not apply to patches which have only local interest such as camporees, Scout-O-Ramas, Scout circus, and other local items. Ron says, "before you sell, compare what I pay to other offers."

> Ron Aldridge
> 250 Canyon Oaks Drive
> Argyle, TX 76226
> (214) 239-3574 days   (817) 455-2519 eves   Fax: (817) 455-5094

★ **Boy Scout items of all sorts** wanted. Of special interest are Order of the Arrow patches (worth $3 to $150+), Eagle and other medals, pins, and items from World Jamborees 1920-1951 (worth $50 to $300). Interested in games, postcards, and books and uniforms before 1950. No camping items, tents, mess kits, canteens, etc.

> Doug Bearce
> PO Box 4742
> Salem, OR 97302
> (503) 399-9872

★ **Boy Scout items,** Eagle awards, and Order of the Arrow patches (marked O.A., Lodge, or W.W.W.). "I'll pay from $1 to $100 for most, though some very scarce items may bring $1,000 or more. I need a photocopy, although you may send what you have for sale to me and if we can't agree on a fair price, I will return it and pay shipping costs both ways." He does not want handbooks printed after 1915, first aid kits, neckerchief slides, belt buckles, knapsacks, tents, or camping gear.

> Greg Souchik
> PO Box 133
> Custer City, PA 16725
> (814) 362-2642   Fax: (814) 362-7356

★ **Girl Scout memorabilia.** Wants to buy pre-1960 catalogs, postcards, magazines, uniforms, equipment, and other items. Handbooks before 1921 only. Send Xerox™ or photo. Do not send items without prior arrangement.

> Jerry King
> 8429 Katy Freeway
> Houston, TX 77024
> (713) 465-2500

RELIGIOUS ITEMS

★ **Relics of the Saints.** This buyer seeks "first class relics" of Catholic Saints. A "first class relic" is a tiny fragment of bone displayed in a reliquary, a small metal or wooden container with a glass cover. It should include the Saint's name. "Second class relics" are fragments of something worn or used by a Saint, and not of particular interest. Please send a photocopy or brief description including the Saint's name. You may mail your relic on approval, and your mailing costs will be reimbursed whether he purchases your item or not. Hal notes that relics are not to be sold, but that he will "make a donation to any church or charity you name in exchange. I assure you, I will care for your relic and treat it with proper respect," Hal vows.

> Hal Miller
> 240 East Evergreen Avenue
> Philadelphia, PA 19118

★ **Crucifixes, medals, Stars of David, and other symbols from any religion.** Wants a wide variety of items...interesting, unusual, precious, sentimental...anything you want preserved or displayed. Donated crosses and other items are preserved with your family name or other identification of your choice. "I can't afford to buy things as all my money is being set aside to build a religious museum. I'm hoping people will donate their items so they are preserved and cared for properly. I'm looking for an angel to subsidize a museum of religious artifacts and symbols." Send a stamped self-addressed envelope if you'd like an offer, response to a donation, an answer to a question regarding crosses, or simply more information about his goals.

> Ernie Reda
> 3997 Latimer Avenue
> San Jose, CA 95130

★ **Protestant religious items** including old **Bibles**, **hymnals**, bronze statues, old pictures and prints, **oil paintings, engravings**, watercolors, books, autographs, and more. Gene asks you give a standard description, send Xerox™ copies or photos and estimate the age of what you have. Give standard bibliographic entries for any books.

> Gene Albert, Jr.
> 12324 Big Pool Road
> Clear Spring, MD 21722
> (301) 842-2401   Fax: (301) 733-5669

Don't forget your Stamped Self-Addressed Envelope when you write. Use a long #10 folded into thirds for best results.

★ **Religious music, poetry and dance.** Wants hymnals, cantorial or choir music, religious poetry, sacred music, oblongs, indexes, books, magazines, leaflets, and original manuscripts (typed or handwritten, whether published or not) of religious music, poetry and dance notation or directions. May be in any language, English preferred. May be mixed collections of religious and secular music. Since these are "for use, not display, the appearance is unimportant" but items must be complete. Values range from 25¢ to $400. He does not want prose, blank verse, or secular music and has little interest in hymnology, data/discussions about music, dance, poetry, social causes, or religious topics. Doesn't buy duplicates, and offers to trade. Give the exact title, edition or revision number, latest copyright date, editor or compiler, and indicate the total number of religious music or verse selections or number of pages. This non-profit group encourages donations.

David Whitney, The Pealing Chord
8 Ellen Drive K.T.
Wyoming, PA 18644
(717) 696-2218

★ **Methodist items** including histories, biographies, photos of preachers or churches, diaries, letters or manuscript material about Methodism, prints, posters, sheet music, copies of the *Discipline* and *Hymnal* printed before 1850 as well as all Methodist publications such as *Christian Advocate* from any year any edition, especially Southern. Also wants personal items of preachers, bishops or prominent laity such as canes, hats, gloves, etc. Does not want Sunday School material, holy cards or general material like a postcard of the Holy Land."

Rev. Kenneth Brown
243 South Pine Street
Hazleton, PA 18201
(717) 454-1468

★ **Pentecostal religious items** including histories, biographies of preachers or leaders, photos of churches or services, sermons and sermon notes, and anniversary items from holiness and Pentecostal churches such as mugs, plates, etc. Will buy oils, napkins, snake handling boxes, and identified hymnals, Bibles and disciplines of denominations. Also wants any and all books, periodicals, and tracts on the subject of sanctification, holiness, perfection, second blessing, speaking in tongues, faith healing and healers, or snake handling and will buy single issues or bound volumes of Pentecostal magazines. Does not want Sunday School items, pictures of the Virgin Mary, etc., but is looking for historical books, documents, photos and artifacts only.

Rev. Kenneth Brown
243 South Pine Street
Hazleton, PA 18201
(717) 454-1468

★ **Chautauqua and camp meeting revivalism.** "I'm seeking any and all materials related to Chautauqua and camp meeting revivalism including posters, stereoviews, postcards, photographs, letters, diaries, magazines, prints, souvenirs, etc. I'll even buy artifacts like lanterns, pulpits, signs and the like, but am primarily interested in items that are identified as to the preachers and/or dates involved. **I** *do not* **buy** items like old Bibles, Sunday school postcards, photos of churches and the like, or any Scouting items." Brown is editor of *Camp Meeting Challenge*, historian for the National Camp Meeting Association and author of *Holy Ground: A Study of the American Camp Meeting*, available for $42.

> Rev. Kenneth Brown
> 243 South Pine Street
> Hazleton, PA 18201
> (717) 454-1468

★ **Missionary correspondence** from Protestant or Catholic missionaries in Asia, Africa, South Pacific and South America. The envelope must be intact as it is the stamps and cancellations (covers) that are of primary importance. Advisable to first phone or send a photocopy of the envelope by mail or fax. Repays post on items sent on approval.

> Bruce Lewin, Bridgewater Onvelopes Collectibles
> 680 Route 206 North
> Bridgewater, NJ 08807
> (908) 725-0022   Fax: (908) 707-4647

★ **Judaica,** especially silver religious items and old books. Use standard bibliographic information for books. Send a photo of religious items, and include all markings found on the piece.

> Jay Brand
> PO Box 871
> Reynoldsburg, OH 43068
> (614) 868-8655

★ **Israel, Palestine, and the Holocaust.** What have you? It could be worth your time to make an inquiry.

> Harvey Dolin
> 5 Beekman Street #406
> New York, NY 10038
> (212) 267-0216

★ **Sacred books, including Bibles before 1800, Books of Common Prayer, the Koran**, and other unusual, beautiful or early sacred book.

> Ron Lieberman, Family Album
> Route 1 Box 42
> Glen Rock, PA 17327
> (717) 235-2134   Fax: (717) 235-8042

★ **Shakers and other utopian groups.** "I buy and sell early and current (to 1970) books, hymnals, manuscripts, photos, and other ephemera by or about the Shakers and related utopian and communal groups. Particularly interested in 18th and 19th century items related to the American Shakers. An 1808 1st edition of *Testimony of Christ's Second Appearing* can bring $1,000, and other works can bring even more. Pamphlets for and against the Shakers printed in Ohio, Kentucky or surrounding states during the 1800-1840 period are of particular interest." Full bibliographic information on books is required, including full description of the condition. A photo or Xerox™ is suggested for other items. He produces periodic catalogs of items for sale. Cost: $4.

> David Newell
> 39 Steady Lane
> Ashfield, MA 01330
> (413) 628-3240   Fax: (413) 628-3216

★ **Shaker artifacts and ephemera.** "I specialize in Shaker books, pamphlets, photographs, and ephemera. I also buy and sell small Shaker artifacts such as bottles, sewing boxes, baskets, seed boxes, and the like. Four times a year, I publish a catalog of Shaker items for sale. If you have something to sell me, generally all I need is a photo or photocopy to come to a decision."

> Scott DeWolfe
> PO Box 425
> Alfred, ME 04002
> (207) 490-5572

★ **Shaker furniture, books, diaries, and letters.** Will buy in any condition. Please write and describe what you have.

> James Williams
> HCR 01   Box 23
> Warrensburg, NY 12885
> (518) 623-2831

★ **Mormonism.** Buys all types of books, photos, letters, and other paper ephemera related to Mormons.

> Warren Anderson
> America West Archives
> PO Box 100
> Cedar City, UT 84720
> (801) 586-9497

★ **Watchtower Society literature, books and other memorabilia** from before 1930 are wanted. He'd like to hear from you if you have anything pertaining to the Watchtower Society, Tower Publishing, the International Bible Students Assn (IBSA), Pastor C.T. Russell, or George Storrs. Books of particular interest include N.H. Barbour's *Three Worlds* (1877, $200 "or a great deal more in fine condition"), J.H. Paton's *Day Dawn* (1880, $200+), C.T. Russell's *The Object & Manner of Our Lord's Return* (1877, $500+), J.F. Rutherford's *Man's Salvation from a Lawyer's Viewpoint* (1906, $500+), and various books by George Storrs. The special Watchtower Edition of *Human Linear Bible* (1902) is a $500 and up prize. Numerous magazines, Journals, and Reports **from before 1930** are sought, including *Watchtower, Golden Age, Herald of the Morning, Bible Examiner,* and*Overland Monthly.* This 35 year veteran collector/researcher wants to hear about **anything you have from before 1930**, books between 1930 and 1940, and nothing after 1950. Dealers should price their goods. Amateurs may request an offer from this 35 year veteran collector/dealer.

> Jeffrey Neumann
> PO Box 171
> Wadsworth, OH 44282
> (330) 334-1784

★ **Watchtower Society publications and ephemera** including *Golden Age, Consolation,* and *Awake* magazines, *Millennial Dawn* books, *Watchtower* books before 1927, items related to **Pastor Russell**, and any pre-1940 Jehovah's Witness literature.

> Mike Castro
> PO Box 72817
> Providence, RI 02907

★ **Mystical arts, crystal balls, tarot cards,** and ephemera related to astrology, spiritualism, pyramids, palmistry, Yoga, numerology, psychic research, Atlantis, Tibet, UFO's and the like.

> Dennis Whelan
> PO Box 170
> Lakeview, AR 72642

★ **Angels.** "I'll buy church type angels made of plaster or chalk, the bigger the better." Send a photo with dimensions.

> Gwen Daniel
> 18 Belleau Lake Court
> O'Fallon, MO 63366
> (314) 978-3190 anytime gdaniel@mail.win.org

Angel figurines are sought by a buyer on p. 456

CHRISTMAS, EASTER & HALLOWEEN

★ **Holiday collectibles**, notably items associated with **Christmas**, **Halloween** and to a lesser extent non-religious **Easter**:
* Halloween **Jack O'lanterns** (at $10 an inch if mint);
* Halloween, Christmas, or Easter candy containers made in Germany of papier mache or composition (no glass);
* **Santa related figures**, especially bisque;
* **Halloween postcards** ($4 to $8);
* **Bubble lights** if working, at $2 to $4 each;
* **Woolly animals**, especially sheep and goats.

Things must be in fine condition for resale. She does not want Japanese made Santas from 1935 to the present, nor does she buy any Christmas item of plastic. She is not interested in Halloween masks, or costumes. No Santas in magazine ads. Give a detailed description or good sharp photo. "Will buy one item or 50."

Jenny Tarrant
Holly Daze Antiques
4 Garden View
St. Peters, MO 63376
(314) 397-1763 any time

★ **Holiday collectibles**, notably items associated with **Christmas**, **Halloween** and to a lesser extent **Easter**, including **decorations** from before 1920, and related items like:
* **Figural ornaments**, made of paper, tinsel, pressed cardboard, cotton batting, glass or other material;
* **Board games** with lithographed boxes depicting Santa;
* **Santa toys** and **other ephemera:** anything based on St. Nick, including advertising, banners, greeting cards, paintings, die-cuts, chromoliths, and prints;
* **Die cut children's books** 1880-1900 about Santa;
* **Litho on tin candle holders** for Christmas trees;
* **Halloween candy containers** in glass or papier-maché;
* **Papier-maché or composition Easter rabbit candy containers** of rabbits wearing clothes..

He does not want *anything* made of plastic or vinyl, nor anything made after 1920. There are many reproductions of Santa items, some of which are quite valuable and require an expert to authenticate. This 25 year veteran requests a photo or photocopy of what you'd like to sell.

Dolph "Father Christmas" Gotelli
PO Box 188977
Sacramento, CA 95818
(916) 456-9734   Fax: (916) 457-1559

★ **Greeting cards from any holiday, 1840-1910.** Nothing later. Everything must be in suitable condition for resale. No postcards.

 Madalaine Selfridge
 33710 Almond Street
 Wildomar, CA 92595
 (909) 674-9221

★ **German glass Christmas ornaments,** shaped like animals, people, and cartoon characters, made before 1920. Also wants painted cotton ornaments, paper Dresdens, and old **candy containers** shaped like Santa. Also buys pre-1930 **postcards** and **photos of Christmas events** plus pre-1960 **department store Santas** with children.

 Jim Bohenstengel
 PO Box 623
 Oak Park, IL 60303
 (708) 524-8870

★ **Early handmade folk art Christmas decorations.**

 Louis Picek, Main Street Antiques
 PO Box 340
 West Branch, IA 52358

★ **Christmas tree ornaments.** Buys a variety of antique ornaments:
- *Kugel* ornaments;
- Glass birds with spun glass wings, tails, or crests;
- Czech beaded ornaments with satin glass rings;
- Birds perched in glass rings;
- Unusual strings of glass beads;
- Spun glass and paper decorations;
- Chandelier or fantasy ornaments (where two or three small bells, pine cones, or other items hang from a larger ornament);
- Delicate and unusual figural ornaments;
- Catalogs and manufacturer's sales literature in any language.

He wants a good description and if you still have the box, the information on it. "I generally avoid plastic items, and items newer than the mid 1950's." He requests return privilege if things aren't as described.

 David Speck
 35 Franklin Street
 Auburn, NY 13021
 (315) 252-8566 eves

★ **Electric Christmas decorations** including figural light bulbs, pre-1940 items only, please. Send photo.

 Cindy Chipps
 4027 Brooks Hill Road
 Brooks, KY 40109
 (502) 955-9238 Fax: (502) 957-5027

★ *Matchless Wonder Stars* **Christmas lights.** "I'll buy all stars, working, dead or broken. Even empty boxes have value." This historian wants all factory wholesale literature and price sheets, as well as store display stands. He also buys other *Matchless* products plus **any old light sets that twinkle or bubble** by *Paramount, Sylvania, Alps, Royal, Peerless, Mazda, Majestic* and others. Especially wants nice boxed light sets by *Propp* and *Clemco*. He wants a good description and if you still have the box, the information on it. "I generally avoid plastic items, and Christmas lights later than the mid 1950's." Although he buys dead bulbs (except *Sylvania* fluorescents), he requests return privilege if things aren't as described.

> David Speck
> 35 Franklin Street
> Auburn, NY 13021
> (315) 253-8495 days

★ *Hallmark* **figural ornaments** from 1973-1986. Excellent condition only. In original box preferred. No ball ornaments.

> Sharon Vohs-Mohammed
> PO Box 7233
> Villa Park, IL 60181
> (630) 268-0210

★ *Hallmark* **Christmas ornaments**, one or a collection, are sought by this 10 year veteran collector/dealer. Especially ornaments signed by the artist or issued for a special event or convention. Ornaments issued "first in a series" are especially desired mint and in original box. Also wants car series, Frosty Friends, pedal cars, planes, and Here Comes Santa. Says he'll pay $400 for First Rocking Horse series mint in box. Does not want round ornaments or any ornaments that are not part of a series (such as Sister, Brother, Friend, Dad, Teacher, etc.). Please give the year the item was made, its condition, and the condition of the box. "I'll buy entire collections, no matter how big."

> Ken Wright
> 4780 Old highway 7
> Shawnee, KS 66226
> (913) 441-0665 eves   Fax: (913) 441-6485

★ **Christmas collector's plates and ornaments**, but only (1) *Royal Copenhagen* plates; (2) *Wedgwood Jasperware* plates; (3) *Bing & Grondahl* plates; (4) *Waterford* crystal "12 Days of Christmas" ornaments. Indicate the year and whether you have the original box.

> Old China Patterns Limited
> 1560 Brimley Road
> Scarborough, Ontario
> M1P 3G9   CANADA
> (416) 299-8880   Fax: (416) 299-4721

★ **Russian Easter eggs** made of porcelain, solid glass, silvered hollow glass, and other materials. They are characterized by the letters "XB" or XHRISTOS VOSKRECE (Christ is risen) inscribed in paint, enamel, or other material. Value depends upon rarity, authenticity and condition.

> David Speck
> 35 Franklin Street
> Auburn, NY 13021

★ **Halloween.** "I'll buy older paper items, *Dennison Boogie Books*, Halloween pins, jewelry, decorations, etc., but only if they were made before 1945. Nothing new is wanted." Stu is the author of *Halloween in America*, available through him for $35 postpaid.

> Stuart Schneider
> PO Box 64
> Teaneck, NJ 07666
>   (201) 261-1983   Fax: (201) 568-3618

4TH OF JULY MEMORABILIA

★ **Anything with a fireworks company name** on it including:
- Fireworks boxes that held salutes, torpedoes, sparklers, etc. (worth up to $200 each);
- Fireworks, rockets, Roman candles and wooden based items;
- Firecracker packs and labels;
- Salesmen's display boards and samples;
- Fireworks catalogs from before 1969 (often $150 up);
- Paper ephemera: stock certificates, posters, banners, photos, letters, billheads, magazine articles, and other paper about American fireworks companies.

"I would like to hear from any former employee of a U.S. fireworks company. Please include your phone number when you write."

> Barry Zecker
> PO Box 217
> Martinsville, NJ 08836
>   (908) 253-3400 from 9 to 9

★ **Firecracker packs and labels,** especially of Chinese, Macao, and Hong Kong manufacture. Want none marked DOT or UNO336. Buys other fireworks related items such as firecracker cannons, cap canes, torpedo and salute boxes, catalogs and salesman's display boards. "I do appraisals and can store and import legally from all countries. Please send Xerox™. I pay postage both ways on all approvals."

> Hal Kantrud
> Route 7
> Jamestown, ND 58401
>   (701) 252-5639 eves   hal.kantrud@daktelco.com

★ **Firecracker labels.** "I'll buy pre-1940 labels with aviation, space, atom bomb, animal, and Americana themes." Also fireworks catalogs. Send a photocopy of what you have. No modern labels.

> Stuart Schneider
> PO Box 64
> Teaneck, NJ 07666
> (201) 261-1983   Fax: (201) 568-3618

★ **Fourth of July fireworks**, firecrackers, and firecracker labels. Wants "anything prior to the early 1970's, especially packs of *Golliwog, Picnic, Tank, Oh Boy, Typewriter, Blue Dragon, Golden Bear, Green Jade, Santa Claus, Dwarf, China Clipper*, and many others." He wants most of these badly enough to pay $50 or more per pack! NOTE: if your package or label contains the letters DOT and/or "Contents do not exceed 60 mg," he's probably not interested. He eagerly buys catalogs of fireworks too. Photocopy when possible.

> William Scales
> 130 Fordham Circle
> Pueblo, CO 81005
> (719) 561-0603

VALENTINE'S DAY

★ **Valentines.** Wants early die-cut and elaborate valentines made before 1910, but buys others "if reasonable." Please, no postcards.

> Madalaine Selfridge
> 33710 Almond Street
> Wildomar, CA 92595
> (909) 674-9221

★ **Valentines** dating from 1889 to about 1920, but only the three dimensional fold-out stand-up type.

> James Conley
> 2758 Coventry Lane NW
> Canton, OH 44708
> (330) 477-7725

★ **Fine Valentines,** including handmade valentines from before 1940, interesting mechanical valentines, lacy 8" x 10" cards, large fan shaped TOKEN OF LOVE cards from the 1800's and anything unusual. Pays $25-$50 for folding ships, planes, and better fans. Photocopy what you wish to sell. NO children's 1¢ valentines from any era.

> Evalene Pulati, Valentine Collector's Association
> PO Box 1404
> Santa Ana, CA 92702
> (714) 547-1355

MISCELLANEOUS

★ **Hand bells.** Wants rare and unusual hand bells including:
- Figural bronze or brass;
- Oriental, especially with enamel;
- Historical, religious, and town crier's;
- Glass, especially colored glass;
- Silver, especially highly decorated, including rattles;
- Porcelain and china, such as *Royal Beyreuth*;
- Mechanical or tap bells that are unusual.

Does not want large bells, but will consider any unusual small hand bell except school bells, cow or other animal bells, sleigh bells, "collectible series" bells, and bells made in India. Give the size, weight, color, and markings. Photo a good idea. She offers five different books on bells priced from $11 to $14. A brochure about bells is available.

    Dorothy Anthony
    World of Bells
    802 South Eddy
    Fort Scott, KS 66701
        (316) 223-3404

★ **Large bells,** especially cast bronze church, mission, train, boat, and school bells are bought, sold and installed. The country's largest dealer in used bells buys and sells a wide range of bells, but is not interested in glass bells or "the little ting-a-ling type." Write or call if buying or selling larger bells. You will be expected to state the price you want for your bell as he does not give free appraisals or make offers.

    R.C. Brosamer's Bells
    207 Irwin Street
    Brooklyn, MI 49230
        (517) 592-9030   Fax: (517) 592-4511

★ **Items that look like something they're not.** "I am always looking for the odd, the unusual, and the curious, and don't hesitate to buy things that require an explanation. I like pens that look like mummies, dice cups that look like bullets, cigarette lighters that look like guns or pencils, compacts that look like 8-balls or watches, and what have you. Most of these things are not of great value, but the variety is endless, so describe what you have carefully, include a Xerox™ when you can, and I will make an offer. I like anything that isn't what it seems to be."

    Betty Bird
    Antiques, Etc.
    107 Ida Street
    Mt. Shasta, CA 96067
        (916) 926-2231

★ **Miniatures.** "I buy miniatures that will fit in a doll house (but not limited to doll house things). I also want children's size dishes, castor sets, hats in hat boxes, and almost anything else that is child size but not necessarily created for children." She cautions you to bear in mind that this takes in a vast area, and there are many reproductions (which she does not want). Mint condition is a must. "I love tiny things that are odd and unusual."

> Betty Bird
> Antiques, Etc.
> 107 Ida Street
> Mt. Shasta, CA 96067

★ **Carved shells,** especially cowrie shells with the Lord's Prayer, personalized messages and/or dates, cities, foreign places with pictures (often sold as souvenirs), or events such as World's Fairs. "I buy any condition, any age, but do not want current souvenir shells made in the Philippines with zodiac signs and poor carvings of dolphins or fish done as souvenirs for coastal towns. I will buy modern items, but the quality of the carving must be exceptional." Values range from $5 to $50 or more.

> Vicki Tori
> 711 Oak Drive
> Capitola, CA 95010
> (408) 479-7711

★ **3-D movies, slides, magazines and other items** including:
  • Any 3-D cameras, viewers, and projectors;
  • *Viewmaster* views from before 1982;
  • *Tru-Vue* filmstrips and viewers, but not *Tru-Vue* cards;
  • 3-D color slides from the 40's;
  • 3-D magazines and comic books from the 1950's;
  • Stereoviews, especially of movie related subjects.

He would pay $300 for the stereoview card set from the 20's sold in Germany called "The Making of the Hunchback of Notre Dame" but has no interest in (1) stereoviews that are printed rather than actual photos, (2) stereoviews of scenery, (3) cartoon subjects, or (4) *Viewmaster* reels that are damaged or dirty. He needs to know the brand and model of equipment and the title, subject, and catalog number of reels and stereoviews. If you have original packet envelopes, boxes, instructions or other paper, make certain to note the fact. When offering views, you should understand that most of them are worth only $1-$5.

> Chris "Dr. 3-D" Perry
> 7470 Church Street #A
> Yucca Valley, CA 92284
> (619) 365-0495

★ **Missouri Health buttons.** Buttons were issued annually from 1926 to 1974 and are found in various configurations with various ribbons attached. Most desirable are the issues of 1943-45 which were made of paper and/or plastic instead of metal. No damaged, stained, or faded buttons are wanted. Please Xerox©.

Karen Ferguson
1010 Tarsney Lane
Buckner, MO 64016
(816) 650-5671

★ **Peace symbols** from the late 1960's and early 70's. "I'm looking for jewelry, rings, watchbands, dogtags, belts, and anything unusual depicting the black and white symbol called a "chickenfoot" by detractors. Condition is very important, and items must not show damage or wear. Send a description, Xerox™, and asking price.

Judy Polk Harding
1701 60th Street
Des Moines, IA 50322
(515) 279-7099 voice and fax   THEFIVEJS@aol.com

★ **Yellow smile faces** from 1968 to 1975. "I want cups, pins, luggage, handbags, ice buckets, drinking glasses, cookie jars, flower pots, you name it. Smiley faces appeared on just about everything imaginable." Condition is very important, and items must not show damage or wear. Send a description, Xerox™, and asking price.

Judy Polk Harding
1701 60th Street
Des Moines, IA 50322
(515) 279-7099 voice and fax   THEFIVEJS@aol.com

★ **Badges, buttons, emblems or ribbons of all types**. This includes, but is not limited to, political buttons, **union & labor items**, old and new movie and cartoon items, fast food pins, **fire and police badges**, military medals, **Olympic pins**, and items given by gasoline companies and airlines, including wings. "I'll buy them all, common or rare, big quantities or small. Since the average reader doesn't have my 20 years experience, I will look at all items or Xerox copies of them and give an honest opinion."

Fred Swindall, Button Exchange
111 NW 2nd
Portland, OR 97209
(503) 224-0678 days   (503) 234-2454 eves

NOTE: Buttons and badges are popular items and there are many buyers throughout this book. Look in the index under: buttons, badges, pop culture, tobacco, Olympics, sports, fire, unions, military, and specific companies. Ted Hake on p 132 is author of 4 books on buttons. Can you find the celebrity button buyer?

★ **Puzzle bottles.** "I'll buy bottles that contain unusual items such as chairs, carved human figures, etc. I do not buy ships in bottles. Things in undamaged condition only, please." Photo suggested.

    Barry Friedman
    PO Box 55492
    Valencia, CA 91385
    (805) 255-2365

★ **Corn collectibles.** "I'll buy almost anything related to corn:
- **Pottery** shaped like corn (except *Shawnee*) or with corn patterns, especially Majolica and pottery by *Stanford* or *Vallona Star*;
- **Glassware** shaped like corn or with corn patterns;
- **Lamps** and other objects with corn motif or patterns;
- Corn **planters, planter plates** and **shock tyres**;
- Corn **shellers**, hand held, box mounted and free standing;
- Corn **seed company advertising** signs and catalogs;
- **Paper goods**, letterheads, correspondence, etc., related to corn seed or tools, with particular interest in small regional companies rather than *DeKalb* or *Pioneer.*;
- **Cloth corn seed sacks**.

Books, government documents, Agricultural Experiment Bulletins, and general farm magazines with articles about corn are **NOT** wanted. Items should be made before 1950. "If in doubt, ask, because previously unknown items are found regularly." State your item's condition, and if it is for sale what you would like for it. Include an SASE. This corny stuff is wanted by the editor of the Corn Items Collectors Association Newsletter (*The Bang Board* available along with membership for only $15/year). She has been a corn collector for more than 20 years.

    E. Eloise Alton
    613 North Long Street
    Shelbyville, IL 62565
    (217) 774-5002

★ **Occupied Germany.** Seeks a wide range of figures, china, toys, children's games, Christmas ornaments, kitchen items, tools and other items marked as having come from US ZONE, BRITISH ZONE, FRENCH ZONE and USSR OCCUPIED. Items should be described clearly and be in good condition. A photo is helpful.

    Larry L. Krug
    Americana Resources
    18222 Flower Hill Way #299
    Gaithersburg, MD 20879
  (301) 926-8663   Fax: (301) 926-7648   larry.krug@amres.com

☆ **Electric and pre-electric vibrators and hand held massagers.** "I especially like those with metal casings rather than plastic, those with hand-cranks, and vibrators with wooden bodies, handles or parts. Not interested in battery operated devices. You won't make a fortune selling to me, but your item could reside in the world's only vibrator museum and will be happier than in your attic." No *Oster* vibrators which are worn on the back of the hand. Describe, give numbers, and indicate whether the box is present and describe any attachments or instructional inserts. Will buy items which do not work but are not physically broken. Joani owns a large specialty sex toy and book store, and offers catalogs of sexual self-help books and sexual aids.

> Joani Blank
> Good Vibrations Vibrator Museum
> Box 863
> Emeryville, CA 94662

★ **Sealing wax seals.** "We collect virtually any type of material or motif. While we are happy to look at (and sometimes buy) nice traditional pieces such as sterling art nouveau or agate seals, we are really seeking larger more unusual desk type seals. Upon occasion, we buy desk sets which include seals. Generally, we buy only items in perfect condition. We don't want fob seals, modern seals, or Oriental chops." To sell your seal you'll need good close up photos with notes about size, materials, and anything important that doesn't show in the photo. Include any pertinent history. If your seal is for sale they're happy to make offers. There may be a fee for formal appraisals.

> Eileen & Irwin Prince
> 3500 West DePauw Blvd. #2015
> Indianapolis, IN 46268
> (317) 334-9200 days   (317) 255-1913 eves   Fax: (317) 228-3355

★ **"Old Ironsides" memorabilia.** "I want relics of all types from the United States Frigate Constitution ("Old Ironsides"). These bronze or wood items items include: ash trays, dishes, anchors, cannons, etc., all marked THIS MATERIAL WAS TAKEN FROM US FRIGATE CONSTITUTION.

> Tim O'Callaghan
> PO Box 512
> Northville, MI 48167
> (810) 449-2652

★ **Snowmobile, ski vehicle and *Ski-Doo* toy models, literature, brochures, license plates and photos of them taken before 1970.

> Don Schneider
> PO Box 1570
> Merritt, BC
> V1K 1B8 CANADA
> (604) 378-6421

MISCELLANEOUS FIGURES

★ **Hear no evil, see no evil, speak no evil figurines** are sought by this collector. Although not particularly valuable, she would like to hear from you if you have one for sale, and will make a fair offer. Describe the size, material, any markings on the bottom, and information about where you got it, if possible. Lois also buys some single figurines of monkeys. Most aren't particularly valuable, "but they make me laugh."

    Lois Dwyer
    324 Allen Street
    Syracuse, NY 13210
       (315) 476-1014

★ **Mermaids and mermen.** "I will consider any item, made of porcelain, china, metal, stone, cloth, lace or paper which has a mermaid, merman, or merbaby motif. The item must be old and unusual, but may be advertising, folk art, scrimshaw, jewelry, bottles, fishing lures, and what have you. I DO NOT WANT Japanese bisque, anything new, or anything cracked or broken. Indicate the size, markings, and condition as part of your description. Wants you to set the price.

    Stephanie Schnatz
    17 Tallow Court
    Baltimore, MD 21244
       (410) 944-0819

★ **Billikens.** Naked pot-bellied figures sitting with the bottoms of their feet facing you. Promoted as the god of things as they ought to be, or the god of happiness, luck, etc. Found in a variety of sizes and materials. Wants original 1908-1910 Billikens as featured on flatware, ice cream molds, charms, jewelry, dolls, games, banks, thimbles, toothpick holders, postcards, and all other items in the shape of Billikens. No jade or tusk Billikens, which are more modern items from Alaska.

    Judy Knauer
    1224 Spring Valley Lane
    West Chester, PA 19380
       (610) 431-3477

★ **Golliwogs.** These cartoonish racist Black characters have appeared in many forms since they first arrived in England at the turn of the century. They can be found both store bought and home made, of nearly any material. She particularly wants them as small lead figures. These have been reproduced but "a photo will tell me a lot."

    Marilyn Baseman
    Birdcage Antiques
    PO Box 268
    South Egremont, MA 01258
       (413) 528-3556

★ **Angels.** "I'll buy church type angels made of plaster or chalk, the bigger the better." Send a photo with dimensions.
Gwen Daniel
18 Belleau Lake Court
O'Fallon, MO 63366
(314) 978-3190 anytime gdaniel@mail.win.org

Psycho Ceramics are blobby, cartoony type characters with little bodies, big heads and strange expressions, posed in wacky positions, often with cheap looking cut stones for eyes and body decoration. They are usually marked clearly on the bottom.
Some were made as mugs, ash trays, egg cups and vases; some had paper labels with cute sayings. Most are 4" to 5" tall, although they can be as tall as 10"

☆ **Psycho-Ceramics** and other wacky ceramic figures made by Kreiss & Co. Most Psycho Ceramics are blobby, cartoony type characters with little bodies, big heads and strange expressions. Some were made as mugs, ash trays, egg cups and vases, some of which had paper labels with cute sayings, others had rhinestone eyes, yet others have pipe cleaner antennae. Most are 4" to 5" tall, although they can be as tall as 10" ("which I pay double for"). Tell him about what you have, no matter what it's condition as chips, cracks and repairs are OK on many figures. Kreiss also made ceramic **Beatniks**, a line called **Elegant Heirs** (covered with rhinestones), **Moon Beings** (resemble Dr. Seuss characters) and **Members of the Bar** (drunks and bums), all of which are usually mounted on wooden bases. Also wants **ceramics by Rumph** including mugs, candle holders, toilet paper dispensers, bongs, and other 1970's unusual things.
Mark "Joe Lunchbucket" Blondy
35952 North Valley Court, #207
Farmington Hills, MI 48335
(248) 442-7339 grooveden@aol.com

★ **Bride and groom cake tops.** "I especially want ones from the 1940's and 50's with the grooms in uniform. Also want any top pieces that are marked with a maker's mark, date, patent, or other markings. Anything unusual is also sought, but I don't want children or animals dressed up as brides, nor do I want any contemporary *Lladro* or other "collectible" brides and grooms." A close up photo taken with a 35mm camera is best. Make certain to include any and all markings. Most sell in the $30 to $50 range, but a few will bring twice that.

Dede Evans
209 Homer Avenue
Palo Alto, CA 94301
(415) 321-3149   Fax: (415) 329-0136

★ **Bride and groom cake tops.** "I collect German bisque bride and groom sets from the 1890's through the 1940's. Some of my favorites are still mounted on the icing cake top platforms. Paint and condition are very important to me. Clear close up photos are important to show subtle differences and detail since they all sound pretty similar over the phone." You set the price. If it's fair, she says she'll pay it.

Linda Vines
PO Box 43721
Upper Montclair, NJ 07043

★ **Mannequins** from the Victorian era to the 1950's. "I'll buy heads or full body figures, in any size. I do not want plastic items, reproductions, or anything modern. Please send me a photo."

Gwen Daniel
18 Belleau Lake Court
O'Fallon, MO 63366
(314) 978-3190 anytime   gdaniel@mail.win.org

★ **Hands.** "I'll buy wooden hands with fingers that move, generally used as glove stretchers, and **Palmistry hands** showing lines, zones, and mounds. I'm looking for wood or ceramic, not paper items."

Don Gorlick
PO Box 24541
Seattle, WA 98124

Don't forget to include a Self-Addressed Stamped Envelope. Use a long #10 envelope folded into thirds for best results.

EPHEMERA OF FAMOUS PEOPLE

★ **Celebrity yearbooks.** Celebrities of both yesteryear and today are sought in high school yearbooks. Politics, show biz, music, arts...If you went to school with anyone famous or infamous and have a yearbook with their picture, here's where you go to sell it. Typical prices start at $100 but can be higher for rare annuals with stars they need. "Our primary interest is in the celebrity's senior year and senior year photo, but will consider earlier if those aren't available." Their current "Most Wanted List" includes oldies like 1900 Groton, 1901 Independence Missouri HS, 1945 West Lake School for Girls, and 1947 Miss Porter's School, all of which will bring you $1,000 or more. Newer books include 1978 Collegiate HS in NYC and 1987 Buckley (Sherman Oaks, CA) which are worth $300. They do not want college yearbooks, nor do they want books that are mildewed or seriously damaged. If you do not know whether anyone famous is in your book, write to the Poppels, giving the name of the school, the city and state, and the year published. Please include a long SASE, for which they will also send you a list of books from your area they'd like to find. Great for serious yardsalers and pickers. They would also like to hear from you were a HS friend or teacher of someone who became famous.

> Seth Poppel
> Yearbook Archives
> 38 Range Drive
> Merrick, NY 11566
> (516) 867-6280   Fax (516) 546-4128   Sethpoppel@aol.com

★ **Celebrity memorabilia.** "I buy, sell and collect personal belongings of **entertainment stars and historical figures**, including **movie costumes**, props, and autographed photos. I'm not interested in most mass produced items, except very rare items like movie posters." Your description should include what the item is, its condition, and its history, including how you came to own it. Make certain to describe what authentication you have.

> Richard Wilson
> Norma's Jeans
> 3511 Turner Land
> Chevy Chase, MD 20815
> (301) 652-4644   Fax: (301) 907-0216

★ **Carrie Nation memorabilia** including vinegar bottles in her caricature, souvenir hatchet pins, photos, tickets to lectures, *The Hatchet*, newspaper articles about her, and *anything* else. You find it and you've got a buyer here if it's in any decent condition at all.

> Steve Chyrchel
> 25 Kansas
> Eureka Springs, AR 72632
> (501) 253-9150 voice and fax

★ **Stalin, Hitler, and Mussolini** items, especially those from the 1920's and 1930's, are bought. Wants documented personal effects, autographs, letters, photos and some magazine and newspaper accounts. Also **Al Capone** and **other Chicago prohibition era figures,** both good guys and bad guys, including gangsters, police chiefs, State attorneys, FBI men, Elliott Ness, etc. Particularly interested in Capone and will pay from $50 to $1,000 depending on what you have, its condition, and its documentation. If offering personal items such as clothing, guns, jewelry or letters, you should phone and be prepared to discuss.

Michael Graham
33133 O'Plaine Road
Gurnee, IL 60031
(897) 263-6285

★ **John "Johnny Appleseed" Chapman memorabilia** including books and personal items. He's looking for artifacts from the real Johnny Appleseed, not the Disney cartoon character.

Frederic Janson, Pomona Book Exchange
Highway 52
Rockton, ON
L0R 1X0 CANADA

★ **Commodore Matthew Perry material** including autographs, letters, and manuscripts, especially any artifacts or documents related to his expedition to Japan. Also all **Lafcadio Hearn** books, ephemera.

Jerrold Stanoff, Rare Oriental Book Co.
PO Box 1599
Aptos, CA 95001

★ **Frank Lloyd Wright material** including drawings, furniture, letters, photographs, books, smaller publications, and other ephemera.

J.B. Muns' Fine Arts Books
1162 Shattuck Avenue
Berkeley, CA 94707
(510) 525-2420

★ **Horace Greeley memorabilia** of all types, especially campaign buttons from 1872 (worth $30 to $3,000) and copies of the *NY Tribune* newspaper from 1840 to 1872. If you know of other journalists who've run for public office and have materials from their campaigns, please contact him. Send a picture or photocopy. Dealers must price your goods. Amateur sellers may request an offer. "I am very selective."

Walter Brasch
Department of Journalism
Bloomsburg University
Bloomsburg, PA 17815
(717) 389-4565 days   Fax: (717) 389-2094

★ **Samuel Gompers ephemera** from before 1886 is sought, particularly items related to his career as a cigar maker or an NYC union officer, but please inquire about *any* Gompers item.

> Tony Hyman
> PO Box 3028
> Pismo Beach, CA 93448
> (805) 773-6777   Fax: (805) 773-8436   thyman@tobacciana.com

★ **Lillie Langtry memorabilia** including photos, cigarette and trade cards, letters, programs, posters, tickets, costume or set sketches, and cosmetics issued under her name. Wants a wine label produced on Langtry Farms, 1889-1906, worth up to $500. Langtry was also known as Langtree, the Jersey Lily, Lady Lillie de Bathe, Mrs. Jersey, and Emilie Charlotte Le Breton. In addition to his interest in Mrs. Langtry, he also wants material on **Edward Langtry** and **Freddie Gebhard(t)**.

> Orville Magoon
> PO Box 279
> Middletown, CA 95461
> (707) 987-2385 days   Fax: (707) 987-9351

★ **John Steinbeck** memorabilia, signed limited editions, first editions, first printings by subsequent publishers, appearances in anthologies, spoken word records and tapes, film and theater memorabilia, and things owned by him. Does not want book club editions, items in poor condition, or fakes. If a book originally had a dust jacket, slipcase, box or wrap-around, then it should still be present. Be specific about what you have, giving complete bibliographic information.

> James Dourgarian, Bookman
> 1595-A Third Avenue
> Walnut Creek, CA 94596
> (510) 935-5033

★ **Mark Twain memorabilia**, autographs, photos, stories about, books about, and especially first editions of his books, "but no books that are falling apart." Include the color of the cover when providing standard bibliographic information.

> Duane and Eunice Bietz
> 6461 SE Thorburn
> Portland, OR 97215
> Fax: (503) 233-1602

★ **Jack London memorabilia, books** and **personal effects.**

> Winifred Kingman
> Jack London Bookstore
> PO Box 337
> Glen Ellen, CA 95442
> (707) 996-2888   (707) 996-4107

★ **Edgar Rice Burroughs and characters.** Wants rare items related to stories and characters created by Edgar Rice Burroughs, including:

- Hardback books, reprints with dust jackets or 1st editions with or w/out dust jackets (1st editions in dj's of *Tarzan of the Apes Return of Tarzan*, or *Princess of Mars* are worth $2,000+;
- Pulp magazines, 1912 to 1919, featuring ERB stories;
- Original *Tarzan* art by Ray Kuenkel, J. Allen St. John, Hogarth, Frank Schoonover, and Hal Foster;
- Autographed items by ERB or by early movie Tarzans;
- Toys, games and premiums before 1950;
- Movie posters and lobby cards before 1945.

Does not want reprint hardbacks without dust jackets, paperbacks, recent comic books, or anything in poor condition. Make certain to include the publisher when describing a book. Give your phone number. Dealers must price your goods, but amateurs may request an offer.

> Jim Gerlach
> 2206 Greenbrier Drive
> Irving, TX 75060
> (214) 986-5233

★ **Sherlock Holmes items and specific related Victoriana.** "Please call me if you have **anything written about or showing** Sherlock Holmes, Dr. John Watson or author Sir Arthur Conan Doyle. This includes **all memorabilia**, books, photos, movies, magazines, comics, ads, busts, ceramics, records, tapes, pipes, play books, scripts, etc., no matter where or when made. Also wants scientific apparatus and instruments, books, weapons and **anything else made between 1850-1900 that was mentioned in Holmes stories**. "I don't want currently published books containing just the regular 56 short stories and the 4 novels. However, if the book contains the stories plus commentary, analysis, notes, etc., then I would indeed be interested. If in doubt, please call." He adds, "Yes, it's my real name"

> Rev. Sherlock Holmes
> Private Letter Box 3
> Worcester, MA 01613
> (508) 754-9907

★ **Sherlock Holmes.** Wants "anything related to Sherlock Holmes or **Sir Arthur Conan Doyle**" including figurines, drawings, autographs, posters, photos, etc. Also wants items from **actors who have played Holmes** including Basil Rathbone, Peter Cushing and Jeremy Brett.

> Robert Hess
> 559 Potter Blvd.
> Brightwaters, NY 11718
> (516) 665-8365

ANIMAL COLLECTIBLES

★ *Royal Doulton* **flambe animal figurines.** Hundreds of different animals, both wild and domestic, are to be found in these attractive red pottery figures which range from 2" to 14" in size. They are still made today, so it's the older figures that are most sought after and bring the best prices. Have the figure(s) in front of you when you call this 20 year veteran collector. Or send a good description.

> Ed Pascoe
> 101 Almeria Avenue
> Coral Gables, FL 33134
>   (800) 872-0195   Fax: (305) 445-3305

★ *Royal Doulton* **animal figurines.** "I'll buy any, large or small, as long as they are marked ROYAL DOULTON and are in perfect condition. "Look for a number with the letters HN or K. Tell me the number and I'll make an immediate cash offer."

> Carol Payne
> Carol's Gallery
> 14455 Big Basin Way
> Saratoga, CA 95070
>   (408) 867-7055

★ **Camels.** Seeks prints, paintings, sculptures, and whatever you have, with a few exceptions. "I am not interested in small wood, or leather camels or in anything to do with *Camel* cigarettes. Please send photo or Xerox™ copy, along with the price wanted and your phone number. All letters will be answered promptly."

> Charlie Stewart
> 900 Grandview Avenue
> Reno, NV 89503
>   (702) 747-1439

★ **Zebras in many different forms,** including porcelain, carvings, paintings, folk art, etc. To be of interest, an item must be of a zebra, not just zebra striped. Please, no hides or parts of dead zebras.

> Dave Galt
> 302 West 78th Street
> New York, NY 10024
>   (212) 769-2514

★ **Musk oxen figurines, prints, book plates, and other small ephemera,** 1750-1930. Especially wants postcards, cigarette silks, trading cards, pottery, stamps and other small paper items. Will pay up to $100 each for illustrations from *History of Quadrupeds* (1781) or *Arctic Zoology* (1784) both by Thomas Pennant.
Ross Hartsough
98 Bryn Mawr Road
Winnipeg, MB R3T 3P5, CANADA

★ **Wild boar ephemera.** "I'll buy paintings, bronzes, ceramics, advertising, anything featuring the wild European boar or its American counterparts, the peccary or javelina." Describe condition.
Henry Winningham
3205 South Morgan Street
Chicago, IL 60608

★ **Snakes, turtles, frogs, lizards, alligators and other reptile and amphibians.** Wants paintings and prints, wood carvings, ceramics, bronzes, stained glass, postcards, jewelry, folk art, pens, snake canes, stamps, posters, tribal art and gargoyles with reptile designs. Also wants **zoological artifacts like turtle shells or snake skulls**. Please send a good description or photo and phone number.
Mark Miller
PO Box 52261
Philadelphia, PA 19115
(215) 464-3561 voice and fax   70176.1153@compuserve.com

★ **Old butterfly collections** in Riker mounts, glass-topped drawers, or in paper triangles. He's trying to preserve lost species found only in antique collections, as well as supplying butterflies to museums and collectors worldwide. His personal favorites as swallowtails, the Solomon Islands version of which can be worth $900. Send photos of the collection or, if you can, a species list. He DOES NOT WANT endangered or protected species, butterflies with paper bodies or coffee trays or other items made from butterfly wings. A long business size envelope with 64¢ postage will get you *How to Butterfly Garden*.
Marc Schenck
The Butterfly Zoo
1151 Aquidneck Avenue
Middletowne, RI 02842
(401) 849-9519 7pm - midnight ET   Fax: (401) 847-2970

HORSE COLLECTIBLES

★ **Books, prints, and paper ephemera about horses.** "I buy books, prints, and paper *only*, but I buy on all horse related topics: polo, horse-back riding, carriage driving, sidesaddle, draft horses, horseshoeing, veterinary, etc." Buys horse farm catalogs, brochures, posters, prints of riding and recognized horse breeds, books (1st editions in dust jackets only), magazines, postcards (if horse is named), stud books, and breed registers. "I don't buy common books still in print, book club editions, *Diseases of the Horse,* books on racing or horse race betting, or books with highlighting or underlining in the text. Please, I am not in the market for figurines, bronzes, or anything other than books, prints and paper about horses. Your items must be in fine condition for resale."

Barbara Cole
October Farm
2609 Branch Road
Raleigh, NC 27610
(919) 772-0482   Fax: (919) 779-6265

★ **Breyer plastic model horses** and other animals in good to excellent condition, without breaks or heavy scratches. "I'm interested in singles and in whole collections. I'm especially looking for *Breyer* horses of a different color, such as blue or gold, and am a little more lenient in condition for rarities. I pay up to $400 for rare colors, though most *Breyer* horses are worth from $10 to $60. Horses should be at least five inches tall and not made in Hong Kong." Describe your horse thoroughly, including the position in which it's standing or laying and the position of the feet, the color, and any mold information your might find on the bottom." She requests you include your phone number.

Leslie Baldwin
706 Pan Am Avenue
Naples, FL 34110
(941) 566-8412

★ **Hagen-Renaker porcelain horses and other animals**, as long as they're at least two inches tall. "I look for ones in good to excellent condition, but will consider animals with breaks. I'm interested in singles and in whole collections. Most *Hagen-Renaker* horses are worth from $10 to $60 but a few rare ones can reach $300, so please describe your horse thoroughly, including what it is, the position in which it's standing or laying and the position of the feet, the color, and any mold information your might find on the bottom." She requests you include your phone number.

Leslie Baldwin
706 Pan Am Avenue
Naples, FL 34110
(941) 566-8412

CAT COLLECTIBLES

★ **Cat items of all sorts,** especially high quality porcelain, paintings, carvings, prints, Orientalia, needlework, pottery, jade, ivory, jewelry, cookie jars, calendars, Art Deco, advertising, steins, medals, doorstops, bronzes, crystal, postcards, playing cards, toys, etc. Buys some cartoon cats (**Felix , Sylvester, Kliban** cats) but does not want any Garfield figures or reproductions in any form. Also she does not buy chalk figures, or anything broken or damaged.

Marilyn Dipboye
33161 Wendy Drive
Sterling Heights, MI 48310
(810) 264-0285

★ **B.Kliban cat items** of all types, including figurines, candy dishes, banks, salt and pepper sets, mugs, cookie jars, cat feeders, kitchen and bath towels, framed pictures, stuffed animals, curtains, comforters, mugs, candle holders, magnets, place mats, etc. Ceramic items should be marked TASTESETTER/SIGMA. "I don't need sheets, soiled towels or broken items although I will consider ceramic items with small chips. Note that **I want black and white cats**, not black, white and gray cats as those are newer. These are relatively inexpensive items, so please set the price you would like. Values can be from $5 to $100 depending on the item."

Sue Lucente
115 Marbeth Avenue
Carlisle, PA 17013
(717) 249-9343

★ **Felix the Cat** pictured on china, or anything else, as long as it's from the 1930's or before. She is not interested in any of the Felix items reproduced in the 1950's. Please include a clear photo as she will be able to tell old from new in most cases.

Marilyn Baseman
Birdcage Antiques
PO Box 268
South Egremont, MA 01258
(413) 528-3556

Don't forget to include a Self-Addressed Stamped Envelope. Use a long #10 envelope folded into thirds for best results.

DOG COLLECTIBLES

★ **Dog related collectibles** "especially figurines, jewelry and post-cards, but everything doggy considered." Russian Wolfhounds and Greyhounds are favorite breeds, especially in porcelain. Size, material, and markings are key elements in description, along with the breed if you know dogs well enough to tell.

> Denise Hamilton
> 899 Latta Brook Road
> Elmira, NY 14901
> (607) 732-2550

★ **Dog art and ephemera.** Wants many different quality items:
- Dog figurines by well known porcelain companies from England, Germany, Denmark, Austria and America as well as a few others, especially artist signed pieces;
- Ceramics representing purebred dogs in lifelike colors; these are usually of lesser quality than the above, but are often signed or labeled;
- Bronzes of dogs, especially signed;
- *Wedgwood* dog plates by Marguerite Kirmse;
- Woodcarvings by ANRI of Italy;
- Oil paintings or etchings of purebred dogs;
- Cigarette cards of purebred dogs;
- Kennel club, dog show, or dog club medallions pre-1920 which have a lifelike representation of a dog on them;
- Other interesting three dimensional items depicting dogs.

"I am not interested in chalkware, Staffordshire, toys, doorstops, cast metal souvenir items, plastic, celluloid, poor quality items, or books, nor do I buy paper items other than etchings and cigarette cards. Figures must be lifelike portrayals of purebred dogs." Photo is preferred, along with the size and manufacturer. The condition is very important. All scratches, chips, flakes, breaks and imperfections must be noted.

> Sharlene Beckwith
> Exclusively Dogs!
> PO Box 1858
> Upland, CA 91785
> (909) 946-1544 days   Fax: (909) 949-4796

★ *Morton Studio* **figurines of dogs, wild animals or people.** These heavy ceramics are almost always marked on the bottom. Size, color, and shape are needed, along with condition.

> Denise Hamilton
> 899 Latta Brook Road
> Elmira, NY 14901
> (607) 732-2550

★ **Bull terriers and dog fighting.** Especially wants prints, paintings, and statuary. Books on dog fighting also wanted.

> Ron Lieberman
> RD #1   Box 42
> Glen Rock, PA 17327
>   (717) 235-2134   Fax: (717) 235-8042

★ **Animated dog items.** "I buy dog items that move or are functional such as clocks, watches, toys and pop-up books. If it's got a dog on it and it moves or does something useful, drop me a line."

> Mel Rosenthal
> 5 The Strand
> New Castle, DE 19720
>   (302) 322-8944

★ **Pet license tags, rabies tags, and all other metal tags related to animals.** Especially interested in Illinois tags. Especially wants tags pre-1900 for which he pays $15 and up.

> Rich Hartzog
> PO Box 4143 BVT
> Rockford, IL 61110

★ **Dog license tags** including: (1) tags from any state if they are shaped like the date of issue ($7-$25); (2) tags from anywhere in the world pre-1910 ($4-$100); (3) all NY tags issued before 1918 $5-$150); and (4) NY Conservation Dept. tags, 1917-35 (15-$50). Most tags before 1900 start at $25 and those before 1880 start at $40.

> James Case
> 10189 Crane Road
> Lindley, NY 14858
>   (607) 524-6606

WET CRITTER COLLECTIBLES

★ **Whales and dolphins.** Interested in images of whales and dolphins that occur in books, photos, postcards, stereoviews, art of all types (paintings, prints, sculpture), advertising, posters, stamps, coins, money, toys and games. Also interested in film footage (including home movies) of whales and recordings of whale sounds. Will also buy whale bones, baleen, and other whale artifacts. "We already have most items made after 1975." Send "a detailed description, including a photo" asks this collector-dealer-nonprofit organization.
>Steve King
>Whales & Friends
>PO Box 2660
>Alameda, CA 94501
>(510) 769-8500   Fax: (510) 865-0851

★ **Tropical fish tanks, equipment and ephemera.** Wants old books, magazines, catalogs directly related to tropical fish, as well as "pet shop" or turtle magazines and other paper relevant to the hobby. Photocopy what you have. Priced items preferred but will make offers.
>Gary Bagnall
>3100 McMillan Road
>San Luis Obispo, CA 93401
>(805) 542-9988   Fax: (805) 542-9295

★ **Goldfish ephemera**, such as old food containers, literature, magazines, advertising for related items. What have you?
>Thomas McKinnon
>PO Box 86
>Wagram, NC 28396
>(910) 369-2367

★ **Oyster memorabilia.** Got anything related to oysters? Cans, figurines, what have you?
>Sheldon Katz
>211 Roanoke Ave.
>Riverhead, NY 11901
>(516) 369-1100

★ **Oyster related items** such as oyster cans, signs, posters, trade cards, labels, pinbacks, and what have you. Does not want oyster plates or reproduction signs. Describe the condition. Dealers, price your goods. Amateurs may ask for offers.
>John Baron
>2928 Marshall Avenue
>Cincinnati, OH 45220
>(513) 751-6631   Fax: (513) 763-5372

IF YOUR ITEM IS RELATED TO TRANSPORTATION, BUSINESS OR THE PROFESSIONS, IT WILL PROBABLY SELL.

If it has anything to do with business, manufacturing, advertising, sales or commerce...someone collects it.

Some of these items are obscure, so there isn't a great deal of competition for them, and prices stay relatively low. But small sums add up to substantial amounts of money. On the other hand, some items listed on the nest 100 pages sell for $10,000. You don't want to confuse the two.

You are not qualified to judge what something is worth. If you aren't absolutely certain what you have and what its current market value is, you should turn to experts in Trash or Treasure 8 to help you. *I've brought you the best in transportation, advertising and business buyers. Someone here will be just right for you.*

To sell your transportation, business, advertising or profession related item, your description should include:

   (1) What it is you wish to sell;
   (2) What product or business it's associated with;
   (3) What it depicts;
   (4) What material(s) it is made from;
   (5) Its size, shape, and color (especially colors of glass);
   (6) Markings embossed (raised) or incised (stamped in);
   (7) Information contained on an ID plate;
   (8) Accurate information regarding condition.

*The history and artifacts of some American industries is being preserved by fewer than a half dozen people, who can be difficult for you to find. **Trash or Treasure** sometimes puts you in touch with the only person in the country willing to buy what you have!*

AUTOMOBILES

★ **American and European cars** 1920 - 1970 in unrestored condition, as well as parts and accessories for those cars. "I prefer convertibles and two-door models, but will purchase unusual or limited production four-door models if very complete and original. **Pre-1940 race cars, sports cars and hot rods** are also very interesting to me." Buys accessorie, add-ons like skirts and sunvisors amd speed or high performance quipment. Also buy collections of older auto items like **ornaments**, mascots, **literature**, shop **signs**, etc. This 31 year veteran dealer says to tell him the year, make, model, body style, and number of cylinders "as a good place to start." He warns that "scratched or faded original paint is far more desirable to a restorer than a cheap repaint, so sell your car as it sits, don't try to fix it up." Include your phone #.

David "old car nut" Tomlinson's Collectible Cars & Parts
4739 Valley Boulevard
Los Angeles, CA 90032
(213) 222-4611 days   Fax: (213) 223-0752

★ **Old and antique cars and car parts.** "I buy and sell all types of antique cars and parts, foreign and domestic, as well as related materials such as parts, **service manuals**, advertisements and promotional **toys**." He specializes in **antique, classic, custom (hot rods), exotic and kit cars**, especially 1964 1/2 through 1968 *Mustangs* and *Shelbys*. Your description should include the type of item, and if a car, a description, including year, make, model, mileage, colors, and a brief history. Note its condition. "A color photo is helpful." Will make offers, but only if you intend to sell. Don't bother this busy 13 year veteran if you're only price fishing. Operates a national computer database on which you can advertise autos and cycles for sale or wanted, complete with color photos! Call for info.

Gregory Janaczek, Janaczek Engineering
Route 1 Box 1594
Gouldsboro, PA 18424
(717) 842-2277

★ **Books, catalogs and advertising for guns and automobiles** from before 1940. This well know author writes on those topics, appraises guns and autos, and acts as a consultant, helping folks sell automobiles lucratively. **If you own an antique, classic, or sports car and need help deciding how and where to sell it**, Balderson may be the best place to begin. His *Price Guide to Collector Cars (8th ed)* is $17 in stores as is his price guide to collectible firearms.

Robert Balderson
2830 Arden Way #110
Sacramento, CA 95825
(916) 974-7733

★ **Sports and race cars, 1950-1989.** We want cars used for slalom, **drag racing**, auto cross, and particularly road racing events. Most interested in obtaining German, Italian and British factory team cars, but well prepared amateur driven cars are also of interest. Will buy in any condition, but must be complete.

> Paul Dunlop
> PO Box 6269
> Statesville, NC 28687
> (800) 227-1996

★ **Classic American and foreign automobiles.** One of the nation's largest auctioneers of high quality foreign and old domestic automobiles. If you have anything fast, sleek, limited production, or unusual, give Cole a call and discuss putting it up for sale in California's lucrative automobile market. Also *Corvettes, T-Birds*, older convertibles, and fine condition high quality American cars of the 1950's and 1960's. "Don't sell your old car for too little."

> Rick Cole Auction Co.
> 7447 La Jolla Blvd.
> La Jolla, CA 92037
> (818) 506-6533

★ **Race car "speed equipment"** to hop up automobiles from the 1930's, 40's, 50's, and 60's. Whether factory equipment or aftermarket, if it's designed to make a car go faster, and you want to sell it, give Dale a call. He'd especially like to find early *Ford* flathead engine cylinder heads, intake manifolds, and camshafts. 1955 to '58 *Chrysler* aftermarket intake manifolds or valve covers will bring top prices. He personally does not want complete cars, complete engines, or "any items that can't be shipped U.P.S." But, if you have these things for sale, you might inquire as he adds, "I do have quality buyers for this type item." Describe what you have, including manufacturer and date, when possible. Dale publishes *RPM*, a monthly catalog which includes 30 pages of classified ads for folks buying and selling speed parts. You can subscribe for $20 a year.

> Dale Wilch
> 2217 North 99th
> Kansas City, KS 66109
> (913) 788-3219   Fax: (913) 788-9682   RPM@internetMCI.COM

★ **Automobiles made between 1940 and 1969** if well maintained and low mileage, especially a *Cadillac* convertible from the 1950's or 60's. "I'd keep it as long as I live!" Also buys **automotive related signs**: auto sales and service, gasoline, motor oil, etc. Also **auto toys**.

> Gus Garton, Garton's Auto
> 5th and Vine
> Millville, NJ 08332

AUTOMOBILE EPHEMERA

★ **Paper ephemera, advertising, and promotional items associated with automobiles,** trucks, buses, campers, taxis, auto racing, police cars, ambulances, and hearses. Jay operates a large mail order business selling **transportation memorabilia of all sorts** and always needs clean old catalogs, promotional items, emblems, models given away by car dealers, auto company service pins, owner's manuals, and other small items associated with any form of vehicle. Will buy U.S. and foreign items, and multiples of some things. Will accept boxes sent on approval and "will make immediate offers to buy." Include your phone number. Does not want shop manuals, parts lists, and magazine ads.

Jay Ketelle
3721 Farwell
Amarillo, TX 79109
(806) 355-3456   Fax: (806) 355-5743

★ **Automobile related memorabilia** including promotional give-aways, **owner's manuals**, repair manuals, radiator emblems and caps, dial type tire gauges, fancy gear shift knobs, car clocks, **spark plugs**, horns, dash panels, brass speedometers, **DAV keychains**, automobile **magazines**, plant employee badges, canceled checks from auto companies, **stocks and bonds**, porcelain or leather license plates, driving awards and anything you can imagine having to do with automobiles except magazine ads.

Joseph Russell
455 Ollie Street
Cottage Grove, WI 53527
(608) 839-4736 eves

★ **Automobile sales catalogs, brochures, owner's manuals** and **repair guides** printed by the auto company. Wants material for all cars and trucks, American or foreign, especially pre-1970. No magazines, clipped ads, *Motor's Manuals, Chilton's Manuals*, or books not printed by the auto company. Also buys **auto dealer promotional items** including signs, salesman's awards, and the like. "Please send me a list of each item by year and make. If a list is not practical, give me a count by decade, such as 'so many brochures from 1950 to 1959,' etc."

Walter Miller
6710 Brooklawn Parkway
Syracuse, NY 13211
(315) 432-8282   Fax: (315) 432-8256

★ **Hot Rod and custom car magazines** from 1940-1964.

Don Schneider
PO Box 1570
Merritt, BC
V1K 1B8 CANADA

★ **Books, magazines, and factory literature about cars**, trucks, motorcycles, and bicycles. Also buys newsletters and magazines produced by automobile clubs devoted to one particular make of vehicle or another. Documents related to vehicle history 1895-1990 also purchased.

> Ralph Dunwoodie
> 5935 Calico Drive
> Sun Valley, NV 89433
> (702) 673-3811

★ **Books, catalogs, and owner's manuals**. Books may be on automobiles, auto history, racing, biography, auto travel, etc. Not interested in technical and repair manuals. Give standard bibliographic information, and note condition of cover, pages, spine, binding, and dust jacket. Also buys some photos of cars.

> David King's Automotive Books
> 5 Brouwer Lane
> Rockville Center, NY 11570
> (516) 766-1561   Fax: (516) 766-7502

★ **Automobile dealership ephemera** including signs for any make of automobile, sales literature, and what have you from the period 1930 to 1970. Nothing newer. No reproductions. SASE a must.

> Gus Garton, Garton's Auto
> 5th and Vine
> Millville, NJ 08332
> (609) 825-3618

★ **1932 *Chevrolet*** parts, accessories and paper ephemera including ads, showroom literature, catalogs, repair manuals, and what have you. As long as it's from a 1932 Chevy car or truck, he wants it.

> Reed Fitzpatrick
> PO Box 369
> Vashon, WA 98070
> (206) 567-4391 eves 5-7 Pacific

★ ***Delorean* items**. Wants "anything and everything related to John Z. Delorean and the *Delorean* car," including parts, newspaper clippings, magazine articles, posters, photos, commercials, certificates, and company greeting cards (worth $125 each!). Also items about the *Delorean* used in *Back to the Future* movies except bubble gum cards which are common. "The original Delorean sales brochure and John D's *On a Clear Day* are widely available; don't waste your time."

> Everen T. Brown
> PO Box 296
> Salt Lake City, UT 84110
> Fax: (801) 364-2646

★ *Ford* **Motor Company.** Buys and sells "almost anything" having to do with Ford Motor Company or Henry and Edsel Ford. Particularly interested in *Ford* aviation and *Ford* display and exhibition items from various World's Fairs up to 1964.

> Tim O'Callaghan
> PO Box 512
> Northville, MI 48167
> (810) 449-2652

★ *Ford* **Motor Company memorabilia** and other items related to Ford automobiles: postcards, books, photos, Christmas cards, sheet music, records, pens, pins, china, silverware, menus, sales literature, joke books, and what have you. Also wants items related to Henry Ford. Has a special interest in sales literature from 1928 to 1936.

> Cliff Moebius
> 484 Winthrop Street
> Westbury, NY 11590
> (516) 333-3797   Fax: (516) 333-1712

★ *Ford* **parts,** 1932 to 1967, that are new and unused, including fenders, grill assemblies, radiators, etc. Does not want reproduction parts.

> Gus Garton, Garton's Auto
> 5th and Vine
> Millville, NJ 08332
> (609) 825-3618

★ *Willy's* **automobile items** from 1933-42, including parts, showroom literature, shop manuals, dealer promos and signs. Also interested in 1950's and 60's *Willy's* drag racing items, photos of drivers, meets, etc. He emphasizes he has "no interest in jeep items" or any reprints.

> David Facey, Auto-Ads
> 7015 Klein Road
> Lakeland, FL 33813

★ *Volkswagen* **related memorabilia,** literature, toys, etc. "My preference is for older bug related items, with spilt window bug and oval window bug toys and memorabilia the most desirable. However, any old VW items are of interest." Many foreign made toys are worth from $100 to $400 each, with some others, including some plastic ones, bringing even more! Does not want recent toys, *Avon,* or toys made in China. To sell toys, give the size, color, maker, and condition, noting whether you have the original box. Best to Xerox™ other items.

> Mike Wilson
> 23490 SW 82nd Street
> Tualatin, OR 97062
> (503) 638-7074 eves

★ *Buick* **promotional items.**
Alvin Heckard
Route #1 Box 88
Lewistown, PA 17044
(717) 248-7071

★ *Mercedes* **and** *Rolls-Royce* radiator mascots and other parts, accessories, manuals, and literature made before 1960.
Joseph Weber
604 Centre Street
Ashland, PA 17921
(717) 875-4401 from 3 to 5 p.m.

★ *Rolls-Royce* **advertising,** pamphlets, cards, toys, and other information. Has particular interest in all models from the years 1957 through 1962, *Princess* through *Silver Cloud.*
Richard Melcher
PO Box 1812
Wenatchee, WA 98807
(509) 662-0386

★ **Parts and ephemera for** *Gardner* **autos.** Buys parts, hubcaps, mascots, owner's manuals, and the like. Will pay $75 for a single brochure on the front drive 1930 *Gardner.*
Robert Owen
PO Box 204
Fairborn, OH 45324

★ **Radiator and hood ornaments** from autos before WWII, whether factory original or accessories. Does not want broken items or reproductions. Also buys catalogs, brochures, and advertising related to hood ornaments. Give a photo or detailed description.
Sy and Ronnie Margolis
17853 Santiago Boulevard #107-210
Villa Park, CA 92861
(714) 974-5938   Fax: (714) 921-0731

★ **Odd looking spark plugs.** "I'll buy as many as you have, the odder looking the better." He especially wants those with priming cups. No *AC* or *Champion* plugs.
Joseph Weber
604 Centre Street
Ashland, PA 17921
(717) 875-4401 from 3 to 5 p.m.

★ **Tire and tube repair kits cans** made of paper or tin. The older and more colorful the better. Photocopy what you have, please.

> Ed Natale, Jr.
> PO Box 222
> Wyckoff, NJ 07481
> (201) 848-8485   Fax: (201) 891-4252

★ **Car jacks.** "I'm a Baptist minister who owns more than 2,000 car jacks. I collect them, but also supply jacks to collectors and restoration shops. I am interested in buying:
  • Old bumper jacks with round or little I-beam upright shaft;
  • Small jacks with names of early car manufacturers on them;
  • Small screw jacks with protrusions like little shark's teeth;
  • Any unusual screw jack.
Please send a photo or drawing with the dimensions along with any patent dates or other numbers. I've been doing this for 14 years, and don't mind providing approximate values of jacks or making offers." No modern jacks, *Volkswagen* jacks or jacks with big screws.

> Larry Olson
> 4125 56th Street
> Des Moines, IA 50310
> (515) 278-8487

★ *Firestone Tire Company* **promotional items** especially those shaped like tires including tire ashtrays, clocks, pen holders, cigarette cases. Also radios shaped like batteries, and other figural selling aids. List everything printed on the tire and on the insert. Does not want domestic ashtrays made after 1950. Pays $20-$35 for most items.

> Wayne Ray
> 10325 Willeo Creek Trace
> Roswell, GA 30075
> (770) 998-5325

★ **Tire company promotional items** especially **tire ashtrays**, tire clocks, pen holders, radios, globes, *Tires* magazines, tire catalogs, and other literature and promotional items. "Will pay $50 for any original *Michelin* or *Overman* rubber tire ashtray." Also want foreign tires and those issued for promotions. Long priced wants list available.

> Jeff McVey
> 1810 West State Street #427
> Boise, ID 83702
> (208) 342-8447

★ **Tire ash trays** all sizes, colors, makes and ages, new or old.

> Don Schneider
> PO Box 1570
> Merritt, BC
> V1K 1B8 CANADA

★ **Factory original automobile AM radios** 1926-1962. Only AM-FM from 1963-77. Wants brand and model number. Also **auto wheelcovers** (not hubcaps), 1950 to the present. Tell the make, model, condition, and quantity. Include your price, phone number and hours to call.

> John Sheldon
> 2718 Koper Drive
> Sterling Heights, MI 48310
> (810) 977-7979 days   Fax: (810) 977-0895

★ **Mobile homes, trailer coaches, trailers and related ephemera.** "We're interested in full size trailers, motor homes and post war trailer coaches (early mobile homes) in good to excellent condition made between 1925 and 1959. Please send photos of the inside and outside of your vehicle along with an SASE for our offer." Also **all ephemera related to motor camping** including photos, articles, license plates, salesmen's samples, models, toys, amateur or professional film, sheet music, advertising, brochures, postcards, and promotional material of all sort, including that for *Volkswagen* campers. Todd & Kristin operate *Lost Highways*, a club magazine filled with photos, memories and ads from the heyday of trailering and motor camping. Sample issue $6. Compete information for a long SASE.

> Todd & Kristin Kimmell
> PO Box 43737
> Philadelphia, PA 19106
> (215) 925-2568

★ *Mullins Red Cap* **Trailer** literature, parts, and advertising.

> Cliff Moebius
> 484 Winthrop Street
> Westbury, NY 11590
> (516) 333-3797   Fax: (516) 333-1712

★ **Engine rebuilding equipment** and tools for working on antique auto, marine, truck, tractor, and stationary engines made by *KR Wilson, Kent Moore, Hempy-Cooper, Waterbury Simplicity, Van-Norman, Peterson* and others. Especially wants original equipment for Babbitt bearings including production equipment, smaller equipment for motorcycles and larger equipment for stationary engines. Please give the make, model, and power required. Indicate if it works or not, whether it has been modified, and what accessories are available. Not interested in home made equipment or items that have been "super modified."

> Shawn R. Aldrich
> Aldrich Engine Rebuilding
> 352 River Road
> Willington, CT 06279
> (860) 429-3111

LICENSE PLATES

★ **License plates before 1920,** especially **undated** plates made of leather, brass, or porcelain. Will buy old collections or accumulations. Describe condition carefully, including damage, chips, and crazing. He offers to answer questions about license plates and says, "If I don't want your plates, perhaps I can find someone who does." Gary is secretary of the Automobile License Plate Collector's Association and a valuable source of information.

    Gary Brent Kincade
    PO Box 7
    Horner, WV 26372
        (304) 269-7623 days   (304) 842-3773 eves

★ **License plates.** Will buy any good condition pre-1935 plate plus collections or accumulations of plates:
- **Undated** or those made of porcelain, leather, or wood;
- Any U.S. pre-1915;
- Southern and South-western plates pre-1935;
- All Alaska, Hawaii or foreign plates before 1950;
- All motorcycle plates pre-1950;
- All plates issued on or for Indian reservations;
- Personalized plates "with cute names or phrases";
- Any pictorial plates;
- **Mini plates** from DAV, *Goodrich, Wheaties,* or *Post* cereals;
- **Car club emblems** such as AAA, especially foreign or pre-1925;
- **Chauffeur's badges** in good original condition, pre-1940;
- Ordinary plates in near new condition will bring 25¢ to $5 (for hard to find ones).

List the type of item, place of origin, date, number, condition, quantity, and price (if possible). "If you don't like what I offer for your license plate, I'll let you run a free ad in my *License Plate Corner* magazine so you can try to sell it for more."

    George Chartrand
    PO Box 334
    Winnipeg, MB
    R3C 2H6 CANADA
        (204) 774-1186

★ **Porcelain license plates** from U.S. and Canadian cars, trucks, and motorcycles before 1923. Also wants early **photos and photo postcards of vehicles clearly showing readable plates.** Pays especially well for plates from Southern and unpopulated Western states. Does not buy painted metal plates. Photocopies suggested.

    Rodney Brunsell
    55 Spring Street
    Hanson, MA 02341

★ **License plates** from anywhere in the world, but primarily Washington and Alaska. "I'll buy singles or accumulations. Unusual plates such as mobile home, taxi, trailer, state representative, etc., are particularly welcome." Also buys **plates that carry an advertising message** and fasten just above or below a license plate. Brass plaques, **auto club insignias**, and the like are of interest too. "When you contact me, I want to know the state, year and type of plate. Photocopy if you can."

    Reed Fitzpatrick
    PO Box 369
    Vashon, WA 98070
       (206) 463-3900 8am to 4pm

★ **License plates of all types** from anywhere especially early porcelain plates. "I am happy to receive inquiries even regarding common items. If I am not interested I will gladly refer readers to someone else or try to help out in other ways." Give the name of the issuing agency, type of plate, material from which it was made, the date, and its condition. Note any repainting or repair. Fluent in Spanish and French.

    Andy Bernstein
    43-60 Douglaston Parkway #524
    Douglaston, NY 11363
       (718) 279-1890   (407) 793-8422

★ **Expired obsolete license plates of all types and varieties** from anywhere. "I'll buy almost anything and everything ever used for registration or identification on a motor vehicle, front or back, domestic or foreign, from the earliest days of motoring up to and including current issues." Porcelain plates from before 1920, especially from less populous states, city and local issues and home-made plates bring the biggest premiums. Values depend on type of plate, numbers, rarity, condition, and degree of collector interest. He encourages you to write about *any* plate you think might be unusual, as long as you include a Xerox™ or clear color photo and a SASE. If a porcelain plate has a maker's name on the back, include that information. This long time collector/dealer asks that you also include your evening phone number.

    Dave Lincoln
    PO Box 331
    Yorklyn, DE 19736
       (610) 444-4144

★ **License plates from Missouri, Kansas, and Colorado.** Also wants other states from the years 1936, 1976, and 1989. Also **miniature key chain license plates** produced by *B.F. Goodrich* or the DAV. Provide a list of the items you have and the price you'd like.

    George Van Trump, Jr.
    PO Box 260170
    Lakewood, CO 80226
       (303) 985-3508

★ **License plates.** "I specialize in buying and selling all types of license plates, especially porcelains, early issues, error plates, motorcycle plates and other unusual plates from any country. I will buy one plate or an entire collection." This twenty year veteran collector says you may "write, call or e-mail any question about plate identification. I'm glad to help." Xerox™ is a good way to describe a plate.

> Drew Steitz
> PO Box 222
> East Texas, PA 18046
> (610) 791-7979 voice and fax   PL8Seditor@aol.com

★ **British Columbia license plates** before 1922 in any condition. Later BC plates will be considered if unusual, as will pre-1960 Yukon plates, Canadian **motorcycle** plates, and BC chauffeur's badges.

> Don Schneider
> PO Box 1570
> Merritt, BC
> V1K 1B8   CANADA
> (604) 378-6421

★ *B.F.Goodrich* **and DAV keychain license plate tags.** Pays 50¢ to $1 each, depending on age and state. The older the better.

> Dennis Schulte
> 8th Avenue NW
> Waukon, IA 52172

BUSSES & TROLLEYS 349

BUSSES, TROLLEYS & TAXIS

★ **Bus industry memorabilia** from 1935 to the present is wanted, including models, toys, banks, post cards of busses and terminals, time tables, bus manufacturer sales brochures, bus drivers' manuals, uniforms, driver's badges, promotional items, coach logos, bus industry trade magazines, and china, crystal, and flatware with bus company logos. This charter coach company owner will even consider actual **full size _Greyhound_ style buses.** Please send a good description of the item and its condition for a fair offer. Regularly issues a catalog of bus related items for sale.

    Charles Wotring
    Royal Coach
    911 Conley Drive
    Mechanicsburg, PA 17055
       (717) 691-1147 Fax: (717) 691-6623

★ _Greyhound_ **and** _Trailways_ **bus memorabilia.** Wants a wide range of items, such as cap badges, driver awards, etc., but mostly interested in toy _Greyhound_ and _Trailways_ busses, and _Greyvan Moving_ truck toys. Prefers a picture or photocopy. No magazine ads, timetables, postcards or posters, but he does want internal company data like garage locations, driver assignments, and organizational directories.

    Eugene Farha
    PO Box 633
    Cedar Grove, WV 25039
       (304) 340-3308 days Fax: (304) 347-4800

★ **Memorabilia from buses, taxis, hearses, ambulances, and any other public conveyance** before 1960 including emblems, badges, licenses, license plates, advertising, promotional giveaway trinkets, operator's manuals, sales literature, etc. May be foreign or U.S. as long as they are old and genuine. Will accept items sent on approval.

    Jay Ketelle
    3721 Farwell
    Amarillo, TX 79109
       (806) 355-3456 Fax: (806) 355-5743

★ **Bus, trolley, and streetcar memorabilia** pre-1940 including photos, artifacts, driver's badges, caps, bus emblems, route maps, and advertising. Has particular interest in Florida companies but says "I will consider any item if the seller describes it well and attaches a price."

    Sam LaRoue
    5980 SW 35th Street
    Miami, FL 33155
       (305) 237-7478

TRASH OR TREASURE

★ **Taxi cabs.** "If it pictures an American taxi cab, I'll buy it," says Henry, who seeks a wide variety of taxi related items. Also seeks unbuilt pre-1970 plastic **model car kits depicting antique cars**.

> Henry Winningham
> 3205 South Morgan Street
> Chicago, IL 60608
> (312) 847-1672

MOTORCYCLES & EPHEMERA

★ **Motorcycles and motorcycle parts.** "I'm in the market for all American made parts for American motorcycles." Give marks and numbers when appropriate in your description. "I pay all shipping costs. I'm in the parts business and will travel to pick up large lots."

> Robert Fay, Rusted & Busted Bob's
> Star Route Box AF
> Whitmore, CA 96096
> (916) 472-3132

★ *Harley-Davidson* **motorcycles, parts, and all other ephemera**. All types, all sizes, all things *Harley*. Ads, posters, **leathers**, cast iron toys, you name it. "If you got something great, I'll pay the price."

> Danny Perkins
> 17927 River Court
> Pierrefonds, PQ
> H9J 1A2 CANADA
> (514) 624-8515 Fax: (514) 624-8942

★ **Old European and Japanese motorcycles** with a particular interest in *Moto Guzzi* cycles. He would like the name of the manufacturer, the year, model and an accurate description of condition. "Very good photos" are requested. This 30 year veteran does not buy any Japanese motorcycles made after 1968. No exceptions.

> Michael Harper
> Harper's Moto Guzzi
> 32401 Stringtown Road
> Greenwood, MO 64034
> (816) 697-3511 Fax: (816) 566-3413

★ **Motorcycle memorabilia** including advertising, giveaway trinkets, watch fobs, and other items, both foreign and domestic, pre-1960. "I will accept boxes sent to me on approval and will make immediate offers to buy." Pledges to repay your postage if his offer not accepted.

> Jay Ketelle
> 3721 Farwell
> Amarillo, TX 79109
> (806) 355-3456 Fax: (806) 355-5743

★ **Motorcycles and motorcycle ephemera** from before 1920. Wants advertising, factory sales catalogs, manuals, magazines, pins, fobs, trophies, medals, and related items.
> Herb Glass
> Route #1   Box 506-A
> Pine Bush, NY 12566
> (914) 361-3657

★ *Can-Am* **motorcycle parts and ephemera** including *Rotax* motors, brochures, decals, gloves, leathers, goggles, and anything else marked CAN-AM. This motorcycle is made by *Bombardier* of Canada.
> Don Schneider
> PO Box 1570
> Merritt, BC
> V1K 1B8   CANADA
> (604) 378-6421

★ **Pre-1970 motorcycles** and motorcycle literature, manuals, magazines, postcards, toy and related items.
> Don Olson
> PO Box 245
> Humboldt, IA 50548

★ **Motorcycles and motorcycle parts.** Wants *Harley-Davidson, BSA, Indian* and *Vincent* brands, not Japanese cycles. Your description should include the type of item, and if a cycle, a description, including year, make, model, mileage, and a brief history. Note its condition. "A color photo is helpful but doesn't replace seeing the actual item." Will make offers, but only if you intend to sell. Don't bother this busy 13 year veteran if you're only "price fishing." Runs a computer database on which you can advertise cycles for sale or wanted. Call for info.
> Gregory Janaczek
> Janaczek Engineering
> Route 1   Box 1594
> Gouldsboro, PA 18424
> (717) 842-2277

★ **Motorcycle club/gang memorabilia** including photos, patches, pins, news clippings, business cards..."anything." Also buys **cans of motorcycle oil**, full or empty, "in all sizes and vintages." He notes that he'll pay from $50 to $200 for *Indian* and *Harley Davidson* cans and $20 each for oil can banks. Ed is the President of the American Iron Motorcycle Club and issues both wants and for sale lists.
> Ed Natale, Jr.
> PO Box 222
> Wyckoff, NJ 07481
> (201) 848-8485   Fax: (201) 891-4252

BICYCLES & EPHEMERA

★ **Bicycles made before 1900** and associated memorabilia, medals, pins, LAW souvenirs, awards, ribbons, photos, whatever. Please send photo or Xerox™ copy, along with the price wanted and your phone number. All letters answered promptly.

    Charlie Stewart
    900 Grandview Avenue
    Reno, NV 89503
      (702) 747-1439

★ **Bicycles and everything related to them** including:
- Deluxe men's & boy's bicycles 1880-1960;
- Highwheeler bicycles by any manufacturer;
- All men's and women's hard tire safety bicycles;
- All *Harley Davidson* or *Indian* bicycles;
- All *Schwinn* bicycles with tanks and balloon tired bikes from 1933 on especially those with speedometers built into the handlebar crossbrace and Aerocycle, Autocycle and Motobike;
- All aluminum bikes by *Monarch SilverKing, Wards-Hawthorne;*
- All deluxe bikes with mechanical suspension systems and all bikes with rear suspension;
- *Schwinn Stingray, Orange Krates, Apple Krates, Lemon Peelers, Pea Pickers,* etc. with 5 speed or coaster brakes;
- Fiberglass streamlined bikes by *Bowden, Sherrell,* etc.
- Motorized bicycles, including *Whizzers* and *Monarch Twins;*
- All bicycle parts, accessories, clocks, etc., including trophies;
- Catalogs, advertising, signs, and the like.

Prices can be serious. He offers $5,000 for the early model Sears *Elgin Bluebird* and up to $5,000 for some hi-wheelers. He DOES NOT WANT reproductions or homemade, mismatched "phonied up" bikes and definitely no 1959 or newer girl's middleweight bikes with 24 or 26 x 1.75 tires. He requests you give the make, model (if known), tire size (printed on side of tire), sex and color of the bike, and a photo whenever possible. "Please don't call on the 800 line if you do not have a bike to sell. If you want to chat or reminisce, use the other line."

    Michael "Bike Mike" Kaplan
    Funtiques
    Box 476
    Lexington, MA 02173
  (800) 336-BIKE   (617) 862-3344   Fax: (617) 861-6230

★ **League of American Wheelmen memorabilia** is sought by this expert 20 year veteran collector who buys pins, medals, ribbons, magazines, etc., from 1880-1955. You might try him for general **early bicycle memorabilia** as well. Not interested in anything after 1955.

> Walley Francis
> PO Box 6941
> Syracuse, NY 13217
> (315) 478-5671   wfrancis@mailbox.syr.edu

★ **Balloon tire bicycles** made between 1934-1960 in new or mint condition only, especially *Schwinn, Shelby, Monarch, Columbia,* or *Elgin* (Sears Roebuck). Please include a photo.

> Gus Garton, Garton's Auto
> 5th and Vine
> Millville, NJ 08332

☆ *Whizzers* **and balloon tire bicycles** are wanted. *Whizzers* are motor driven bicycles, some of which were factory built, others made from kits with a belt drive attached to the rear wheel. If you're selling a *Whizzer*, include the serial number as part of your description, which ideally should include a sharp photo of the vehicle. The bicycles he wants have tires sized 20", 24", or 26" x 2.125". Especially looking for a 1933 *Schwinn Aerocycle* or a 1938-39 *Shelby Speedline Airflow.* "The longer and weirder the bicycle's tanks are, the more I want them." Also buys **signs and shop fixtures**, including old brake parts cabinets, literature, and advertising. He does not want middleweight bikes with 1.75" tires or plain bikes with no tanks. Send a photo with description.

> Alan Kinsey
> 1035 68th Street #1
> West Des Moines, IA 50266
> (515) 266-8352   geswhosbac@aol.com

★ **Bicycle license tags,** often called "sidepath licenses," from any state as long as they are dated before 1930. Value ranges from $20-$100 depending on the age, condition and place of issue.

> James Case
> 10189 Crane Road
> Lindley, NY 14858
> (607) 524-6606

> *"Collectible bikes usually have tires sized: 26"x1.125", 24"x2.125" or 28"x1.5" and are especially good if colored red or blue."*

SHIPS & THE SEA EPHEMERA

★ **Fine marine antiques of all types** including but not limited to:
  • **Paintings** and **prints of boats**, ships and the sea, 1700-1900;
  • **Navigational instruments** from the 19th century, sextants,
      telescopes on tripods, marine clocks, compasses, etc.;
  • **Photographs** of **whaling**, yachting, ship launchings, and
      identified parts in the 19th or early 20th century;
  • **Journals, logs** and **out-of-print books** about whaling, **yachting**,
      clippers, "but only in resellable condition";
  • **Wood carvings** such as figureheads, pilot house eagles,
      name boards, and tail boards;
  • **Scrimshaw** teeth and sailor's whimsies, inlaid boxes, **crimpers**,
      bone swifts, and tools, but only genuine quality old pieces;
  • **Paper** and other ephemera including deck plans, broadsides,
      ship's china...anything rare, interesting and in fine condition;
  • **Artifacts** related to **lighthouses** and the **Life Saving Service.**
Generally buys only 19th century items. He does not want fakes, altered items, modern scrimshaw, boxed compasses, or ship's telegraphs
unless they are small, very early, or historically important. Description
should include dimensions, note of repairs or restoration, history and
price ("if you can"). He specializes in forming and liquidating collections and issues interesting catalogs of items for sale.
>   Andrew Jacobson's Marine Antiques
>   PO Box 2155
>   South Hamilton, MA 01982
>   (508) 468-6276

★ **Nautical instruments** by American and foreign makers including
brass sextants, wood octants, spyglasses, pocket sundials, cased navigating devices, as well as map drawing tools. Must be made before 1890.
>   Jonathan Thomas, Scientific Americana
>   1208 Main Street North
>   Southbury, CT 06488
>   (203) 263-2233

★ **Model sailboats.** "I'll buy wooden models that are at least 18"
long, made of wood, with rigged canvas sails. May be up to 8' high. I
prefer them to have stands. I'm looking for their decorative value so
am not particularly looking for famous boats, ship builder's models,
and other high ticket items. Send a picture of what you have, please."
Should be in fine or readily restorable condition.
>   Joan Brady
>   834 Central Avenue
>   Pawtucket, RI   02861

★ **Ship models,** particularly identified 19th century American, English or French vessels. "I also deal in 20th century high quality models of all types: sail, steam, liners, yachts, and **pond models**." Also buys **builder's half models**, including 19th century American or British hulls, exceptional 20th century hulls, and all yacht models. Does not want reproductions, or items which have been heavily "restored" or otherwise altered. Please give the dimensions, age, condition, history, and price. "If you want an appraisal, I must examine the object personally, and there is a fee, although I will give 'ball park' verbal estimates on routine items, with the understanding there is no legal responsibility or liability."

> Andrew Jacobson
> Marine Antiques
> PO Box 2155
> South Hamilton, MA 01982
> (508) 468-6276

★ **Whaling industry artifacts.** "I'm looking for anything related to the American whaling industry, including scrimshaw, tools, and early copies of *Moby Dick*, especially the 1851 first edition."

> Greg "Dr. Z" Zemenick
> 1350 Kirts Blvd. #160
> Troy, MI 48084
> (810) 642-8129   Fax: (810) 244-9495

★ **Steamship memorabilia** including china, silver, ashtrays, whistles, locks, lanterns, badges, signs, uniforms and caps, calendars, posters, route maps, and numerous similar items. **He does not want** paper ephemera after 1910, low value paper goods, fake or altered items or big heavy tools, nor does he buy items that are shabby or missing important parts.

> Scott Arden
> 20457 Highway 126
> Noti, OR 97461
> (541) 935-1619 from 9 to 9 Pacific time

★ **Ocean liner memorabilia** from all companies, especially paper items such as deck plans, menus, booklets, and passenger lists from *Cunard, French, German, White Star, Italian, Canadian, Dutch,* and all others. "We do not buy reproductions or items that are strictly 'travel' interest, such as brochures describing Paris. You may send items on approval as we cannot make offers based only on your description."

> Alan Taksler
> New Steamship Consultants
> PO Box 30088
> Mesa, AZ 85275
> Fax: (602) 807-3624   Ships@indirect.com

★ **Ocean liner memorabilia,** deck plans, postcards, paintings, posters, and anything relating to passenger ship travel especially from "disaster ships" such as the *Titanic, Lusitania, Normandie* or *Andrea Doria.* After 1945, only maiden voyage items wanted. Ken produces a large illustrated catalog for $15.

  Ken Schultz
  PO Box M-753
  Hoboken, NJ 07030
   (201) 656-0966 Fax: (201) 418-8640

★ **Canadian steamship ephemera** before 1950 such as deck plans, calendars, stock certificates, bonds, fancy letterheads, envelopes, etc. Seeks *Canadian Pacific* steamships, *BC Coast* steamships, and others.

  Michael Rice
  PO Box 286
  Saanichton, BC
  V8M 2C5 CANADA
   (604) 652-9047

★ **Steamship ephemera collections** dating pre-1960, including menus, programs, deck plans, posters, etc., from either American or European lines. Promises a quick answer to all inquiries.

  George Theofilies, The Miscellaneous Man
  PO Box 1776
  New Freedom, PA 17349
   (717) 235-4766 days Fax: (717) 235-2853

★ **Licenses for ship masters, mates, pilots, and engineers.** Wants those issued by the U.S. Coast Guard and the Steamboat Inspection Service. Please photocopy. Also wants boat license stickers and decals from any state or agency.

  Bill Smiley
  PO Box 361
  Portage, WI 53901
   (608) 742-3714 eves

★ **Lighthouses, U.S. Coast Guard**, and **sea rescue services**, pre-1940. Wants all types of ephemera.

  Robert Glick, Columbia Trading Co.
  1 Barnstable Road
  Hyannis, MA 02601
 (508) 778-2929 Fax: (508) 778-2922 nautical@capecod.net

★ **Hardhat diving gear** and old two hose SCUBA regulators.

  Thomas Szymanski
  5 Stoney Brook Lane
  Stratham, NH 03885
   (603) 772-6372

★ *Chris Craft* **boats and ephemera.** "I buy vintage *Chris Craft* run-abouts and utility boats, as well as owner's manuals, engine manuals, and other literature including sales catalogs, service bulletins, and ad-vertising. Artwork, photos and factory models of *Chris Craft* are may also be of interest. We don't want reproductions, copies, or kid's mod-els." When describing a boat, give the year of manufacture, the model, length, power, condition, and degree of originality. For other items, the age and condition. Wilson is Executive Director of the *Chris Craft* An-tique Boat Club and editor of its newsletter, *The Brass Bell*, available with club membership of $25/year.

Wilson Wright
217 South Adams Street
Tallahassee, FL 32301
  (904) 224-5169 days   Fax: (904) 224-1033

★ **Boating memorabilia** especially items related to Gar Wood, the man and his boats, 1923-47, but also *Chris Craft, Century, Lyman* and *Truscott*. Buys sales literature, catalogs, **boating magazines**, photo-graphs, and parts, like spot lights, dash board instruments, steering wheels, windshield brackets, etc., made before 1950.

Tony Mollica
110 Cherry Hill
Dewitt, NY 13214
  (315) 446-5654

★ **Outboard motors.** "I'll buy outboard motors, boat and sales litera-ture, and engine manuals from before 1940. Also **boating magazines**, book, and other ephemera with **information about** marine engines, outboard motors, **yachts, canoes, treasure hunting, Arctic voyages**, and **boat building**." Nothing after 1940 please. When you describe outboard motors, give serial number and tell whether the engine is fro-zen or turns over. Offers wants list and catalog of items for sale.

Robert Glick, Columbia Trading Co.
1 Barnstable Road
Hyannis, MA 02601
  (508) 778-2929   Fax: (508) 778-2922   nautical@capecod.net

★ **Outboard motors, 1940-1960.** "I'm especially interested in motors by *Flambeau, Neptune, Martin 200* and any racing outboards made in the United States, such as *Mercury* and *Champion*. If you send me a photo of your old outboard motor along with an SASE, I'll identify it for you, and if it's something I can use, I'll make an offer." Peter is the **author** of *The Old Outboard Book*.

Peter Hunn
Antique Boat Museum
750 Mary Street
Clayton, NY 13624

AIRPLANE & AIRLINE ITEMS

☆ **Aviation history.** These relatively new dealers in aviation equipment and history want authentic military and antique flying equipment, parts, props, engines, wheels, armaments, suits, overhaul manuals, helmets, goggles, jackets, survival gear, maps, photographs, histories, toys, artwork, jewelry, etc. If it's genuine, old, and aviation, they probably want it. They do not buy reproductions or items that have been altered. Please supply data found on the manufacturer's ID tag, a condition statement, and what you know of the item's history. Photo suggested and will be returned. A sample of their interesting catalog is $1. They say, "a satisfied customer is our number one goal."

> Norm & Bev Smith
> Aviators World
> 3000 Airway #125
> Costa Mesa, CA 92626
> (714) 540-5656   Fax: (714) 540-5610

★ **Airplanes and old airplane parts,** early flight equipment, books, magazines, photos, etc., are sought by the 6,000 members of *The Antique Airplane Association.* Write what you have for sale in the way of early air memorabilia, and President Taylor will forward your letter to a member who is looking for what you have to sell. The Association is the parent organization of the Air-Power Museum and Bob is empowered to accept tax deductible donations of significant and interesting items from the history of air flight.

> Bob Taylor
> Antique Airplane Association
> 22001 Bluegrass Road
> Ottumwa, IA 52501
> (515) 938-2773 days

★ **All early airplane memorabilia** including propellers, instruments, badges, flight awards, tools, manuals, emblems, accessories, china, checks, bonds, and virtually any good quality early item.

> Joseph Russell
> 455 Ollie Street
> Cottage Grove, WI 53527
> (608) 839-4736 eves

★ *Pan Am's China Clipper* and all **Chinese airline memorabilia, 1925-45,** including caps, uniforms, medals, photos, diaries, badges, posters, and what have you.

> Gene Christian
> 3849 Bailey Avenue
> Bronx, NY 10463
> (718) 548-0243

★ **Concorde and SST items.** "Everything related to the Concorde or SST is of interest, including newspaper reports, magazines articles, advertisements, autographs of people influential in building the planes, models larger than 24", jewelry, videotapes of commercials, china, silver, parts, old seats, gifts given away on flights and commemorative menus. No everyday menus, underarm portfolios, airline magazines, or duty free catalogs are wanted, nor is the video *How They Fly the Concorde.* Send a Xerox™ and "an honest description."

> Everen T. Brown
> PO Box 296
> Salt Lake City, UT 84110
> Fax: (801) 364-2646

★ *Ford* **tri-motor airplane memorabilia.** Wants aviation sales brochers and literature as well as airline ads and timetables picturing the *Ford* Tri-Motor airplan from 1926-1930's. Also wants aviation engine and parts manufacture literature featuring *Fords.* "Will pay $200 for Ford Airplane Co. factory badge, $25 to $100 for most other items."

> Tim O'Callaghan
> PO Box 512
> Northville, MI 48167
> (810) 449-2652

★ **Commercial airline memorabilia** including pilot and stewardess wings, hat emblems, **display models**, anniversary pins, **playing cards, postcards**, buttons, flight schedules, **kiddie wings**, and almost anything else old and unusual from the airlines. Especially ephemera from *Northeast Airlines, Delta, Chicago and Southern* and *Western Airlines.*

> John Joiner
> 173 Green Tree Drive
> Newnan, GA 30265
> (770) 502-9565

★ **Pan-Am airlines and affiliates** ephemera wanted including toys, playsets, schedules, brochures, premiums, posters, photos, postcards, advertising, and other memorabilia. Other companies include **Panagra, Panair de Brasil, C.N.A.C., Pacific Alaska, Aeromarine, and N.Y.R.B.A.** Especially wants items from the Clipper ships of the 1930's. Does not want kiddie wings, pilot wings, swizzle sticks, uniforms, glasses, or china. Give a complete description including dimensions. Describe the logo or make a photocopy.

> Robert Horn
> 345 East 73rd Street
> New York, NY 10021
> (212) 371-1511   Fax: (212) 223-4911

★ **Commercial airline memorabilia** including:
  • **Insignia:** pilot wings, pilot cap badges, stewardess wings, service
    pins, award pins, commemorative pins, badges, jewelry, and
    ground personnel cap badges, uniform patches, etc. He does
    NOT want military items or international pilot or stewardess
    insignia;
  • **Dining service items:** glassware, silverware, serving pieces, cups,
    butter pat plates, nut dishes, salt and pepper shakers, etc., from
    before 1980. He does not want broken, chipped, cracked or
    damaged china and glassware, but "average wear is OK;"
  • **Airline kiddie items:** junior pilot wings, junior stewardess wings,
    junior flight certificates, junior pilot and stewardess patches,
    junior log books, etc. He DOES NOT want plastic kiddie wings
    from *Delta, Northwest, Northwest Orient, United, American,
    TWA, Continental, Alaska Air, Eastern, Midwest Express,
    PSA, Piedmont, RAA, Republic, Southwest, Sun Country*, or
    the red on white *Midway*;
  • **Airline paper:** inaugural flight certificates, commemorative art
    work, ticket jackets, seat back packets, **first flight envelopes**,
    inaugural flights covers, dinner menus, timetables, safety
    cards, seat occupied cards, annual reports, log books, **photos**,
    etc. He does not want items in poor condition, although lesser
    condition may be acceptable for 1930's items;
  • **Other items: lighters**, plane models, advertising and marketing
    giveaways, etc. He buys complete decks of **airline playing
    cards**, but decks after 1960 must be sealed and unopened.
"If you wish to sell it, you have to describe it. A Xerox™ copy can
often answer a lot of questions and save you a lot of writing. You do
not need to list every defect but you should provide an estimate of the
condition. Sometimes I may need additional information concerning
markings, colors, condition, etc. I do and will make offers to amateurs.
I expect dealers to provide accurate information and the selling price."
William is the **author** of *Kiddie Wings and Other Things*, available
from him for $18 postpaid.

William Gawchik
88 Clarendon Avenue
Yonkers, NY 10701
(914) 965-3010   Fax: (914) 966-1055   panam314@aol.com

★ **Helicopter, vertical flight, gyro-copter, jet-pack and experimental aircraft.** Buys everything: objects, photos, printed items, specs, blueprints, advertising for them or using them, paintings, prints, toys, and "anything else, military or civilian, in any age or condition" related to flight other than in standard fixed-wing aircraft. Rick is also interested in photos of Presidents or other celebrities with their helicopters.

    Rick Bohr
    12865 NE 85th Street #239
    Kirkland, WA 98033
      (206) 828-9417

★ **Manufacturer's model planes used at travel agencies** and airport counters. Send several photos with dimensions of the wing span and the length of the fuselage. Include your asking price. Please include your day and evening telephone numbers. Also buys wooden airplane propellers from early aircraft.

    Charles Martignette
    PO Box 293
    Hallandale, FL 33008
      (954) 454-3474

★ **Airline pilot and stewardess wings and hat badges** pre-1970. Also **stewardess uniforms** pre-1965 *if they are complete.* Looking for pilot and stewardess wings from the 1940's and 50's from airlines such as *Mohawk Airlines, Northeast Airlines, Inland Airlines, Pioneer Air Lines, Empire Airlines, Colonial Airlines, Chicago and Southern Airlines, Mid-Continent Airlines,* others. Also **metal desk models of airliners** (travel agent type) from 1940-70. No military items. Photocopies helpful.

    Charles Quarles
    204 Reservation Drive
    Spindale, NC 28160
  (704) 286-2962   (704) 245-7803 eves   Fax: (704) 286-3224

★ **Desk display models of aircraft, rockets and missiles** from various manufacturers such as *Convair, General Dynamics, Douglass, Lockheed,* and others. Models created by Topping are preferred but all will be considered. All models should have their original stands.

    Bob Keller
    Starline Hobbies
    PO Box 38
    Stanton, CA 90680
        (714) 826-5218 days   Email: GQYGOIA@prodigy.com

★ **Zeppelin, blimp** and **dirigible memorabilia** including anything shaped like, or about, the giant gas bags such as photos, paper ephemera, postcards, china marked "LZ," stereocards, timetables, books, souvenirs, stamps and covers, training films, toys, games, and Christmas ornaments. Especially wants pieces and parts of zeppelins. No repros, repainted or restored items, homemades, or fakes. "I am a historian not a dealer."

> Zeppelin
> PO Box 2502
> Cinnaminson, NJ   08077
>   (609) 829-3959

★ **Balloons, airships and zeppelin memorabilia,** relics, and historical ephemera. "Anything from 18th century to WWII, including books, prints, miniatures, flight manuals, uniforms, pieces, photos, etc., even pre 1940 children's toys. Early American ballooning is our specialty and we pay top dollar for porcelain, jewelry, snuff boxes, etc. with representations of early ballooning. We do not buy magazines or newspapers. Please give a full description or standard bibliographic info.

> Christopher Lynch
> Velhalk Aerostation
> PO Box 24
> Glens Falls, NY 12801
>   (518) 793-8262 voice and fax

★ **Aviation magazines, pilot's handbooks**, and **overhaul manuals** dating from before 1940.

> Alan C. King
> PO Box 86
> Radnor, OH 43066

★ **Aviation models and toys** including desk models, travel agency and airline promotional display models, wind tunnel and manufacturer display models, ID and **recognition models**, and aviation toys of all types, including friction floor toys and battery operated toy airplanes. Seeks airplanes, **helicopters, missiles and rockets**, with civilian or military markings. He does not want plastic or wood kid's model kits or home-made items. Tell him the material from which it's made, the size, the type of stand and all markings. Indicate any and all missing or broken parts.

> Larry McLaughlin
> 17 Seventh Avenue
> Smithtown, NY 11787
>   (516) 265-9224

SPACE MEMORABILIA

★ **Space memorabilia.** "Anything and everything, with special emphasis on the U.S. space program. I prefer items issued by NASA, larger items, autographs, models, spacesuits, and objects that have been in space and would like to find unopened box of *Pillsbury's* space food sticks. No newspapers. Please Xerox© and give accurate description."
Everen T. Brown
PO Box 296
Salt Lake City, UT 84110
Fax: (801) 364-2646

★ **Memorabilia of all early rocket research** including "newsletters, journals, books, magazines, reports, studies, correspondence, drawings, films, blueprints, photographs and any other documentation from France, Germany, UK, USSR or the US regarding speculation, research, development and implementation conducted by any amateur, military, or civilian group or any individual pertaining to rockets, missiles and space travel, 1900-1960." He especially wants "any material from WWII pertaining to work done at Peenemunde, Germany, by Wernher Von Braun, which led to the V-2 and rocket weapons. Also any material having to do with Robert H. Goddard and the experiments he conducted in Worcester, MA, and Roswell, NM, during the 1920's through the 1940's." He is not interested in science fiction or Pop Culture figures like *Buck Rogers* but does want speculative articles that are scholarly or serious.
Randy Liebermann
2820 Lee Oaks Place #102
Falls Church, VA 22046
(703) 560-5790   Fax: (703) 560-6003   lunarcity@aol.com

★ **Space shot memorabilia** including souvenirs such as magazines, buttons, autographs, etc. Especially wants "internal" souvenirs such as special medallions, mission patches, models, etc., produced for people directly involved with some space "event" such as a launching or completion of construction. Also internal documents such as manuals, flight plans, charts, and so on. Also hardware, pieces of spacecraft, and other items discarded as part of mission preparation or completion. Also video tapes of launchings or reports from space. Does not want recent items which NASA still sells such as slide sets, T-shirts, etc.
Mike Smithwick
450 Navaro Way #109
San Jose, CA 95134
(408) 383-0627

RAILROAD MEMORABILIA

☆ **Almost anything related to American railroads** especially dining car china, silverware, glass, marked lanterns, and marked brass locks. Pays $20-$85 for sugar tongs or spoons marked with railroad names. Make certain your description includes dimensions and all marks and logos. Rick does not want date nails, books, or model trains. This 34 year veteran (president of railroad collector organization) answers questions from amateurs with or without things to sell. Info on clubs, railroad collectors shows, etc., sent on request. SASE appreciated.

> Richard Wright
> West Coast Rick's
> PO Box 4894
> Diamond Bar, CA 91765
> (909) 681-4647 eves

★ **Railroad items** including dining car china, silverware, lanterns and lamps, stock certificates, engine builder's plates, ticket dating machines, depot signs, advertising, postcards of depots, brochures and timetables pre-1940, historical documents, hat and cap badges, wax seals, Express Company signs, annual passes from before 1920, and books, manuals, and guides. Nothing newer than 1959. "I do not want magazines, receipts, letters, checks, tin cans, oilers, buckets, photographs, bells, whistles, tools, date nails, tokens, insulators, buttons, tickets, watches, belt buckles, record books, or correspondence." This 30 year veteran requests your phone number.

> Fred Arone
> The Depot Attic
> 3 Vista Place
> Hartsdale, NY 10530
> (914) 693-5858 any time

★ **Railroad and Express Company memorabilia** including dining car china, silverware, ashtrays, playing cards, paperweights, brass lamps and lanterns (including unmarked ones), locks, badges, switch keys, builder plates, steam whistles, caps pre-1960, uniforms pre-1920, railroad pocket watches if in perfect condition, pre-1916 timetables, posters, and calendars. Also *RR Cyclopedia*, dictionaries or other reference books published by *RY Gazette, Simmons-Boardman, Moody,* or *Poors* pre-1950. No large tools, large oil cans, spikes, low value paper, junky or damaged items, or material other than U.S. or Canadian. No "overly cleaned" or replated items. This 26 year veteran dealer always needs new merchandise.

> Scott Arden
> 20457 Highway 126
> Noti, OR 97461
> (541) 935-1619 from 9 to 9 Pacific time

★ **Canadian railroad memorabilia** from before 1950, especially *White Pass and Yukon Railway, Grand Trunk Railway,* and *Canadian Pacific,* among others. Cannot use lanterns or hardware items.
>Michael Rice
>PO Box 286
>Saanichton, BC
>V8M 2C5 CANADA
>>(250) 652-9412 eves. Please, no daytime calls.

★ **Railroad dining car memorabilia** including china, silver, glassware, menus, and anything else. Items without markings as to the railroad are "worthless" to him.
>Charles Goodman
>636 West Grant Avenue
>Charleston, IL 61920
>>(217) 345-6771

★ **Chesapeake & Ohio Railroad memorabilia** of all sorts, as long as it features of of the two cats, "Chessie" and "Peake." A photocopy or photo is appreciated. No repros. SASE please. "I do not make offers."
>Charles Worman
>PO Box 33584 (AMC)
>Dayton, OH 45433
>>(513) 760-1873

★ **Memorabilia from Arkansas railways** including *Eureka Springs Railway, St. Louis and North Arkansas Railroad, Missouri and Arkansas Railroad*, and the *Missouri and North Arkansas Railroad.* "I'll buy advertising, passes, china and silver, photos, switch locks and keys, lanterns, tickets, bills of lading, stock certificates, etc."
>Steve Chyrchel
>25 Kansas
>Eureka Springs, AR 72632
>>(501) 253-9150 voice and fax

★ **Railroad maps** from before 1900. Please Xerox™.
>Dario Dimare
>1 Elda Road
>Framingham, MA 01701
>>(508) 877-0958 eves   Fax: (508) 877-4474

Don't forget to include a Self-Addressed Stamped Envelope. Use a long #10 envelope folded into thirds for best results.

★ **Railroad date nails and other small railroad items** such as lanterns, locks, and keys. Will buy almost any date nails (nails about 2.5" long with a date on the head). If you describe the shape of the head, the number, and whether it is incised or raised, he says he's glad to tell you what you have. Dick is a collector with limited storage so is interested only in small fine items.

> Dick Gartin
> 619 Adams Drive
> Duncanville, TX 75137
>   (214) 296-8742 anytime

★ **Date nails** used by railroads, telephone, telegraph, and power companies to record when their ties or poles were placed in service. Most, but not all, have either round or square heads and have numbers (or other symbols) either raised or indented on the head. Nails may be steel, copper, or aluminum. Although there are many common nails, there are also nails worth $50 up so describe what you have and Jerry will make an offer. Jerry is editor of *Nailer News* a brief bimonthly newsletter for nail collectors.

> Jerry Waits
> 501 West Horton
> Brenham, TX 77833
>   (409) 830-1495

★ **Railroad books** of all types, especially locomotive, car builders, maintenances of way, signal dictionaries, and *Poor's Manual of Railroads*, pre-1920. Also other items, especially from **Central RR of New Jersey's Blue Comet,** such as pre-1920 annual passes, uniform buttons and pins. Wants all **brass RR padlocks with raised letters**.

> Dan Allen
> PO Box 917
> Marlton, NJ 08053
>   (609) 953-1387 eves

Almost any item marked with the name of a railroad, airline, shipping company, bus, etc., has a market if in good condition. Describe what you have carefully, noting all names, numbers and dates which appear. Chips, cracks, tears and other damage should be described. Photos are helpful as are photocopies.

Don't forget your S.A.S.E.

GOVERNMENT SERVICES

★ **School, teacher, and student memorabilia** from before 1920, especially diaries, postcards, photographs, teaching certificates, teacher souvenirs, rewards of merit, report cards, letters, student assignments, and books having to do with teaching or operating schools. No student textbooks except those from before 1860. Has particular interest in ephemera associated with New England educator **Samuel Read Hall** (1795-1877), a prominent early textbook author.
>   Tedd Levy
>   PO Box 2217
>   Norwalk, CT 06850
>   (203) 852-9864   Fax: (203) 855-7750

★ **Civilian Conservation Corps (CCC)** memorabilia such as belt buckles, scarves, uniforms, sweetheart pillows, china, etc., which run $15 and up. Items marked with the unit camp number are the most desirable, especially the sleeve unit patches designed by the individual camps, worth $25 up. Honor awards will bring $150 each, more if found complete with original ribbon in good condition. Send photo, sketch or photocopy of what you have, along with your asking price.
>   Tom Pooler
>   PO Box 1861
>   Grass Valley, CA 95945
>   (916) 268-1338

★ **Civilian Conservation Corps (CCC)** memorabilia including uniforms, awards, footlockers, tools, photos, art, crafts, manuals, camp scrip, official records, diaries. "I'll buy just about anything you find at prices ranging from $10 to $5,000." Please, no WPA or other agencies.
>   Ken Kipp
>   Box 116
>   Allenwood, PA 17810

★ **U.S. Post Office memorabilia** including steel postmarking devices, locks and keys, uniform badges and buttons, scales, marked handguns, and postcards depicting post offices. Many other items are also wanted, but not postage stamps. If you have a postmarking device to sell, make an imprint. His large illustrated wants list can be had if you send first class postage on a large self addressed envelope. "Please, only offer me obsolete items no longer in use."
>   Frank Scheer
>   12 East Rosemont Ave.
>   Alexandria, VA 22301
> (703) 549-4095 eves Fax: (703) 836-1955   fscheer@email.usps.gov

FIRE FIGHTING EPHEMERA

★ **Fire fighting antiques** such as early leather fire helmets, leather fire buckets with paintings on them, speaking trumpets with fancy engraving, early fire nozzles from hand operated pumpers, fire department lanterns that burn kerosene or whale oil and have two color glass globes, gold or silver presentation badges, etc. **Anything from the Chicago Fire Department** from before 1940. Very old fire alarm boxes, wood cased fire gongs, fire alarm registers, and other old equipment marked *Gamewell, Star, Moses Crane, American*, or *U.S. Police & Fire* is wanted by this veteran fire fighter.

> Larry Meyer
> 4001 Elmwood Avenue
> Stickney, IL 60402
> (708) 749-1564

★ **Wood cased fire station gongs.** "I'll buy any wood cased fire station gong, working condition or not, made by *Gamewell Fire Alarm Telegraph Co., Star Co., Moses Crane Co.*, or other manufacturer. Gongs have wooden cases, glass doors, and key wind movements." Also wants literature describing gongs or photos of fire station watch desks showing a wall gong.

> Gary Carino
> 805 West 3rd Street
> Duluth, MN 55806
> (218) 722-0964

★ **Fire and casualty insurance company memorabilia,** especially reverse on glass signs and automobile bumper and grill tags that have an insurance company's name. Your description should include the name of the insurance company, size, material, and condition. "Best to send a photo, along with the dimensions." If he doesn't want your item, he will give you the name of another collector who might be interested in what you have, whenever possible. No life insurance items.

> Byron Gregerson
> PO Box 951
> Modesto, CA 95353
> (209) 523-3300

Check the index for other buyers of insurance items.

★ **Badges, lanterns, helmets** and other old fire department items. Have a special interest in fire items, including paper, from Cincinnati.

> Stan Willis
> 3029 Burning Tree Lane
> Cincinnati, OH 45237
> (513) 351-3441 days   BADGES@TSO.cin.ix.net

★ **Fire Department antiques and fire alarm equipment,** especially fire alarm boxes and **wood cased gongs** in any condition and quantity (would like to buy entire systems or collections). Will also buy extinguishers, nozzles, bells, lanterns, helmets, badges, **fire grenades**, **fire related toys**, and catalogs. Your description should give all markings, dimensions, and any history of the piece you know. Make sure you include your phone number and best time for him to call.
Stan Zukowski
1867 Ellard Place
Concord, CA 94521
(510) 687-6426

★ **Fire fighting and fire insurance ephemera** including, but not limited to, fire grenades, awards, helmets, buckets, axes, **badges, toys**, fire marks, fire insurance signs, advertising items, nozzles, apparatus parts, alarm equipment, **photos**, lanterns, **extinguishers**, **postcards**, books, salesmen's samples, models, etc., especially from pre-1900. Nothing made after 1940 is of interest.
Ralph Jennings, Jr.
301 Fort Washington Avenue
Fort Washington, PA 19034
(215) 646-7178 eves

★ **Glass fire grenade bottles** in any color if embossed with a brand name and "fire grenade." He is particularly interested in finding those with the name of a railroad. He does not want glass bulb grenades from the 1940's that are filled with carbon tetrachloride. List the color, size, and all defects, especially chips, cracks, or damage to any labels.
Larry Meyer
4001 Elmwood Avenue
Stickney, IL 60402
(708) 749-1564

★ **Medals awarded to firefighters** for valor, service, longevity, participation in an event, or as a prize in a competition. They may be from any country and any period, especially pre-1920. He does not want fire convention medals from various states. A Xerox™ copy will describe the medal and accompanying paper. Dealers price your goods.
David Cerull
PO Box 992
Milwaukee, WI 53201

DOCTORS & DRUG STORES

★ **Unusual medicines and things claiming to act like medicines.**
"I'll buy pills, liquids, mixtures, devices and things promoted to cure ills or bring on better health. I'll consider items whether they work or not, whether scientific or crackpot, drab or colorful, sincere, absurd, or ridiculous. I'll even buy brand new items if they are odd or come with an interesting story."
   • **Bottles and containers**, empty or full of pills and powders;
   • **Bottling and filling materials**;
   • **Advertising flyers** and trade cards of all sorts for medicines;
   • **Medical catalogs**;
   • **Health devices, real or quack**, such as vaporizers, electric
      gadgets, etc., the more unusual the better;
   • **Any product that makes a health claim** such as tobacco,
      mineral water, etc.;
   • **Books and booklets**, serious or humorous, on medicines;
   • **Medical teaching devices**.
"I'd like as complete a description as possible, including the item's age, condition, price, and what you feel to be its unique characteristics."
   August Maymudes
   10564 Cheviot Drive
   Los Angeles, CA 90064
      (310) 839-4426 eves   Fax: (310) 839-2021

★ **Medical and apothecary (drug store) equipment** from before 1900 including **doctor's instruments**, bleeding bowls, leech jars, apothecary tools, pontiled and embossed **patent medicine** bottles, especially with colored glass and all labels (will pay from $500 to $6,000 for fine ones), patent medicine tax stamps 1860-80, and all patent medicine advertising in *any* form especially signs, clocks, tins, and 3-dimensional papier-maché figures. A 26 year veteran collector/dealer, he'll pay from $150 to $3,000 for leech jars and to $1,500 for figures.
   Jerry Phelps
   8012 Deronia Avenue
   Louisville, KY 40222
      (502) 425-2561

★ **Medical instruments such as monaural stethoscopes, ear trumpets and conversation tubes,** brass anesthesia masks from the drop ether days, all bleeders, especially mechanical, and old dental instruments if made from wood or ivory.
   Lucille Malitz, Lucid Antiques
   PO Box KH
   Scarsdale, NY 10583
      (914) 636-7825

★ **Medicine, dentistry, apothecary and quackery** of all sorts:
  • Surgical tools with wood or bone handles or in boxed sets;
  • Bleeding instruments, leech jars and cupping sets;
  • **Electric quackery,** including belts, boxes, helmets, etc.;
  • **Stethoscopes** with woven tubes and hard rubber bells;
  • Ear trumpets;
  • **Homeopathic medicine** cases;
  • Apothecary cases, pill rollers, **medicine bottles, mortars and pestles,** and bottles with gold painted labels;
  • Tooth extractors;
  • **Phrenology heads;**
  • **Eyeglasses** with telescoping ear pieces or wide loops;
  • Hanging signs for opticians;
  • **Microscopes** and microscope lamps;
  • **X-Ray tubes** and other oddly shaped vacuum tubes;
  • **Medical books,** 1600 to 1900, the earlier the better;
  • **Planetarium models.**

Send photos or photocopies of what you have for sale. Make a Xerox™ of eyeglasses as he does not want 20th century eyeglasses (they have nosepads). Give standard bibliographic information on all books. Always include your phone number so he can phone you if he needs to ask questions before purchase.

> Jon Lewin
> 622 Raleigh Avenue #3
> Norfolk, VA 23507
> (804) 625-6732

★ **Microscopes and other medical or scientific instruments.** "I'll buy pre-1900 microscopes by the following makers: *Zentmayer, Grunow, Bullock, McAllister, Gundlock, Tolles, Queen, Pike* and *Charles Spencer.*" Give the maker's name and serial number. Describe overall condition of the instrument, case, and accessories. "Don't clean or polish anything," he warns.

> Dr. Allan Wissner
> PO Box 102
> Ardsley, NY 10502
> (914) 693-4628

★ **Medical, dental and apothecary antiques and curiosities** up to and including World War II. Pre-sterilization instruments and sets before 1870 are most desirable and have wooden, bone, or ivory handles that make great hideaways for bacteria but have wonderful workmanship. Complete sets of cased instruments are wanted. Quack items such as electric belts, rejuvenators, blood letting bowls, medical electrical instruments, phrenology, homeopathy, xray tubes, microscopes, leech jars, and the like. Eye-glasses and lens testing sets from before the Civil War are wanted, but not later. **Wanted ephemera includes:**
- Instruments, percussion hammers, hearing aids, stethoscopes, etc;
- Posters and broadsides;
- Photographs with medical, dental or apothecary themes;
- Letters and manuscripts;
- Poison books;
- Medical school admission cards;
- Red Cross items of all sorts;
- Nursing items;
- Drug store items, apothecary display pieces, show globes, pill rollers, medical files, etc.;
- Any relics of wartime medicine of the Civil War and before;
- Narcotics related items before 1910;
- Dental sets, tooth keys, etc.

"We are not interested in furniture, cabinets, laboratory glassware or large equipment as we run a mail order business. Generally, the earlier the item, the higher the price paid. To sell something, describe what you have, its measurements, maker, condition and history, if known. We prefer you to set the price, but will make fair offers as long as you don't engage us in a bidding war." Their *Antique Medical Instruments* is available for $16, and includes a price guide.

Ruth Wilbur & C. Keith Wilbur, MD
The Doctor's Bag
397 Prospect Street
Northampton, MA 01060

★ **Stethoscopes.** "I'll buy antique and unusual physician's stethoscopes, both monaural and binaural." Give all markings, patents, etc., with your description and photo.

Chris Papadopoulos, MD
1107 Chatterleigh Circle
Towson, MD 21286
(410) 825-9157

★ **Old quack medical devices** which shock, spark, buzz, vibrate, or do nothing at all. Most devices were built into fancy boxes with dials, wires, hand electrodes, plated terminals, coils, and levers. Other devices consisted of therapeutic gloves, brushes, charms, and the like. There is an extensive list of brand names he seeks but he does not want common massage vibrators, violet rays, and *Electreat* devices. He also buys books, catalogs, pamphlets, and other paper ephemera promoting quack electrical items or other therapeutic gimmicks. Keller prefers you price your item but will make offers.

> Leland Keller
> 1205 Imperial Drive
> Pittsburg, KS 66762

★ **Phrenology items** including heads showing trait lines, or numbered zones on the head, posters, and wall hangings. No books.

> Donald Gorlick
> PO Box 24541
> Seattle, WA 98124
>   (206) 824-0508

★ **Phrenology, homeopathy and other non-mainstream medical practices** are sought, as are items related to **medical quackery and cures**. "We are NOT interested in furniture, cabinets, laboratory glassware or large equipment as we run a mail order business.   Generally, the earlier the item, the higher the price paid. To sell something, describe what you have, its measurements, maker, condition and history, if known. We prefer you to set the price, but will make fair offers as long as you don't engage us in a bidding war."

> Ruth Wilbur & C. Keith Wilbur, MD
> The Doctor's Bag
> 397 Prospect Street
> Northampton, MA 01060

★ **Chiropractic equipment and books** especially electronic diagnostic gear or items from the Palmer College/School. Pre-1960 only, please.

> Mel Rosenthal
> 5 The Strand
> New Castle, DE 19720
>   (302) 322-8944

★ **Medical items and quackery.** Wants pre-1900 medical advertising, **patent medicine** ads and displays, and devices and ads related to medical quackery of any sort, except "I don't need any more violet ray machines." Send a good description; photocopy paper items.

> W.H. Marshall
> PO Box 1339
> Melrose, FL 32666

★ **Medical books and ephemera.** Wants quality items including books from before 1840, medical broadsides, pamphlets, hand colored illustrations, stereo views, letters, documents, and catalogs. "I'll pay well for quality material," he states.

    Ivan Gilbert
    Miran Arts & Books
    2824 Elm Avenue
    Columbus, OH 43209
        (614) 421-3222   Fax: (614) 421-3223

★ **Medical books and journals published from 1850-1900**, especially *Lancet*. Also a **doctor's bag**, medical and surgical instruments, including a professional quality microscope.

    Rev. Sherlock "Yes, it's my real name" Holmes
    Private Letter Box 3
    Worcester, MA 01613
        (508) 754-9907

★ **Optical supplies and equipment**: buys old, rare and unusual testing devices, trade signs, eyeglasses, eyeglass cases, quack devices, medicines for eye care, and "anything optical." Give the maker's name, serial number, and description of the piece.

    Tom Baltrusaitis
    Optical Museum
    214 North Main
    Hannibal, MO 63401
        (573) 221-2020 voice/fax

★ **All human glass eyes** in any size or color, rights or lefts.

    Donald Gorlick
    PO Box 24541
    Seattle, WA 98124
        (206) 824-0508

★ **Unusual eye cups.**

    W.T. Atkinson
    1217 Bayside Circle West
    Wilmington, NC 28405

★ **Dental cabinets, instruments, and catalogs,** but only before 1920.

    Peter Chu, DDS
    5470 Folkestone Drive
    Dayton, OH 45459
        (513) 435-6849

★ **Twins, multiple births, and freak parasitic twin births.** This dedicated nurse archivist wants photos, newspaper clips, souvenirs, personal information, and *anything* statistical, scholarly, or informative. If you are one of a multiple birth, this is the lady who will preserve the experience. She always wants first hand information from multiples about their lives. *She does not want* undated clippings or items that have been damaged by pinning, pasting, or taping. When describing scrapbooks, make certain to note whether the clippings are dated. "My collection is not a hobby but a full time job in research, internationally recognized for its accuracy and extent, a source of factual information for physicians, researchers, and news media of all types." She has been at it since 1939, but Miss Helen always appreciates help, especially people sending clippings from local papers and obscure magazines about twins (you **must** tell where it came from and the date). Especially wants **photos and other Dionne quints** items. This is a labor of love and scholarship, not profit, so keep your expectations reasonable and help this elderly researcher gather data.

"Miss Helen" Multiple Birth Museum
PO Box 254
Galveston, TX 77553
　(409) 762-4792

★ **Veterinary items** of all types from before 1930, including:
  • **Veterinary patent medicine** bottles, tins and cardboard packages with original contents (colorful, pictorial items bring the most money usually);
  • Veterinary signs, posters, **calendars** and display items;
  • Store **display cabinets** by Dr. Daniels, Dr. Lesure, Pratts, Dr. Claris, Humphrey's, Columbia or Sergent's dog medicines or other over the counter purveyors of animal remedies;
  • **Paper ephemera** including booklets, trade cards, letterheads, receipts, **almanacs** and other items of veterinary interest;
  • Giveaways including celluloid mirrors, tip trays, decks of cards, pinback **buttons**, watch fobs and the like of particular interest with many items worth up to $300;
  • Wooden packing crates for veterinary medicines;
  • **Photos of veterinarians**, vet hospitals or vet colleges.

Among things he DOES NOT want are items from after 1930, screw top bottles, damaged or heavily stained items, or items that have been repaired. Reproductions are of no interest. Please send an accurate description, including size, color, and amount of damage. Include your phone number. This 15 year veteran collector is editor of *Veterinary Collectibles Roundtable* newsletter, published six times a year for $20.

Michael Smith, DVM
7431 Covington Highway
Lithonia, GA 30058
　(770) 482-5100 days   Fax: (770) 484-1304

DRUG STORE ITEMS

★ **Patent medicine advertising.** "I'll buy 19th century advertising, trade cards, almanacs, booklets, postcards, posters, sheet music, tokens, and giveaway items related to any patent medicine. I have a particular interest in *Antikamniea* and *Kilmer's Swamp Root* items. In trade cards, I am looking for 'private' cards, made for one manufacturer, not stock cards with overprints. Please send a photocopy or send the item itself on approval." Walker recently wrote*The Snake Oil Syndrome: Patent Medicine Advertising*, a colorful well-done book available from the author for $44.

A. Walker Bingham
19 East 72nd Street
New York, NY 10021
(212) 628-5358   Fax: (212) 628-4936   NickEnamel@aol.com

★ **Drug store memorabilia** including apothecary bottles and displays, show globes, pill rollers, prescription files, full boxes, bottles and containers of patent medicines, and just about anything else small and fine condition, including **related advertising, and catalogs** related to medicine or the drug store business. "We are not interested in furniture, cabinets, laboratory glassware or large equipment as we run a mail order business. Generally, the earlier the item, the higher the price paid. To sell something, describe what you have, its measurements, maker, condition and history, if known. We prefer you to set the price, but will make fair offers as long as you don't engage us in a bidding war."

Ruth Wilbur & C. Keith Wilbur, MD
The Doctor's Bag
397 Prospect Street
Northampton, MA 01060

★ **Almanacs published by patent medicine companies, between 1840-1920.** Many of these pay $20-$30. If you have many of them to sell it is advisable to have his detailed wants list. There were dozens of almanac companies that are wanted. He does not want any of the three most common almanacs: *Swamp Root, Hostetters*, or *Ayers*. No foreign language editions, either. The only almanacs he wants are printed before 1920. Please don't offer medical booklets, pamphlets, cookbooks, or paper items other than almanacs.

Rodney Brunsell
55 Spring Street
Hanson, MA 02341

MEDICINE & POISON BOTTLES

★ **Dark blue medicine and poison bottles.** Bottles must be cork tops, not screw tops. Particularly looking for bottles which held salts by *John Wyeth and Bro.* that have dose caps, contents, and paper labels. Also want *Warner's, Mulford's,* and other cobalt blue and green bottles complete with contents and labels. Pays $60+ for *Kickapoo* bottle with original stopper. No bottles marked TAIWAN or WHEATON or modern milk of magnesia. Give the color, size, and embossed letters or designs, and note existence of chips, cracks, labels, screw threads, etc.

>Adrienne Escoe
>4448 Ironwood Avenue
>Seal Beach, CA 90740

★ **Poison bottles.** Early poison bottles usually came in distinctive shapes and colors, so they could be readily identified, even in the dark. Many are marked with skull and crossbones, and others will say USE WITH CAUTION. Those with original labels and contents are of particular interest, and a blue bottle shaped like a skull with the word POISON on the forehead could bring you $1,000 or more. This veteran collector notes that there is a ceramic reproduction of the skull bottle which is of no interest. Condition is of "extreme importance" to bottle collectors. Chips, cracks, bruises, stains, weak or faint embossing can all affect the value of a bottle. Please give the height of your bottle after examining it carefully for any damage. Bottles with screw tops are not wanted.

>Tim Denton
>113 St. James Street South
>Waterford, ON
>N0E 1Y0 CANADA
>(519) 443-4162

BOTTLES

★ **Bottles.** "I'll buy American bottles from *before* 1900 which have complete labels or interesting embossing. I prefer bitters, historical flasks, and barber bottles, but will consider cures, ink, patent medicine, figures, liquors, beer, soda, bar decanters, fruit jars, poisons, and miniatures. They may be clear, aqua, green, amber, blue, or milk glass in color." Bottles are *not* wanted if there is a side seam which goes from the base of the bottle to the top of the lip, or if they have screw tops (except canning jars). Bottles which do not have seams or which have seams that end before the neck of the bottle are usually old enough to be worth an inquiry. Age alone does not make value, though. Combinations of color, shape, embossing, and rarity are what makes a bottle worth money. Because color of bottles is so important in determining value, a clear accurate photo is essential when selling bottles. A rubbing of the embossing is advised. Dimensions should be included. Do not offer bottles which have cracks or chips. He will make offers to amateurs only. Dealers must set their price. Steve's one-page *Guide to Bottle Dating* is yours for only $1 and an SASE.

> Steve Ketcham
> PO Box 24114
> Minneapolis, MN 55424
> (612) 920-4205

★ **Bottles.** "I buy antique bitters, figurals, historical flasks, poisons, cures, inks, sodas and mineral waters, fruit jars, whiskeys, free blown and pattern molded bottles, three mold bottles, decanters, and other forms. I'm looking for unusual colors and rarities, and will pay very well for them. I also want **advertising, trade cards, posters, boxes, display cases, tokens, tins, signs, etc., related to antique bottles,** or picturing old medicines and whiskey bottles." Nothing made after 1910 or marked WHEATON NJ. *Jim Beam* type collectible ceramics have no interest. Please send a sharp color photo. Note the size and all chips and cracks, no matter how tiny. If you know the item's history, please share it. Dealers price your goods. Amateurs may ask for an offer.

> Mike Waters
> 3947 Old Columbia Pike
> Ellicott City, MD 21043
> (410) 465-8095 eves   Fax: (301) 470-4148

★ **Bottles and bottle company ephemera** of all types such as calendars, brochures, and signs. *Gayner Glass Co.* is of special interest, as are Salem squats, a type of New Jersey soda bottle.

> Charles McDonald's Bottle Museum
> 4 Friendship Drive
> Salem, NJ 08079
> (609) 935-5631

★ **Early American bottles.** Buys a wide range of glass bottles, including bitters, campaign bottles, figurals, whiskey flasks and **glass jugs with handles.** Wants glass bottles with agricultural symbols, flags, sunbursts, portraits of national heroes, and the like, or bottles in the shape of log cabins, cannons, lighthouses, pigs, etc. Many of these items are worth in excess of $1,000. **Pottery pig bottles** are also wanted, but no *Jim Beam* type whiskey bottles.

     Robert Daly
     10341 Jewell Lake Court
     Fenton, MI 48430
        (810) 629-4934   ldaly1@aol.com

★ **Early American bottles and historical flasks.** Wants hand blown figural bottles or those with embossed figures and portraits. Will pay $3,000 for *"The American System"* flask depicting a paddle wheeler. Also wants **figural bitters bottles** and hand-blown, pontil marked, **colored ink** and **medicine bottles.** Burt also buys **rare fruit (canning) jars** complete with lids, round and **colored milk bottles** and mineral water bottles. No cracks, chips, or bad stains are acceptable. Burt advises reading McKearin's *American Glass* to see bottles which attract top dollar. No machine made bottles or reproductions.

     Burton Spiller
     49 Palmerston Road
     Rochester, NY 14618
        (716) 244-2229

☆ **Early U.S. and Canadian medicine and beer bottles,** both glass and pottery. Has a particular interest in the patent medicine bottles of *G. W. Merchant* of Lockport, NY. Also wants mineral waters, **poisons, barber shop bottles, pottery mini jugs, and some sodas.** Buys **trade cards, advertising, billheads,** and other items associated with makers or users of bottles in **Western New York state.** No cracks, chips, scratches or bad stains are acceptable. Offers made only on bottles shipped for inspection. If offer is refused, it's the seller's responsibility to pay return postage.

     Sven Stau
     851 Harlem Road #11
     West Seneca, NY 14224
        (716) 823-0470

★ **Bottles from California and the old West.** "I'll buy **whiskey, medicine,** food and other bottles from the days of miners, loggers, and cowboys in the West. I especially like bottles with the names of California towns and companies on them." He wants **whiskey bottles with pictures** embedded in the glass, which bring from $100 to as much as $2,500 for a *California Club* bottle. "Bottles without names or designs embossed in the glass are generally

"If your bottle says FEDERAL LAW FORBIDS THE RESALE... it isn't old enough to be of interest to collectors."

valueless to collectors as are most cracked or chipped ones." Tell him what it says on your bottle, what color it is and what condition it is in, particularly regarding neck chips.

John Goetz
PO Box 1570
Cedar Ridge, CA 95924
(916) 272-4644

★ *Flaccus, Hunter and Exwaco* **bottles and jars** with colorful labels. All West Virginia food companies from before 1910 are wanted. Has special interest in food jars, bottles, and crocks from the above, but buys **any jars marked as made or used in Wheeling or Wellsburg, WV**. Give the color of the glass and its size. Report *exactly* what is written on the jar or crock, and note any cracks, chips, or unwashable stains. They will pay $200 for a *Flaccus* stoneware water cooler.

Tom and Deena Caniff
1223 Oak Grove Avenue
Steubenville, OH 43952
(614) 282-8918

LAW ENFORCEMENT MEMORABILIA

★ **Law enforcement memorabilia** such as badges, patches, night-sticks, handcuffs, and restraints from all types of law enforcement officers including fish and game, railroad security, sheriffs, marshals, constables, Indian police, city police, and other. Also likes studio **portraits of law enforcement officers**. Make a photocopy of the front and rear of your badge or photo and give its history if you can. No security company, college police, or "gun show" brass badges. Include any wording or numbers you find on handcuffs or leg irons.

> Gene Matzke
> Gene's Badges
> 2345 South 28th Street
> Milwaukee, WI 53215
> (414) 383-8995 (414) 645-8288

★ **All items related to imprisonment, locking and restraint** including handcuffs, shackles, ball & chains, leather restraints, straight-jackets, prison uniforms and antique or unusual **padlocks**. Also wants magician's escape locks, lock picks and books about lock picking. Well known dealers in magic and escape devices offer their catalog for $2.

> Joe and Pam Tanner
> Tanner Escapes
> 3024 East 35th
> Spokane, WA 99223
> (509) 448-8457 voice and fax

★ **Law enforcement badges, handcuffs, and leg irons** from anywhere in the U.S., the older the better. Also police department photos and histories, especially from Ohio. Mention whether your item works and has a key.

> Stan Willis
> 3029 Burning Tree Lane
> Cincinnati, OH 45237
> (513) 351-3441 days BADGES@cin.ix.net

★ **Handcuffs, leg irons, torture and execution devices, and electric chairs,** both authentic and reproduction. Also wants photos of these devices in use. Please photocopy any photographs you want to sell.

> Harvey Lee Boswell
> Palace of Wonders
> PO Box 446
> Elm City, NC 27822
> (919) 291-7181

★ **Northwest Mounted Police items** from before 1950. Also the Royal Northwest Mounted Police, the Royal Canadian Mounted Police, the BC Provincial Police, or the Alberta Provincial Police. Especially awards and medals, cap badges, collar badges, uniforms, and law enforcement items marked with the initials of one of these agencies. He does not want tourist "Mountie" items.

> Michael Rice
> PO Box 286
> Saanichton, BC
> V8M 2C5 CANADA
> (250) 652-9412 eves only

★ **Law enforcement memorabilia from prohibition era Chicago** including photos, police bulletins, warrants for arrests, court transcripts, police uniforms (1920's only), badges, and personal items from police chiefs Garrity, Fitzmorris, Collins, Hughs, and Russell. Only well documented personal effects with value dependent upon authenticity and story accompanying the item. Tell how you obtained them.

> Michael Graham's Roaring 20's
> 33133 O'Plaine Road
> Gurnee, IL 60031
> (847) 263-6285

★ **Convict memoirs and other prisoner memorabilia** from any era from any American prison. This retired prison psychologist is interested in staff, convicts, and the prisons themselves. He'll buy letters from prisoners, prison script and tokens, prison newspapers, photos and postcards depicting the inside or outside of prisons (with women's prisons especially rare and desirable), sheet music about prisons or prisoners, and prisoner folk art. Prisoners of special note are many, including men like Ed Morrell (Folsom and San Quentin at the turn of the century), Donald Lowrie (wrote *My Life in Prison* for the *San Francisco Call Bulletin*), Jake Oppenheimer (2nd longest death row prisoner), Sir Harry Westwood Cooper (widow swindler and famous forger who created his own prison passes), Jack Black (highwayman, skilled burglar and hard core convict), and Christopher Evans and George Sontag (who together ran a gang of train robbers in the 1890's). Books, writings, and other items related to wardens Thomas Mott Osborne and Lewis Lawes at Sing Sing is another special interest. Do you know or have anything about these people, or anyone else in prison or running a prison? If so, Jack wants to hear from you.

> Jack Fleming
> 1825 Vine #2
> Berkeley, CA 94703
> (510) 526-4565

★ **Jail, prison, and law enforcement memorabilia,** with emphasis on all types of restraints, including U.S. or foreign military, third world, and Eastern European. Wants handcuffs, ball and chains, manacles, leg irons, thumb screws, nippers, iron claws, and comealongs. Also wants literature from manufacturers, copies of *Detective*, a peace officer trade magazine, and patent information on locks and restraints. Wants to find magician's key rings as well as restraint keys marked with the maker's name. He says now is a particularly good time to sell.

> Larry Franklin
> 3238 Hutchison Ave.
> Los Angeles, CA 90034
>   (310) 559-4461

★ **Paper related to law enforcement** before 1920 including wanted posters, warrants, subpoenas, letters, court documents, complaints, etc. Will consider **anything signed by sheriffs, U.S. Marshals, or judges**.

> Warren Anderson
> America West Archives
> PO Box 100
> Cedar City, UT 84721
>   (801) 586-9497

★ **Fingerprinting equipment.** "I'll buy old police fingerprinting equipment including *Bertillon* equipment and especially books and magazines concerning fingerprinting."

> Kathy Saviers
> 1230 Hoyt Street SE
> Salem, OR 97302
>   (800) 852-0300   Fax: (503) 588-0398
>   75464.20543@compuserve.com

BUSINESS CARDS & OTHER PAPER

★ **Business cards.** "I'll consider buying business cards that are unique, unusual, or have an interesting story. Cards from exotic or unlikely materials such as stainless steel, plastic, papyrus, tin, etc., and cards from celebrities. Looks for creativity, which is "timeless," so will consider anything imaginative in shape, color, message, or material. "I love cards that make you laugh." Photocopy what you have if possible, otherwise describe as best you can. Some **trade card collections** will be considered if they are suitable for resale or auction. Avery is president of the American Business Card Club. SASE a must.

> Avery N. Pitzak
> PO Box 460297
> Aurora, CO 80046
>   (303) 690-6496

★ **Business cards of all types.** "We buy business cards before 1960. We even buy cards that are damaged or written upon if they are rare ones. We also buy **paper items such as bill heads that are directly related to business cards**. We will pay postage on items sent to us on approval, but you must write first." Some business cards have high value like Mathew Brady, Benjamin Franklin, and some other famous people. He emphasizes that chromolith (color printed) cards were stock items issued in large quantities. Photocopies are the best description. Jack edits *The Business Card Journal*.

> Jack Gurner
> 116 Dupuy Street
> Water Valley, MS 38965
>   (601) 473-1154   jgurner@watervalley.net

★ **Illustrated commercial paper** from before 1950: envelopes, bills, invoices, posters, letterheads, booklets from any companies as long as they're in good condition and picture the product, company headquarters or some other illustration. Also buys similar paper with military and patriotic illustrations. Quality of the illustration, its rarity, colors and the condition of the paper all play a part in determining value. Prices range from a dollar or two up to $25. Jeff has no interest in paper related to hotels, but "I will consider other common categories." He does not buy anything removed from magazines or newspapers. A Xerox™ is the best description. Inquire about sending on approval.

> Jeffrey Meyer
> Turn-of-the-Century Enterprises
> 425 North B Street
> Arkansas City, KS 67005
>   (800) 520-0025   Fax: (316) 442-2340

See note regarding commercial paper on next page.

★ **Trade catalogs and piles of business letters and other illustrated commercial paper,** pre-1920, from manufacturers, wholesalers, and retailers. "The earlier the better," says Jim. Most common catalogs bring from $5-$10, but "we have paid as high as $400 for some." Please check that all pages are present as you list the company name, the type of products, size and number of pages, and the type and number of illustrations. Photocopies are helpful. Mention *Trash or Treasure* for a free copy of Jim's catalog of catalogs.

> Jim Presgraves
> Bookworm & Silverfish
> PO Box 639
> Wytheville, VA 24382

★ **Trade catalogs** for consumer products. "These are exciting peeks into their time, giving the unvarnished truth about their era. Prices vary from two figures (most catalogs are $10-$90) to over $10,000 for rare and desirable ones."

> Ivan Gilbert
> Miran Arts & Books
> 2824 Elm Avenue
> Columbus, OH 43209

A note to sellers of illustrated commercial paper:

When selling catalogs, trade cards and other commercial paper, it might prove profitable to offer your items to specialists in the particular topic being advertised in or on your item. Cigars, insurance, tobacco, jewelry, toys, soft drinks are among many specialties with collectors eager for commercial paper.

★ **Catalogs from Sears, Montgomery Wards** and other mail order companies. "The older the better," but will buy through the 1960's.

> Douglas Cowles
> 2966 West Talara Lane
> Tucson, AZ 85742
>   (602) 297-9062

★ **Trade cards,** especially better quality and specialized collections. Especially interested in clipper ships, mechanical banks, *Currier & Ives*, metamorphic and mechanical, and other better items. Will pay $300 up for fine cards depicting mechanical banks, and $150+ for clipper ships. No interest in damaged, common cards, or stock cards with no company name. Must actually see an item in person before making offers. No phone appraisals or evaluations of items not for sale.

>Russell Mascieri
>13 Running Water Court
>Medford, NJ 08055
>   (609) 953-7711   Fax: (609) 953-7768

★ **Advertising trade cards** for chewing gum and **insert cards** issued by candy, gum, bakery, beverage, cereal or tobacco companies. "Photocopy your cards and tell me what you want for them, or I welcome approvals, pay all postage, and respond within 48 hours of receipt. Condition is important as I do not collect trimmed cards, badly creased or otherwise battered items."

>William Nielsen
>PO Box 1379
>Brewster, MA 02631
>   (508) 896-7389

★ **Employee photo ID passes.** All photo ID badges are wanted, especially celluloid buttons with pin backs. Rich pays $3 each except for older ones. Don't bother to inquire, just drop your badge in the mail.

>Rich Hartzog
>PO Box 4143 BVT
>Rockford, IL 61110

When you ask someone for information or an offer, include a long business size #10 envelope, address it to yourself, and put a stamp in the corner. This is a Self-Addressed Stamped Envelope (SASE). If you do not include an SASE, you are telling buyers not to bother answering your letter.

"If my help isn't worth an envelope and stamp to the seller," said one expert, *"it's not worth my time."*

OFFICE MACHINES

★ **Unusual antique typewriters and adding devices.** Wants items dating between 1870 and 1920. Look for typewriters with odd designs, curved keyboards, no keyboards, pointers, or more or less than the standard four rows of keys. The most desired machine is a *Sholes & Glidden,* worth as much as $5,000 in outstanding condition. Give the make and model number if it can be found on the machine, the serial number, and "an in-focus photo." Rehr will provide you with a free checklist to help you describe your typewriter to him. Also buys **ribbon tins** and **early literature and catalogs of typewriters.** Darryl also has an interest in small early hand-held **adding machines, calculators and calculating devices**. "I'll send you an evaluation of your typewriter if you send me a good sharp photo, or tell me the make, model, and serial number and include a long SASE." The Early Typewriter Collector's Association is $20 per year and includes an interesting illustrated newsletter. For more information about the Association, send a long SASE. Rehr is **author** of *Antique Typewriters and Office Collectibles.*

Darryl Rehr
Early Typewriter Collectors' Association
2591 Military Avenue
Los Angeles, CA 90064
(310) 477-5229   Fax: (310) 268-8420   dcrehr@earthlink.net

If you recognize the brand name on your typewriter, collectors probably don't want it. Remington, Smith-Corona, Oliver *and* Underwood *are common, and not of interest to collectors.* IBM *electrics are not wanted either.*

★ **Typewriters** made before 1910, especially those with fancy or strange mechanisms, such as the *Sholes & Glidden* from the 1870's which strikes from below so the typist can't see her work. "I'm always willing to give you an opinion about a machine if you send a picture or good description."

Joseph Weber
604 Centre Street
Ashland, PA 17921
(717) 875-4401 from 3 to 5 p.m.

*When you look at a typewriter
ask yourself the following questions:*

Does it have four rows of keys?
Does it have or take a ribbon?
Can I see the key hit the paper?
Are the keys English alphabet?

Did you answer yes to all?
If so, collectors don't want it.

★ **Typewriters and adding devices** before 1920 that are odd in appearance, with unusual printing mechanisms or keyboards. This includes typewriters with no keyboards, but with a pointing device which typed letters one at a time. Adding machines with slide levers and rotary hand cranks to perform calculations are preferred. Also want **sales literature** for office machines before 1920. "I do not want *Remington, Underwood, Royal, Oliver, LC Smith, Corona* or other machines made after 1920. A photo is a must. If we agree on a price, I'll have the machine picked up at your home so you don't have to worry about shipping." A long SASE will bring you a wants list.
> Anthony Casillo
> 325 Nassau Blvd.
> Garden City South, NY 11530
> (516) 742-4919 eves   Fax: (516) 489-6501

★ **Check writers and protectors** pre-1910 in working condition. May be home, office, or hand held models. No machines by *Todd, F & E Lightning, Hedman, Paymaster,* or *Safeguard.* Also **antique staplers** and **paper fastening tools.** Not interested in anything that uses modern staples. "Older machines use wire or unusual staples or fasten paper without staples. Both kinds are wanted."
> William Feigin
> 45 West 34th Street #811
> New York, NY 10001
> (212) 736-3360   Fax: (212) 594-8327

☆ **Telegraphones and other unusual magnetic recorders, especially wire.** Not interested in *Webster* or *Silvertone* machines. SASE a must.
> Harold Layer
> PO Box 27676
> San Francisco, CA 94127

★ **Calculating devices before 1915** and associated ephemera including catalogs and advertising. Wants mechanical calculators such as arithmometers, generally in wooden cases. Brand names to look for include *Autarith, Baldwin, Calculmeter, Grant, Madas, Spalding, Thomas,* but interested in anything odd. Also rotary machine, heavy devices operated by a crank, and other types of calculators including **slide rules** (if they don't have patent numbers). He buys comptometers with wooden cases as well as **planimeters**, devices for measuring area on maps. Give a photo or sketch of what you have plus describe markings, serial numbers, etc. Weight and dimensions helpful. Photocopy your paper goods.
> Robert Otnes
> 2160 Middlefield Road
> Palo Alto, CA 94301
>   (415) 324-1821 eves

★ **Cash registers made of brass or wood,** especially early wooden registers with inlaid cabinets, dial registers, or multiple drawers. Also registers that ring only to $1. He also buys brass or glass AMOUNT PURCHASED signs that were on top of registers, including electrified ones. Clocks marked "NCR" on the face are also of interest, as is literature about registers. Machines can be in any condition since he uses damaged machines for parts. Give both the brand name and model number of your machine and include the serial number. Provide your phone number so Ken can make arrangements to pick up your machine. Nothing after 1917, or with a serial number higher than 1,700,000.
> Ken Konet
> 17 Hortense Place
> St. Louis, MO 63108
>   (314) 361-7975   Fax: (314) 361-7982

★ **Decorative resellable things found in the offices** of doctors, dentists, undertakers, blacksmiths, watchmakers, gunsmiths, locksmiths, opticians, jewelers, mines, hotels, brothels, police stations, prisons, firehouses, asylums, saloons, roadhouses, arcades, breweries, boat wrights, etc., including **furniture**, **cash registers**, display counters, **tools**, and the like. He requests a complete description indicating all wear or broken parts. If you know the item's history, it is helpful. Photos of larger items and photocopies of smaller ones are recommended. "I'd rather buy an entire store or business than a single item. No lot is too large. I will respond to any honest inquiry for help to evaluate an item that is actually for sale."
> Larry Franklin
> 3238 Hutchison Avenue
> Los Angeles, CA 90034
>   (310) 559-4461

★ **Stock market tickers, books, and other memorabilia** having to do with speculation, panics, commodities, cycles, and other activities pre-1940. Also turn of the century prints depicting the stock market, and **stock market magazines** pre-1935.

> R.G. Klein
> PO Box 24A06
> Los Angeles, CA 90024

★ **Banking relics, bank safes, money bags**, bullion and stage coach boxes, *Wells Fargo and Co.* or *Railway Express* locks, assay office items, scales, and **three fingered lock boxes** (which cut off your fingers if you put them in the wrong holes to open the box). Wants things before 1900. Not interested in paper.

> Larry Franklin
> 3238 Hutchison Avenue
> Los Angeles, CA 90034
> (310) 559-4461

★ **Safes.** "I'll buy small house type, pre-1910, black, cream or Burgundy colored safes, usually decorated with gold pinstriping and small painted vignettes. I also want early catalogs, photos, and other paper ephemera related to the use of safes, and would love to find a salesman's sample safe. I'll pay the cost of shipping safes via UPS."

> Greg "Dr. Z" Zemenick
> 1350 Kirts Blvd. #160
> Troy, MI 48084
> (810) 642-8129   Fax: (810) 244-9495

★ **Embossers and company seals** in interesting forms or made of less common material such as whalebone. Special interest in unusual companies and occupations. "I'll pay $25 to $250 for figural examples."

> Greg "Dr. Z" Zemenick
> 1350 Kirts Blvd. #160
> Troy, MI 48084

★ **Mimeograph memorabilia.** Advertising, instructions, service manuals, etc. If it's very *old* and about mimeos, he may be interested.

> Walley Francis
> PO Box 6941
> Syracuse, NY 13217
> (315) 478-5671

★ **Time clocks.** Give the brand name, model number and condition.

> Steve Chyrchel
> 25 Kansas
> Eureka Springs, AR 72632
> (501) 253-9150 voice and fax

CALCULATORS & COMPUTERS

★ **Calculators and adding machines.** They want to buy almost anything that calculates except models made in the past 15 years. Pocket calculators from the 1970's sell for pennies at yard sales but may be worth $10 to $50. You can tell these from new models because these calculators typically are fairly thick, more than a half inch, and have a hole in the side for a wall power adapter. These are wanted even if the adapters are missing. Desk-top calculators are also wanted, but NOT the kind that prints on paper tape. **Early microcomputers** such as those made by MITS-Altair and Scelbi are also wanted. Please send the maker and model number along with a self addressed stamped envelope. Bruce and Jan claim they'll try to beat any offer you have. Watch for their upcoming book listing the value of 1200 calculators.

Bruce and Jan Flamm
10445 Victoria Avenue
Riverside, CA 92503
Fax: (909) 353-5625

★ **Portable electronic calculators** are wanted. Wants to buy items that are battery or nicad powered with "non-modern" LCD displays or with "displays that light up (LED, nixie tube, fluorescent digits) from about 1970 to 1978." He especially wants manufacturers like M.I.T.S., Busicom, Adler, Decimo, Sinclair, Melcor and Omron and calculators that were not marketed in the United States. He emphasizes that he seeks portable machines, not those that are powered exclusively by being plugged into the wall. Tell him the maker, model number, type of display if you can, some of the functions included, the power source and the condition. Most calculators from this period are worth from $10 to $20. Guy produces the newsletter for the International Association of Calculator Collectors, available from him for just $16 a year. You may request a sample for three 32¢ stamps.

Guy "Mr. Calculator" Ball
14561 Livingston Street
Tustin, CA 92780
Fax: (714) 730-6140   mrcalc@aol.com

☆ **Microcomputers and computer literature** including just about anything: machines, literature, catalogs, you name it, if it's from the pre-*Apple* pre*Radio Shack* days (before 1977). Look for *Mark-8, Sphere, Scelbi, Intel* and other machines created for "do it yourselfers."

Harold Layer
PO Box 27676
San Francisco, CA 94127

SCIENTIFIC INSTRUMENTS

★ **Slide rules.** Seeking early and unusual rules used for general calculation, carpentry, logging estimates, tax calculations on alcoholic beverages, chemical analysis, mechanical and electrical engineering, cement calculations, etc. Generally does not want simple slide rules with white painted surfaces and numbers printed over them although there are a *few* specialty ones such as musical scales that would be desirable. Please send manufacturer, model number, condition and whether it has a case or not. A Xerox™ would be very helpful. Dealers set your price, but genuine amateurs may request an offer. SASE.

> Dr. Wayne Feely
> 1172 Lindsay Lane
> Rydal, PA 19046
> (215) 884-5640   Fax: (215) 884-8660

★ **Scientific and technical devices** from before 1910 such as microscopes, surveying instruments, **computing devices**, stock tickers, planetariums, **typewriters**, precision **clocks**, mining and mineralogical instruments, **medical and surgical instruments** (before 1875), devices used in physics demonstrations and precision instruments related to **telegraphy**, navigation, and watch making. Items preferred when in their original cases. Does *not* want items made after 1910, items in poor condition or common items. Xerox™ all written information accompanying the device, tell anything you know of the item's history, and include a photo and an SASE.

> Dale Beeks
> PO Box 117
> Mt. Vernon, IA 52314
> (319) 895-0506   (800) 880-5178

★ **Scientific instruments** and microphones. Please send a picture and give a good description. List all writing and marks that might identify the manufacturer. Has been buying these items for 40 years.

> Dr. Tom Perera
> 11 Squire Hill Road
> North Caldwell, NJ 07006
> (201) 226-9185   (802) 767-3265 in July or August

★ **Scientific and scholarly instruments** and devices of the more ordinary 19th century nature such as barometers, world globes, scales, periodic tables chart, **chemical bottles**, **test tubes**, flasks, stands, other chemistry equipment, chemical balance, spirit lamps, **microscope**, syringe, **magnifying glass**, etc. "Yes, it's my real name"

> Rev. Sherlock Holmes
> Private Letter Box 3
> Worcester, MA 01613
> (508) 754-9907

★ **Microscopes.** "I buy antique microscopes, old microscopes, old **toy** microscopes, microscope parts, microscope books and any microscope accessories. American made early microscopes are my favorite, but I collect absolutely all microscopes from ancient to modern and never met a microscope I didn't like. I have over 1,500 microscopes but still want yours. Even if it's incomplete or a duplicate, I guarantee to buy it for a reasonable price." There is one exception. "I usually do not want small black toy microscopes marked JAPAN unless they are unusual." Please give the maker's name and serial number. It is helpful is you send a photo.

> Randy Watson, MD
> 545 SE Oak Street #D
> Hillsboro, OR 97123
> (503) 297-7424 eves   Fax: (503) 681-0925

★ **Scientific instruments** by American and foreign makers including brass sextants, wood octants, spyglasses, telescopes, pocket sundials, surveying instruments, cased navigating devices, microscopes as well as map drawing tools and what have you. Must be made before 1890.

> Jonathan Thomas, Scientific Americana
> 1208 Main Street North
> Southbury, CT 06488
> (203) 263-2233

★ **Antique surveying instruments** including compasses, transits, levels, wire link measuring chains, circumferentors, semi-circumferentors, railroad compasses, and solar compasses. Items may be wood, brass, or wood and brass. "Also have interest in **mathematical and philosophical instruments** of the past." Give all names and numbers found on the body or lens.

> Michael Manier
> PO Box 100
> Houston, MO 65483
> (417) 967-2777 anytime   Fax: (417) 967-3026

TELEPHONES

★ **Telephones and phone company memorabilia** including:
- Pay phones with 3 coin slots;
- Candlestick and cradle phones;
- Bakelite phones, especially in colors;
- Wood wall phones;
- Character phones of the 70's;
- Parts for any of the above;
- Signs and advertising;
- Literature of all sorts before 1920;
- Magazines from before 1900 with phone ads.

No modern or electronic phones. They offer *History and Identification of Old Telephones* with 6,000 pictures of old phones for $58.

> Ron and Mary Knappen
> Phoneco
> 19813 East Mill Road
> Galesville, WI 54630
> (608) 582-4124 Fax: (608) 582-4593 Phonecoinc@aol.com

★ **Telephones made before 1905,** many types of coin phones, nickel plated candlestick phones, porcelain signs featuring phones, telephone watch fobs, pocket mirrors, and similar phone related items. **Also** *Gamewell* **fire alarms.** No paper. "A photo is worth 1,000 words."

> Paul Engelke
> Key Telephone Company
> 23399 Rio Del Mar Drive
> Boca Raton, FL 33486
> (561) 338-3332

★ **Telephones made before 1930.** His wants list and parts catalog's handy numbered illustrations will help you describe what you want to sell. Also buys **telephone directories** pre-1950, "the earlier the better."

> Gerry Billard
> Old Telephones
> 21710 Regnart Road
> Cupertino, CA 95014
> (408) 252-2104

★ **Novelty telephones** shaped like products, food, drinks, household items, media stars, comic characters, etc. Tell whether it has its cord, its original box, and whether it works. Describe how much surface wear appears on the phone.

> Bob Roberts
> PO Box 152
> Guilderland, NY 12084

INSULATORS

★ **Glass insulators,** one or a collection. As with most collectibles, color, shape and condition are all important. Even though most threaded insulators have little value, there are a few that can put thousands of dollars in your pocket. Colored insulators are usually better than clear or aqua. Certain brand names will be more valuable than others, so photos and a good description are essential. Make sure to include all names or numbers embossed on the insulator. His colored wants list will help you decide what you have.   He also buys pre-1900 insulator or telegraph books, maps, or catalogs.

> Dario Dimare
> 1 Elda Road
> Framingham, MA 01701
>   (508) 877-0958 eves   Fax: (508) 877-4474

The most common glass insulators are threaded and made of clear or aqua glass. So is the most valuable one. Get expert advice.

Insulator collectors want to know:
  • *Whether there is embossing on the insulator. If so, what does it say.*
  • *Does it have threads?*
  • *What is its condition...any cracks or chips?*
  • *The color is particularly important. Blue is like a Milk of Magnesia bottle. Green is like a 7-Up bottle. Any other shades are usually described as "aqua" or "greenish aqua." White means like the color of milk. If it has no color, it is called "clear."*

★ **Rare glass insulators.** Describe the color, dimensions, embossing, whether it has threads, and its condition. Requests you describe insulators using numbers found in McDougald's two volume *Insulators*, available for free at your public library or from Linscott, complete with price guide, for $75 (foreign orders are $85 in U.S.D.). No damaged insulators are wanted. Color of your insulators is particularly important. For information send a long SASE.

> Len Linscott
> 3557 Nicklaus Drive
> Titusville, FL 32780
>   (407) 267-9170

TELEGRAPH

★ **Telegraph keys.** "I prefer old and unusual but I will buy any telegraph keys. Send an SASE for an illustrated wants list showing prices I pay for keys, up to $500+ for keys from the Civil War era. Please send a picture and give a good description. List all writing and marks that might identify the manufacturer. I will consider purchasing any other telegraph items you might have as well." Has been buying telegraph keys for 40 years.

> Dr. Tom Perera
> 11 Squire Hill Road
> North Caldwell, NJ 07006
> (201) 226-9185   (802) 767-3265 Jul/Aug
> pererat@alpha.montclair.edu

★ **Telegraph instruments and ephemera** before 1900 such as keys, sounders, relays, and wood or porcelain signs. Of special interest are lineman's sets, clockwork driven registers, and stock tickers with or without glass domes. Toys and instruments marked *Signal* or *Menominee* are not desired. Likes early telegrams sent on companies other than Western Union and Postal. A photo or sketch is appreciated but "a call to our 800 number may be all that's needed to identify your item."

> Roger Reinke, Brasspounder
> 5301 Neville Court
> Alexandria, VA 22310
> (703) 971-4095   (800) 348-0294

★ *Western Union* and *Postal Telegraph* instruments and ephemera. List all markings on items for sale. No cracked or damaged pieces.

> Charles Goodman
> 636 West Grant Avenue
> Charleston, IL 61920
> (217) 345-6771

★ **Telegraph instruments** if old, complete, and professional quality, especially from railroads.

> Scott Arden
> 20457 Highway 126
> Noti, OR 97461
> (541) 935-1619

PRINTING

★ **Letterpress printing items** including:
- **Printing presses**, but *only* unusual presses before 1900;
  has particular interest in an *Akorn* hand press for which
  he'll pay $2,000 and a *Lowe* table top press for which
  he'll pay $300.
- Printer's wooden or metal **type**, borders, cuts and dingbats
  from before 1900; has interest in ornate metal type from
  Ryan Type Foundry and wooden type from *Wm. Page*.
- **Catalogs** of printer's type (called type founder's specimen
  books) from before 1918; pays $300+ for catalogs from
  California Type Foundry and *Johnson Type Foundry*.
- **Equipment for molding or making antique type**.

Describe the condition well. Estimate the date whenever possible.
Give information on the title page of catalogs, information on the name
plates. If you have type, make a proof printing if you can. Dave is not
interested in 20th century lead type, large newspaper presses, *Chandler
& Price* platen presses, or any *Linotype* machines and mats. Dave is
Director of the Amalgamated Printers Ass'n and collected for 35 years.

David Peat
Peat's Press
1225 Carroll White
Indianapolis, IN 46219

★ **Table top printing presses.** "I'll buy table top and other small,
amateur and toy printing presses, used by boys, businesses and tradesmen for do-it-yourself printing between 1865 and 1910."   Brands to
look for are *Lowe, Home, Novelty, Bonanza, Giant* and others. Those
that print 3x5 or smaller are preferred, but unusual other presses will be
considered. He also buys **catalogs**, folders, instruction books, etc. for
printers before 1900. He does not want *Kelsey* presses. Send a picture
which shows detail if at all possible. The name, model, dimensions,
condition, and size of area it can print should be included in your letter.
Jim has collected for 35 years and prints limited editions as a hobby.

James Weygand
Box 215
Nappanee, IN 46550
(219) 773-4832

ARCHITECTURE & BUILDING ITEMS

★ **Architectural antiques,** including fireplace mantles, doors, stair railings and posts, large chandeliers, wall sconces, garden statuary, gargoyles, gates, large quantities of iron fencing, leaded and stained glass windows and doors, ecclesiastical items (benches, pulpits, etc.), bathroom fixtures, toilets and the like. Please send complete details and measurements along with a photo. They do not buy jewelry, china, small figurines, appliances, or reproductions. These folks have 19 years experience helping people find unusual items for remodeling.

> Architectural Antiques
> 801 Washington Avenue North
> Minneapolis, MN 55401
>   (612) 332-8344   Fax: (612) 332-8967

★ **Architectural antiques.** If you have mantles, stained glass windows, chandeliers, iron fencing or gates, garden statuary, and other architectural relics, it may be profitable to give this giant dealer a call.

> United House Wrecking
> 535 Hope Street
> Stamford, CT 06906
>   (203) 348-5371

★ **Stained or beveled glass windows.** Send photos of the window, note all cracks or missing pieces, and include your phone number.

> Carl Heck
> PO Box 8416
> Aspen, CO 81612
>   (970) 925-8011

★ **Architect's renderings** and other paintings of skyscrapers, houses, and other buildings.
Charles Martignette
PO Box 293
Hallandale, FL 33008
(954) 454-3474

★ **Blueprints for buildings or machines** before 1920.
Jim Presgraves, Bookworm & Silverfish
PO Box 639
Wytheville, VA 24382

★ **Display cases and lighting fixtures,** especially from old drugstores. Wants early counter-top display cases with original glass, especially revolving cases, bow-front cases, and double tower cases. Also wrought iron or tin **lighting fixtures**, especially from commercial buildings. List all damage and give all data on maker's plate. Nothing after 1900.
Jerry Phelps
8012 Deronia Avenue
Louisville, KY 40222
(502) 425-2561

★ **Ornate doorknobs and other builder's hardware from 1870 to 1940.** Ornate lock sets, hinges, doorbells, knockers, door handles, bin pulls, **mail boxes**, mail slots, etc. May be brass, iron, wood, porcelain, glass, or other material, but must be ornately decorated. No plain porcelain or common octagonal glass knobs are wanted, but colored glass may bring a premium. "The decoration is the thing. I like state seals, railroads, Indians, and knobs that can be attributed to a particular building. Sets of knobs routinely bring $20-$30, but get my offer before you sell, as some can bring $300 each. Send SASE for my illustrated wants list. Photocopies speed offers. I must have a photo, Xerox™ or rubbing. Don't clean them. Paint and corrosion are not a problem for me."
Charles Wardell
PO Box 195
Trinity, NC 27370
(910) 434-1145

★ **Antique doorknobs.** "I am looking for antique doorknobs, escutcheon plates and old catalogs published by hardware companies. I co-edit the club's newsletter and can locate door hardware, lock sets, hinges, knockers, doorbells, etc., for restoring period homes, or put you in touch with dealers in your area. I will give you an honest appraisal of your hardware if you send photos/photocopy along with an SASE.
Loretta Nemec, Antique Doorknob Collectors of America
PO Box 126
Eola, IL 60519
(630) 357-2381   Fax: (630) 357-2391

OLD TOOLS

★ **Old tools of the trades and crafts** especially wooden and metallic planes, folding rulers, chisels, levels, saws, plumb bobs, scribes, spokeshaves, hammers, squares, axes, trammel points, measuring devices, drills, bit braces, marking gauges, wrenches, fancy tool boxes, and hand or foot powered machinery. Also wants advertising items and hardware store displays, catalogs ($200+ for pre 1900), and documents. Does not want car mechanics' tools, electric tools, agricultural and farm tools, or any "reconditioned" ones. Give all markings. Watch for an ivory plow plane made in Ohio, because "I'll pay $10,000 for one." John will accept select consignments at 10% commission for inclusion in his good looking quarterly newsletter on tools. John produced *Antique & Collectible Stanley Tools: A Guide to Identity and Value*, a detailed 455 page illustrated guide which you can obtain from him for $25. He also publishes *The Stanley Tool Collector News*.

> John Walter, The Old Tool Shop
> 208 Front Street
> Marietta, OH 45750
> (614) 373-9973

★ **Joiner's planes and other tools.** "I'll buy planes or any pre-1900 paper ephemera about them. I'll also buy, and pay retail prices for, fancy old woodworking hand tools."

> Richard Wood
> PO Box 22165
> Juneau, AK 99802
> (907) 789-8450 voice and fax   akrare@alaska.net

★ **Corn planting and harvesting tools** including hand held corn **planters**, **planter plates**, **shock tyres** and **corn shellers** (hand held, box mounted and free standing). Items should be made before 1950. State condition, and what you would like for it. Include an SASE.

> E. Eloise Alton
> 613 North Long Street
> Shelbyville, IL 62565

★ **Large pairs of scissors** used by tradesmen at work: carpet layers, paper hangers, upholsterers, etc. Any over 8" long may be of interest, especially if you can give a history of its use. "I'm looking for scissors that helped people earn a living." Pays from $5 to $35 for shears. Trace the shears on paper, include any names or numbers. SASE. Catalogs depicting industrial/workman's scissors from any period are also wanted. No kitchen shears or household scissors are wanted.

> Tim Burns
> 11 Oak Lane
> Stevens, PA 17578
> (717) 336-3399   Fax: (717) 336-3339

ELECTRICAL DEVICES

As a rule, it's a good idea not to plug in any early electric device. Insulation breaks down over time and could cause a short, hurting you or damaging the equipment. Damage could make it worthless. Let the experts deal with it.

★ **Electrical apparatus, tubes, test equipment, open frame motors, generators,** switch board meters, knife switches, **neon signs, fans,** Tesla coils, **quack medical devices** (Violet Ray, etc.), **unusual clocks,** etc., as well as books on radio and electrical theory and practice. Give info from the item's ID plate, and include a sketch or photo.

    Hank Andreoni
    504 West 6th Street
    Beaumont, CA 92223
      (909) 849-7539

★ **Early electrical meters, gauges, and other apparatus** made by *Thompson-Houston,* or of the 133 cycle type. Also early direct current watthour meters, type CS, manufactured by *G.E.* Any very old unusual electrical items will be considered by this veteran collector and electrical museum owner. Give him the information found on the item's ID plate, measurements and weight. "I prefer the seller to set the price. I may need to see the item before buying."

    Tommy Bolack
    Electric Museum
    PO Box 2059
    Farminton, NM 87499
      (505) 325-7873

★ **Motors** (1880-1920). "I'm seeking very old 'open frame' motors with everything exposed, nothing enclosed. Names to look for include *Crocker-Wheeler, Holtzer-Cabot, C&C, Roth & Eck,* and others. I also buy old toy electric motors with names like *Ajax, Lil Hustler, Voltamp, Knott, Elbridge,* and catalogs of electric motors printed before 1905. I no longer make offers. You must price what you have."

    Steve Cunningham
    3200 Ashland Drive
    Bedford, TX 76021
      (800) 991-0165   Fax: (800) 991-0166

PACKAGING & ADVERTISING

★ **Advertising signs, calendars, posters, display pieces,** packaging, and small giveaway items. "We prefer food, soda, coffee, hunting and fishing, veterinary, medicines, sporting goods, gasoline and autos with nice color pictures, especially those featuring celebrities. Items related to *Planters* peanuts are especially sought, with some bringing $1,000+. Condition is vital in advertising items, so please don't offer items in only fair condition. We prefer to see photos of the items along with accurate description of size, flaws, blemishes, etc." This large regional auctioneer issues semi-annual catalogs for absentee auctions.

> William Morford
> Wm. Morford Auctions
> Route 2
> Cazenovia, NY 13035
> (315) 662-7625   Fax: (315) 662-3570

★ **Advertising signs and gaming machines.** Signs on paper, cardboard, and especially tin, advertising whiskey, beer, tobacco, and other home and personal products. Items must be old and in very fine condition to be of interest to this well known auctioneer.

> James D. Julia Auctions
> PO Box 830
> Fairfield, ME 04937
> (207) 453-7904   Fax: (207) 453-2502

★ **Advertising signs, posters, trays, calendars** and other items including tip trays, die cut cardboard signs, trade cards, match holders, etched glasses, and tin or glass advertising display pieces. Things must be interesting, colorful, old, original, and in perfect or near perfect condition. "Although I will consider any products, I am particularly interested in **beer, whiskey, soda, patent medicine, food, and tobacco** items which feature colorful pictures of pretty girls, children, sporting scenes, animals, or products. I DO NOT buy signs without interesting pictures nor do I buy reproductions." Send a good quality photo, dimensions, and a statement of condition. Steve will make offers to amateur sellers only. Dealers must set their price. Include an SASE.

> Steve Ketcham
> PO Box 24114
> Minneapolis, MN 55424
> (612) 920-4205

★ **Advertising**, store stock, **signs, catalogs**, fixtures and especially items not intended for the general public from:
- General stores, especially cereal boxes;
- Pharmacies;
- Soda fountains, especially *Coca-Cola*;
- Trades and professions such as barber, lawyer, doctor;
- Fast food restaurants before 1970.

"I do not buy anything associated with beer or liquor, nor do I buy damaged items or bottles without labels." Photos are preferred as condition is critical in pricing and evaluating anything having to do with advertising or packaging. Interested in how you obtained your item.

> Dale Stolldorf, The 1905 Emporium
> PO Box 112
> Richmond, IL 60071
>   (815) 678-4414

★ **Trade signs from various businesses** including pawn shops, watch makers, jewelers, etc. "I'll pay large sums of money for American wooden carved trade signs."

> Greg "Dr. Z" Zemenick
> 1350 Kirts Blvd. #160
> Troy, MI 48084
>   (810) 642-8129   (810) 244-9426

★ **Three-dimensional advertising trademarked character displays from stores.** "I buy plaster, composition, plastic, vinyl and wooden store figures depicting cartoonish advertising characters. Items wanted are store displays and statuettes, promotional banks, figural ash trays, and bobbing head dolls. I'm particularly interested in items of the 1940's through the 1970's. Some character examples include *Speedy Alka Seltzer, Reddy Kilowatt, Elsie the Cow, Philip Morris's* Johnny, the *Esquire* man and the *Pep Boys* figures. Please provide a good description, paying close attention to damage. I prefer dealers to price goods, but will make offers to amateur sellers." Warren's *Advertising Character Collectibles* and *What a Character!* are available in stores.

> Warren Dotz
> 2999 Regent Street
> Berkeley, CA 94705
>   (510) 652-1159   Fax: (510) 540-0325

★ **Motion display advertising,** especially by *Baranger*. These are small pieces, under 3' high, usually with animated people advertising watches from the 1930's and 40's, but other products are also found.

> Frank Novak, Modernica
> 7366 Beverly Blvd.
> Los Angeles, CA 90036
>   (213) 683-1963   Fax: (213) 683-1312

★ **Neon advertising clocks and signs,** 1920-50. Buys those entirely of neon as well as those with "reverse painting on glass" that are lit by neon. Prefers smaller sizes that can be safely shipped via UPS. His favorite clocks and signs are "point of purchase" which sit on counter tops, although he buys wall models, too. He is particularly interested in signs with neon glow tubes made by AMGLO. Also buys **signs that bubble, create optical illusions, or are animated.** Value is based on visual appeal so a photo is essential. Does not want new neon beer signs, plastic signs of any sort, or signs lit by fluorescent tubes.

> Roark Vane
> 6839 Havenside Drive
> Sacramento, CA 95831
>   (916) 392-3864   NeonClock.aol.com

★ **Colorful tin cans, signs, trays, match holders and pocket mirrors** advertising beer, whiskey, soda pop, medicines, tobacco, and food such as peanuts, peanut butter, tea, coffee, and the like. Especially likes rare peanut butter pails and 1 lb. coffee cans from New York companies. Nothing rusty or damaged, please. Describe colors. Photocopy please. All items must date before 1930.

> Burton Spiller
> 49 Palmerston Road
> Rochester, NY 14618
>   (716) 244-2229

★ **Tin cans which held any product,** but only those that are small, printed on the tin and in very fine condition. Typical products are aspirin, condoms, coffee (sample sizes only), cosmetics, needles, shoe polish, typewriter ribbons and the like. He does not want any tins after 1940 or "anything common, including *Tums, Anacin, Bayer Aspirin* and Kee-Lox typewriter tins." It is suggested that you send a Xerox™ of what you have. This 18 year veteran collector is among the few buyers found in this guidebook who insists you set the price wanted. However, he does offer to send you a 20 page list of over 2,000 items with the prices he will pay. This list is available for a #10 or larger SASE with three stamps. David is co-author of *Encyclopedia of Advertising Tin Cans, Smalls, and Samples*, available from him for $30.

> David Zimmerman
> 6834 Newtonsville Road
> Pleasant Plain, OH 45162
>   (513) 625-5188

★ **Advertising or satire in the form of currency.** Also advertising printed on any Confederate or foreign currency. Send a Xerox™ of both sides, and quote a suggested price.

> Robin Ellis
> 14555 Blanco Road
> San Antonio, TX 78216

★ **Porcelain enamel signs,** 1880-1950, advertising any U.S. bicycles, automobiles, motorcycles, gasoline, oil, soda pop, food, soap, clothing, telephones, telegraph, money orders, etc. Likes all types of porcelain signs, including those with **neon trim, thermometers,** and the like, especially interesting figurals. Pays most for multiple color signs depicting animals, people, products, or fancy logos. Condition is very important. He is not interested in repros (look for brass grommets in the hanging holes). No signs bigger than 8 feet long or high. "I want a close up photo, dimensions, and any information the seller has on the item's background. Make certain to include your home phone."

> Robert Newman
> 10809 Charnock Road
> Los Angeles, CA 90034
> (310) 559-0539

★ **Porcelain signs advertising Canadian products**. Wants porcelain enamel signs, but warns that those with brass grommets in the corners are reproductions and not wanted. Will consider some U.S. products.

> Don Schneider
> PO Box 1570
> Merritt, BC
> V1K 1B8 CANADA
> (604) 378-6421

★ **Food packages from 1960's and 70's** especially **cereal and snack cracker boxes** and colorful empty **TV Dinner cartons**. "I also buy some jars with original labels and tops from this same period, the more colorful the better. Send and SASE for my free color flyer picturing my wants." Describe condition and send a clear photo or Xerox© copy.

> Paul Scharfman
> Chic-a-Boom
> 6817 Melrose Avenue
> Los Angeles, CA 90038
> (213) 931-7441   Fax: (213) 930-2990

★ **String cracker boxes** for children's crackers made by *Sunshine, Loose-Wiles* and other companies. "We buy from any companies as long as the boxes are pictorially interesting and in fine condition before 1960. Boxes should have Disney characters, Andy Gump, Popeye, the Katzenjammer Kids, goldfish, animals, etc. If someone could find us one with the Dionne quints on it, it would set a record price."

> Liz and Dick Wilmes
> 38W 567 Brindlewood
> Elgin, IL 60123
> (847) 697-9679   Fax: (847) 742-1054

★ **Pet food packages** including tins, boxes, bags and bottles which held **food for any dog, cat, bird, turtle**, etc., from 1910 to 1970. Describe condition by making a good Xerox© copy.

> Paul Scharfman
> Chic-a-Boom
> 6817 Melrose Avenue
> Los Angeles, CA 90038
> (213) 931-7441   Fax: (213) 930-2990

★ **Sunglasses** made between 1920 and 1970 if still on their original counter display cards.

> Paul Scharfman, Chic-a-Boom
> 6817 Melrose Avenue
> Los Angeles, CA 90038
> (213) 931-7441   Fax: (213) 930-2990

★ **Tin plates** from the turn of the century depicting women and/or advertising. Plates were usually printed by *Meek, Beech* or *Shonk*. Plates must be in fine condition. Photos are almost essential.

> Lisa Van Hook
> PO Box 2666
> Spring Valley, CA 91979
> Fax: (619) 470-3430   Badblu22@aol.com

★ **Typewriter ribbon tins.** "I'm interested in any typewriter tin in good condition. I especially want tins made to hold ribbon wider than 1/2" and boxed sets of tins. Large quantities eagerly accepted, but no cardboard boxes of any type." Please send a photocopy.

> Darryl Rehr
> 2591 Military Avenue
> Los Angeles, CA 90064
> (310) 477-5229   Fax: (310) 268-8420   dcrehr@earthlink.net

★ **Salesmen's samples** and other well-made miniatures of real objects. "If your item is in miniature, all parts to scale, and complete, it can be well worth your while to contact me. A sample barber's chair, for example, is worth $10,000 to me. So is a *Wooten* desk sample. Other samples are worth from $300 to $5,000. I'm not interested in doll house miniatures, but want to hear about just about any other small well-crafted items. Since I am writing a book on salesmen's samples, I would like to hear from you even if your piece is not for sale." A photo is almost essential. Include dimensions. Note all repairs. Describe any marks or labels. Describe the case and its condition.

> John Everett
> PO Box 126
> Bodega, CA 94922
> (707) 876-3513

★ **Tin can and box making and labeling.** "I'll pay you cash for anything having to do with the history and processes of making cans, boxes, and labels of any kind before World War II. I want **label collections, printer's proofs, artist's sketch books, and salesmen's samples of cans, boxes, and labels** with special interest in items before 1910. Information, photos, and other ephemera from the people who created cans, boxes and labels, and those who made them, sold them, and used them. Xerox™ what you have whenever possible. Trade directories, instruction manuals, procedures books, job descriptions, and the like are sought. Unusual original historical photos always wanted."

Tony Hyman
PO Box 3028
Pismo Beach, CA 93448
(805) 773-6777   Fax: (805) 773-8436   thyman@tobacciana.com

★ **Canning machinery, catalogs and tools** of the *Ferracute Machine Company* of Bridgeton, NJ, are sought by this researcher who also wants anything related to company founder **Oberlin Smith**. The Oberlin Smith Society is particularly interested in advertising, catalogs, small presses, medals and tokens, but will consider anything related to FMCo or Smith himself. The OSS is a 501(c)(3) organization and seeks donations, too.

James Gandy
Oberlin Smith Society
Route #2   Box 109
92 River Road
Bridgeton, NJ 08302
(609) 451-8580

★ **Advertising paperweights made of cast iron.** Must advertise a product or service. "I am primarily interested in figural items, but will purchase some non-figurals. Must be in excellent condition, preferably will all original paint. I am also interested in **other cast iron items: shooting gallery targets, water sprinklers, and advertising.** I do not buy reproductions. Nor to I want damaged items, even if they have been repaired." Photo is important, along with dimensions. "All inquiries answered and photos returned."

Richard Tucker
PO Box 262
Argyle, TX 76226
(817) 464-3752   Fax: (817) 464-7293
Email: millwt@pop.intex.net

ADVERTISING FOR VARIOUS INDUSTRIES

★ **Coffee cans with pictures printed onto the tin** are wanted, especially tall one pound cans with slip tops. No vacuum (key open) cans are wanted. $500 to $1,000 each will be paid for *Army & Navy, Blue Parrot, College Town, Convention Hall* (green or yellow only), *Festall Hall, Mayflower* or *Town Crier.* Most paper label cans are not as desirable and bring a substantially smaller selling price. Send the name of the tin, height and diameter, and state whether the condition is like new or scratched and worn. The *Luzianne* can is common, worth about $15.

> Tim Schweighart
> 1123 Santa Luisa Drive
> Solana Beach, CA 92075
> (619) 481-8315

★ **Cigar advertising boxes, labels and tins,** especially boxes featuring nudes, sports, gambling, comic characters, and other colorful scenes. Also **gambling devices, trade figures, or signs related to cigars.** Also tin **tobacco cans** and boxes. Photocopy the inside lid of boxes you'd like to sell. Long SASE will bring you a priced illustrated wants list. Don't want items covered with cigar bands except as a gift. Nothing in poor condition. Will pay $400+ for *Asthma Cure, Cheez It* or any xxx rated box. *Handbook of American Cigar Boxes,* an illustrated limited edition, is available for $17.95 postpaid with price guide.

> Tony Hyman
> PO Box 3028
> Pismo Beach, CA 93448
>   (805) 773-6777   Fax: (805) 773-8436

★ **Gun and ammunition related advertising.** "I buy posters, calendars, envelopes with ads, cardboard shotshell boxes, gunpowder cans, pin back buttons, glass target balls, catalogs, etc., but I am only interested in items produced by a gun or ammunition maker (not secondary vendors) before 1940."

> Ron Willoughby
> 1072 Route 171
> Woodstock, CT 06281
> (860) 974-1226   Fax: (860) 974-1226   swillo@neca.com

★ **Gun company advertising depicting cowboys, cowgirls or cattle.** Advertising from other products considered, but particular interest in items with Western orientation. Also wants all **original art for gun and ammunition company ads**. Please send color photo.

> Johnny Spellman
> 10806 North Lamar Blvd.
> Austin, TX 78753
>   (512) 836-2889 days   (512) 258-6910 eves

★ **Stove company samples and toy stoves.** Wants salesmen's sample stoves, particularly made by *Majestic, Quick Meal, Engman-Matthews* and *Home Comfort*. Desirable toy stoves include *Dolly's Favorite* and all models of *Buck's Jr.* Also wants toy cooking utensils that accompany these stoves (skillets, Dutch ovens, and especially tea kettles up to 4" high) by such makers as *Wagner Ware* and *Griswold*. Dimensions and condition are helpful but a "picture is usually all I need."

> Ed Hullet
> 5200 North Lorraine
> Hutchinson, KS 67502
>   (316) 662-9381

★ **Monarch Stove Company sample.** "I'm looking for a 32" tall miniature *Monarch* kitchen stove finished in porcelain enamel. Will consider in any condition."

> Marilyn Wren
> PO Box 3025
> Blaine, WA 98231
>   (360) 354-1903

★ **Round Oak Stove Company and Simmons Hardware Company** items, especially the *Keen Kutter* brand items put out by Simmons. "I will buy just about anything put out by these companies, such as calenders, tools, postcards, store displays, advertising and the like. Would love to find the Indian figure that stood atop the Round Oak stoves." He does not buy stoves, razors, or axe heads. SASE a must.

> Dennis Schulte
> 8th Avenue NW
> Waukon, IA 52172
>   (319) 568-3628

★ **Bread end labels.** These labels, mostly from the 1950's, came with many different pictorial themes, from cowboys to movie stars, space to baseball, James Bond to Howdy Doody and all are collectible. Prices for rare labels can reach as high as $200 for basketball labels, with most others in the $5 to $30 each range. Also wants posters, label albums, and advertising referring to label issues and collecting. He does not buy labels from *Wonder Bread, Tip Top*, and other labels that are not part of a collectible series. Unless you have very large quantities of labels, your best bet is to Xerox™ them. Don wrote *Bread End Labels Illustrated Price Guide*, available for $18.

> Don Shelley
> PO Box 11
> Fitchville, CT 06334
>   (860) 887-6163

☆ **Salmon cans and labels** from Alaska, Canada, or the lower 48. Also buys postcards, letterheads, and views of canneries, fish traps, etc. Only items dating from before 1960 are wanted. Send Xerox™ for offer. You have his authorization to send items on approval.

> W.E. "Nick" Nickell
> 710 North 102nd Street
> Seattle, WA 98133

☆ **Fruit and vegetable labels** from Washington, Oregon, California and Florida. Buys and sells singles, bulk quantities, and collections of can, crate and barrel labels having to do with agri-business. Will buy fruit crate labels still attached to boxes! Will buy all companies, but has a particular interest in **Sunkist**™ and will buy reamers and other items marked with that company, including postcards, trade cards, and other paper ephemera. Pat's informative *Collector's Guide to Fruit Crate Labels* and *International Price Guide to Fruit Crate Labels* are available for $42 each, or both for $75.

> Pat Jacobsen
> PO Box 791
> Weimar, CA 95736
> (530) 637-5923

★ **Florida citrus labels.** Also wants advertisements and other paper related to the Florida citrus industry. Jerry is co-author of the lovely and informative *Florida Citrus Crate Labels: An Illustrated History*, available from him for $39.

> Jerry Chicone
> PO Box 547636
> Orlando, FL 32854

★ **Popcorn memorabilia** including boxes, cans, crates, brochures, catalogs, old **machines**, parts of machines, *Creator's* steam engines, and everything else related to popcorn.

> Jack Cory
> 3395 West Pink Place
> Las Vegas, NV 89102
> (702) 367-2676   Fax: (702) 876-1099

★ **Advertising for medicine and whiskey companies.**

> Robert Daly
> 10341 Jewell Lake Court
> Fenton, MI 48430
> (810) 629-4934

★ **Glass candy and other product jars** with company names printed or embossed on the jars. Typical companies include *Necco, Life Savers, Sunshine, Lays, Toms,* and many others. Must have lids. Your description should include a photo.

> Richard and Barbara Reddock
> 914 Ilse Court
> North Bellmore, NY 11710
>   (516) 826-2032 eves

★ **Chewing gum related items** from before 1970 (wrappers, display boxes, signs, advertising) from companies such as *Wrigley's, Adams, Beechnut, Clark* and others. "I have a special interest in pre WWII items. Gum packs from that period can be recognized because they do not have an ingredient list on the pack. Rare packs of gum, such as *Wrigley's* licorice are worth $50 and up.

> David Welch
> PO Box 714
> Murphysboro, IL 62966
>   (618) 687-2282   Fax: (618) 684-2243

★ **Veterinary advertising** of all types from before 1930, including patent medicine bottles, tins cardboard packages, signs, posters, store display cabinets, calendars, display items, booklets, trade cards, letterheads, receipts, almanacs, mirrors, tip trays, decks of cards, pinback buttons, watch fobs, wooden packing crates for veterinary medicines andphotos of veterinarians, vet hospitals or vet colleges. Among things he DOES NOT want are items from after 1930, screw top bottles, damaged or heavily stained items, or items that have been repaired. Reproductions are of no interest. Please send an accurate description, including size, color, and amount of damage. Include your phone number. This 15 year veteran collector is editor of *Veterinary Collectibles Roundtable* newsletter, published six times a year for $20.

> Michael Smith, DVM
> 7431 Covington Highway
> Lithonia, GA 30058
>   (770) 482-5100 days   Fax: (770) 484-1304

★ **Seed corn company advertising, premiums and giveaways** including signs, posters, catalogs, brochures, pin-back buttons, mirrors, badges and what have you. State your item's condition, and if it is for sale what you would like for it. Include an SASE. This 20 year veteran is editor of *the Bang Board*, the Corn Items Collectors Association's newsletter, available along with membership for only $15/year.

> E. Eloise Alton
> 613 North Long Street
> Shelbyville, IL 62565
>   (217) 774-5002

ADVERTISING FOR SPECIFIC COMPANIES

★ **Junk food character premiums and the boxes that advertise them** from 1950-1980 kid's junk food such as cookies, candy, cereal, ice cream, drink mixes, and snacks. "Characters I buy in include *Choo Choo Charlie, Quisp, Quake, Cap'n Crunch, Milton the Toaster, Mr. Bubble, Frankenberry, Count Chocula, Marky Maypo, Twinkles, Trix Rabbit, Mr. Wiggle, King Vitamin, Freakies, Farfel* and other cartoon ad trademarks. Products include *Jiffy Pop, Mr. Chips, Fizzies, Funny Face, Cocoa Marsh, Bosco, Scooter Pies, Bugs Bunny Cookies, Nestle's Chiller, Kool Aid, Otter Pops, Kool Pops, Royal Pudding, Keds, P.F. Flyers, Big Shot Syrup* and especially discontinued oddball products. Will buy **watches**, toys, puppets, figures, banks, fan club kits, T-shirts, and especially store displays such as posters, stand-ups, animated displays and large 3-D figures. "I don't want fast food, generic products with no premium or character." Give condition, your phone number and best hours to call.

> Roland Coover, Jr.
> 1537 East Strasburg Road
> West Chester, PA 19380
> (610) 692-3112   Fax: (610) 738-9108

★ *Cracker Jack* **products,** packaging, prizes, point of sale advertising, etc., from before 1940. Not interested in plastic prizes from the late 1940's to the present, or anything marked "Borden Co." Also items associated with *Angelus* marshmallows, *Chums, Checkers, Reuckheim and Eckstein* and *Reliable* candies. Wes prefers you to Xerox™ what you have, or simply mail him your prizes for his offer. SASE required. Do not call at home.

> Wes Johnson, Sr.
> 106 Bauer Avenue
> Louisville, KY 40207
> (502) 899-3030 extension 228 days only

★ *Cracker Jack* **prizes, advertising** and related items, including tins, jars, store advertising, point of sale, and dealer items from any of the following companies: *Checkers Confections, Angelus Marshmallows, Chums Confections, Shotwell Mfg. Co., Rueckheim Bros.* and *Eckstein Co*. He does not want anything marked BORDEN CO. Note any obvious signs of wear. Price if you can.

> Edwin Snyder
> PO Box 156
> Lancaster, KY 40444
> (606) 792-4816

★ *Planter's Peanut* **memorabilia.** "I'll buy all rare or unusual items" with particular interest in any and all figural, 3-D *Mr. Peanuts* such as:
- Wooden jointed doll;
- "Blinker" with lighted eye;
- "Tapper" which taps on a window;
- Scale made of cast iron and aluminum, 4' high;
- Rubber squeeze toy about 8" tall;
- *Mr. Peanut* hand puppet;
- Fence sitter, cast iron, 42" high;
- Parade costume and anything papiermaché;
- Any tin displays and 5# and 10# peanut tins;
- Unopened key wind tins of peanuts;
- Cardboard display boxes peanuts came in;
- Wooden shipping boxes;
- Old jars with peanut finials.

Does not want reproductions or anything made after 1970 or any cardboard boxes that candy bars came in. No broken or incomplete items. Send a photo and complete description, including condition of the surface and paint. Enclose an SASE for picture return. Richard is author of *Planter's Peanut Advertising and Collectibles*.

> Richard and Barbara Reddock
> 914 Ilse Court
> North Bellmore, NY 11710
>   (516) 826-2032 eves

★ *Planter's Peanut* **memorabilia** from before 1970 including:
- Unopened key wind tins;
- Display items, statues, signs, and jars;
- Banks and other giveaways.

"I'm interested in anything rare or unusual. Send a description and the price wanted."

> Glenn Grush
> 5344 North Collingwood Circle
> Calabasas, CA 91302
>   (818) 880-6200   Fax: (818) 880-6500

★ *Elsie the Cow* **and other** *Borden's* **ephemera** including games, toys, cookbooks, comic books, cups, glasses, Xmas cards, employee magazines, neon signs, postcards showing the milk plants, magazine ads (especially from 30's medical magazines), milk bottles, trade cards and paper ephemera of all types. Also buys milk bottles and advertising from Du Page County, Illinois. Describe and price your items.

> Ronald Selcke
> PO Box 237
> Bloomingdale, IL 60108
>   (630) 543-4848 eves

★ *California Raisin* **anything:** figures, videos, records, paper products, fan club items, etc. Buys singles, multiples or collections. Wants only licensed CALRAB items.

> Ken Clee
> PO Box 11412
> Philadelphia, PA 19111
>   (215) 722-1979

★ *The California Raisins.* "We're avidly seeking *California Raisin* PVC (hard plastic) characters, especially the 3" ones. We don't need any more of the 2 1/2" *Hardee's* releases. We are particularly interested in obtaining licensed raisin-related items such as boxed sets, games, mugs, plush toys, display stands, pencils, magnets, clocks, etc., and will consider any licensed product with *California Raisins* on it. Preference is given to items that are mint in the original package."

> George and Pam Curran
> PO Box 713
> New Smyrna Beach, FL 32170
>   (904) 760-6600   Fax: (904) 760-5004

☆ **Arbuckle Coffee Company items** such as trade cards, advertising, receipts, coffee cans, and other ephemera. Send a Xerox™ if you'd like an offer. You have his permission to send items on approval.

> W.E. "Nick" Nickell
> 710 102nd Street
> Seattle, WA 98133

★ *Sunshine Biscuits* **and Loose-Wiles ephemera** including tins, boxes, signs, display racks, novelties, games, calendars, pin back buttons, trade cards, invoices, stationery and "things we have yet to imagine." Buys items from all brands produced by *Sunshine* or its predecessor, *Loose-Wiles Company*. These companies made potato chips, cookies, crackers, marshmallows, pretzels, candy, and several cereals. "We especially want uncut sheets of stuffed animal toys (worth $150 each), *Ann Hathaway* cookie tins ($250) and neckties advertising their products ($25 up)." Complete descriptions include size, shape, condition, what is pictured, and a photograph or photocopy of the best and worst side. "I will discuss an item with a seller on the phone but prefer a letter with pictures and SASE. I will not agree to purchase nor can I make an offer to buy or appraise an item without seeing it in person. I pay or reimburse for postage on anything I request be sent for inspection."

> Liz and Dick Wilmes
> 38W 567 Brindlewood
> Elgin, IL 60123
>   (847) 697-9679   Fax: (847) 742-1054

★ *Walgreens Drug Store* **products and ephemera.** "I'll buy a wide range of products marketed by this national chain between 1901 and 1960, including non-prescription drug and health aids, candy, tobacco, coffee, toys and what have you.

Items were sold under many different brand names including: *Walgreens, Myers, Union Drug, Keller, Glide,Valentine, Carrel, Amoray, Ladonna, Olafsen, Orlis, Triomphe, Hill Rose, CRW,* and others. I'm especially interested in finding *Walgreens* tin cans for coffee and other products. I do not want any product marked with the words AGENCY or WALGREEN AGENCY, nor do I want heating pads, water bottles, or ice caps." To sell to this 10 year veteran collector, you need to tell him what you have, and its size, color, and condition. Indicate whether you have the original box or not, and give the original selling price, if it's marked on the container.

"There are only a few collectors of Walgreens *so there isn't a lot of competition. But some items are quite rare and I'd love to hear from you if you have one."*

> Gordon Addington
> 260 East Chestnut #2801
> Chicago, IL 60611
> (312) 943-4085

★ *Beech-Nut* **items** including any glass container with excellent paper labels, especially catsup, mustard, chili sauce, sliced beef, bacon, ginger ale, sarsaparilla, peanut butter, and jams. Also wants spaghetti cans, gum or candy store display racks, tin or cardboard advertising, biscuit or cookie containers, souvenirs, Christmas boxes, postcards of factories, and anything else. Describe the condition. Include photo when possible. Dealers, price your goods; amateurs may ask for an offer if they don't know an item's value.

> Bruce Van Evera
> 94 Montgomery Street
> Canajoharie, NY 13317
> (518) 673-3522

★ *Larkin Soap Company* **items.** "I'll buy items made by or relating to the *Larkin Company,* including products, trade cards, catalogs, advertising, calendars and other paper items. If the item says LARKIN, I'm interested. I want info about the *Larkin* administration building designed by Frank Lloyd Wright and would love to find dedication programs, etc." Please make sure you describe condition.

> Jerome Puma
> 78 Brinton Street
> Buffalo, NY 14214
> (716) 838-5674

★ *Big Jo Flour* and Wabasha Roller Mill items. "I'll buy anything *Big Jo*, and will consider any other advertising, large or small, related to Wabasha, MN." She does not want flour items other than that one brand and mill.

      Carla Schuth
      Route 2 Box 6
      Wabasha, MN 55981
         (612) 565-4251

★ **Blue bell paperweights** used as promotional items by the phone company. Values range from $30 to $1,500 so it's worth getting yours checked out. Also buys bell weights by the TPA (Telephone Pioneers of America). Give the color, embossing, and condition. She wrote *Blue Bell Paperweights* available with update and addendum for $17.

      Jacqueline Linscott
      3557 Nicklaus Drive
      Titusville, FL 32780
         (407) 267-9170

★ *Coleman* **products**, either U.S. or Canadian made, such as lamps, lanterns, irons, heaters, torches, parts, parts racks, tools, shipping boxes, advertising literature, salesmen's samples, hats and shirts with *Coleman* logo, repair manuals and what have you. He does not want clippings from old magazines or camping products other than *Coleman*. Pictures are helpful if you don't know the item's proper name or catalog number. Describe condition. Dealers price your goods. Amateurs may request offers.

      Ernest Hiatt, S.T.A. Shop
      3404 West 450 North
      Rochester, IN 46975
         (219) 223-3232   Fax: (219) 223-2842

★ *Arm & Hammer* and *Cow Brand* **Baking soda ephemera** including advertising cards, posters, tins, jars, premiums and give-aways, invoices, company correspondences and anything historical or unusual marked with those brand names. Soda and Saleratus tins and pre-1950 packages are wanted. Soda box cards are worth from $1 to $10, point-of-sale advertising up to $200 and posters with dowels or metal strips are worth from $100 to $500. He does not want magazine ads and soda boxes made after 1950. Photos or photocopies are preferred. Give the size, material and condition. John is author of *Church & Dwight Advertising and Soda Box Cards* available from him for $22.50

      John Hodge
      4032 Lawngate Drive
      Dallas, TX 75287
         (214) 380-8539

INSURANCE COMPANY ITEMS

★ *State Farm Insurance Company* **memorabilia,** 1922-52. He wants all items marked with their 3 oval emblem depicting a car, fire helmet, and cornucopia. Also selected items marked with either the home office or an old car. He buys ashtrays, pocket knives, pencils, tape measures, signs, stationery, and everything else. He does not want anything marked with the three ovals and the words AUTO, LIFE and FIRE.

> Ken Jones
> 100 Manor Drive
> Columbia, MO 65203
> (573) 445-7171

★ *Prudential Insurance Company* ephemera, especially pre-1920 calendars. Also wants postcards, pens, key rings, paperweights, policies, advertising material, and other ephemera from other life and casualty companies. Make a Xerox™ of your item.

> Mike Sawrie
> PO Box 1228
> Sedalia, MO 65301
> (816) 584-6262 days   (816) 827-6399 eves

★ **Fire service and fire insurance items** such as badges, histories of insurance companies, pre-1900 fire insurance policies, firemarks, signs, advertising, and postcards. Doesn't want anything except fire related items, and nothing modern. Please quote books that are fire related.

> Glenn Hartley
> 2859 Marlin Drive
> Chamblee, GA 30341
> (404) 451-2651

★ **Anything relating to fire insurance companies** before 1940. Wants firemarks, illustrated policies, advertising, signs, and giveaways. Does not make offers, so price what you have.

> Ralph Jennings
> 301 Fort Washington Avenue
> Fort Washington, PA 19034

**Nearly all advertising giveaways
are also purchased by dealers
in Pop Culture, pp 132-139**

COCA-COLA

☆ *Coca-Cola* **advertising.** "I'll buy pre-1969 calendars, trays, small signs, syrup bottles, clocks, thermometers, menu boards, ashtrays, playing cards, lighters, and just about anything else free of rust or wrinkles that says *Coca-Cola*." Loves to find salesman's sample coolers and dispensers. Describe condition carefully and include a photo. Does not want magazine ads, reproduction trays, or bottles of any sort including commemorative. There's one exception to the "no bottles" as he wants a straight sided bottle from Buchheit Bottling Company in New Decatur, but it must have *Coca-Cola* written in script.

Terry Buchheit
214 South Moulton Street
Perryville, MO 63775
(573) 547-5628

★ *Coca-Cola* **memorabilia** from before 1945, including fancier *Coke* items with pretty girls and lots of color especially cardboard cutout signs and back bar decorations. He will pay up to $5,000 for pre-1900 calendars. Pays well for metal tins, trays, and signs. Magazine ads are wanted only if before 1932. No commemorative bottles, please.

Randy Schaeffer, C-C Trayders
611 North 5th Street
Reading, PA 19601
(610) 373-3333   Fax: (610) 683-4633   schaeffe@kutztown.edu

★ *Coca-Cola* **advertising** of all type before 1940. Buys cardboard cut-outs, festoons, and calendars, but has most interest in small items such as watch fobs, openers, pocket knives, pocket mirrors, coupons, letter heads, and the like. "I'll pay premium prices for all advertising for *Coca-Cola* chewing gum." Thom says he "will be glad to help you evaluate the worth of your *Coca-Cola* items."

Thom Thompson
123 Shaw Avenue
Versailles, KY 40383
(606) 255-2727 days   (606) 873-8787 eves

★ *Coca-Cola* **ephemera.** Wants pre-1960 signs, clocks, calendars, bottles and carriers, dispensers, machines, uniforms, etc. Will consider any item that reads "Drink *Coca-Cola*." Those that read "Enjoy *Coca-Cola*" are new. Please include your phone number.

Marion Lathan
1188 Fire Tower Road
Chester, SC 29706
(803) 377-8225

If your item says "Enjoy Coca-Cola" it's too new to be collectible.

OTHER SOFT DRINKS

★ *7-Up* and *Howdy* **memorabilia.** "If it's from 1930's, 40's or 50's and has *7up* or *Howdy* on it, please contact me. If I'm not interested in your item, I may know someone who is. Watch for Howdy Company's *Bib-Lable Lithiated Lemon-Lime Soda* which later became *7-Up.* Not interested after 1960, but buys older good condition items, whether big, little, paper, neon, working or not...but the older the better.
    Don Fiebiger
    1970 Las Lomitas Drive
    Hacienda Heights, CA 91745
    (562) 693-6484

★ *Pepsi-Cola* **items** that are small, genuine, and in fine condition are wanted by this *Pepsi* VP, primarily ashtrays from the 1940's and 50's ($10-$20), cone top cans, bottle carriers from the 1930's and 40's made of paper, pre-1960 cigarette lighters ($5-$100), jewelry like pins and tie clasps from the early 1900's ($5-$200), bottle openers, buttons, postcards, radios (worth up to $350), rulers, toys, vendor caps from the 1940's to 60's ($15-$75), trays from before 1910 ($200 to $1,000), and other small items. "I shy away from large signs and buy few paper items, although I don't mind answering questions for people with older items they may wish to sell. If I don't want something, I often know someone who does. I do not buy reproductions or anything made after 1970." Send a photo or Xerox™ and note all damage.
    John Minges
    PO Box 7247
    Greenville, NC 27835
    (919) 756-4303 eves   Fax: (919) 758-5566

★ *Dr. Pepper* **memorabilia** including signs, fountain items, pinback buttons, serving trays, calendars, jewelry, clocks, toys, clothing, games, and what have you. Especially wants very early bottles with "blob tops or bowling pin shapes, and embossed bottles with DR. PEPPER written in script on the bottom of the bottle. I don't buy new stuff such as found at flea markets, but if you're not sure, send an SASE and your description of the item." Give him the colors, dimensions, and condition.
    Bob Thiele
    620 Tinker Avenue
    Pawhuska, OK 74056
    (918) 287-3845 eves

★ **Ice chests and advertising from off-brand soda pops.** Send description, photo, and price desired as he will not make offers to anyone.
    Andy Fulks
    PO Box 92
    Whitestown, IN 46075

★ *Hires Root Beer* **memorabilia** pre-1930 in fine to mint condition. Wants trays, dispensers, and signs. No syrup extract bottles or reproductions of any *Hires* items.

> Steve Sourapas
> 1212 9th Avenue West, Unit #2
> Seattle, WA 98119
>   (206) 282-9922

★ *Moxie* **memorabilia.** Wants signs, fans, toys, advertising posters, metal trays, and other pre-1940 items associated with this old time soft drink. Will buy *Moxie* bottles only if the name of a town is part of the inscription. Bowers is the author of *The Moxie Encyclopedia*, a 760 page illustrated history available for $19.95.

> Q. David Bowers
> PO Box 1224
> Wolfeboro, NH 03894
>   (603) 569-5095

★ **Soda pop cans** pre-1965, especially small local brands. Will buy quantities of rare cans, but no rusty cans are wanted by this 10 year veteran collector-dealer. "Some light spotting and aging is natural. I require cans be sent before a final purchase offer is made because condition so greatly affects the value and I need to examine cans closely."

> Tony Steffen
> 1115 Cedar Avenue
> Elgin, IL 60120
> (847) 428-3150 days   (847) 741-9684 eves   Fax: (847) 742-5778

★ **Soda pop bottles with painted labels** (called ACL's or applied color labels) are wanted, particularly minor bottling companies anywhere in North America. "I think I have West Virginia well covered, but I'm buying bottles from anywhere. Would love to find a three colored *Uncle Tom's Root Beer* from California. Please describe the color of the glass, all colors that are on the label and the exact wording "so I can make the best offer."

> Gary Brent Kincade
> PO Box 7
> Horner, WV 26372
>   (304) 842-3773 eves   (304) 269-7623 days

★ **Bottle caps** from soda pop. The world's largest collector of them still seeks early collections. Not interested in singles, unless you have something unusual like a prototype, error, etc.

> Danny Ginsberg
> 26753 Basswood Avenue
> Rancho Palos Verdes, CA 90274
>   (310) 378-1821

SODA FOUNTAIN MEMORABILIA

★ **Soda Fountain memorabilia** especially historical ephemera related to soda fountain operations such as **photographs, trade catalogs,** bills and **letterheads,** recipe and formula books, **trade magazines** (like *Soda Dispenser* and *Soda Fountain*), and the like. Also wants **19th century soda fountain items** such as **hand crank milk shakers, crockery root beer mugs,** straw dispensers *with glass feet or tops,* **pink ice cream soda glasses,** and **colored banana split dishes with feet.** Especially interested in *True Fruit* and other advertising from the *J. Hungerford Smith Co.* of Rochester. The favorite find of this 20 year veteran collector would be an equipment and supplies catalog from before 1870. He does not want syrup well inserts for fountains, nor does he want match book covers, cup holders, trinkets, anything made of plastic, or anything related to the ice cream industry. "Please give as much reasonable detail as possible. A photo or photocopy is helpful." Dealers should price goods; amateurs may request offer. SASE a must.

> Harold Screen
> 2804 Munster Road
> Baltimore, MD 21234
> (410) 661-6765   sodaftn@aol.com

★ **Ice cream and soda fountain memorabilia:**
- **Postcards** depicting ice cream or soda fountains, ice cream trucks, factories or any other ice cream topic (any year);
- **Photographs** of soda fountain interiors;
- Letterheads, envelopes and other **paper** with ice cream images;
- **Magazines** from soda fountain and ice cream trade, pre-1930;
- **Trade cards** with ice cream parlors, freezers, or soda fountains;
- **Catalogs** pre-1920 (except *Mills* #31);
- **Advertising giveaways,** fobs, buttons, tape measures, etc.

Allan buys a wide range of ice cream related items, but says his focus for the last few years has been on postcards with historical photos. He buys nothing damaged or made after 1945. He does not make offers, and requests you price what you have.

> Allan "Mr. Ice Cream" Mellis
> 1115 West Montana
> Chicago, IL 60614
> (312) 327-9123   MELLIS@ENTERACT.COM

★ *Dixie* **ice cream cup picture lids** and other memorabilia 1930-54 including premium pictures and offers, albums, scrapbook covers, ads, and company literature. Also buys some non-*Dixie* pictorial ice cream cup lids such as *Tarzan* or American Historical Shrines series.

> Stephen Leone
> 94 Pond Street
> Salem, NH 03079
> (603) 898-4900   Fax: (508) 837-5029

RESTAURANT & FAST FOOD MEMORABILIA

★ *McDonald's* **items.** Seeks unusual *McDonald's* items including:
- Wacky cups, made of plastic, singles or the set ($10-$15 each);
- Cigarette lighters by *Bently, Zippo* or *Maroman* (up to $20);
- Matchbooks of all types ($1 to $5);
- Ashtrays (some of which are worth $5);
- Hamburglar doll from the early 70's with purple and white stripes, yellow tie, 15" tall with narrow black mask and ugly face (up to $100 depending on condition);
- Stuffed Ronald McDonald doll with slash mark logo on the pockets, very round face and printed curly hair (up to $100);
- *Lego* Ronald McDonald that was part of a store display;
- *Barbies* test marketed in 1990;
- Anything unusual, including pencil sharpeners, maps, phones, postcards, wooden yo-yo's, among other things.

"These are a few key pieces on most collector's wants lists. We do not want Happy Meal toys or boxes dated after 1990 and very few dated after 1987. We also do not want any of the common glasses & cups that were put out nationally." They warn my readers that "most McDonald's collectors are average people without much extra cash. None of us can afford to buy all the stuff offered to us. McDonald's collecting is still a very affordable hobby, one reason it is so popular. An "old" McDonald's item is from the late 60's. The oldest toys date from the 1970's. The hobby is so new that a great many things have never been cataloged yet, and we love it when someone offers us something we've never heard of before. When someone calls us, we ask enough questions to determine exactly what they have and its condition so we can give an accurate estimate of value whether we wish to buy it or not. If people write us, an SASE is a must." John is a collector who also conducts auctions of McDonald's items and offers to auction high quality items offered by readers.

John Larsen
523 3rd Street
Colusa, CA 95932
(530) 458-4769

Collectibles of fast food chains are part of "Pop Culture" and have become very popular. Things you got free may find a buyer.

McDonald's is the most popular, but other restaurant collectibles are on the rise.

★ *McDonald's* **memorabilia** including:
  - **Employee uniforms** with the M logo;
  - **Paper goods** including boxes, place mats, napkins, flyers;
  - **Displays and promotions** such as signs, decals, posters;
  - **Anything in foreign languages**;
  - **Not for public items** such as ID cards, newsletters, bulletins,sales and procedures manuals, and worksheets;
  - **Fixtures, signs, and lights**.

Does not want items currently available in all restaurants. Take a photo of larger items please. Matt does not buy for resale, but hopes to build a *McDonald's* museum and put them on public display. Offers free appraisals if you send an SASE.

> Matt Welch
> PO Box 30444
> Tucson, AZ 85751
>   (520) 886-0505   Fax: (520) 722-3607

★ *McDonald's* **restaurant memorabilia** including Happy Meal toys, boxes, sacks, advertising pieces, postcards, **paper items**, **uniforms**, cups, **glasses**, mugs, pins, buttons, jewelry, **foreign items**, clocks, watches, displays, rings, retail items, games, clothes, shoes, special convention items, letters, newsletters, and other public and company items. Not interested in "common items which appear in Happy Meals nationwide." Your description should include what it is, the color, size, any trademarks, dates, and condition. Meredith **wrote** *Price Guide to McDonald's Happy Meal Collectibles*, available from the author for $31 postpaid. The McDonald's Collectors Club offers a 10 page monthly newsletter on collecting McDonald's items available for $25.

> Mr. Meredith Williams
> PO Box 633
> Joplin, MO 64802
>   (417) 781-3855   Fax: (417) 624-0090

★ **Fast food chain ephemera including kid's meal toys and boxes** from before 1988. Also crew pins, displays, and other fast-food related items that are odd or unusual. He's interested in chains like *Wendy's, Sonic Drive-In, Arby's, Burger King, Roy Rogers, Hardees, Carls Jr., What-a-Burger*, and other similar.

> Ken Clee
> PO Box 11412
> Philadelphia, PA 19111
>   (215) 722-1979

Don't assume that what you have is common. Many fast food chain collectibles have limited distribution, and may in fact have been given away in only a few restaurants. Rare doesn't always translate into great value, but it can!

★ *Bob's Big Boy* **restaurant memorabilia,** ceramic ashtrays and salt and peppers, cups or dishes with logos, lunch boxes, game boards, toys, comics, figurines, and other unusual pieces. Please write or fax with a description, noting all repairs. Dealers must set the price they want; amateurs may request offers. Vinyl plastic doll banks are not wanted.

> Glenn Grush
> 5344 North Collingwood Circle
> Calabasas, CA 91302
>   (818) 880-6200   Fax: (818) 880-6500

★ *Bob's Big Boy* **items,** especially menus, lamps, matches, ashtrays, salt and pepper shakers, and nodders. No plastic banks.

> Steve Soelberg
> 29126 Laro Drive
> Agoura Hills, CA 91301
>   (818) 889-9909

★ *Coon Chicken Inn* **memorabilia** of all kinds that features Blacks.

> Diane Cauwels
> 3947 Old South Road
> Murfreesboro, TN 37128
>   (615) 896-3614   (615) 896-3614

★ *Isaly's Dairy* **ephemera.** Wants badges, bibs, bottles, calendars, clocks, dishes, milk and ice cream cartons, mugs, signs, straw holders, and other advertising from this dairy/deli chain from PA and Ohio.

> Brian Butke
> 2640 Sunset Drive
> West Mifflin, PA 15122

Glasses given away by restaurants are becoming quite collectible, with a few of them at $50 each. Look under "glasses" in the index for more buyers.

A reminder: the people in this book are often very busy professionals, working with no staff to help them answer letters. Many of them travel a great deal. One important buyer sets up at more than 50 antique shows a year. On the other hand, another top buyer told me, "I'm a lonely old man, and I love getting mail. So I always answer it the day it arrives."

Be patient. If you own something spectacular, you'll get quick response from everyone. My own mail is often months behind because there are so many demands upon my time.

HOTELS & MOTELS

★ **Items from famous Chicago hotels** and their shops. Wants furniture, menus, stationery, fixtures, signs, etc., from places like the *Lexington, Metropole, Hawthorne Inn, Hawthorne Smoke Shop*, and *Scholfields Flower Shop*.

> Michael Graham
> 33133 O'Plaine Road
> Gurnee, IL 60031
> (847) 263-6285

★ **Youth hostel ephemera** such as handbooks, pins, magazines, etc.

> Walley Francis
> PO Box 6941
> Syracuse, NY 13217
> (315) 478-5671

When you ask someone for information or an offer, include a long business size #10 envelope, address it to yourself, and put a stamp in the corner. This is a Self-Addressed Stamped Envelope (SASE). If you do not include an SASE, you are telling buyers not to bother answering your letter.

"If my help isn't worth an envelope and stamp to the seller," said one expert, *"it's not worth my time."*

FARMS, HORSES & TRACTORS

★ **Wagons, carriages and commercial horse drawn vehicles,** in whole or in part. Buys carriage lamps, dashboard clocks, wagon tools, nameplates, wheel making machines, coachman's and groom's clothing, jacks, tack room fixtures, whip racks, wagon odometers, hitching post statuary, rein clips, wagon seats, wagon poles, **veterinary tools**, lap robes, life size harness maker's horses, **zinc animal heads**, and anything else related to carriages and wagons. Offers from $500 to $2,500 for lamps marked *Studebaker, Brewster,* or *Healey.* Also buys **goat and dog carts.** If your item is old, genuine, and in good condition you may ship it on approval. No harnesses, please. Don will send you a thick illustrated wants list if you send him a long SASE with four stamps on the envelope.

> Don Sawyer, West Newbury Wagon Works
> 40 Bachelor Street
> West Newbury, MA 01985
>   (508) 346-4724 days   Fax: (508) 346-4841

★ **Horse bits.** "I buy old iron, brass or silver horse bits (mouthpieces) especially custom or unusual ones. I also want old decorative **glass pictorial bridle rosettes**. Old catalogs that picture bridles, bits, and other tack are also wanted."

> Jean Gayle, Three Horses
> 7403 Blaine Road
> Aberdeen, WA 98520
> (360) 533-3490

★ **Tractor memorabilia** including all sorts of paper ephemera and small trinkets given away as advertising promotion by tractor makers and dealers, such as watch fobs, pens, cigarette lighters, etc. You may ship on approval if it's old, original, and clean.

> Jay Ketelle
> 3721 Farwell
> Amarillo, TX 79109
>   (806) 355-3456

★ **Tractor, farm machinery, and gasoline engine paper ephemera** including pre-1940 manuals, catalogs, parts books, in-house publications, and sales literature. Also buys farm magazines such as *Implement Record, Farm Machinery & Hardware,* and *Farm Mechanics.* Also buys "giveaways" such as signs, ashtrays, buttons, etc. associated with any farm machinery. No textbooks or reprints are wanted. Please indicate the color of the item and the price you'd like.

> Alan C. King
> PO Box 86
> Radnor, OH 43066

★ *J.I. Case Tractor Company* **memorabilia** including tractors and implements, toy tractors, advertising signs, catalogs, books, and anything else marked *J.I. Case.* If you want to sell an **old** *Case* **tractor** make certain to tell them where it is presently located.

Ed and Carla Schuth
Route 2   Box 6
Wabasha, MN 55981
(612) 565-4251

★ *John Deere* **items**, especially portable **gasoline engines**. He also buys **corn shellers**, watch fobs, advertising, pump jacks, or **older farm equipment**. "If you have anything *John Deere*, contact me."

Gary Voigt
4010 Glendale Drive
Excelsior, MN 55331
(612) 474-3540 eves

★ **Windmill ephemera,** especially cast iron windmill weights, display model windmills and salesman's sample windmills. He does not want reproductions, damaged or repaired items, items with new paint, or "short tail horse" windmill weights. Also **cast iron tractor hood ornaments.** Please send a color photo, your phone number, and the price range you'd like to get.

Richard Tucker, Argyle Antiques
PO Box 262
Argyle, TX 76226
(817) 464-3752   Fax: (817) 464-7293

★ **Ice harvesting tools** are wanted, but "I have all the common ones." Buys crescent saws, house axes, and paper goods related to the history of ice. In general, most tongs, pikes, plows, and markers are not of interest, but some rare styles and makers *are* wanted, so you are encouraged to send a photo and maker's name. "Please, I don't need house signs which tell the ice man to stop." Phil lectures on ice harvesting and other 19th century practices, and heads the New England Tool Collectors Association, dues for which are $5/yr.

Philip Whitney
303 Fisher Road
Fitchburg, MA 01420
(508) 342-1350

★ **Poultry industry items** including, but not limited to, egg cartons from before 1955, egg scales ($25-$60), stoneware chick waterers and feeders ($40-$80), books before 1940, and egg shipping containers and carriers. Does not want cracked or chipped stoneware or tops with no bottoms, nor does he want rusted scales, plastic egg cartons, or wooden folding egg carriers. Identify all labels or marks, patent numbers, etc. "A nice close up photo would be helpful."
   Roland Pautz
   371 Lincoln Street
   San Luis Obispo, CA 93405
      (805) 543-2049   rpautz@thegrid.net

★ **Corn planting and harvesting tools** including hand corn **planters**, **planter plates**, **shock tyres**, **corn shellers** (all types), and cloth **corn seed sacks**, all from before 1950. I DO NOT WANT books, government documents, Agricultural Experiment Bulletins, and general farm magazines with articles about corn. "If in doubt, ask, because previously unknown items are found regularly." State your item's condition, and if it is for sale what you would like for it. Include an SASE. Eloise edits the Corn Items Collectors Association's newsletter, available with membership for only $15/year.
   E. Eloise Alton
   613 North Long Street
   Shelbyville, IL 62565
      (217) 774-5002

MILK & DAIRY EPHEMERA

★ **Round milk bottles with dairy names** embossed or printed on them. Square bottles OK if amber colored or from any Western states. Nothing worn, cracked, or chipped is wanted.
   Leigh Giarde
   PO Box 2243
   Redlands, CA 92373
      (909) 792-8681

★ **Dairy creamers** made of glass with the names of dairies embossed or printed on are sought. He does not want ceramic creamers or those without names. Also **milk bottles** with cop tops, baby tops, or war slogans, but only in excellent condition.
   Ken Clee
   PO Box 11412
   Philadelphia, PA 19111
      (215) 722-1979

★ **Milk or dairy industry items marked with the name and address of a dairy** including old and unusual bottles, advertising, toys, and signs, especially from institutional bottlers such as prisons, colleges, railroads, hotels, and the like. Any bottles with character endorsements (sports, *Hopalong Cassidy*, etc.) are wanted with cartoon characters particularly desirable (Disney bottles bring $100+ each). Bottles and posters with WWII slogans are also sought. Unusually shaped bottles with faces or heads or those made of colored glass are always wanted, as are creamer size bottles marked with the name of a dairy, hotel, or restaurant. Bottles with glass lids, tin handles or lids and pour spouts can go as high as $300. Just about anything related to *Borden's* or their *Elsie the Cow* **trademark** is wanted, especially their ruby red bottles which bring from $700-$1,000 each. "I'll buy **catalogs of bottle makers** which show design variations offered." Large items like cream separators, churns, milk cans, and the like are not wanted. "If in doubt about the authenticity of what you own, feel free to call or send me a good photo. I will verify what you have and answer your questions about it, if you include a Self-Addressed Stamped Envelope."

"You can never give too much information when describing condition. List all flaws, chips, scratches, tears or cracks. I can give you a good appraisal only if you give me a good description."

    Ralph Riovo
    686 Franklin Street
    Alburtis, PA 18011
    (610) 966-2536

★ **Milk bottle caps** of all kinds used on the old glass milk bottles. The flat, plug type, caps that fit inside the top of the bottle are preferred especially those from Southern and Western States, small local dairies, and Washington DC. Other caps of note are special issue caps, those made to advertise products or support the War effort, and those with holiday messages. Older collections or accumulations of caps are the most desirable, bringing $1 to $3 each. "I also want advertising and free samples from cap companies, but have no interest in pogs, nor do I want huge quantities of any one cap (I'll buy tubes, but not cases)." Photocopies are good, but even better is a sample of each cap, with the number you have of each written on the back lightly in pencil.

    David Wampler
    1808 Hidden Harbor Road
    Hixson, TN 37343
  (423) 843-1693   (423) 875-7315   dwampler@mindspring.com

MINING

★ **Mining and blasting items**, including carbide lamps, candlesticks, safety lamps, tools, handbooks, tool catalogs, blasting cap tins, detonators, etc. He only wants items marked with a manufacturer's name, but warns "do not clean or wire brush your item, as I want them as is, not cleaned." Value depends on maker and condition, so give a good description including all names and marks. *Justrite* and *Autolite* lamps are not wanted if made after 1900. No repros. Photo suggested.

Anthony Glab
Sun Ray
4154 Falls Road
Baltimore, MD 21211
(410) 235-1777   Fax: (410) 889-1937   glab@aol.com

★ **Mining items** including safety lamps, oil wick cap lamps, carbide lamps, blasting cap tins and blasting machines, candle holders, and hundreds of other small tools, photos, souvenirs, and advertising items related to mining. Will even buy ore carts and buckets. Also wants ribbons, banners, and badges from the **United Mine Workers** (UMWA) and the Western Federation of Miners (WFM). Dave says he's willing to pay you in cash if you prefer.

David Crawford
1308 Halsted Road
Rockford, IL 61103
(815) 637-6720

★ **Coal company scrip, stocks and bonds,** and **cap lamps** worn by miners when underground.

"Tip" Tippy
22 Cottonwood Lane
Carterville, IL 62916

★ **Colorado mining memorabilia 1859-1915** including photos, paper ephemera, stocks, maps, stereoviews, advertising, and small souvenirs, especially from towns of Cripple Creek, Victor, Central City, Leadville, Breckenridge, Idaho Springs, Telluride, etc. Also books about Colorado mining and any city directories pre-1915. No interest in "flatland cities" like Denver or Colorado Springs, nor in Colorado tourist attractions and parks. No photos unless a mine or mining town is featured.

George Foott
6683 South Yukon Way
Littleton, CO 80123
(303) 979-8688

★ **Mining ephemera,** especially pre-1920 mining stock certificates, photographs of mining operations (but only if they are dated and identified), and postcards depicting mining. No coal mining is wanted. Buys books on mining and select other mining-related material.

>Russell Filer Mining
>13057 California Street
>Yucaipa, CA 92399
>(909) 797-1650

When you have tools to sell, don't even consider cleaning them. Collectors do not want things that have been scrubbed with a wire brush or rust removing solvent.

ROCKS, FOSSILS & CAVES

★ **Meteorites.** Many types exist, and he wants them all, rough or smooth, large or small. Look for rocks that are especially heavy, or with signs of melting or with rust. A freshly fallen meteorite often has a thin black skin, called "fusion crust." If you have a rock that attracts a magnet, you may have a meteorite. "A strong magnet on a string will swing towards all meteorites, which makes this one of the best preliminary tests. Other excellent field tests for meteorites include checking for rust, and filing off a tiny corner to look inside for bright metal or metal flakes. If you think you have found a meteorite, please send a small, dime-sized piece for me to examine along with a description and photo of the entire specimen. If you wish to have the sample returned to you, you must enclose return postage. All non-meteorite samples without return postage are discarded. If I suspect your sample is a meteorite, I will contact you, so be sure to enclose your name, address and phone number along with all samples." Rare forms of meteorites can be surprisingly valuable.

>Robert Haag
>PO Box 27527
>Tucson, AZ 85726
>(520) 882-8804   Fax: (520) 743-7225

★ **Rock, mineral, and fossil collections** are wanted, as are samples of gold, silver, and copper, particularly samples associated with Western mining. Pays in any form you prefer.

>David Crawford
>1308 Halsted Road
>Rockford, IL 61103
>(815) 637-6720

☆ **Fossils of fish, large trilobites or shark's teeth** such as those that are found on Florida's West coast beaches. "I prefer to buy in bulk, and want only those in near perfect condition. are wanted.
    Sven Stau
    851 Harlem Road #11
    West Seneca, NY 14224
       (716) 823-0470

★ **Cave or cavern memorabilia** before 1950, including books, magazine articles, pamphlets, prints, postcards, etc. "Any items that would make a contribution to the history of a particular cave or area such as journal entries, deeds, wills, maps, tickets, and advertising, are of interest." Common souvenirs and chrome postcards are not desired.
    Jack Speece
    711 East Atlantic Avenue
    Altoona, PA 16602
       (814) 946-3155 eves

★ **Caves or cavern memorabilia of all sorts.** "I'll buy anything old or unusual pertaining to caves or caverns worldwide" including photos, brochures, postcards, souvenirs, silver spoons, plates, etc. Does not want anything after 1940, and prefers items from before 1900.
    Gordon Smith
    PO Box 217
    Marengo, IN 47140
       (812) 945-5721

★ **Cave-related items** from before 1950, including post cards with real photos, souvenir plates and paperweights, signs, etc., related to either wild or show caves. Has particular interest in items related to the Floyd Collins rescue in Sand Cave, KY, including souvenirs sold at the event, books on the topic, songs recorded about it, etc. A good description should include all markings. Photo suggested.
    Anthony Glab
    Sun Ray
    4154 Falls Road
    Baltimore, MD 21211
       (410) 235-1777   Fax: (410) 889-1937   glab@aol.com

FRUIT, TREES & LUMBER

★ **Canning machinery, catalogs and tools** of the *Ferracute Machine Company* of Bridgeton, NJ, are sought by this researcher who also wants anything related to company founder **Oberlin Smith**. The Oberlin Smith Society is particularly interested in advertising, catalogs, small presses, medals and tokens, but will consider anything related to FMCo or Smith himself. The OSS is a 501(c)(3) organization and seeks donations too.

> James Gandy, Oberlin Smith Society
> Route 2   Box 109, 92 River Road
> Bridgeton, NJ   08302
> (609) 451-8580

★ **Everything about fruit and vegetable growing, packing and canning** is wanted, such as labels, photographs, postcards, magazines, buttons, ribbons and giveaway trinkets of all types. Wants all sorts of paper ephemera from various organizations and events promoting fruit and vegetable growing and packing. Buys **orange juicers, reamers and extractors** from major packers, if company name is impressed.

> Pat Jacobsen
> PO Box 791
> Weimar, CA 95736
> (916) 637-5923

★ **Everything about fruit raising and varieties before 1900,** including illustrated books, magazine articles, ceramic tiles depicting fruit, postcards, prints, folders, and greeting cards depicting apples. Especially wants books and paper with color plates or descriptions of fruit varieties. May be in any language.   No tropical fruit, or anything later than 1940. This veteran horticulture experimenter wants **cuttings from uncommon tree fruit varieties** you have on your farm. He wants temperate climate fruits, especially apples, but also pears, plums, quinces and medlars. Also buys **books on fruit propagation** which were printed before 1920.

> Fred Janson
> Pomona Book Exchange
> Highway 52
> Rockton, Ontario
> L0R 1X0   CANADA

★ **Lumber company and store tokens, scrip, stocks and bonds.** Please make a photocopy of your items.

> "Tip" Tippy
> 22 Cottonwood Lane
> Carterville, IL 62916

OIL COMPANY MEMORABILIA

★ **Oil company memorabilia from the 1920's** including advertising of all sorts, giveaways, stationary, point of purchase advertising, signs, pump globes, etc. Also seeks informative material such as early gas station **photos, trade publications,** and the like, from any company, as long as it's generally from the 1920's era. This 20+ year veteran collector does not want reproductions of any sort. Give him the name of the company, and a description of the item you have.

> Bill Allard
> 1801 Fernside
> Tacoma, WA 98465
> (206) 565-2545

★ **Gasoline and oil company advertising and promotional items from local, regional and independent oil companies** and dealers *only*. "I'll buy gas pump globes, banks shaped like oil cans or gas pumps, salt/pepper shaped like gas pumps, thermometers, transistor radios shaped like oil cans or gas pumps and small cans of oil. He is not interested in paper items, large signs, reproductions, or national brands like *Mobil, Shell, Esso, Phillips, Conoco, Amoco, Texaco* etc. Describe the condition, and include a description of decals or labels.

> Peter Capell
> 1838 West Grace Street
> Chicago, IL 60613
> (312) 871-8735

★ **Gasoline and oil company signs** in porcelain or enamel. Also buys some other petroleum advertising.

> Gus Garton, Garton's Auto
> 5th and Vine
> Millville, NJ 08332
> (609) 825-3618

★ *Mobil Oil* **memorabilia** including anything picturing the red horse. Also collecting service pins given to *Mobil* employees. Also buys porcelain signs from *Gargoyle, White Eagle*, and *Magnolia* gas and oil. No repros...and Billie says she has enough globes. She insists that the seller set the price wanted as she and Bob do not make offers for additions to their herd.

> Bob and Billie Butler
> 1236 Helen Street
> Augusta, KS 67010
> (316) 775-6193

★ **Oil cans in all sizes, all types, and all materials,** including brass, aluminum, glass, tin, graniteware or plastic. Wants everything from small sewing machine size up to and including railroad oil cans, advertising cans, and novelty cans.   Pays $10-$25 for a graniteware can especially with the name WHITE on it, $10-$15 for most others, more for railroad cans.   Not all desirable cans have names on them. Make a sketch. If it is a pump can, tell Robert whether the pump works.

    Robert Larson
    3517 Vernal Court
    Merced, CA 95340
       (209) 723-7828

★ **Oil cans from Canada,** especially British Columbia oil in tin cans, and any quart oil cans related to motorcycles.

    Don Schneider
    PO Box 1570
    Merritt, BC
    V1K 1B8 CANADA
       (604) 378-6421

★ **Oil company credit cards** and pocket **calendars** are purchased. You may send your items for his immediate offer and a return check.

    Noel Levy
    1109 Silent Glade Road
    Owings Mills, MD 21117
       (410) 363-9040

When you ask someone for information or an offer, include a long business size #10 envelope, address it to yourself, and put a stamp in the corner. This is a Self-Addressed Stamped Envelope (SASE). Use a long envelope because many buyers will send you information which won't fit into smaller envelopes. If you do not include an SASE, you are telling buyers not to bother answering your letter if they are not interested in what you have to sell. Buyers find it annoying when you do not include one. If you annoy buyers, they will quit offering their services for free.

BARBERSHOP ITEMS

★ **Decorated shaving mugs** depicting the owner's occupation, trade, or hobby above or below his name. Also hand painted personal occupational barber bottles. Since each was custom made, they must be evaluated individually. Also **salesman's sample barber chairs** made in porcelain or wood. No Japanese reproductions or "Sportsman's Series" mugs from the 1950's.

> Burton Handelsman
> 18 Hotel Drive
> White Plains, NY 10605
>   (914) 761-8880   Fax: (914) 428-2145

★ **Barbershop memorabilia,** including:
- Decorated **shaving mugs** with original owner's name and picture of any occupation, vehicle, fraternal order, animal, etc.;
- Fancy barber bowls, bottles, and waste jars;
- **Catalogs** of barber supplies or equipment;
- **Salesmen's sample barber chairs,** and much more.

Powell both collects and deals so buys a wide range of fine items or accepts them on consignment. Include a tracing or close up photo. New shaving mugs are not wanted. This well known historian is the only member of the Barber's Hall of Fame who isn't a barber.

> Robert Powell
> PO Box 833
> Hurst, TX 76053
>   (817) 284-8145

**See also: razors and knives and advertising
for buyers of this type of material.**

*I do not at this time have a buyer for
ordinary household shaving mugs
that are not decorated with advertising
or with the owner's picture or occupation
or other interesting subject matter.
Simple florals without the owner's name
are not of interest.*

How to sell guns, weapons and military items.

You're likely to own these items so I've supplied premium experts to help you dispose of them properly. If your item is collectible, you'll find a buyer here.

To describe most military items, *follow the basics: material(s) from which it is made, color(s), dimensions, serial numbers and other marks, what you know of its history, and the item's condition. If it's supposed to do something, does it do it? Are all parts and pieces there? Is it for sale or do you "just want a price"? It may be easier to photocopy small items.*

When you offer a uniform *for sale, you should describe all insignia and ribbons. They will decide the uniform's value. Your uniform should be in good condition. Buyers will forgive moth holes in a Revolutionary War outfit but not in most WWII uniforms.*

When describing a sword, dagger or bayonet *measure from end to end and from the tip of the blade to the handle guard. Measure the width of the blade where it attaches to the handle guard. List every word or number found on the blade, hilt, or handle. Trace or photocopy any decoration on the blade or sheath. Describe the condition of the scabbard or sheath. Treat knives and swords as fragile objects. Mishandling can be costly.*

To sell a gun make sure it is not loaded *before anything else. Gun buyers want to know the make, model, serial number, caliber or gauge, barrel length, type and percent of finish, type of stock or grips, mechanical condition and condition of the bore. List all marks inside and out and note dings, defects and alterations.*

The buyer will tell you how to ship your items. *When rare or valuable weapons are involved, the buyer may prefer to pick them up personally or arrange for pick up.*

Buyers prefer to obtain military items from the veteran who owned them, or from a direct heir. Counterfeits abound...especially of leather jackets and Nazi items.

GUNS

★ **American percussion and early cartridge firearms,** both long guns and revolvers, 1840-1920. "I'll buy guns by any maker, but especially *Colt, Winchester, Remington, Marlin, Smith & Wesson, Manhattan, Sharps, Stevens,* and *Bacon.* I like to buy derringers of all types, especially those that are particularly small or short barreled, those that are very large caliber (.41 cal. up), or those which take metallic cartridges. I also like finding any pocket size pistols made by *Colt, Remington, Bacon, Marston, Moore, National, Reid, Terry, Warner,* and *Williamson,* among others." Pays $300 to $3,000 for these guns. Wants photos or photocopies of both sides of the weapon and all markings and numbers found anywhere on the gun.

> Steve Howard
> Past Tyme Pleasures
> 101 First Street #404
> Los Altos, CA 94022
>   (510) 484-4488 eves

★ **Antique and modern firearms.** "I'll buy a wide range of items, from Civil War carbines, Indian Wars guns, trap doors, rolling blocks, cap and ball, etc., to early *Winchester, Marlin, Savage* and *Remington.*" This 25 year dealer also buys some *Colt* **handguns.** If your gun or rifle is pre-1964 and all wood and metal surfaces are original and unrestored, it might be worth a call. Although he buys *Krag, Springfield* and others for parts, he does not want reworked guns or reproductions. Rudy offers a catalog of guns for sale.

> Rudy Dotzenrod
> 752 7th Street
> Wyndmere, ND 58081
>   (701) 439-2646

★ **Guns and gun collections** of all types. "I'm always searching for **Gattling guns.**"

> Ed Kukowski
> Ed's Gun House
> PO Box 62
> Minnesota City, MN 55959
>   (507) 689-2925   Fax: (507) 689-4286

★ **Antique weapons of all types** including guns, swords, uniforms and other high grade military goods. Holds regular cataloged auctions of high grade guns.

> James D. Julia Auctioneers
> PO Box 830
> Fairfield, ME 04937
>   (207) 453-7904   Fax: (207) 453-2502

★ **Pinfire and other antique fire arms** are sought in any condition including cheap guns suitable only for parts. Provide a general description and all names, dates, and other numbers you find on the gun. If the parts of the gun have serial numbers, tell him whether the numbers match. This important 40 year historian says, "I'm retired now and don't buy many guns, but I own a big research library and am happy to answer questions, give free advice, and help you find a buyer."

Larry Compeau
5262 Old Franklin Road
Grand Blanc, MI 48439
(810) 694-2705

Any gun buyer wants to know the make, model, serial number, caliber or gauge, barrel length, type and percent of finish, type of stock or grips, mechanical condition and condition of the bore. Describe all marks inside and out, list alterations, and note dings and defects.

★ **American guns** from before 1890, especially those with historic association. No interest in reproductions. If possible, send a clear photo of the item and write down all markings found anywhere on it. If it is a pistol, please make a photocopy, or draw a pencil outline. Mention any broken or missing wood, metal that is pitted, parts missing, etc. Does it work? Worman wrote two books on firearms of the American West and was firearms editor of *Hobbies* magazine for sixteen years. SASE please. "I do not make offers."

Charles Worman
PO Box 33584 (AMC)
Dayton, OH 45433
(513) 760-1873

★ **High grade shotguns, double rifles, and big bore rifles**, whether English, Italian, or American made. Guns must be in original condition. "I do not want broken or damaged guns, paramilitary weapons, clunkers or guns you can buy at your local gun shop. I will pay up to $100,000 for rare sporting guns, but a personal physical inspection is essential before any purchase." Your first contact by mail or phone should include the brand name, serial number, caliber or gauge, length of the barrel, a description of any markings stamped on the metal or wood parts, and a statement of condition. The history of the gun is useful. If writing, include your phone number.

Francis Lombardi II
PO Box 181-TH
Syracuse, NY 13208
(315) 685-9806

★ **Black powder antique guns** made in Western New York State. Makers of interest include *Artis, Cutler, Ellis, Gardner, Lefever, Marsley, Miller, Plimpton, Southerland, Walker, Wood* and several others. Antique guns only.

> Alan Stone
> PO Box 500 or 5170 County Road 33
> Honeoye, NY 14471
> (716) 229-2700

★ **Revolvers (pistols).** "I'll consider any antique or collectible firearms to build my dealer's inventory or to enhance my personal collection, but my special interests are:
- Serial number one guns, antique or modern;
- *Smith & Wesson* revolvers;
- Antique engraved revolvers;
- Old West firearms;
- Guns owned by famous individuals.

"I can travel if needed. Confidentiality assured. I try to be considerate and helpful in cases of divorce, bankruptcy, and estate liquidation. I can pay immediately or arrange auction or consignment sales. I'm interested in unusual or oddball older guns that many other collectors avoid. Honest wear and alterations from the period of use are OK, but do affect the value of the piece. I will consider heavily worn, broken, or refinished items only if they are rare or have documented historical connection. I am not interested in fakes, reproductions or modern guns. If offering an historic gun, quality of documentation is important. Send a copy of documentation and what you will swear to in a notarized affidavit. A personal inspection is required before final offer, especially on finely engraved guns. Please don't offer anything stolen or illegal. I won't buy it." Specific regulations govern shipment of firearms. Jim has the necessary licenses, but check for shipping instructions. If you don't want to sell your gun but want an informal appraisal, Jim charges only $1 each to appraise most handguns. Interesting catalog available. Jim is co-author of *Standard Catalog of Smith & Wesson.*

> Jim Supica, Jr., Old Town Station Ltd.
> PO Box 15351
> Lenexa, KS 66285
> (913) 492-3000   Fax: (913) 492-3022   OldTownSta@aol.com

Any gun buyer wants to know the make, model, serial number, caliber or gauge, barrel length, type and percent of finish, type of stock or grips, mechanical condition and condition of the bore. Describe all marks inside and out, list alterations, and note dings and defects.

★ *Colt* **pistols with factory engraving.** "I'll buy single action *Colts* in 95% or better original condition, if they predate WWII and have factory engraving." Give the serial number when you write, and, if possible, a good close up photo of the artwork. Some newer single actions are also wanted. Also wants **guns from outlaws and lawmen** if they have proper documentation. All early **memorabilia from the *Colt* company,** including all advertising and literature are wanted, including *Coltrock* brand products and the boxes they came in.

> Johnny Spellman
> 10806 North Lamar
> Austin, TX 78753
>   (512) 836-2889 days   (512) 258-6910 eves

★ *Colt* **pistols and** *Colt* **Firearms Mfg Co. ephemera** including all correspondence on factory letterhead, pamphlets and brochures by *Colt*, empty black and maroon boxes that *Colt* guns were packed in, instruction sheets and manuals, and "anything else pertaining to *Colt* products." John wants *Colt* factory catalogs, 1888-1910, for which he pays from $40-$500+. 1910-1940 catalogs bring $20-$100. John also buys plastic and electrical items marked *Coltrock*.

> John Fischer
> 10950 West Pico Blvd.
> Los Angeles, CA 90064
>   (310) 474-2567

★ *Newton Arms Co.* **guns and other memorabilia** from this progressive 1916-18 gunsmith. "I'll buy rifles, catalogs, **loading tools**, letters, stock certificates, cartridges, and any other paper or memorabilia from the *Newton Arms Co.* or the *Buffalo.Newton Rifle Corp.* I will pay $5,000 for a .276 *Newton* rifle or a rifle in .280, .33 or .40 (.400) calibers if in mint condition, and look for **unusual *Newton* cartridges**. I will gladly pay a finder's fee for *Newton* guns I buy. I'll take anything signed by Chas. Newton but nothing marked *Buffalo Newton Rifle Co.* Any items other than guns must be original condition."

> Bruce Jennings
> 70 Metz Road
> Sheridan, WY 82801
>   (307) 674-6921

★ **Junk guns and gun parts** in any condition. "I'm in the parts business and will travel to pick up large lots." Wants nothing having to do with current guns. Describe all markings and numbers. Bob is available for insurance appraisals of fire damaged gun collections.

> Robert Fay
> Rusted & Busted Bob's
> Star Route Box AF
> Whitmore, CA 96096
>   (916) 472-3132

★ **Old double barrel shotguns** are wanted in any condition. "I will buy any double barrel made before 1940, including parts guns and wall-hangers. Your trash is my treasure." Give the maker, model, condition, amount of bluing, rust, missing parts, engraving, etc." Charles has been in business since 1937.

> Charles Black, Gundoctor
> 512 Coman Street
> Athens, AL 35611
> (205) 230-3773

★ *Iver Johnson* **products and memorabilia** including **guns, bicycles, catalogs**, etc. Special wants include engraved presentation guns and awards and any other unusual *Iver Johnson* item. This 30 year veteran collector does not want "common handguns in less than mint condition." Send a complete description, including a sketch or photo. Prefers seller to price, but will make offers.

> Charles Best
> 11523 Pinevalley Drive
> Franktown, CO 80116
> (303) 660-2318

★ **Brass military shell casings.** "I want to buy the casings for shells and projectiles in 37mm and larger sizes. Particularly wants an 8" Navy shell. I'll buy shell casings of all weapons, all nations."

> Charles Eberhart
> 3616 N.E. Seward
> Topeka, KS 66616
> (913) 235-1016

★ **Ammunition and exploding devices** including grenades, mines, bombs, and fuses of all type, from the beginning of time to the present. "We buy everything from stone cannon balls to the **smart weapons** used in Operation Desert Storm. Also want books, films, reports, and videos about ordnance in any format or language." Schmitt's family has been making ammunition since 1849, so he particularly wants things marked with the *Crittenden* name. He is willing to pay $2,000 for a **.69 caliber** *Crittenden and Tibbals* **Rimfire cartridge**. He wants the measurements, condition, and all markings on what you have, preferring you also include a photo. He has no interest in store stock items. Schmitt is a contributing editor of two gun magazines and involved with cleaning up explosive ordnance from the Iraq/UN war.

> J. Randall Crittenden Schmitt
> Court House Station
> PO Box 4253
> Rockville, MD 20849
> (301) 946-2643

SHOOTING COMPETITION

★ **Single shot target shooting rifles** made between 1850 and 1915. "I want *only* those rifles and no other guns. I DO NOT want shotguns, skeet/trap guns, military or National Guard weapons, police guns, or rifles designed for hunting." If you have one to sell, include the maker and any information found on the barrel, sight or elsewhere on the rifle, including serial numbers. A photo of your item is helpful. Also buys anything associated with target shooting and target shooting organizations here or in Europe, 1850-1915.

    Allen Hallock
    PO Box 2747
    San Rafael, CA 94902
        (415) 924-1967   arh@earthlink.net

★ **National Rifle Association (N.R.A.)** shooting medals and literature showing or describing N.R.A. shooting matches and medals.

    Charles Best
    11523 Pine Valley Drive
    Franktown, CO 80116

★ **Target Shooting Organization memorabilia** from Switzerland, Germany or the U.S. Called *SchuetzenVereins*, they existed primarily from the Civil War period to World War One. He seeks medals, trophies, banners, painted targets, photographs, match programs, posters and other items. "I DO NOT want military, National Guard, police, trap or skeet shooting, shotgun, hunting or recent (after 1915) material, nor does he want souvenir Swiss medals or coins" but if it says SCHUETZEN on it send a full description, including any engraving or maker's marks, and the condition of the item. A Xerox™ or photo is helpful as most items are unique. He also buys single shot target shooting rifles.

    Allen Hallock
    PO Box 2747
    San Rafael, CA 94902
        (415) 924-1967   arh@earthlink.net

WAR & WEAPONS

★ **Anything military.** "My specialty is WWII paratrooper items from the U.S., Germany, and Japan, but **I will buy any military items from the Roman Empire to current issue Operation Desert Storm**. I buy small items like dog tags and big items like tanks, so look in the attic and give me a call." This 30 year veteran collector does not want reproductions or fakes but will consider anything you find in that trunk in your attic such as flags, uniforms, helmets, equipment, guns, daggers, hats, shoes, medals, jewelry, boats, jeeps, tanks. "I buy anything military." Take a photo if you can and tell him whatever history you know about the item(s) you have. "If you want to know what something is worth, but you can't take a photo, or find writing to be difficult," he says, "give me a call and I'll be happy to talk to you." If you write, make sure you include your phone number as I do 90% of my business over the phone.

> Michael Burke
> Kats Militaria
> 906 Chambers Ridge
> York, PA 17402
>   (717) 840-4156

★ **Revolutionary War through the War of 1812 items** including:
- **Artillery shells** and solid shot from 2" to 7" in diameter;
- **Cannon** or mortar barrels in any size, brass or iron;
- **Tomahawks** or belt axe heads;
- Triangular **bayonettes** or plug bayonettes;
- **Trade beads** or other Indian artifacts of this period;
- **Flintlock** military muskets, usually .50 caliber or larger;
- Belt buckles, shoe buckles, plates, buttons, etc.;
- Wooden **canteens** of all types;
- Leather pouches for ammunition or personal items;
- **Swords, daggers, and belt knives**;
- Halberds, spontoons, pikes, and linstocks.
- Anything similar to the above.

He is not interested in reproductions of these items, or in any books about the Revolutionary War era. "A photo is best, but a complete, accurate description is helpful. As much as possible, give the history of the item. Asking price is helpful but not necessary."

> Larry Jarvinen
> 313 Condon Road
> Manistee, MI 49660
>   (616) 723-5063

★ **Primitive weapons from around the world.** Also trade beads from various cultures.
> David Boone
> Boone Trading Company
> 562 Coyote Road
> Brinnon, WA 98320
> (360) 796-4330   Fax: (360) 796-4511

★ **Boer war items**, with particular interest in carvings made of cedar wood. Describe thoroughly.
> Ernest H. Roberts
> 5 Corsa Street
> Dix Hills, NY 11746
> (516) 7805 days   (516) 586-1462 eves   Fax: (516) 346-7823

★ **Mexican War** (1846-48) photos and documents are sought.
> Johnny Spellman
> 10806 North Lamar
> Austin, TX 78753
> (512) 836-2889 days   (512) 258-6910 eves

★ **Civil War artifacts, Union and Confederate** are wanted, including autographs of important military and civilian personalities, documents, photos, diaries, books, manuals, soldier's letters, personal items, campaign histories, regimental histories, G.A.R. or Confederate Veteran items. Has a particular interest in the battles of Gettysburg and Antietam. Provide a detailed description of items, especially condition.
> Stan Clark, Jr., Military Books
> 915 Fairview Avenue
> Gettysburg, PA 17325
> (717) 337-1728   Fax: (717) 337-0581

★ **Civil War artifacts** including guns, knives, documents, swords, and **prisoner of war items**. No repros. It is important to indicate any markings. SASE requested. "I do not make offers."
> Charles Worman
> PO Box 33584 (AMC)
> Dayton, OH 45433
> (513) 760-1873

★ **Civil War paper items** such as soldier's letters and diaries, documents, envelopes, stamps, maps, prisoner of war items, currency, script and photos. Specializes in Confederate items, especially stampless envelopes (covers). "I do not deal in reproductions."
> Gordon McHenry
> PO Box 1117
> Osprey, FL 34229

★ **Civil War items**, especially uniforms. Buys muskets, pistols, swords, photographs and sundry items including bottles and excavated artifacts related to the war. Also buys other military items up through World War II. Nothing later.

Will Gorges Antiques
2100 Trent Blvd.
New Bern, NC 28560
(919) 636-3909 days (919) 514-5548 eves   Fax: (919) 637-1862

★ **G.A.R. china, mugs, and spoons.** Any pieces marked G.A.R. (Grand Army of the Republic).

Don McMahon
385 Thorpe Avenue
Meriden, CT 06450
(203) 238-3434

★ **United Confederate Reunion (UCV)** badges, buttons, and ribbons.

Peggy Dillard
PO Box 210904
Nashville, TN 37221
(615) 646-1605 eves

★ **Civil War regimental histories** and first person narratives.

Jim Presgraves
Bookworm & Silverfish
PO Box 639
Wytheville, VA 24382

★ **Indian War veterans material.** Anything from National Indian War Veterans, Order of Indian Wars of the United States and any similar organization: membership certificates or cards, medals, convention ribbons, photos, etc. Call or send complete details. Up to $5,000 paid.

Thomas Pooler
PO Box 1861
Grass Valley, CA 95945
(916) 268-1338

★ **Military books of World War I, World War II and Korean War** on the air, land and sea. First editions in dust jackets preferred. Some rare titles will be purchased in lesser condition. Provide standard bibliographic information, including printing data found on the title page or reverse. No book club books and no paperbacks.

Edward Conroy
SUMAC Books
Route 1 Box 197
Troy, NY 12180
(518) 279-9638 voice and fax

★ **Afro-American militaria** especially unit photos in any condition, unit history books, holiday menus, unit insignia, shoulder patches, medals, scrapbooks, or what have you. "If you want an offer, send it for my examination. I pay all postage, both ways."
>Lt. Col. Wilfred Baumann
>PO Box 319
>Esperance, NY 12066
>(518) 875-6753

★ **Black militaria.** "I will buy any and all items specific to African-American participation in wars from the Revolution through Vietnam, especially named medals, uniforms, equipment, documents, photos, and prints, as well as **books** dealing with Black military history; "I have a particular interest in the **Buffalo Soldiers and the Tuskegee Airmen**. Rare or one-of-a-kind items with strong provenance connected to a Black historical event are most desired. "I don't want books, sheet music, stereo cards or postcards, or any reproductions." Send a description, including the condition. You may set the price wanted or request offers. I buy, sell, and trade.
>Elizabeth Meaders
>94 Mersereau Avenue
>Staten Island, NY 10303
>(718) 727-0703

★ **Military items.** "I'll buy most military items, if original, especially WWI, WWII Airborne (paratroopers), military aviation and glider operations, and **Vietnam**. I do not want reproductions of WWII German items." Give the origin of your piece. Photograph expensive items.
>Robert Thomas, Jr.
>Thomas Militaria
>1926 West Trask Avenue
>Santa Ana, CA 92706
>(714) 971-2258   Fax: (714) 971-1531

★ **Military souvenirs from WWI to Vietnam** from any country: books, documents, medals, uniforms, manuals, daggers, swords, guns, patches, flags, and "any other war souvenirs you find." Send a Photo or Xerox™ along with a description of all markings. SASE.
>Gaal Long Jr.
>Route 1 Box 40
>Sardis, MS 38666
>(601) 487-2457

★ **Regimental and Battalion unit flags** from all nations and periods of history. "I'll also buy flag related items such as U.S. Army spear pole tops, color woven flag cords and tassels, engraved battle honor rings and battle streamers, canvas issue flag cover bags, and close up or **parade photos** showing unit flags." No national flags or reenactment group flags. Please make a sketch of the flag, noting size and material. Ben can provide info about unit flags if you send an SASE.

> Ben Weed
> PO Box 4643
> Stockton, CA 95204

★ **Cloth shoulder insignia** of divisions, regiments, brigades, and units from the Civil War to Vietnam. WWI U.S. and German insignia are of special interest. He prefers to buy directly from the veteran or family. Condition is important. This 25 year veteran does not want repros.

> Hank McGonagle
> 26 Broad Street
> Newburyport, MA 01950
> (508) 462-2354   (617) 594-1596

★ **Military medals and decorations** from all countries and periods. Also any documents or certificates related to military awards, medals and decorations. He prefers to buy directly from the vet or his family. Condition is important, and a photocopy is requested.

> Hank McGonagle
> 26 Broad Street
> Newburyport, MA 01950
> (508) 462-2354   (617) 594-1596

★ **Medals, Decorations, and Orders** for military gallantry and other campaign medals of the U.S. and British Empire, 1780 to the present. Especially wants U.S. Medals of Honor and **British Victoria Crosses** and U.S. Purple Hearts for WWII officially named to the Navy and Marines. Does not want reproductions. Photocopy both sides.

> Alan Harrow
> 2292 Chelan Drive
> Los Angeles, CA 90068

★ **U.S. Military medals** with the recipient's name engraved. Offers to buy Purple Hearts, Distinguished Service Cross, Distinguished Flying Cross, Air Medals, Silver Star, Navy Cross, and Medals of Honor. Send photocopy of the engraving or the name of the recipient. Also any supporting documents.

> Gary Hullfish
> 16 Gordon Avenue
> Lawranceville, NJ 08648
> (609) 896-0224   Fax: (609) 896-2040

★ **Military newsreel and training films** from WWII on any military, naval, or aviation subject. British, American, Canadian, German, or Russian, but must be 16mm sound films shot 1939-45. Films may be training, propaganda or documentary. Buys military aviation films 1903-1985, especially WWI, Korean Conflict, and Vietnam. Give complete title, producer, length and defects. If possible, describe the contents. Nothing damaged. Also buys **military magazines.**

>Edward Topor
>4313 South Marshfield Avenue
>Chicago, IL 60609
>(312) 847-6392

★ **General Douglas MacArthur memorabilia** of all types is wanted. "I'll buy books, scrapbooks, autographed items, pictures, documents, toys, dolls, medals, coins, any item with 'I shall return' or 'I have returned' on it, buttons, statues, and any item documented as having belonged to MacArthur." Gaal also wants "letters or phone calls from anyone who knew MacArthur at any period of his life and can tell me stories about him. Please send a Xerox™ if you'd like an offer.

>Gaal Long Jr.
>Route 1   Box 40
>Sardis, MS   38666
>(601) 487-2457

★ **War crimes trial articles from Nurnberg or Japan** including jewelry, insignia, patches, etc. "Please give a ballpark price for your item."

>Jerry Keohane
>16 Saint Margaret's Court
>Buffalo, NY 14216

★ **Women's service uniforms from WWII**, plus any other items related to the women's military during that war.

>Bruce Updegrove
>Route 5 Box 546
>Boyertown, PA 19512
>(610) 369-1798

U.S. NAVY, MARINE CORPS & MARITIME SERVICES

★ **Merchant Marine, Coast Guard and the U.S. Maritime Service** photos, uniforms, medals, flags, discharges, etc.

>Harvey Lee Boswell, USMR Ret.
>PO Box 446
>Elm City, NC 27822

★ **U.S. Navy memorabilia** including postcards, ship postmarks and documents, matchcovers, cruise books. Describe. Pricing appreciated.
> Frank Hoak III
> PO Box 668
> New Canaan, CT 06840

★ **U.S. Marine Corps memorabilia** of all kinds including recruiting posters and materials, books, photos, belt buckles, cigarette lighters, steins, mugs, documents, autographs, postcards, **trench art**, bronzes, and **John Philip Sousa** ephemera. Also buys **toy soldiers, trucks, and planes** with Marine markings. Describe or make a photocopy.
> Dick Weisler
> 5307 213th Street
> Bayside, NY 11364
>   (718) 626-7110 days   (718) 428-9829 eves

★ **U.S. Marine Corps everything.** Anything used and/or worn by Marines from 1776 to 1946, such as **uniforms, medals**, helmets and weapons. Also buys unit histories, documents and **recruiting posters**. Wants photos of Marines at war, work, or play, especially amateur photos. Also wants trench art created by Marines and souvenirs of war brought home by Marines. Tell what you can of the item's history.
> Bruce Updegrove
> Route 5   Box 546
> Boyertown, PA 19512
>   (610) 369-1798 eves

★ **U.S. Marine Corps ephemera** including recruiting posters, other artwork, postcards, autographs, letters written by Marines, and "almost any" Marine related book, including signed books by or about Marines, personal memoirs, unit histories, campaign histories, biographies, fiction, juveniles, children's books and poetry. "I would especially like a set of monographs written by Marine Major Edwin McClellan in 1925, in book or mimeographed form." He is not interested in book club editions or in books "in questionable condition." To sell your Marine Corps books, give standard bibliographic information, including number of pages, size, and whether or not it has a dust jacket. This 10 year veteran distributes four catalogs a year of military books for sale. "If you are actually selling, give us a call, but we don't have time for casual inquiries or information seekers. Sorry."
> Stan Clark, Jr.
> Stan Clark Military Books
> 915 Fairview Avenue
> Gettysburg, PA 17325
>   (717) 337-1728   Fax: (717) 337-0581

THE AIR WAR

★ **Japanese and German pilots and planes.** "I buy all items related to Japanese and German wartime aviation and pilots including equipment, uniforms, float vests, boots, gloves, parachutes, etc. I'd especially like to find aircraft fuselage pieces with Japanese or German markings and airplane gauges, radios, and parts." Please don't contact him unless you are willing to sell what you have. This 20 year veteran collector pledges "a very nice purchase offer" if you're actually selling.
> Stuart Tamaru
> Box 4095
> Torrance, CA 90510
> (310) 320-8130

★ **Army Air Force A2 flight jackets,** AAF pocket insignia, sterling silver military aviation wings and WWI enlisted men's round collar discs. Nothing later than the Korean War. "Please give a ballpark asking price for any item you offer."
> Jerry Keohane
> 16 Saint Margaret's Court
> Buffalo, NY 14216

    "If the seller did not get the jacket from the veteran
or his family, it is probably not old."

★ **WWII leather or cloth aviation jackets** with squadron patch and/or painted artwork on the back, from any branch of the service, any branch of aviation. Needs information on jacket label, condition of the jacket and its patches or art, plus details about the art. Photo helpful. Does not want currently made flight jackets with antiqued paintings or patches. Clue: If the zipper isn't marked as being *Talon* brand, the jacket isn't old. Buys documented **WWII Flying Tiger memorabilia, squadron patches and histories** and photos of **airplane nose art.**
> Gary Hullfish
> 16 Gordon Avenue
> Lawranceville, NJ 08648
> (609) 896-0224   Fax: (609) 896-2040

★ **Airplane identification models,** 1940-1970. Also promotional models, travel agency models, and **squadron and bomb group unit histories**. When writing, copy all info printed on the plane.
> John Pochobradsky
> 1991 East Schodack Road
> Castleton, NY 12033
> (518) 477-9488

TANKS & HEAVY WEAPONS

★ **Tanks, artillery, armored vehicles and machine guns and their parts and accessories.** "We are a Federally licensed machine gun manufacturer and dealer, and seek to buy registered operational machine guns and other military equipment, including **muzzle loading cannon** and **Gattling guns.** We buy machine gun parts and accessories including, but not limited to, barrels, buttstocks, magazines, clips, drums, bipods, tripods, mounts, loading machines, linkers, armorer's kits, etc. We are particularly interested in mounts for *Maxim* machine guns and will pay $150+ for them. We will buy **most anything made in the 19th or 20th centuries.** Parts and guns do not have to be in perfect condition. We will look at all items, but clear photos are a must. A VHS video is even better. Include dimensions and condition of accessories. Copies of any accompanying paperwork or manuals are helpful. If, after inspection, our offer is unacceptable, I will pay shipping both ways." Not interested in toys, miniatures, stolen firearms or U.S. Army manuals.

> Greg Souchik
> T.M.P. Company
> PO Box 133
> Custer City, PA 16725
>   (814) 362-2642   Fax: (814) 362-7356

★ **Half tracks, armored cars, tanks, Gattling guns,** howitzers, and cannons, especially a *FT-17 Renault* (M1917) tank in any condition. Larry will arrange for transporting what you have. Also wants:
- **U.S. women's uniforms** and accessories, WWI or WWII but only in fine condition;
- **Hard hat diving** equipment and related items including catalogs;
- *Mercedes Benz 500K* or *540K* autos between 1930 and 1945;
- **German military staff cars;**
- **Military aircraft** from any country pre-1946.

Provide all the information printed on the machine's data plates. In most cases when you are trying to sell large equipment, a few photographs from different angles would be recommended.

> Larry Pitman
> Zanzibar War Museum
> 5424 Bryan Station Road
> Paris, KY 40361
>   (606) 299-5022   Fax: (606) 299-4522

THE HOME FRONT

★ **MIA/POW bracelets** stamped with the name and rank of a soldier in Vietnam, and the date he was listed as missing in action or became a prisoner of war. Pays $8 each. Prefers to have the original certificate which came with the bracelet. Call or write before sending the bracelet.

> Judy Polk Harding
> 1701 60th Street
> Des Moines, IA 50322
> (515) 279-7099 voice and fax   THEFIVEJS@aol.com

★ **Rationing material** worldwide. CSU owns most American items, buys only paper and "wants many foreign posters and other items." No U.S. ration books are needed.

> Tammy Lau
> Head of Special Collections
> Madden Library
> Calif. State University at Fresno
> Fresno, CA 93740
> (209) 294-2595   Fax: (209) 278-6952   tammy_lau@csufresno.edu

★ **Ration tokens.** Pays 2¢ each for red tokens, 3¢ each for blue. After the first 250, he pays 1¢ each. Pays "much more" for error tokens. Ship for his inspection and check.

> Rich Hartzog
> PO Box 4143 BVT
> Rockford, IL 61110

★ **Patriotic embroidery.** "I want embroidered or hand stitched cotton or silk American or Confederate flags, patriotic or military themes, American eagles, and similar, especially turn of the century items with Marine Corps themes. Nothing made after 1960 is wanted, nor is anything with serious holes, tears, or insect damage." Photo is suggested.

> Stan Clark, Jr.
> 915 Fairview Avenue
> Gettysburg, PA 17325
> (717) 337-1728   Fax: (717) 337-0581

FOREIGN ARMIES

★ **Napoleonic arms and armor.** This 30 year veteran collector/dealer in Western ephemera requires you to send a photo and complete description and your asking price. No fakes or reproductions are wanted.
>Pierre Bovis
>The Az-Tex Cowboy Trading Co.
>PO Box 13345
>Tucson, AZ 85732
>   (520) 318-9512   Fax: (520) 318-0023

★ **Canadian military medals and cap badges.** "I'll buy all cap badges with the initials CEF on them, or badges with a number and the words OVERSEAS BATTALION and CANADA or CANADIAN on them. I'll buy any war or period. Look for name, rank and military unit on the rims of medals as some are worth $1,000+." Answers all inquiries.
>Michael Rice
>PO Box 286
>Saanichton, BC
>V8M 2C5 CANADA
>   (250) 652-9412 evenings only. Please no day calls.

★ **Military items of Great Britain or Commonwealth nations.** "I'll buy hat, collar or shoulder badges, headdresses, uniforms, field equipment (belts, packs, pouches) and **edged weapons**. Particularly seek Scottish bagpipers' headdress and badges, kilts and sporrans (leather kilt purses), dirks, and knives." 45 year collector will consider 1910-1945 items from other countries, especially cloth patches. No fakes or repros. Describe the material the item is made from, colors, etc. Note if anything seems to be missing and chips, dents, moth holes, stitch marks, corrosion, fading, stains and polish wear. Photocopy.
>Charles Edwards
>Pass in Review
>PO Box 622
>Grayslake, IL 60030
>   (847) 223-2332

★ **Military items from the Coldstream Guards.** The museum wants to buy uniforms, equipment, badges, and miscellaneous items used by the British Coldstream Guards. Other British Army ephemera may be of interest. A full description includes dimensions, materials, and age. Indicate anything you believe to be unique. Donations acknowledged. No U.S. items are wanted.
>Ernest Klapmeier
>Coldstream Guards Living History Museum
>83 South La Salle Street
>Aurora, IL 60505
>   (630) 801-1696 voice and fax

★ **French or British military forces** overseas, British Indian Native States forces, Spanish or **French Foreign Legion**, Abraham Lincoln Brigade, Camel Corps, Free French and Vichy forces, French forces in China, Devil's Island, White Russian forces, Chinese Customs Service, Chinese bandits or pirates, China Navigation Company, international settlements in China, Chinese airlines, and similar topics. Wants badges, banners, **medals**, photos, certificates, souvenirs, etc. Material about American volunteers or **famous soldiers of fortune** of any nationality is particularly welcome. No repros of Devil's Island folk art or souvenirs produced by the Foreign Legion Veteran's Home.

> Gene Christian
> 3849 Bailey Avenue
> Bronx, NY 10463
> (718) 548-0243

★ **Nazi notables** especially Heinrich Himmler, commander of the SS and Gestapo. Wants items given by or to Hitler, Goering, Goebbles, Hess, etc., including promotion and award documents, letters, trophies, **uniforms** or **medals**. "I am generally not interested in any item you or a member of your family did not personally bring back from overseas." He prefers you to write, describe what you have, make a photocopy, and include your phone number and an SASE.

> Thomas Pooler
> PO Box 1861
> Grass Valley, CA 95945
> (916) 268-1338

★ **German war memorabilia** from WW I and WW II. Buys edged weapons and selected other quality items of German war memorabilia. He is not interested in reproductions or in "lesser condition" items. Please send a photo, sketch, or photocopy. He requests you set the price you have in mind, but will make offers to amateurs who are selling. Send $7 for one of his catalogs of items for sale. For $28 you can subscribe to his quarterly newsletter on military collecting. Johnson is an internationally known appraiser and author of fourteen books (send for his catalog). "Our firm offers the largest selection of Imperial and Third Reich swords and daggers in the world."

> LTC (ret) Thomas Johnson
> Johnson Reference Books
> 312 Butler Road, Chatham Square Office Park #403
> Fredericksburg, VA 22405
> (540) 373-9150 Fax: (540) 373-0087 Email: ww2daggers@aol.com

★ **German, Japanese, and Italian military** wanted, especially daggers and dagger parts, swords, medals, badges, spike helmets, flagpole tops, etc. Pays $50 up for **German WWII helmets** complete with liner. "I will also buy flags, but the bigger the flag, the less they're worth. You may write, giving me your phone number. Take a photo or send insured for cash offer." This is a hobby for Dick, so he says that he's happy to help people if they send him an SASE. Makes offers only on items for sale. Also interested in U.S. military patches.

Dick Pankowski
PO Box 22
Greendale, WI 53129
(414) 421-7056 days   (414) 421-5212 eves

★ **Japanese and German WWII military items** including swords, guns, daggers, medals, helmets, field caps, hats, field equipment, all uniforms and footwear, camouflage netting, diaries, insignia, maps, photos.,,you name it. If you intend to sell, send this 20 year veteran collector a brief description along with your phone number and address.

Stuart Tamaru
PO Box 4095
Torrance, CA 90510
(310) 320-8130

★ **German and Italian WWII military items** including flags, swords, guns, daggers, medals, helmets, field caps, hats, insignia, uniforms and footwear, belt buckles, diaries, maps, photos, you name it. "I also buy items from European collaborator countries such as Hungary, Slovakia, Croatia, etc. I particularly enjoy buying from the family of the vet who brought the item back." If you intend to sell, send this 19 year veteran buyer a good description along with your phone number and address. Indicate how much of the original paint remains on painted surfaces. Describe whether blades show evidence of rust or sharpening? "I don't want reproductions but will sometimes buy items in poor condition if priced accordingly. Many items have been faked, and some fakes are quite good."

John Telesmanich
PO Box 62
East White Plains, NY 10604
(914) 949-5519

As a general rule, don't clean your souvenirs. Amateur cleaning can turn a $300 item into scrap.

JAPANESE SWORDS

★ **Japanese swords, daggers, spears, armor and other Samurai items**, especially fine swords and daggers, and sword and dagger parts. Ron will send you a checklist to help you describe a sword for sale. An SASE is appreciated. Please photograph your sword laying alongside its scabbard. Ron is an internationally known collector who has been studying Japanese swords for twenty years. He will be pleased to determine the quality of your sword and to make you an offer for it. No other guns, bayonets, or non-Japanese swords and daggers are wanted.

> Ron Hartmann
> 5907 Deerwood Drive
> St. Louis, MO 63123
> (314) 832-3477

★ **Japanese swords.** A brief description is adequate. Give the length of the sword's blade as part of your description. "I am more than happy to discuss prices with people who contact me with items they intend to sell. I would like to avoid callers who are just trying to find out what something is worth. If you're actually selling, I'll make a very nice purchase offer."

> Stuart Tamaru
> PO Box 4095
> Torrance, CA 90510
> (310) 320-8130

★ **Japanese swords and daggers,** fighting issue or dress type. He prefers to buy directly from the veteran or family, and wants information about your weapon's history. This 25 year expert appraiser offers free appraisals of all edged weapons to private parties.

> Hank McGonagle
> 26 Broad Street
> Newburyport, MA 01950
> (508) 462-2354   (617) 594-1596

If a Japanese sword has a blade 26 1/2" long and has serial numbers it is probably an enlisted man's sword from WWII and worth around $100 or so. One reader discoverd that the sword on her rec room wall was from the 13th century and worth over $10,000. Another bought a sword at a yard sale for $100 and resold it to one of these buyers for $5,000.

SWORDS & KNIVES

★ **American swords from 1789-1902.** Especially wants swords with presentations or inscriptions to military persons with dates and rank, either etched or engraved on the blade or on the metal part of the scabbard. Inscribed Civil War swords are particularly desirable. The best makers marks are *Ames, Starr, Roby, Rose, Widman, Horstmann,* or *Glaze.* It is most important for sellers to send a very good drawing or photo of the hilt handle (guard and grip) of the sword. List all markings on the blade. Indicate the type of metal the guard is made from (brass, iron, aluminum), the type of grip or handle (ivory, bone, metal, wood, leather covered wood, or plastic). Note if the scabbard or sheath is included, and the condition of the sword and scabbard (rust? pitting?), and whether the scabbard is dented. Indicate the width of the blade at the handle, the length of the blade, and any engraving or etching. This 30+ year collector and dealer is interested in most swords, including early fakes and reproductions as long as the seller knows that the price will be considerably less than for an original. Common original swords are also purchased for resale. Ron is curator of the Tampa Veteran's Memorial Museum and author of two books on swords.

> Ron Hickox
> Antique Arms & Militaria
> PO Box 360006, Dept. T
> Tampa, FL 33673
> (813) 968-1571   Fax: (813) 744-5678

★ **American swords and large knives** from before 1900. Please describe thoroughly, including any numbers or writing found on the weapon. Photocopy the knife and of the sword handle if you can. Otherwise photograph it or make a good sketch. No fraternal, lodge or ceremonial swords, please. SASE requested. "I do not make offers."

> Charles Worman
> PO Box 33584 (AMC)
> Dayton, OH 45433
> (513) 760-1873

★ **British and American military knives** from WWI and WWII especially British Commando daggers, *Wilkinson Sword* fighting knives (marked FS FIGHTING KNIFE), and American special unit fighting knives. Value ranges from $50 to $1,500 depending on rarity, condition and its scabbard. It is very important for you to copy every word and symbol on the blade, handle, guard, and scabbard. John does not want bayonets that attach to the end of a rifle.

> John Fischer
> 10950 West Pico Blvd.
> Los Angeles, CA 90064
> (310) 474-2567   (818) 902-1375

★ **German & other European swords, daggers and other military** items from 1870-1945 (1933-1945). Will buy both common and rare variations, with etched or with plain blades. Especially wanted are swords and daggers with inscriptions giving name, date, and military unit etched on the scabbard or blade. It is most important for sellers to send a very good drawing or photo of the hilt handle (guard and grip) of the sword. List all markings on the blade. Indicate the type of metal the guard is made from (brass, iron, aluminum), the type of grip or handle (ivory, bone, metal, wood, leather covered wood, or plastic). Note if the scabbard or sheath is included, and the condition of the sword and scabbard (rust? pitting?), and whether the scabbard is dented. Indicate the width of the blade at the handle, the length of the blade, and any engraving or etching. Ron is curator of the Tampa Veteran's Memorial Museum and author of two books on swords.

Ron Hickox
Antique Arms & Militaria
PO Box 360006, Dept. T
Tampa, FL 33673
(813) 968-1571   Fax: (813) 744-5678

★ **German swords, knives, daggers, and bayonets** from WW I and WW II. Also buys selected other quality items of German war memorabilia. He is not interested in reproductions or in "lesser condition" items. Please send a photo, sketch, or photocopy. He requests you set the price you have in mind, but will make offers to amateurs who are selling. Send $7 if you'd like one of his catalogs of items for sale. For $28 you can subscribe to his quarterly newsletter on military collecting and collectibles around the world. Johnson is an internationally known appraiser, author of fourteen books on edged weapons, and can provide you a catalog of available reference books.

LTC (ret) Thomas Johnson
Johnson Reference Books
312 Butler Road
Chatham Square Office Park #403
Fredericksburg, VA 22405
(540) 373-9150 Fax: (540) 373-0087 Email: ww2daggers@aol.com

★ **U.S. and German swords, bayonets and daggers,** fighting issue or dress type. Other countries also purchased. He prefers to buy directly from the veteran or family, and wants information about your weapon's history. This 25 year expert appraiser offers free appraisals of **all military swords** and edged weapons to private parties.

Hank McGonagle
26 Broad Street
Newburyport, MA 01950
(508) 462-2354   (617) 594-1596

HOW TO FIND OUT IF YOUR MONEY
IS AS VALUABLE AS YOU HOPE

Everyone seems to have old coins or bills tucked away in a drawer. Now's the time to find out if you have something good to cash in. I've got some fine folks from the world of collectible money standing by to help.

*Valuable coins and bills exist, and they do turn up in strang places on occasion, but **your bills and coins will probably not have collectors panting.** Since some unusual things do have value, including a few foreign bills, it might be worth your while to check out what you have.*

***Photocopying makes it possible to check the value of your money easily and quickly.** If inquiring about modern currency, it is important to note the color of the Treasury seal to the right of the portrait on the face of each bill. Colors can be blue, green, red, brown, gold, or yellow. Value differs by color.*

***If you want an idea of your coins' value without anyone knowing what you have,** it's easy to do. Use A Guide Book of United States Coins by R.S. Yoeman. Called "The Red Book" it gives average selling prices of coins. Yoeman's Handbook of U.S. Coins ("The Blue Book") gives prices dealers pay for coins. These can be borrowed from most libraries. If you own anything that catalogs over $50, get expert advice. Coins valued under $10 will find few takers.*

***Amateur sellers overestimate condition.** Yoeman's books contain information you should read about coin grading, because amateurs over-estimate condition of coins and bills. Buyers will grade severely. A spot of wear at the tip of an eagle wing can cost 50% of a coin's value.*

*The coin world has attracted more than its share of shady characters. **Never sell coins, watches or jewelry to someone buying out of a motel room.** You get much less than you would from well-established dealers. Deal with folks in here instead.*

TRASH OR TREASURE HAS MADE MILLIONS FOR ITS READERS

ANTIQUITIES & OLD COINS

★ **European antiquities from prehistoric days to 1500 AD.** Wants relics and artifacts from Europe, particularly the British Isles, but all regions of Europe are wanted. Items may be of stone, bone, pottery or metal, and include **swords** made of bronze or iron, bone harpoon heads, **pottery, blown glass, Celtic coins, Roman weaponry, Viking** and Celt jewelry, **Scottish Highlander** items and other interesting antiquities. Especially wants pre-600 AD flint **arrowheads**, stone or bronze **axe heads**, and pottery. Does NOT WANT Roman, Greek or Etruscan pottery, figures, coins or other art from these cultures, but will consider their fine weaponry and jewelry. Tell him whatever you can about your item's history. Photos are helpful "and at a minimum, I need a tracing, sketch or Xerox™ copy."
>   Charles Ray
>   The Keltoi
>   PSC 813, Box 169
>   FPO, AE 09620

Ray's is a military address, and correct as printed.

★ **Coins and antiquities, especially Biblical, Greek, and Roman.** Ancient artifacts including Egyptian, Greek, Roman, and Biblical pottery, glass and relics. **Nothing made after 1000AD is wanted.** This 20 year veteran collector wrote *Guide to Ancient Jewish Coins* and other books, and issues periodic catalogs of relics for sale. He does not buy prints, rugs, weavings, or drawings of Biblical topics. He does not want reproductions, pictures, or drawings. Ancient artifacts *only.*
>   David Hendin
>   Amphora
>   PO Box 805
>   Nyack, NY 10960

☆ **Spanish pieces of eight.** Wants *reales* minted in Spanish or South American mints **dated between 1732 and 1772.** Seeks coins with globe and pillars on one side and shield and crown on the other. No pitted shipwreck coins. All coins must be shipped for examination before offers can be made as there are many reproductions. Postage both ways is the responsibility of the seller.
>   Sven Stau
>   851 Harlem Avenue #11
>   West Seneca, NY 14224
>   (716) 823-0470

COINS & PAPER MONEY

★ **Coins or paper currency from anywhere** especially silver or gold.
> Dr. Robert Hiett, Maple City Coin
> PO Box 47
> Monmouth, IL 61462
>   (309) 734-3212   Fax: (309) 734-8083

★ **Coin collections of all types,** "from pennies to gold." Also individual gold coins, medals, and artifacts. Also pre-1930 U.S. banknotes and commemorative coins. No pennies after 1955, nickels after 1939, dimes, quarters, and halves after 1964, or silver dollars after 1936.
> Ron Aldridge
> 250 Canyon Oaks Drive
> Argyle, TX 76226
>   (817) 455-2519 eves   Fax: (817) 455-5094

★ **Paper money.** "I buy all U.S. paper money issued before 1929, all **Confederate money** and all broken bank notes from any state. I especially want **items made of ground up paper money**, and will pay 60% of retail. I recommend making photocopies of bills you'd like to sell."
> William Skelton, Highland's Vault
> PO Box 55448
> Birmingham, AL 35255
>   (205) 939-3166 extension 3   (205) 939-1178

★ **Paper money.** "We'll buy **any foreign and obsolete U.S. and Confederate banknotes**. We will buy currency in any condition and quantity in order to supply fellow collectors in all parts of the world. We deal by mail only but telephone calls are welcomed. We will buy collections as well as single notes, but we do not want U.S. currency after 1928." A description should include the date, denomination, and the country of issue. A photocopy is the best way to describe currency. With his available research library, he is "able to identify and appraise any banknote ever issued."
> Josef Klaus, World Wide Notaphilic Service
> PO Box 5427
> Vallejo, CA 94591
>   (707) 644-3146   (707) 643-8616   Fax: (707) 643-3806

★ **All foreign paper money.** "I'll buy collections, accumulations, dealer's stock, hoards, rarities, **German inflation currency**, specimens, printer's proofs, banknote presentations, sample **books** and entire **numismatic libraries**." Will travel. Has been buying since 1964.
> AMCASE
> PO Box 5473
> Akron, OH 44334
>   (330) 867-6724

★ **U.S. Coins and paper money.** Wants estates, collections and accumulations of early **U.S. silver and gold coins**, paper money, and all other U.S. coins from 1793-1900. This nationally known dealer has been around for 40 years, and will travel to see large lots and better collections. Send a list and description. Photocopy suggested.

> Littleton Coin Co., THCC
> 253 Union Street
> Littleton, NH 03561
> (603) 444-5386

★ **Printed or manuscript items relating to coins, currency, medals, tokens, or counterfeiting.** Especially scholarly books on coins from any period or language. Also **numismatic periodicals** and catalogs of coin auctions pre-1940 in any language. Also **counterfeit detectors and bank note reporters** issued in the U.S., 1820 - 1900. No modern works or general surveys of numismatics. Makes offers on better items.

> George Frederick Kolbe
> PO Drawer 3100
> Crestline, CA 92325
> (909) 338-6527   Fax: (909) 338-6980

★ **Items made from macerated (ground up) currency** by the mint, including statues, plaques, postcards, shoes, hats, etc., which have a small tag reading, THIS ITEM MADE OF US GREENBACKS REDEEMED AND MACERATED BY THE US GOVERNMENT. Describe damage carefully.

> Donald Gorlick
> PO Box 24541
> Seattle, WA 98124
> (206) 824-0508

★ **Red coin books** printed before 1954.

> James Williams
> HCR 01   Box 23
> Warrensburg, NY 12885
> (518) 623-2831

★ **Wooden money.** First used in 1931, it comes in two forms, flat like bills and round like coins. Round pieces from civic celebrations bring 10¢ to $5. *Sambo's* and *McDonald's* bring 25¢ to $1.50 (but only if they have the city printed on the coin). Flat money from Tenino, WA, is $35 to $50, while other flat pieces bring $1 to $35. Please send a photocopy of your money and SASE for an appraisal. Boughton is the author of two books on wooden money of NY state (both for $7).

> Norm Boughton
> PO Box 93262
> Rochester, NY 14692
> (716) 292-0128 eves   Fax: (716) 292-6513

ERROR COINS & ELONGATES

★ **Mis-strike and error coins created by the U.S. Mint.** Under most circumstances, it is best to send a good clear pencil rubbing or photocopy for evaluation if you wish an offer. Also **paper currency issued before 1930.** Include photocopy and SASE for free appraisal.

>Neil Osina
>Best Variety Coin Center
>358 West Foothill Blvd.
>Glendora, CA 91741
>(818) 914-2273

★ **Elongated coins** dated before 1960. Also buys the machines and the dies to make them. "I'll pay well for scarce items I want."

>C.J. "Gus" Meccarello
>Elongated Coin Museum
>1572 Bowmans Trail
>Lakeland, FL 33809

★ **Elongated coins.** If what you have is pre-1930, ship it for an offer, but *do not* ship COD. Hartzog pays $1-$5 and up for elongates before 1940. Large collections especially wanted.

>Rich Hartzog
>PO Box 4143 BVT
>Rockford, IL 61110

COUNTERFEITING DEVICES

★ **Coin scales and anything used to detect counterfeit money,** coins or currency, including coin detectors, scanners, grids, magnifiers, Detectographs and other devices to check weight, thickness or diameter of coins. Also any scale with markings in amounts, such as "20 dol., 10 dol., 5 dol." Names to look for: *Ewing, Herpers, Fairbanks, McNalley, MBT, Rice, Statler, Meyers* among many others.

>Donald Gorlick
>PO Box 24541
>Seattle, WA 98124
>(206) 824-0508

Coin scales do not have pans or weights like a gold scale. They do have some method of weighing a coin, and another for testing thickness.

★ **Coin scales, coin detectors, and counterfeit detectors.** Will buy the devices and/or books about them and the processes of counterfeiting and counterfeit detecting. Buys items outright or may accept on consignment for auction.
> Rich Hartzog
> PO Box 4143 BVT
> Rockford, IL 61110
> (815) 226-0771   Fax: (815) 397-7662

CREDIT CARDS

★ **Credit cards** from any source, paper or plastic, are desired. "Send items for immediate offer and check. I pay postage both ways."
> Noel Levy
> 1109 Silentglade Road
> Owings Mills, MD 21117
> (410) 363-9040

★ **Credit cards.** "I'll pay a flat $2 each for credit cards, charge plates, and charge coins made of celluloid, metal, paper or plastic, U.S. or foreign, as long as they are not abused. Ship the cards you have for my prompt payment." ATM and sample credit cards are worth very little, about 25¢ each, if that.
> Lin Overholt
> PO Box 8481
> Madeira Beach, FL 33738

★ **Credit cards.** "I've collected credit cards for over ten years and am seriously interested in buying both the older metal charge cards and modern plastic cards. Please ship any quantity of used or new cards. I pay $4 up for older metal charge cards and will pay *at least* $15 for any metal one I need for my own collection. Pre-1980 plastic cards bring $1 up, and those before 1970 average $2. More paid for local businesses, unusual types, etc. Post-1980 cards are worth 50¢ each, a few bring more. I will also reimburse your postage. Please ship for my check."
> Rich Hartzog
> PO Box 4143 BVT
> Rockford, IL 61110

STOCKS, BONDS & FISCAL PAPER

When people ask for "fiscal paper" they mean documents having to do with money, including stocks, bonds, checks, mortgages, scrip, IOU's, revenue stamps, and the like. Collectors buy fiscal paper for the elaborate pictorial engravings called vignettes. Fiscal paper is also sought if signed by famous people or if it is pre-1850. Values range from $1 to $500 with most selling for under $30.

★ **Stocks and bonds from around the world** issued before 1930, especially ornate 19th century transportation or mining certificates. Please send a Xerox© copy of what you wish to sell. This 30 year veteran stock expert cautions, "It is important that you not sell uncanceled certificates issued in your own name or in a family member's name without first having us check their value. These certificates could be worth much more if the company has changed names or left assets when it was liquidated. There are billions of dollars waiting to be claimed by people who believe their stocks are worthless."
Micheline Masse
Stock Search International
10855 North Glen Abbey
Tucson, AZ 85737
(800) 537-4523   Fax: (520) 544-9395   stocksrch@aol.com

★ **Stocks, bonds, and other fiscal paper worldwide**. "I want to buy old bank checks, drafts, certificates of deposit, promissory notes, bills of exchange, U.S. postal money orders, postal notes, warrants, etc., just about every type of fiscal document which represents an order to pay from any country from 1500 to 1902 for bank instruments and up to 1933 for anything from Montana. Values vary widely, so all I can say is that I pay from $5 to $500 per piece. I do not buy plain checks without vignettes, nor do I buy receipts." Clear photocopies required. "I prefer sellers to place a price on their items, but I will make offers. I do not do appraisals except for a fee." His *Catalogue of Nevada Checks, 1860-1933* is available from him for $21 postpaid.
Douglas McDonald
PO Box 5833
Helena, MT 59604
(406) 449-8076   gypsyfoot@aol.com

★ **Fiscal paper** including **rare currency (U.S. and foreign)**, checks, stocks and bonds, certificates of deposits, books on money, other items. He is particularly expert in **California currency, national currency and Mexican currency.** Doesn't want items after 1935 or any kind of reproduction. A photocopy will often do, but "I'll usually request to see the item in person before making an offer."

>Lowell Horwedel
>PO Box 2395
>West Lafayette, IN 47906
>>(317) 583-2784 Fax: (317) 583-2763

★ **Stocks and bonds,** especially decorative stocks from pre-1900 railroads and gold mines. "Although these are our main areas of interest, we would like to see photocopies of any and all stocks and bonds that you might have, and will promptly give you a free appraisal/offer." Generally, nothing after 1940 unless you have 5,000 or more of them.

>Richard Urmston
>Centennial Documents
>PO Box 5262
>Clinton, NJ 08809
>>(908) 730-6009 Fax: (908) 730-9566

★ **Elaborately illustrated stocks and bonds.** All are wanted but have particular need for pre-1920 railroads, mining, telegraph, aviation, oil, and automobiles. Also stocks from unusual companies like a maker of life rafts. Items pre-1870 given special consideration. Especially want Western paper with autographs of important people like Rockefeller, Carnegie, Gould, James Hill, U.S. Presidents, and other recognizable people. "Send a photocopy and an SASE for fast payment."

>David Beach's Paper Americana
>PO Box 2026
>Goldenrod, FL 32733
>>(407) 657-7403 Fax: (407) 657-6382

★ **Stocks and bonds** issued in the United States before 1910, especially mining, railroads, or unusual companies. "I am not interested in stocks that were never issued and are unsigned. Stocks and bonds must have an original company seal."

>Phyllis Barrella
>Buttonwood Galleries
>3082 Eger Place
>New York, NY 10465
>>(718) 828-0649

★ **U.S. stocks and bonds,** issued before 1930, especially mining, railroads, energy and automobiles. Signed, illustrated, used documents are desired, with premium paid for Western items before the Civil War with interesting vignettes. Plain items are not of interest unless before 1850 or signed by someone famous. Send Xerox™ of what you have. His six sales catalogs a year cost $15.

> Warren Anderson
> America West Archives
> PO Box 100
> Cedar City, UT 84720
> (801) 586-9497

★ **U.S. and Canadian stocks and bonds,** especially railroads, mining, oil, shipping, automotive, aviation, expositions, and others. Also stocks or bonds signed or owned by someone famous. Also seeks documents with a **printed revenue stamp.** This past president of the Bond & Share Society also wants all pre-1800 certificates from any company.

> Bob Kluge
> American Vignettes
> PO Box 155
> Roselle Park, NJ 07204
> (908) 241-4209

★ **All paper items printed with fancy engraved illustrations by security printers,** including railroad passes, semi-postals (advertising stamps), souvenir cards, and annual reports. Security printers include the Bureau of Printing and Engraving, U.S.P.S., American Bank Note Co., Canadian Bank Note Co., and Homer Lee Bank Note Co. Wants to find *Annual Reports* of American Bank Note Co. and other security printers and engravers.

> Robin Ellis
> 14555 Blanco Road #1301
> San Antonio, TX 78216
> (210) 492-8157

★ **Fiscal paper from South Carolina** before 1910, especially from the city of Charleston.

> Bob Karrer
> 17 Wentworth Street
> Charleston, SC 29401

HOW TO SELL TOKENS & MEDALS

Collecting tokens is popular because they are inexpensive. Most retail for 25¢ to $3. Have an expert look at your tokens as a few are worth $500. Tokens are difficult to evaluate on your own because more than 300 books are in print about tokens and tiny differences can mean a lot. The following definitions should help you describe "a little round thing" to a potential buyer.

__Coins__ are money issued by governments. Most modern coins contain the name of the issuing agency, the denomination, and the date of issue.

__Exonumia__ means all coin-like objects that aren't money. It refers primarily to tokens, but has come to include medals, orders, decorations, plaques, awards, ribbons, and the like. Dealers of exonumia often sell advertising mirrors (they were frequently trade tokens) and other small collectibles as well.

__Tokens__ are money substitutes, often marked with a value, such as "good for 5¢ in trade." Tokens were issued by local businesses usually for advertising. Sometimes they were issued because no legal coinage was available.

__Medals__ are "any piece of metal marked with a design or inscription, made to honor a person, place or event," according to one of our buyers. Medals vary in size and shape, although most are round. Medals larger than 3" in diameter are usually called __medallions__. Small rectangular medals are called __plaquettes__ and larger ones, meant to hang on the wall, are __plaques__.

__Orders__ and __decorations__ are an important separate category, generally related to diplomacy and the military. They are often worn around the neck or on sashes across the wearer's breast.

__Military medals__ are emblems of honor normally made with ribbons so they can be worn. __Badges__ have a top pin or device, with or without a ribbon, so they too can be worn. Both usually have a medallic device hanging from them (what amateurs think of when someone says "medals").

__Ribbons__ are commemorative items, printed with information about the event commemorated. They are usually associated with lodges, fraternal organizations, conventions, and the like.

Whichever one of these you have, make a pencil rubbing or a photocopy and let the buyers tell you exactly what you own and what they'll pay. Buyers of just about anything will also be interested in medals and tokens related to their specialty.

TRASH OR TREASURE

TOKENS & MEDALS

★ **All types and quantities of tokens, medals, ribbons, badges, and related items.** Some old tokens are common, but others can be worth $1,500+ each if they picture a ship, trolley, horse car, ferry, or stagecoach. Look for the words DEPOTEL, BAGGAGE, HOTEL, OMNIBUS, DRAYAGE, DEPOT TO HOTEL, and similar wordings. He buys trade tokens, medals of all sort, hard times tokens, Civil War tokens, **transportation and toll tokens** especially with pictures on them, amusement tokens, telephone tokens, sales tax tokens, **any token or medal made from another item**, **medals related to medicine or the arts** and humanities, **love tokens, World's Fair medals** and elongated coins, **G.A.R. badges** and tokens, **Indian peace medals** ($1,500 up), **slave tags, Canadian** tokens and medals, **military awards and medals,** counterstamped coins, and just about everything similar

We sell bags of 2,500 modern tokens with cut-out letters for $99, so you can see they are not worth much."

to the above including advertising mirrors and **Franklin Mint token sets.** There are millions of varieties, and condition plays an important role in value. If what you have is pre-1930, simply ship it to him for an offer, but do not ship COD. Hartzog will send you a check for the lot. "We cannot make individual offers on a long list of material. Our offers are for the entire lot as we want to purchase everything. We are not interested in pricing your material for you to sell to others, sorry!" He claims to pay higher prices than anyone else. If your collection is very early, very large, or very valuable, phone collect and Hartzog will make arrangements to see what you have. Hartzog can auction your materials for you if you prefer. A sample of his auction catalog is available for $3. Hartzog's lengthy wants list shows prices and is recommended. Also **Franklin Mint and other private mint issues.** "I will purchase all bronze, silver and gold singles, sets and other items such as plates, bronzes, etc., in any quantity. Many silver or gold pieces are worth substantially above issue price. Bronze tokens and medals are worth less than their issue price, most of them under 25¢ apiece. I pay reasonable prices for all modern mint items. Since I do not specialize in *Franklin Mint* items, do not ship them without inquiring first. State the price you want, or request my offer. If my offer is not accepted, I do not pay return postage on modern mint medals that have been shipped." There is little market for *Franklin Mint* items, so it's best to contact Rich first by phone or letter so you fully understand their value or lack of it.

Rich Hartzog
World Exonumia
PO Box 4143 BVT
Rockford, IL 61110
(815) 226-0771

★ **Tokens and medals of all kinds and countries** including transportation tokens, advertising tokens, gambling tokens, merchants' GOOD FOR tokens and the like. All old coin-like items are purchased as well as related items such as elongated or encased coins, engraved coins, pre-1900 dog licenses, advertising **pocket mirrors**, political buttons, and stage or movie money. Steve pays $10 to $250 for **old original hobo nickels (buffalo nickels with the Indian head reengraved into another face)**. Award and commemorative medals from Fairs are also wanted. Photocopies are usually the best way to describe what you have. No large modern fantasy tokens are wanted. No Franklin Mint medals. No modern arcade tokens. Steve runs mail auctions of tokens and medals and has written books on amusement tokens, U.S.A. tokens, Scouting tokens and lucky souvenir coins, all available from the author at very reasonable prices.

> Stephen Alpert
> PO Box 66331
> Los Angeles, CA 90066
>   (310) 836-2482   Fax: (3120) 836-5691

★ **Transportation or toll tokens** for bridges, toll roads, ferries, horsecars, depot hacks, and early streetcars. Tokens *must* be made of metal or plastic. Cardboard tokens are wanted *only* if round, *not* square or rectangular. HOTEL TO DEPOT or TRANSFER LINE tokens are worth $25-$100, more if pictorial. A token reading I GIBBS BELLEVILLE & NEW YORK USM STAGE//GOOD FOR ONE RIDE TO THE BEARER would be worth $1,500 in nice condition.

> Rev. John Coffee
> PO Box 1204
> Boston, MA 02104
>   (617) 277-8111

★ **Medals and medallions from Canada, Britain, and other English speaking countries** issued for coronations, jubilees, town celebrations, victories, fraternal groups, achievement, athletics, and especially military valor medals awarded to Canadians. Also **love tokens** engraved with names, initials, dates, pledges, and the like from around the world especially pre-1900. Also merchant's GOOD FOR **trade tokens** from Canada, Britain and English speaking countries. Also buys **Canadian paper money** dating before 1937, singles or collections.

> Michael Rice
> PO Box 286
> Saanichton, BC
> V8M 2C5 CANADA
>   (250) 652-9412 eves and weekends only

★ **Medals and tokens of all sorts** are wanted by this 22 year veteran dealer. Identify what the token or medal is made from, and provide a photocopy or a good rubbing. "I buy them all," he says.

> Bill Williges
> PO Box 1245
> Wheatland, CA 95692
> (916) 633-2732

★ **U.S., British, and Soviet valor decorations** and war medals. **Foreign awards given to Americans** are of great interest, especially Soviet World War II orders and decorations. All items *must* have supporting documentation of the award to U.S. personnel. Hlinka also buys all letters, certificates, or documents pertaining to valor awards. He seeks a U.S. Medal of Honor awarded between 1917 and 1970. He encourages you to photocopy both sides of medals and supporting paperwork. Hlinka has been dealing in medals for 40 years and has been an officer in various collectors' societies.

> Peter Hlinka
> PO Box 310
> New York, NY 10028
> (718) 409-6407

★ **Medals, decorations, and orders,** especially military gallantry awards from U.S. and England, but will consider **all governmental awards** from any Western nation. No Asian awards, please.

> Alan Harrow
> 2292 Chelan Drive
> Los Angeles, CA 90068

★ **Indian War medals, badges and awards** issued by the U.S. government, states, or veteran's groups. An Indian scout's Medal of Honor can be worth $20,000. Other items from $100 to $10,000. "No offers based on phone calls or photos. Items must be seen. Ship insured with record of delivery. Your postage will be reimbursed."

> Thomas Pooler
> PO Box 1861
> Grass Valley, CA 95949

★ **U.S. medals of all kinds** particularly historical, art and award medals of the 19th and early 20th century. This 25 year veteran offers $4,000 for the Teddy Roosevelt inaugural medal by Saint Gaudens and $2,000 up for silver Indian peace medals.

> H. Joseph Levine
> Presidential Coin & Antique Co.
> 6550-I Little River Turnpike
> Alexandria, VA 22312

★ **Medals commemorating or depicting Black Americans.** "I'll buy medals, medallions, badges, or tokens relating to, or depicting, Afro-Americans or including the words NEGRO, COLORED or BLACK-AMERI-CAN. Items may be positive or negative in tone. I'll pay $1,200 for the Franklin Mint set of 70 American Negro Commemorative Society medals." Tell him the material (silver, bronze, or aluminum), the size in millimeters, and inscriptions on both sides.

> Elijah Singley
> 2301 Noble Avenue
> Springfield, IL 62704
>   (217) 546-5143 eves   (217) 786-2251

★ **Tokens, medals, and exonumia (non-money coinage) from Georgia** including "good for" tokens issued by merchants, saloons and lumber companies, encased and **elongated coins**, advertising and com-memorative medals and tokens, including those issued for the 1895 Atlanta Cotton States Exposition, and any agriculture awards and medals from Georgia state fairs, the earlier the better.

> R.W. Colbert
> 4156 Livsey Road
> Tucker, GA 30084
>   (770) 938-2596

★ **Animal rescue, heroism, school attendance or truant officer's** medals, badges and certificates.

> Gene Christian
> 3849 Bailey Avenue
> Bronx, NY 10463
>   (718) 548-0243

HOW TO SELL VALUABLE STAMPS

Only a few 20th century U.S. stamps have substantial value, but stamped and unstamped envelopes and letters dating before 1910 may be worth hundreds of dollars! Value is affected by the stamp, the cancellation, the carriers, and where it was mailed from and to.

Buyers of early letters are often interested in postmarks. Examine them with an eye toward historic places, vanished cities, and unusual cancellations as on board a riverboat, airplane, or military ship. Canadian buyer Mike Rice tells of a U.S. antique dealer who sent him two items and a bill for only $4. "If that dealer had taken your advice and asked me to make an offer, I'd have paid $300 for them. The postcard she sent me has the only known cancellation from a post office that was only open for a few months."

Empty envelopes sell, but an enclosed letter with interesting contents will add to the value. Decorated stamped envelopes sell too. Condition is crucial, although envelopes that have been opened messily can still find a buyer if the postmark and stamp are undamaged.

Letters about travel, Indians, mining, colorful people, disasters, famous events, business, military service, personal history, and the like, especially those which give details, are best. Someone looking for stamps paid $20 for a box of envelopes at a Beverly Hills yard sale. Letters in those envelopes were resold to experts for $267,000!

Don't be surprised if most foreign stamps turn out to have little value. Enough valuable ones do exist, however, to make it worth your while to check them, especially when they are on interesting envelopes. If you own a few foreign stamps you can look them up in Scott's Standard Postage Stamp Catalogue. U.S. stamps are in Scott's Specialized Catalogue of United States Stamps. Both are available at most public libraries. If you own many stamps, you are facing a tedious chore. **Trash or Treasure** *will be faster and more efficient.*

STAMPS

☆ **U.S. and foreign stamp collections and accumulations** are wanted
by this 35 year veteran dealer who buys:
- **Albums** from any country or from mixed countries;
- **Stockbooks** and **unsorted boxfuls** of duplicate stamps;
- **Old envelopes** with stamps from any country;
- Mint sheets and blocks;
- Old **revenue (tax) stamps** on documents of all kinds;
- **Duck hunting** and fishing permit stamps, mint or used,
  especially on licenses;
- Stamp-like labels and seals of all kinds;
- **Postal related souvenirs** including booklets, cards, and
  stamp announcements;
- **Philatelic reference books** from any period or country in
  any language;
- **Stamp magazines** pre-1945;
- **Worldwide stamp catalogs** pre-1925;
- **Philatelic (stamp) auction catalogs** pre-1945;
- **Photos or real photo postcards** of mail carriers, mail trucks,
  post offices, and mail delivery.

"If in doubt, include it! I must be one of the last people who collect
EVERYTHING in stamps and stamp-related items." Doug says stamp
collecting has many variations and specialties, and that even the most
common looking items
(especially envelopes with
unusual markings) may
have value. "Because of
their nature and sheer
numbers, stamps must be
sent for my inspection.
You must call first, because I can give you clear
shipping instructions and
help you eliminate heavy
items that have no value,

"Three errors made by amateurs:
   *(1) Cutting stamps off
envelopes and documents;*
   *(2) Improperly storing and
handling mint stamps;*
   *(3) Forgetting that labor costs of
preparing stamps for resale will
affect how much money you are
paid. It's very costly to make your
piles into attractive packages."*

such as newer stamp catalogs, 3-ring notebooks, and empty albums. I
can give you guidance on how to ship stamps to prevent damage and
preserve value. Return postage must be included with your shipment.
Never send things UPS or FedEx. Inquiries should include an SASE if
you wish an answer."

Douglas Swisher
PO Box 52701
Jacksonville, FL 32201
   (904) 744-5493

★ **Stamp collections mounted in albums.** No interest in accumulations of loose stamps. Call for instructions.

> Myron Ross
> Heroes & Legends
> 28884 Roadside Drive
> Agoura Hills, CA 91301
> (818) 991-5979   Fax: (818) 735-0802

★ **U.S. or foreign stamp collections** from before 1960.

> Ron Aldridge
> 250 Canyon Oaks Drive
> Argyle, TX 76226
> (214) 239-3574 days   (817) 455-2519 eves   Fax: (817)455-5094

★ **Stamps from any country in any quantity.** "We'll buy everything you have," says Harvey, who has been dealing by the mail since 1934. He wants collections of singles, plate blocks, sheets, covers and rarities. If you have a large or valuable collection, Harvey Dolin & Company will come to your home. Smaller collections may be shipped to them for their cash offer. "Your satisfaction is always guaranteed," say their ads. Dolin buys **stampless letters** (dating before the first U.S. stamps in 1843, or after), **Confederate stamps and envelopes, Wells Fargo envelopes,** and **Duck Hunting stamps.**

> Harvey Dolin & Company
> 5 Beekman Street #406
> New York, NY 10038
> (212) 267-0216

★ **Envelopes with stamps mailed in the Orient.** Buys nearly all envelopes with stamps mailed in China, Tibet, Korea, Hong Kong, Nepal, Mongolia and Japan. Advisable to first phone or send a photocopy by mail or fax. Pledges to pay post on items sent on approval.

> Bruce Lewin
> Bridgewater Onvelopes Collectibles
> 680 Route 206 North
> Bridgewater, NJ 08807
> (908) 725-0022   Fax: (908) 707-4647

REVENUE & SPECIAL TAX STAMPS

★ **Federal and state revenue and special tax stamps** including document stamps and all stamps used to show that taxes had been paid on a product. Special tax stamps are large and look like licenses to engage in various occupations, such as liquor dealer, cigar salesman, wine maker, etc. Some of these issues, notably 1875, 1877, 1879, 1883, and 1885, are available in large quantities and sell for very little. Photocopies are strongly urged by this 30 year veteran buyer.

> Hermann Ivester
> 5 Leslie Circle
> Little Rock, AR 72205
>   (501) 376-7788   (501) 225-8565 eves

★ **U.S. Internal Revenue special tax stamps,** licenses and permits for making and selling beer, liquor, wine, tobacco, cigars, margarine, firearms, opium and marijuana. Also for businesses such as brokers, pawnbrokers, dentists, lawyers, etc. No stamps from between 1873 and 1885 with punched holes are wanted. Also wants state stamps and licenses for any business, activity, or product including hunting and fishing. **USDA export stamps** and certificates for meat products are also sought.   **Ration coupons for gas, fuel oil and sugar** are wanted, but no war books (1,2,3, or 4) or any red or blue tokens. "Photocopies are very helpful."

> Bill Smiley
> PO Box 361
> Portage, WI 53901
>   (608) 742-6349   (608) 742-3714

★ **U.S. Internal Revenue (tax) stamps** on documents of all kinds.

> Douglas Swisher
> PO Box 52701
> Jacksonville, FL 32201

HOW TO SELL PAINTINGS AND PRINTS: GET EXPERT ADVICE.

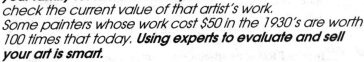

Paintings and prints that look sloppy, amateurish or depressing to you may be snapped up for big dollars. Each year, a few turn up in private hands that end up being worth $10,000 or more and $1,000,000 finds do happen. **If a painting has been passed down in your family for more than 60 years,** *check the current value of that artist's work. Some painters whose work cost $50 in the 1930's are worth 100 times that today.* **Using experts to evaluate and sell your art is smart.**

Researching art is work. So many paintings were created by unknowns, the vast majority of what you own will not be listed, cataloged or pictured. **Unsigned works or those by unknown artists seldom sell for more than $200, but you want to be very careful that it is indeed not signed. Check the back too for dates or stickers.**

To sell a print, *give the dimensions of the entire sheet and of the printed area. List all signatures, dates, and other information. Photocopy whenever practical. Prints signed and numbered in pencil are more likely to have value. Some prints like Currier & Ives have developed cult status and sell for $100 to $5,000 up! Photocopy if possible.*

To sell paintings, sculpture, or folk art, *a good 35mm photo is essential, along with dimensions. Take a close-up of the signature if possible.* **Folk art** *includes items made by untrained amateurs, done with style, vigor, form and color. Anything hand-crafted in decorative ways may qualify. Quality pieces bring thousands of dollars.*

Art from places other than the U.S. and Europe *is doing well. Prices are rising fast for South Pacific masks, bowls and shields. Mexican and South American paintings and folk arts have hit record prices within the last year and Oriental items remain strong.*

WARNING: *If you have a painting you think valuable, showing it to many dealers and auctioneers in hopes of getting ever higher prices is likely to do the opposite.* **Paintings often diminish in value in proportion to the number of people to whom they are offered.**

ART BY COMMERCIAL ILLUSTRATORS

★ **Original illustration art for mystery, detective, horror, science fiction, adventure and fantasy magazines**, pulps, and paperbacks. "I want the original paintings created to illustrate these covers as well as black and white pen and ink illustrations for the stories inside." Seeks artists like Roy Kuenkel, J. Allen St. John, Paul, Frank Frazetta, Stromberg, Olson, and others, especially those that depict known characters like the Shadow, the Spider, Doc Savage, Tarzan, etc. Does not want covers, prints, or reproductions. Send a photo, including the dimensions, and the name of the artist if you can read the signature.

> Jim Gerlack
> 2206 Greenbrier Drive
> Irving, TX 75060
> (214) 986-5233

★ **Original paintings for American magazine covers and story illustrations,** 1900 to date. "I'll buy art for magazines and stories in the following genres: aviation, western, fantasy, science fiction, adventure, erotica, detective, mystery, and movie." Also buys **art for pin-up calendars, advertising campaigns, and paperback book covers with similar themes.** These covers were generally vividly painted on 24" x 30" canvas. Rough sketches for cover or story art can also have value. Sellers should send a photo of the art, the dimensions and an accurate description of the condition (any soil, holes, dents, scratches). Note the signature, in the unlikely event there is one. Check the back of the painting for exhibit or publishing history. Most pulp paintings are worth $500 to $2,000, depending upon the artist, subject and condition, although a few covers bring up to $10,000. Jim is a popular artist and comic book illustrator who wrote two books on the history of comics.

"Don't ever guess what is and isn't worth something. Send us pictures and let us evaluate it for you."

> Jim Steranko, Supergraphics
> PO Box 974
> Reading, PA 19603
> (215) 374-7477

★ **Original paintings by American illustrators for magazine covers,** magazine story illustrations, or advertising, 1910-1980, including artists such as **Norman Rockwell** and all his contemporaries. Also original art for magazine or calendar pin-ups. Has special interest in sexual or sentimental themes (children, dogs, families, patriotism, etc.).

> Charles Martignette
> PO Box 293
> Hallandale, FL 33008
> (954) 454-3474

★ **Printed illustrations by well known 20th century artists** such as Maxfield Parrish, the Leyendecker Bros., **Norman Rockwell**, Rolf Armstrong, Vargas, Petty, Rose O'Neill, Mucha, Erte, Grace Drayton, Will Bradley, and Coles Phillips. Wants **original art, prints, posters, advertising, calendars, magazines, and books**, 1895-1930. Especially Maxfield Parrish and pin-up calendars, 1920-1960. Give dimensions and condition of your print, and tell what book, magazine, calendar, etc., it came from. Denis does not want "free appraisals, pen pals, or time wasters." He is the author of price guides for print artists and edits *The Illustrator Collector's News*, available for $17 a year.

> Denis Jackson
> PO Box 1958
> Sequim, WA 98382
> (360) 683-2559   Fax: (360) 683-9708   ticn@daka.com

★ **Maxfield Parrish paintings, watercolors, pen and ink sketches, letters, and 1st printings** including art prints, *Edison Mazda* calendars, *Brown & Biglow* prints and calendars, posters, books, playing cards, games, novelty items, and other advertising. She emphasizes she is not interested in "new prints" or reproductions of the first printings. This 18 year veteran dealer says she will pay $20,000 and up for paintings, $1,500 for a *Mother Goose in Prose* 1st edition from 1897, and from $800 to $3,500 for some posters and calendars, especially 1918, 1919, and 1920. "I need to know the size, color, and if there is any damage to the piece such as brown spots or water stains. It is helpful if you call with the piece in front of you."

> Michelle Ferretta, Maxfield Parrish Collectables
> 1314 Oak Street
> Alameda, CA 94501
> (510) 522-1823

★ **Maxfield Parrish paintings,** calendars (all years), complete books, full decks of playing cards, original prints, autographs and unusual advertising items. Not interested in book fragments or modern reproductions. Describe condition.

> Debra Buonaguidi
> 540 Reeside Avenue
> Monterey, CA 93940
> (408) 375-7345

★ **Original art and prints by F. Earl Christy** who specialized in beautiful society women. Wants his work on covers from movie and women's magazines, advertising, fans, blotters, calendars, postcards, and anything else illustrated by Christy.

> Audrey Buffington
> Box 386
> South Thomaston, ME 04858
> (207) 594-2683

★ **Paintings and prints by R. Atkinson Fox, Maxfield Parrish, and Icart.** Claims she'll pay "top cash" for Parrish art prints and *Edison Mazda* calendars illustrated by Parrish. She emphasizes that she has no interest in Icart reproductions, "only original etchings." Please state size and condition and if possible send a photo. Dealers price your goods. Amateurs may request an offer.

    Christine Daniels
    135 East Shiloh Road
    Santa Rosa, CA 95403
    (707) 838-6083

★ **R. Atkinson Fox prints wanted.** "I'll buy prints, calendars, postcards, or anything else with artwork by R. Atkinson Fox." Please telephone or send a photocopy.

    Pat Gibson
    38280 Guava Drive
    Newark, CA 94560
    (510) 792-0586

★ **Illustration art by Philip Goodwin** on trays, **calendars**, posters, and advertising. He can provide a detailed wants list of magazines, illustrations, books, and other items to dealers who send an SASE.

    Jim Combs
    417 27th Street NW
    Great Falls, MT 59404
    (406) 761-3320

★ **Sketches, drawings, and paintings by Philip Boileau and Robert Robinson,** American 20th century illustrators. Boileau is known for his 1900-1917 paintings of attractive women done for private customers, magazine covers, and other commercial purposes. Robinson worked commercially from 1907-1952 also on magazine covers and other commercial work. Please provide Bowers with a good close up color photo and as much information about the work as you can.

    Q. David Bowers
    PO Box 1224
    Wolfeboro, NH 03894
    (603) 569-5095

★ **Commercial printed art by J.G. Scott** who specialized in cute round faced children. Most of his work is signed JG SCOTT and can be found on the covers of women's magazines, advertising blotters and calendars from the 1920's and 30's. His unsigned work appears on Valentine's Day cards printed by the *Gibson Co.*

    Robert Stauffer
    3235 Mudlick Road SW
    Roanoke, VA 24018
    (703) 774-4319

★ **Charles M. Russell memorabilia.** "I'll buy just about anything illustrated by Russell: trays, posters, books, magazines, calendars, etc., as well as personal items, autographs, and other Russell memorabilia.
Jim Combs
417 27th Street NW
Great Falls, MT 59404
(406) 761-3320

★ **Original art for advertising and calendars** especially airlines, automobiles, gasoline, tires, soft drinks or whiskey. Especially likes paintings for ads for *Coke*, alcohol, movies, tobacco products, and other culturally significant items and events. If in doubt, call.
Charles Martignette
PO Box 293
Hallandale, FL 33008
(954) 454-3474

PAINTINGS & PRINTS BY SUBJECT MATTER

★ **Paintings of 18th and 19th century American political figures** or historic events. Please send a photo along with a copy of the painter's signature if there is one. Only fine condition original oils or watercolors are wanted. No paper prints, engravings or pictures torn from books.
Rex Stark
49 Wethersfield Road
Bellingham, MA 02019
(508) 966-0994

★ **Engraved portraits and photographs of famous people** in all walks of life. Will consider items loose or in books. Photocopies make the best descriptions.
Kenneth Rendell
PO Box 9001
Wellesley, MA 02181
(617) 431-1776   Fax: (617) 237-1492

★ **Paintings and prints depicting smoking.** Buys prints, paintings, and other items with a tobacco theme before 1940. Prefers smaller paintings but all sizes, all media, and all nationalities considered. Buys pre-1930 illustrations, prints, advertising, signs, posters, photographs and other items. **Special interest in cigars**, but anything tobacco considered. Buying for resale and for his personal collection.
Tony Hyman
PO Box 3028
Pismo Beach, CA 93448
(805) 773-6777   Fax: (805) 773-8436   thyman@tobacciana.com

★ **Paintings depicting depression era America**, the scenes, lives and times of the 1920's, 30's and 40's, especially those which involve political, social or economic issues or events. Send photo.
David Zdyb
PO Box 146
Dingmans Ferry, PA 18328
(717) 828-2361

★ **Paintings of cowboys, Indians or Eskimos.** Please send a photo for a prompt response. It's helpful if you can read the signature. Dealers, price your goods; amateur sellers may request an offer.
Barry Friedman
PO Box 55492
Valencia, CA 91385
(805) 255-2365

★ **Paintings of early California.** Claims she'll pay "top cash." Please state size, condition and name of the artist. If possible send a photo. Dealers price your goods. Amateurs may request an offer.
Christine Daniels
135 East Shiloh Road
Santa Rosa, CA 95403
(707) 838-6083

★ **Paintings and prints depicting boats** including whaling, yachting, racing, working, etc., are sought by this well known dealer in marine antiques. Give the dimensions, history, and a careful account of any damage or restoration. Photo suggested. Will give "ball park" estimates of value on ordinary items, but appraisals are for a fee.
Andrew Jacobson
PO Box 2155
South Hamilton, MA 01982
(508) 468-6276

★ **Paintings and prints depicting automobiles** before 1930. Also photos from before 1930. He does not want magazine ads of any type. "A Xerox™ or photo is a must."
David Bausch
252 North 7th Street
Allentown, PA 18102
(610) 432-3355   Fax: (610) 820-9368

★ **Prints and illustrations of flowers, children & beautiful women** including **calendars, yard-longs**, and books before 1919.
Linda Gibbs, Heirloom Keepsakes
10380 Miranda
Buena Park, CA 90620

PAINTINGS & PRINTS

★ **Paintings, limited edition graphics and 3-D (sculptural) art** by listed artists, folk artists old and new, both American and **Oriental**. Give the size in inches, condition, and the medium (oil, watercolor, wood, marble, etc.). Include a photo, and if possible, a close-up photo of the signature.

      Ivan Gilbert
      Miran Arts & Books
      2824 Elm Avenue
      Columbus, OH 43209
          (614) 421-3222   Fax: (614) 421-3223

★ **Paintings by listed artists of all types and periods,** including 20th century. This first rate auction house regularly handles works of art from $1,000 to $100,000 and may be the perfect outlet for your better quality paintings. Send a photo, give the dimensions, describe any damage and note any signature.

      James D. Julia Auctions
      PO Box 830
      Fairfield, ME 04937
          (207) 453-7904   Fax: (207) 453-2502

★ **Paintings, prints, and photographs made by artists listed in** *Who Was Who in American Art.* Although he's primarily interested in American Impressionism, Peter will consider a wide range of works from 1800-1950, as long as the artist is listed. Among the types of artwork in which he has a special interests are:

- **Art depicting competitive rowing** ($500-$1,500);
- **Color woodblock prints**, particularly the *White Line* prints of the Provincetown, MA, printmaker group ($500-$2,000);
- **Paintings and prints by American women artists** of any period ($500-$10,000+);
- **Photos of Abraham Lincoln** ($500-$10,000).

Does not want wood engravings from *Harper's, Leslie's*, and other newspapers or magazines. Send photograph and the dimensions. Falk's company, Sound View Press, publishes the *Art Price Index*, one of the basic reference books for the art world. This $199 book contains prices paid in the last year for more than 200,000 works of art.

      Peter Falk
      170 Boston Post Road
      Madison, CT 06443
          (203) 245-2246   Fax: (203) 245-3589

★ **Oil paintings** of any size, particularly American before 1940. Provide this veteran art dealer and appraiser with the name of the artist, the size, and a sharp photo of the painting, both front and back. He is not interested in newer paintings.

Robert Anderson, Aaron's Fine Antiques
1217 Broadway
Fort Wayne, IN 46802
(219) 422-5184

★ **Paintings by artists from Ohio, Kentucky, and Indiana** with a special interest in Cincinnati artists who worked between 1850 and 1950. Buys especially work by Blum, Twachtman, Hurley, Sawier, Weis, Vogt, Wessel, Selden, Casinelli, Duveneck, Sharp, Farney, Nourse, Potthast, Volkert, as well as selected other American and European artists. Please send a good clear photo of items for sale. If in doubt, telephone. Have your work in hand when you do.

Riley Humler
Cincinnati Art Galleries
635 Main Street
Cincinnati, OH 45202
(513) 381-2128   Fax: (513) 381-7527

★ **Artist's and designer's sketchbooks** before 1970. Has a particular interest in California artists, American art and artists, and creator's of modern decorative arts such as glass, furniture and ceramics before 1970. Alan writes monthly columns on art, and is author of *Art for All* ($17.95) and *Buy Art Smart* ($17.95), both available from him.

Alan S. Bamberger
2510 Bush Street
San Francisco, CA 94115
(415) 922-3580

★ **Damaged art of all kinds** is wanted. "If people send a good sharp photo I will make an offer on paintings, sculpture, and movie posters that have been damaged but are still in restorable condition." SASE will bring a free evaluation.

Alan Voorhees' Art Restoration
450 Breesport Road
Horseheads, NY 14845
(607) 739-7898   Fax: (607) 733-8550   VoorheesBS@aol.com

If you are not trained to recognize valuable art get expert advice. Mistakes can be costly.

PRINTS

★ **Prints, American and European.** Buys a wide range of prints. topical prints are of more interest than scenics. Give a complete description, including size of image, size of sheet, colors, and any and all information printed or written at the bottom of the print. Newman operates the oldest and largest antique print source in New York City and one of the essential places to shop for prints for study or decor. A long time family business.

> Kenneth Newman
> The Old Print Shop
> 150 Lexington Avenue at 30th Street
> New York, NY 10016
> (212) 683-3950

★ **Prints, fine and decorative** are bought and sold by this veteran high quality bookseller. He particularly seeks:
- **Prints signed by the artist**, from any period, in b/w or color;
- **Decorative color prints** printed prior to 1900, including costume prints, botanicals, and other subjects;
- **Scientific and scholarly prints** prior to 1880;
- **Decorative b/w prints** in the fields of history, architecture, etc.
- **Portraits** of the famous and infamous.

Give them as much of the following information as you can: the title, artist, publisher, any dates, size of the paper and size of the print itself. If possible, make a Xerox™ if you can do so without damaging it. Open daily with 60,000 items in stock and 25 years of experience.

> James & Mary Laurie
> Booksellers
> 921 Nicollet
> Minneapolis, MN 55402
> (800) 774-1114   (612) 338-1114   Fax: (612) 338-3665

★ **Prints, engravings, chromoliths, and woodcuts** before 1900 on many topics including city scenes of the U.S. and Canada, natural history (birds, bugs, fish, and animals), military uniforms, fashion, the old West, children, expositions and fairs, disasters, mining, Indians, and Oriental life in America. "These are very difficult to buy by mail, and must be examined under high magnification to set a fair price." If your print is framed, he believes "it is wise to remove the print from the frame in order to find the publisher and date of publication." Indicate the size of the image and the size of the paper on which it is printed. Include an SASE.

> John Rosenhoover
> 100 Mandalay Road
> Chicopee, MA 01020
> (413) 536-5542

★ **Chromoliths and hand colored prints** on topics of natural history (birds, bugs, fish and animals), military, medicine, old West, Indians, costumes and fashion, Negroes, sports, and Art Nouveau. Wants pre-1900 prints only, but does buy 19th and 20th century **advertising art and labels** on similar themes or with other attractive pictures. Describe fully for this major graphics dealer, known for paying high prices for quality items. Joe is author of two books on advertising labels.

> Joe Davidson
> 5185 Windfall Road
> Medina, OH 44256
> (330) 723-7172

★ **Prints by artists listed in** *Who Was Who in American Art.* Peter will consider a wide range of works from 1800-1950, as long as the artist is listed. He particularly wants **color woodblock prints**, especially the *White Line* prints of the Provincetown, MA, printmaker group and any **prints by American women artists** of any period. Does not want wood engravings from *Harper's, Leslie's,* and other newspapers or magazines. Send photograph and the dimensions. Falk's company, Sound View Press, publishes the *Art Price Index,* one of the basic reference books for the art world. This $199 book contains prices paid in the last year for more than 200,000 works of art.

> Peter Falk
> 170 Boston Post Road
> Madison, CT 06443
> (203) 245-2246   Fax: (203) 245-3589

Prints of all types are also sought for their subject matter by historians in many fields. When looking for a buyer, make certain to check the section on illustration prints and paintings on pages 478 to 482.

Print buyers want to know the size of the image and the size of the paper on which it is printed. They also want to know everything that is printed at the bottom of the print. If there is a penciled signature, make a Xerox™ copy of it. Make certain to mention any damage, tears, stains, or little brown spots.

If you are not trained to recognize valuable art get expert advice. Mistakes can be costly.

WOODBLOCK PRINTS

★ **Woodblock prints by European, American and Canadian artists** (1895-1950) in color or black and white. He buys only pencil signed prints created and signed by the artist whose work they are. Particular interests include:

- **Landscapes and marinescapes by** the widely traveled artist **Arthur Wesley Dow** of Ipswitch MA. His prints are signed but unnumbered, usually 5x7 inches or smaller, and can be worth $1,000 and more.
- **Prints by Provincetown printers,** especially "white line prints" characterized by blocks of color separated by white lines. These run in size from 3x4 inches to 16x20, but are mostly from 5x7 to 8x10 inches. Values run from $1,000 to $15,000.
- **Prints with Oriental subjects,** but only those by Western, often British, artists. People to look for include Bartlett, Hyde, Keith and Lum.

"Woodblocks are rectangular with sharply defined borders. When printed in color, a slight registration problem is often apparent. They are usually signed in pencil outside the image area."

"I do not want Oriental prints from Japan and the Far East or wood engravings from *Harper's Weekly* or other magazines and newspapers. Nor do I generally buy woodblock illustrations from books." If your print is loose and unframed, a photocopy is quick and accurate. If you feel you have one of these valuable prints, the expense of a color copy may be justified. If your print is framed, try to get a good photograph by shooting outdoors in open shade. Thomas makes offers *if your item is genuinely for sale*, but is not interested in doing free appraisals. In business for 17 years, Thomas issues annual catalogs of art for sale and will send you an illustrated wants list if you send a #10 (long) envelope.

Steven Thomas, Inc.
PO Box 41
Woodstock, VT 05091
(802) 457-1764   Fax: (802) 457-1764

★ **Japanese woodblock prints.** "I buy woodblock prints by Paul Jacoulet, but I will also consider other artists. Send a clear color photo with dimensions and a general description of condition." Bob is a private collector.

Bob Block
PO Box 233
Trumbull, CT 06611
(203) 380-1920

WALLACE NUTTING

★ **Wallace Nutting pictures, books, furniture and memorabilia.**
Among Nutting pictures, Mike particularly wants interiors, scenes with
people, animals, and houses. He does not want single pictures of common
exteriors of apple blossoms, country lanes, trees, lakes, and ponds,
although he will take these as part of a large collection. Collections are
preferred, but single pieces will be considered. No size is too large.
Mike says he'll travel anywhere to view collections of considerable
size and diversity. When describing pictures, give the title, frame size,
and condition. When describing **books** give standard bibliographic information, including title, edition, color of the cover. Mike will either
buy outright or consider accepting your items on consignment for one
of his Nutting auctions. The 4th edition of Mike's *Price Guide to Wallace Nutting Pictures* is available from him for $17 postpaid.

Michael Ivankovich
PO Box 2458
Doylestown, PA 18901
(215) 345-6094

★ **Wallace Nutting pictures, books and other ephemera,** including
furniture, lamps, wooden dishes, postcards, calendars, and greeting
cards designed, built, or used by him. "Especially interested in pictures
with indoor scenes and those which include people or animals. Not
interested in recent items, or things that are damaged or otherwise in
less than very good condition," says this 7 year veteran Nutting dealer.

James Buskirk
Eleanor's Hand Tinted Photos
3009 Oleander Avenue
San Marcos, CA 92069
(619) 599-1054

*High prices are being paid for good items
in today's art world, even though the market
is generally depressed. This is a very volatile
time, and tastes are changing as a result of
the movement of baby boomers into the market.*

*Personally, I believe their impact will be felt for
a long time, so I'm selling any piece of art that I
consider surplus that I don't feel has boomer-appeal.*

*If you get a good offer for something, remember,
prices do not always go up over time. Artists and styles fall in
and out of favor.*

FOLK ART

★ **American folk art** such as:
- **Wood carvings**, **whirligigs**, and **decoys;**
- Old **weathervanes** of any and all materials;
- **Quilts** in fine, unworn condition;
- **Hooked rugs** with pictorials rather than patterns;
- **Handmade dolls** of wood and/or cloth;
- **Folk paintings of children** and animals;
- Figural 19th century **pottery;**
- **Fishing decoys** in fine condition and good provenance;
- **Architectural figurals** such as cherubs and gargoyles,
- **Game boards** in original finish;
- **Indian art,** rugs, baskets, pottery, pipes, and other artifacts.

No damaged or repaired pieces. Send a photo and SASE. Include complete description, dimensions, and condition.

Louis Picek, Main Street Antiques
PO Box 340
West Branch, IA 52358
(319) 643-2065

★ **Folk art.** "We seek quality American one-of-a-kind pieces in very good condition. We prefer old, but also buy contemporary and outsider art, as well as a few old factory made items. We seek items with good form, especially quirky, humorous and colorful pieces such as:
- **Tramp art chip carved pieces**, the bigger the better;
- Carvings that are whimsical, folksy, interesting or unusual;
- **Quilts,** especially very old, funky, graphic patriotic, Amish, Black made, album, coarse;
- **Samplers;**
- Circus and **side show banners** and signs;
- Recycled **oddities made of found objects** like bottle caps, match sticks, ice cream sticks;
- Hand made items such as trade signs, barber poles, game boards, hitching posts, toys, and what have you.

Unusual depictions of people, places and animals are preferred. "We do not want 'cute' items like sunbonnet girls, most factory made items, damaged items, or things that are recently repaired or repainted (unusual or old repairs may be OK)." Description should include colors, size, materials, and history of the piece. "We want at least one good photo. Other photos of damage and details are helpful. Dealers should price their goods, but amateurs may request offers."

Matt Lippa and Elizabeth Schaaf
Artisans
PO Box 256
Mentone, AL 35984
(205) 634-4037   artisans@folkartisans.com

★ **Folk art** including painting, sculpture, weaving, wood, etc., including **American Indian, Oriental, African, or Eskimo** art. Provide the dimensions, condition, and photos. Condition critical. Special interest in current "outsider art." Contact Ivan only if your item is for sale.

> Ivan Gilbert
> Miran Arts & Books
> 2824 Elm Ave.
> Columbus, OH 43209
> (614) 421-3222   Fax: (614) 421-3223

★ **Tramp art** items made from cigar boxes or fruit crate wood which has been layered into edge-notched pyramids. Typical items include boxes, picture frames, doll furniture, banks, and wall pockets. Collects interesting or unusual boxes, especially pedestal form, but will buy any good example for resale. Intact condition and original finish are important. Information about origin is a plus. He does not want items made from ice cream sticks, matches, wood burning or 'crown of thorns.' A photo is essential. Will also buy historical documents related to tramp art, such as old photos of makers with their work, patterns, etc.

> Michael Cornish
> 92 Florence Street
> Roslindale, MA 02131
> (617) 323-6029

★ **Prisoner of war straw figures** woven or plaited by French prisoners during the early 1800's. Other documented prisoner art from the 19th century, including **ivory carvings**, are sought.

> Lucille Malitz
> Lucid Antiques
> PO Box KH
> Scarsdale, NY 10583
> (914) 636-7825

★ **Fraktur birth and baptismal certificates** dating before 1900. These certificates are usually, but not always, printed with hand done watercolor decoration. Some are totally freehand drawn manuscripts. Most are written in German, but some are in English. Prefers colorful watercolor birds and flowers that are "folksy" rather than formal. These are wanted in any condition. Inquire by removing your fraktur from any frame and sending a photocopy, including the name of the printer. Do not make any repairs with tape or glue no matter how carefully. Make sure the copy is clear and readable.

> Louis Picek
> Main Street Antiques
> PO Box 340
> West Branch, IA 52358
> (319) 643-2065

★ **American needlework samplers** made before 1850. "I prefer samplers, whether framed or unframed, to be in good condition with the name and date of the maker. I am particularly interested in those which contain poetry, but buy all types. These are valued between $300 and $3,000 depending on the nature of the work, quality of workmanship, and condition. I am not interested in those made after 1860 or those based on punchpaper mottoes." Give the name, date and condition, including a description of anything stitched other than the usual alphabets and numbers. He lectures on early samplers and is forming a club for those with similar interests.

> Peter Cifelli
> PO Box 2160
> Los Gatos, CA 95031
> (408) 529-9797 voice and fax days   (408) 395-4050 eves

★ **Mourning pictures** in watercolor or embroidery. These are characterized by willow trees, tombstones, birth and death dates, weeping women, etc. These are often for famous people, presidents, generals, etc. Those honoring "nobodies" are more rare and desirable. Will pay at least $100 and as much as $300-$400 for better ones.

> Steve DeGenaro
> PO Box 5662
> Youngstown, OH 44504

★ **Samplers**, both U.S. and English, from before 1850, including mourning samplers and needlework pictures. Clear photo is essential, along with dimensions and the item's history as you understand it. Books on American and/or British needlework are also sought. Give standard bibliographic information.

> Donna Litwin
> PO Box 5865
> Trenton, NJ 08638
> (609) 275-0996   Fax: (609) 275-1427

★ **Folk art weavings worldwide,** including rugs, saddle blankets, tapestries, ponchos, and other old, fine, and rare pieces. Will consider Oriental, Middle Eastern, European, Indian, and South American fine quality rugs and other weavings. Also **Eskimo and American Indian weavings**. In addition to weavings, he buys **needlepoint, paisley shawls, and hooked rugs**. Nothing after 1920 or machine made.

> Renate Halpern Galleries
> 325 East 79th Street
> New York, NY 10021
> (212) 988-9316

★ **Quilts that are graphically artistic** made before 1940 especially made before 1900. Cotton, wool, and silk quilts all have value if made well but children's size quilts are best if they do not have children's subject matter. Solid color materials and small calico patterns are most desirable. Large patterns cut into small pieces usually make the quilt of no interest. All quilts should be in mint condition, with at least six stitches per inch, preferably more. No holes, tears, stains, thin spots when held to light, fading, soft from too much washing, and no patched repairs. A photo is very desirable. Herb says he will pay $5,000 for an album quilt made between 1840 and 1860, $15,000 for an album quilt from that same period made in Baltimore, and $600 up for navy blue and white quilts in excellent condition. Herb does not make offers.

Herbert Wallerstein Jr., Calico Antiques
611 North Alta Drive
Beverly Hills, CA 90210
(310) 273-4192   Fax: (310) 273-1921

★ **Patchwork quilts made by African-Americans,** especially unusual or improvisational quilts. Provide a full photo of the quilt, a statement of condition, and all information you can about its history. "I'll also buy **fabric sample books**, especially of printed cottons."

Eli Leon
5663 Dover Street
Oakland, CA 94609

★ **Patchwork quilts** of all types made before 1930, including ones that have some damage. Please send a photo which shows the colors and pattern, along with a description of condition. Also buys **ribbon pictures** (small, usually framed, 8"x10" or so, patchwork pictures made from dimestore ribbons in the 1920's and 30's).

Bird In the Cage
118 King Street
Alexandria, VA 22314
(703) 549-5114

★ **Quilts** made by hand before 1950 in any condition. "I'm looking for rare patterns like U.S. Flag, albums, samples, and pictorials, but I also buy common patterns like starts, wedding rings, flower gardens, etc. Prices are from $200 to more than $1,000 for U.S. flag quilts. I do not buy quilts made with synthetic fabrics." He wants to know the pattern, size, condition, and age if you know it. A photo is needed.

Michael Council
250 West Hubbard Avenue
Columbus, OH 43215
(614) 299-9099 voice & fax

★ **Mexican weavings,** including serapes, saltillos, rugs, and other pre-1940 items. Excellent condition only. It is essential that you include a photo and the dimensions.

> Barry Friedman
> PO Box 55492
> Valencia, CA 91385
>   (805) 255-2365   BarryF@fishnet.net

How do you tell ivory from bone from plastic from celluloid? Bone has fine brown specks. Plastic sometimes has air bubbles or pits. Ivory has grain like fine wood. Celluloid is very smooth and can be melted with a hot pin.

★ **Ivory items of all sorts,** including Eskimo and Oriental carvings, scrimshaw, ivory tusks (elephant, walrus, whale, hippo, etc.), dresser sets, poker chips, dice, and billiard balls. Dave does not want ivory jewelry, letter openers, or sewing and crochet tools, nor does he buy bone or synthetic objects. If you are selling tusks, give the length around the outside curve, and the diameter at the large end. He asks you to use a flashlight to carefully inspect for cracks in the hollow end. Follow standard description form. A sample catalog is $1. Please list your phone number and best time to call.

> David Boone
> Boone Trading Company
> 562 Coyote Road
> Brinnon, WA 98320
>   (206) 796-4330   (800) 423-1945   Fax: (206) 796-4511

★ **Figures and native carvings made of ivory.** Ivory can be elephant, walrus, whale, hippo, wart hog, or narwhale, but he wants ivory art, not small useful items like pins, combs, spoons, brooches and toothpicks. Picture is a necessity, and he prefers you to set a price. Terry also buys **primitive and pre-Columbian artifacts.**

> Terry Cronin
> 207 Silver Palm Avenue
> Melbourne, FL 32501

★ **African or South Pacific tribal art** including masks, weapons, musical instruments, jewelry, household objects, bowls, furniture, feather work, textiles, and "almost anything else that was made for tribal use and not for the tourist trade." Especially old collections including artifacts with elaborate decoration and animal, human, or spirit figures. High quality tribal art can bring as much as $100,000 so is worth inquiry. Does not want items made after 1970, ebony carvings, tourist items, or figures of natives holding spears. A photograph is essential and Jones would like to know where the item was collected.

    Charles Jones
    African Art
    6716 Barren Inlet Road
    Wilmington, NC 28405
        (910) 686-0717   Fax: (910) 686-1313

Buyers generally do not want any art from Mexico or South America without good provenance (history). The markets of that region have been flooded with modern imitations for nearly a century. Skill of the local artisans remains high, so it is hard for anyone but an expert to attest to the age of a piece...and they get fooled too, especially evaluating items made of clay. Objects made of precious metals and stones are harder to fake and less likely to come to you. Many art dealers are concerned about grave robbing and disruption of ancient sites.

★ **Pre-Columbian art** in all media: ceramic, stone, wood, textiles, and gold. Requests photos of the front and back of each piece, measurements, a description of condition, and information on where you got it. This collector-dealer has been in business for seven years.

    Jack Bond
    Kent Bond Gallery
    11301 North 56th Street #10
    Tampa, FL 33617
        (813) 988-2132

★ **Pre-Columbian pottery from Mexico or Peru** are sought, but *only* if documented and authenticated. Collections preferred. A photograph is essential and Jones would like to know where the item was collected or obtained, and any other history of the piece.

    Charles Jones
    6716 Barren Inlet Road
    Wilmington, NC 28405
        (910) 686-0717   Fax: (910) 686-1313

ORIENTALIA

★ **Antique Japanese netsuke, inro, and other art** including pouches, pipes and pipe cases, ivory and wooden statues, Japanese lacquer, metalwork, cloisonne, paintings, and ceramics. Will pay $10,000 up for ivory and wood 18th and 19th century netsuke and $1,000 for netsuke inlaid in various materials. No roughly carved pieces, manmade materials, or factory pieces bought in hotel lobbies, airports or gift shops. If you provide clear close-up photographs of your netsuke from all angles and an exact drawing of the signature, Denis will make an offer if interested. He has been president of the Netsuke Dealer's Association for 15 years, has written extensively on the topic, and is a member of the Appraisers Association of America. He does formal appraisals for a fee.

 Denis Szeszler
 Antique Oriental Art
 PO Box 714
 New York, NY 10028
 (212) 427-4682 Fax: (212) 860-4426 szeszler@juno.com

★ **Fine quality Oriental antiques** with special emphasis on Japanese netsuke, inro, lacquer, and fine Chinese porcelains. Marsha buys, sells, and collects all types of Oriental antiques from early ceramics to late 19th century items including furniture, Japanese swords, sword fittings, jade carvings, and jewelry. Many small ivory and wood carvings are worth between $1,000 and $10,000. Modern or reproduction items are not wanted, nor are silk robes decorated with dragons brought back by WWII soldiers. Marsha is a senior member of the American Society of Appraisers, specializing in Oriental art, and will appraise for a fee. She will also help amateur sellers with fine items genuinely for sale if you take a good photo, give the measurements, and draw or photocopy all markings or signatures found on the bottom.

 Marsha Vargas
 The Oriental Corner
 280 Main Street
 Los Altos, CA 94022
  (415) 941-3207 Fax: (415) 941-3297

★ **Modern Oriental prints.** Please send a Xerox™ copy, dimensions, and a description of condition.

 Eric Matthies
 PO Box 470965
 San Francisco, CA 94147
  (415) 921-6604 Fax: (415) 563-4957

SCULPTURE & FIGURINES

★ **Bronzes and porcelain figures** prior to 1935. Describe all marks and give dimensions and colors. A photo is highly recommended.

> Arnold Reamer
> PO Box 26416
> Baltimore, MD 21207
>   (410) 944-6414   (410) 486-8412   Fax: (410) 265-7877

★ **Bathing beauties and "naughties" figurines.** Wants small bisque or porcelain figurines, 1900-1940, which are nude, in bathing suits, in their underwear, stockings, or dressed in lace. They are finely modeled and in coy poses. Some had actual mohair wigs. Naughties were hollow figurines, often of children or women, intended to be filled with water so they peed or squirted out of their breasts. Other naughties appeared to be innocent figurines until lifted up or turned over, displaying a risque (often explicit) side. "I am especially interested in finding Black naughties or bathers with a wig, but I am interested in *all* fine examples of bathing beauties and naughties. I am also looking for old catalogs, advertisements, and other information about them. Bathing beauties and naughties can range anywhere from less than $100 to over $1,000 depending upon the rarity, pose, and quality of execution." She is also interested in fine quality **mermaids**, as well as original advertisements or catalogs featuring bathing beauty figurines or related items. No Japanese figures or reproductions. Generally does not want damaged pieces, but will consider extraordinary figures with minor damage. Size and pose is important so accurate measurements and a sketch or photo is almost essential. Include your phone number. Will buy only if you grant right of refusal after inspection. If you too collect these figures, please call. She'd love to meet you. Sharon has written *Naughties, Nudies and Bathing Beauties,* available from her for $20.

> Sharon Hope Weintraub
> 3613-F Las Colinas Drive
> Austin, TX 78731
>   (512) 323-9639

★ *Art Metal Works* **figures of humans or animals:** ashtrays, bookends, incense burners, and the like, especially those marked ART METAL WORKS, RONSON, or LVA. Send a sharp photo of what you have along with an SASE. In your description indicate the condition of the paint, including what percent remains. No cracked or damaged items wanted. Will pay premium price for Art Metal Works catalogs. All brochures and advertising which pictures the line is wanted.

> Urban Cummings
> 1231 Parkinson Avenue
> Palo Alto, CA 94301
>   (415) 328-0329

★ **Beautiful nude women** in bronze, alabaster or marble. Also any **sculpture with romantic themes.** Please send a photo, dimensions and your asking price.

Charles Martignette
PO Box 293
Hallandale, FL 33008
(954) 454-3474

★ **Female figurines, especially nudes** in bronze or porcelain in Art Deco or Art Nouveau styles. Wants work of fine makers without repairs. No figurines of children or from Limited Edition series. She does not make offers, expecting you to price what you have.

Madeleine France, Past Pleasures
PO Box 15555
Plantation, FL 33318
(954) 921-0022 days   Fax: (954) 584-0014

★ *Royal Doulton* **figurines and character jugs** are purchased by this well known dealer who has been in business for 20 years. "No collection is too large or too small," he says, encouraging you to "call toll free as long as you have the name and HN number of the figurines and the name and size of the character jugs." Pascoe is especially interested in the rarest items, since they maintain a computer list of collectors worldwide who are looking for specific types of figure. Ed lectures frequently in the U.S. and England, and has edited price guides to these popular figures. He is not interested in buying dinnerware, and does not do pattern matching.

Ed Pascoe
Pascoe & Co.
101 Almeria Avenue
Coral Gables, FL 33134
(800) 872-0195   (305) 445-3229

★ **John Rogers statuary.** If you have a gray or putty colored plaster grouping of figures, check for the signature JOHN ROGERS, often accompanied by NEW YORK and a date. These Victorian figural groups can be from 12" to 48" high, with most just under 2' tall. Themes are Civil War, Americana, theater, etc., with a few comic. A few are made of material other than plaster, such as parian or bronze. Perfect condition is always best, but he will buy damaged pieces, as he is a restorer of Rogers' work. He needs to know the name of the piece (which is always found on the front of the base) and the condition of the putty colored paint. Prefers you to telephone him with your statue in front of you.

Bruce Bleier
73 Riverdale Road
Valley Stream, NY 11581
(516) 791-4353 (call collect)

★ **Kewpie figurines of German bisque.** These 3"-5" figures are most interesting in action poses with cats, toys, brooms, ducks, etc. Look for German figures to be marked O'NEILL on the back. Doesn't want figures made in Japan or elsewhere. Must be mint: no damage or repairs.

> Linda Vines
> PO Box 43721
> Upper Montclair, NJ 07043
> (201) 748-4990

★ **Snow Babies.** "I'll buy German 'Snow Babies' (china children in pebbly snow suits 1"-3" high), especially jointed Snow Babies and 'action' Babies with animals or engaged in some activity." Also buys **small German bisque or papier mache Santas** dressed in felt with fur beards. Doesn't want items from Japan or Taiwan, nor does she want damaged or faded items or anything newer than 1940. Give the size and markings, if any, and note all damage, no matter how minor. No offers or free appraisals. She expects you to look them up in price guides and says she pays "50%-75% of book value."

> Linda Vines
> PO Box 43721
> Upper Montclair, NJ 07043
> (201) 748-4990

★ *Noritake* **human and animal figures** are wanted by this well known glass auctioneer and porcelain collector.

> Tom Burns
> PO Box 608
> Bath, NY 14810
> (607) 776-7942

FIGURINES & LIMITED EDITIONS

★ *Heubach* **porcelain or bisque figurines and other items** including children's tea sets, trays, religious items, and anything else. Draw a picture of the mark, and give all colors. Frances is cataloging every *Heubach* product made and she'd like to hear from anyone who owns anything unusual by Gebruder Heubach, even if it is not for sale.

> Frances Sanda
> 5624 Plymouth Road
> Baltimore, MD 21214

★ *Hummel* **figurines** with full bee and crown markings preferred, though some later ones considered. Please give complete information concerning condition and an accurate drawing of all markings on the bottom. Price fishing is discouraged by this nationally known dealer who cautions that dealers can seldom use more common items, so can pay little if they buy them at all. "When you are ready to buy or sell *Hummels*, contact me, especially with rare items!" He is available to restore glass and porcelain, including your damaged *Hummels*.

> Donald Hardisty, Don's Collectibles
> 3020 East Majestic Ridge
> Las Cruces, NM 88001
> (505) 522-3721   Fax: (505) 522-7909

★ *Hummel* **figurines** with the crown or full bee marks. Also wants *Goebel* vases, figurines, half dolls, wall plaques and monks in red robes. Also *Hummel* calendars from 1950 through 1975. Also *Precious Moments* **figurines** with the triangle or hourglass mark or with no mark at all. All *Hummels* must be marked. Please give all marks and numbers and note whether or not you have the original box. Please don't offer *Hummel* plates, bells, or anything that is chipped or cracked.

> Sharon Vohs-Mohammed
> PO Box 7233
> Villa Park, IL 60181
> (630) 268-0210

★ **Hummel-look-alike figures designed by Erich Stauffer.** Please give a detailed description of the figure's activity and props. Especially wanted are nuns, angels, two piece perfume girls, animals, and wall plaques. Height is important, as is the style number and complete mark found on the base. These are usually marked either DESIGNED BY ERICH STAUFFER, ARNART or ROYAL CROWN. Does not make offers.

> Joan Oates
> 685 South Washington
> Constantine, MI 49042

★ **Lladro Spanish porcelain figurines** that are no longer available through retail stores. Please note that some figures have been in continuous production for more than 20 years so the age is not important. "We are particularly interested in pieces created exclusively for the Lladro Collector's Society since 1985 and in the 21 "special event" figures created since 1991. There are approximately 100 other popular figures for which we will make offers." All Lladro figures are marked on the bottom with the Lladro trademark. Original boxes are important and the value of your piece is less if you do not have it. If you have the original box, the identification number will be on the box and "this tells me everything." If you do not have the box, the height in inches is a very important part of your description, as is the number and sex of the figures and any damage. "Lladro has produced a less expensive, lower quality, line of porcelain called NAO. We do not buy these at all." Write for their current catalog of Lladro and other fine items for sale.

Clark and Charlotte Sanchez
Sanchez Collectibles Consultants
1555 East Glendale Avenue
Phoenix, AZ 85020
(602) 277-1661   Fax: (602) 241-0702   sanchcol@primenet.com

★ *Goebel* **figurines of cats.** "I don't want cats other than *Goebel* or *Goebels* other than cats." Include marks and numbers on the bottom.

Linda Nothnagel
Route 3 Box 30
Shelbina, MO 63468
(573) 588-4958

★ *Osborne Ivorex* **plaques.** These 3-D plaster wall plaques were made between 1899 and 1968. In addition to plaques, the company made statuary of people and buildings, jewelry boxes, and other small items. Subject matter of the plaques includes individual characters to large cathedrals. Sizes range from a few inches to over a foot, with 3"x5" and 6.5"x9" being two popular sizes. Some premium items are factory framed in wood. Some poor quality repros exist. Most, but not all, *Ivorex* plaques are marked A/O (Arthur Osborne) on the lower right or left corner. In the 1930's they began marking them on the back with a three line ink stamp with the company name and copyright. Small vertical oval and rectangular plaques sometimes have markings on the lower rim. Values range from $30 up, with a few reaching $200. Andy wants to hear from other collectors for purposes of starting a club.

Andy Jackson
501 Falcon Lane
West Chester, PA 19382
(610) 692-0269   Fax: (610) 272-7040

★ *Erphila* German figurines, teapots and other ceramics, which are usually marked. Size, color and form are needed. Photo a good idea.

> Denise Hamilton
> 575 Latta Brook Road
> Elmira, NY 14901
> (607) 732-2550

★ *Pen Delfin* **rabbits.** This mail order dealer in *Pen Delfin* is always looking for rabbits, especially those retired before 1980. Quality is important. Please no damaged, chipped or smudged items. Asking price helpful, but not necessary. Note the figure's name on the bottom.

> George Sparacio
> PO Box 791
> Malaga, NJ 08328
> (609) 694-4167 eves

★ **Angel figurines** made of china, generally 3" to 7" tall are wanted. Made by various companies including Lefton, Napco, Enesco, Norcrest and Kelvin among others, these 1950's and 60's angels have the days of the week, months of the year, or signs of the zodiac on them and the figures are usually holding something appropriate to that day, month or sign (October holding a pumpkin, for example). They may also have a flower or birthstone. Some of these angels are incorporated into bells, planters, salt and pepper shakers, and the like. These older angels are made of hard fired glossy china, not the softer bisque (which he does not want). Most are in the $15 to $20 range, but a handful will bring twice that. He does NOT want angels playing musical instruments or other angel figures except those described, nor does he want broken or glued items. Give the name of the maker and any numbers stamped on the bottom of the figure. If this info isn't available, a photo is a must.

> James Atkinson
> 555 East School Street
> Owatonna, MN 55060
> (507) 455-3340 eves

★ **Swarovski Austrian crystal animals** but only the ten Collector's Club pieces: lovebirds (1987), woodpeckers (1988), turtledoves (1989), dolphins (1990), seals (1991), whales (1992), elephant (1993), kudu (1994), lion (1995) and unicorn (1996). The more recent the piece, the more plentiful and the lower the price. The original box and certificate is "almost a must" with Swarovski crystal. Write for their catalog of Swarovski and other fine items for sale.

> Clark and Charlotte Sanchez, Collectibles Consultants
> 1555 East Glendale Avenue
> Phoenix, AZ 85020
> (602) 277-1661   Fax: (602) 241-0702   sanchcol@primenet.com

★ *Sebastian* **miniatures** by P.W. Baston including commercial issues, limited editions and private commissions. "Ask me about any *Sebastian* miniatures because some common ones have rare variations." Give the title of the piece, the color of the label (if any), and the condition. Jim buys and sells miniatures and can help you obtain custom made miniatures for promotions or fundraising purposes.

Jim Waite, Blossom Shop Collectibles
112 North Main
Farmer City, IL 61842
(309) 928-3222   (800) 842-2593

★ **Collector's plates.** The Ernst family is one of the nation's larger dealers in collector's plates. If you have plates to sell, they will help you in one of two ways, (1) by outright purchase of those they can sell promptly or (2) by selling your plates on consignment (in the more likely event you own plates in less demand). They charge 20% of the item's selling price for this valuable service. When you call or write, they will send you complete information plus specific instructions on how to pack and ship your plates safely. The Ernsts have been in business for 27 years and are listed in Dun & Bradstreet.

Ross and Ruth Ernst
Collectors Plates
7308 Izard
Omaha, NE 68114
(402) 391-3469

★ *Bossons* **artware** including heads, wall plaques and figures. These are made of plaster or *Stonite*, a vinyl/stone mix marketed as *Fraser-Art.* "We buy figures that are still available, but mostly seek discontinued figures, worth $85 up." There are *Bossons* look-alikes, but only figures marked BOSSONS CONGLETON ENGLAND COPYRIGHT are wanted. Slightly damaged figures will be considered by this authorized *Bossons* dealer and repairman. "If you want to buy or sell *Bossons*, contact me."

Donald Hardisty
Don's Collectibles
3020 East Majestic Ridge
Las Cruces, NM 88011
(505) 522-3721   Fax: (505) 522-7909

★ *Bossons* **artware** including heads, wall plaques and figures. "We're only looking for the discontinued ones. They need not be perfect as I am a restorer of *Bossons.* Almost all are signed on the back in the plaster. The name of the piece is frequently inscribed on the bottom at the cross-section of the neck.

Bruce Bleier
73 Riverdale Road
Valley Stream, NY 11581
(516) 791-4353

HOW TO SELL PAPER ITEMS

*If you are handling an estate, closing a business, or have piles of family papers and photos, **read this section carefully.** Piles of papers can be piles of dollars.*

Paper is bought for one of two reasons:
(1) It is pretty, and collectible because it is, or
(2) it is historically interesting and informative.
Some paper is bought for both reasons.

Popular papers are postcards, photographs, catalogs, bills and letters, autographs, posters, and advertising. Minor types include menus, blueprints, scrapbooks, maps, labels, etc. Values of these range from a few cents to a few thousand dollars. Some photos bring even more. A $50,000 photo was sold at a Hudson River yard sale for $5. The dealer who bought it, resold it for $15 to someone who decided to ask an expert what he had.

Historical data is not often worth a lot of money, but **Trash or Treasure** *buyers will preserve what you have. Please, never to throw away paper with prices, formulas, processes, or descriptions of people or travels.*

Sports, movies, music, transportation, liquor, tobacco, business and Pop Culture paper is easiest to sell. You'll find buyers in the next few pages ready to buy a wide range of items. Don't give up if you don't find a buyer your first try.

***Condition is critical** for buyers of paper. Don't clean paper yourself. It is easy to do more harm than good. Let the buyer do it.*

***Describing paper is usually easy.** Photocopy it! If your item is too large to fit on a machine, take multiple copies and tape them together or go to a commercial copy center where larger machines are available.*

***Important tip:** unless you are certain your item is both rare and desirable, do not go to a great deal of effort to make photocopies of big piles of paper. Write to the buyer first, expressing a willingness to make copies if desired.*

MISCELLANEOUS PAPER

★ **Rare documents** from the time of papyrus to the present. Buys collections of letters, manuscript (hand written) material, land grants, photograph collections, diaries, hand colored maps, atlases, and "anything unusual in paper."
> Ivan Gilbert, Miran Arts & Books
> 2824 Elm Avenue
> Columbus, OH 43209
>   (614) 236-3222   Fax: (614) 236-3223

★ **Rare documents in all fields,** from autographs to stock certificates, from song sheets to pardons and passes, including handwritten documents, maps, and "most any other unusual paper items." Gordon buys lots of all sizes, from single items to entire estates.
> Gordon McHenry
> PO Box 1117
> Osprey, FL 34229
>   (941) 966-5563   Fax: (941) 966-5563

★ **Accumulations of paper items** especially stocks and bonds, but also buys bills, checks, and letters with "pretty vignettes." Buys some **Western, circus,** and **magic posters** as well. Does not buy anything made after 1940. If you have a collection of family or business correspondence, phone with your items in front of you.
> David Beach
> Paper Americana
> PO Box 2026
> Goldenrod, FL 32733
>   (407) 657-7403   Fax: (407) 657-6382

★ **Accumulations of paper items** related to business, finance, mining, or transportation before 1920. Buys stocks, bonds, billheads, advertising, land grants, maps, diaries, letters, photographs and other printed and manuscript items. Will consider all collections related to military, mining, railroads, energy, banking, express companies, law enforcement, and other topics generally associated with the old West.
> Warren Anderson
> America West Archives
> PO Box 100
> Cedar City, UT 84720
>   (801) 586-9497

*Paper items, billheads, maps and
the like are bought by man collectors.
The index helps you get the best deal.*

★ **Manuscripts and printed documents with interesting content.**
These need not be signed by anyone famous. "I particularly like
colonial American documents from before the Revolutionary War, but
will consider material from all periods. Please describe the contents
and why you think the item is unusual." Photocopy advisable.

>Chris Wilson
>8101 Revatom Court
>Dunn Loring, VA 22027
>(703) 698-7073

★ **Amateur poetry in autograph books, friendship books, sketchbooks, journals and diaries.** If what you have was written after 1870,
he is not interested at all. Please give any names, dates, and places
mentioned, and mention any watercolor or other embellishment, including fancy calligraphy. Making Xerox™ copies seems like a good idea.
He is author of *Early American Poetry: Voices of New England Youth*,
available from him for $19.

>Peter Cifelli
>PO Box 2160
>Los Gatos, CA 95031
>(408) 529-9797 voice and fax days   (408) 395-4050 eves

★ **Pictorial calendars of all types and products** (except those with
the spiral binding in the middle) dating before 1979. "I buy **all years,
all subjects**, for resale. Calendars must be in condition good enough to
frame" with no writing on the pages. Especially want Victorian die cut
calendars, pin-up girls, and advertising before 1940. The value of calendars is based on the picture, the artist, the condition of the paper, the
product being advertised, and the age. Newer calendars are available at
very reasonable prices. She does not want calendars with common or
unattractive pictures, damage, writing, or religious themes. A description of a calendar should include its size and condition, noting any
damage. Include all printed information on the calendar and note who
the artist is, if the picture is signed. Tell what month the calendar starts
with. "Sending a Xerox™ of the calendar is the best way to get a quick
sale at a fair price." Dealers must price their goods, but amateurs may
request an offer. Appraisals are for a fee.

>Elizabeth Pensoneau
>The Calendar Girl
>72 Brighton Road
>Springfield, IL 62702
>(217) 793-5586 eves and weekends

*Paper items are bought by many people.
Use the index to get the best deal possible.*

★ **Scrapbooks** with diecut embossed scrap from the Victorian era, **trade cards and prints**. Also wants collections of loose die-cut, embossed **Victorian paper**, especially Santas, snow angels, and children. Also wants **cards from any holiday**, 1840 to 1910. Nothing later. Everything must be in suitable condition for resale. No postcards.
> Madalaine Selfridge
> 33710 Almond Street
> Wildomar, CA 92595

★ **Scrapbooks of Victorian era trade cards.**
> Russell Mascieri
> 13 Running Water Court
> Medford, NJ 08055
> (609) 953-7711   Fax: (609) 953-7768

★ **Children's illustrators.** "I want **prints**, **calendars**, **trade cards**, **magazine covers** and books with color illustrations from 1920-1940 by children's illustrators like Frances Brundage, Maud Humphrey, Ida Waugh, Torres Bevins, Mabel Attwell, Rose O'Niell, Grace Drayton, Bessie Pease Gutmann and similar artists of that period."
> Madalaine Selfridge
> 33710 Almond Street
> Wildomar, CA 92595
> (909) 674-9221

★ **Collections of labels, stickers** and **poster stamps** pre-1960. Wants collections of colorful, smaller graphics of all types, even if many are duplicates. Immediate answer if you include your phone number.
> George Theofiles
> PO Box 1776
> New Freedom, PA 17349

★ **Paper puzzles in any printed format.** "I'll buy crosswords, mathematical puzzles, rebuses, tangrams, brain teasers, picture puzzles, etc. The format can be a book, magazine, pamphlet, broadside, trade card, or newspaper, but I do not want 'hidden image' puzzles or those that are too juvenile, intended for small children." In general, he is most interested in items from before 1950, the earlier the better, although value depends on the quality of the puzzle and the rarity of the material. He also wants material about the history of puzzles, directories of puzzles, and "anything with the byline 'Sam Loyd,' a famous turn of the century puzzlist." Give the date and condition, and describe the puzzle or state its objective. No jigsaw puzzles.
> Will Shortz
> 55 Great Oak Lane
> Pleasantville, NY 10570
> (914) 769-9128 voice and fax

★ **Bookplates,** primarily before 1930. Bookplates are decorative printed ID plates which identify the owner of a book. Send a Xerox™ of the plate(s) you have and the price wanted. Does not make offers.

> Lewis Jaffe
> 1919 Chestnut Street #1117
> Philadelphia, PA 19103
> (215) 568-9253   Fax: (215) 568-6768

★ **Passports** and some other travel documents, pre-1940 American or foreign. Documents must be complete: nothing missing, removed or torn. Photocopy the page with the owner's description and inside pages that have been used. "No overpriced passports owned by celebrities."

> Dan Jacobson
> PO Box 277101
> Sacramento, CA 95827

★ **U.S. Consular and foreign service stamps on passports, visas,** or documents of any type, 1906-1955. Send photocopy.

> H. Ritter
> 68 Heatherwood
> Norristown, PA 19403
> (610) 539-5755

★ **"Dirty letters."** This long time erotica buyer wants sexy or risque letters 1800-1975, ideally with the original envelope if mailed. May be hand written or typed. "Even better if photos or other items mailed with the letters are still there."

> Charles Martignette
> PO Box 293
> Hallandale, FL 33008
> (954) 454-3474

PAPER DOLLS

★ **Paper dolls of all types.** Wants to buy antique paper dolls and toys, especially those by Tuck. Also wants books of paper dolls dating before 1960, magazine dolls from adult or children's publications and newspaper comic strip dolls from the 1930's and 40's such as *Flash Gordon* and *Brenda Starr*. May buy cut dolls if neatly done. Please give name, date if possible, book number and mention any writing on the front or back of the doll, the box, or the book. Can also use tinsel and antique crepe paper for making paper doll ornaments.

> Madalaine Selfridge
> Hidden Magic Doll Museum
> 33710 Almond Street
> Wildomar, CA 92595

*"Dolls that have been cut out are sellable as long as their
arms and legs aren't bent. Do not mend with tape!
If you own paper dolls, it is absolutely essential you do not
attempt to repair any tears, stains, creases. Don't tape dolls,
Don't color paper dolls. Don't press dolls.*

*When offering books of paper dolls for sale, it's helpful to buyers
if you give the name of the book, the publisher, and the date.
Many of these books have catalog numbers printed on the front
or back. Give that number too.*

Remember, dealers and collectors can't make offers on
what they don't understand.

★ **All types of paper dolls, cut or uncut,** one or a collection as long
as they're pre-1960. Sellers should list paper dolls by name, if possible,
and indicate whether they are cut or not. Photocopies of the doll are
helpful. "I will identify your dolls for a reasonable fee."
> Fran Van Vynckt
> 7412 Monroe Avenue
> Hammond, IN 46324
> (219) 931-6813

★ **Paper dolls and paper toys** of all kinds, cut or uncut, from boxed
or book sets, newspapers, magazines, cereal boxes, etc. Especially
wanted are paper dolls of real people. If you really want to sell your
dolls, indicate names, dates, and quantity, and whether cut or not. Also
indicate condition, mentioning bends, tears, missing parts, and tape.
No need to photograph or photocopy any more than the doll (not the
whole set). Will buy some rare sets even when damaged, and buys
some current items, but no *Betsy McCall* sheets. For 23 years, Loraine
has published *Celebrity Doll Journal*, a quarterly available for $7/year.
> Loraine Burdick, Quest-Eridon Books
> 413 10th Avenue Court NE
> Puyallup, WA 98372

★ **Paper toys, figures, and buildings,** especially toys and models by
Builtrite, but interested in any paper dolls and soldiers in good condition. In business for more than 20 years, The Paper Soldier publishes a
large and informative catalog for $5.
> Barbara & Jonathan Newman
> The Paper Soldier
> 8 McIntosh Lane
> Clifton Park, NY 12065
> (518) 371-9202   jmnewman@worldnet.att.net

MAPS & GLOBES

★ **Maps**. Many different types of maps are wanted by this specialty dealer, especially U.S. areas pre-1920 and worldwide prior to 1900. Particular interests include:
- **Books with maps**: atlases, geographies, travel guides, gazeteers, land surveys and explorations prior to 1900;
- Wall maps before 1920;
- **Pocket maps** with folding covers, case maps which fit into cases, and other maps separately published (not as part of a book of maps) before 1920;
- **Hand drawn maps**, especially battlefields;
- City plat maps before 1900;
- Texas, the Southwest and Southeast maps before 1900;
- Decorative maps;
- Geologic maps;
- Railroad maps, especially of the entire world, USA or the US Southwest before 1920;
- **Bird's eye views of cities**;
- **Globes of the world** before WWII, especially those with unusual or decorative stands;
- **Games and puzzles** pre-1960, including jigsaw, based on maps.

Please do not offer atlases or geographies after 1900. Description should include the author or map maker, the title or area depicted, the latest date on the map, the size, whether or not it is colored, and the condition, especially noting anything missing.

Murray Hudson
Antiquarian Books & Maps
109 South Church Street
Halls, TN 38040
(800) 748-9946   Fax: (901) 836-9017

☆ **Maps and atlases** before 1890 wanted, particularly those showing the present day United States. Maps and books that are damaged, torn, moldy, or bug eaten are worth a small fraction of those in fine condition. Maps are worthless if laminated, dry mounted or glued to cardboard or Masonite. Best to send your map on approval but description will suffice if you include the title, date, mapmaker, size and condition. No reproductions wanted.

Charles Neuschafer
New World Maps
Apple Hill Road
Bennington, VT 05201
(802) 442-2846   Charlieneu@aol.com

★ **Atlases and maps** before 1880 from anywhere in the world, as long as they are in very good or better condition. When describing maps, give the topic of the map, publisher, date of publication and anything else written in the map's legend. Include the size of the paper and the size of the map itself. For atlases, give standard bibliographic information: author, title, place published, publisher, all dates of publication and a description of the cover, binding, pages, and dust jacket. Please, no book club books, textbooks, or anything in poor condition. Open daily with 60,000 items in stock and 25 years of experience.

> James & Mary Laurie
> Booksellers
> 921 Nicollet
> Minneapolis, MN 55402
> (800) 774-1114   (612) 338-1114   Fax: (612) 338-3665

★ **U.S. maps and atlases before 1870**.
> Joe Davidson
> Antiquarian Graphic Society
> 5185 Windfall Road
> Medina, OH 44256
> (330) 723-7172

★ **U.S. maps and atlases before 1870.**
> Frank Klein
> The Bookseller
> 521 West Exchange Street
> Akron, OH 44302
> (216) 762-3101   Fax: (216) 762-4413

★ **Atlases with colored plates** before 1870 as long as they deal in whole or in part with the United States. It is important that double page plates should not have a white area separating the plate into two sections. Also interested in **commercial atlases prior to 1925** and **books of all types with foldout maps** in black and white or color, but they must be before 1870. Groups of loose color plate **maps** are also considered. Include dimensions with standard bibliographic information. Note tears, erasures, foxing, etc. If you have a book with many maps, give the number of maps in color and in b/w.

> John Rosenhoover
> 100 Mandalay Road
> Chicopee, MA 01020

★ **London, England, and European maps,** 1850 and 1900, especially *Ordnance Survey Map.* Also a pull down **wall map** showing America from that same period. "Yes, it's my real name"
>Rev. Sherlock Holmes
>Private Letter Box 3
>Worcester, MA 01613
>(508) 754-9907

★ **Maps of any Asian country:** Japan, China, Korea, Vietnam, Siam, Tonkin, Cambodia, Laos, Malaya, Singapore, Indonesia, Philippines, Burma, Formosa, Taiwan, Tibet, Mongolia, Manchuria, New Guinea, or anywhere else in Southeast Asia and the Far East. Maps before 1930 only, please. Photocopies are appreciated.
>Jerry Stanoff
>Rare Oriental Book Co.
>PO Box 1599
>Aptos, CA 95001
>(408) 689-0203   Fax: (408) 689-0204

When describing an atlas or book of maps, use Standard Bibliographic Information consisting of: Title, author, publisher, city where published, and date when published.

★ **Globes of the world,** especially globes made of glass (not plastic) covered with paper with interior lights that shine through, globes with black oceans, globes with revolving planets, etc. Anything unusual or before 1940 (map will show Palestine) considered. Send photo, including stand. Give height and circumference. Condition critical.
>Jay Novak, Modernica
>7366 Beverly Blvd.
>Los Angeles, CA 90036
>(213) 933-0383   Fax: (213) 683-1312

★ **Globes and models of the solar system** are wanted by this recent but large dealer in them. He especially wants 19th century globes, both desk and floor models, and points out that some globes made in pairs between 1500 and 1850 can be worth $100,000 or more. He does not want globes made after WWII (look for Israel). Give the maker, diameter, material it's made from, and condition.
>Jonathan Blackman, The Yellow Room
>511 North Robertson Blvd.
>Los Angeles, CA 90048
>(310) 274-3190

ROAD MAPS

☆ **Road maps** given away by gas stations, state highway departments, automobile clubs, and various tourist offices. Will consider all dates, but pre-1970 is preferred. Most maps are relatively low value, bringing $1 to $3 each if dated between 1930-1970, but a pile can add up, and some maps do bring more than those prices. Maps that are damaged, torn, moldy, or bug eaten are not wanted, although those with routes marked are "not a problem." He requests you send your maps on approval via 4th class book rate. Personal inspection is needed, since most maps are undated except for "secret codes" used by the printers.

> Charles Neuschafer
> New World Maps
> Apple Hill Road
> Bennington, VT 05201
> (802) 442-2846   Charlieneu@aol.com

★ **Road maps,** particularly from the 1920's and 30's. "I like city maps, state maps, and regional maps, foreign or domestic." Must be in good condition. Also will buy old official State Highway Department maps, the earlier the better. Noel says you may send your items for his immediate offer and a return check. Will buy large quantities, too.

> Noel Levy
> 1109 Silent Glade Road
> Owings Mills, MD 21117
> (410) 363-9040

AUTOGRAPHS

★ **Letters, signed photos and signatures of famous people** in any category: Presidents, Hollywood, NASA, sports, Civil War, art, music, literary, scientific, historical, rock and roll, theater, aviation, old West. Also interested in old handwritten diaries, collections of letters from the not-so-famous, handwritten recipe books, and anything written while traveling across America. Wants California and New Orleans letters from 1800-1870. Offers $1,000 for signed **Buddy Holly photo**. Please photocopy what you have. No autopen or printed signatures.

> Michael Reese II
> PO Box 5704
> South San Francisco, CA 94083
> (415) 641-5920

The signatures of politicians other than U.S. Presidents are worth little. Movie and TV stars since 1960 are also of little value, with a few exceptions such as Marilyn Monroe and James Dean. The same is true for musicians, with only a few bands and individuals having value.

The value of any autograph is highly influenced by the context. Handwritten letters are most desirable, especially when written concerning important events or personal thoughts of the famous.

Plain autographs on blank white cards are the least desirable but will still find some market, especially for important people.

★ **Autographs, signed books, and rare documents in all fields.** Particularly wants U.S. Presidents and first ladies and "investment quality items." Wants handwritten letters of Presidents while in office, particularly of William Henry Harrison and James A. Garfield, whose letters could be worth as much as $50,000! No facsimile or secretary signatures. "It is usually necessary to see the actual item, particularly in order to make a firm offer." Their monthly catalog is free. Larry and Mike are authors of *From the President's Pen: an illustrated Guide to Presidential Autographs,* available from them for $25.

> Michael Minor and Larry Vrzalik
> Lone Star Autographs
> PO Drawer 500
> Kaufman, TX 75142
> (214) 932-6050 from 10 to 10   Fax: (214) 932-7742

★ **Autographed letters and documents** from ancient times to modern day in all fields. Significant **medieval documents** and manuscripts are always of interest. This 28 year veteran dealer does not want autographs obtained by writing celebrities, modern politicians, or movie stars. A photocopy is strongly suggested.

> Kenneth Rendell
> PO Box 9001
> Wellesley, MA   02181
>   (617) 431-1776   Fax: (617) 237-1492

★ **Handwritten documents and letters of famous Americans.** "We particularly want Washington, Adams, Jefferson, Franklin, Hancock, and Lincoln, and specialize in U.S. Presidents." Famous scientists, inventors, authors and musicians are also sought. Note all imperfections.

> Steve and Linda Alsberg
> 9850 Kedvale Avenue
> Skokie, IL 60076
>   (847) 676-9850

★ **Historical documents signed by U.S. Presidents.** "I'll buy land grants, military and civil commissions, ship's papers, passports, appointments of judges, postmasters, ambassadors, etc. I search for clean documents with no holes, stains, tape or trims. Every mark, fade, crease or wrinkle *must* be described accurately."

> Richard Lechaux
> 658 South Fort Valley Road
> Fort Valley, VA   22652
>   (540) 933-6305

★ **Autographs in all fields** with a particular emphasis on Presidents and political, military, and historical figures. He does not want Hollywood or TV people after 1940. "The more information the better. Describe what it is written on, whether faded or bright, whether written in pen or pencil, and the wording of any inscription."

> Chris Wilson
> 8101 Revatom Court
> Dun Loring, VA 22027
>   (703) 698-7073

★ **Autographs and manuscripts of importance** by Presidents or important historical figures. Wants the old, rare, and valuable only.

> Ivan Gilbert
> Miran Arts & Books
> 2824 Elm Avenue
> Columbus, OH 43209
>   (614) 421-3222   Fax: (614) 421-3223

★ **American and foreign autographs in all fields throughout Western history,** including politicians, Presidents, signers of the Declaration of Independence, music and the arts, literature, the military, and scientists. Will buy one or collections. This 20+ year veteran is not interested in unsigned documents of any sort.

Robert Batchelder
1 West Butler Avenue
Ambler, PA 19002
(215) 643-1430   Fax: (215) 643-6613

★ **Checks autographed by any famous person** are wanted, especially bounced checks. He'll pay from $750-$3,500 for checks he especially wants from Henry Ford, Harry Houdini, Greta Garbo, Buddy Holly, President Taylor, Gerald Ford, Lyndon Johnson, Al Capone, Richard Nixon, Charles Chaplin, President Tyler, and others. He also buys pay orders, certificates of deposit, and other small size **financial documents**. Send a fax or photocopy. "I want to know the condition, the date, whether the check is signed or endorsed, and the color of the check. If the seller has a price in mind, please quote it up front. If the seller has no idea of value, then I will make him a fair quote."

Olan Chiles
1892 Avenida Aragon
Oceanside, CA 92056
(619) 724-2339   Fax: (619) 726-4964

★ **Famous people's signatures on manuscript documents, maps, photographs,** and other early paper. Has particular interest in Southern and Civil War figures and in letters signed by James McHenry, Washington's Secretary of War.

Gordon McHenry
PO Box 1117
Osprey, FL 33559
(941) 966-5563

★ **Historic early American autographed documents,** old sailing ship's papers, letters with historic content, bonds and stock certificates.

Earl Moore
PO Box 243
Wynnewood, PA 19096
(610) 649-1549

★ **Composers, musicians and singers of classical music.** Buys signed photos, letters, musical notations, etc. No free appraisals.

J.B. Muns, Books & Fine Art
1162 Shattuck Avenue
Berkeley, CA 94707
(510) 525-1126

★   **Composers, musicians, opera singers, and movie stars** from the late 1800's to the 1950's. Prefers to buy signed photos, letters with important content, or musical quotes. "We are not interested in the autographs of current performers, but will pay very well for first class older items. Condition is important. We request photocopies and prefer to see the item in person, especially when large collections are involved." Will make offers for amateurs. Dealers, price your goods.

   Bill Safka and Arbe Bareis
   PO Box 886
   Forest Hills, NY 11375
      (718) 263-2276   Fax: (718) 263-2276

★   **Autographs of Hollywood stars** and other famous people. "If they were famous enough for you to recognize, I probably want their autograph." Tom urges you to get a quote from him, and points out that lots of stories in the popular press about autographs and their values are not accurate. Prefers autographed 8" x 10" b/w photos. Does not buy severely damaged items. "Since autographs and photos are subjective, please send me a Xerox™ of what you have for sale." Tom publishes *Celebrity Address Book, 6th ed.*, and is interested in obtaining home addresses you might know. Tom prefers you to set the price wanted but will make offers. His autograph catalog costs $3, *Celebrity Address Book* is $25. SASE is essential if you want an answer. They charge a fee for appraisals and authentication of celebrity autographs.

   Thomas Burford
   Celebrity Access Publications
   20 Sunnyside Avenue #A241
   Mill Valley, CA 94941
      (415) 389-8133   103632.156@compuserve.com

★   **Autographs of celebrities and "newsworthy persons"** including photos, letters, checks, or other documents signed by mass murderers, assassins, spies, heads of state, royalty, rock stars, and other famous and infamous persons. Examples: Arafat, Jackie Kennedy, Madonna, Michael Jackson, David Berkowitz, John Hinkley, etc. Not interested in printed signatures or autopens. Photocopies are a must if you want an offer. "If I cannot tell from your copy whether the signature is authentic, it will be necessary to ship it for my inspection. Before I buy items, I expect the seller to sign a statement guaranteeing that they own the item in question and that there are no liens against it."

   Sheldon Kamerman
   World Wide Auctioneering Group
   466 11th Street #F
   Lakewood, NJ 08701
      (908) 363-6161 weekends

HOW TO SELL POSTCARDS

*Postcards are bought for the photograph, message, artist, stamp, and the postmark. Real photo cards (black and white real photos of people, places or events) are among the most sought. If you have a card that pictures any business, occupation or vehicle, the folks interested in those topics will pay more for the card than will a postcard dealer or collector. **Scenics picturing rivers, trees, mountains, lakes and the like, are seldom wanted, and worth only a dime or so.***

If you want to sell postcards, you have two choices: (1) Send them on approval or (2) send photocopies. Because most of my readers have postcards, and many buyers want them (all through the book), I'm giving you guidelines on how to identify the various types of cards, and how to evaluate their condition.

TYPES OF POSTCARDS

EARLY **"PIONEER ERA"** CARDS: Cards from the mid 1870's to 1900. Until 1893 cards had no pictures other than advertising. These cards are wanted for the postmark as much as for the card.

POSTCARDS: In 1901, "real photo" cards were introduced. A black and white or sepia photo is on one side of the card and the address on the reverse. Messages were not allowed on the address side, so pictures were often defaced by messages.

DIVIDED BACK CARDS: Cards used between 1907 and 1914 are called "divided back" cards because the message was written on the left and address on the right, thus preserving the picture. Real photo cards often have divided backs. Very collectible.

WHITE BORDER CARDS: From around 1915 to 1930, most postcards had a white border around the picture. Desirable, but less so.

LINEN CARDS: During the Depression and WWII (1930-45), postcards had a textured surface, like linen. Inks from this period were usually bright. The colored printed photographs were usually of poor quality with little detail. Much less valuable.

CHROME CARDS: Modern brightly colored, slick surface postcards made since WWII. Their colors are vivid, the details are sharp, and the cards are of little interest to collectors.

Postcard buyers are fussy about condition. Poor condition cards seldom have a buyer, and prices drop dramatically for anything less than "excellent" condition. That's why dealers and collectors want to see your cards before paying for them.

If you have a large quantity of cards, my advice is to ship them on approval after first contacting the potential *Trash or Treasure* buyer. Check whether the postcard buyer wants you to contact them first. Most do!

HOW TO DESCRIBE CONDITION

MINT: A perfect card, as it comes from the press. No marks, bends or creases. No writing or postmarks. Rarely seen.

NEAR MINT: Like mint but very light aging or very slight discoloration from being in an album for many years. Not as fresh looking as mint.

EXCELLENT: Card looks like mint with sharply pointed corners (no blunt or rounded corners). It may not have any bends or creases. May be used or unused, but writing and postmark are only on address side, with clean fresh picture side.

VERY GOOD: Corners may be just a bit blunt or rounded, or it might have an almost undetectable crease or bend that does not detract from overall appearance of picture side. May have writing only on the address side.

GOOD: Corners may be noticeably blunt or rounded with noticeable but slight bends or creases. May be postally used or have writing, but only on the address side.

AVERAGE: Creases and bends more pronounced. Corners more rounded. Or it may have writing in margins on picture side, or the postmark may show through from address side but not on main portion of picture.

POOR: Card is intact, but has excess soil, stains, or heavy creases. Or it is written on the picture side, or has a cancel that affects the picture. Salable only if a very rare and desirable card.

SPACE FILLER: Poor condition, perhaps with torn or missing corners or breaks in the picture surface. Cards in this condition are neither desirable nor valuable.

POSTCARDS

★ **Postcard collections, pre-1930,** especially American street views, disasters, railroad stations, fire departments, and diners. He also buys cards depicting foreign royalty, expositions, snowmen, full length Santas, and pre-jet commercial aircraft. Does not want foreign views, scenery, parks, woods, mountains, lakes, and flowers. Does not want damaged cards or those which have been pasted in albums. "If your cards are not for sale, or if my offer is not accepted, I will appraise your cards at a cost of only one postcard of my choice for each 100 cards I appraise." Cards must be shipped for inspection for purchase or appraisal. John runs auctions, postcard shows, and heads the Postcard History Society. He can supply you with many interesting free or low cost items regarding postcard collecting. For more information send a stamped return envelope for his "Postcard Opportunity" sheet. John is President of the International Federation of Postcard Dealers.

> John McClintock
> PO Box 1765
> Manassas, VA 20108
> (703) 368-2757 10am to 10 pm Eastern

☆ **Postcard albums and collections,** the older the better, in very good condition only. Interested in all topics, but does not want damaged cards. Joan conducts mail auctions and sells on approval. Wants to know the number of cards, condition, and types of subjects pictured. She's been a collector for nearly 50 years!

> Jo Ann Van Scotter
> 4730 NW 10 Court #318
> Plantation, FL 33313
> (954) 583-8228

☆ **Postcards, American and foreign,** all subjects, used or unused, if before 1950. "I'll pay competitive prices for better single cards or will buy collections, box lots, accumulations, etc."

> Sheldon Dobres
> 4 Calypso Court
> Baltimore, MD 21209
> (410) 486-6569   (800) 342-5983 days

Postcard buyers are among the fussiest customers you'll have when it comes to condition. They usually want to see what you have before sending money.

★ **Picture postcards** before 1950 are sought by this paper dealer, who does not buy chrome cards of any type or subject matter.

> Mike Rasmussen
> PO Box 726
> Marina, CA 93933
> (408) 759-0259   Fax: (408) 422-1529

★ **Postcards worldwide,** used or unused, before 1950, from any country, but especially from the U.S. and Canada. Wants street scenes, buildings, occupationals, sports, transportation, and people. Doesn't want water, forests, trees, mountains, deserts, etc. Also buys some pictorial "greetings." Pays 25¢ to $5 for most postcards, but a few European cards drawn or painted by famous illustrators can bring $100 up. No quantity too large. "Prompt payment if you send your cards on approval; unwanted cards are returned." Neil makes payment in the currency of the seller.

> Neil Hayne
> PO Box 220
> Bath, ON
> K0H 1G0 CANADA
> (613) 352-7456

★ **Canadian and English postcards** from before 1930, new or used. "I'm particularly interested in real photo views of small towns and interesting social history. I'll pay excellent prices for real photo cards of British Columbia or Yukon street scenes. I can not use damaged cards or boring mountain scenery. You may send cards on approval for my offer, and I'll pay the postage." Will pay in U.S. funds.

> Michael Rice
> PO Box 286
> Saanichton, BC
> V8M 2C5 CANADA
> (250) 652-9412 eves only. Please, no day calls.

★ **Canadian postcards** from Ontario, Saskatchewan, Alberta, and Newfoundland provinces. Want small town views, events, railroad stations, politics, buildings, and transportation. No scenics. Nothing after 1930. "A photocopy of the item is almost essential."

> Peter Cox
> 480 Boix Street
> Espanola, ON
> P5E 1A7 CANADA
> (705) 869-2441 winter   (705) 859-2410 summer

If you have postcards to sell and you didn't read the introduction to this section on postcards, turn to page 518 now. It's important.

POSTERS

★ **Posters of all types**. This 30 year veteran dealer says, "I'll pay top prices for any printed poster done before 1960, especially WWI and WWII, film, travel, theater, circus, and transportation (ocean liner, railroad, and air). Also buys poster books, periodicals, and photos of posters being printed or posted. Include your phone number.
> George Theofiles, Miscellaneous Man
> PO Box 1776
> New Freedom, PA 17349
> (717) 235-4766 days

★ **Posters of all types, 1880-1950**, all countries and subjects, especially U.S. posters from WWI and II and 1890-1910 American advertising. Army recruiting posters by Christy and Flagg from WWI bring $500 to $1,500. No reproduction posters are wanted.
> George Dembo, The Poster Master
> PO Box 657
> Chatham, NJ 07928
> (201) 701-0713   Fax: (201) 701-0713

★ **American posters of WWI.** No foreign, repros, or damaged items. Give the main slogan, the size, the artist if known, and the condition.
> Ken Khuans
> 155 Harbor #4812
> Chicago, IL 60601
> (312) 642-0554

★ **Rock and roll concert posters** from the 1960's. Must give the name of the bands, where they are performing, the date, and the price of admission. Send a photo.
> Bill and Linda Montgomery
> 12111 SE River Road
> Milwaukee, OR 97222
> (503) 652-2992

Rock concert posters will be of interest to Rock & Roll buyers as well as Pop Culture dealers. Some of these from San Francisco sell for many thousands of dollars. ❖

★ **Wild psychedelic black light fluorescent posters** (1960's - 70's), but only in perfect condition. Send photo along with your asking price.
> Judy Polk Harding
> 1701 60th Street
> Des Moines, IA 50322
> (515) 279-7099 voice and fax   THEFIVEJS@aol.com

HOW TO SELL PHOTOGRAPHS

Unidentified portraits typically have little value. But those same portraits will find buyers quickly if the sitters are in uniform or holding tools or weapons. Photos of officials, workers, events, outdoor city scenes, parades, stores, vehicles and uniforms will always find a buyer among collectors trying to learn more about an industry or era.

To sell a photo, Xerox© what you have. Condition of the photo and its mat are both important to a buyer. Note banged corners, stains, and the like. If the photo is faded, make certain you indicate that fact, as photocopies tend to make photos look better than they are.

TYPES OF PHOTOGRAPHS

DAGUERREOTYPES: 1839-1854, recognizable by a silvery image on glass. The leather and early plastic cases are often worth more than the photo. Outdoor and city views are rare. Large "Dags" can be valuable. Do not clean them and do not leave them exposed to sunlight.

AMBROTYPES: Photos on a glass negative backed with dark paper to make a positive image. Mid-19th century. Subject matter is the key to value. These often come in elaborate cases.

ALBUMEN PHOTOGRAPHS: Paper prints before 1890 usually used egg albumen in preparation of the image surface.

TINTYPES: Cheap popular portraits, 1858-1910, printed on sheets of black tin. Also called ferrotypes. Subject matter is the key to value. Pictures not taken in a studio are usually more valuable.

CARTES DE VISITE (CDV): Photos on card stock measuring 2.5" x 4" popular between 1860-1890, often found in albums.

CABINET CARDS: Photos on 4" x 7" cards, usually studio shots with the photographer's name at the bottom. These are found with pictures of celebrities, Presidents and generals.

STEREOVIEWS: Cards containing two shots of the same subject to give a 3-D effect seen through a viewer. Views before 1890 are larger, flat, have colored mounts (yellow, pink, etc.) and generally no printing on back. Later views have curved gray mounts (*Underwood* is common). Newest, and worthless, are colored printed stereoviews. Older views will often be curved, the result of being stored with newer cards.

SNAPSHOTS. Printed in b/w on thin paper, popular from 1920-1960, when color pictures and slides became the photo of choice.

PHOTOGRAPHS

★ **Photographs,** especially signed 19th and 20th century images, also tintypes, Daguerreotypes, ambrotypes, cartes de visite, cabinet photos, albumen prints, stereoviews, silver prints, platinum prints, cyanotypes, and photo albums. His list of "fine subjects" includes: banjo players, Russians, kids playing marbles, Brooklyn, photographers, auto racing, nudes, military, Civil War, funny photos, Lincoln, John Wilkes Booth, unusual photos, WWII, **mug shots**, writers, artists, Philadelphia, famous people, Hawaii and Samoa in the 19th century, Indians, mining, Orientals, sports, aviation, people at work and pre-1915 images. No ordinary studio portraits, and no photo equipment is wanted. Photocopy both sides of your photo and price what you have for sale.

>Richard Rosenthal
>4718 Springfield Avenue
>Philadelphia, PA 19143
>(215) 726-5493   Fax: (215) 726-5926

★ **Rare old photographs,** cased photos, stereoviews, etc., especially work by important Western photographers such as Jackson, Curtis, and others. Also buys books with actual photos tipped (pasted) in. Buys **modern computer generated art photos** also. Send Xerox™ copy.

>Ivan Gilbert
>Miran Arts & Books
>2824 Elm Avenue
>Columbus, OH 43209
>(614) 421-3222   Fax: (614) 421-3223

If you have photographs of events, businesses, industry, or sports, you might find it profitable to deal with specialists in those subjects as they are often your best buyers. It could put more $$$ in your pocket to read the chapter dealing with the subject matter of your photo.

★ **Photographs,** especially Daguerreotypes, ambrotypes, tintypes, stereoviews, and round *Kodak* snapshots. Would love to find photos of photographers at work, photos containing microscopes, photos related to speech and hearing and photos of Pittsburgh and Allegheny County, Pennsylvania. Buys complete unpicked photo albums.

>Nicholas Graver
>276 Brooklawn Drive
>Rochester, NY 14618
>(716) 244-4818

★ **Interesting photographs of all types** including Daguerreotypes, ambrotypes, tintypes, cabinet cards, CDV's, albumen prints, real photo postcards and stereoviews. Indicates a willingness to pay high prices for a wide range of photos including the following categories:
- **Civil War soldiers** and scenes;
- **Presidents** and famous 19th century persons, especially Lincoln;
- Street or riverfront scenes;
- **Cowboys** and **Indians**;
- **Sports**, **circuses**, and other amusements;
- **Crime scene** photographs;
- **Photographers** in the studio or in the field;
- **Artists** and **sculptors**;
- **Nudes**, both artistic and erotic;
- **Portraits of ordinary people** in CDV or Daguerreotype form that are very sharp and in fine condition;
- **Travel albums** with mounted albumen photos (America, Egypt, and the Far East are preferred), but not albums of black construction paper with mounted snapshots unless the subject matter is extraordinary;
- Extraordinary portraiture, s**trange people**, people in costume, side show performers and early soft focus art photography'
- **Children or adults posed with unusual objects**;
- **Bizarre** and **unusual** subject matter including **death portraits**;
- **Political or other public events**.

Has special interest in the Civil War, **Lincoln** and fine Daguerreotypes. All photos must be undamaged and not faded. Do not ask about printed or halftone reproductions. Make a Xerox™ copy of your photo for this relatively new collector/dealer who pledges prompt answers and competitive prices.

    Tom Harris
    223 East 4th Street #14
    New York, NY 10009
        (212) 420-9121

★ **Daguerreotypes, ambrotypes and tintypes** of children, families, animals, architecture, Indians, Civil War, military, or anything out of the ordinary. "I will buy complete **family albums** with photos from the 1800's, but DON'T WANt loose individual ordinary portraits, unless the person sitting for the photo is identified." Indicate any inscriptions or markings as well as any damage. Dealers must price their goods. Amateur sellers may ask for help. "Please, I do not want any empty albums or photos taken after 1900."

    Ed Clark
    Texas Photo Center
    215 W. Camp Wisdom #6
    Duncanville, TX 75116
  (972) 780-5735 Fax: (972) 780-0937 camera35@aol.com

★ **Stereoview cards** "in nearly all categories" are sought. He points out that there are two types of stereo cards, printed and photographic, and that he wants only photographic views of:
- **Famous people**;
- **Ships, sailboats, riverboats**, wharfs, etc.;
- **Railroads**, street cars, cable cars, etc.;
- **Airplanes**, blimps, balloons, etc.;
- **Automobiles**, fire engines, bicycles and other vehicles;
- Military, especially the **Civil War**;
- Western lore, **cowboys**, **Indians**, mining, etc.;
- **Music, bands, theatrical scenes**, etc.;
- **Street scenes** from any city or town;
- **Occupationals** - people at work, especially photographers.

"I want any cards that capture a bygone era, people at leisure, at home, children playing, costumes, furniture, and the like. In addition to U.S. views, I will buy fine condition photos of Canada and Europe. Please describe your cards briefly, telling the subject matter and condition."

Steve Jabloner
7380 Adrian Drive #23
Rohnert Park, CA 94928
    (707) 795-3081   jabloner@marin.cc.ca.us

★ **Stereoview cards,** particularly older Western scenes, transportation, mining, **Mt. Lowe**, fires, **high wheel bicycles**, famous people, **Civil War**, and early **California**. "But I buy most common stereos, too," but for a lot less. He particularly wants **stereos of Lincoln** published while Lincoln was alive. If you want to sell your cards, Chuck wants to know the subject of the card quite specifically, an accurate description of condition, and the publisher. If you have a price you want, say so. He does not want cards *printed* in color or in black and white.

Chuck Reincke
2141 Sweet Briar Road
Tustin, CA 92780
    (714) 832-8563 eves   Fax: (714) 832-8563

★ **Stereoviews, U.S. and foreign,** that are real photos pasted on cards, not printed in color. Especially wants the odd and unusual, old West, occupations, photographers and their equipment, Indians, Civil War, nudes, ships, railroads, whaling, stores, factories, street vendors, circus, and many more topics. Send an SASE for his informative handout and wants list which gives much greater detail. **Scenery** is of interest only from Western states or exotic foreign countries. All views must be in fine condition to be considered for purchase. Send a Xerox™ of both sides of the card if writing is on the back.

Russell Norton
PO Box 1070
New Haven, CT 06504
    (203) 562-7800

★ **Bizarre photos,** such as freaks, dwarfs, lynchings, slaves, public punishment, and what have you. Especially interested in photos of **death, especially post-mortem photos, but also mourning photos, executions, lynchings, and embalming and medical photos with doctors and cadavers.** Likes photos of the family gathered around the deceased. Worth from $10 to $100+ for the very early and unusual.

> Steve DeGenaro
> PO Box 5662
> Youngstown, OH 44504
> (330) 757-7735

★ **Stereoviews showing the development of the early West, 1860-1900:** expeditions, **railroad construction**, freighting in the Sierras, maritime scenes, **Indian portraits** and culture, **mining, logging**, and **early small town scenes** as well as **San Francisco.** Particular interest in Custer, Teddy Roosevelt, Mark Twain, Bret Harte, John Sutter, artist Albert Bierstadt, and all early **photographers and their equipment**. The latter will bring "hundreds of dollars" in excellent condition. Also wants paper advertising from early western photographers. Not interested in faded views or those with damaged mounts. No lithographed views, only real photos in excellent condition.

> Jim Crain
> 131 Bennington Street
> San Francisco, CA 94110
> (415) 648-1092 eves

★ **Daguerreotypes** of famous people, Negroes, outdoor scenes, military, freaks, animals, people working or with tools, nudes, ships, fire engines, railroads, old West, balloons and disasters. premium for very large ones. Describe the picture, give the dimensions and describe the case and its condition.

> Russell Norton
> PO Box 1070
> New Haven, CT 06504
> (203) 562-7800 11 a.m. to 8 p.m. any day

★ **Original photos of Lincoln.** "I'll buy photos of Lincoln taken from life and printed before 1866. Will also purchase the Ayers photos of Lincoln printed in the 1880's and 1890's. I'll also buy photos of Lincoln look-alikes." No photos of prints, statues, or Abe's house. Send a photocopy of what you have. "Serious sellers only, please."

> Stuart Schneider
> PO Box 64
> Teaneck, NJ 07666
> (201) 261-1983   Fax: (201) 568-3618

★ **Photos of cowboys, Indians,** and related subjects, including cattle drives, early Texas towns, outlaws, lawmen, the Geronimo expedition (especially those taken by C.S. Fly), and the Mexican War. All types wanted, including stereo. Please send photocopies.

> Johnny Spellman
> 10806 North Lamar
> Austin, TX 78753
> (512) 258-6910 eves   (512) 836-2889 days

★ **Photos of old Western personalities**, Wild West Show characters, armed cowboys and cowgirls, trappers and scouts dressed in buckskin, famous lawmen, armed Indian braves, and death views of outlaws. This 25 year veteran pays from $200 to $2,500 depending on the subject and type of photo. Excellent condition items before 1920 only. He does not want postcards, Indian women, children, cattle drives, or general Western views. Must send a clear Xerox™ of what you have. Dealers, price your goods. Amateurs may request an offer.

> Emory Cantey, Jr.
> Our Turn Antiques
> 1405 Ems Road East
> Fort Worth, TX 76116
> (817) 737-0430 voice and fax

★ **Photos of famous people, outdoor scenes and "the odd and the unusual"** taken before 1910/ Will buy Daguerreotypes, ambrotypes, tintypes and cartes de visite in fine condition. Send a photocopy.

> Chris Wilson
> 8101 Revatom Court
> Dunn Loring, VA 22027
> (703) 698-7073

★ **Photographs and engravings of famous people** in all walks of life. Will consider items loose or in books. Please photocopy.

> Kenneth Rendell
> PO Box 9001
> Wellesley, MA 02181
> (617) 431-1776   Fax: (617) 237-1492

★ **Photos of Indians and Eskimos,** especially the work of Edward S. Curtis. Also buys real photo postcards on the same theme. Please send photocopies for a prompt response. Dealers, price your goods, but amateur sellers may request an offer.

> Barry Friedman
> PO Box 55492
> Valencia, CA 91385
> (805) 255-2365   BarryF@fishnet.net

★ **Photographs of people with guns.** Has a particular interest in Civil War and Western scenes but wants hunters, soldiers, sailors, Indians, and cowboys. All types of early images are considered, including cdv's, cabinet cards, tintypes, Daguerreotypes, etc. Send a photocopy of any image you want to sell, except those on Daguerreotypes, the cased photos with a mirror finish. SASE please. "I do not make offers."

    Charles Worman
    PO Box 33584 (AMC)
    Dayton, OH 45433
       (513) 760-1873

★ **Photos in memorial matts** (ordinary portraits mounted in memorial matts after the person died). Memorial matts have printed or embossed angels, doves, Gates of Heaven, etc., and mottoes like "Free at Last."

    Steve DeGenaro
    PO Box 5662
    Youngstown, OH 44504
       (330) 757-7735

★ **Photos of the Dakotas, Minnesota, Wyoming, and Montana** from before 1930 in any format, including real photo postcards, especially those marked DT, DAKOTA TERRITORY, DAK or SOUTH DAKOTA. Buys single items or collections. Is often as interested in the photographers as the subject matter of the photo. Photocopies are recommended. If your items are in fine condition, you may ship them on approval.

    Robert Kolbe
    1301 South Duluth
    Sioux Falls, SD 57105
       (605) 332-9662

Watch for revenue stamps on the back of Civil War era cartes de visite and other photos. Most are common, but a few are quite valuable. Buyers of revenue stamps may be found on page 433.

HOW TO SELL CAMERAS

You may find it hard to recognize the earliest Daguerreotype cameras because they look like wooden boxes without a lens. They are quite valuable. So are hidden ("detective") cameras, popular in the late 1800's. Multi-lens cameras, panorama cameras, and other early oddities will also sell quickly.

If you want to sell a camera, provide the following information in your first letter:

(1) Brand name, and model name if you know it;
(2) All numbers on the body of the camera;
(3) The name of the brand of lens, and any numbers and other information printed around the front circumference of the lens;
(4) Whether or not the camera works;
(5) Whether or not the camera seems to be complete;
(6) Whether the case and camera are covered with wood, metal, leather or cloth...and its condition;
(7) Whether or not the camera has a folding cloth or leather bellows; if it does, the bellows' color;
(8) A list of accessories with the camera, such as lenses, boxes, instructions, etc.

Kodak cameras with built in flash are not collectible, but many brand-name German and Japanese 35mm cameras from the 1930's, 40's and 50's are. A few of them bring prices above $1,000. They are well worth your time.

Don't try to clean your camera or the lens. *You're not helping...and you may cost yourself money. If there is old film in the camera, do not remove it. Whenever selling any equipment or mechanical devices, the less you do, the better off you are.*

CAMERAS

★ **Cameras.** "I'll buy complete camera collections or camera shops."
Has a special interest in:
- **35mm rangefinder cameras** by *Leica, Nixon* and *Canon;*
- **1940's-50's SLR cameras** by *Nikon, Zeiss, Konica* and others;
- **16mm movie cameras** by *Angenieux, Arriflex, Beaulieu, Bolex*
    and *Mitchell* only (no 8mm cameras are wanted);
- *Polaroid* models 180, 190, and 195 ONLY;
- **3-D** cameras and all accessories and advertising;
- **Subminiature cameras**.

Harry offers free appraisals of these, but does not want to hear about
your Brownies, built-in flash cameras, plastic cameras, black box cameras, folding cameras with black bellows, or 16mm home movie cameras and projectors, please. These have no value to collectors.

  Harry Poster
  PO Box 1883
  South Hackensack, NJ 07606
(201) 794-9606 Fax: (201) 794-9553 hposter@WORLDNET.ATT.NET

★ **Unusual and early cameras** including panoramic cameras, wide
angles, subminiatures, hidden cameras, and oddly shaped or novelty
cameras such as those shaped like cartoon or advertising characters.
When writing, include all names and numbers found on the lens. If the
camera is unusual, make certain to take a picture of it or make a good
sketch. Jim is author of *Collectors Guide to Kodak Cameras* and *Price
Guide to Antique and Classic Cameras.* SASE required.

  Jim McKeown
  Centennial Photo
  11595 State Road 70
  Grantsburg, WI 54840
   (715) 689-2153

★ **Cameras of brass, chrome, or wood** made before 1948. Anything
interesting photographic, be it camera, book, or what have you, will be
considered, including pre-1930 **photo magazines**, pre-1948 catalogs,
and other ephemera. *No Polaroids.* Provide any numbers or names
anywhere on the object. Describe condition of wood, leather, or metal.
Must include an SASE. Free evaluation if you include an SASE.

  Alan Voorhees
  Cameras & Such
  450 Breesport Road
  Horseheads, NY 14845
(607) 739-7898 Fax: (607) 733-8550 VoorheesBS@aol.com

★ *Kodak* **cameras, advertising, and memorabilia.** "I'll buy only pre-1930 cameras in near mint condition, especially those with original cardboard or wooden cartons. I'll also buy just the empty cartons!" Frank's list of cameras he seeks is too long to print here, but if you deal in cameras or if you have an old *Kodak*, it might be worth picking up his wants list. He also wants a *Kodiopticon* **slide projector**, and cameras made by companies absorbed by *Kodak* including *Poco, Columbus, Ludigraph, Kameret* and **Rochester Optical's** *Empire State View* camera. *Kodak* newspaper and magazine advertising before 1930 may also find a buyer, as will counter top advertising, posters, signs, wood framed pictures of people using *Kodaks*, and any of the hundreds of items with the *Kodak* logo. "If it says *'Kodak'* on it, I want to know about it. That includes books which use *Kodak* as part of the title, advertising in foreign languages, instruction books, stock certificates from any camera company, *Kodak* annual reports, and anything else that is old, in fine condition and related to *Kodak*."

Frank Storey
194 School Lane
Linthicum, MD 21090
     (410) 850-5728 eves   KKSFTS.aol.com

★ **Cameras** are wanted, but only the rare, unusual, or very early (pre-1880), especially stereo, multiple lens, and panoramic. Cameras hidden inside other objects are of great interest, as are the very small cameras called subminiatures. Not interested in *Kodak, Ansco,* or *Polaroid.* Give make, model, and names and numbers printed around the lens.

Russell Norton
PO Box 1070
New Haven, CT 06504
     (203) 562-7800

Most Kodak *and* Polaroid *still cameras have little if any value, although commemorative, colored, and very early* Kodak *cameras are worth inquiry. 16mm home movie cameras and projectors have little value.*

  **Whenever selling any equipment
or mechanical devices,
the less you clean, repair or adjust
the better off you are.**

VIEW-MASTER & 3-D EQUIPMENT

★ *View-Master* **reels and equipment** made by *Sawyers* or *GAF*, the companies that owned *View-Master* before 1980. Will buy single reels, 3-pack reels, cameras and accessories, *Stereomatic 500* projectors, and the blue Model B viewer (worth $100 to him). Also buys some *Tru-Vue* and other 3-D items. Pays from 25¢ to $50 per reel, with top money going to 3-D movie preview reels and reels of commercial advertising for popular products. The more obscure 3-reel packets (such as those for *The Munsters* or *The Addams Family*) can bring good money. Does not want any cartoon reels or any damaged, broken, or worn items. Give numbers on the reels and state their condition. If you have anything from View-Master that was intended for in-house or factory use and not for the public, make certain you inquire as it might be valuable.

> Walter Sigg
> PO Box 208
> Swartswood, NJ 07877

★ **3-D cameras, reels, and other** *View-Master* **equipment,** including flash, close up lenses, cases, film cutters, 3-D projectors, library boxes, adjustable viewers, and old order lists from *Sawyers* or *GAF*, the manufacturers of *View-Master*. Wants early views with blue backs, view reels that look like they're hand printed, Belgian made scenic views, pre-1970 U.S., and scenics of other continents. "I don't want children's cartoon reels made after 1950 or any scratched or damaged reels." The reel number and copyright date are more important info than the title.

> Robert Gill
> PO Box 485
> Allendale, NJ 07401
>   (201) 934-7754   Fax: (201) 934-7754

★ *View-Master* **and 3-D (two lens) cameras and accessories** including viewers, projectors (2 lens), manuals, and books. Brands include *Airequipt, Realist, Kodak, Wollensak* and other makers. Stereo cameras are worth $200 to $2,000, and many viewers are $100 each, especially the focussing viewer and stereo projector. "I'll pay 20¢ to $20 for most *View-Master* reels and packets, and some are worth more."

> Harry Poster
> PO Box 1883
> South Hackensack, NJ 07606
(201) 794-9606   Fax: (201) 794-9553   hposter@WORLDNET.ATT.NET

DON'T THROW AWAY OLD SOUVENIRS!

Collectors of "places" want a wide range of items. Many of the buyers in the next 16 pages are historians of their region and focus on photos and old documents, while others are just having fun collecting colorful doodads.

Value will be determined by the content of the photos and documents, along with age, scarcity and desirability. The value of photos and documents generally ranges from $5 to $50. Particularly rare and important photos will bring more, sometimes in the many thousands of dollars. Few photos fall in this category.

Some collectors seek products made in or traditionally associated with the region of the country in which they live. Great Lakes shipping, Western mining, Florida citrus, and the like. A few collectors want it all, including art native to their area, guidebooks, minor paper ephemera, stocks, photos and trinkets.

I have arranged buyers into geographic regions of the country in an effort to make it easier for you to find them.

HIGHWAY SOUVENIRS

★ **Souvenirs from diners and drive-in theaters on the Lincoln Highway** and other items related to that road. Looks for ashtrays, calendars, guidebooks, lapel pins, maps, matchbooks, postcards, menus, and toys like miniature drive-ins. The Lincoln Highway was known as Route 30 to Wyoming and Route 40 or 50 from there to San Francisco.
>
> Brian Butke
> 2640 Sunset Drive
> West Mifflin, PA 15122

★ **Pennsylvania Turnpike, National Road (US 40), Lincoln Highway (US 30) and The Mother Road (US 66) memorabilia** of all kinds including maps before 1950 for my personal collection. What have you? Please photocopy or send a photo with your description.
>
> J.C. Keyser
> PO Box 937
> Powell, OH 43065
>   Fax: (614) 436-4760 after 5 Eastern

★ **Trailer park memorabilia.** "If it moved down a highway and you could live in it, we're interested" including auto campers, mobile homes, motor homes, VW campers, and specialty vehicles designed for various professions. Everything about the vehicles, the gear and the parks they stayed in, 1900 to 1970, is wanted: magazines, brochures, photos, film footage, personal reminiscences, stories, models, toys, salesmen's samples, matchbook covers, sheet music, postcards, articles, advertisements, signs, ID plates, license plates and hubcaps. Please send a photo or Xerox™ of what you have. Todd & Kristin operate *Lost Highways*, a club, archive, and magazine filled with photos, reminisces, ads, etc. from the heyday of trailering and motor camping. Sample issue $6. Compete information for a long SASE.

> Todd & Kristin Kimmell
> Box 43737
> Philadelphia, PA 19106
> (215) 925-2568

NORTHEASTERN EPHEMERA

★ **Wooden Adirondack souvenirs.** "I'll buy the weird and the wonderful! I'm seeking items made in the Adirondacks and sold all over America, usually stamped with the name of the place where they were sold." The distinguishing feature of these rustic wood souvenirs is the maker always left some bark on the piece. He wants **lamps, mugs, tankards, picture frames, smoker's stands, clocks, plaques, inkwells, towel racks, wishing wells,** and just about anything else except nut bowls and salt and pepper shakers. Many of these items had decals of Indians on them and better pieces had carvings of big game animals like moose or bears. He will also buy **miniature canoes and canoe paddles** and other birch bark items of all types. All items must be completely undamaged. Price and describe fully in your first letter.

> Barry Friedman
> PO Box 55492
> Valencia, CA 91355
> (805) 255-2365   BarryF@fishnet.net

★ **Great Barrington, Massachusetts, and Berkshire County souvenirs** including pictorial china, spoons, cups, postcards, photos and especially souvenir china from the years 1900-1930. Towns to look for are Housatonic, Van Deusenville, Risingdale, Egremont, North Egremont, Stockbridge and Sheffield.

> Gary Leveille
> PO Box 562
> Great Barrington, MA 01230

★ **Ocean Grove, New Jersey, memorabilia** including souvenirs, maps, photos, postcards, books, glass, porcelain, and anything else from this camp meeting seaside resort located south of Asbury Park. "I want everything, including beach, hotels, auditorium, etc."

> Norman B. Buckman
> PO Box 608
> Ocean Grove, NJ 07756
> (800) 533-6163

★ **Hoboken, New Jersey memorabilia** including paper, books, photographs, postcard, prints, maps, articles, letterheads, labels, and any manufactured item with the word HOBOKEN molded or printed on it. "We buy almost everything, no matter how trivial, including **personal reminiscences of early Hoboken residents** for inclusion in various local histories we are writing." You have the Hans's permission to ship any early Hoboken item on approval. They pay postage both ways.

> Jim and Beverly Hans
> PO Box M-1220
> Hoboken, NJ 07030
> (201) 653-7392

★ **Souvenir china** from many New York State cities and towns is sought, especially Rochester, LeRoy, Batavia and Thousand Islands. "I also buy quality pieces from Florida, California, New Mexico and all New England states." He seeks creamers, vases, toothpick holders and other forms with scenes from the cities and towns depicted in multicolors. This pre WWI German china is particularly desirable in cobalt blue. Nothing chipped or cracked, please.

> Burton Spiller
> 49 Palmerston Road
> Rochester, NY 14618
> (716) 244-2229

★ **Coney Island souvenirs** including Dreamland, Luna Park, and Steeplechase. He particularly wants pitchers, glasses, dishes, and other cream colored diamond and peg pattern custard glass marked CONEY ISLAND. SASE appreciated.

> John Belinsky
> 84 Day Street
> Seymour, CT 06483
> (203) 888-2225

SOUTHERN EPHEMERA

★ **Tennessee small town souvenirs.** Buys a wide range of items including bottles, stoneware jugs of all sizes, real photo postcards of street scenes, merchant tokens, phone books, business letterheads (especially general merchandise stores), small size flour sacks, calendar plates, manufacturers' catalogs, miscellaneous souvenirs marked *Wheelock* or *JonRoth, Germany* on the reverse. No *Coca-Cola* bottles or current *Jack Daniels* reproductions, please. A typical complete description will be enough: size, material, colors, marks, and condition. Make certain to mention any cracks or chips, no matter how small.

> Paul Jarrett
> 611 West Main
> Waverly, TN 37185
> (615) 296-3151

★ **Tennessee ephemera** wanted, including trade tokens, medals, pins, badges, real photo postcards of small towns, city business directories and phone books printed before 1950, Civil War tokens, city and county histories, and items from **the Tennessee Centennial Expo of 1897.** This major token collector asks that you describe your item well, including its condition. He is not interested in modern reproductions.

> Joe Copeland
> PO Box 4221
> Oak Ridge, TN 37831
> (423) 482-4215

★ **Dawson Springs, Kentucky souvenirs from their Mineral Well Springs** including jugs, mugs, pottery, glass, pitchers, and plates. These souvenirs usually have a decal showing a hotel or the Mineral Well. "I will pay $150 for a wire handled white crockery jug which says SALOON on it." He is not interested in anything made after 1930, including reproductions made by *Jack Daniels*. Make certain to mention any cracks or chips, no matter how small.

> Paul Jarrett
> 611 West Main
> Waverly, TN 37185
> • (615) 296-3151

★ **Southern souvenir china, glass or silver spoons** from before 1920 with pictures of old buildings, streets, resorts or celebrations. Photo or description, the trademark, and exact condition required. SASE a must.

> Abbie Bush
> Elkader, IA 52043-0503
> (319) 245-2128

★ **Panoramic group photos** taken in North or South Carolina.
>   Lew Powell
>   700 East Park Avenue
>   Charlotte, NC 28203
>   (704) 358-5229

★ **Charleston, Georgetown and Kingstree South Carolina items**
such as letters and envelopes, maps, tokens, medals, souvenir spoons,
books, pamphlets, postcards, stock certificates and other fiscal paper.
Also any South Carolina item related to the Confederacy, the SC Interstate, and the West Indian Expo of 1901-02.
>   Bob Karrer
>   17 Wentworth Street
>   Charleston, SC 29401

★ **Great Smoky Mountains National Park** in NC and TN, before
1970. "I'll buy guidebooks, maps, photos, brochures, pamphlets, and
similar paper ephemera including b/w real photo cards. Also souvenirs,
especially plates and glassware associated with the Park. Also interested in similar items for the towns of **Gatlinburg and Townsend, TN,
and the Cherokee Indian Reservation, in NC.** Not interested in any
color postcards or in any materials from Chattanooga or Lookout
Mountain," Photocopies appreciated.
>   Doug Redding
>   16532 Baederwood Lane
>   Rockville, MD 20855

★ **Georgia, South Carolina, and Florida paper pre-1870** that is
related to **slavery, the Civil War**, indentures, King's grants, state
grants, wills, or historically interesting topics. Georgia is of particular
interest and documents can bring $100-$500 depending upon contents.
>   John Parks
>   203 Tanglewood Road
>   Savannah, GA 31419
>   (912) 925-6075

★ **Eureka Springs, Arkansas souvenirs and paper ephemera.**
Wants informative or colorful paper, plates, cups, spoons, etc., from
this resort capitol of the Ozarks. Only pre-1930 items in fine condition.
>   Sheryl Baker
>   Bank of Eureka Springs
>   PO Box 309
>   Eureka Springs, AR 72632
>   (501) 253-8241

★ **Eureka Springs, Arkansas, before 1920.** "Anything wanted from souvenirs to advertising, photographs to books, but I'll especially buy any information, maps, lawsuits, newspaper reports, etc., on the early land disputes in Eureka Springs. Also the Eureka Springs railroad. Also have strong interest in **Dr. Norman Baker's Cancer Hospital** in the Springs in the 1930's and will buy all ephemera related to it."

> Steve Chyrchel
> 25 Kansas
> Eureka Springs, AR 72632
> (501) 253-9150 voice and fax

★ **Florida historical paper and memorabilia,** especially items from Fort Jefferson, Florida.

> Gordon McHenry
> PO Box 1117
> Osprey, FL 34229
> (941) 966-5563 Fax: (941) 966-5563

★ **Florida items.** Wants to buy **everything** relevant to history of Florida, but only items made before 1930. including: **maps**, postcards, stereoviews, souvenir china and spoons, paintings and prints, books, pamphlets, RR China, transportation schedules, license plates, stampless postal covers, etc. Please send this 30 year veteran researcher a "detailed description including condition." Note that most souvenir china brings from $15 to $35, the same price as real photo post cards.

> Douglas Hendriksen
> PO Box 21153
> Kennedy Space Center, FL 32815
> (407) 867-2551 days (407) 452-0633 eves

★ **Orlando, Florida, memorabilia.**

> Jerry Chicone
> PO Box 547636
> Orlando, FL 32854
> (407) 298-5550 Fax: (407) 290-2717

★ **Coral Gables, Florida, souvenirs and advertising,** especially items related to land sales in that area.

> Sam LaRoue
> 5980 SW 35th Street
> Miami, FL 33155
> (305) 237-7478 Fax: (305) 237-7534 SAM@mdcc.edu

MIDWESTERN EPHEMERA

★ **Ohio memorabilia,** especially books, manuscripts, maps and photographs, from before 1900. Particularly interested in local history prior to the Civil War, especially in the Akron area.
  Frank Klein, The Bookseller
  174 West Exchange Street
  Akron, OH 44302
    (330) 762-3101   Fax: (330) 762-4413

★ **Wisconsin small town main street postcards.** "I have two lists. One has about 1,200 towns I have. The other has about 1,800 towns I don't have. I'm glad to send one or both to anyone who is interested and sends a long SASE."
  Leo Smith
  1831 Folsom Street
  Eau Claire, WI 54703
    (715) 832-6188

★ **Waukesha, Wisconsin memorabilia.** Waukesha was noted for its spring waters and a number of food products, so keep your eyes open for all sorts of things marked as being from Waukesha.
  W.E. Schwanz
  S. 45 W22339 Quinn Road
  Waukesha, WI 53186
    (414) 542-8586   (414) 333-9127

★ **Michigan and the Great Lakes** ephemera and historically interesting paper goods of all types from that region.
  Jay Platt, West Side Book Shop
  113 West Liberty
  Ann Arbor, MI 48104
    (313) 995-1891

★ **Midwestern souvenir china** from before 1920, especially from Iowa. "All good items from all Iowa towns, especially Colfax, Clayton and Elkader are sought." Send a long SASE for her wants list.
  Abbie Bush
  Elkader, IA 52043
    (319) 245-2128

★ **Iowa souvenirs.** "Always interested in all Iowa souvenirs, especially china. Towns of Colfax, Ackley and Sibley are particularly wanted, but all nice Iowa pieces will be considered."
  Mary Yohe
  6827 South Juniper
  Tempe, AZ 85283
    (602) 820-7442

★ **Humboldt or Rutland, Iowa,** pictorial postcards and advertising from those two towns.

> Don Olson
> PO Box 245
> Humboldt, IA 50548

★ **Iowa trade tokens and dog licenses.**

> Dennis Schulte
> 8th Avenue NW
> Waukon, IA 52172
>   (319) 568-3628 before 10 p.m.

★ **Rockford, Freeport, and Belvidere Illinois tokens, medals,** buttons, badges, ribbons, and other small flat collectibles. Also banks, early signs, coffee tins, bottles, etc. Loves to find larger items marked as being from Rockford. No paper or cardboard items.

> Rich Hartzog
> PO Box 4143 BVT
> Rockford, IL 61110
>   (815) 226-0771

★ **Dakota Territory, South Dakota, North Dakota, Minnesota, Wyoming, and Montana photographs and small ephemera** from before 1930 in any format, including real photo postcards. Wants all historically or pictorially interesting paper ephemera, advertising, letters, books, bottles, and small objects. Especially wants items marked DT, DAKOTA TERRITORY, DAK or SOUTH DAKOTA. Buys single items or collections. Is often as interested in the photographers as the subject matter of the photo. Photocopies are recommended. If your items are in fine condition, you may ship them on approval.

> Robert Kolbe
> 1301 South Duluth
> Sioux Falls, SD 57105
>   (605) 332-9662

When writing about these generally inexpensive items, include an envelope addressed to yourself with the appropriate postage. If you are sending pictures and it takes two stamps, it will take two stamps to return them. Always indicate whether you want pictures returned.

I called these "generally inexpensive," but there are valuable photos, catalogs, bottles, and china out there...items worth more than $100 each. That's why I always advise getting advice from people you find in **Trash or Treasure.**

WESTERN EPHEMERA

★ **Western U.S. paper ephemera** (1840-1920) related to the military, early forts, ghost towns, Mormons, railroads, mining, banking, cowboys, Indians, lawmen, cattle, courts, and financial matters. Buys letters about the West, autographs of famous Westerners, and most illustrated pre-1920 Western documents such as checks, stocks, and the like. Subscription to his 6 annual sales catalogs is $15.
> Warren Anderson
> America West Archives
> PO Box 100
> Cedar City, UT 84720
> > (801) 586-9497

★ **Western and Midwestern U.S. paper ephemera** from pre 1910, including photos, pamphlets, view books, travel and tourism documents and promotional materials. Does not want Calif, Oregon or Washington. No postcards, please.
> Ron Pearson
> 10620 Creekmere Drive
> Dallas, TX 75218
> > (214) 321-9717

★ **Dallas and Ft. Worth ephemera** pre-1910, including photographs, pamphlets, documents, and promotional materials. Also wants **Texas State Fair.** No postcards, please.
> Ron Pearson
> 10620 Creekmere Drive
> Dallas, TX 75218
> > (214) 321-9717

★ **Colorado mining memorabilia,** 1859-1915, especially Cripple Creek and all other mining towns and camps and the railroads that served them. Wants photos, stereoviews, advertising, letterheads, billheads, brochures, pamphlets, mining papers, stock certificates, maps, badges, candlesticks, souvenirs, and other small items marked with the name of one of these towns. Photos should be of mining, railroad, or downtown activities, not people or scenery. Albums with numerous photos eagerly sought, as are business or mining directories and books on Colorado mining. Does not want *anything* from the flatland Colorado towns like Denver, Pueblo or Colorado Springs, nor anything from state or national parks. Give whatever info is printed or written on the backs of photos.
> George Foott
> 6683 South Yukon Way
> Littleton, CO 80123
> > (303) 979-8688

★ **Maps of Texas** from before 1900. Also trail driving maps.
Johnny Spellman
10806 North Lamar
Austin, TX 78753
    (512) 836-2889 days   (512) 258-6910 eves

★ **Colorado and Wyoming memorabilia** from 1860 to 1930. Wants
real photo and advertising postcards, souvenirs, "good for" trade tokens, stereoviews, envelopes and letterheads, fancy whiskey bottles,
posters, calendars, trade cards, political buttons, ephemera from the
Leadville Ice Palace, *any* item from the 1908 Democratic National
Convention held in Denver, items from military forts, and items from
fairs, rodeos, and Cheyenne Frontier Days. All items *must* be from
Wyoming or Colorado within the 1860-1930 time frame. "I do not want
items from National Parks, items after 1930, newspapers, or magazines.
Please give a complete description." He emphasizes, "Please do not
send unsolicited items."
Edward Marriott
9191 East Oxford Drive
Denver, CO 80237
    (303) 779-5237   Fax: (303) 733-2479

★ **Nevada, Death Valley, and San Bernardino County ephemera**
before 1930 is wanted including books, newspapers, magazines,
diaries, letters, maps, promotional brochures, "and anything else
printed or written on paper." Also stereoviews, merchant tokens, dog
tags, hunting licenses, photos, postcards and what have you. He
requests prices but will make offers.
Gil Schmidtmann
Route #1 Box 371
Mentone, CA 92359
    (909) 794-1211

★ **Las Vegas, Nevada souvenirs and memorabilia** from before 1980.
Buys gambling tokens and chips, casino playing cards, match covers,
postcards, stationery, plates, **ashtrays**, buttons, pins, charms, menus,
business directories, showroom programs, magazines with stories about
Las Vegas history, prints, photos, maps, room key tags, and other
minor trinkets and **souvenirs**. Also interested in photos of Las Vegas
celebrities. Will consider other ephemera from this desert playground.
Marc Weiser
PO Box 28730
Las Vegas, NV 89126
    (702) 871-8686

★ **All Montana memorabilia** from before 1950 is wanted, including maps, photos, postcards, stationery, tokens, and other ephemera but especially items related to banks and finance including bank bags, letterheads, documents, stocks, checks and scrip.

>Douglas McDonald
>PO Box 5833
>Helena, MT 59604
>>(406) 449-8076   gypsyfoot@aol.com

★ **Montana memorabilia of all types**, with a particular interest in Great Falls, and its breweries and famous saloons like *The Mint* and the *Silver Dollar*. Among Montana items he wants are:
- Photos of saloons, cowboys, Indians, etc.;
- Tokens;
- Advertising from Montana companies, saloons and breweries;
- Books and paper ephemera from Montana Territory.

This 25 year veteran prefers you to set the price you want, but you may ask for offers if you provide a good description.

>Jim Combs
>417 27th Street NW
>Great Falls, MT 59404
>>(406) 761-3320

★ **Montana, New Mexico, Nevada, Utah and Wyoming** souvenirs are wanted including china, glass, sterling silver, postcards, pottery, and other small items originating in those states. SASE for wants list.

>Abbie Bush
>PO Box 503
>Elkader, IA 52043
>>(319) 245-2128

★ **Idaho, Montana, and Washington items** including trade tokens, postcards, letterheads, calendars, buttons, ribbons, wooden nickels, stocks, match holders, calendar plates and other advertising china. Pays $1-$3 for postcards with postmarks from obscure post offices. Pays $2-$10 for cards of small towns he can use. Nothing after 1930.

>Mike Fritz
>PO Box 160
>Rathdrum, ID 83858
>>(208) 687-0159

★ **Oregon related items**, especially small items marked with the name(s) of Oregon cities or places. "A photo or good Xerox is a must."

>Fred Swindall
>111 NW 2nd
>Portland, OR 97209
>>(503) 224-0678 days   (503) 234-2454 eves

★ **Yakima County, Washington, items.** "I buy pre-1950 photos, phone books, newspapers, directories, souvenirs, promotional booklets, and postcards, but no chrome faced postcards." Yakima HS yearbooks from pre-1910, 1933-34, and 1953-54 are also wanted.   If in doubt, send for his wants list of 28 towns he seeks.

    Ron Ott
    10 North 45th Avenue
    Yakima, WA 98908
        (509) 965-3385

★ **San Francisco Bay area ephemera** pre-1910, especially related to the 1906 quake. Photos, diaries, letters, family mementos, and the like are wanted with emphasis on unusual. Ron has particular interest in items associated with schools and education before 1906 and in meal tickets and other items related to life in relief camps immediately after the disaster. No newspapers, postcards, or checks. Ron heads the S.F. History Ass'n and can accept tax deductible gifts from any period.

    Ron Ross
    1982-A Fulton Street
    San Francisco, CA 94117
        (415) 752-9704   Fax: (415) 863-8265

★ **Central California beach towns** of Pismo Beach (also spelled Pizmo/Pizmu), Shell Beach, Oceano, Avila Beach, Port San Luis, Cambria, Los Osos, and Morro Bay. Especially photos and stereoviews, but will consider anything interesting. Please Xerox™ what you have.

    Tony Hyman
    PO Box 3028
    Pismo Beach, CA 93448

★ **San Gabriel Valley, California, items.** Wants pre-1930 items from any San Gabriel Valley towns: Arcadia, Temple City, El Monte, San Gabriel, Baldwin Park, Rosemead, Pasadena, Covina, San Marino, Monrovia, Duarte and Azusa. Also wants anything related to **Emperor Norton** and **Lucky Baldwin**. He suggests you ship your items to him via UPS at 650 West Duarte, #309, to get his offer.

    SC Coin & Stamp Co., Inc.
    PO Drawer 66180
    Arcadia, CA 91066
  (800) 367-0779   (818) 445-8277 in LA Co.   Fax (818) 445-8278

★ **San Diego, California, memorabilia** including postcards, pamphlets and photographs.

    Ralph Bowman's Paper Gallery
    5349 Wheaton Street
    La Mesa, CA 91942
        (619) 462-6268 voice and fax

ALASKA & YUKON EPHEMERA

☆ **Alaska and Yukon memorabilia.** Wants real photo postcards, salmon cans and labels, advertising mirrors, matchbook covers, trade tokens, ashtrays, cards, maps, dishes and brochures about Alaska, Alaskan industry and Alaskan steamshipping. "You name it and I want it." Will be happy to answer any questions about Alaska collectibles. Send a Xerox™ copy if you'd like an offer. You have his permission to send pre-1940 Alaska and Yukon items on approval.

> W.E. "Nick" Nickell
> 710 North 102nd Street
> Seattle, WA 98133

★ **Alaskan memorabilia.** "I'll buy nearly anything old about Alaska, the Yukon, or the Polar Region including postcards, books, photographs, stereoviews, lantern slides, letters, maps, souvenirs, china, spoons, and miscellaneous ephemera. I buy for resale, and seldom buy items newer than 1945."

> Richard Wood
> Alaska Heritage Bookshop
> PO Box 22165
> Juneau, AK 99802
> (907) 789-8450 voice and fax   akrare@alaska.net

★ **Alaska and Yukon historical items.** "I buy old photos, postcards, books, embossed **bottles**, magazines, artifacts, art prints, license plates, train and steamer brochures, Alaska Yukon Expo and items related to Klondike history. Give description, condition, date of origin, and what cities, towns, or regions are featured. Do not send items unsolicited.

> Reed Fitzpatrick
> PO Box 369
> Vashon, WA 98070
> (206) 567-4391 eves 5-7 Pacific

When you ask someone for information or an offer, include a long business size #10 envelope, address it to yourself, and put a stamp in the corner. This is a Self-Addressed Stamped Envelope (SASE). Use a long envelope because many buyers will send you information which won't fit into smaller envelopes.
If you do not include an SASE, you are telling buyers not to bother answering your letter if they are not interested in what you have to sell. "If my help isn't worth an envelope and stamp to the seller," said one expert, "it's not worth my time and money either."

HAWAIIAN ITEMS

★ **Hawaiian items** that can be resold in a shop specializing in Hawaiian souvenirs, photos, menus, lithographs, paintings, fiction and non-fiction books, magazines devoted to Hawaii (especially *Holiday*), post-cards, souvenirs, salt and pepper shakers, hula lamps, hula dolls and nodders, bolts of material and Hawaiian **ukeleles**. The more colorful the better. Does not want other islands, items after 1970, Hawaiian shirts, vinyl hula dolls, C&H dolls, damaged postcards, or paper with parts or pages missing. Items must be in condition for resale. Your description should include dimensions and a brief history. Not interested in hearing about anything that you are not willing to sell now. Some items, especially art, will have to be examined before final payment,

Susan Mast
849 Almar Avenue #C-270
Santa Cruz, CA 95060
(800) 366-9816 Voice or Fax: (408) 423-7001

★ **Hawaii, South Seas and Samoa ephemera.** Wants:
- **Books** before 1920 about Hawaii, written by Hawaiians, or printed in Hawaii;
- **Magazines** from 1940 or earlier with stories of Hawaii;
- **Paintings and prints** of Hawaii, the South Pacific, or Asia;
- Printed ephemera of any type before 1920 about these areas;
- Oriental block prints, tapa cloth, ethnographic carvings from the South Pacific, and any other art of this region of the world;
- **Photographs** of Hawaii, South Pacific or Asia before 1940;
- **Postcards** mailed from, or depicting, this region;
- Diaries or manuscripts about this area;
- **Whaling** souvenirs;
- Jewelry, pottery, and jade from these areas.

And other memorabilia from Hawaii or the South Pacific, as long as it's pre-1920. Send insured. No Hula dolls or Hawaiian shirts.

Bernie Berman
755 Isenberg Street #305
Honolulu, HI 96826
(808) 941-8639

★ **Hawaiian items** before 1970, including art by Mundorff, Halepua, Tip Freeman, or Oda, usually in bamboo frames. Any 1960's or older surfing items, **ukeleles**, cruise line menus, paper leis, books, photos, **hula girl figures**, and tikis. "I am not a dealer. I'm decorating my house. What do you have that will fit in? Please call me."

Wayne Babcock
4846 Carpenteria Avenue
Carpenteria, CA 93013
(805) 684-8148

FOREIGN EPHEMERA

★ **Canadian items:** calendars, stock certificates, bank notes, old letters in original envelopes, fancy letterheads, all Canadian railway, merchants' tokens from Western Canada, Canadian military or law enforcement, and postcards of BC, Yukon, NWT, AB, SK, and Newfoundland. Nothing after 1950, please. No road maps, tourist brochures, and postcards of tourist attractions or scenery. Prefers items be sent on approval or a photocopy made and included in your letter.
> Michael Rice
> PO Box 286
> Saanichton, BC
> V8M 2C5 CANADA
> (250) 652-9412 evenings and weekends only

★ **Panama Canal Zone and the Isthmus of Panama memorabilia** including postcards, letters, stamped envelopes, scrapbooks, tokens, medals, maps, coins, stamps, and everything else including souvenirs. Especially likes pre-1915 picture postcards with cancellations from obscure Canal Zone post offices. "I usually offer to buy anything Isthmus related." Bob is the long time editor of a journal for Isthmus collectors and promises to send a sample to readers who send a long SASE.
> Bob Karrer
> 17 Wentworth Street
> Charleston, SC 29401

★ **Bermuda ephemera** including photographs, stereoviews, real photo postcards (worth up to $100), travel brochures, hotel stationery, luggage labels, guide books, maps, posters, phone directories, china plates with scenes of Bermuda, sterling silver souvenir spoons, and books. Does not want items after 1950. Describe "well enough for me to know exactly what I am buying." Dealers, price your goods.
> Ernest Roberts
> 5 Corsa Street
> Dix Hills, NY 11746
> (516) 7805 days   (516) 586-1462 eves   Fax: (516) 346-7823

★ **Cuban memorabilia** before Castro including coins, stamps, money, historical documents, postcards, souvenir spoons, maps, stocks and bonds, lottery tickets, cigar bands, military decorations and insignia, "or any other collectible items including those related to the Spanish domination of the Island." He'll pay from $80-$400 for the 10, 20 and 50 peso bank notes of 1869. There is a 1916 coin and a 1944 banknote each worth more than $50,000, so it could pay you to look.
> Manuel Alvarez
> 1735 SW 8th Street
> Miami, FL 33135
> (305) 649-1176

★ **Brazil.** Books, photos, and paper ephemera from the colonial period through 1945. Especially interested in travel and exploration books with early information about Rio de Janeiro and/or the Amazon. Also wants letters and diaries of military personnel who served in Brazil during WWII or in the Joint Brazil-U.S. Military Commission. Material may be in any language. Please include your phone number.

>Lee Harrer
>1908 Seagull Drive
>Clearwater, FL 34624
>>(813) 536-4029 evenings

☆ **Philippine Islands.** "I'll buy postcards, photos, books, magazines, maps, and other paper items, especially real photo postcards from Manila or elsewhere in the Philippines. I don't want coins, stamps, paper money, or books on the Spanish American War."

>Michael G. Price
>PO Box 468
>Michigan Center, MI 49254
>>(517) 764-4517   mgprice@acd.net

★ **Antarctic and Arctic ephemera** especially books but also diaries, posters, photographs, letters, pamphlets and *Aurora Austrailis*, the Antarctic newspaper 1907-09. Will buy any clean copies of the latter.

>Jay Platt
>West Side Book Shop
>113 West Liberty
>Ann Arbor, MI 48104
>>(313) 995-1891 days

★ **Arctic and Antarctic exploration items:** diaries, journals, articles, newspaper accounts, and memorabilia from expeditions. Send Xerox.

>Everen T. Brown
>PO Box 296
>Salt Lake City, UT 84110
>>Fax: (801) 364-2646

★ **Greenland, Pitcairn Island, Hudson's Bay, Canada, Mexico, and other countries' ephemera** especially tokens and medals, but other small items, especially before 1930 are likely to be of interest. Your best bet is to photocopy what you have.

>Rich Hartzog
>World Exonumia
>PO Box 4143 BVT
>Rockford, IL 61110
>>(815) 226-0771

★ **Switzerland ephemera** including books, medals, badges, emblems, postcards from before 1930, travel brochures, luggage labels, boxed stereoviews, trade cards, maps, prints posters and other collectibles. Please send Xerox© copy and SASE for offer.

> Donald Tritt
> 4072 Goose Lane
> Granville, OH 43023
> (614) 587-0213 eves

★ **Lapland and Lapp/Sami culture** from before WWII, including maps, postcards, travel brochures, photographs, and some books. He requests a detailed description of the content and condition, a Xerox™ when practical or the item on approval. Contact before sending things.

> Mel Olsen
> 8605 East Sage Road
> Wentworth, WI 54874

☆ **Imperial Russian antiques** and memorabilia whether civil, military, or religious. Buys and sells pre-1917 Russian:
- Orders, decorations, badges, buttons, medals, and other militaria;
- Porcelains, bronzes, prints, icons, paintings and graphic arts;
- Coronation and other commemorative memorabilia.

Items are bought for cash or brokered. "Please send a clear photo or photocopy and details, including price wanted." Mail order catalog and appraisal services available. No Soviet items, nor does he want samovars or hammered brassware.

> Timothy Miller
> American Russian Trading Co.
> PO Box 33191
> Decatur, GA 30033
> (404) 633-1172 artco@mindspring.com

☆ **Asian books and paper ephemera:** books, maps, photos, prints and paintings on Japan, China, Korea, Vietnam, Tonking, Siam, Cambodia, Laos, Burma, Malaya, Singapore, Indonesia, Philippines, Formosa, Taiwan, Tibet, Mongolia, Manchuria, New Guinea, South-East Asia and the Far East.

> Jerry Stanoff
> Rare Oriental Book Co.
> PO Box 1599
> Aptos, CA 95001
> (831) 689-0203 Fax: (831) 689-0204 jgs@rareorientbooks.com

HOW TO SELL MAGAZINES

People are attracted to magazines for many reasons. Some buy for the covers and illustrations. Others look for early articles or advertising relevant to their hobby. Some folks just collect magazines!

To describe items for sale, give the name and date of the magazines and note all tears, creases, address stickers, writing, or anything else affecting the cover or contents. If you have many issues, list them, counting only those with covers and pictures intact, no water damage, and no mildew smell. Describe the condition of a typical issue.

If you offer a magazine to someone because of an article contained in it, give the name and date of the magazine, the author of the article, and the number of illustrations. It's a good idea to photocopy the cover.

Collectors who buy books, magazines, photos, maps, postcards and other paper items tend to be fussy about condition. Don't overestimate the condition of a magazine. What you think of as "normal wear" can be "serious damage" to any paper collector. If you you find a magazine with pictures cut out, it's likely that others in the pile will also be cut.

DESCRIBING CONDITION OF MAGAZINES

VF (very fine) = fresh, bright copy without flaws except for minor aging of paper;

F (fine) = bright copy with very minor wear and only minute cover tears or creases;

VG (very good) = cover and spine wear, tiny tears and creases, minor chipping , browning of paper;

G (good) = obvious cover and spine wear, discoloration, water stains, pieces missing, tears up to 1" long;

FA (fair) = tight and complete, but longer creases, tears, rubbing, fading, and/or store stamps or dates;

P (poor) = many defects, serious damage, well worn; referred to as a "reading copy," not as a collectible.

MAGAZINES

★ **Volume 1, Number 1 (first issue) magazines,** newspapers, comic books, or miscellaneous publications including newsletters, catalogs, fan publications, etc. Also buys pre-publication issues, dummies, proofs and premier issues. "When I don't buy, I will try to help the seller find someone else who might."

    Stan Gold
    7042 Dartbrook
    Dallas, TX 75240
    (972) 239-8621   Fax: (972) 239-9622   record@unicomp.net

★ **Most magazines in quantity** if before 1950 and most newer **movie, fashion** and quality **photography** magazines. Has a particular interest in erotica, nudity, and spicier men's publications except *Playboy* and similar general newsstand magazines. Give quantity of each title and a description. They don't want *National Geographic* after 1910, *Reader's Digest* after 1930, *Life* after 1936, *Arizona Highways* after 1940, or *American Heritage* hardcovers. One of the largest magazine dealers, they will pick them up if you have a truckload.

    The Antiquarian Bookstore
    1070 Lafayette Road
    Portsmouth, NH 03801
    (603) 436-7250

★ **Women's, children's, theater, motorcycle, farm, and many other illustrated magazines, including pulps, 1895 to 1930.** Titles such as *Collier's, Esquire, Vogue, Saturday Evening Post, Vanity Fair, American* and others are wanted. Buys **movie and men's adventure** magazines up to 1960. Does not want magazines from 1970's or 80's. Give the date, condition, and price you'd like. Most of these magazines do not have extreme value. Denis publishes *The Illustrator Collector News* ($17/year), offers a large catalog of magazines for sale, and produces many reasonably priced price guides to magazines and magazine illustrators. Send SASE for info. Denis makes his information available in many different publications. He does not give free appraisals. "I'm happy to talk to you if you're seriously buying or selling, but I don't have time for pen pals or time wasters."

    Denis Jackson
    PO Box 1958
    Sequim, WA 98382
       (360) 683-2559   Fax: (360) 683-9708   ticn@daka.com

★ **Movie magazines** before 1960 in very good uncut condition.

    Claude Held
    PO Box 515
    Buffalo, NY 14225

★ **Bound volumes of illustrated fashion and other magazines** including *Graham's, Godey's Ladies Magazine,* and others published before 1880. Wants *Craftsman* (1900-1915), *Ladies Home Journal, Delineator, Woman's Home Companion, Vogue* and *Saturday Evening Post* from 1910-1922. Condition is important. Note cracks, tears, foxing. Include SASE for answer.

    John Rosenhoover
    100 Mandalay Road
    Chicopee, MA 01020

★ **Men's outdoor magazines.** "We are active and good buyers in need of magazines on hunting, fishing, archery, hunting dogs, and guns. We buy *Stoeger Shooter's Bibles* (1924-1949), *Gun Digests* (1944-1962) and gun and fishing tackle catalogs (1850-1949). We will currently purchase all fine copies, including current years, of *Guns, Man at Arms, Gun Report, Gun World, Arms and the Man, World & Recreation, Rifle, Shooting and Fishing, Shooting Times, American Angler, Handloader, Guns and Ammo* and certain issues of other similar magazines. Special wants include *Chicago Field* (1876-1880), *Forest & Stream* before 1930, *Sports Afield* before 1932, *Field and Stream* before 1920, *Outdoor Life* before 1920 and others. We need magazines in fine condition, both covers as originally attached, with no bad musty smell, and nothing cut out. Sometimes in the case of very old and scarce magazines we can use them in less than fine condition. Don't ship anything in advance as our wants change over time."

    Lewis Razek
    PO Box 1246
    Traverse City, MI 49684
       (616) 271-3898   Fax: (616) 947-4724

★ **Men's outdoor magazines** including *Field & Stream, Outdoor Life* pre-1920, and *Sports Afield* before 1932.

    Thomas McKinnon
    PO Box 86
    Wagram, NC 28396
       (910) 369-2367

★ **Hot Rod and custom car magazines** from 1940-1964. Wants the small 5" x8" size. Must have cover and no pages removed.

    Don Schneider
    PO Box 1570
    Merritt, BC
    VIK 1B8 CANADA

★ *Sports Illustrated* and other sports magazines from before 1970.

    Gary Alderman
    PO Box 259164
    Madison, WI 53715

★ *Billboard, Cashbox* and *Record World* **magazines.** "I'll buy one or a truckload as long as they're fine clean complete issues with good covers between 1930 and 1979."

    Paul Scharfman, Chic-a-Boom
    6817 Melrose Avenue
    Los Angeles, CA 90038
        (213) 931-7441   Fax: (213) 930-2990

★ **Magazines about diving and underwater activities.** Buys foreign and domestic magazines such as *Skin Diver, Aquarius, Diver, Scuba Times, Sport Diver, Ocean Realm,* etc. No books, hardcover or soft. Also interested in old Mike Nelson *Sea Hunt* comic books and *Primus* comic books.

    Thomas Szymanski
    5 Stoney Brook Lane
    Stratham, NH 03885
        (603) 772-6372

★ **Negro magazines** such as *Sepia, Jive,* and *Tan* from the 1940's and 1950's. Must be complete with good covers.

    Paul Scharfman
    6817 Melrose Avenue
    Los Angeles, CA 90038
        (213) 931-7441   Fax: (213) 930-2990

★ **Scandal and exploitation magazines** from 1952-1973 including but not limited to *Behind the Scenes, Bunk!, Celebrity, Exposed, Hollywood Tattler, Hush-Hush, Inside Story, The Lowdown, Naked Truth, Sensation, Top Secret, TV Scandals, Untold Secrets,* and *Whisper.* "I'll pay $35 each for complete issues of *Inside Stuff* from the 1930's." Also wants **Police Gazette** in good condition, especially bound. Nothing current, soiled, damaged or with pages clipped. Give title, date, and volume.

    Gordon Hasse
    PO Box 1543 Grand Central Station
    New York, NY 10163-1543
        (212) 885-3619 days   (212) 996-3825 eves

★ *Esquire* **magazine,** 1933-1959. Also buys *Playboy* **pre-1960** only, *True,* and complete years of *Cosmopolitan, McCalls, Vogue, Ladies Home Journal, Woman's Home Companion, Redbook,* **Saturday Evening Post,** *Country Gentlemen* and *Collier's.* List the years and the condition of the covers and magazines. Do they smell musty?

    Charles Martignette
    PO Box 293
    Hallandale, FL 33008

★ *Architectural Digest* and similar architecture picture magazines. Please give the issue date or issue number and describe the condition. "I don't want magazines with no pictures or with pictures cut out."
Gary Bart
620 Siena Way
Los Angeles, CA 90077
(310) 471-6980   Fax: (310) 471-1910

★ *TV Guide* and other TV log magazines, 1948-1970. Selected U.S. issues from 1971-1996 and Canadian issues 1977-1996 are also purchased. Also wants early local editions, and all weekly newspaper TV supplement magazines from any period. Issues of NY City's *Television Guide* from 1948 are worth $25-$50 each. Note if there is a mailing label on the cover, and if it affects the picture.
Jeffrey Kadet
PO Box 20
Macomb, IL 61455
(309) 833-1809

★ *Humorama* magazine. Pays $1 and up. Give dates and condition.
Jeff Patton
3621 Carolina Street NW
Massillon, OH 44646

★ **National Geographic Society publications of all types.** Buys magazines, books, maps, article reprints, atlases, pictorials, school bulletins, advertising, invitations, slides, videos, postcards, and calendars produced by the NGS. Also buys materials published by other companies with articles about the NGS, which spoof the NGS, are funded by the NGS, or in any way refer to the NGS. He particularly wants pre-1913 magazines, NGS books such as that on Machu Picchu ($1,000) and the complete advertising brochure sent to prospective members in 1888. He'll pay $5,000 for a Vol. 1, No. 1 magazine. **No magazines after 1959.** He encourages buyers and sellers to call.
Nick Koopman, Collectors Exchange
10600 Lowery Drive
Raleigh, NC 27615
(919) 870-8407   Fax: (919) 870-8416   KoompanN@ix.netcom.com

★ *New Yorker* **magazines and covers.** "I pay the following.

1970's	$1-3	1960's	2-3	1950's	3-5
1940's	5-8	1930's	5-15	1920's	25 up

"I do not buy damaged magazines or those stamped by libraries. To sell, give the issue date and the condition of the magazine and cover."
Alvin Golub
1659 West 7th Street
Brooklyn, NY 11223
(718) 339-0237

★ **Crossword and other puzzle magazines** before 1970. "It doesn't matter if they're filled in." Give the name, date and condition. The first 18 issues of *The Eastern Enigma* are worth $1,000.

Will Shortz
55 Great Oak Lane
Pleasantville, NY 10570
(914) 769-9128 voice and fax

★ **Magazines about the fruit or printing industry,** 1860-1960, such as *Modern Packaging, Better Fruit, Calif Citrograph, Blue Anchor, Modern Printing, Skookum News, Pacific Bottler, California Farmer* and other publications from the produce and printing industries.

Pat Jacobsen
PO Box 791
Weimar, CA 95736
(916) 637-5923

PULP MAGAZINES

★ **Pulp magazines.** Buys many types, especially hero, superhero and character pulps such as *The Shadow, The Spider, Doc Savage, Captain Hazard, Captain Zero, The Wizard, Wu Fang,* etc. Also aviation pulps like *G-8, Dusty Ayres, Battle Aces* and similar titles. Other collectible pulp categories are detective, spicy, terror, and odd like *Gun Molls* and *Speakeasy Stories.* Not interested in romance or Westerns. Give the title, date, and overall condition. Include your phone number. Please don't ask about comic books or family magazines like *Post, Life* or *Readers Digest.* Also buys **items related to pulp magazines and characters** including pins, badges, rings, membership cards, art, displays, and autographs of writers and artists.

Jack Deveny
6805 Cheyenne Trail
Edina, MN 55439
(612) 941-2457

★ **Pulp magazines** (1896-1950). This 35 year veteran collector dealer says he'll buy a wide range of magazines but has a particular interest in detectives. He asks that you contact him with the specifics of what you have. Xerox™ copies of the covers is a good idea. He requests dealers set their fair price, but will make an offer to amateur sellers.

J. Randolph Cox
PO Box 226
Dundas, MN 55019
(507) 646-3598 days   (507) 645-5711 eves   Fax: (507) 646-3734

★ **Pulp magazines.** Buys nearly 1,000 titles: **adventure, aviation, crime and detective, hero, mystery and menace, Western, science fiction and fantasy, romance, spicy, sports, confession,** and others. Give the title, date, and condition of each magazine, with emphasis on the condition and graphic appearance of the cover.

> Jim Steranko
> PO Box 974
> Reading, PA 19603
> (215) 374-7477

★ **Pulp magazines.** Buys mystery, detective, spicy, adventure, superhero and character pulps such as *The Shadow, The Spider, Gun Molls, Dime Detective, Doc Savage, Black Mask,* and similar crime and Terror pulps. Not interested in romance or Westerns. Give the title, date, and overall condition. Include your phone number. Offers $1,000 for the October 1912 *All Story* in very good condition.

> Claude Held
> PO Box 515
> Buffalo, NY 14225

Pulp magazines are lurid fiction magazines popular in the teens, twenties, thirties, and forties. As you can tell from reading about these three buyers, they came in many titles. They were usually approximately 6 1/2″ x 10″, printed on newsprint, and had colorful covers.
The paper and covers are often very fragile today because they used such poor paper stock. Handle them with care, as some can be quite valuable. I found two magazines in an old barn, sent them off, and got the easiest $30 I ever made.

HOW TO SELL NEWSPAPERS

Newspapers seldom sell for much money, *even if they're over 100 years old. A whole year of the London Gazette from 1800 is only worth about $300. Some newer years are much more valuable as value in part is determined by what historic events happened that year.*

Some 19th and early 20thcentury publications are important, however, because they contain the first printing of stories by famous writers.

In some cases, it is artwork found in the papers which has itself become collectible. The newspapers that are always welcome are illustrated weeklies like Harper's and Leslie's from 1855-1900.

To describe a paper you wish to sell give the name, city, date, number and size of pages, and mention any significant stories.

If the newspapers are bound, indicate the type and condition of the binding (leather or boards, loose, split, leather crumbling, etc.). If it is a small town 18th or 19th century paper, a photocopy of the masthead is suggested.

When offering 19th century illustrated papers, make certain they are complete as the value drops significantly if important pictures are missing.

Tell the buyer about tears, rips, stains, cut outs, and foxing (brown spots). If the paper is dry, brown, orbrittle, it is seldom of value unless it's before 1750 or the only known copy of a title.

NEWSPAPERS

★ **Newspapers related to the Lincoln assassination and other newspapers with historic content.** "I've been collecting for about 30 years and for the past dozen have been editor and publisher of *Collectible Newspapers*, the Journal of the Newspaper Collectors Society. I will make purchase offers on any Lincoln assassination related newspapers ("If you have an April 15, 1865 *New York Herald* it is almost certain to be a reprint. If you have other collectible newspapers, I will forward to other buyers (libraries or private parties) who specialize in the area of interest of your paper (most people specialize). When writing about newspapers, include the title of the paper, date, historic content in the paper, noting stains, tears and any defects. You are encouraged to send a long SASE for information about the Society. Rick is author of *Index of American Newspaper Editions known to have been Reprinted* ($8 ppd) and *New York Herald April 15th 1865 Lincoln Assassination Reprints* ($5 ppd).
> Rick Brown
> Newspaper Collectors Society
> Box 19134
> Lansing, MI 48901
> (517) 887-1255 www/serve/cp,/ephemera/historybuff.html

SAMPLE DESCRIPTION

Philadelphia Inquirer, April 28, 1865. Capture and death of John W. Booth, front page coverage, solid condition, no stains, tears or damage. Folded.

★ **London newspapers** published between 1850 and 1900.
> Rev. Sherlock "Yes, it's my real name" Holmes
> Private Letter Box 3
> Worcester, MA 01613
> (508) 754-9907

★ **Newspapers of historical significance** especially relative to Lincoln's speeches or death, George Washington, the Revolution, the Civil War, colonial America, early Illinois and the Chicago fire. Buys individual issues of historical significance or bound volumes. Buys all *Harper's Weekly* and *Frank Leslie's Illustrated*, 1855-1916.
> Steve and Linda Alsberg
> 9850 Kedvale Avenue
> Skokie, IL 60076
> (847) 676-9850

★ **Newspapers covering any important event before 1945.** Also all half year bound runs of pre-1870 papers, especially from Southern U.S., **Confederate** states, early West, or anywhere in the U.S. pre-1800. Wants specialty papers covering the women's movement, labor, railroads, abolitionism, temperance, or the Civil War. Also **illustrated newspapers** like *Harper's, Leslie's, Ballou's, Southern Illustrated News, London Illustrated News*, etc. Also bound volumes of British newspapers and magazines pre-1700 (although he will buy later issues if historically significant). Also issues of any American magazine before 1800. Pays $100 each for newspapers before 1730 but notes that many reprints exist so they need to be authenticated. No 20th century items except mint condition reports of important events. No severely defective papers.

> Phil Barber
> PO Box 8694
> Boston, MA 02114
> (617) 492-4653   Fax: (617) 868-1534   user1.channel1.com

★ **Bound volumes of American and European illustrated newspapers dated 1850-1910** including *Harper's Weekly, Leslie's, Illustrated London News, Judge, Vanity Fair, Das Plachate, Puck*, and the like. Prefers to buy in large quantities. Prepared to buy entire libraries.

> Joe and Susie Davidson
> 5185 Windfall Road
> Medina, OH 44256
> (330) 723-7172

★ **Bound volumes of illustrated weekly newspapers** such as *Puck, Harper's, Scientific American* and others, but before 1890 only. Loose stacks considered but single copies are not wanted. Fine condition only.

> John Rosenhoover
> 100 Mandalay Road
> Chicopee, MA 01020
> (413) 536-5542

★ **Confederate newspapers.** Any paper printed in the South during the War. Give the name, place and date on the masthead.

> Peggy Dillard
> PO Box 210904
> Nashville, TN 37221
> (615) 646-1605

TIPS ON SELLING OLD BOOKS

Books have been printed in the hundreds of millions. Valuable ones exist, but most are destined for yard sales and thrift shops. There are some surprises, though, none greater than the astonishing value of detective first editions from 1920-1960.

__Buyers look for books__ on specific topics, by specific authors, published by certain publishers, illustrated in a particular manner, from a particular period or country, and of a specific type, such as leather bound or first edition.

__When writing to potential buyers__ about a book, provide what we call "Standard Bibliographic Information."
- *Title as on the title page, not as on the spine;*
- *Author, publisher, and place of publication;*
- *All printing and copyright dates;*
- *Number of pages;*
- *Type and approximate number of illustrations.*

A Xerox© machine can capture that in seconds; copy the title page, back of the title page and dust jacket.

__Remember, a book has parts.__ Describe the condition of each part: (1) cover, (2) spine, (3) binding, (4) pages and (5) dust jacket. Tell the buyer about bookplates, writing, and all damage. __Don't offer books that are damaged or not the buyer's specialty as listed in__ Trash or Treasure. Books with missing pages, covers off, bindings collapsing, water stains simply aren't wanted unless they're before 1800.

__The amount a dealer will pay for books__ depends upon his customers and present stock, the rarity of your offering, current market, and his cash flow at that moment. Read the next fifteen pages and try selling on your own. Many people report being pleasantly surprised by selling books local dealers told them were worthless.

__Books can be shipped__ Special 4th Class Book Rate which permits three pounds for around two dollars. However, books are fragile and may be damaged in transit. It only costs $1 or so more to send a book first class. Since the buyer is paying for shipping, use the faster, safer method.

BOOKS

★ **Large collections of good books,** especially:
  - **Collections of books on a single topic**, such as Michigan history, the Civil War, theology, golf, Indians, art, architecture, etc.;
  - **Books with color plates**;
  - **Leather bound books**;
  - **Autographed books** by famous authors.

Catalogs are issued periodically. If you want to sell, give standard bibliographic information. One of the nation's largest used and rare booksellers, John does not buy *Reader's Digest* books, *National Geographic* magazines, book club editions, textbooks of any kind, encyclopedia sets, or anything in poor condition.

> John K. King Books
> 901 West Lafayette Blvd.
> Detroit, MI 48226
> (313) 961-0622   Fax: (313) 963-9138

★ **Various fine and early books,** including:
  - **Incunabula**, hand written books before 1501;
  - **European books** before 1600;
  - **English books** and manuscripts from before 1700;
  - **American books before 1800**;
  - **Books published in Pennsylvania** before 1810 in English or 1830 in German. Especially seeks items printed by Benjamin Franklin in Philadelphia, the Brotherhood in Ephrata, or the Saurs (Sower) in Germantown;
  - **Fine leather bound books** in sets;
  - **Books with fore edge paintings**; "Let us hear about all fore edge paintings, no matter what era;"
  - **Books illustrated in color**, especially chromoliths before 1900;
  - **Books on China or Japan** if scholarly and illustrated;
  - **African exploration and development** and materials devoted to problems faced by less developed countries today;
  - **Arabic studies** including material relating the spheres of Moslem influence, both ancient and modern. Buys important books in Arabic and related languages;
  - **Urban studies** including all aspects about any cities anywhere and in all eras;
  - **City view books of buildings and streets of cities worldwide.**

Make certain to include count of pages and photos in your description. Photocopy the title page. In business for 20 years, Ron offers a series of fine catalogs.

> Ron Lieberman, Family Album
> Route #1   Box 42
> Glen Rock, PA 17327
> (717) 235-2134   Fax: (717) 235-8042

★ **Fine and antiquarian books,** pamphlets, and original manuscripts, especially illustrated books, including children's. Has a special interest in **old medical books and paper.**

    Ivan Gilbert, Miran Arts & Books
    2824 Elm Avenue
    Columbus, OH 43209

★ **Any book, pamphlet, almanac, magazine, or tract printed in English speaking America before 1800.** "Books need not be complete nor necessarily in good condition. We will purchase damaged books or even fragments." If you own a book without a title page that you believe to be very old you may send them the book for identification. It's always best to write first, though, and if possible send them a photocopy. The Haydn Foundation for the Cultural Arts is a non- profit public institution.

    Michael Zinman, Haydn Foundation
    495 Ashford Avenue
    Ardsley, NY 10502
    (914) 693-0400

★ **Any type of book from art and archery to Zen and zoology.** This important Florida dealer prefers rare books but is interested in a wide variety of topics and subject matter, especially **limited edition books by fine presses** such as Derrydale, Kelmscott Press, Black Sun Press, Grolier Club, Grabhorne Press and the like. He does not buy school books, encyclopedias, medical texts, Book of the Month Club editions, or reprints of famous novels. "Only tentative evaluations are possible without seeing your book." Give all bibliographic information.

    Steven Eisenstein, Book-A-Brack
    6760 Collins Avenue
    Miami, FL 33141
    (305) 865-0092

★ **Books.** A selection of books is sought, including:
- **Books signed** by U.S. Presidents, authors, sports celebrities stars;
- **Mystery first editions;**
- **Cookbooks** before 1920;
- **Children's books**

Books must be in fine condition and complete with dust jackets if origi- nally issued with them. Torn or missing pages, writing, water damage, missing covers or other damage is not acceptable as this specialty deal- er buys these for resale to collectors. Give standard bibliographic in- formation, including edition number.

    Barbara Ruppert, Alcott Books
    5909 Darnell
    Houston, TX 77074
    (713) 774-2202 before 6pm

★ **Fine quality books from all periods** are wanted. "My book buying is guided by the belief that the quality of a book comes from both the content and from the physical book itself. The books I seek are generally first or early printings or are examples of high quality hand made private press bookmaking. I am particularly interested in buying books in the fields of **art, architecture, Americana and the West, science and medicine, literature and literary criticism, travel and exploration, philosophy and religion, and world history**, but will consider any high quality book. I am always looking for examples of **fine binding, printing and illustration**, especially books signed by Zaehnsdorf, Sangorski and Sutcliffe, Riviere, and other fine binders. Some fine private press books to look for include Kelmscott Press, Ashendone Press, Doves Press, Cranach Press, Nonesuch Press, Arion Press, and Golden Cockerel Press, among others. **Books signed by the author or illustrator** are also of particular interest to me as are Chagall's *Illustrations for the Bible* and *Drawings for the Bible*, Harold Bell Wright's *To My Sons,* pre-1800 copies of *The Book of Common Prayer*, pre-1955 *Alcoholics Anonymous* books, and the Limited Editions Club books, especially *Lysistrata* and *Ulysses*. I do not want book club editions, *Reader's Digest* books, dictionaries or encyclopedia sets after 1850, Bibles after 1750, and incomplete sets of books. I generally prefer the seller to set the price, but if you want an offer, you should provide all information on the title page and copyright page. Make a photocopy of these two pages if you can do so without damaging the book. Describe the binding and format, and the condition of the cover, binding and pages." Don't forget your SASE.

    Paul Melzer, Fine & Rare Books
    12 East Vine Street
    Redlands, CA 92373
        (909) 792-7299   pmbooks@eee.org

 Standard Bibliographic Information" consists of: Title, author, publisher, city where published, date when published, and copyright date.

★ **Leather bound books.** "I'll buy decorator leather bound books in quantity for $3 to $5 each. Not interested in fine first editions, just old books with little other value. Must have good spines and covers, but can be in any language from any period, as I want them only for their decorator potential. Call if you've got a bunch of them."

    Joan Brady
    834 Central Avenue
    Pawtucket, RI 02861

★ **Collectible and scholarly books and art in all fields.** Book and other items this high quality shop seeks include, but are not limited to:
- Books **printed in Europe before 1600**;
- Books **printed in America before 1700**;
- **Important literary works** in first, limited or illustrated editions;
- Illustrated books **by noted artists**;
- Modern **1st editions**;
- Fine and limited editions;
- **Scholarly**, significant books in **art**, **architecture**, **photography**, travel, exploration, **music**, psychology, **religion**, history, science, and other fields.
- **Atlases** and individual maps;
- **Prints** signed by artists from any period;
- Decorative prints prior to 1900.

Please, no book club books, textbooks, or anything in poor condition. Give standard bibliographic information: author, title, place published, publisher, all dates of publication and a description of the cover, binding, pages, and dust jacket. Open daily with 60,000 items in stock. Will buy individual books and entire collections.

> James & Mary Laurie, Booksellers
> 921 Nicollet
> Minneapolis, MN 55402
> (800) 774-1114   (612) 338-1114   Fax: (612) 338-3665

★ **Sporting books.** "We are always interested in purchasing sporting books on hunting, fishing, bird dogs, archery, guns and gun collecting, game animals and birds, books by the Derrydale Press, and many more. We purchase for stock, so there is no delay. We do ask that if you quote a book to us, you wait until you hear from us. We answer all quotes even if we do not buy them. We are good active buyers and ask that you keep our wants in mind. Among many authors we seek are Frank Forester, Havilah Babcock, Robert Ruark, Archibald Rutledge, Robert Traver and Corey Ford." Provide standard bibliographic info.

> Lewis Razek, Highwood Bookshop
> PO Box 1246
> Traverse City, MI 49685
>   (616) 271-3898   Fax: (616) 947-4724

Publishers have many different ways of making their first editions. Some do it in code. Many make it easy buy listing the printing near the bottom on the front or back of the title page. Look for a string of numbers which usually start around 10 and count backwards. Whatever the lowest number is...that's the number of the printing you have.

★ **Books about art, architecture, photography and design** written before 1970. Has a particular interest in California artists, American art and artists, and modern decorative arts such as glass, furniture and ceramics (1890-1970). Alan writes the nationally syndicated "Art Talk" column, and is author of *Art for All* ($17.95) and *Buy Art Smart* ($17.95), both available from him or at your local bookstore.
> Alan S. Bamberger
> 2510 Bush Street
> San Francisco, CA 94115
> (415) 922-3580

You are more likely to have valuable books when you own a private library of hundreds on a single topic. Never break up a private library on a particular topic without help. All fiction, even if fairly recent, should be checked out if it is by a famous author and has its original dust jacket.

★ **Jewish and Hebrew books**, particularly illustrated material pre 1920. Anything printed or photographic related to Jewish history in the U.S. or Europe before WWII may be of interest including photo albums, cookbooks, diaries, scholarly books, and the like. This 25 year veteran buyer says that if your book is printed in any language you can't read, simply Xerox© the front and back of the title page. If your book is in English, provide a Xerox© or standard bibliographic information including the condition of cover, binding and pages.
> Elliot Brill
> 505 8th Avenue
> New York, NY 10018
> (212) 695-1996   (800) 562-9911   Fax (212) 695-3860

★ **Asian books, maps, photos, and prints** on Japan, China, Korea, Vietnam, Tonkin, Siam, Cambodia, Laos, Burma, Malaya, Singapore, Indonesia, Philippines, Formosa, Taiwan, Tibet, Mongolia, Manchuria, New Guinea, South-East Asia and the Far East. Has a special interest in **books illustrated by Japanese woodblocks**.
> Jerry Stanoff
> Rare Oriental Book Co.
> PO Box 1599
> Aptos, CA 95001
> (408) 689-0203   Fax: (408) 689-0204

★ **Reference books on any topic published in England, 1850-1900.**
Science, medicine, geology, electricity, geography, poisons, toxicology,
Great Britain, Law, criminal history, boxing, anatomy, bee-keeping,
etc. Special wants include *Lloyd's Register of British & Foreign Shipping, History of British Birds, Crockford's Clerical Directory, Gazeteer
of the World, Morris's Directory, Kelly's Post Office Directory, Whi-
taker's Almanack, The Holy War, History of the Holy Warre,*   Also
King James Bible from that period. Any book that might be in the fictional Sherlock Holmes' private library will be considered. Give title,
author, date of publication and condition.

> Rev. Sherlock "Yes, it's my real name" Holmes
> Private Letter Box 3
> Worcester, MA 01613
> (508) 754-9907

★ **Books on the following subjects:**
 • **Russian and East European Royalty**, especially Romanovs;
 • **Russian Revolution;**
 • **World Wars I and II** in Europe and in Asia;
 • **Aviation** and air wars;
 • **Korean War;**
 • **Tibet and environs;**
 • **Soviet Union, Eastern Europe, Communism, Socialism.**
First editions in dust jackets preferred. Some rare titles purchased in
lesser condition. Provide standard bibliographic information, including
printing data found on the title page or reverse. No book club books
and no paperbacks.

> Edward Conroy
> SUMAC Books
> Route 1   Box 197
> Troy, NY 12180
> (518) 279-9638 voice and fax

★ **Books about reptiles and amphibians** including snakes, turtles,
crocodiles, lizards, frogs, etc. Prefers older, illustrated volumes as well
as scientific monographs. Would pay $1,000 for Holbrook's *North
American Herpetology* in fine condition. Not interested in books still
in print, biology textbooks, children's and juvenile titles published after
1960 (but will consider early ones) or Ditmar titles greater than $5.
Please send a photo of unusual items and give complete bibliographic
info. A computer bulletin board about reptiles is at (215) 698-1905.

> Mark Miller
> Herp-Net
> PO Box 52261
> Philadelphia, PA 19115
> (215) 464-3561 voice or fax   70176.1153@compuserve.com

Publishers have many different ways of making their first editions. Some do it in code. Many make it easy buy listing the printing near the bottom on the front or back of the title page. Look for a string of numbers which usually start around 10 and count backwards. Whatever the lowest number is...that's the number of the printing you have.

★ **Books about wine.** "I'll buy hardcover books intended for resale to dealers and collectors. I prefer older, less well-known titles but will consider all offers of books in good shape. Give author, title, publisher, year of publication(s), edition, and a detailed description of condition. I do not buy paperbacks, price guides to bottles of wine, wine tasting notes, and travel guides of wine regions. I will buy some cookbooks which emphasize wine, especially those which are colorful and have eye appeal." He especially wants to find fine condition 19th Century wine books in very good condition.

> Warren R. Johnson
> Second Harvest Books
> PO Box 3306
> Florence, OR 97439
> (800) 928-5206

★ **Books on gambling.** "We can give anyone information as to whether their book or gambling paraphernalia has value if they write, call, or preferably fax us." Not a bad bet, since Howard has been described elsewhere as the man who "knows more about gambling literature than anyone else alive."

> Howard Schwartz
> Gambler's Book Club
> 630 South 11th Street
> Las Vegas, NV 89101
> (702) 382-7555 (2 to 5pm)   (800) 522-1777   Fax: (702) 382-7594

★ **Social etiquette (manners) books** for adults, children, or teens, especially first editions. Very good condition preferred, but unusual titles will be considered in lesser condition. Please do not inquire about cookbooks or health books. Give this 20 year veteran collector standard bibliographic information. Free appraisals.

> LuAnn Gavula
> 20 Barrington Bourne
> Barrington Hills, IL 60010
> (847) 658-1500

★ **Hollywood biographies** of all types in hardcover with dust jacket.
> Edward Conroy , SUMAC Books
> Route 1 Box 197
> Troy, NY 12180
> > (518) 279-9638 voice and fax

★ **Genealogy books.**
> James Williams
> HCR 01 Box 23
> Warrensburg, NY 12885
> (518) 623-2831

★ **Alcoholics Anonymous books** earlier than 1975. Nothing later.
Will pay $50 to $100 each for 1939 to 1954 first editions. Does not
want 3rd editions, plain books or those in poor condition. Describe the
dust jacket, date, and printing number.
> Clark Phelps
> 390 K Street
> Salt Lake City, UT 84103
> > (801) 364-4747

★ **Occult and mystic science,** astrology, magic, numerology, alche-
my, palmistry, spiritualism, pyramids, tarot, Yoga, Atlantis, UFO's,
ESP, and anything else metaphysical. "I'll also buy art, posters, cards,
games, antique crystal balls, and other mystical and occult ephemera.
I'll buy one or one thousand, if in fine condition."
> Dennis Whelan
> PO Box 170
> Lakeview, AR 72642

★ **Technical books and paper ephemera,** pre-1910. He wants books
on trades, machines, manufacturing and technical processes.
> Jim Presgraves
> Bookworm & Silverfish
> PO Box 639
> Wytheville, VA 24382

*Standard Bibliographic Information" consists of
title, author, publisher, city where published,
the date of publication and the printing
number whenever possible.*

☆ **Technical and trade books** on all topics, especially:
- **International Correspondence School** (I.C.S.) reference;
- **I.C.S. Technical library**;
- International Textbook Company (I.T.C.) library;
- Early **architecture books about wood construction**;
- **Audel manuals**;
- Books on **blacksmithing, tin work, wood working**, etc..

Make a photocopy of the title page if possible. Otherwise provide standard bibliographic information. Describe condition of cover, binding, pages. Self-addressed stamped envelope, please. He requests that items be shipped US Post Office via special 4th class book rate, not UPS.

> Jack Zimmerly
> RD #4   Box 58
> Reynoldsville, PA 15851
> (814) 375-0781

★ **Crossword puzzle books.** It doesn't matter if the puzzles are filled in, as long as the books are hardcover and before 1955. Give standard bibliographic information.

> Will Shortz
> 55 Great Oak Lane
> Pleasantville, NY 10570
> (914) 769-9128 voice and fax

★ **Pre-1970 crossword and other word puzzle books,** hard or soft cover, even if written in. Especially wants Simon and Schuster hardcover puzzle books 1924-60. Give the complete title, date, and series number, and how much of the book has been filled in. No crossword dictionaries, but does buy **crossword magazines**. Wants list sent for large SASE. Stan also buys pre-1970 **board games** if they are in good condition with no missing pieces. No common games, though.

> Stanley Newman
> American Crossword
> PO Box 69
> Massapequa Park, NY 11762

Standard Bibliographic Information" consists of
title, author, publisher, city where published,
the date of publication and the printing
number whenever possible.

BOOKS BY PARTICULAR PUBLISHERS

★ **Books published by the Limited Editions Club.** "I'll buy all years, all titles, as long as they are in fine condition in a fine box. I'll also buy Club ephemera including monthly letters, prospectus, etc." Only *Lysistrata* and *Ulysses* are acceptable without original box. Also buys **Heritage Press** books, **Encyclopedia Britannica** published after 1990, and **Encyclopedia Judaica** (any edition). Please describe fully.
>   Lee and Mike Temares
>   50 Heights Road
>   Plandome, NY 11030
>   (516) 627-8688   Fax: (516) 627-7822

★ **Roycroft and other high quality small press books,** especially editions of less than 500 with hand tooled binding and/or hand painted illumination or illustration. Buys the books of 60 small hand presses of the 1890-1920 era (dealers are encouraged to send an SASE for his list). He does NOT want "Little Journeys to...," *Scrapbooks* or *Notebooks* published by Roycroft. Give the title, date, material of binding, unusual characteristics, and the condition if you want an offer. A Xerox™ is a good idea.
>   Richard Blacher
>   209 Plymouth Colony/Alps Road
>   Branford, CT 06405

★ **Tower Publishing Company books** and other books and printed ephemera related to the **Watchtower Society** from before 1930. He'd like to hear from you if you have anything pertaining to the Watchtower Society, Tower Publishing, the International Bible Students Assn (IBSA), Pastor C.T. Russell, or George Storrs. Books of particular interest include N.H. Barbour's *Three Worlds* (1877, $200 "or a great deal more in fine condition"), J.H. Paton's *Day Dawn* (1880, $200+), C.T. Russell's *The Object & Manner of Our Lord's Return* (1877, $500+), J.F. Rutherford's *Man's Salvation from a Lawyer's Viewpoint* (1906, $500+), and various books by George Storrs. The special Watchtower Edition of *Human Linear Bible* (1902) is a $500 and up prize. Numerous magazines, Journals, and Reports **from before 1930** are sought, including *Watchtower, Golden Age, Herald of the Morning, Bible Examiner,* and*Overland Monthly.* This 35 year veteran collector/researcher wants to hear about **anything you have from before 1930**, books between 1930 and 1940, and nothing after 1950. Dealers should price their goods. Amateurs may request an offer from this 35 year veteran collector/dealer.
>   Jeffrey Neumann
>   PO Box 171
>   Wadsworth, OH 44282
>   (330) 334-1784

★ **Fine quality small press books from all periods** are wanted. "My book buying is guided by the belief that the quality of a book comes from both the content and from the physical book itself. I seek high quality hand made private press bookmaking. Some fine private press books to look for include Kelmscott Press, Ashendone Press, Doves Press, Cranach Press, Nonesuch Press, Arion Press, and Golden Cockerel Press, among others. I do not want book club editions, *Reader's Digest* books, dictionaries or encyclopedia sets after 1850, Bibles after 1750, and incomplete sets of books. I generally prefer the seller to set the price, but if you want an offer, you should provide all information on the title page and copyright page. Make a photocopy of these two pages if you can do so without damaging the book. Describe the binding and format, and the condition of the cover, binding and pages." Don't forget your SASE.

    Paul Melzer
    Fine & Rare Books
    12 East Vine Street
    Redlands, CA 92373
        (909) 792-7299   pmbooks@eee.org

Standard Bibliographic Information" consists of title, authon, publisher, city where published, the date of publication and the printing number whenever possible.

★ **Fine quality limited editions from all periods** are wanted, especially important literary or scholarly works, or those illustrated by important artists. Please, no book club books, textbooks, or anything in poor condition. Give standard bibliographic information: author, title, place published, publisher, all dates of publication and a description of the cover, binding, pages, and dust jacket. Open daily with 60,000 items in stock. Will buy individual books and entire collections.

    James & Mary Laurie
    Booksellers
    921 Nicollet
    Minneapolis, MN 55402
  (800) 774-1114   (612) 338-1114   Fax: (612) 338-3665

BOOKS WITH MAPS & ILLUSTRATIONS

★ **Books illustrated with color pictures before 1890** depicting plants, animals, birds, fish, Indians, sports, cowboys, medicine, military, buildings, costumes, fashion, or advertising. Standard bibliographic data is requested.

> Joe and Susie Davidson
> 5185 Windfall Road
> Medina, OH 44256
> (330) 723-7172

★ **Books illustrated with full page b/w illustrations,** including steel engravings, etchings, copper plates, and woodblocks. Wants views of the U.S. and Canada, North American Indians, explorations and Western America, animals, art, railway surveys, pre-1880 fairs and Centennials, architecture, Civil War, and pre-1860 Hawaii (Sandwich Islands). Indicate size along with standard bibliographic information. Note tears, foxing, etc. Count the number of illustrations.

> John Rosenhoover
> 100 Mandalay Road
> Chicopee, MA 01020
> (413) 536-5542

★ **Books illustrated with color plates before 1899,** especially German before 1895, American natural history (plants and animals) before 1870, and Indians. Especially wants **books illustrated by** Kate Greenaway, Arthur Rackham, Jessie Smith, K. Nielson, Wyeth, W. Crane, Maxfield Parrish, Pogany, Dulac, Newell, Maud Humphrey, Remington, Erte, or Harrison Fisher. Books must date between 1890 and 1926. Give standard bibliographic information, noting tears, erasures, foxing, etc. Count and indicate the number of illustrations in color and in b/w.

> John Rosenhoover
> 100 Mandalay Road
> Chicopee, MA 01020

★ **Used and rare books, manuscripts** and **maps.** "We specialize in **U.S. maps and atlases before 1870**, books on the military, aviation, lighter-than-air craft and Ohio subjects. We also have interest in obtaining old **bookbinding tools** and equipment."

> Frank Klein, The Bookseller
> 174 West Exchange Street
> Akron, OH 44302
> (330) 762-3101   Fax: (330) 762-4413

FICTION

★ **Detective and mystery 1st editions** in hardcover or paperback. Also biography, reference, and bibliography related to the detective/mystery genre. Wants Dashiell Hammett and Raymond Chandler and other classics, and authors like Tony Hillerman, Sue Grafton, Robert Block, and other popular contemporary writers in 1st editions with dust jackets. Computerized for modem access.

Richard West's Booking Agency
PO Box 406
Elm Grove, WI 53122
(414) 786-8420

★ **Large 20th century fiction collections.** If you have many hundreds of hardback fiction books with their original dust jackets, give him a call. Has strong interest in **John Steinbeck, Wallace Stegner, Richard Brautigan and Jack London** signed limited editions, first editions, first printings by subsequent publishers, appearances in anthologies, spoken word records, tapes, film and theater memorabilia, and things owned by him. Does not want book club editions or items in poor condition. If a book had a dust jacket, slipcase, box, or wrap-around as originally issued, these items should still be present. Be specific about what you have for sale, giving complete bibliographic information and a full description. No interest in paperbacks or contemporary remainders.

James Dourgarian
Bookman
1595-A Third Avenue
Walnut Creek, CA 94596
(510) 935-5033

★ **Books by Jules Verne** are wanted in British, French and American editions. Most interested in buying first or other early editions, or editions of lesser known titles such as *Clovis Dardentor, Mathias Sandorf* and *Foundling Mick*. Also interested in appearances of Verne in the Seaside Library or Lakeside Library dime novels. "If you find an old edition of any work in good shape, you might send a quote." Give full title, copyright date(s), publisher, the type and number of illustrations and a complete statement of condition of the cover, binding, and pages.

Dana Eales
2447 Delta Drive
Uniontown, OH 44685
(330) 699-5341   ealesd@newreach.net

★ **Books by Harlan Ellison,** U.S. or foreign. Will consider mint condition paperbacks or fine hardcovers with dust jackets. Especially wants U.S. first editions, numbered editions, and autographed copies. Wants to find *Sex Gang*, written under his Paul Merchant pseudonym.

    Edy Chandler
    PO Box 20664
    Houston, TX 77225
       (713) 531-9615

★ **Books by Stephen King, Anne Rice or Larry McMurtry.** Want first editions, foreign editions, and uncorrected proofs. Books must be in fine condition and complete with dust jackets. Torn or missing pages, writing, water damage, missing covers or other damage is not acceptable as this specialty dealer buys these for resale to collectors. Give standard bibliographic information, including edition number.

    Barbara Ruppert
    Alcott Books
    5909 Darnell
    Houston, TX 77074
       (713) 774-2202 before 6pm

★ **Beat Generation poets and authors.** Wants first edition books and records by Allen Ginsberg, Jack Kerouac, Kenneth Rexroth, and others who symbolized "The Beat Generation" of the 1950's, especially in San Francisco. State condition, date, and how the item was stored.

    Richard Synchef
    16 Midway Avenue
    Mill Valley, CA 94941
       (415) 381-4448 days   Fax: (415) 381-4145

★ **Science fiction hardcover 1st editions** only. Autographed books are of particular interest. Also interested in trade paperbacks issued at the same time as the hardcover editions. "Please, no book club editions (these are usually marked on the dust jacket). No ex-library books and nothing in poor condition. Please note I am not interested in fantasy. Only science fiction. Fantasy involves witches, warlocks, wizards, dragons, magic and is usually set in a Pre-Industrial Revolution technology." When describing your book remember to give complete bibliographic information.

    David Kveragas
    1943 Timberlane
    Clarks Summit, PA 18411
       (717) 587-3429 eves

★ **Dime novels and serial story papers.** Dime novels were paper covered books issued between 1860 and 1915, reprinted into the early 1930's. Serial stories began in the late 1830's and continued into the 1920's. There are many he seeks, especially Nick Carter stories. Make a photocopy of the cover. J.R. is the editor of *Dime Novel Round-Up*, the newsletter for dime novel collectors. He requests dealers set the price wanted, but will make a purchase offer to amateur sellers.

> J. Randolph Cox
> PO Box 226
> Dundas, MN 55019
> (507) 646-3598 days   (507) 645-5711 eves   Fax: (507) 646-3734

★ **Paperback books** from before 1960, but only in mint or near mint condition. Give title, publisher, catalog number (usually on the spine), cover price, and edition or printing number.

> James Williams
> HCR 01   Box 23
> Warrensburg, NY 12885
> (518) 623-2831

Book buyers want to know standard bibliographic information: title, author, publisher and place of publication, all dates of printing or copyright, number of pages, the illustrator, and approximate number of illustrations. Describe condition of the cover, spine, binding, pages and dust jacket. Note bookplates, writing, and all other damage.

CHILDREN'S BOOKS

★ **First editions of children's books** in very good condition. Wants books illustrated by Mabel Lucie Atwell, Jessie Wilcox Smith, Charles Robinson, Maxfield Parrish, Charles Folkard, Maurice Sendak, Edward Gorey, and Ralph Steadman, among others. Can send you a wants list.

> Joel Birenbaum
> 2765 Shellingham Drive
> Lisle, IL 60532
> (630) 637-8530

★ **Children's books** including:
- *Dick and Jane* **readers** in all their forms, including flash cards;
- **Boys' and girls' series books** like *Nancy Drew, Hardy Boys, Tom Swift,* and many others as long as they are in fine condition and have original dust jackets;
- **Judy Bolton and other modern children's** books in fine condition with dust jackets;
- *Little Black Sambo, Nicodemus, Little Brown Kokos* and other stories about black/negro children;
- *Oz* books by Baum and others;
- *Uncle Wiggily;*
- *Uncle Remus;*
- **Books with high quality illustrations**, especially by Parrish, N.C. Wyeth, J.W. Smith, T. Tudor, Pogany, Rackham, Pyle, Potter, Lenski, Gruelle, Nielson, Dulac, Crane, Ward, and other prominent illustrators;
- Books that have won the Newbery or Caldecott Award;
- Children's **pop-up books** from before 1940;
- Old **Mother Goose** and Father Goose stories.

Books must be in fine condition and complete with dust jackets if originally issued with them. Torn pages, writing or crayoning, water damage, missing covers or other damage is not acceptable as this specialty dealer buys these for resale to collectors. Give standard bibliographic information, including edition number.

Barbara Ruppert
Alcott Books
5909 Darnell
Houston, TX 77074
(713) 774-2202 before 6pm

★ **Children's books,** American or English, from the 1400's to 1925, including **educational books** such as McGuffey's readers.

Ron Graham
8167 Park Avenue
Forestville, CA 95436
(707) 887-2856

★ **Children's series books.** Must be in dust jacket if issued that way. Especially seeking the last 3 or 4 titles in any series. Describe condition of dust jacket. Better if you Xerox™ both sides.

Lee and Mike Temares
50 Heights Road
Plandome, NY 11030
(516) 627-8688   Fax: (516) 627-7822

★ **Juvenile series books** like the Hardy Boys, Nancy Drew, Motion Picture Girls, etc. in good condition, especially with dust jackets. Please give standard bibliographic information and a Xerox™ copy of the jacket if it has one. Note the condition of the spine, cover, and pages. He requests dealers set the price wanted, but will make an offer to amateur sellers.

> J. Randolph Cox
> PO Box 226
> Dundas, MN 55019
> (507) 646-3598 days (507) 645-5711 eves Fax: (507) 646-3734

★ **Children's school books** from before 1910. Please give standard bibliographic information and make a Xerox™ of the cover if possible.

> Douglas Cowles
> 2966 West Talara Lane
> Tucson, AZ 85741
> (602) 297-9062

Book buyers want to know standard bibliographic information: title, author, publisher and place of publication, all dates of printing or copyright, number of pages, the illustrator, and approximate number of illustrations. Describe condition of the cover, spine, binding, pages and dust jacket. Note bookplates, writing, and all other damage.

★ **Thornton W. Burgess and Harrison Cady books** and ephemera. Does not want any of their books published by *Grosset & Dunlap*.

> Stephen Kruskall
> PO Box 418
> Dover, MA 02030

★ *Little Golden Books* **and other children's literature.** "I primarily deal in *Little Golden Books, Wonder Books, Elf Books, Bonnie Books, Cozy Corner, Friendly* and *Tell-A-Tale.* These were mass production items, so I'm looking for fine condition ones only. Please give the title, catalog number (it it has one), cover price, and condition. If you know what edition you have, please tell me. I don't buy *Little Golden Books* with a 5 digit catalog number (eg., 124-33) as these are too new." Steve wrote the comprehensive *Collecting Little Golden Books,* available from him for $25.

> Steve Santi
> 19626 Ricardo Avenue
> Hayward, CA 94541
> (510) 481-2586

Friedman, Barry 6, 7, 75, 97,
260, 297, 299, 301, 321,
483, 494, 528, 535
Fritz, Mike 544
Fuchs, Danny 146
Fulks, Andy 419

G

Galt, Dave 253, 330
Gandy, James 407, 433
Gartin, Dick 366
Garton, Gus 339, 341, 342,
353, 434
Gatanis, Gary 230, 243
Gavula, LuAnn 568
Gawchik, William 360
Gayle, Jean 426
Geisman, Grant 150
George, Joan 51
Gerlach, Jim 147, 329, 479
Gewalt, Marjorie 105
Geyer, Lynn 262, 266
Giarde, Leigh 428
Gibbs, Linda 74, 80, 81, 483
Gibson, Pat 481
Gilbert, Ivan 282, 285, 374, 385,
484, 491, 505, 515, 524, 563
Gill, Robert 533
Gilleeny, Peter 270
Ginsberg, Sam 304
Ginzberg, Danny 420
Glab, Anthony 113, 430, 432
Glass, Herb 351
Glick, Robert 356, 357
Glickman, Sid 197
Godek, Matt 232
Goetz, Albert 25
Goetz, John 380
Gold, Stan 138, 552
Goldstein, Lee 233
Golub, Alvin 555
Goodman, Charles 365, 396
Gordon, Steve 263
Gorges, Will 446
Gorlick, Don 111, 205, 302, 325,
373, 374, 463, 464

Gotelli, Dolph 108, 313
Govig, Valerie 110
Goyda, Michael 242
Graham, Michael 259, 264,
294, 295, 305, 327, 382, 425
Graham, Ron 209, 577
Graver, Nicholas 524
Gregerson, Byron 368
Griffin, Mark 48
Gronowski, Richard 124, 129
Gronsky, Michael 146
Grush, Glenn 413, 424
Gumtow, Alan 52
Gurner, Jack 384
Gutzke, Kim 193, 205, 219

H

Haag, Robert 431
Hakal, Ed 200
Hake, Ted 132, 292
Hall, George 168
Hallock, Allen 443
Halpern, Renate 8, 298, 492
Hamburg, Bill 115, 126, 135
Hamburg, Loretta 33
Hamer, Beverly 206
Hamilton, Denise 74, 334, 502
Hammerman, Jay 237
Hampton, David 280
Handelsman, Burton 436
Hannan, Steve 72
Hans, Jim & Beverly 536
Hanson, Rick 125
Harding, Judy 19, 64, 75, 78,
84, 221, 320, 453, 522
Hardisty, Donald 500, 503
Hardy, Art 188
Harper, Michael 350
Harrer, Lee 549
Harris, Tom 525
Harris, Warren 24
Harrison, Robert 252
Harrow, Alan 448, 472
Hartley, Glenn 417
Hartmann, Ron 457
Hartsough, Ross 152, 331

TRASH OR TREASURE

THINGS YOU CAN SELL **617**

TRASH OR TREASURE IS NOT ONLY ABOUT MONEY.

Getting things into the hands of collectors may help you preserve your family's heritage.

Many of the buyers in Trash or Treasure are also historians, authors, museum curators, editors, and other archivists who preserve American culture by protecting, studying, and writing about its artifacts. You own those artifacts.

If you and your family are not prepared to properly store, care for, and preserve them, they could be lost or permanently damaged. Photos, letters, catalogs, diaries and "family things" which deal with life and business in a different era should get into the hands of those who can insure the items and their story will survive. Many people have sold or given photographs of their ancestor's cigar stores or factories to me because they know their family's legacy will be appreciated, preserved, and written about.

ELL-A-GRAM from one of Tony Hyman's readers

TO: _____

FROM: _____
_____
Phone: ( ) _____

e the following item:

ember to include the (1) shape, (2) colors, (3) dimensions, and (4) all names, dates, and marks.

ondition is:

ips, creases, cracks, dents, scratches, rips, tears, holes, stains, fading, and foxing.
nissing pages, parts, or paint. Describe any repairs that have been done.

he item is for sale for $_____ plus shipping.

he item is for sale. I am an amateur seller and would like you to make an offer.

he item may be for sale if the price is sufficient. Would you like to make an offer?

he item is not for sale, but I am willing to pay a fee to learn its value.

st you to evaluate the item, I am enclosing a:
ple ☐Photocopy ☐Photo ☐Tracing ☐Sketch ☐

rtify that, to the best of my knowledge, the item is genuine and as described.
5 day examination period during which the item may be returned for any reason.

_____ Date: _____

☐ _____ ☐ _____

BUYER'S RESPONSE:

Dr. Hyman and Treasure Hunt Publications make every effort to bring you the latest most reliable information possible. If you know of additional address of phone number changes, please share them with other readers by notifying us. Remember, when a recording says a phone number is 'No longer in service' or has been'disconnected' it often means the area code is changed. Ask your operator for assistance.

PAGE	BUYER & CHANGES
307+	Aldridge, Ron: home and fax area code now (940)
7+	Applebaum, Steve: moved; call: (817) 337-1561
138+	Blondy, Mark: new phone (248) 442-7339
309+	Brown, Rev. Ken, moved and is temporarily unreachable.
7+	Bueschel, Richard, has died.
269	Cairo, Terry & Karen: area code now (630)
170	Cleveland, Dwight: area code now (773)
497	Cummings, Urban: area code now (650)
328+	Dourgarian, James: area code now (925)
267	Elliott, Richard: area code now (978)
129+	Jacobsen, Pat: area code now (530)
367	Levy, Tedd: phone now (203) 899-2910
188	Mancina, Dean: area code now (562)
327+	Stanoff, Jerry: area code now (831)
134	Tumbusch, Tom: area code now (937)
496	Vargas, Marsha: area code now (650)

PAGE	ADDITIONS
214+	Clee, Ken: <waxntoys@aol.com>
237	Fitzpatrick, Reed: <reed369@aol.com>
36	Smith, David: <david@panman.com>

Addresses last updated 8-5-98